P9-EGM-514

Eleanor
Roosevelt

Eleanor

Roosevelt

VOLUME ONE

1884–1933

Blanche Wiesen Cook

VIKING

VIKING
Published by the Penguin Group
Viking Penguin, a division of Penguin Books USA Inc.,
375 Hudson Street, New York, New York 10014, U.S.A.
Penguin Books Ltd, 27 Wrights Lane,
London W8 5TZ, England
Penguin Books Australia Ltd, Ringwood,
Victoria, Australia
Penguin Books Canada Ltd, 10 Alcorn Avenue, Suite 300,
Toronto, Ontario, Canada M4V 3B2
Penguin Books (N.Z.) Ltd, 182–190 Wairau Road,
Auckland 10, New Zealand

Penguin Books Ltd, Registered Offices:
Harmondsworth, Middlesex, England

10 9 8 7 6 5 4 3 2 1

PHOTOGRAPH CREDITS
Pages iv–v: UPI/Bettmann; iv (insert): The Bettmann Archive.
In photo section, pages 8 (top) and 14 (top): Pach Bros./Bettmann;
10: Bachrach Studios; 12 (below): Roy Karten; 13 (top): New York
Times Pictures; 16 (below): Jessie Tarbox Beals, courtesy of the
Franklin D. Roosevelt Library; 17 (top): Dagmar Schultz; 17 (below):
G. W. Harting, courtesy of the Franklin D. Roosevelt Library; 21
(below): Keystone Press; 23 (top): Capitol Press; 23 (below right):
Underwood & Underwood/Bettmann; 24: UPI/Bettmann. All
other photographs courtesy of the Franklin D. Roosevelt Library.

LIBRARY OF CONGRESS CATALOGING IN PUBLICATION DATA
Cook, Blanche Wiesen.
Eleanor Roosevelt, Volume One 1884–1933 / Blanche Wiesen Cook.
p.   cm.
Includes bibliographical references and index.
ISBN 0-670-80486-X
1. Roosevelt, Eleanor, 1884–1962.   2. Presidents—United States—
Wives—Biography.   I. Title.
E807.1.R48C66   1992
973.917′092—dc20
[B]   87-40632

Printed in the United States of America
Set in Simoncini Garamond
Designed by Amy Hill

"The big question before our people today is whether we are to be more material in our thinking, judging administrative success by its economic results entirely and leaving out all other achievements. History shows that a nation interested primarily in material things invariably is on a downward path. Great wealth has ruined every nation since the day that Cheops laid the corner stone of the Great Pyramid, not because of any inherent wrong in wealth, but because it became the ideal and the idol of the people. Phoenicia, Carthage, Greece, Rome, Spain, all bear witness to this truth."

—Eleanor Roosevelt, 1927

"It takes courage to love, but pain through love is the purifying fire which those who live generously know."

—Eleanor Roosevelt, 1 April 1939

Preface and Acknowledgments

THIS BOOK WAS IN PART MADE POSSIBLE BY A MOVE-ment—led and informed by women and men who have in the past twenty years transformed the craft of biography and enlarged the contours of our learning traditions. I am proud to be part of this movement that removed women from the margins of our culture and placed them at the center of their own lives, and our field of vision. However embattled we remain, the new poetry, literature, and scholarship have enabled us to ask bolder questions about the nature of identity, relationships, and power—as they concern individuals and society.

Eleanor Roosevelt is one of the most admired and controversial women in world history, but her life was for many years obscured by closed archives and court biography. She seemed then a mythic character, larger than life and not quite human. There seemed actually to be no story beyond her dutiful marriage and her valiant precepts, both already well detailed.

Between 1958 and 1962, I met Eleanor Roosevelt several times in my capacity as president of the student government of Hunter College and then as vice-president for student affairs of the National Student Association. Each time the experience felt charged: The room simply changed when she walked into it—one felt the air fill with her vibrancy. After each meeting, there was conversation and tea. Eleanor Roosevelt was still, as she had been for so many decades, an adviser to students—an optimistic galvanizing force for activism and political commitment. She might have been one of the first heroes of the new feminist movement as it emerged during the 1970s on that account alone. But her papers were closed, and we were actually discouraged from considering Eleanor Roosevelt as a woman with independent power.

Then, in 1978, everything changed. When the Lorena Hickok papers were opened, we all learned that there were many more dimensions to Eleanor Roosevelt's life. Although her friendship with Lorena Hickok was at first taken out of context and treated meanly, the fact of a world of relationships long denied, of a hard-won struggle to live life fully, and with a flair for adventure, created for me the challenge that became this biography: Who in fact was Eleanor Roosevelt? What were the sources of her strength? What did she really think? What of the great range of her own writings? How did she actually spend her days?

To some extent this book is "a life and times" of Eleanor Roosevelt and her generation: an historical reconsideration of the events that served to define a life, a life that served to define events. To appreciate the struggles that Eleanor Roosevelt faced enables us to understand the struggles we continue to face, the political alternatives available, and the fact that on the road to political decency and personal dignity there have been no final victories.

In 1984, during a centennial celebration of ER's life, Joseph P. Lash said that Eleanor Roosevelt is infinite and timeless. Because I also believe successive generations will find additional questions to ask, different issues to explore, new interpretations to forge, I have made every effort to avoid historiographical quibbles and biographical arguments. Where I have given in to temptation, I have relegated the issue to the endnotes, along with sources and tangential historical detail.

During the decade that I researched Eleanor Roosevelt, new documents appeared and previously closed or "lost" archival sources were opened, and my gratitude to various archivists and librarians is profound. At the Library of Congress, I am as always grateful to David Wigdor. At Columbia University, I want to thank Ron Grele, director of Columbia's Oral History Project, and the ever-helpful archivists of Columbia's special collections. At the United States Archives, I am especially grateful to Milton Gustafson and the Diplomatic archivists who, along with Bill Slany, historian of the United States Department of State, helped me locate ER's entire human-rights record; indeed, the entire U.S. human-rights record for 1946–53—long closed, classified, and forgotten. At the FBI, I am thankful for historian Susan Rosenfeld Falb's many courtesies during the various Freedom of Information requests I have made over the years. At John Jay College I want especially to thank Eileen Rowland and Marilyn Lutzker.

At Oyster Bay, I want to thank John Gable, director of the Theodore Roosevelt Association; and Wallace Dailey, the curator of the Theodore Roosevelt Collection at the Houghton Library, Harvard University, which includes a vast treasure of new materials concerning ER's paternal family. Indeed, during the 1980s, the size of that collection has almost doubled. Most of my work on this project was done at the Franklin Delano Roosevelt Library in Hyde Park, New York, a most congenial research facility. I appreciate particularly the knowledgeable and generous assistance of Frances Seeber, Susan Elter, Mark Renovitch, and Paul McLaughlin.

For the use of Eleanor Roosevelt's correspondence with Isabella Selmes Ferguson Greenway King, at the Arizona Historical Society in Tucson, her son John Greenway and archivist Adelaide Elm offered most cordial assistance.

For the Esther Lape Papers in their private collection, and for their hospitality in Phoenix, I am grateful to Lape's friends Harold Clarke and Bert Drucker. For other Lape papers and many memories, I appreciate the contributions of medical historian Patricia Spain Ward, whose work on and friendship with Esther Lape is so important to our understanding of this long-ignored pioneer for health care in America.

Regarding Esther Lape, I am also grateful to Michael Sonino, Olga Bendix, and especially Margaret (Peggy) Bok Kiskadden, whose candor and political acumen enabled me to appreciate the manifold textures of the extended Lape-Roosevelt circle.

Above all, I want to thank Maureen Corr, ER's last secretary and Esther Lape's friend, for all her valuable memories, her sage advice, and an incomparable tour of Lape's estate, Saltmeadow, and home and office in Westbrook, Connecticut. Also for their hospitality during that visit, I want to thank my friends Jay and Jane Gould.

Countless people agreed to interviews, and a full bibliography will appear at the end of Volume Two of this biography. But I particularly want to thank ER's friends and family members who took significant time to meet with me.

Joseph Lash, Trude Lash, and Edna Gurewitsch were unfailingly gracious, and their insights concerning a wide range of still-controversial issues and relationships greatly enhanced my understanding. Edna Gurewitsch, for example, told me that she had it harder than many women: They might have Marilyn Monroe for a rival, she had Eleanor Roosevelt. The insights and memories of ER's granddaughter, Anna Eleanor Roosevelt Dall Seagraves ("Sisty"), were particularly helpful and I am very grateful for the hours she took out of her very busy schedule. ER's sons cordially took time during several centennial celebrations we all attended in 1984 to share with me additional memories, and I am grateful to Elliott, James, and FDR, Jr. To Franklin III (Frank Roosevelt), my deep gratitude for his support for this project, and his memories.

I am grateful to Henry Morgenthau III and Daniel O'Day for their memories of their mothers, Elinor Morgenthau and Caroline O'Day; to Ralph Disbrow Burghardt, regarding his mother, Alice Disbrow; and to Richard Disbrow and William Disbrow for their assistance and memorabilia of their aunt and sister, Alice Disbrow; to Patricia Schepps Vaill and Annis Eastman Fuller Young for their memories of Todhunter; to Vivian Cadden, Estelle Linzer, Carol Lubin, Dorothy Height, Virginia Durr, Alger Hiss, Justine Wise Polier, Ruth Gruber, and Pauli Murray for their various recollections of Eleanor Roosevelt over time.

During the course of my research I was assisted by several graduate students and friends who photocopied articles and documents, and found obscure or out-of-print books and journals in Washington, New York, Hyde Park, and Cambridge. I am profoundly grateful to Melanie Gustafson, Phyllis Lewis, Deborah Aguayo-Delgado, Elizabeth Lorde-Rollins, Susan Heske, Scott Sandage, Mindy Chateauvert, and Betty Maset. I also want to thank my friends Lisa Breskin Rudikoff and Ben and Judy Kohl for those convivial evenings in the Hyde Park area.

Over the years there were many conversations with FDR's biographers who generously shared with me their insights or research. I want to thank: Ted Morgan, Geoffrey Ward, Alfred B. Rollins, Arthur Schlesinger, Jr., and especially James MacGregor Burns, who said emphatically: "Be Bold. Above all: Be Bold."

During ER's centennial year, the conveners of the conference at San Diego, Jess Flemion and Colleen O'Connor, enabled many of us to meet together, and contribute to *Eleanor Roosevelt: An American Journey.* Also, the effort to create *Without Precedent,* an anthology of new work on Eleanor Roosevelt, edited by Joan Hoff-Wilson and Marjorie Lightman, led to many meetings, discussions, panels, and shared insights; I am very grateful to each of the participants, all of them at work on different aspects of ER and the issues that faced her generation, and ours. For their work, and our stimulating and provocative conversations I want specifically to thank Susan Ware, Lois Scharf, Bill Youngs, Maureen Beasley and Elizabeth Israels Perry.

Personally I am indebted to my family, friends, and colleagues who have lived with me and this book for over ten years.

On the East End I want to thank Phyllis Wright, who helped me make the transition from fountain pen to word processor; Deborah Ann Light for the many kindnesses of her office facilities; and Sandy Ferguson, her assistant, for her accessibility and computer knowledge. I also want to thank Lyla Hoffman for asking those most difficult questions.

My agent, Charlotte Sheedy, always more than an agent, a friend and adviser, has been forceful and encouraging from the beginning.

My original editor at Viking, Amanda Vaill, was for a decade a great help as this project unfolded and changed shape. I appreciate her wit and large vision, her encouragement and support over time. My new editor, Nan Graham, and her staff, notably Gillian Silverman, have carried through with valuable insights, and I am very grateful to them. I also appreciate Viking's astute and precise copy editors, Terry Zaroff and Kate Griggs; and the enthusiasm of Scott Edward Anderson.

My colleagues and friends at John Jay College, CUNY, have been an unfailing source of support and collegiality. I want especially to thank President Gerald Lynch, former vice-president John Collins, former dean and history chair John Cammett, and my students—both at John

Jay and the Graduate Center. In particular, I want to thank William P. T. Preston, whose many feats of friendship included a tour of ER's childhood environs—the North Shore estate area around Meadowbrook, Hempstead, and Roslyn—and an informative visit with his cousin Betty Babcock, whose mother was one of ER's rivals in New York State politics.

Over the years, Gerald Markowitz and Alice Kessler-Harris have been unfailing sources of historical vision and knowledge. I want to express my heartfelt gratitude to them for reading the entire manuscript of the once combined volumes with diligence and discernment.

Daily, my life has been enhanced by that community of scholars and biographers, poets, activists, and writers, without whom this book would not be possible. Their work has informed my own, their friendship has sustained me and emboldened my quest. In addition to those named above, I appreciate those friends and colleagues who read parts of this manuscript and enhanced in various ways this project over time: Clare Coss, Audre Lorde, Berenice Carroll, Frances Clayton, Michelle Cliff, Sandi Cooper, Judith Friedlander, Alvia Golden, Sharon Good, Lucille Field Goodman, Gloria I. Joseph, Phyllis Kriegel, Susan Koppelman, Frederica Leser, Deborah Ann Light, Jane Marcus, Midge Mackenzie, Jean Millar, Connie Murray, Adrienne Rich, Patsy Rogers, Carroll Smith-Rosenberg, Amy Swerdlow, Leslie Weisman; members of the Biography Seminar at the New York Institute of the Humanities, especially: Deidre Bair, Louise Bernikow, Louise DeSalvo, Richard Goldstone, Elizabeth Harlan, Carolyn Heilbrun, Fred Karl, Eunice Lipton, Honor Moore, Sue Schapiro, Aileen Ward, and Elizabeth Wood; and the women of Gay Women's Alternative, especially Marge Barton.

In particular for their unfailing support, I am profoundly grateful to my family, Sadonia Ecker Wiesen, Marjorie Doris Lessem, Daniel Wayne, Douglas Jed, and Clare M. Coss, who—in addition to everything else—read each draft and informed this book with her clarity, style, and vigor. Their support made this work possible when there were so many other battles to wage, so many waves to ride, so much else to do.

—Blanche Wiesen Cook
The Springs, October 1991

Contents

Eleanor Roosevelt

Introduction

"**H**er very presence lit up the room."

"She was the ugliest woman I ever saw."

"She was the most beautiful woman I ever met."

"Her voice could shatter glass; and she was so unbearably righteous."

"She changed my life, just by caring."

"Once Eleanor Roosevelt decided to ice you out you could be frozen to death."

"You don't think she was really smart, do you? I mean, she hardly understood the New Deal, and knew nothing about foreign policy."

"We were warned: If you behaved that way and said those things you'd wind up like Eleanor Roosevelt—too tall, too unattractive, too strident for any man."

"You could never invite her to dinner. You would never know quite who she would bring along—Blacks, Jews, Sapphists in slacks, rude communist youths. It was so unsettling."

"We have already had a woman in the White House. Everybody knows she was president; that was why he was called Franklin D'Eleanor Roosevelt."

"She was so open to young people, and to social and cultural changes. Even when young people became disrespectful and began wearing the oddest clothes and using foul language, Eleanor Roosevelt remained completely unruffled. She used to say: 'There are only two unacceptable four-letter words, Hate and Wars.' "

"People always made fun of her physical incapacities, and made her out to be rather awkward and feeble. But shortly after the war, I was living in Greenwich Village and we all had those long green corduroy skirts, country-style skirts, and quite the rage after all those war years without cotton. I was running for the Fifth Avenue bus, which had that marvelous open-air roof, and all of a sudden there was this long-legged woman with quite a stride running for that bus. She was much faster than I was, and I really noticed because she was wearing that same skirt. She hopped on just as the bus pulled out, and held out her long arm and with a very firm grip pulled me aboard. And I got on right into the smiling face of Eleanor Roosevelt."

"The thing is, she was so modest. She never thought of herself as exceptional or extraordinary or important. Whenever we traveled, she was genuinely surprised that people made a fuss. Once, when she returned from a tour to promote the United Nations, we landed in an airport that had laid down a red carpet and there were children with flowers and quite a display, and she said: 'Oh, look! Somebody significant must be flying in.' "

~

DURING THE DECADE I RESEARCHED AND RECONSIDERED Eleanor Roosevelt, I learned that even today, more than a hundred years after her birth and thirty years after her death, nobody is neutral about Eleanor Roosevelt. There are those who mock the person, focus on her teeth and voice and other cartoon characteristics, long before they reveal how much they despise her politics, most notably her interest in civil rights and racial justice, or in civil liberties and world peace.

Many judge her naïve because she supported "causes" and was "taken in" by united-front communists and radicals. Still others believe that she was never "duped" by radicals but actually supported united-front communists and causes, and was for decades a considerable security risk. John Edgar Hoover kept a running record of Eleanor Roosevelt's every word and activity from 1924 (when she supported the United States' entrance into the World Court and that "un-American" body the League of Nations) until her death. Indeed, ER's vast FBI file is one of the wonders of modern history.

The vigor of contempt and rage elicited by Eleanor Roosevelt continues to frame much of the discourse about women with power, access to power, or the appearance of power.

In many ways Eleanor Roosevelt remains a bellwether for our belief system. A woman who insists on her right to self-identity, a woman who creates herself over and over again, a woman of consummate power and courageous vision continues to challenge our sense of what is acceptable and what is possible. To this day, there is no agreement as to who Eleanor Roosevelt was, what she represented, or how she lived her life. Her friends and her detractors have made extravagant claims of goodness and mercy, foolishness and naïveté. She has acquired sainthood and been consigned to sinner status. Many of us, especially those of us born daughters in a world that encouraged daughters to sit along the sidelines of action, are drawn to her because of her vision and her commitment to an activist's life. She continues to haunt our memories and inspire our days, because she never gave up on life; she never stopped learning and changing. She worked to transform our world in behalf of greater dignity and more security for all people, for women and men in equal measure.

As I contemplated Eleanor Roosevelt's life, my interest in her grew. Even when her selection of words, her political decisions, her personal choices caused me to wonder or wince, or even to cringe, I recognized at every stage of her life a purposeful journey: to become brave, to communicate and to act upon what she understood.

~

BORN INTO A FAMILY RAVAGED BY THE DISEASE OF ALCO-holism and self-destruction, ER was forever attracted to people who evoked her father. She believed that we were "born to be used"; and she never minded being "used" by those who required help, or support, or simply encouragement. If her illusory father dominated many of the choices she made in her romantic life, she specifically refused to emulate the lives of her mother and her aunts. Determined to be active rather than idle, determined to be neither depressed nor long-suffering, ER turned to her great teacher, Marie Souvestre, who introduced an alternative way of being—assertive, independent, and bold.

Over time, ER mastered her teacher's special counsel: "Never be bored; and you will never be boring." For ER, every day was busy, exciting, full; and she always credited Marie Souvestre for her essential understanding of her full capacities. ER considered her school years in England (1899–1902) the "happiest years of my life," and believed that "whatever I have become since had its seeds in those three years of contact with a liberal mind and strong personality." During the 1920s, ER returned to a community of women who helped restore a sense of ambition that she had suppressed in the first decade of her marriage.

A political woman in a world ruled by men, Eleanor Roosevelt was frequently embattled. But she always agreed with British activist Emmeline Pethick-Lawrence, who said: "The only life worth living is a fighting life." A team player, surrounded by allies and hard-fighting friends, ER understood that politics was not an isolated, individualist adventure.

For all the cavils, the criticisms, and the jokes, for all her own limitations, Eleanor Roosevelt was, and is, among the most admired women in United States history. For the past ten years, the question of whether she merited admiration or censure has seemed to me far less interesting than the process of re-creating a life that has so very much to tell us about survival and activity, consciousness and change.

~

As I CONSIDERED THE PEOPLE IN ER'S LIFE WHO ENHANCED her endless quest, and accompanied her remarkable journey, her refusal to be stopped by critics and cartoonists, by enemies and rivals, her refusal even to allow occasions of betrayal and cruelty to restrain her optimism, I sensed a great and passionate commitment to life and to loving that many associate with spirituality.

For some, religion and spirituality are about sin and damnation, repression and restriction, fundamental laws to be accepted without interpretation. For others they are about community and connectedness. For some, spirituality is love, and above all a sense of responsibility, enabled by love. Eleanor Roosevelt frequently spoke and wrote about what spirituality meant to her: She participated in an undefined ethic that embraced the world community. It was not about fear and damnation, or about specific knowledge or duty. Rather: "In the infinite extent of the universe it is a direction of the heart."

This is not to imply that Eleanor Roosevelt was more a mystic than an activist. For almost fifty years, she was a very tough politician entirely at home in the smoke-filled rooms where deals were made on a daily and nasty basis. Above all, she was the leading woman politician, actually the women's "boss" of the Democratic Party. Although she later denied her share of power and influence, throughout her lifetime she was honored for her role by the women she most immediately influenced and empowered. One gets a sense of ER's political understanding in the timeless advice she offered to women working in politics in 1936:

You cannot take anything personally.

You cannot bear grudges.

You must finish the day's work when the day's work is done.

You cannot get discouraged too easily.

You have to take defeat over and over again, and pick up and go on.

Be sure of your facts.

Argue the other side with a friend until you have found the answer to every point which might be brought up against you.

Women who are willing to be leaders must stand out and be shot at. More and more they are going to do it, and more and more they should do it.

Above all, ER insisted: Every political woman needs "to develop skin as tough as rhinoceros hide!"

~

IN *TOMORROW IS NOW*, HER LAST BOOK, PUBLISHED POST-humously in 1963, she wrote that "there is no more liberating, no more exhilarating experience than to determine one's position, state it bravely and then *act boldly*." Action creates "its own courage"; and courage, she always believed, was as contagious as fear.

Her commitment to a life of engaged political action involved the most pressing and controversial issues of the twentieth century: women and power, race and class, war and peace; issues of justice, economic security, and human rights. Her views changed slowly over time. She became an antiracist activist, although she began her public career steeped in the sensibilities of the Old South, filled with distorted and ugly images of blacks and Jews. The distance she traveled on issues of race, gender, and class, her ability to stand up for what she believed, involved conscious struggle.

The 1920s was a decade of dramatic transition that shaped the course of all subsequent changes in ER's life. Politically the postwar world was realigned; and personally ER's life was momentarily shattered by her discovery of her husband's affair with her own friend and social secretary, Lucy Mercer. Their marriage endured an agonizing reappraisal that profoundly affected ER's temperament. She abandoned timidity, and a matronly caution that had made her seem remote, occasionally austere. She proceeded to meet new people, make new friends, and open her life to new adventure.

After 1920, she joined the world of postsuffrage feminist activists, notably Esther Lape and Elizabeth Read, who lived in Greenwich Village. Like Louis Howe—the only friend she fully shared with FDR—ER's best friends were public women and men, concerned as she was with the great events of political life. One of her first intimates, Howe encouraged and supported ER's personal and public quests. His counsel and advice, with that of Lape and Read, enabled her to realize the full range of her political interests and skills. Later, other friends—like Nancy Cook, Marion Dickerman, and Caroline O'Day—involved her in publishing, teaching, and business enterprises. Some, like Bernard Baruch, protected her from the treachery of political sharks and financially supported the social causes that most moved her. Others, like Earl Miller and Lorena Hickok, were there for her alone, and devoted themselves to her interests. Bodyguard and squire, Miller protected ER, filled her home with music and laughter, built her a tennis court, and taught her to dive. Hick was responsible for ER's decision to hold affirmative-action press conferences, for women journalists only, and encouraged ER to write what became one of the most popular syndicated columns in the country, "My Day."

ER's friends influenced her politically, as she influenced them: Mary McCleod Bethune, Walter White, Lillian Smith, and Pauli Murray moved her further along the road in the civil-rights struggle than she might otherwise have traveled. Her young friends in the leadership of the antifascist student movement—notably Joseph Cadden, Trude Pratt, and Joseph Lash—allowed her to consider the dimensions of radical antifascism, and to understand the perils of communist loyalties with more personal concern than she otherwise could have done. Her own shift away from a rather crude anti-Semitism and casual race consciousness depended significantly on her friendships with radical Jewish students, as well as with her contemporary friends Elinor and Henry Morgenthau, and with Carrie Chapman Catt, who in August 1933 organized a Christian Woman's Protest Against the Atrocities Suffered by Jews in Hitler's Germany. ER's crusade for freedom during and after the fascist era is a story of perseverance, and the greatest integrity.

～

SUSTAINED AND EMBOLDENED BY HER INTIMATE FRIENDS AND the wide-ranging feminist network of activist women and political men who accompanied her throughout the White House years and beyond, ER became nonconformist and followed the impulses of her own vision, and the needs of her own heart.

As I considered Eleanor Roosevelt, it was necessary to confront certain stereotypes that have limited our understanding; to turn the prism, refocus the lens, and widen the scope. A vastly enhanced picture emerges. She was a dutiful wife, and also a submissive daughter-in-law. She was an unprepared and unhappy mother, and a daughter devoted to an illusory father. She was also a woman in struggle, dedicated to modernity. A feminist leader and competitive politician, she was a woman with power who enjoyed power. She was, in her own words, "an adventurer":

> Learning and living. But they are really the same thing aren't they? There is no experience from which you can't learn something. . . . And the purpose of life, after all, is to live it, to taste experience to the utmost, to reach out eagerly and without fear for newer and richer experience.
>
> You can do that only if you have curiosity, an unquenchable spirit of adventure. The experience can have meaning only if you understand it. You can understand it only if you have arrived at some knowledge of yourself, a knowledge based on a deliberately and usually painfully acquired self-discipline, which teaches you to cast out fear and frees you for the fullest experience of the adventure of life. . . .
>
> I honor the human race. When it faces life head-on, it can almost remake itself. . . .

Eleanor Roosevelt wrote those words in January 1960, at the age of seventy-six. In *You Learn by Living,* a collection of reflective essays, she intended to explain her life's philosophy. She was moved, after all, by "an avid desire" to "experience all I could as deeply as I could."

Although she was at the center of a movement of feminists and activists during her own lifetime, Eleanor Roosevelt has only belatedly been reclaimed by contemporary feminists. When, during the first years of the 1970s, a new feminist awakening sought to rediscover the contributions of our foremothers, suffragist, philanthropist and lifelong activist Esther Lape wrote ER's daughter Anna and several others with dismay: Why do these new feminists celebrate Jane Addams, Carrie Chapman Catt, Lillian Wald, and fail even to recognize Eleanor Roosevelt?

To Esther Lape, who died in 1982 at the age of one hundred, the work and vision of an entire feminist community—a circle of intimate friends connected to Eleanor Roosevelt—seemed to be trivialized and ignored. It was in fact an historical outrage, born of closed archives, court biography, misogynist interpretation, misinformation. As in the case of the women of Bloomsbury, ER's British contemporaries, the work and the words were in the hands of sons and surrogate sons who rarely sought to address or even recognize the complex relationships of very complex lives. They tended to praise the fathers, condemn the mothers, and misunderstand the others. It would be easy to blame the sons and surrogate sons for the failure of our historical record, but that would be only partly accurate. ER, as much as Virginia Woolf or Vita Sackville-West, played a role in what we were allowed to know.

Marriages hid romances; romances were discreet and buried in archives; archives were until recently closed. Although ER kept much of the historical record, the private details of her life with others and with FDR were entirely obscured in three volumes of memoir and several autobiographical essays. With certain exceptions, such as FDR's momentous affair with Lucy Mercer, ER's appointed heirs follow her lead: If a subject appeared in her books, it appeared in theirs.

ER's memoirs were understated, self-deprecating, monuments to discretion and silence. Written during and immediately after the White House years, they reveal extremely painful truths about her own childhood, but nothing of her relations with her husband. Her friends, his friends, the intensity of love and affection that made their lives so complex and extraordinary are erased. More than that, ER never missed an opportunity to discount her influence, to minimize her power, and to discredit her work. As a young social investigator and settlement-house worker before her marriage, she did a bit—but "I feel sure I was a very poor teacher." She implied that she was lazy and capricious: "I rather imagine that by spring I was quite ready to drop all this good work and go up to the country and spend the summer in idleness and recreation!"

And so Eleanor Roosevelt consciously, determinedly, joined that historical tradition about which Muriel Rukeyser wrote:

What would happen if one woman told the truth about her life?
The world would split open.

ER herself gave us all the images of homeliness, helplessness, and inadequacy that have since become the clichés of her life. She created for the future a picture of rectitude and quietly encountered duty, of constant if not thankless service to her husband, children, and grandchildren. She told us nothing of her political ambitions or of the intimate details of her private life. And virtually every book written subsequently caters to her own presentation.

~

NOW RECENTLY OPENED ARCHIVES, ER'S FBI AND STATE DEpartment documents, and access to the letters of long-ignored friends give us another set of facts by which to interpret a woman's life. More than twenty years after her death, we discovered that for decades, ER had had a very full private life, well known to her husband, her mother-in-law, her children, and many of the scores of people who shared her intimate life and her public work.

If her heirs followed her lead and honored her discretionary code, they can hardly be faulted. But the continual almost hysterical reactions to the intimate life revealed in her correspondence (a correspondence she carefully preserved for the historical record) suggests another pattern: Our generation is as prudish as our "Victorian" forebears when faced with the real lives of historically significant women.

For over twenty years, women historians and literary critics have insisted upon the connection between the personal and the political. In the words of Virginia Woolf: "The tyrannies and servilities of the one, are the tyrannies and servilities of the other." In thinking about the personal and the political in the life of Eleanor Roosevelt, I have turned frequently to the writings of Virginia Woolf. The two were contemporaries, and they had much in common. For years their power, the complexities of their lives, and their feminism were denied to us. Even during national conferences held to celebrate her centennial year in 1984, the feminist aspects of ER's life and work were angrily rejected. Indeed, an "Eleanor Roosevelt Mobile" toured the country stripped of any photographs of her closest women friends and displayed the banner headline "Eleanor Roosevelt Was an Antifeminist."

Without her essential vision, the forcefulness of her political activism, and the details of her intimate life, Eleanor Roosevelt has been lost in an historical lie. Above all we have been denied access to that core subject so intriguing to students of life, that place where sex and power converge.

The issue of sex and power is assumed to be central to the lives of great men. When looking at the lives of great women, we continue to divide the world into saints and sinners, and we make assumptions based on race and class, even looks. White, Protestant, aristocratic, and "unattractive" women are not supposed to flourish in the political arena, and are not presumed to have sex or independently passionate interests. Regarding these women, all questions concerning that wondrous crossroads of sex and power have been traditionally disallowed.

We have tended to constrict the range of historical inquiry about women, failing even to ask life's most elemental questions. We have been encouraged to disregard the essential mysteries of a woman's life: What is energy and where does it come from? How do we channel energy—to write, to organize, to love? How do we acquire courage, develop vision, sustain power, create style? What is the connection between chronic undiagnosed illness, depression, suicide, and the refusal to acknowledge the fullness of a woman's capacities, her right to love and to lead?

Until recently, historians and literary analysts have preferred to see our great women writers and activists as asexual spinsters, odd gentlewomen who sublimated their lust in their various good works. But as we consider their true natures, we see that it was frequently their ability to express love and passion—and to surround themselves with likeminded women and men who offered support, strength, and emotional armor—that enabled them to achieve all that they did achieve. The fact is that our culture has sought to deny the truths and complexities about women's passion because it is one of the great keys to women's power.

Born in 1884, ER reached adulthood long after Queen Victoria was dead. Nevertheless, all explanations of her life have continued to assure us that she was limited by her Victorian upbringing, confined to her Victorian sensibilities. Even in 1984, a contemporary historian assured us that ER "was imprisoned in the cage of her culture."

To "encage" Eleanor Roosevelt seems to me a remarkably limited reading of a woman's life. It is not simply the language one revolts against; it is the failure to consider a woman's wants and needs, including her range of choice and freedom to have, or not to have, sex; it is the failure to consider the nature of passion, lust, and love in a woman's life.

The "true" Victorian woman was assumed to be virtuous, compliant, passive, dependent, and childlike. She was meant to have neither influence nor authority. For her, pursuing a college education was as dangerous as riding a bicycle, or a horse astride. Our culture's seemingly endless devotion to the Victorian woman is actually more about mindlessness than about sexlessness. The Victorian woman was, above all, deprived of the capacity for free thought and independence. A simple and compliant figure, she ran from ambition and refused the trappings of power.

Now nothing shatters the myth of the angel in the house, the fragrant spirit in the garden, so fundamentally as the appearance of the independently passionate woman, who chooses her mate, her partner, her lover, for reasons of her own, and according to the needs and wants of her own chemistry. The myths of Victorian prudery and purity have been history's most dependable means of social control. Class-bound and gender-related, obscured by privets and closets and vanishing documents, establishment lust has followed the dictates of establishment culture: traditionally for men only.

Eleanor Roosevelt has been a persistent victim of this effort at social control. Portrayed as a Victorian wife and mother, she has been rendered a saint without desire, an aristocratic lady without erotic imagination. We have even been told that she birthed six children because she knew nothing about the "facts" of life. But then we learn that she was a lifelong member of the Birth Control League. We have been told, over and over again, based exclusively on her daughter's casual observation, that ER considered "sex an ordeal to be borne." Beyond the fact that such a remark raises the question of FDR as a lazy and selfish lover, ER maintained a dedicated optimism concerning love: She encouraged the romances of her young friends and children, supported their divorces, provided safe havens for trysts and liaisons, and expressed relief when they stepped out of painful marriages and into new relationships. Not unlike her own mother-in-law, but with a vastly different emphasis, Eleanor Roosevelt could be quite meddlesome.

After a period of intense self-discovery, during World War I, ER forged for herself new and intimate friendships with two lesbian couples, Esther Lape and Elizabeth Read, and Nancy Cook and Marion Dickerman. Later her relationships with Earl Miller and Lorena Hickok were erotic and romantic, daring and tumultuous, though so many letters have been lost or destroyed that the full dimensions of her love will remain to some degree a mystery of interpretation. Most grievously, all of Earl Miller's long, daily letters, written from 1928 until ER's death in 1962, have disappeared without a trace.

How, then, do we assess ER's intimate life? We might begin by acknowledging that the disappearance of so many documents was not an accident, but rather a calculated denial of ER's passionate friendships. In the case of her demonstrated ardor for Lorena Hickok, the denials have been high-strung and voluble; and ER's romantic love for her younger friend Earl Miller, which began when she was forty-five and he thirty-two, has been dismissed almost without hesitation.

And yet it is now clear that ER lived a life dedicated to passion and experience. After 1920 many of her closest friends were lesbian women. She honored their relationships, and their privacy. She protected their secrets and kept her own. Women who love women, and women who love younger men have understood for generations that it was necessary to hide their love, lest they be the target of slander and cruelty. For over a century, scandal and love have seemed so entwined that it has been merely polite to love in private. The romance of the closet, and the perspective of the fortress, became necessary barricades against bigotry and pain.

In the closet, romance between women developed its own ceremonies: coded words and costumes, pinky rings and pearls, lavender and violets. The closet allowed one to avoid embarrassed smiles, discomfort, a friend's disdain, a parent's shock, a child's confusion. For some the closet was lonely and disabling. For others it was entirely satisfying and intensely romantic—its very secrecy lent additional sparkle to the game of hearts. The romance of the closet had a life of its own.

Public women of Eleanor Roosevelt's generation, long protective of their private lives, see nothing particularly valuable about our insistence, today, on greater openness. I was told quite frankly during one interview: "I have been in the closet for sixty years; why the hell should I come out for you?" During another interview, a veteran British journalist exploded: "Listen, you young reporters are wrecking everything. We had much more fun before it all started coming out." Both women believed that hateful stereotypes followed in the wake of trivializing labels. Ultimately, they argued, the public woman, no matter how talented or independent, could not be free outside the closet, and the potential for scandal threatened work, publication, and influence.

Over the years, in Greenwich Village and at Val-Kill, Eleanor Roosevelt created homes of her own, with members of her chosen family, private, distinct, separate from her husband and children. Even as First Lady, ER established a hiding house in a brownstone walk-up that she rented from Esther Lape in Greenwich Village, at 20 East 11th Street. Away from the glare of reporters and photographers, she stepped outside and moved beyond the exclusive circle of her heritage to find comfort, privacy, and satisfaction. In conventional terms, ER lived an outrageous life.

She never considered her friends or her friendships secret or shameful. Her family and her friends lived in one extended community. For decades, there was Eleanor's court and Franklin's court, which included Missy LeHand, his live-in secretary and companion. After ER's death, her friends might deny one another, in private or in print. But during her lifetime, they had to deal with one another. They sat across from one another at Christmas and Thanksgiving. They were invited to the same parties, and the same picnics.

Although ER never wrote a word for publication about the stirrings of her heart, she purposefully saved her entire correspondence with both Lorena Hickok and Esther Lape. After her death, Hickok and Lape sat around the open fire at Lape's Connecticut estate and spent hours burning letter after letter. To date, no correspondence between Esther Lape and her lifetime companion, Elizabeth Read, has been found. Although Lape had agreed to be interviewed by an archivist for ER's oral-history project, she changed her mind and sealed her interview. After Hick's death, her sister burned another packet of letters found in her home. What is left is sufficient to detail a thirty-year friendship marked by the most intense ardor for at least six years, but what has been lost is immeasurable: not only the Lape letters, but ER's correspondence with Earl Miller and Nancy Cook; the letters between Nancy Cook and Marion Dickerman; and all of Caroline O'Day's correspondence, covering a lifetime of activism and three terms as member of Congress at large.

With the documentary record in tatters, we cannot be certain about what ER felt or believed on subjects about which she remained forever elusive. We can only conclude, with Virginia Woolf: "When a subject is highly controversial—and any question about sex is that—one cannot hope to tell the truth. One can only show how one came to hold whatever opinion one does hold."

Eleanor Roosevelt never lived a sheltered or protected life. The "Victorian" world of her father, and subsequently her young uncles and aunts, involved alcoholism, adultery, child molestation, rape, abandonment. ER grew up with scandal, understood its nuances, and hated it. For years she lived according to a code of her own design created to avoid the kind of suffering she knew as a child. But by 1918 she understood that there was no code on earth that could protect her or her family against scandal and pain. So she opted for self-fulfillment and meaningful work. She pursued the course of her convictions, and determinedly ignored all the attacks made against her.

In February 1942, when her public activities as one of the most outspoken women in American public life, and her friendship and support for young radicals and Jews, were much in the headlines, ER wrote to novelist Fannie Hurst: "I am indifferent to attacks on me, but I hate to see other people hurt. However I intend to go on fighting for the things in which I believe, and will undoubtedly furnish plenty of ammunition for attacks."

ER confronted every issue that traditionally served to diminish a woman's life. She never succumbed to malaise or chronic illness; she triumphed over anorexia; and she consciously rejected suicide. She could be cold, passive-aggressive, and impatient. Never permitted to cry in public as a child, she scolded her children and grandchildren when they seemed to her emotionally self-indulgent. She once became very annoyed at a child who seemed to be crying all over the White House halls, and insisted he find a bathtub to sit in until he was through. When her own emotions were riven, she went off by herself and spent hours walking or sitting in a park. She was rarely direct or confrontational. If she ever shouted in anger or hurt, there is no record of it. For many years, however, she was accompanied wherever she went by dogs trained by Earl Miller to protect his "Lady." They snarled and barked; growled and jumped; tugged and nipped; finally, they bit people with such ferocity they had to be sent away.

ER did on several occasions take to her bed in anguish and depression. But the migraines that had plagued her adolescence and the first decade of her marriage subsided as the life she carefully knit together began to serve her: one life, one weave, dedicated to experience, adventure, and power.

But it was not power over others that she sought. Her experiences as a woman caused her to appreciate the elements of empowerment, of shared power in partnership with others. Her lifelong capacity to identify with individuals and groups in need, mistreated, misunderstood, or despised had its origins in her own struggle.

Eleanor Roosevelt was a woman of principle who understood the vagaries of politics and competition. And she always advised her friends: "If you have to compromise, be sure to compromise up!" She personally carried her commitment to liberty, individual freedom, equal rights, civil rights, and human dignity into tiny villages and hamlets as well as into the citadels of government authority.

During the first White House years, she struggled to create a New Deal for women as well as for men, and was among the first to see race relations as the primary issue America would have to confront if it were to move into its future as a united, liberal, and progressive nation. Long before her husband and most of his advisers, she publicly connected white supremacy in the United States with white supremacy in Hitler's Europe. To fathom North America's failure to respond to the Holocaust, it is necessary to reconsider Eleanor Roosevelt's early and lonely public opposition to racism in the United States, as well as her own crusade against fascism in Spain and in support of Jewish refugees from Europe—which is discussed in Volume Two of this biography.

After the White House years, Eleanor Roosevelt devoted her life to the achievement of human rights worldwide. The United Nations' Declaration of Human Rights promised dignity, political influence, and economic security to all the people of this planet. It was adopted on 10 December 1948 largely as a result of the vision, stamina, and personal diplomacy of ER, then the United States' representative to the United Nations.

For Eleanor Roosevelt, a sense of urgency for a Declaration of Human Rights was created by the Holocaust, by the victims beyond tally of that Social Darwinist category Hitler introduced into the mainstream of world politics: "Lives that are not worth living." Eleanor Roosevelt was among the first civilian witnesses to speak with Holocaust survivors, to tour concentration camps, to consider the needs of the future as mandated by that historical moment. And she wondered: "When will our consciences grow so tender that we will act to prevent human misery rather than avenge it?" In an article for *The Annals of the American Academy,* she wrote that history "clearly shows that we arrive at catastrophe by failing to meet situations—by failing to act where we should act. . . . [The] opportunity passes and the next situation always is more difficult than the last one."

ER touched the imagination of people everywhere, because she included in her vision people of all economic and social classes. The magnetism of her profound sincerity caused people to believe, with her, that there was hope for a more generous future. There was really nothing radical about her views, or her efforts. But it is amazing how radical simple decency has been made to seem.

Just as slavery mocked for so many years the Declaration of Independence, so did racism and the coils of the Cold War mock the

Declaration of Human Rights. During Dwight D. Eisenhower's administration, all efforts in behalf of international peace and human rights,
especially economic and social rights, were condemned as suspicious,
if not overtly communistic. President Eisenhower, who privately opposed the excesses of Senator Joseph McCarthy, publicly mocked ER
and noted in 1954 that opposition to the U.N.'s human-rights agreement
was an effort "to save the U.S. from Eleanor Roosevelt."

When ER was removed from her official tour of duty at the U.N.,
she walked across First Avenue and offered her time and energy to the
American Association for the United Nations. From 1953 to 1962, she
traveled around this country and around the world with her message
of peace and human dignity. ER understood that it would take as much
energy and vision, as much money and dedication, to win a war for the
intrusion of morality and decency into the international arena as it would
to win any other war.

In 1958, she wrote:

> Where, after all, do universal human rights begin? In small
> places, close to home—so close and so small they cannot be seen
> on any maps of the world. Yet they *are* the world of the individual
> persons; the neighborhood . . . ; the school or college . . . ; the
> factory, farm or office. . . . Such are the places where every man,
> woman and child seeks equal justice, equal opportunity, equal dig-
> nity without discrimination. Unless these rights have meaning there,
> they have little meaning anywhere. Without concerned citizen action
> to uphold them close to home, we shall look in vain for progress
> in the larger world.

After FDR's death on 12 April 1945, ER contemplated a return to
"private" life. But she was urgently moved by the great unfinished
agenda that faced the postwar world. After a lifetime of struggle to find
her own role, she was fearless and unencumbered. Although she refused
to run for political office, maintaining that women were still insufficiently
organized, she agreed to serve on the United States' first delegation to
the United Nations General Assembly. She called her memoir of the
postpresidential years *On My Own*, and as she embarked for London

told reporters: "For the first time in my life I can say just what I want. For your information it is wonderful to feel free."

For the rest of her days, she traveled the world in order to bear witness, to write, and to speak out: "One must never turn one's back on life. There is so much to do, so many engrossing challenges, so many heartbreaking and pressing needs."

Esther Lape, Lorena Hickok, and Earl Miller remained constant and steady companions. A most surprising assortment of friends, including Bernard Baruch, proposed marriage. But ER's life was increasingly dedicated to world politics, and her younger friends, Trude and Joseph Lash, Adlai Stevenson, and her last great friend, physician, and traveling companion, David Gurewitsch. She remained the subject of occasional criticism, and continued to attract controversy. While Secretary of State John Foster Dulles called her "more subversive and dangerous than Moscow," her own vigorous anticommunist activities astounded many. She agreed to do TV commercials for money, and her friends and enemies were finally united in disapproval. ER noted the difference: Her friends were sad that she had besmirched her reputation; her enemies were glad that she had besmirched her reputation. She taught at Brandeis University, hosted a monthly television program on the "prospects of mankind," and chaired John F. Kennedy's Presidential Commission on the Status of Women, which heralded the contemporary feminist movement; and she campaigned for world development.

Long before most of America's leadership appreciated the changing needs of this planet, ER did. She opposed the growing reliance on armaments and military solutions, and during the last weeks of her life wrote a column anticipating what remains today the primary challenge of our time:

> It has always seemed to me that we never present our case to the smaller nations in either a persuasive or interesting way. I think most people will acknowledge . . . that we have given far more military aid to these nations than economic aid. It is not very pleasant to palm off this military equipment on people who really are not looking for it. . . .
>
> In view of this, why don't we offer them something they really

want? For one thing, most of them would like food. Many of them
. . . know that wider training of their people is essential . . . and
hence a primary need is aid to their education system. . . .

Until her death on 7 November 1962, ER was committed to a liberal
vision. In *Tomorrow Is Now* she looked to the future with pragmatic
optimism. But for the future to be "more rewarding," she concluded,
the United States needed to resurrect with conviction and daring the
good American word "liberal," "which derives from the word *free*. . . .
We must cherish and honor the word *free* or it will cease to apply
to us."

~

ELEANOR ROOSEVELT'S PERSONAL AND POLITICAL JOURNEY
reflects the full range of the complex tides of the twentieth century. She
addressed the most controversial issues of state, none of which have
become any less pressing. She made the noblest values seem globally
achievable, and she believed particularly in the power of people, community by community, and in the power of ideas to transform society.
She wrote that social change required that ideas be faced with imagination, integrity, and courage. That was how she lived her life.

1. Ancestry and Heritage

THE FIRST WORDS OF ELEANOR ROOSEVELT'S MEMOIRS are: "My mother was one of the most beautiful women I have ever seen." That declaration represented an unending reproach and longing that defined the terms of her unfinished relationship with her mother, Anna Livingston Ludlow Hall, who died at twenty-nine, when Eleanor was only eight.

Anna Hall considered manners more important than feelings, and beauty most important of all. From the beginning, she made Eleanor feel homely and unloved, always outside the closed circle that embraced her two younger brothers. Anna mocked her daughter's appearance and chided her manner, calling her "Granny" because she was so serious, even at the age of two. Before company Eleanor was embarrassed to hear her mother explain that she was "a shy and solemn child." And, ER wrote, "I never smiled." From her earliest days her mother seemed to consider her doomed to social failure. And for her mother, social success was everything.

Anna was proud of her family lineage. Her maternal grandmother was Elizabeth Livingston Ludlow, a granddaughter of Chancellor Robert R. Livingston. ER remembered the matriarch vividly. Domineering and imperious, she walked with a long cane, which she banged and pointed insistently, and she always got her way. She and her relatives, the Clarksons and DePeysters, had ruled the Hudson River Valley since the seventeenth century.

New York's first Robert Livingston had sailed from Scotland in 1673, allied himself with French and Indian traders, married a Schuyler, befriended a provincial governor, and was sufficiently diplomatic to be ceded a land grant in 1686 that established him as the first lord of the manor of Livingston, 163,000 acres spanning Dutchess and Columbia counties. His grandson Philip Livingston was a signer of the Declaration of Independence. His great-grandson Robert Livingston, as chancellor of New York, presided over the inauguration of President George Washington in 1789.

Philanthropic and public-spirited, the Livingstons were also leaders of that small circle that became Knickerbocker Society. In fact, the first known effort to list America's nascent social aristocracy was made by Sara Van Brugh Livingston, who married John Jay, later to become the United States Supreme Court's first chief justice. Her dinner and supper lists, compiled beginning in 1787, were largely limited to her cousins— Alsops, Cadwaladers, DePeysters, Van Rensselaers, Van Hornes, and always other Livingstons—who continued to marry one another generation after generation, but her lists did also include over a dozen physicians and clerics. Subsequent enumerations, made by more narrow-minded folk, tended to eliminate such self-created gentry.

Shortly after the Civil War, when the new wealth of the industrial revolution provided too many aspirants to the upper reaches of society and confused the standards for entry, a Southern fop named Ward McAllister decided to codify America's aristocracy once and for all. He made distinctions between "Nobs" (old families), "Swells" (acceptable new families), and "Parvenus" (unacceptable new families). In 1872, he organized the first of Ward McAllister's "Patriarch" balls. Twenty-five illustrious Knickerbockers were chosen to sponsor this annual charity ball, and each Patriarch was asked to invite four ladies and five gentlemen of similar Patriarchal status. The Knickerbocker Society thereby numbered 250. But Ward McAllister's chief sponsor, his "Mystic Rose," was Mrs. William Astor—Caroline Webster Schermerhorn Astor— whose ballroom comfortably contained four hundred people. So it was that "The 400," as they were forevermore known, came to be assembled by Ward "Make-a-lister." The names of Mr. and Mrs. Valentine G. Hall, as well as their eldest daughter, Miss Anna Hall, are found on one of the first "400" lists ever published. Later, however, Anna Hall Roosevelt and several of her cousins and friends decided that the Patriarchs, and even Mrs. Astor, had become too democratic, and held a series of Monday and Tuesday dinner dances at Sherry's, then society's most fashionable restaurant and supper club, as well as a variety of alternative cotillions and assemblies, whose even more restricted guest lists better fitted their idea of society.

ER scorned the unregenerate elitism of her mother's family. But she failed to recognize that her father shared virtually all of their social inclinations. As ER reflected on her heritage during the last years of her life, she wrote:

> My father, Elliott Roosevelt, charming, good-looking, loved by all who came in contact with him, had a background and upbringing which were alien to my mother's pattern. . . . I doubt that the background of their respective lives could have been more different. His family was not so much concerned with Society (spelled with a big S) as with people, and these people included the newsboys from the streets of New York and the cripples whom Dr. Schaefer, one of the most noted early orthopedic surgeons, was trying to cure.

ER romanticized her father, remembering herself as "perfectly happy" whenever she was with him. She saw him as the very opposite of her mother. The fact is that when Anna Rebecca Hall married Elliott Roosevelt, he was both an eligible and ardent member of her society.

Anna was seventeen when her father, Valentine Hall, died in 1880. A dour, hypochondriachal country squire who boasted Irish roots and a phenomenal fortune, he was a religious zealot whose primary interests were satisfied by his own live-in theologian. Unlike many of his Knickerbocker colleagues, he never worked to increase the family fortune, considering his father's commercial success sufficient. After all, he was a partner (and the husband of his partner's daughter) in the firm of Tonnele and Hall, which had "unlimited credit" throughout the world and large real-estate holdings in one of the most booming and valuable neighborhoods in New York City, Sixth Avenue from 14th to 18th street.

Valentine Hall's wife and six children lived in dread of his rages, in thrall to his power, in service to his whims. Oak Terrace, the spacious family home overlooking the Hudson River, five miles north of the village of Tivoli, was a joyless place despite its virgin woods, its tennis courts, its exuberant plantings, its well-trained horses, and its extensive library. It was remembered as a solemn place, devoted to prayer and consternation. There were so many sins, and so many sinners to worry about. In this space laughter was scorned and frivolity despised. The Hall town house at 11 West 37th Street in Manhattan was also dreary, though it did occasionally host some of society's more glamorous entertainments. When the family was at home alone, however, its dark narrow rooms were filled with silence and each meal was a somber event.

However pious, Valentine Hall was not a recluse. He was an active member of society, and conscious of its requirements. Though he would not permit his wife to handle money or to shop in public, he ordered a lavish array of clothes and accessories sent to the house so that she and their daughters would have the opportunity to make appropriate selections. Mrs. Hall and the older girls were always stylishly attired in the best and most expensive fashions. Appearances for women eclipsed education, and the girls were tutored—in religion, music, and a hint of usable literature and language. They were above all taught to dance, and to walk correctly. The two oldest sisters, Anna and Elizabeth (known as Tissie), were known for their regal bearing, achieved by grueling hours of back-straightening hikes up and down the River Road with sticks across their shoulders, held by the crooks of their elbows.

When Valentine Hall died suddenly at the age of forty-six, an iron and forbidding hand was removed. Mary Livingston Ludlow Hall, who was a decade younger than her husband and had always been treated as one of the children, did not know the first thing about accounts, household management, or how to raise a family. Seventeen-year-old Anna, who seemed to share her father's religious principles, as well as his sense of propriety and discipline, tried for a time to maintain a semblance of order. But her siblings were wild and unruly, very young and very needy. Her young brothers, Valentine and Edward, twelve and nine, were uncontrollable; Edith (known as Pussie) was seven, and little Maude was only three. Anna's efforts at control were exhausting and futile. It was not at all the sort of life a belle was meant to lead.

After a year of that ordeal, she was pleased to meet the dashing, well-traveled, if somewhat eccentric Elliott Roosevelt. "I am just pining for excitement," Anna wrote Elliott. They announced their engagement in June 1883 at Algonac, the Delano home, at a party given by Laura Delano, Sara Delano Roosevelt's younger sister and one of Anna Hall's best friends.

~

THERE HAD ALWAYS BEEN SOME COMPETITION BETWEEN THE Oyster Bay branch of the Roosevelt family, from which Elliott Roosevelt descended, and the Hyde Park/Poughkeepsie branch, to which Sara Delano Roosevelt belonged by marriage. But all Roosevelts shared a common ancestor. Claes Martenszen van Rosenvelt (Nicholas son of Martin of the Rose Field) and his wife, Jannetje Samuels Thomas, landed in New Amsterdam during the 1640s. For generations the Roosevelts prospered, lived comfortably, gave to charity, married one another or their closest neighbors, and continued to broaden their financial base, if not their geographical horizon. For over a century, in fact, the Roosevelts all seemed to live, work, court, and build new homes within the confines of the neighborhood between South Street and the family business center on Maiden Lane in downtown New York.

Merchants and patriots, the Roosevelts served the revolutionary cause with distinction. As time passed, they built increasingly large homes, moved uptown, diversified their interests (from sugar-refining to hardware to plate glass to real estate and banking), and served as city aldermen and in the State Assembly and Senate.

Isaac Roosevelt, born in 1726, was known as the first American Roosevelt because he was the first to conduct his business in English and, later, because he supported George Washington, as Isaac the Patriot. He helped to found the New York Chamber of Commerce, became president of the Bank of New York, the second bank chartered in America, and built the first large-scale sugar-refinery in Manhattan, importing his raw sugar from the West Indies.

By 1800, there were over fifty Roosevelt families. Some endowed hospitals, others simply amassed ever-larger fortunes. All worked hard and lived well. James, only son of Isaac, purchased a four-hundred-acre farm in what was then the country: the property ranged from Fifth Avenue to the East River, from 110th Street to 125th Street. Wanting to become a gentleman farmer, he built stables and bred horses, cut much of the timberlands and cleared the land. But the soil was too rocky for profitable farming, and in 1819 he sold the land for $25,000 and moved north, to Poughkeepsie, becoming the first Roosevelt to leave New York City's merchant arena for the life of a country squire. One of James's many sons (he had three wives) was named Isaac, after his grandfather; he graduated from Princeton and Columbia's College of Physicians and Surgeons. But Isaac abandoned medicine to tend and extend the family estate. Eventually he married Mary Rebecca Aspinwall, the eighteen-year-old niece of his second stepmother, Harriet Howland Roosevelt. A year later, in 1828, their son, James, was born. This James Roosevelt became Sara Delano's husband—and Franklin Delano Roosevelt's father.

While Isaac the Patriot's Dutchess County descendants were cultivating their gardens, their New York City merchant cousins were buying land on Long Island and becoming known as the Hempstead and Oyster Bay Roosevelts. The Oyster Bay Roosevelts traced their lineage not to Isaac but to Cornelius Van Schaack Roosevelt and Margaret Barnhill, a Philadelphia Quaker.

Cornelius Van Schaack (CVS) Roosevelt achieved a virtual monopoly of the plate-glass importing business and bought real estate all over New York City. In addition, CVS became a director of the new Chemical Bank, and was eventually named one of the five richest men in New York. During the 1830s, CVS moved his family north to 14th Street (to what is now Union Square), and built a suitable summer residence in Oyster Bay, on Long Island Sound. His four sons (a fifth died in childhood) all had distinguished careers, in law, banking, diplomacy, and politics. Theodore Roosevelt, CVS's youngest son and father of the future president, was born in 1831. Like his brothers, Theodore was a businessman, reformer, and politician. He managed the family's plate-glass business until the firm moved entirely into finance.

Known as Greatheart, Eleanor Roosevelt's grandfather Theodore was the first humanitarian in the family. Disturbed by the increasing number of poor and homeless, Theodore Roosevelt, Sr., was a pioneer in the creation of New York's charities. He helped found the Children's Aid Society and organized a Newsboys' Lodging House. He supported efforts to train and find work for blind people. He became vice-president of the State Charities Aid Association and joined the board of United Charities. Inspired by his eldest daughter's need for medical care and physical therapy, he founded the Orthopedic Hospital. He also helped to found the Society for the Prevention of Cruelty to Animals, sponsored Miss Slattery's Night School for Little Italians, and helped to create the Metropolitan Museum of Art and the Museum of Natural History. He gave generously of his time as well as his money. Theodore Roosevelt spent every Sunday evening with the newsboys of New York City, every Monday evening visiting families in distress, and frequently visited the Orthopedic Hospital. Over time, he encouraged his children—Anna (Bamie), Theodore, Jr., Elliott, and Corinne (nicknamed Pussie— like Anna Hall's sister Edith—and later known as Conie)—to do the same.

He was also one of the most dashing men in New York society. He loved to dance and to party. Above all, he loved to careen through Central Park driving a four-in-hand at reckless speeds.

In 1853, Theodore Roosevelt, Sr.—though an abolitionist like his brothers—became the first Roosevelt to marry into a slave-owning Southern family. Martha ("Mittie") Bulloch grew up—with fourteen brothers, sisters, stepbrothers and stepsisters, and half-brothers and half-sisters—in Cobb County, Georgia, on former Cherokee lands made famous when gold was found there in 1830. The Cherokee Indians, who had already converted to Christianity and lived peacefully alongside their European neighbors, were forcibly removed and embarked on "the trail of tears"—a long westward march during which thousands died. Nine years later the town of Roswell was created by Mittie's parents and several other prominent Savannah families, on a hilltop along the Chattahoochee River. Bulloch Hall was not magnificent by local standards—but it was congenial, with four Doric columns supporting a splendid veranda that overlooked Virginia cedars and magnolias, giant oaks and mimosa. Behind this grand façade, family passions and intrigues were played out with increasing, if relative, poverty.

When Mittie married Theodore Roosevelt, her widowed mother (Martha Stewart Elliott Bulloch) and her sister Anna (Annie) moved with her from Georgia to the dark New York town house on East 20th Street to which her marriage brought her. She was eighteen—beautiful, passionate, and deeply in love—but she missed her pastoral Georgia home. When she had children, she filled their heads with images and tales of her Southern childhood—wild and romantic stories of love and loss, tales of high adventure on the turbulent seas, and blood-curdling stories of nighttime horror in the cruel and smoky swamps. Duels were fought; ships were wrecked; slaves were torn apart by wild cougars.

The violence and brutality of slavery had always been a part of Mittie's life. At Bulloch Hall there were nineteen slaves, including a butler and a coachman, a head housekeeper and a cook, as well as a personal nurse and a "little black shadow" for each child. The child consigned to Mittie slept on a straw mat on the floor of her bedroom, was at her side at all times, available to run errands—and presumably to play. But play among children under slavery was a dangerous thing. Mittie's brother Daniel Stewart Elliott was sent away to Europe for a year after he killed his "little black shadow" in a temper.*

The Civil War was a time of divided passions in Theodore Roosevelt's family. His wife was a Southern patriot, as were his wife's mother and sister, who had joined Mittie in New York City only reluctantly, and for reasons of economic need (Mrs. Bulloch had to sell four slaves to pay for her daughter's lavish wedding). Though their politics differed, Theodore welcomed his wife's relatives, who were warm, devoted, cheerful, and actually much needed in the Roosevelt household, especially after the birth of their first child, Anna (known as Bamie, and later as Bye) on 18 January 1855. The intensive care the fragile baby required

---

* Mittie's life in Georgia, at least circumstantially, was not unlike that of Margaret Mitchell's Scarlett O'Hara, and Bulloch Hall was not unlike Tara. In fact, in 1923, Mitchell, a young reporter for the Atlanta *Journal,* toured Bulloch Hall before writing *Gone With the Wind,* which was to become one of Eleanor Roosevelt's favorite books, so well did it capture, she believed, the atmosphere of her Southern family.

became the primary responsibility of Theodore and his mother-in-law, since nineteen-year-old Mittie spent months in bed depressed after her daughter's birth.

Although Grandmother Bulloch longed to return to Georgia, she was "unwilling to leave" her increasingly dependent daughter, and granddaughter Bamie, whose early efforts to walk revealed that she had Pott's disease, a form of bone tuberculosis that resulted in curvature of the spine and was at that time treated with a heavy steel brace. On 27 October 1858, another baby, Theodore, Jr., was born; then on 28 February 1860, Elliott was born; and Corinne arrived in September 1861, while the Civil War raged. With four needy toddlers and Mittie's heart torn apart, the Civil War was devastating for the Roosevelts of East 20th Street.

Grandmother Bulloch cried for three days when Port Royal fell in November 1861. She announced that she would rather die than live under a triumphant Yankee government. In October 1864, at the age of sixty-five, Martha Bulloch died after she learned that two of her sons had been killed before Richmond fell, and before she could learn that her beloved Roswell had been spared during Sherman's sweep through Georgia.

It was rumored that Mittie hung a Confederate flag out the window every time the South won a victory, and everybody knew that she and her family sent packages of contraband supplies (woolens, cosmetics, food) through the Yankee blockade via the Bahamas to relatives and friends in Georgia. Two of Mittie's brothers, James and Irvine Bulloch, were great Southern heroes. Captain James Bulloch was sent on a secret mission to England, where he designed and helped build the famous *Alabama* raider on which Irvine served with distinction until it was torpedoed.

While the Bulloch brothers fought for the Confederacy, Theodore Roosevelt—like Anna Hall's father, Valentine—hired a substitute to take his place in the Union army, for $300, which at the time satisfied the draft law. But there was no way of buying exemption from the effects of the war on his family. The right of the rich to hire the poor to do their fighting and dying during the Civil War led to the New

York City draft riots of 1863; it also influenced Theodore's son's life. Subsequently shamed by his father's failure to fight, TR became fanatical about the need for heroic military adventure.

By the end of the war, the Roosevelt household was in shambles. Mittie spent weeks in bed with unknown maladies marked by palpitations and heart pain. Young Theodore was haunted by nightmares and monsters, headaches and stomach upsets, and on occasion, an acute case of asthma, which completely incapacitated him. America's most robust president was, for many years, a maladjusted and miserable little boy. Undersized and underweight, he relied on his younger brother, Elliott, for physical protection. But Elliott too suffered from an undiagnosed disorder and fainting spells, which some of his relatives subsequently called epilepsy. Like Theodore, Corinne also had chronic but less severe asthma.

Of the children, only Bamie, Theodore, Sr.'s favorite, was free of self-induced or psychosomatic ailments. Young as she was, Bamie emerged in this period as the responsible mother-surrogate she would remain throughout her life, to the great good fortune of her siblings and her mother—who with the years had become more and more eccentric. Always forgetful and late, Mittie was now fanatic about cleanliness, and would only wear white. Not only dirt but color disturbed her. She took several baths a day, each requiring two full tubs of water—one to wash and one to rinse. Years later, Bamie recalled that her mother never went to town in the summer without "veils and dust coat, and . . . brown paper cuffs so that not a single speck of dust or smudge could touch her."

However odd Mittie was, she did become more functional after the death of her mother. When the Civil War ended, she redecorated and refurnished East 20th Street, became a leading society hostess, and assumed responsibility for her children's education, hiring new tutors for them, and taking them on a series of tours to Europe to free the spirits and enlarge the mind. In 1870 she sent Bamie off to Les Ruches, Europe's most prestigious school for aristocratic girls, located in a great park near Fontainebleau. Les Ruches's headmistress, the learned and powerful Marie Souvestre, was to figure prominently in the lives and education of several young Roosevelt women, including Eleanor.

The family's first grand tour, of 1869–70, functioned not only as a remarkable journey in behalf of language and culture but as a family reunion with the Bullochs, who had been denied amnesty and remained in exile in Liverpool after the Civil War.

This tour of the continent also revealed some startling attitudes about people and society that no survey of Theodore Roosevelt, Sr.'s charitable activities could possibly have suggested. In his *Diaries of Boyhood and Youth,* Theodore Roosevelt, Jr., noted on 14 December 1869, for example, that they climbed hills and visited castles. During a scenic lunch, "beggars came round." Father "hired one to keep off the rest," and then the family had "fun" when they tossed cakes to a crowd of beggar "boys, girls, and women."

> We tossed the cakes to them and I fed them like chickens with small pieces of cake and like chickens they ate it. Mr. Stevens kept guard with a whip with which he pretended to whip a small boy. We made them open their mouths and tossed cake into it. For a "Coup de Grace" we threw a lot of them in a place and a writhing heap of human beings. We drove on very soon in the moonlight. It was beautiful. . . . We made the crowds that we gave cakes to give three cheers for the U.S.A. before we gave them cake. . . .

A week later, on 4 January 1870, the Roosevelts went from Vesuvius to the baths of Nero, to the temples of Diana, Mercury, and Venus— where "Father tossed pennies" to the beggar children, and when a boy transgressed a rule made by Papa, "he whipped him till he cried and then gave him a sou."

After the family returned to the United States, Mittie for the first time took personal charge of her older son's effort to improve his physical capacities. Young Theodore was humiliated by his undersized and scrawny body, and was determined to best his younger brother. For months Mittie accompanied her sons to a gymnasium, where they lifted weights, heaved themselves over and under and around parallel bars, and pummeled punching bags and each other. Eventually she had a gymnasium fully outfitted on the back porch of 20 East 20th Street, where she continued to direct the proceedings.

Elliott enjoyed these bodybuilding exercises, but Theodore regarded them as sacrosanct. They enabled him to act out his wildly competitive feelings toward his taller, better-looking, more popular younger brother: "As athletes we are about equal; he rows best; I run best; he can beat me sailing or swimming; I can beat him wrestling or boxing; I am best with the rifle, he with the shotgun, &c, &c." Theodore's commitment to competition with Elliott marked their relationship far into the future.

For years the leader of the two, Elliott Roosevelt was also the most congenial child in the family. As a boy, Elliott had been considered "decidedly pretty." At two, he spoke more clearly than Theodore, and was a better athlete. "Little brother was big brother"—gracious, kind, and always generous. Eleanor Roosevelt often told the story of her father's first demonstration of generosity, which occurred when he was seven years old. One frosty evening near Christmas, Elliott went for a walk and returned without his new and much-treasured overcoat. When asked where it was, he explained that he had given it away "to a small and ragged urchin who looked cold."

By all accounts, Elliott was the most favored of the Roosevelt children. Called Nell, after the understanding, compassionate, and long-suffering little girl in Charles Dickens's *Old Curiosity Shop,* Elliott was unmarred by his brother's "aggressive egotism." Neither overbearing nor strident, he seemed always capable and charming.

But in adolescence new traits began to appear in Elliott's character—a troubling quest for pleasure, a casual sense of purpose, an inclination toward poetic introspection. Once the family geography began to change, it changed very rapidly. In 1872, thirteen-year-old Theodore Roosevelt was presented with a "double barrelled breech loading shotgun" by his father. That present revealed that young Theodore was severely myopic. Nobody had ever noticed that his range of vision had throughout his childhood been somewhat less than thirty feet. It was not until he complained that his brother and friends were always shooting things he had not noticed that spectacles were ordered. They changed his life. "I had no idea how beautiful the world was." With his spectacles and his gun, Theodore embarked on a life of killing—especially birds. During the winter of 1872, the family sailed in a luxurious *dahabeah* up the Nile. Young Theodore went off each morning to return with dead birds—ten, twelve, eighteen at a time, larks, doves, ringed plovers, large cranes, hawks, pelicans, geese—which the young naturalist proceeded to stuff. His parents were so pleased by his preoccupation with such "splendid sport," and delighted to see that his asthma had vanished, that they endured the reek of formaldehyde and other noxious chemicals. While Theodore went off to shoot, Elliott went off by himself in a small boat, which had been his present that Christmas. Alone with his notebook, he wrote verse and stories and contemplated the silence.

~

CHANGES IN THE BALANCE OF POWER BETWEEN ELLIOTT AND Theodore became even more apparent on the family's return to New York in 1873, when the Roosevelts moved from East 20th Street into their new home at 6 West 57th Street, located in what was then the northernmost neighborhood of the city. Theodore, Sr., found it "glorious to be able to go into the country at once from our door." Theodore also decided to join his brothers in the family compound at Oyster Bay in the summer of 1874. During this otherwise idyllic period, Elliott began to develop disturbing symptoms of a serious but never diagnosed condition. He fainted and had seizures. That summer, when Elliott was fourteen and Theodore, Jr., sixteen, Elliott was no longer the leader, the stronger. He confided a range of fears to his father, fears that had begun to emerge when he encountered difficulty studying German in Dresden the year before. He could not keep his mind upon his studies, and he feared he would never succeed in his father's business. "What will I become when I am a man?" Weren't there already "a very large number of partners in the store?" "I think Teedie would be the boy to put in the store if you wanted to be sure of it." Elliott wanted to be "as good as you," he wrote his father, "if it is in me. But it is hard."

Believing that travel would cure all trouble, Theodore, Sr., took Elliott for a holiday in England for the autumn season. While visiting the Bullochs, Elliott had the most severe attack to date. Theodore wrote Mittie:

It came from overexcitement but of so natural a kind that I foresee it will be very difficult to guard him from it. A pillow fight was perhaps the principal cause. . . . It produced congestion of the brain with all its attendant horrors of delirium, etc. The doctor says that there is no cause for anxiety as it is only necessary to avoid all excitements for 2 or 3 years and he will entirely outgrow it. He is perfectly well again now, but of course weak and confined to his bed. . . . Ellie's sweetness entirely won the heart of the doctor as it has that of all the servants here. . . .

The worst time was at night, when Elliott feared being alone. Theodore wrote his wife, "He is nervous although he stoutly denies it. He sleeps in my bed." Theodore suggested that when they returned it would be best for the two boys to share "the large bed in the back 3d story room. . . . I should be afraid to leave [Elliott] alone." In a subsequent letter to his older son, Theodore told him that his letters gave Ellie joy. "His first inquiry is if there is anything from Teedie. . . . You will have to assume more of the responsibilities of elder brother when we return. Ellie is anticipating all sorts of pleasure with you that he will not be able to realize, and it will require much tact on your part not to let him feel his deprivations too much. . . ."

Elliott also wrote Teedie to explain his condition. "It is so funny, my illness." The doctor had called it "hysteria." And so, Elliott wrote, "it comes from the nerves and therefore is not at all serious, but my body is getting so thin . . . , and my arms as well as my legs look like I have the strength of a baby. I jump involuntarily at the smallest sound and have a perpetual headache and [am] nearly always in low spirits. . . ."

Whatever was wrong with Elliott, whether he had a brain tumor or epilepsy, whether he was having a sexual coming-out crisis as he entered adolescence, or whether he was the one who acted out the emotional turbulence of his family, we will never know. But travel far away from his family and the rugged outdoor life did seem temporarily to heal him.

In 1875, however, Elliott decided he wanted to join his cousin and best friend, Archibald Gracie, at Saint Paul's School in New Hampshire. He applied himself and, according to Cousin Archie, "studied hard and late." But in October, he had a dreadful attack during Latin class. Without "the slightest warning," he wrote his father, "I had a bad rush of blood to my head." The pain was intolerable, and "I can't remember what happened. I believe I screamed out." In December, Archibald Gracie wrote to his mother that Elliott's "brother came up to take him home."

Elliott did not remain at home. At fifteen he was sent off to Texas with family friends, in order to rough it on the frontier. But the experience made him feel like a fraud. He wrote his father that it seemed "just a sell my being down here. . . . it's a very pleasant one but a sell nevertheless, for I feel well enough to study and instead here I am spending all your money . . . as if I was ill."

Elliott's writings during this period reveal a remarkable gender confusion. He referred to himself as a woman on the range, and wrote stories about himself in which he was disguised as a woman. However androgynous, Elliott was sent to Texas to do precisely what his brother most longed to do—hunt buffalo and other big game. He spent all day in the saddle, and was delighted by the "rough and tumble chaps" who befriended, and tempted, him. He wrote his father that he had not yet "taken a drink or a smoke" though he wanted at least to smoke. On the Texas frontier Elliott enjoyed himself "just as much as anyone ever enjoyed anything." However much this exacerbated young Theodore's obsession to best his brother, TR was always proud of this aspect of his brother's youth. He dedicated *Hunting Trips of a Ranchman* to that "keenest of sportsmen and truest of friends, my Brother, Elliott Roosevelt." TR explained that his brother "was in at the death of the great Southern herds in 1877, and had a good deal of experience in buffalo-hunting, and once or twice was charged by old bulls but never had any difficulty in either evading the charge or else killing the brute as it came on."

~

WHILE ELLIOTT GALLOPED ABOUT THE WILDERNESS, THEO-dore achieved his first social successes at Harvard, taking on the airs and costume of a well-dressed dandy. Although he evidently never learned to eat with any propriety, causing his good friend Cecil Spring-

Rice to remark subsequently that Teddy had "a variety of curious habits" (one of which was "to eat chicken like a wild animal"), he was, nevertheless, elected to the best clubs, including the exclusive Porcellian, and took great care to associate with the right people. On 15 October 1876, he wrote his family that he chose his friends entirely from the "gentleman sort." This was slow going, however, since he knew nothing of anyone's "antecedents." "On this very account, I have avoided being very intimate with the New York fellows."

The family took young Theodore's Harvard doings seriously and tried to protect him from familial tensions, including and especially his father's final illness. For three months, Elliott and his sisters cared for and nursed their father during his slow and tormented death from intestinal cancer. According to Corinne, "Elliott gave unstintedly a devotion which was so tender that it was more like that of a woman, and his young strength was poured out to help his father." Theodore, on the other hand, was shielded so successfully from this trauma that when he learned of his father's death he was devastated by the shock of it, and never forgave Elliott for not warning him of its imminence.

Afterward, Elliott agonized over his failure to contact his father's firstborn son during the fourteen-hour deathbed ordeal. While his uncles watched the dead, he was haunted by his neglect. "I lay down on the sofa in Father's dressing room but not to sleep, if only I didn't have to meet Theodore tomorrow and tell him all, and I promised if there was danger to have him there, may God forgive me."

Theodore "Greatheart" Roosevelt died at the age of forty-six on 9 February 1878. But he had been failing for some time, and had entertained thoughts of death years before, when he wrote his wife: "I feel so glad to think I have done something in life for I fear I am becoming old and lazy now. Tell Teedie and Ellie they must be prepared to take my place."

He might well have named Bamie and Corinne, who were at least as capable. But without the vote, acknowledged influence, or authority, Theodore's daughters were able to do little besides support their brothers' careers. Though Bamie and Corinne both worked politically behind the scenes and contributed significantly to American public life, they were denied access to work of their own. It galled Bamie in particular, but all the Roosevelt women expressed discontent.

One evening in March 1881, as they sat in Mittie's room, they talked about their own lives and ambitions. Bamie said she would have preferred to live in "more stirring times," when strong women had real power. Corinne wrote to her fiancé, Douglas Robinson, about that evening: "What a splendid queen she would have made. . . . With you and Teddy as prime ministers and Elliott as master of ceremonies, [Bamie] might have ruled the world!"

Eleanor Roosevelt and TR's daughter Alice were particularly inspired by Bamie. Both agreed that she would have been president had she been a man.

Denied a position of public power, Bamie nevertheless had a great influence on the political life of the country while her brother Theodore was president.

Elliott, however, was becoming increasingly mercurial and distracted—haunted and pulled by a need to escape into frivolity and excessive drinking.

2. Elliott and Anna

D ESPITE ELEANOR ROOSEVELT'S PRIVILEGED AND DIS-
tinguished heritage, her childhood was a time of anguish and
tragedy. If she was "born into a secure golden world," it was
also in the end a world shattered by disappointment, alcoholism, and
betrayal.

Anna Hall Roosevelt was twenty when she gave birth to Eleanor, a
year after she and Elliott married. Uneducated and self-indulgent, determined to cast off the limitations of her own dour childhood, and the
responsibilities she had shouldered after her father's early death, she
wanted little more than to enjoy society's youthful rituals—the round
of dances and dinners, tennis, and the hunt—available as one traveled
with the seasons from New York to Long Island to Newport. Anna was
entirely unprepared for life's sharp corners. And she knew little, if
anything, about meeting the needs and demands of her dashing and
troubled husband.

Long-suffering, apparently helpless, occasionally desperate, Anna
Hall protected and excused her husband for as long as she could. She
became bitter in the process and had very little energy for anyone else.
Overwrought and frequently exhausted, she continued, in vain, to seek
release and comfort in society's extravagances. Unable to find any real
comfort anywhere, and under ever-increasing pressures from her desperate family situation, Anna forged a hard, untouchable armor that
warned those around her to keep their distance. Once forged, that

armor seemed to her firstborn daughter created expressly for her.

As completely as she felt scolded and scorned by her mother, Eleanor felt understood and loved by her father. He encouraged his little daughter to excel, to be courageous and bold. He promoted her interests and her education. He wanted her to be self-reliant and self-fulfilled. Eleanor adored her father, but she never knew when he would abandon her, emotionally or literally. At least once, when she was six or eight, she was left standing under the canopy of his club when he had flown in for a drink and forgotten his "little Nell." There she stood waiting, holding several of his dogs on their leashes outside the Knickerbocker Club for over six hours. Finally, she saw her father, unconscious, carried out. Yet she kept waiting until a kind doorman escorted her home.

Like most children of alcoholics, Eleanor felt that she could never do enough to protect her parent, to care for him, to ward off danger, to change or try to control the situation. But she never knew when his eruptions of rage, self-pity, or despair might occur. With him, the world was always on the verge of spinning out of control, leaving her insecure and powerless. Over the years, in a variety of ways, ER re-created her father in her imagination. She brooded over his letters, romanticized his flamboyant life, and continually enhanced and intensified memories of what were only fleeting moments. The father she loved so absolutely and unconditionally was in part her own creation.

Exactly when Elliott lost his lifelong race against the effects of alcohol is unclear, but the problem began sometime during his adolescent years on the Western frontier. Almost two years after their father's death, Elliott and Theodore embarked on a jolly summer's hunting spree through the "Wild West" of Illinois, Minnesota, and Iowa. Although they never reached the "real west," beyond the Minnesota-Dakota border, they had a splendid jaunt, took incomparable risks, and almost drowned when their overloaded rowboat capsized. They hunted and met exciting frontier folk, all of whom—women and men—were attracted by Elliott's easy manner.

Their trip was marked by regular visits to Chicago, to rest and restock. There Theodore wrote a letter to Corinne that was to haunt the family's future:

We have come back here after a weeks hunting in Iowa. Elliott revels in the change to civilization—and epicurean pleasures. As soon as we got here he took some ale to get the dust out of his throat; then a milk punch because he was thirsty; a mint julep because it was hot; a brandy smash "to keep the cold out of his stomach"; and then sherry and bitters to give him an appetite. . . . Elliott says these remarks are incorrect and malevolent; but I say they pay him off for his last letter about my eating manners.

Actually, it was then still TR's health that concerned his family. Given over to dramatic bouts of asthma and "cholera morbus," he never knew when an attack would keep him up all night gasping for air, or doubled over with cramps and discomfort—"very embarrassing for a lover," he once confided to Corinne after a trip with his future wife, Alice Lee. What nobody knew was that TR had been told by a college physician during a routine examination the previous March that he had serious heart trouble and should spend his life quietly, without physical exertion of any kind. He kept this consultation secret, and vowed to live his life as vigorously as humanly possible.

TR and Alice Lee were married on his twenty-second birthday, 27 October 1880. Elliott postponed a long-planned trip to India to stand by his brother—TR had told him that, if he would not be his best man, he would have no other. The ceremony at the Unitarian Church in Brookline, Massachusetts, and the reception at the Lee home were full of flowers and sunshine, resplendent with joy. Soon after, in November, while his newly married brother remained at 57th Street with his "little pink wife" and his family, all of whom adored Alice Lee, Elliott Roosevelt embarked on a hunting trip that took him around the world. Bored, without ambition or plans, he had decided to spend part of his inheritance on a year of total self-indulgence in order to find himself. He hunted elephants and tigers and had an incomparable adventure.

From the beginning, he was treated like royalty by countless friends who dedicated themselves to his care. En route to England, he wrote his "Dear Little Mother: Everybody on board has been very kind and good to me, Mr. and Mrs. James Roosevelt, of Hyde Park (who pass for my aunt and uncle) particularly so. While I am in London their rooms are to be home."

Sara Delano and James Roosevelt were inclined to favor Elliott. They had, after all, been introduced to each other the previous April by his mother and his sister Bamie, who was Sara's dearest friend. James, then recently widowed and over fifty, had fallen in love with and proposed marriage to Bamie, who was young enough to be his daughter. But Bamie did not reciprocate his feelings. Mittie cleverly invited him to dinner with Bamie's friend Sara Delano, who was tall, beautiful, and imperious and, at twenty-six, resolved to remain a "spinster." At Mittie's, Squire James "never took his eyes off" Sara, and within the month he invited Mittie, Bamie, and Sara to his home at Springwood, in Hyde Park on the Hudson. Like Theodore and Alice Lee, Sara Delano and James Roosevelt were married in October 1880, and they spent their honeymoon aboard the *Germanic,* where they grew even closer to Elliott, whom they subsequently asked to be godfather to their son, Franklin Delano Roosevelt.

Elliott began his journey to India via England and Italy, learning Hindustani en route.

When Elliott finally arrived in India, he was surrounded by friends, many of them his chums from New York, and all of them hard-drinking, fast-living, dedicated sportsmen accustomed to luxury and service. Elliott was twenty and impressionable. It "was all too Arabian night-like." He was fascinated by the endless colonial privileges of the ruling classes, stunned by the trappings of imperial splendor, and appalled by the poverty but not particularly adverse to the servility of the impoverished classes. In fact, he rather swooned over the manners of "the quiet service—no sound of boots for the boys go without them, and the clothes make no noise. They are certainly wonderful servants. . . ." At a dinner for six in his honor, "each man has his own servant to wait on him and a boy to keep him cool. . . ." Still, he made a point of endearing himself to his host's servants, since he believed "that true judgment comes from below. . . ." And he was genuinely disturbed by their political and social situation. "The more I see of India the much more ready I am to lift up my hand and hold my breath for the future development of the world."

One of the first Americans to travel extensively throughout India and make an effort to understand its complexities, Elliott was also an enthusiastic shopper. He sent home as many of the totems of his travels and hunting expeditions as he could: hides and skins, rugs and tapestries, tiger teeth, carved boxes, and vast quantities of gold and silver. Clearly it was from her father that Eleanor derived her enthusiasm for buying and giving presents. Like him, ER would buy with precise thoughtfulness presents in great number for all of her friends and an amazing number of relatives. As Elliott wrote his mother, "I think to buy pretty things is one of the greatest pleasures in the world don't you?"

Elliott decided to return home to attend his sister Corinne's marriage to his friend and partner, Douglas Robinson. Although his time in India was thrilling, he had a profound fear of becoming isolated, unwanted, or neglected, forgotten even by his family. He earnestly courted approval, and when Corinne wrote that she both needed and wanted him to return for her wedding, he was overcome with sentiment: "I cried like your own dear little self and a perfect 'Baby' when you called me 'Father Brother.' "

Elliott began his journey home via Ceylon and China. He was ready to return, since he had been in delicate health for months. Indian fever, a mysterious and recurring malady, had wrecked his sport through the summer of 1881, from May to August, and was to plague him for the rest of his life. But his letters remained stoic and jaunty. In Ceylon he "picked up an awfully jolly little European servant. . . . I've no doubt we make a very rummy couple traveling together but all the men say he is the best servant they ever saw. . . ."

Within months of his return to New York, Elliott met and fell in love with Anna Rebecca Hall. In February 1883, Elliott wrote his thoughts on "My Love" in his diary. Rambling, romantic, repetitious, and maudlin, Elliott's diary glorified women as God's own pure invention of inspired and unselfish devotion to their male kin.

"When my worship for women began," he wrote, "I cannot tell." Perhaps it was when his "poor little Mother turned to me . . . called me her loving son and only comfort." Perhaps it was when he realized that his "two sisters unselfishly and with thoughts often only for us boys" laid aside their own lives and dedicated themselves to "our interests, our lives." Elliott's reverence for the women of his family was complicated by his fear, disdain, distrust, and hatred for "the life and character of the generality of women that I have met." Over time, in his travels, he had been hurt and disappointed by, and "learned" a "contempt" for, "thoughtless" women and "really bad women."

Now, however, in Anna Hall he had at last found "a Sweet Hearted, a true, loving Earnest Woman who lives the life she professed. Womanly in all purity, holiness and beauty an angel in tolerance, in forgiveness and in faith—My Love Thank God our Father—And in her true promise to be my wife I find the peace and happiness which God has taken from me for so long."

For Elliott, Anna Hall embodied perfection. He romanticized and mystified his fiancée—to the point of being torn by self-doubt. "She seems to me so pure and so high and ideal that in my roughness and unworthiness I do not see how I can make her happy. . . . How can any single love make up for the lavish admiration of the many."

For her part, Anna Hall also had doubts about their impending marriage. She worried that his exaggerated visions of her perfection would inevitably be disappointed. She feared his sudden explosions of jealousy. She was concerned about his morose and mercurial moods, which caused him to disappear for days, behind the locked door of his room, writing, drawing, smoking. Was he drinking as well? She did not ask, and the possibility was not mentioned.

Anna Hall did not agree to be Elliott's bride immediately. Though flattered by the vigorous pursuit of one of the most popular men about town, who had just returned from a rare round-the-world adventure, she feared his unpredictability. Eventually, however, like so many of the women of their circle, she found Elliott irresistible. Unlike Theodore, who hopped when he danced and howled when he laughed, Elliott was attractive, suave, and correct. Marriage to him promised a life of comfort, glamour and joy, a path beyond her responsibilities to her widowed mother and younger brothers and sisters. But she was not unmindful of what even then seemed certain risks, the danger of unnamed but enormous challenges.

On 8 August, shortly after their engagement was announced Anna wrote to reassure Elliott, who was in a morose mood.

All my love and ambition are now centered in you. . . . I shall indeed always tell you everything and shall not be happy unless I feel that all your troubles, joys, sins and misfortunes are to be mine too. Please never keep anything from me for fear of giving me pain or say to yourself "there can be no possible use of my telling her." Believe me, I am quite strong enough to face, with you, the storms of this life and I shall always be so happy when I know that you have told and will always tell me every thought, and I can perhaps sometimes be of use to you. . . .

I think for the future as far as I am concerned, you will have to bury [your] fierce doubts. . . .

She was nineteen; he was twenty-three. Yet the heavy, solemn tones of their correspondence reveal a specific absence of the kind of carefree, youthful gaiety they both craved.

After their engagement, Elliott's favorite aunts—Ella Bulloch (Irvine's wife) and Annie Gracie—wrote letters of congratulations in tones of such overwhelming relief that one pauses to wonder about his actual condition even in July 1883. Aunt Ella, for example, wrote: "This happiness of yours seems the direct answer to so many prayers! & I feel as if God must through it have brought you so near to him! Out of darkness into light, & joy & perfect faith again—."

Aunt Gracie (Annie Bulloch married New York banker and realtor James King Gracie) had noted in her journal that she had gone to church when Elliott returned from India in March 1882, to pray to God "to cure him." "Ellie is very ill." Ecstatic about his engagement, she warned him: "You must be very pure and very true now that you have secured the right to guard, love and cherish so sweet a girl as Anna—"

The New York Times on 2 December 1883 featured the "Roosevelt-Hall Wedding" on page 3, calling it "One of the most brilliant weddings of the season." Elliott Roosevelt and Anna Livingston Ludlow Hall represented the pinnacle, the very essence, of New York's younger society. They were the people Edith Wharton described in *The Age of Innocence*, that "little inner group of people who, during the long New York season, disported themselves together daily and nightly with apparently undiminished zest." Although Elliott had been best man and ringbearer when TR married Alice Lee, Theodore was neither best man nor even usher at Elliott's wedding. He was merely listed as one of the guests, along with scores of Astors, Gracies, Haddens, Halls, Livingstons, Ludlows, Swans, Vanderbilts, Hoyts, Tuckermans, Leavitts, Sloans, Bigelows, and Roosevelts.

This wedding was to be the last time the Roosevelts ever again gathered for a joyous occasion. Only two months later, on 14 February 1884, Mittie Bulloch Roosevelt and Alice Lee died within hours of each other, quite suddenly, Mittie of typhoid fever, Alice Lee of Bright's disease, or nephritis, which had gone unnoticed until the birth of her daughter, Alice, on 12 February.

Once again, as at the death of his father, Elliott was the son at home and in attendance, and once again, Theodore, unaware that there was any trouble, was absent. Then a New York State assemblyman, TR had remained in Albany on pressing business after receiving a first telegram that informed him he was the proud father of a healthy and beautiful baby girl. Only hours later, Elliott dispatched a second quite different telegram to his brother, and to Corinne and Douglas Robinson, who had taken a trip to Baltimore. When the Robinsons arrived in New York, Elliott greeted them at the door with a dreadful expression that distorted his face, and a message of horror: "There is a curse on this house! Mother is dying, and Alice is dying too."

Surrounded by her four children, all summoned by the sudden transformation of what had appeared to be an ordinary cold, Martha Bulloch Roosevelt died at three in the morning. Alice, just a floor away in the 57th Street house that had so recently seemed a home of increasing bounty and good fortune, died eleven hours later, at two in the afternoon. Mittie was forty-eight, Alice twenty-two. There was a double funeral service, and they were buried together in the family plot at Greenwood Cemetery in Brooklyn. The family was stunned by the shock, devastated by their losses.

Everything was changed. Elliott especially had considered his "little Motherling" his own particular charge. She had been his anchor. The struggle he had been waging against the effects of the fever he had contracted in India, and against his recurring bouts of depression, now intensified as never before.

He was for a time inconsolable, and drank with abandon. Anna, in her first month of pregnancy when the deaths occurred, was given over to her own despondency and fear. The months that followed were tense, unrelieved by any healing intimacy.

Then, on Saturday, 11 October 1884, Anna Eleanor Roosevelt was born, and the first hint of gladness returned to the troubled family. By all accounts, including her own, ER was greeted by her father with unalloyed joy. To him, she wrote, "I was a miracle from heaven." But to her mother she seemed, practically from infancy, wanting and unlovely.

Always correct and generally aloof, Anna Hall Roosevelt was not a woman of spontaneous emotion. The problems in her marriage caused her to become even more walled off from her feelings, as she struggled to ignore as much as she could and hoped always to notice less, to care less, to feel less hurt. Since to love a child is to open oneself to the most profound feelings, little Eleanor could only have seemed a threat to Anna's quest for composure. From the first she was the recipient of her mother's coldest attentions.

By contrast, Elliott Roosevelt doted upon his daughter, while his wife increasingly received the scrappier end of his attentions. He spent hours and days, entire weeks, cavorting with his friends. Even when working in New York on real-estate ventures with his brother-in-law and partner, Douglas Robinson, or in finance with his Uncle James King Gracie, he spent hours at such favorite watering holes as the Knicker-bocker Club. Then there were weekends, and frequent holidays, when all care was suspended for the pleasures of the hunt. Elliott rode to the hounds at Hempstead and played polo at Meadowbrook. Anna was not idle, but she was increasingly bored, lonely, discontent. During the spring and summer, she spent most of her time at her mother's house in Tivoli, while Elliott remained in New York and at Meadowbrook. She had no appetite; she had frequent and monumental headaches; she took to her bed for days at a time. She wrote her husband that he had ruined even her ability to sustain a tennis game: "My dear Elliott I have just come in from playing tennis and my hand is shaking so that I can hardly form a letter. Do you know that I think your influence on me must be a very weak living one. I used to be able to play tennis all day,

& now before I am through with one set I am *perfectly exhausted.* All I seem to be capable of is sitting still."

Anna's letters were full of her distress: "Though I have no news dearest Elliott, yet I sit down to write you as usual. . . . I am really not the same strong girl I used to be. . . . All I can do is sleep & yet I feel I must not give in to it too much. . . . It comes to me more & more every day how much of my liberty I have given up to you. . . ."

While Anna languished at Tivoli, with her mother, five younger siblings, infant daughter, and visitors who neither attracted nor interested her, Elliott partied frantically, with distressing consequences. Anna said only that she hoped Elliott might change his ways, and suffer less.

> Poor old Nell I was so awfully sorry for you last night. . . .
> Please remember your promise not to touch any champagne tonight.
> It is poison truly & how I dread seeing you suffer. I am still hoping
> you may change your mind & come home this afternoon. Do take
> care of your dear, dear self. Ever most lovingly Anna.
> PS Ask any one you like for Thanksgiving night. . . . Do come back
> in less pain.

Anna too enjoyed parties, and she organized countless charity balls. She was the founder and creative director of an "Amateur Comedy Club," in which she, her brother Valentine Hall, and their friends Elsie de Wolfe and "the Misses Lawrence and other well-known amateurs made histrionic successes." She liked activity, and she enjoyed engaging company. But she was embattled. More and more, she hid her rage within the confines of headaches and ennui. She became impatient and distraught. Above all, Anna was irritated by her solemn daughter, Elliott's "Little Nell," who looked about her with sorrowful eyes reflecting fully the feelings her mother could not express.

For years Anna went about resolutely covering up the situation with a layer of threadbare gaiety. She missed Elliott awfully when he was away, even though she could not stand his progressively wanton condition when they were together. They made and broke promises to each other on a regular basis. "Have you had any doubts since you left? Try to remember that I do love you and will always be true and loyal.

Goodbye again darling Boy. Goodbye from your loved Baby Wife . . ."

She worried about his health; she wondered about his activities. He rarely returned when he promised to do so. There were growing hints of scandal. She spent more and more time alone. The situation was untenable. Finally, during the spring of 1887, they decided that a change of climate, scene, and society might restore Elliott's health and their sagging marriage. Accompanied by two-and-a-half-year-old Eleanor, Eleanor's nurse, and Anna's sister Tissie (Elizabeth Hall), they boarded the *Britannic* on their way to Europe for an extended tour of the Continent.

The first day out, in the fog, the *Celtic,* an incoming steamer, rammed their ship. Suddenly they were surrounded by screams of agony and hideous sights of carnage. One child lost an arm, another child was beheaded. Many passengers were killed, hundreds injured. Elliott helped his wife, sister-in-law, and the baby nurse into a lifeboat, and then called for little Eleanor, clinging frantically to a crewman, to be dropped into his waiting arms. But Eleanor would not let go. She screamed and cried. The din all about her was terrifying. Her abiding memory was her profound fear of being dropped from the deck into her father's arms. The crewman finally freed her fingers, and Eleanor always remembered that fall, the feel of plummeting from the deck high above into the pitching lifeboat below, surrounded by "cries of terror" and shouts for help.

While newspaper accounts verify Eleanor's recollections of the fearsome din, the sight of blood and dismembered limbs, Anna Hall wrote Bamie a strangely tranquil letter of the turmoil: "The strain for a few minutes when we all thought we were sinking was fearful though there were no screams and no milling about. Everyone was perfectly quiet."

Eleanor's ship-board trauma was compounded when her parents embarked again for England, leaving her with the Gracies at Oyster Bay. Anna explained that Eleanor simply refused to join them, she was so afraid of the ocean. Anna and Elliott evidently seized the excuse to leave their two-and-a-half-year-old daughter at home. Without the immediate opportunity to face her terror again, the accident left Eleanor with a fear of heights and water that was connected to a lifelong sense of abandonment. If she had not cried, if she had not struggled, if she had not been afraid, if she had only done more and been better, she would be with her parents. This theme would be repeated again and again in her young life.

But her parents were off on a different mission, more than a holiday, and it was easier for them to have Eleanor safe in the caring company of "gentle and patient Aunt Annie Gracie, my dearly loved great-aunt." Aunt Gracie wrote Corinne that "our sweet little Eleanor" was "so little and gentle & had made such a narrow escape out of the great ocean that it made her seem doubly helpless & pathetic to us." She asked several times where "her 'dear Mamma was, & where her Papa was, & where is Aunt Tissie?' " When she was told that they had gone to Europe, she asked, " 'where is baby's home now?' I said 'baby's home is Gracewood with Uncle Bunkle & Aunt Gracie,' which seemed to entirely satisfy the sweet little darling. But as we came near the Bay . . . she said to her uncle in an anxious alarmed way 'Baby does not want to go into the water. Not in a boat.' "

Anna wrote from Paris that her first separation from her daughter was painful. "I do so long for her, but know it was wiser to leave her." And Elliott, she wrote, seemed vastly improved. Elliott indeed sounded ebullient. On 19 June, he wrote, "Dearest old Bye: If you had only been with us our joy would have been complete."

The Hall sisters, as always, were greatly admired. Anna's splendid features and luminous blue eyes inspired painters and poets. On one occasion, poet Robert Browning asked merely to gaze upon her as she had her portrait painted. "Tissie was too jolly for anything, and Anna they fell down and worshipped. She certainly never has looked so perfectly lovely or seemed so strong and well." Elliott sounded proud and happy to report that the "two girls are having that kind of a dissipated time buying dresses, hats and the Lord know what that I don't know what will become of mine or the Hall mother's credit if I don't get them into less tempting quarters soon. . . ."

On 8 July, Elliott wrote again to Bye: "We have had a glorious time. In England the girls took like wild fire and they really had a great success." He also boasted that he had "persuaded Anna to give up the

Italian Lakes and arranged a very good September in Scotland. It is selfish of me I know but I think she will enjoy it too really when once there. . . . Anna has been having a headache for six hours. . . ."

Evidently Elliott never connected his wife's headache with his cavalier insistence that they go to Scotland rather than the Italian lakes. Anna had acquiesced with the mildest of protests, and then took to her bed in agony. However pleasant their European sojourn may have been, nothing really changed. When they returned, full of promises and plans, Elliott rejoined Uncle Gracie's banking firm, and they purchased ten acres of rolling hills, virgin woodlands, and verdant meadows for a home in Hempstead, which would allow him to be closer to the Meadow Brook Club at Westbury. While their large and impressive house was being built, they rented a place nearby in order to supervise the details.

~

BY THE SPRING OF 1888 THEODORE ROOSEVELT WAS APPALLED by Elliott's dedication to the sporting life. Increasingly he blamed Anna, whom he now regarded as "utterly frivolous" and responsible for Elliott's habits. TR wrote Bye: "I do hate his Hempstead life. I don't know whether he could get along without the excitement now, but it is certainly very unhealthy, and it leads to nothing."

However much TR criticized Elliott, he shared his brother's competitive mania. He too rode to the hounds with total disregard for life and limb. He too finished the hunt, generally in the lead, no matter what the cost. Once, he remounted his horse even after it had smashed into a wall, leaving him with an arm broken in several places and a bloodied face in which shards of his eyeglasses were embedded. After several more jumps, the bones of his arm slipped down, causing it to resemble "a length of liverwurst." TR boasted that he looked "like the walls of a slaughterhouse." Still he came in just behind the huntsman. As he wrote to Henry Cabot Lodge: "I don't grudge the broken arm a bit. . . . I'm always ready to pay the piper when I've had a good dance; and every now and then I like to drink the wine of life with brandy in it."

The hunt took place on his birthday weekend in 1886, on what would have been the sixth anniversary of his marriage to Alice Lee.

Since her death, their little daughter, Alice, had been raised by her Aunt Bye; that evening was the first time in months that the two-and-a-half-year-old Alice Roosevelt had seen her father, and the vision served for years as the metaphor of their relationship. She had awaited his return at the stable with Auntie Bye. As soon as he saw his daughter, his dashing hunting-jacket torn to shreds, his head and face bleeding profusely, his arm dangling limply at his side, he jumped off his horse and ran toward her. But little Alice ran in horror. When TR caught her and held her, his bloody face grinning down into her frightened eyes, "I started screaming at this apparition and he started shaking me to shut me up, which only made me scream more. So he shook more." According to Alice, it went on that way throughout much of her life.

Later that same night, his face blistered and bruised and his arm in splints, TR presided over the Hunt Ball. Edith Carow—a childhood friend whom he was soon to marry—was his guest of honor.

On 6 November 1886, TR and Bye sailed for England for his wedding to Edith. Aboard ship TR met Cecil Spring-Rice, an instant and profound friendship developed, and TR persuaded the dapper British diplomat, who bore an amazing resemblance to Elliott, to stand as his best man on 2 December.

Whatever this substitution may reveal about TR's and Elliott's relationship, they had become almost deadly rivals. On 29 July 1888, Elliott competed with his brother in a polo match between Oyster Bay and Meadow Brook. According to Corinne, the game was uneventful until "Theodore rushed after Elliott at terrific speed as he took the ball downfield. There was a thump of horseflesh as brother tried to ride brother out. Suddenly—no one saw how—Theodore was thrown, and knocked unconscious." TR "neither moved nor stirred, and seemed like a dead man" for several minutes. He was dazed for hours, and did not fully recover for several days. His wife, Edith Carow Roosevelt, who witnessed the game without noticeable upset, had a miscarriage a week later.

The frantic pace of the summer of 1888 continued unabated as did the separations between Elliott and Anna. Elliott spent two weeks with Arch Rogers, racing on Rogers's boat, the *Bedouin*. Anna was in Newport with the Fred Vanderbilts, and then at the E. D. Morgans', where, Elliott wrote, "I am to join her tonight. I am staying at Meadow Brook Club during the week and spent one night with Aunt Annie, to see little Eleanor. . . ."

"Newport has been very gay Anna tells me. A lot of private dances . . . any number of dinners too. Meadow Brook won all the polo games and cups. . . ."

While Elliott was racing on the *Bedouin,* Anna wrote from Oyster Bay, where she was visiting TR and Edith:

My dearest old Nellie Boy I am waiting anxiously to see the papers to see if you reached New London safely. We are having lovely weather and are most comfortably settled. I am very lazy and don't come down until nine o'clock and Baby has a splendid time. Yesterday she went to Lewis West's party and this morning is to play on the beach with Alice and then she has lessons with Aunt Annie. . . . Uncle Jimmie [Gracie] wants me to tackle Mrs. James [Sara Delano Roosevelt] for a large subscription for the Orthopedic [the hospital founded by her father-in-law]. I know I shall fail but of course will try. Write when you can. I hope you are enjoying it and find the party sufficiently congenial.

Anna ended her carefree note with an expression of her abiding concern about his health: She wanted Elliott to speak to his friend and physician. "Try and persuade Dr. Lusk to come to town by Sept. 1st. Tell him how worried I am. . . ."

However distressed were the summer and autumn of 1888, in October Eleanor had a delightful birthday. She loved her presents and her party, and Elliott wrote Bye that his cunning little daughter went to bed announcing that she "loved everybody and everybody loved her."

After the Meadow Brook mishap, Elliott had a more serious accident during a charity circus at Larry Waterbury's Westchester estate. That autumn, according to his daughter's later recollections, his "rather gay, sporting life together with his work was beginning to tell on [his] health, and a bad accident when riding in an amateur circus completely broke his nerves." Elliott's leg was broken and set once, then had to be rebroken and reset. In 1937, ER wrote that she remembered that day well, "for we were alone in his room when he told me about it. Little as I was, I sensed that this was a terrible ordeal, and when he went hobbling out on crutches to the waiting doctors, I was dissolved in tears and sobbed my heart out for hours. From this illness my father never quite recovered."

The severe pain, relieved occasionally by morphine, laudanum, and ever-increasing quantities of alcohol, caused Elliott to suffer a nervous collapse.

Nonetheless, on 13 June 1889, Elliott wrote to Bye with unbridled optimism from the Knickerbocker Club. Their new home was almost completed: "Under Anna's ready hand . . . it is rapidly growing not only livable but very cosey and comfortable. . . . Anna is wonderfully well, enjoys everything, even the moving, and looks the beautiful girl she is. Little Eleanor is as happy as the day is long, plays with her kitten, the puppy and the chickens all the time, and is very dirty as a general rule." But there was a warning, indeed, an urgent plea: "I am the only 'off' member of the family and my foot is very bad yet. . . . Do come to us on your return, dear old girl, just for a little while if you can't pay us a long visit and help Anna out. I am no use on my sticks and there is so much that your cool judgment and good taste would help her in. . . ."

In the autumn of 1889, Elliott Roosevelt, Jr., was born, and ER was sent off to Anna's sisters Pussie and Tissie in Tivoli. In their letters of congratulations on the birth of baby Elliott, they wrote of Eleanor's happiness at the news of her little brother: "Totty [ER's nickname] is flourishing." Raised by a French governess, Totty was now given French lessons, which were "progressing, although I am afraid the pupil knows more than the teacher." Eleanor was a golden brown, and played in the sun each day. Pussie wrote: "It is so gorgeous up here now, the trees are one mass of red and gold. I was so glad you were not in that hunt the other day, when Mrs. Mortimer was hurt. What a risk it is every time. But *oh!* What fun! How I wish I were a man. . . ."

~

THE BIRTH OF HIS FIRST SON SEEMS TO HAVE PLUNGED Elliott deeper into depression. He worried about money, and feared that he was doomed to failure. He became suspicious of his wife, and wrote jealous notes suggesting that while he suffered at work in the city she was gay and carefree on Long Island. Throughout the autumn and winter of 1889, Anna patiently tried to comfort him in her letters: "Poor darling old Elliott . . . Please don't worry darling. Start off firmly making up your mind that you will be happy. Say to yourself that *you* know I am true, & that you will trust people. It would make you feel so much happier if you truly could, & I tell you there is *nothing* to fear. Please believe me— And as to success, remember that you are God's child. . . . I seldom worry when I tell Him everything, all my troubles."

As the Christmas season neared and Elliott chose to remain in the city even on weekends, Anna felt increasingly abandoned: "Dearest Elliott, I was so depressed when the carriage came back this afternoon with Douglas in it & without you. I actually sobbed alone in my bed & am beginning again now as I write. . . . I am anxiously waiting for a letter from you tomorrow." Anna begged him to give up drinking and drugs: "I shall never feel you are really your dear old self until you can give up all medicine and wine of every kind. I believe the latter has really led to your great difficulty in giving up morphine and laudanum. That is I believe it irritates and makes your ankle worse, as well as ruining your stomach. Do dearest throw your horrid cocktails away & don't touch anything now you are off for your health you have no business and nothing to trouble you—I wonder if this last is asking too much."

That year, Elliott decided to spend Christmas away from his family, in Bermuda. Left alone for weeks with the children, Anna hemorrhaged and took to her bed on Christmas Day. "I am so *terribly* lonely without you. I do hope you are really getting well. Not simply playing Polo & having a splendid gay old time. Perhaps your letter will tell me all. I was taken unwell Xmas morning, but got up & looked at all the presents with Eleanor. (It was very lonely) Then I kept quiet all day, but went to the News Boys dinner, where all the boys cheered you."

Anna completed her letter the next day, after receiving a note from Elliott in which he acknowledged that he felt "a little homesick." She was relieved to know he thought of them; it was their first Christmas apart. "Eleanor came wandering down when she heard the postman to know if there was a letter from you and what you said. I told her you would not be here for two weeks, & she seemed awfully disappointed but was quite satisfied when I told her you were getting well. . . ."

After his return, Elliott's behavior became so offensive that his sisters, Bye and Corinne, feared even to invite him to dinner parties. Meanwhile, Theodore was thriving. He ran a splendid though ultimately unsuccessful race for mayor of New York, which left him with high hopes for his future; and he worked on Benjamin Harrison's campaign for president, for which he was rewarded with an appointment as a United States Civil Service commissioner. He and Edith were surprised by how very much they really enjoyed Washington society. TR wrote Bye that Edith particularly "likes going round and seeing all the people—queer, social, political and otherwise."

At this point in his life, with his political star rising, TR wanted nothing to do with Elliott. On 24 January 1890, he wrote: "Darling Bye, It is a perfect nightmare about Elliott: I am distressed beyond measure at what you write. No wonder you dread having him to dinners." The nightmare was only beginning. Elliott's disease was consuming him: It challenged love, mocked adventure, destroyed hope.

3. Childhood of Tears
and Loss

FOR MONTHS ELLIOTT BROODED, AND CAST ABOUT FOR cures, relying on Dr. Lusk, who offered sage advice but little practical help. Elliott wanted to return to Europe with his family and he hoped Bye would join them in a trip that would be diverting and healing. Anna remained encouraging and faithful, but grew increasingly remote. Seeking to escape his wild, abusive behavior, as well as his self-pity and remorse, she spent time with her own friends, kept her own counsel, and became more and more emotionally withdrawn. Nobody was allowed to see her suffering. She asked no advice, sought no expert opinion. Her sisters, except for Tissie, were too young to go to for support, and Tissie was preoccupied with her new husband, Stanley Mortimer, and their new home. Her mother was increasingly concerned, and generally distraught. But there was little that she could say, really nothing she could do. Anna was on her own, and she clung desperately to a misplaced faith in Elliott's judgment.

~

ON 30 APRIL 1890, TR WROTE HIS SISTER BYE, WHO REMAINED close to Elliott's struggle. Theodore was in Washington and for months had had virtually no direct contact with his brother but was nonetheless eager to exercise some control over the situation.

I have been *very* glad to get both your recent letters; you are very good to keep us so constantly informed. Yesterday I received a perfectly ordinary letter from poor old Nell himself, it made me feel dreadfully to read it. In response I put in a line or two of . . . advice as I knew how; but of course it will do no good. He *must* leave that fool Lusk and put himself completely in the hands of some first rate man of decision . . . and unless he goes to a retreat he ought to be sent on some long trip, preferably by sea, with a doctor as companion. Anna, sweet though she is, is an impossible person to deal with. Her utterly frivolous life has, as was inevitable, eaten into her character like an acid. She does not realize and feel as other women would in her place. San Moritz would be in my opinion madness; he must get away [from the] club and social life. For you to go to Europe with them, under their guidance, would in my opinion be simple folly. Somebody must guide them; merely to follow them round would be nothing. . . .

TR wanted dramatic action to be taken. "Half measures simply put off the day, make the case more hopeless, and render the chance of public scandal greater. . . ." There is little in TR's letters at this time to indicate any real concern for Elliott, for his health, his well-being, his emotional needs or those of his family. He expressed only a vague contempt for Anna, who seemed so long-suffering, so "Chinese" in her "moral and mental" stand, which was beside and in support of her husband.

As during his adolescent trips west and his hunting voyage to India, Elliott imagined he might again escape and prove himself worthy in exile. The Elliott Roosevelts left for Germany during the summer of 1890. Their last days in New York were tense and bitter. Elliott felt abused and rejected by everyone in his family except Bye. On 21 July 1890, Elliott wrote his sister from Berlin: "For Bye only/Dearest old Bye, Your sweet note to me and your letter to Anna have both been received. You were very good to us as you always are. . . . Continue it all to her, our noble beautiful Anna. But I am not going to speak of this all again even to you. I am too sad & need no friends."

They did not stay in Germany long, continuing on to Italy, where

Eleanor Roosevelt remembered "my father acting as a gondolier, taking me out on the Venice canals, singing with the other boatmen, to my intense joy." ER loved her father's voice, and, "above all, I loved the way he treated me. He called me 'Little Nell' after the Little Nell in Dickens' *Old Curiosity Shop*. . . . Later he made me read the book, but at that time I only knew it was a term of affection, and I never doubted that I stood first in his heart."

Indeed, Elliott wrote proudly to "Dear Anna's Mother": "Eleanor is so sweet and good [with her younger brother] and really is learning to read and write for love of its making it possible to tell him stories. . . ." Together, Elliott and little Eleanor adored "the lovely music on the Canal in decorated Gondolas . . . , the delight that Eleanor and I have taken in the Lido Shore, wandering up and down looking over the blue Adriatic watching the gray surf and catching little funny crabs." But, he told his mother-in-law, "I am not, I fear, particularly well. . . ."

~

ELLIOTT HAD IN FACT BECOME IRASCIBLE, DEMANDING, thoughtless, and even cruel. He stormed and raged, then wept uncontrollably. Though his little daughter was generally protected from his most obnoxious outbursts, she did recall one unhappy incident, for which she blamed herself:

"I was given a donkey and a donkey boy so I could ride over the beautiful roads. One day the others overtook me and offered to let me go with them, but at the first steep descent which they slid down I turned pale, and preferred to stay on the high road. I can remember still the tone of disapproval in [my father's] voice." "I never knew you were a coward," he said to the five-year-old Eleanor, then he galloped ahead and left his daughter alone to ponder her failure.

All the way back, she contemplated her father's anger, and the fact that fear had caused her to disappoint him. It seemed never to occur to her, even years later, that her father's expectation had been unreasonable, and his impatience cruel. Evidently he did not pause to consider his daughter's hesitation at the steep height, so reminiscent of the dreadful day their ship sank three years before when Eleanor was dropped into the lurching lifeboat. ER recalled only that she had to conquer fear.

After Italy, the family returned to Germany, where Elliott entered a sanitarium at Graz for a cure. From there they went on to France, and another spa. Their travels and their tastes were expensive, and no treatment seemed effective. They spent over $1,200 a month, which exceeded Elliott's trust income, and they began to invade the family capital. In France, Anna began to prepare for the birth of her third child.

During much of this time, Anna remained outwardly optimistic. Often alone with her children, she struggled to provide a stable and entertaining environment. But her imaginative powers and her faith began to waver as Elliott's spirits grew more chaotic. By October, his depression had become overpowering, and finally, at Innsbruck, he seemed suicidal. In desperation, Anna turned to Bye for help:

> Elliott has been a perfect angel since he left Arles & he never tried to take anything more which I think shows how very much better he is & how much more control over himself. But Bamie I have *never* been so worried about him as for the past week he is settled into a melancholy from which nothing moves him. . . . He says you and Uncle Jimmy both told him he has irretrievably disgraced himself, which he knows you think true, so he says he cannot go home, & there is no future for him, besides which he feels that as long as he stays with us, he injures the children & myself. I was so worried I stayed another three nights fearing his mind would flee away. Yet he is as well in every way as you & I. He is the saddest object I have ever seen & so good & penitent. Ask Theodore to write him praising him for keeping straight & pulling himself together & you write me in the same vein. I am afraid he might suspect my telling you if you both write him. He also believes there is something dreadful awaiting us in the near future.

Elliott's fear of "something dreadful awaiting us" was more than prescient. Just at this time, a servant named Katy Mann, who had been employed by Anna, took legal steps to claim that she was now pregnant with Elliott's child. Evidently Katy Mann and Anna were to deliver their babies at about the same time. At first TR refused to believe Katy Mann's charges, and was profoundly relieved when Elliott denied the story absolutely. Still, TR feared the consequences of his brother's alcoholism, and he wanted him confined. If there was any hint of relapse, "he *must* go into an asylum. It is both wrong and foolish for Anna to go on living with him, and having the children with him, while he is in such a state, for he is then either insane and should be confined, or else not insane, and therefore acting with vicious and criminal selfishness."

Matters worsened when Katy Mann's charges intensified. TR wrote to Bye, who was with Anna in Paris. "Did Douglas write you that the woman claims to have a locket and some letters of Elliott's? Of course she is lying. Wynkoop is going to try to get at the truth. Whether she will make a public scandal or not no one can tell. . . ."

When Katy Mann responded to Elliott's denial by threatening to go to court and create a public scandal, TR again wrote to Bye that the family—Douglas Robinson and Uncle Gracie in particular—wanted to offer a settlement. Having seen Katy Mann, they agreed that $3,000 or $4,000 should be "allowed," for "the support of the child." TR was told that in any suit of this sort the jury sympathizes with the woman "if she can make out at all a plausible case. The character of the man is taken much into account. If it can be shown that he was apt to get drunk, or to be under the influence of opiates, or to go out of his head and become irresponsible, it would tell heavily against him. . . ." Moreover:

> Katy Mann says she can prove the other servants chaffed her about his being devoted to her, and asked her once if they had not heard his voice in her room. . . .
>
> Elliott must consider whether he is fit to go on a witness stand and be examined as to his whole way of living—his habits. . . . You know what every one who knows him would have to testify to on these points; the more intimate they were with him, the more they loved him, the worse it would be. . . .

TR agreed it would be better for Elliott to pay a "moderate sum than have his reputation shredded in court. Is it not better to be black-mailed than to have blazoned to the world the way he has been acting . . . ?" But he wrote Bye that if after talking with Elliott she were certain that he told the truth "and wish us to push the defense until the last gasp we will do it, public scandal or no public scandal."

In March, Elliott agreed to return to Graz for another effort at a cure. Anna and Bye and the children accompanied him. He also agreed to negotiate a settlement with Katy Mann, although he quibbled about the amount. Whereas at first he had denied that he had had sex with her, he now maintained that it might have happened but he had no memory of it.

~

ON 13 MARCH 1891, BYE WROTE TO TR FROM GRAZ THAT Elliott's health was somewhat restored. He rode on horseback virtually every afternoon, while she and Anna and the children took sleigh rides through the snow. They tried earnestly to enjoy what life offered, the budding springtime just barely greening, with primrose and laurel in great profusion. No matter the weather and the recreations, their lives were in a shambles.

As for his drinking, "Elliott has kept perfectly straight," Bye wrote Edith. But he "is as utterly impossible in every other way as usual which naturally leaves me with no confidence as to what he will do when not in this very quiet spot—it apparently never occurs to his mind for one instant that he is in any way responsible for anything he does, or, for what he brings on Anna. . . ."

Though Anna was only two months from delivering, Elliott had refused to consult with her regarding the travel plans he made, and refused to stop to allow her to rest during the long journey from Vienna to Paris. Indeed, "he was perfectly furious the whole day because the doctor told him Anna must break the journey at least three perhaps four times. . . . He said it was all 'Poppycock' and they could go right through it was so much trouble stopping with children. And so it goes all the time."

Nonetheless, Bye assured Edith that Eleanor seemed content. "Anna gives Eleanor writing lessons daily & she has a French governess in the morning—so she is being tutored. . . ."

TR now believed Katy Mann's story and decided that Anna and the children must be made to leave Elliott. He condemned Elliott as a "flagrant man-swine" who had abandoned all claims to decency and honor. On 20 March, Theodore sent Bye an outraged diatribe. Elliott belonged in an asylum. For Anna to remain with him was "little short of criminal." She ought not to have any more children and those she had should be brought up away from him. "Of course he was insane when he did it; but Anna has no *right* to live with him henceforth."

On 10 May, TR wrote again. In a letter full of civil-service reform, Washington politics, and his own interests and pleasures, he reported: "Douglas is in much apprehension. . . ." Katy Mann would not be easily bought off: "there seems a strong likelihood of an ugly scandal." TR mused, "If only [Elliott] could have lived quietly at Oyster Bay! I suppose such a plan would come too late now; and the same with life in the west."

As the tension over the Katy Mann affair mounted, Elliott became more depressed, and spoke of suicide. Anna and Bye left him in Graz and moved to a small house in Neuilly, near Paris, to await the birth of the new baby. Though filled with confusion, anguish, and fear, Anna tried to appear serene.

In hopes of protecting Eleanor from the bitter emotions that filled the household, she decided to send her daughter to a nearby convent school. During the carriage ride to the convent, Anna, worried about her children's future, turned to Eleanor, and gave her a long, thoughtful gaze that ER always remembered. Eleanor, not yet six, was tall for her age and suffered the fate of most prematurely tall children, who are spoken to too candidly by adults who forget how very young, needful, and vulnerable they still are. Anna took this occasion, when Eleanor was already feeling wretched about her banishment from home, to speak to her of her appearance. Although ER was an appealing child with regular features and positively lovely blue eyes, a full mouth that was not yet marked by protruding teeth, and rather glorious thick long blond hair, her mother saw only that she was not beautiful in the Hall tradition. ER looked like a Roosevelt. After careful scrutiny, Anna told her daughter: "You have no looks, so see to it that you have manners."

Eleanor was miserable at the convent school. She felt abandoned, and like her father somehow in disgrace for unnamed crimes she could not describe, unjustly treated, and entirely forlorn.

Of her agony she wrote only: "The house [in Neuilly] was small, so it was decided to put me in a convent to learn French, and to have me out of the way when the baby arrived. In those days children were expected to believe that babies dropped from Heaven. . . ."

From the depths of her exile ER longed for attention, warmth, and love. One day, she contrived to be noticed: "Finally, I fell a prey to temptation. One of the girls swallowed a penny. The excitement was great, every attention was given her, she was the center of everybody's interest. I longed to be in her place." Eleanor went to one of the sisters and told her that she too "had swallowed a penny." Although the nuns doubted her story, little Eleanor insisted it was true.

I could not be shaken, so they sent for my mother. . . . She took me away in disgrace. Understanding as I do now my mother's character, I realize how terrible it must have seemed to her to have a child who would lie!

I finally confessed to my mother, but never could explain my motives. I suppose I did not really understand them then, and certainly my mother did not understand them. . . .

My father had come home for the baby's arrival, and I am sorry to say he was causing my mother and his sister a great deal of anxiety—but he was the only person who did not treat me as a criminal!

Meanwhile, Anna had ceased to be able to protect Elliott from his family's wrath. TR insisted that Elliott be put away. Nor was she any longer able to protect herself or Elliott from the ravages of his disease. Now he disappeared for days at a time, only to return even more depressed, apologetic, repentant.

Every day brought new details, and each day was worse than the day before. During his wife's confinement, Elliott evidently began an affair with a well-traveled and sophisticated American woman, the mother of two children, Florence Bagley Sherman. Although Anna did not know of this relationship, she was undone by his new behavior, his oddly secretive ways, his unconscionable and ever more frequent disappearances.

Elliott's letters during these dreadful weeks were written mostly to his mother-in-law. They were rhapsodies of an idyllic time: He and Anna walked each morning in the beautiful park of the château. The weather was lovely, and they "read for two hours at a time while the children play." Eleanor was sent to the local school in the mornings, but joined them each afternoon and was pleased to feed the fishes and the ducks. "Sometimes in the afternoon Anna and I drive a jolly little pair of ponies we found at a Livery Stable down along the banks of the Seine or through the grand old forest."

Elliott looked forward to their return to Paris, and concluded: "Mother dear I will take good care of your sweet Daughter *own* darling Anna you may be sure that no accident shall come to her from fault of mine. She is my only friend my precious Wife. The children are so happy and little Boy gets more enchanting every day. Eleanor too I think. Give my love to all. . . ." After the birth of his son Gracie Hall, on 2 June 1891, he wrote, "Dear Mother, all is over and Anna our darling girl is well & the Boy is the biggest thing you ever saw and kissed me like a little bird the first hour of his life. . . . Her pains and all did not take three hours. . . . Bamie was very sweet & the doctor a *wonder.* The little wife looks so sweet & *well.* Good bye Mother . . . Try to love and trust your devoted son in law. . . ."

~

FOR ANTIDOTE TO ELLIOTT'S EFFERVESCENCE, TR HAD THE benefit of Bye's candid accounts and wrote to her on 7 June:

> My own dearest sister, the strain under which you are living is like a hideous nightmare even to hear about. Your last letter in which you describe Anna's hysterical attack due to Elliott's violence, is the most frightening of all. His curious callousness and selfishness, his disregard of your words and my letters, and his light-heartedness under them, make one feel hopeless about him.

TR was adamant: Immediately after Anna's confinement, the family would isolate and institutionalize Elliott. Anna had to be persuaded that the situation was hopeless. Her continued faith in Elliott's ability to recuperate was madness. TR considered it "both maudlin and criminal—I am choosing my words with scientific exactness—to continue living with Elliott. . . .

"Make up your mind to one dreadful scene," he wrote Bye. "Tell him he is either responsible or irresponsible. If irresponsible then he must go where he can be cured; if responsible he is simply a selfish, brutal and vicious criminal. . . . If you need me telegraph for me. . . . But remember I come on but one condition. I come to settle the thing once for all. I come to see that Elliott is either put in an asylum, against his will or not, or else to take you, Anna and the children away and to turn Elliott loose to shift for himself. You can tell him that Anna has a perfect right to a divorce; she—or you and I—have but to express belief in the Katy Mann story. . . ."

As soon as Anna was ready to travel, she, Bye, and the three young children sailed for home. Elliott was left in the asylum at Château Suresnes, near Paris, where he had been before Hall's birth. Their departure was marked by bitterness and resentment on both sides. Elliott later protested that he had been "kidnapped." The rest of that summer of 1891 was devoted to legal details regarding the Katy Mann settlement,* and the legal effort to have Elliott declared incompetent and insane.

TR was now unrelenting. He considered his brother "a maniac, morally no less than mentally." Nobody owed him the least consideration. He must be abandoned, discarded. The only consideration was now the safety of Anna and the children. TR worried that Elliott would "try to kidnap" them. He dreaded also "to think of the inheritance the

---

* Katy Mann had asked for $10,000. Whatever settlement was reached, there is now evidence that Katy Mann received no money, and that whatever money was put in trust for her son was presumed "stolen" by the attorneys. On 26 November 1932, Elliott Roosevelt Mann and his mother wrote ER a letter of congratulations on the election results. ER responded: "I was very interested to receive your letter and to learn that you were named after my father. . . . I shall hope sometime to see both you and your mother." According to Eleanor Mann Biles, the granddaughter of Katy Mann, no invitation was ever extended, nor was any further correspondence answered. See notes, page 510.

poor little baby may have in him." And he wanted Anna to get a divorce. Any other decision would be "criminal." The family had hired an expert on likenesses, who saw Katy Mann's baby and had to conclude that "K.M.'s story is true. . . ." TR was outraged "that Anna should have been so foolish as to insist on Elliott's being sent for when her baby was being born. . . ." But Anna continued to believe that Elliott was curable and refused to get a divorce.

Elliott's capacity for self-delusion also remained endless. Even though he suffered delirium tremens, and was emotionally and physically ravaged, he wrote TR a letter that "dumbfounded" his brother. There was no mention of the bitterness surrounding Anna's departure, or of his wild threats to end all support for his wife and children should they leave. He wrote merely to criticize Bye for being "under the Doctor's thumb."

Elliott's financial threats caused TR to demand a lawsuit that would declare Elliott "incapable of taking care of his property." The effort to declare Elliott incompetent and insane divided the family and shattered their spirits. It coincided with a serious economic crisis, which wrecked TR's finances during the recession of 1891–92. The recession culminated in the panic of 1893, which also blasted many of Elliott's holdings. TR's own economic situation during 1892–93 was so dire that he contemplated the sale of his beloved home on Sagamore Hill above Oyster Bay and feared for the future of his political career. Paper money had become so tight that Edith Roosevelt paid the servants in gold. She also feared that her extravagant household management had contributed to the problem, and decided to compensate by making her own tooth powder out of "ground-up cuttlefish bones, dragon's blood, burnt alum, arris root," and fragrances.

Throughout this entire period, Anna struggled desperately against medical advice, TR's bullying, and what must have been her own doubts to persuade his family that Elliott was curable. She stood virtually alone in her effort to find an alternative and loving approach to Elliott's treatment. Only when Elliott became uncontrollable and vindictive, did she agree to leave him in the Château Suresnes, and consent to TR's suit to establish a trust that would protect her children's financial interests. But she continued to hope for Elliott's recovery, and to worry about his peace of mind. All the legal confusion, the clashes between Elliott's representatives and Theodore's, were "awful, & very bad for E." The tension was so great that she had chronic headaches and even began to shout. She apologized to Bye for one such outburst: "I am awfully sorry I lost my temper & think I must be unbearable & very irritating at present to everyone."

Anna had become completely reliant on Bye's opinion, and was now unsure of her ability to deal with Elliott. She no longer knew how to answer Elliott's letters, and sent her replies first to Bye for advice and scrutiny. If Bye approved them, they were mailed. Anna tried to write Elliott only affectionate sentiments, but even these were sometimes met with baseless rantings, dastardly screeds. "His letter is certainly that of a mad man. First he flings the most abominable charges against me [including marital infidelity—he even demanded to know if baby Hall was really his child]. Then says I am a Noble Woman & he trusts me entirely. What do you think I ought to do. Ask Corinne and Douglas." She could demand that he write to retract each word or "I would try & prove him a dangerous lunatic. And yet his letter is so hopelessly sad & I long to help him, not to make him suffer more. And yet I feel I ought not on his account pass this over again. . . ."

~

AND THERE WERE SO MANY OTHER PROBLEMS. FOR INSTANCE, "I am afraid the wet nurse is giving out." Above all there was the dreadful press coverage. On 18 August the New York *Herald* announced:

ELLIOTT ROOSEVELT DEMENTED BY EXCESSES.
Wrecked by Liquor and Folly, He is Now Confined
in an Asylum for the Insane near Paris
Proceedings to Save the Estate
Commissioners in Lunacy Appointed on Petition of his Brother
Theodore and His Sister Anna
with his Wife's Approval

The headlines screamed her shame, ravaged her family's honor, ruined all hope for privacy. To suffer so in public was simply unbearable. And still she tried to protect Elliott: "I have tried to write Elliott as though I had not seen [the newspaper stories]. Do you think this deceitful? Not right? . . ."

Elliott struggled to salvage his reputation. On 21 August, his letter to the editor in the European edition of the *Herald,* was reprinted in the New York paper, denying that he was the subject of proceedings:

> You publish in your edition today a most astounding bit of mis-information under the title "Is Mr. Elliott Roosevelt To Be Adjudged A Lunatic?" I wish emphatically to state that my brother Theodore is taking no steps to have a commission pass on my sanity with or without my wife's approval. I am in Paris taking the cure at an establissement hydrothérapeutique, which my nerves shaken by sev-eral severe accidents in the hunting field, made necessary. My wife went home at my request to spend the summer with her mother, Paris not being a good place for children during the hot months. I hope you will give this letter as great prominence as you today gave the invention—or worse—of your misinformant.
>
> Elliott Roosevelt
> Paris, 18 August 1891

When his Uncle Jimmie Gracie read his letter in the newspaper, he tried to derail the suit. Although TR remained unwavering, the effort to declare Elliott insane was eventually suspended by quarrels within the family and disagreement among the doctors. Anna had always been less than enthusiastic, and TR could not sustain a public scandal that now lacked even the appearance of family unity.

Weighed down by what TR called "a nightmare of horror," Anna nevertheless made every effort to provide her children a normal and active life. She resumed her social activities, and her charity work. In November, she moved into a new and more comfortable house at 54 East 61st Street. A change of scene, the chance to furnish a new home and resettle, seemed a pleasant diversion. She was closer to Bye's home at 62nd Street and Madison Avenue. Publicly she behaved as if her circumstances were ordinary. But she was frequently depressed, and often took to her bed with excruciating headaches. They were the kind of migraines that ate up her days, and her spirit.

Eleanor recalled that we "lived that winter without my father." She had whooping cough, and a series of colds, as she evidently did each winter; but she was allowed to study with the children of Mr. and Mrs. Cleveland Dodge, "so time did not hang altogether heavy on my hands." Above all, Eleanor felt closer to her mother during that winter than ever before. She sensed that her mother needed her, and wanted her close by. For the first time she felt useful and worthy in her mother's eyes. Eleanor wrote in her memoirs:

> I slept in my mother's room, and remember well the thrill of watching her dress to go out in the evenings. She looked so beautiful, I was grateful to be allowed to touch her dress or her jewels or anything that was part of the vision which I admired inordinately.
>
> My mother suffered from very bad headaches, and I know now that life must have been hard and bitter and a very great strain on her. I would often sit at the head of her bed and stroke her head. People have since told me that I have good hands for rubbing, and perhaps even as a child there was something soothing in my touch, for she was willing to let me sit there for hours on end.
>
> As with all children, the feeling that I was useful was perhaps the greatest joy I experienced.

These moments of intimacy were important to Eleanor. They were the only loving moments with her mother she remembered. The "hours on end" she spent rubbing her mother's headache away did not pass entirely in silence. Did Anna tell Eleanor nothing of her feelings or their origins? The adult Eleanor tells us only:

> Sometimes I woke up when my mother and her sisters were talking at bed time, and many a conversation which was not meant for my ears was listened to with great avidity.
>
> I acquired a strange and garbled idea of the troubles which were going on around me. Something was wrong with my father, and from my point of view nothing could be wrong with him.

One day at Tivoli, while Eleanor was visiting her Great-Aunt Elizabeth Ludlow, "whose house was next to ours but nearer the river and quite out of sight," Mrs. Ludlow discovered to her dismay that her seven-year-old great-niece could not read at all. "The very next day and every day thereafter that summer she sent her companion to give me lessons in reading, and then she found out that I could not sew and could not cook and knew none of the things a girl should know!" The tutor her aunt sent over was an Alsatian martinet named Madeleine— stern, unsmiling, and impatient; ER hated her for years. She did, however, teach Eleanor to sew and to read, but never to cook. Every morning, Eleanor repeated to her mother whatever verse in the Old or New Testament she had read and memorized the day before.

ER surmised that her "mother was roundly taken to task" for her daughter's prolonged illiteracy, but she diligently made up for it. Anna monitored her daughter's lessons for hours each day, corrected her spelling, supervised her reading, and read aloud to her three children every afternoon.

Anna also created a schoolroom on the third floor of her new home, where Eleanor and several children of Anna's closest friends would be systematically tutored. She hired Frederic Roser and his assistant Miss Tomes, who were highly regarded by fashionable society as perfect educators. Steeped in Social Darwinist ethics, devoted to McGuffey's *Readers,* Mr. Roser was rigid and formal, pompous and dapper.

Eleanor craved her mother's approval and sought comfort in her company. But she was continually disappointed. No matter what she did, it was never enough really to please Anna. She remembered instead: "I was always disgracing my mother." Even during those precious hours Anna devoted each afternoon to her children, Eleanor always felt a "curious barrier between myself and these three"—her mother and two baby brothers. "Little Ellie . . . was so good he never had to be reproved," and baby Hall "was too small to do anything but sit upon her lap contentedly." Eleanor acknowledged that her mother "made a great effort for me, she would read to me and have me read to her, she would have me recite my poems, she would keep me after the boys had gone to bed, and still I can remember standing in the door, very often with my finger in my mouth—which was, of course, forbidden—and I can see the look in her eyes and hear the tone of her voice as she said: 'Come in, Granny.' "

Anna's disapproval of her daughter's solemnity reflected her own unwillingness to give in to the grave emotions that devastated her heart. Anna turned aside and rejected the feelings Eleanor's eyes revealed. Every time Eleanor thought back to her mother, she remembered her glib dismissal: " 'She is such a funny child, so old-fashioned, that we always call her "Granny." ' " Eleanor "wanted to sink through the floor in shame."

Anna Hall Roosevelt wanted life to go on. Profoundly alone, she was neither a widow nor a divorcee. She agonized over whether to go to balls, to remain active and social. She confided to Bye: "It is an awful temptation when one feels desperately lonely and wildly furious with the world at large, not to make up one's mind to pay no attention to criticism as long as one does no wrong and to try to get some fun out of the few years of our youth. I hate everything and everyone so and am most of the time so miserable that I feel anything one could do would be a comfort to forget for one moment." She wanted to do what was correct and caring, but the situation was out of hand. She tried to ignore her feelings, and dance through the night. But every day little Eleanor's gaze betrayed Anna's loneliness and desperation.

Moreover, Eleanor was an independent and willful child. Since Anna never took her into her confidence, she created a life of her own. Eleanor understood only that her home was a battlefield. Mother and daughter might have been allies, but Anna's silence discouraged that, and so she became the enemy. Too obedient to be a brat, and too quiet to be much fun, Eleanor sulked, pouted, studied the situation, and seemed to know all. She looked accusingly at Anna. She blamed her mother for her father's disappearance, and for all her unhappiness. The adult Eleanor always believed that it would have been better if her mother had told her more: "If people only realized what a war goes on in a child's mind and heart in a situation of this kind, I think they would try to explain more than they do, but nobody told me anything."

Anna sought instead to protect her children. She had no intention of turning her daughter away from Elliott, of betraying the unquestioning devotion Eleanor felt for her father. It might have been easier for Anna if she had. But, with enormous self-control, even as those clear blue eyes gazed at her with such hatred and misunderstanding, even as they reflected her own pain and suffering, Anna said nothing.

Over time, Eleanor went from solemnity to sullenness; she became stubborn and spiteful. One day, during class, when Anna and several other mothers were present, Mr. Roser called on Eleanor to spell the simplest words, words she knew. She stood to answer but was overcome by a strange sensation that silenced her. She stood there in agony, the room heavy with anxiety and shame, until she was asked to sit down. Her mother took her aside and whispered severely in her ear that she feared to think "what would happen if I did not mend my ways!"

Eleanor did things her mother forbade her to do. She put sugar on her cereal, lied about her behavior, stole candy meant for dinner guests by the entire bagful out of the pantry. When her mother tried to get her to parties with other children, she resisted and burst into wild sobbing. On several occasions, she had utterly unbecoming and embarrassing tantrums in public. As an adult, Eleanor wrote: "I now realize I was a great trial to my mother."

But her mother had far greater trials to endure. During Elliott's stay at Château Suresnes, with his wife and children back in New York, his liaison with Mrs. Sherman deepened. From September 1891 to January 1892, all negotiations regarding Elliott were on hold.

TR wrote to Bye on 2 September: "I fear that Elliott when he comes out would repudiate any agreement, and bring a suit for conspiracy. . . ." Coincidentally, TR went on a hunting excursion in October and "killed nine elk in four weeks." At the same time the murder of two U.S. sailors in Valparaiso made him lust for a preventive war against Chile. He was disgusted when the United States asked merely for an apology. President Harrison's Secretary of State John Hay wrote to their mutual friend Henry Adams that "Teddy Roosevelt . . . goes about hissing through his clenched teeth that we are dishonest. For two nickels he would declare war himself, shut up the Civil Service Commission, and wage it sole."

Spoiling for a fight, on 9 January 1892, TR sailed for France to confront Elliott face to face. After a week of browbeating, moral rectitude, specific threats, and familial blandishments, TR persuaded his brother to create a trust fund for his wife and children, and to return to the United States, where he would be confined in a treatment center for a year, and then prove himself worthy by a period of two or three years' probation marked by meaningful work. During that time he would live alone, apart from his family. One can only imagine the scene. Day after day, hours and hours on end: What would Father think of you? Consider your dear sainted mother. You bring disgrace and disaster upon the entire family. Your wife. Your children. Our good name.

On 21 January, TR wrote Bye: "Won! Thank Heaven I came over. . . ."

Once Elliott agreed, he seemed "absolutely changed." He "surrendered completely, and was utterly broken, submissive and repentant. He signed the deed for two-thirds of *all* his property (including the $60,000 trust); and agreed to the probation. I then instantly changed my whole manner, and treated him with the utmost love and tenderness. I told him we would do all we legitimately could to help him to get through his two years (or thereabouts) of probation; that our one object now would be to see him entirely restored to himself; and so to his wife and children. He today attempted no justification; he acknowledged how grievously he had sinned; and said he would do all in his power to prove himself really reformed. He was in a mood that was terribly touching. How long it will last of course no one can say."

On 28 January, Mrs. Sherman wrote in her journal a different version of Elliott's last days in Paris:

This morning, with his silk hat, his overcoat, gloves and cigar E came to my room to say goodbye. It is all over, only my little black Dick [the dog Elliott had given her], who cries at the door of the empty room and howls in the park, he is all there is left to me. So ends the final and great emotion of my life. "The memory of what has been, and never more shall be" is all the future holds. Now my love was swallowed up in pity—for he looks so bruised so beaten down by the past week with his brother. How could they treat so generous and noble a man as they have. He is more noble a figure in my eyes, with all his confessed faults, than either his wife or brother. She is more to be despised, in her virtuous pride, her absolutely selfish position than the most miserable woman I know. But she is the result of an unintelligent, petty, common timid social life. . . . If she were only large-souled enough to appreciate him.

At some point during Elliott's ordeal, he wrote a curiously revealing suicidal story that takes place in Paris and details the last days of an elegant woman, Sophie Vedder, whose life has been lived for pleasure, and entirely wasted. At the end she is penniless, indebted, and lonely, although surrounded by many friends who offer her help, and try to save her. Written in the first-person voice of a woman, "Was Miss Vedder an Adventuress?" presents Elliott's philosophy of life:

"Live and let live" I say, "Never miss an opportunity of enjoying life, no matter at what cost, and when the end comes, well take it cheerfully. Strauss is going to be played at my funeral, no funeral march for me. Not that I am anxious to die, but I can't help realizing at times that if such an occurrence should happen, neither the world or myself would lose much by the event. . . ."

Sophie Vedder's reflections are interrupted by her friends, who try to cheer her; but she is worried about her finances ("wondering how long one's funds are going to last, takes the edge off of every pleasure in life"), and since she has quarreled with her family she can expect no support from them. Her only chance to survive is to marry old, portly Mr. Johnson. But she remains a woman of principle, and shrinks from a cynical marriage of convenience: "I am a bad, weak woman, and I have committed many sins, but thank God! no one has had to suffer for them but myself."

In a final conversation with Dick Carrington, Sophie Vedder explains that she has no regrets: "My life has been a gamble, I lived for pleasure only. I have never done anything I disliked when I could possibly avoid it. . . . I hoped against hope that something would turn up and pull me through. It was the hope of a gambler. My life has been a pleasant one and I do not regret having acted as I have done. . . ."

After Dick leaves, Sophie sits down at her dressing table, lights two candles, and looks at herself closely in her silver mirror. She looks "like a queen," but it is all over. " 'Poor Sophie, what a frivolous, useless thing you were. Still you never did any one any harm but yourself, and now there will be no one to regret you.' Undoing the leather case she took out a small revolver mounted in silver. 'How pretty it is' . . . A few drops of blood running across her white neck, stained some of the old lace about her throat."

Elliott's story was the fantasy of a maudlin romantic, frankly in love with death, and unconcerned with those who would be left behind. Proud, vain, and shallow, he wrote without any hint of remorse or self-doubt.

When Elliott Roosevelt returned to the United States, he entered the Keeley Center for the treatment of alcoholism, featuring "Dr. Keeley's Bi-Chloride of Gold cure," in Dwight, Illinois. But he was soon distraught. Somehow, he had convinced himself that he would have to endure only a three-month probation away from his family. His ongoing exile surprised him, and he wrote to everybody in the angriest terms. He would agree to it if it were Anna's wish, he said, though he considered it cruel, unwise, unnecessary, "both *wicked* and *foolish*."

TR had persuaded Anna to choose between a long probation and divorce. The plan involved his removal to Abingdon, Virginia, where his brother-in-law, Douglas Robinson, hired him to scout, claim, and settle the vast and uncharted lands he had purchased in a giant speculative mining tract. Although Elliott really appreciated this position, he dreaded the long months away, and felt publicly disgraced by his exile from his family.

Above all, he wanted to see Anna. But now, for the first time, she refused even to talk to him. Elliott appealed to Bye to intervene. "I do want her to see me as I *am*. Not as she last saw me, flushed with wine, reckless and unworthy, but an earnest, repentant, self-respecting, gentleman. That is all I wish except for love's sake to see once more my wife and children after these long weary months. Then I shall go on perfectly quietly and without complaint doing what may please her. . . ."

Desperate to prove himself, Elliott repaid old debts to his sister, and endured without complaint all the agonies of the treatment in Dwight. The other "drunkards" were fine and superior fellows, entirely supportive. "I am on in the third stage of the thing . . . and it combines all the troubles flesh is heir to. . . . All together I am about as uncomfortable as I well can be—But it must mean freedom and success at last Bye. . . ."

As Elliott regained his health, he became increasingly clear-eyed about the ordeal that he had put his family through. In a letter to thank Bye for her birthday note and the books she had sent, he wrote: "As I regain my moral and mental balance I am able to appreciate more fully the hideousness of my past actions and I grow stronger daily in my determination to live rightly and do *anything* required of me by my loved ones. . . . Try and think lovingly and forgivingly of me. . . ."

Elliott left Dwight in the spring of 1892 for Abingdon. He worked hard, and very quickly made a host of new and supportive friends. Throughout the summer, his correspondence with his family was warm, cordial, optimistic. Anna and the children were on their usual rounds at Tivoli and Bar Harbor. Anna wrote regular letters of encouragement and information, but she was not eager to see Elliott, and her tone was fearful. It was too soon to tell. She wanted and needed a longer respite—her reserve of trust and optimism had run dry. She now feared her husband, his wrath, his depression, his inconstancy. Elliott was astonished and felt meanly rejected. Her fears were "groundless," he wrote Bye on 12 June. Could she not see how hard he tried? "I signed a deed securing her and the children. . . . If I had been a bad man does she think this would have been my line of action."

Elliott wanted it understood that it would have been much easier for him to have "thrown off all obligations" and start over again, alone, unfettered. He could have created a new identity, built an entirely new life "in the west, or in some other country." His agreement to Anna's harsh terms—and he believed they were Anna's terms, not his brother's—was simply to show "the very powers of self-control and purpose she wishes me to have."

Elliott's sense of despondency and discouragement were not misguided. Anna had come to dread his company. Their marriage had been a terrible ordeal for her, and her sympathies were threadbare. She was exhausted, fragile, and unwell. She now wanted Elliott to leave her alone.

An extended period of sobriety might have restored her faith and her love for him, but they had run out of time. In November, Anna had an operation. Under the influence of ether, she spoke more clearly than ever before of her despair. She wanted to be done with the long years of disappointment and suffering. She wanted to die. Her mother and her sisters heard her lament, and resolved to keep Elliott away, as Anna wished. Shortly thereafter, she contracted diphtheria and lapsed into semiconsciousness.

While Anna lay dying, her children were sent out of their new home. Eleanor stayed with her godmother, Cousin Susie Parish, and her brothers stayed with Cousin Susie's mother, Anna's Aunt Elizabeth Ludlow. Grandmother Hall left Tivoli to nurse her daughter. And the Roosevelt family's faithful friend, Bye's young Scottish escort, Robert Munro Ferguson, now "sat on the stairs outside [Anna's] room to do any errands that might be asked of him, both day and night."

Anna's final struggle coincided with and mocked Elliott's desperate efforts to prove himself worthy of her. His sister Corinne told Elliott of Anna's words during her surgery, and repeated to him Mrs. Hall's remark that "it was the hidden sufferings expressed which she had controlled for so many months." He wrote daily to Mrs. Hall during the last week of Anna's life—alternating between being frantic with worry, overwhelmed by guilt and outraged by the family's refusal to allow him at her bedside.

On 23 November, he wrote: "It is too awful to me to feel I have forfeited the right to be in my proper place. . . . Oh the misery of my Sin! . . . I am so relieved though to know that you are in charge. . . . Is my wife very ill Mrs. Hall? *Two* trained nurses has such a terrifying sound. . . . If I should be wanted, in mercy forgive and remember that I am a husband and a Father and your son by adoption—though I have failed in many things. . . . I have a *right* in the sight of God to be by my wife's side in case she should wish me. . . . Do please *trust* me. . . ." On 26 November, he said: "Of course I trust you entirely and your words in the telegram 'do not come'—I take as Anna's command. . . . Did she say she wanted to die, that I had made her so utterly miserable that she did not care to live any more—And did you say that was what your poor child had been suffering in silence all these past killing months? How terribly sad— . . ."

Elliott could not believe that his wife's refusal to see him represented her real feelings. On the very day of her death, 7 December 1892, he wrote to Mrs. Hall: "I cannot understand what influence can have been brought to bear upon her to make her feel the way she evidently does to me. I have before me two letters she wrote me the day before she had me kidnapped in Paris . . . and no woman using the terms of endearment she does in them and giving promises of faithful love as she does there could possibly have changed without *outside* influence being brought to bear. . . . It is most *horrible* and full of *awe* to me that my wife not only does not want me near her in sickness or trouble but *fears* me. . . ." Elliott protested that he was worthy of Anna's trust and insisted that he "never did a dishonorable thing, or *one cruel act* towards my wife or children." He understood what Mrs. Hall must be going through, and: "If Anna cares for it give her my love. . . ." While he was writing this letter, he was sent for. But that telegram arrived too late.

Eleanor Roosevelt remembered 7 December 1892 very clearly. She was standing by a window when Cousin Susie Parish told her that "my mother was dead. She was very sweet to me, and I must have known that something terrible had happened. Death meant nothing to me, and one fact wiped out everything else—my father was back and I would see him very soon."

4. Years of Dreams and Longing

ANNA HALL ROOSEVELT DIED TOO QUICKLY, TOO UN-expectedly, to resolve any of the bitter feelings that were left now forever unspoken. Whispers in the ether of her lost life remained a substantial part of Anna Hall Roosevelt's lasting legacy.

Eleanor was only eight when her mother died. She had been abandoned by "the most beautiful woman" she had ever seen. She had never won her mother's approval; and now had lost the chance to prove herself worthy. There would be no adolescent storms during which to work things out. If she had been more jolly, more attractive, more compatible, better behaved, would her mother have lived? Would there have been forgiveness? Whatever remorse she might have felt at her mother's death, Eleanor could not answer those questions—not at eight, not ever. Always too painful, they haunted her life. Buried deep in the labyrinths of emotional memory, they remained untouched, forever available to tug at her confidence and cloud her sensibilities.

Her mother's disapproval dominated Eleanor's childhood, and permanently affected her self-image. With her mother's death, she became an outsider, always expecting betrayal and abandonment. But even at eight she was fiercely proud, determined to prove herself courageous, caring, and worthy of love. For the rest of her life her actions were in part an answer to her mother. If she were really good, then perhaps nobody else would leave her, and people would see the love in her heart.

Eleanor never wrote much about her mother. She did not relate to her mother's bitter situation, even in adulthood, after she knew the facts. And she never acknowledged the sacrifice her mother had made for her, an act of love that allowed Eleanor to maintain her romantic image of her father. Eleanor was never able to credit her mother for the fact that she had protected her sensitive daughter as much she could. Anna Hall Roosevelt had neither betrayed Elliott nor turned her daughter against him.

After her mother's death, Eleanor turned to fantasies for the fulfillment of her emotional needs, and especially to her fantasy of her father, built upon a tapestry of letters and idealized moments of intense joy. About her father's love she was sure: "With my father I was perfectly happy. . . . He was the center of my world and all around him loved him." She cherished above all her memory of the future he described when they were reunited in Grandmother Hall's West 37th Street library after her mother's death. That dark day, Elliott brought light back into her life when, sitting in a big chair, dressed all in black, and looking very somber, he folded her into his arms and spoke so convincingly of their future. She would make a real home for him. They would travel together. "Somehow it was always he and I. I did not understand whether my brothers were to be our children or . . . they would be at school and college and later independent." It was father and daughter, "a life of our own together," with incomparable adventures forevermore.

In 1937, when she wrote her memoirs, ER looked back with affection upon the romantic visions she and her father had forged in their correspondence, out of the tears and longing they both shared. She dedicated her book, in part, "To the memory of my Father who fired a child's imagination."*

~

---

* The other part of ER's dedication was anonymous: "And to the few other people who have meant the same inspiration throughout my life."

SOCIETY MOURNED ANNA REBECCA HALL ROOSEVELT. DEAD at twenty-nine, she was "one of the favorites of New York's social set." New York newspapers carried memorials of her death for days: "One of the gayest of the younger set, she and her husband before his misfortune were particularly intimate with the Astors. . . . Last September at Bar Harbor, she was regarded as the belle of the 'beauty dinner' . . ."

But society carried on. The week after her death, on the occasion of the first Patriarchs' Ball of the season—one of the lavish charity events that ushered in the height of New York's pre-Christmas social whirl—the editor of *The New York Times'* society page breathed a sigh of relief:

> It had been thought that the sad death of young Mrs. Elliott Roosevelt, who, had she lived, would have been one of the patronesses, would have greatly dimmed the brilliancy of the ball, but New York is a large town, and "we are soon forgot" so that the absence of the few who stayed away . . . was hardly noticed. . . .

Only one obituary mentioned anything of Anna Hall's concerned generosity. "Hers was a beautiful character. She was constantly thinking of others." This *New York Times* reporter had recently seen her "instruct her coachman to stop when passing a woman . . . on crutches, an entire stranger to her, and urged her to get in her carriage and she would take her home. . . . How few of the fashionable women of the day would have done so. . . ."

At the time of his wife's death, there had been only two months remaining in the probation period that Elliott Roosevelt's family had imposed on him. But with Anna gone, he had little reason to continue to prove himself, and all his efforts at rehabilitation went quickly to smash. As Eleanor noted in her memoirs, Anna's death represented "a tragedy of utter defeat for him. No hope now of ever wiping out the sorrowful years he had brought upon my mother . . . He had no wife, no children, no hope!"

Mrs. Hall continued to write kindly to Elliott. She sent him letters about his children, details of their activities and accomplishments, and presents of fruit and delicacies she knew he liked. But she had custody of the children, and she did not want Elliott to see them alone. By Christmas, Elliott was drinking again, and by January 1893, there were letters from Abingdon that referred to his old sickness.

But even in the midst of his dissolution, Elliott wrote regularly to Mrs. Hall and his daughter. His stationery was bordered in black for a full inch around. He wrote entertaining letters to amuse Eleanor, and letters of earnest sobriety to impress Mrs. Hall. He made financial arrangements for his children's security and wrote to Mrs. Hall on 26 January 1893 that the various trust funds already established assured an income of $7,500 a year, or $635 a month, and he would send whatever was needed over and above that, "so long as you have as much money as you need for the children's support and they are no drain on you. . . ."

On 20 January 1893, he wrote to Eleanor, "Father's own little Nell," a letter of apology that he had not written sooner, because he had "been very sick, dear, as Auntie Maude and Auntie Gracie will explain to you." This letter, one of Elliott's incomparable compositions, fueled his daughter's fantasies for years to come: There had been, and would be again, wonderful long rides, saddle horses and carts, walks and sleds, "days through the Grand snow clad forests, over the white hills, under the blue skies as blue as those in Italy under which you and I and Little Ellie . . . used to sail over Naples Bay to beautiful Capri. . . ."

Then there was the matter of Eleanor's education. Elliott urged her to work hard at her lessons so that she might achieve that "curious thing they call 'education.'" He suggested that she watch workmen build a house, place "one stone after another . . . and then think that there are a lot of funny little workmen running about in your small head called 'Ideas' which are carrying a lot of stones like small bodies called 'Facts,' and these little 'Ideas' are being directed by your teachers in various ways, by 'Persuasion,' 'Instruction' 'Love' and 'Truth' to place all these 'Fact Stones' on top of and alongside each other in your dear Golden Head until they build a beautiful house called 'Education'— *then!* Oh, my dear companionable little Daughter, you will come to Father and what jolly games we will have together. . . ."

Elliott hoped that in Eleanor's "Education" house she would have "such a happy life." But he warned her "those little fact stones are a queer lot," and that to use them she needed patience with her teachers. Then there were difficult, rebellious, and "stupid, wearisome, trying fact stones. . . ." There would be things she didn't like to do, but ought, and so *"discipline!"* needed to be introduced.

Over time, Eleanor Roosevelt cited discipline as one of the primary forces in her own life; but love was always her motivating principle. And in this letter her father wrote: "Of all the forces your Teachers use, Father and you too, Little Witch, probably like Love best."

Discipline and love became Eleanor's magic charms. To invoke them was to bring back the world of happiness, security, and hope created by her father's letters. And the letters themselves conjured up pictures of him at his writing desk, thinking of her late each night.

As she read and reread those letters, then and in future years, she found messages, teachings, and admonitions she could continue to learn from and take seriously as they changed in meaning to her with the passage of time. In one letter he had written: "I am glad you are taking such good care of those cunning wee hands that Father loves so to be petted by, all those *little* things will make my dear Girl so much more attractive if she attends them, not forgetting the big ones. Unselfishness, generosity, loving tenderness and cheerfulness." Eleanor reread that letter when she was almost sixteen, and was able finally to stop biting her nails.

While Elliott was writing his daughter letters of encouragement and comfort, he was losing his own final battle. It had been a hard winter in Abingdon. He suffered several minor accidents, and endless anguish. After a March visit to New York, he returned feeling isolated and bitter: "I have not found one person in either my wife's or my connection who encourages me . . . when I propose that the Children join their Father. . . ." On the contrary, everyone agreed that his children belonged "with their Grandmother and surrounded by every thing in the way of luxury and all the advantages, both educational and otherwise to which they have been accustomed. . . . I have told my Mother-in-Law that she shall have the children until I feel I *must* have them and when that time comes she has promised to give them up to me—No matter if I am living alone on White Top [in Abingdon] or in Ceylon. . . ." His favorite aunt, who might have championed him, Annie Bulloch Gracie, died unexpectedly after what had seemed nothing more than a routine operation intended to cure her growing deafness. And then came a tragedy that put an end to his hopes to reunite his family. In May, Elliott, Jr., almost four, died after a bout with scarlet fever and diphtheria. On 26 May 1893, Elliott wrote his daughter:

> My own little Nell— We bury little Ellie tomorrow up at Tivoli by Mother's side. He is happy in Heaven with her now so you must not grieve or sorrow. And you will have to be doubly a good Daughter to your Father and good sister to own little Brudie boy [Hall] who is left to us. I know you will my own little Heart. I cannot write more because I am not feeling very well and my heart is too full. But I wished you to know you were never out of my thoughts and prayers for one instant all the time. I put some flowers close by Ellie in your name as I knew you would like me to do. With abiding and most tender devotion and Love I am always,
>
> Your affectionate Father

Eleanor believed that little Ellie would be "safe in heaven" with Mother and Aunt Gracie. She in turn wrote her father a letter of comfort: "Our Lord wants Ellie boy with him now, we must be happy. . . ."

These new losses devastated Elliott. Heartsick and wretched, he broke down completely. In an undated fragment of a letter written during the summer of 1893, he promised Mrs. Hall that he would not try to visit his children in New York, or "come to Tivoli," or "interfere with Little Nell's stay at Newport," or attempt to see them alone at any time. He only asked that, "some time during the summer, convenient to yourself, *you* bring them down either to the City or sea shore where I can see them and enjoy a little love which my heart craves and for lack of which it has broken. Oh—Mrs. Hall I have tried so hard and it has been so lonely and weary and the breakdown seems to me only natural in my strained condition. Above all believe me it was not drunkenness. Let me see you soon please Mother."

The economic depression of the summer of 1893 threatened Elliott's finances and further strained his equilibrium. On 20 August, he wrote to his "Darling little Daughter":

I have had a very trying time of it down here and am now trying to quiet the poor miners in the Coal field who will listen to no one but me, and who are absolutely, for lack of employment, *starving.* There is great distress all through this country and I too have suffered much. I like to think of you as happy and would like to hear the same from your dear sweet lips or read the words from your pen.

Eager to prove what a good and loving father he would be, if only they could be together, he wrote his lonely daughter: "I wish you could be one of the jolly party of little children who ride with me every morning when I am in Abingdon."

Miriam, Lillian and the four Trigg children all on their ponies and horses and the fox terriers Mr. Belmont gave me (to comfort me in my loneliness) go out about sunrise and gallop over these broad fields for one or two hours; we rarely fail to secure some kind of game, and never return without roses in the cheeks of those I call now, my children.

Do you continue to ride? Learn the right way so that I will not have to teach you all over again. . . .

More and more, Eleanor lived almost exclusively in a dream world with her father. There were many other people about, her aunts and uncles, her grandmother and little Hall, there were governesses, French maids, German maids, and tutors. But they were merely interruptions: "They always tried to talk to me, and I wished to be left alone to live in a dream world in which I was the heroine and my father the hero. Into this world I retired as soon as I went to bed and as soon as I woke in the morning, and all the time I was walking or when any one bored me."

Elliott did not see his daughter that summer, but as the autumn approached he considered her birthday. Eager that she, like the children of Abingdon, be able to ride with ease, he sent her a pony, and agreed to give her a cart also, as Mrs. Hall suggested. Elliott urged that Mrs. Hall allow her to keep the pony in town so that she might be able to ride two or three times a week. "It would *please me greatly* if she did. Do let her do so. It was very kind of you to give her the saddle."

Sometime during that autumn, he returned to New York and moved into an apartment at 313 West 102d Street, near Riverside Park. There he lived with his mistress, Mrs. Evans, who cared for him and made every effort in his behalf. But he had embarked on a final self-destructive binge from which nobody could save him. Moreover, Theodore disavowed all interest in his brother and urged his sisters to do the same. Personally, Theodore wrote Bye, his own life in Washington was rhapsodic: "It is very pleasant here now, as most of my friends are back; I have been dining out almost every evening . . . ," most usually in the rarefied circle around Henry Adams, John Hay, and Nannie and Henry Cabot Lodge.

During the week of 11 October 1893 (Eleanor's ninth birthday), Corinne, who was now closer to Elliott than anybody else, wrote Bye in dismay that he had returned without even telling her:

> Eleanor saw him driving in a Hansom the other day and waved at him (this is what the governess says) & he stopped & took her with him to her sewing class. Mrs. Hall was naturally much worried. I told her she ought to tell the governess that when Eleanor is under her care she should not allow her to go *with any one,* not even her father. It is so strange & sad that he should not be able to see his children & yet there seems to be *no other* course. Poor, poor Elliott. If I don't hear from him soon I shall take some means of seeing him. . . .

Eleanor's memory of the drives she took with her father at this time was both thrilling and terrifying, and entirely justified her aunt's and grandmother's apprehensions: Her father was a "fine horseman" who had a spirited hunter "which he decided to break and drive in New York City in a two-wheeled cart." Perched high in the cart,

> we would go on rather mad chases. . . . My father enjoyed every minute of the excitement as he tried to control the spirited horse.
>
> I remember one day his telling me as we progressed around

Central Park in a long line of carriages that if he just said "Hoopla"
to Mohawk, he would try to jump over all the carts around us. I
tried to hide my fears as I murmured, "I hope you won't say it."

Despite several near accidents, and her "abject terror," ER considered "those drives" the "high points of my existence."

In the winter of 1894, Elliott went back to Abingdon. Despite a
return of his old "Indian fever," and an accident during which he
knocked over his reading lamp and burned himself severely, he resumed
his spirited letters, complimenting his daughter on the progress of her
studies—her spelling was now perfect—and commiserating with her
on her dislike of fractions and long division. He warned her against
impatience and urged her to devote herself to her studies, although he
was "pleased to hear of the good times" she had "at the different
parties." He enclosed letters from two little children, Mary and Harold
Sherman, he particularly wanted Eleanor to meet. They were "the children of my dear Friend, Mrs. F. B. Sherman of Detroit. These little
children I saw a great deal of in Paris when we were there—I gave
them my handsome old black poodle—'Dick' . . . You must know these
two dear little friends of mine some day."

Although he shared his New York City apartment with Mrs. Evans,
Elliott had resumed his relationship with Florence Bagley Sherman.
During the summer of 1894, he went to her country home in Annisquam,
Massachusetts. But he was restless, refused to stay in any one place—
and continued to disintegrate.

Eleanor spent much of that summer riding her pony around Tivoli.
Uncle Vallie taught her to jump, but she longed for her father and wrote
him that she wished he "were up here to ride with me." "Give my love
to the puppies and every one else that you know."

On 5 July, the family left Tivoli for Bar Harbor, and Eleanor noted:
"Brudie wears pants now." Eleanor wrote more regularly that summer.
She "had great fun" fishing, and "caught six fish don't you think I did
well for the first time. I am having lessons with Grandma every day and
go to a French class."

On 13 August, Eleanor received her last letter from her father:
"What must you think of your Father who has not written in so long. . . .

I have after all been very busy, quite ill, at intervals not able to move from my bed for days. . . . Give my love to Grandma and Brudie and all. . . . I hope my little girl is well. . . . Kiss Baby Brudie for me and *never forget* I love you. . . ."

During the night of 14 August, only hours after he sent this letter to Eleanor, Elliott Roosevelt died. On 15 August, Corinne wrote to Bye (then in London serving as hostess to her distant cousin James Roosevelt Roosevelt, who had been recently widowed and was first secretary of the U.S. Embassy) that she had left for New York as soon as she received the telegram from Corinne's husband, Douglas Robinson: "Elliott died suddenly last night."

"It was a fearful shock to me though I was not unprepared for some catastrophe, for yesterday I received a letter from William [Elliott's valet] telling me that Elliott had been using stimulants again, and consequently . . . was having delusions. . . ." At first, the delusions "were gentle," and involved his children. He thought he was showing his dogs to his dead son, Ellie. He knocked on a neighbor's door and asked "if Miss Eleanor Roosevelt were at home." When he was told she was not, he said " 'tell her her father is so sorry not to see her' and soon became excited and ran violently up and down stairs." At some point he jumped out of a parlor window. Uncle Jimmie Gracie, a policeman, Douglas Robinson, and Mrs. Evans all tried to calm him. Then he had "one of those convulsive attacks," after which he slept quietly, had a moment of sanity during which he spoke rationally, and died. "The terrible bloated swelled look was gone & the sweet expression around his forehead and eyes made me weep very bitter tears."

"I know it is best," Corinne wrote. "I know it had to come sooner or later. I know it makes his memory possible to his children. I know all, and yet my heart feels desperately sad for the brother I knew, the Elliott I have loved and known, which all that has passed cannot efface."

The next day, Theodore arrived and "was more overcome than I have ever seen him—cried like a little child for a long time. . . ." On 18 August, Theodore wrote his sister Bye to describe the "frightful drinking" of Elliott's last weeks: He "had been drinking whole bottles of anisette and green mint,—besides whole bottles of raw brandy and of champagne, sometimes half a dozen a morning. But when dead the poor fellow looked very peaceful, and so like his old, generous, gallant self of fifteen years ago. The horror, and the terrible mixture of madness and grotesque, grim evil continued to the very end; and the dreadful flashes of his old sweetness, which made it all even more hopeless. I suppose he has been doomed from the beginning; the absolute contradiction of all his actions, and of all his moral even more than his mental qualities, is utterly impossible to explain."

TR wrote with incredulity that Elliott's "house was so neat, and well kept, with his Bible and religious books, and Anna's pictures everywhere, even in the room of himself and his mistress. Poor woman, she had taken the utmost care of him, and was broken down at his death. Her relations with him have been just as strange as everything else."

As sympathetic as he was, TR was nonetheless appalled that plans had been made to have Elliott buried at Tivoli alongside Anna: "I promptly vetoed this hideous plan, Corinne, who has acted better than I can possibly say throughout, cordially backing me up." TR arranged to have Elliott buried instead in Greenwood Cemetery, close to "those who are associated with only his sweet innocent youth, when no more loyal, generous, disinterested fellow lived."

The Halls were virtually overlooked when Theodore arranged Elliott's burial. Only Anna's brother Vallie was able to attend. Mrs. Hall received the telegram announcing the services too late, and the telegram she sent to Uncle Gracie "asking him to order flowers for the children and myself" also arrived too late, which she particularly regretted: "Elliott loved flowers and always brought them to us, and to think not one from us or his dear ones went to the grave with him grieves me deeply." Eleanor recalled that her grandmother did not want her to attend her father's funeral, and so she was denied even that moment with him.

It seemed to TR that Elliott's funeral followed the pattern of his life, with "the usual touch of the grotesque and terrible, for in one of the four carriages that followed to the grave, went the woman, Mrs. Evans and two of her and his friends, the host and hostess of the Woodbrine Inn. They behaved perfectly well, and their grief seemed entirely sincere. . . ."

Like TR, Elliott's sister Corinne deplored his "incongruous" life, "its beautiful & its evil impulses." But over time she dealt with those incongruities with greater acceptance and deeper understanding. She valued Florence Bagley Sherman's letters to her, written immediately after Elliott's death, and a year later; "I've been sadly wondering about his children," wrote Mrs. Sherman, "if they are well and strong—and inherit anything of his charms. . . ."

In 1914, Corinne Roosevelt Robinson published a book of poetry in which the title poem was dedicated to Elliott's New York mistress, Mrs. Evans. A tender exchange had evidently occurred between the two women, and Corinne wrote *One Woman to Another* in Mrs. Evans's voice:

> *Often he told me that you never failed,*
> *And that when others, with averted gaze,*
> *Would have him know his own unworthiness,*
> *Your eyes held only memories of the past. . . .*

Mrs. Evans had confided to Corinne:

> *I was of that strange world you cannot know,*
> *The "half-world" with its glamour and its glare,*
> *Its sin and shame. . . .*

But Elliott had saved her "vagrant and despairing soul," and in turn she had comforted and protected him, and "soon a great and mighty passion grew," and he was "so very good to me."

> *You, who have never known the fierce, hot fumes . . .*
> *How can you judge of him, and how could she*
> *Whose fair white bosom was a thought too chaste*
> *To pillow a repentant weary head?*
> *But I who knew the evil of the world*
> *Could never shrink before so sad a thing; . . .*
> *Only, when in his eyes I read the look*
> *That longed for her, my swift resentment rose; . . .*
> *Then, sometimes, friends of his would come and speak*

Of that fair world of yours, unknown to me,
And afterward he would be lost in gloom. . . .

At the end of their visit, Corinne embraced Mrs. Evans:

What! you would kiss me? Yes, I take your kiss;
We are both women, and we both have loved!

Eleanor Roosevelt grew up to cherish that poem, as she cherished every positive memory of her father.

Immediately after Elliott's death, Mary Livingston Ludlow Hall wrote to Corinne Roosevelt Robinson from Bar Harbor: "No one can feel more deeply for you than I do. . . . You certainly did everything a sister could do, and it must be a great consolation to you now. . . ." Mrs. Hall wanted it understood that she bore no "ill feelings" for Elliott, and thought only of the time before "this trouble came [when] he was the dearest man I ever knew, so gentle, and kind-hearted." She believed that he was not "accountable for his words, or deeds," during his last years, and "it was with deep regret that I tried to keep him from his children, but truly *I was afraid of him,* for I never knew what he would do."

Mrs. Hall was particularly interested in undoing Theodore Roosevelt's precipitous decision to bury Elliott at Greenwood. She had promised Elliott more than a year before his death that he could be buried at Tivoli with his wife and son. He "took such interest in the vault we were going to build, and I planned the vault so that he and his family should be all together. In October we are going to move Anna, Ellie and my immediate family from the present vault to the new one, and I wish you would then allow Elliott to be taken there. Will you please consult Bamie and Theodore, and if possible comply with Elliott's wish and ours." Penned atop this letter, evidently written at a later date and in a different hand, were the words "Elliott was laid by Anna."

Mrs. Hall also wrote Corinne: "I hope you and Bamie will always advise me about the children, for I want them influenced by their Father's family as well as by their dear Mother's." She wrote with concern that Eleanor seemed rather abstracted much of the time. "The poor child has had so much sorrow crowded into her short life she now takes everything very quietly." When she was told of Elliott's death, "the only remark she made was, 'I did want to see father once more.' I think since last winter she felt there was something not right, but I don't believe she realized what it was."

Although Eleanor would later spend considerable time with her Aunts Bamie and Corinne, for several years she was largely isolated from the bustling Roosevelt world of Oyster Bay, spending most of her time at Tivoli. TR was always delighted to see his niece whenever she visited Sagamore, and was so demonstrative that one of his more enthusiastic bear-hugs popped all the buttons off her shirt. But Edith Carow Roosevelt made no particular effort toward Eleanor, inviting her once a year, if that. Though she had been a childhood friend of both Elliott and TR, Edith was herself the daughter of an alcoholic and seemed particularly bitter about Elliott. The week of Elliott's death, Edith wrote her sister, Emily Carow, that, as much as she missed Aunt Annie Gracie, whose recent passing had also been very painful to Elliott, she felt that she "was taken from evil to come. Elliott has sunk to the lowest depths. Consorts with the vilest women, and Theodore, Bamie and Douglas receive horrid anonymous letters about his life. I live in constant dread of some scandal of his attaching itself to Theodore."

Good blood and bad blood was a big issue among Victorian blue bloods. Social Darwinism, that theory of biological determinism that for generations ruined lives and manners, and utterly distorted sensibilities, was then at its peak and may have caused Edith to extend her "dread" to Eleanor. She wrote her mother, "As you know I never wished Alice to associate with Eleanor so shall not try to keep up any friendship between them."

For her part, Mrs. Hall did not approve of the rambunctious Roosevelts of Oyster Bay. She was as eager to protect her grandchildren from the Roosevelt influence as Aunt Edith was to keep Alice (her stepdaughter) away from Eleanor. Except for very irregular visits to Oyster Bay, and an annual Christmas party at Aunt Corinne's, contact between the two families subsided for several years.

Nothing, however, could keep Eleanor away from her father, whom she visited daily in her fantasies—where, for the first time, she was able to end the cycle of broken promises, guilt, and remorse that her parents had been locked into. In the world she created, she was heroic and loved. People paid attention to her, and noticed the good deeds she performed across the fields of the centuries.

Young Eleanor poured herself into her fantasies the first thing every morning. They dominated her waking hours and were continually fueled by the many books she read with such pleasure—novels, history, biography, poetry especially. Many considered Eleanor's life, in the years following her parents' death, somber and spartan—positively Dickensian. But Eleanor was not Oliver Twist (hero of one of her favorite books), and despite the regimentation of Grandmother Hall's way of life, neither Tivoli nor the dark narrow brownstone on 37th Street was quite Bleak House. The countryside around Tivoli, which ER loved in all seasons, was a constant joy to her, providing wide-ranging spaces in which she was free to hide, to read, and to be alone inside her own world. Although the use of the library was unrestricted, her reading was monitored and several books, including *Bleak House,* did disappear while she was reading them. For all the rules, in the space she most wanted to roam, largely within the confines of her imagination, she had the freest rein.

Eleanor was actually quite content during these outwardly dreary years. Her only serious complaint concerned the continued presence in her life of the nurse Madeleine, who bullied her unmercifully, pulled her hair, and cut large holes in the socks Eleanor had darned imperfectly. Evidently Eleanor endured her cruelty in silence for years. Finally, when she was almost fourteen, she confided some unnamed horror to her grandmother, who immediately dismissed Madeleine. The only other servant Eleanor mentioned during this time was Mrs. Overhalse, the laundress, "a cheerful, healthy soul" who taught ER to wash and iron, and seemed a generous confidante: "I loved the hours spent with this cheerful woman."

In 1894, Grandmother Hall was a relatively young woman, still in her early fifties. But she assumed a posture that made her seem quite ancient to Eleanor. Strict and adamant, she spent many hours alone in her darkened room with the windows closed and the shades drawn, emerging only to issue orders, and to conduct the prayer services that began and ended each day. Everyone in the household attended these services, including the entire staff.

Lenient and indulgent with her own six children, who had grown up too fast and too wild, Mrs. Hall now vowed to keep her grandchildren as young, disciplined, and dependent as possible. Eleanor, for example, was made to wear short skirts, hideous black stockings, and outrageously unfashionable high-ankled shoes. Tall for her age and very thin, Eleanor looked ridiculous in these old-fashioned costumes. But her grandmother insisted, and Eleanor never howled in protest. Eleanor's friends were always amazed that she wore the clothes her grandmother insisted upon. But when they complained on her behalf, she silenced them and always defended her grandmother.

In contrast, Eleanor's young aunts and uncles were free spirits who devoted themselves to the happiness of their orphaned niece and nephew. At Tivoli especially, they encouraged Eleanor to ride her pony, play or not play as long as she liked. Tennis champions and superb athletes, her uncles taught her to jump horses and spent hours trying to teach her to play on one of the first lawn tennis courts in the county. They insisted that she learn to shoot their rifles, and they taught her to ride her new bicycle, which gave her even greater freedom. She liked especially the rowboat that she and Aunt Pussie used throughout the warm months to row down the Hudson for the mail and morning papers. While in New York, they encouraged her activities on the playing fields at Central Park. She reveled in each sport, enjoyed competition, and occasionally rendered herself a filthy mess. The Halls did everything possible to ease her pain and influence her life positively.

ER's studies had been erratic; now they were more rigorously pursued. Her posture had also been neglected. Like her mother and her aunts before her, she was made to walk up and down the River Road for hours at a time, with a stick behind her shoulders, hooked at her elbows. Her grandmother and her aunts believed, moreover, that she suffered from a spinal curvature, and she was put into a corrective steel brace for almost a year.

If her grandmother seemed to her contemporaries harsh or capricious, Eleanor wrote of Grandmother Hall with only the deepest warmth and gratitude. The six years that Eleanor spent with her grandmother were a time of welcome constraint, and healing. Although she felt profoundly the lack of a home of her own, she was no longer treated as an unwanted interruption in the day's real business. To Grandmother Hall she *was* the day's real business, the primary focus of attention. Her grandmother gave Eleanor a new sense of belonging, place, purpose. Her needs were no longer neglected; her presence was demanded; punctuality was expected. Out of the chaos and distress of her parental home, Eleanor felt for the first time secure and wanted.

Eleanor especially esteemed her Aunts Maude and Pussie. They always "called out my deepest admiration and devotion. Pussie read with me both prose and poetry, and her reading of poetry gave me my first conception that poetry was sound and rhythm in addition to whatever meaning it might contain. Prose could convey an idea but rarely had the additional quality of music." Whereas Pussie excelled in the arts, ER wrote, Maude had that rare gift, "the art of association with other people. She can appreciate their ability and bring them out." Eleanor considered Maude "one of the truly unselfish souls of this world." "These two aunts were my early loves and few women since have seemed to me to surpass them in beauty and charm."

At Tivoli, she enjoyed a female world dominated by her aunts and their friends, who were solicitous of the little girl's sensibilities. Lonely and romantic, with no friends or neighbors her own age, she turned her attention to the older women who came into her home. In her memoirs, ER described Alice Kidd, later Mrs. George Huntington, who was a "great influence on me in these early years." She spoke with Eleanor for hours on long walks through the woods, seemed genuinely interested in her thoughts and feelings, and evoked in her a new sense of love and trust:

> I thought her one of the most beautiful and certainly one of the kindest people I knew as a child, and if she was expected I would walk half a mile or more to our entrance for the pleasure of driving in with her and seeing her before she was swallowed up by the older people. I was a little self-conscious about this devotion and I doubt if she ever knew or if any of the others knew . . . , how

much I admired her and how grateful I was for her rather careless kindness. But, I learned something then which has served me in good stead many times—that the most important thing in any relationship is not what you get but what you give. It does not hurt to worship at a shrine which is quite unconscious, for out of it may grow an inner development in yourself and sometimes a relationship of real value. In any case the giving of love is an education in itself.

After Anna Roosevelt's death and the sale of her house, the Roser schoolroom attended by Eleanor and her friends was moved to the homes of Eleanor's classmates, who were the daughters of her mother's closest friends: Gwendolyn Burden, Helen Cutting, Margaret Dix, Valerie Hadden, Sophie Langdon, Jessie Sloane, and Ruth Twombly. Eleanor was closest to Gwendolyn Burden, Helen Cutting, and Jessie Sloane, with whom she remained lifelong friends, but all her Roser classmates seem to have felt protective toward Eleanor, and to have fully appreciated her finest qualities, regardless of her odd clothes or introspective manner. They seem, moreover, to have been the first friends to notice her leadership qualities.

Eleanor loved language, and the sound of language, winning medals for the poetry she memorized and the dramatic readings she gave, and impressing her classmates with the intensity of her essays and stories.

Eleanor's adolescent writings ranged from sentimental and moralistic to romantic and fanciful. In one story, she described a dispute between all the most exquisite blossoms in the conservatory as to which flower is "the most beautiful." An elderly woman declares: "As a young girl I loved the violet for it is the flower you picked for me when you told me of your love. Yes I loved it best then. I love it best now. . . ." At which point all the flowers go into a frenzy, and squabble until the violet says: "Why none of us excell. We are all beautiful in our own way. Some are beautifully colored. Others smell sweetly. . . . We were all made well. From this day we are all equal." Eleanor concluded: "The other flowers listened and to some it seemed strange that the flower which had been chosen to excel should say this but they all agreed and from that day they were equal."

"But I always have [loved] and always will love the violet best."

In another story Eleanor portrays "Gilded Butterflies." One is discontented: "Pooh! I'm not going to sit on a daisy always. . . . I am going to know a great deal and to see everything. I won't stay here to waste my life. . . ." Another, "portly old butterfly," comments: "Dear, dear, dear how dreadful it is to be discontented. For my part I'd rather stay where I am. I've seen life. I've met great men and been to large dinners in the crowded cities. . . ." A young beautiful butterfly says: "Dear me I am so tired. I've been to at least six dinners and about as many dances in the last week but then it is such fun." Still another malcontent arrives, bored and bothered with life. "I wish I was dead. There are nothing but daisies and buttercups, never any change. Now if I were only a genius, or rich then I could buy genius!" "Then I heard a soft, lovely voice near my ear so low it was like a whisper. The voice said, 'Child, learn a lesson from the gilded butterflies and be contented in this world and you will find happiness.' "

Eleanor at fourteen eroticized beauty in nature. She sought to capture the essence of a sunset, which she saw as a "siren of the sea who unrolled the glory of her hair." As she sat alone on a dock watching the "fiery red ball" descend, she "saw a beautiful woman rise out of the sea to meet it." The woman held out her arms for that red ball, "as though begging it to come nearer. Then she shook out her golden hair, till the whole sky became golden and as she drew nearer the red light grew softer and softer and blended itself onto her hair as she sank lower and lower . . . , and just as they kissed the water her mass of golden hair fell over her and hid her from my sight and all that was left of the beautiful vision was a fiery ripple of gold on the water. . . ."

Both at Roser's and later, ER celebrated "Ambition": "Some people consider ambition a sin, but well-trained it seems to be a great good for it leads one to do, and to be things which without it one could never have been." Without ambition, Caesar would never have attempted to conquer the world. Without ambition, "would painters ever paint wonderful portraits or writers ever write books."

> Of course it is easier to have no ambition and just keep on the same way every day and never try to do grand and great things, for it is only those who have ambition and who try to do who meet

with difficulties and they alone face the disappointments that come when one does not succeed in what one has meant to do. . . .

But those with ambition try again, and try until they at last succeed. . . .

Eleanor was concerned that ambition might make one "selfish and careless"; the ambitious might push against others, or "tread" on them. But, she asked, was it "better never to be known, and to leave the world a blank as if one had never come"? "It seems to me that we should leave some mark upon the world and not just pass away for what good can that do?" Without ambition, people "would never do anything good."

However hard-working or ambitious Eleanor's school friends may have considered her, she seemed to herself rather wanting in virtue. One night she wrote in her journal:

> *To be the thing we seem*
> *To do the thing we deem enjoined by duty*
> *To walk in faith nor dream*
> *Of questioning God's scheme of truth and beauty.*

It is very hard to do what this verse says, so hard I never succeed. . . . I am always questioning, questioning because I cannot understand & never succeed in doing what I mean to do, never, never. I suppose I don't really try. I can feel it in me sometimes that I can do much more. . . . I mean to try till I *do* succeed.

On another occasion, Eleanor wrote in her "headache journal": "I am feeling cross. Poor Aunti Pussie she is so worried. I am going to try and see if I can't do something for her tonight. I have studied hard. . . . I've tried to be good and sweet and quiet but have not succeeded. Oh my . . ."

Eleanor's days were not all devoted to ambition, study, or the pursuit of virtue, however: She spent endless hours on her back in the green rolling fields around Tivoli reading and dreaming. She was especially fond of a particular cherry tree that not only shaded her summer days but provided a comfortable perch where she could not be seen, as she recalled in a 1941 article on the importance of reading: "I have to this day an insatiable interest in every kind of romance and story which grew I think from the first forbidden tales and novels which I purloined as a child and read as far from the house as possible, perched in a cherry tree where I could eat cherries and watch the approach of any grown up who might disapprove of the type of literature I had chosen."

Eleanor's capacity to lose herself in her reading caused her to miss many meals. Nothing ordinary could be relied upon to "bring me out of the world between the pages." To the young ER all of Longfellow and such poems as "The Wreck of the Hesperus," "The Skeleton in Armor," "Evangeline," and "The Building of a Ship" were favorites—as were Tennyson and Scott: "What young person can read the 'Revenge' or 'Marmion' or parts of 'The Lady of the Lake' and 'The Idylls of the King' without being stimulated to dreams of a different age." The adult ER encouraged every child to share her joy in reading, and to learn French and German as well. At the very least, to "read the Chanson de Roland, Le Cid, some of Dumas, some of Victor Hugo, some of German poetry, Heine, Goethe and some of the more modern German novelists and dramatists. . . . Every child should read the translations of Indian and Chinese poetry. We know too little of the thought of these far distant races and the beauty of imagery in which they hide their precious kernels of thought and philosophy."

Eleanor's grandmother had her tutored in French, German, and music. She studied the piano dutifully until she was eighteen—although, she complained, nobody had bothered to train her ear. But because Aunt Pussie played the piano with "great feeling," ER developed an "emotional appreciation of music" that lasted throughout her life. "Her playing was one of the unforgettable joys of my childhood. I would lie on the sofa in the 37th Street house and listen to her for hours." Her Aunts Tissie, Pussie, and Maude also introduced Eleanor to opera, theatre, and the dance.

During these years, Eleanor attended Mr. Dodsworth's famous dance classes for little ladies and gentlemen. To learn to waltz, and to polka, and to know how to behave in formal fashion in mixed company was essential to her future in society. But she was also given ballet lessons, which she considered a most extraordinary treat. No other girl of her set received such lessons. But her grandmother decided that, because she was so tall "and probably very awkward," she should have them weekly. ER "learned toe dancing with four or five other girls who were going on the stage . . . and talked of little else, and made me very envious." ER loved the ballet, was fascinated by the idea of the stage, and was enraptured by all their stories: "I loved it and practiced assiduously, and can still appreciate how much work lies behind some of the dances which look so easy on the stage."

Eleanor loved the theatre above all. One of her keenest memories during this time was the evening Aunt Pussie took her to see Eleanora Duse. It was the great Italian actress's first trip to the United States, and Aunt Pussie brought Eleanor backstage. It was "a thrill which I have never forgotten. Her charm and beauty were all that I had imagined."

During her early adolescence, ER "would have given anything to be a singer, partly because my father loved to sing, and when he came to the 37th Street house he would sing with Maude and Pussie, and partly because I admired some of their friends who were professional singers. I felt that one could give a great deal of pleasure and, yes, receive attention and admiration! Attention and admiration were the things throughout all my childhood which I wanted, because I was made to feel so conscious of the fact that nothing about me would attract attention or would bring me admiration!"

During the five years between her parents' deaths and her voyage to school in England, her grandmother and her aunts gave Eleanor her first real opportunities to be noticed and appreciated, as she had not been by her mother.

Eleanor Roosevelt's desire to shine, to perform with excellence, and to be admired was to be even more fully realized following an announcement her grandmother made one day: "Your mother wanted you to go to boarding school in Europe. And I have decided to send you, child." Elliott and Anna had met Marie Souvestre, Bye's former teacher, when they were in Paris with Bye in 1891, and Anna was vastly impressed by the woman whom Bye always named, after her father, as one of the most profound influences in her life. Eleanor's Roosevelt aunts had also encouraged Mrs. Hall to send her to Allenswood immediately after Anna's death.

Despite Bye's conviction that Eleanor would be happiest at Allenswood, Mrs. Hall had at first refused to send Eleanor away to school, and preferred to keep her under closer supervision at Tivoli. By 1899, however, Tivoli no longer seemed a calm, pastoral retreat. ER's young Uncles Eddie and Valentine (Vallie) were ever more unpredictable— and alcoholic. Mrs. Hall decided that Tivoli had become too wild and frivolous for her granddaughter. That summer, when she invited Eleanor into her sitting room to announce her decision, she had already written to Marie Souvestre, who replied: "Believe me as long as Eleanor will stay with me I shall bear her an almost maternal feeling. First because I am devoted to her Aunt [Bye] Mrs. Cowles, and also because I have known both the parents she was unfortunate to lose."*

Eleanor embarked on this new phase of her life with great anticipation and excitement. She left for Allenswood in 1899, when she was fifteen.

* ER's Aunt Bye (Anna Roosevelt Cowles) married Commander Sheffield (Will) Cowles in London in 1895. She surprised the family by her sudden marriage at the age of forty to her forty-nine-year-old "Mr. Bearo," a naval attaché to the United States embassy. Members of her family were put out by her unexpected marriage, most notably Rosy Roosevelt, who lost his diplomatic hostess.

5. Allenswood and Marie Souvestre

E LEANOR SAILED FOR ENGLAND ACCOMPANIED BY HER Aunt Tissie—Elizabeth Livingston Hall—who with her husband, Stanley Mortimer, a famous art-collector and portrait-painter, had lived in England for many years. Close to Eleanor's parents, they were associated with the fox-hunting Meadow Brook set. During the 1890s, the Mortimers built a sixty-room English Tudor manor on their 101-acre estate in Roslyn, Long Island—with Gothic gables, a bright Spanish tiled roof, imported stained-glass windows for the library, and Della Robbias in the stable.

During her five years at Tivoli, Eleanor had not seen the Mortimers often, but they became close while she was at Allenswood. Aunt Tissie (as well as Mademoiselle Souvestre) introduced ER to new experiences, new places, new people: Claridge's Hotel in London, where ER would often stay in the future; the Passion Play at Oberammergau; Saint-Moritz; the Austrian Tyrol, which ER always considered "one of the loveliest places in the world." Tissie was "always kindness itself to me," recalled ER. She was "very beautiful," and "felt more at home in Europe and in England than she did in the United States. . . . She had many friends in that little London coterie known as 'The Souls.' She was one of the people that the word 'exquisite' describes best." Eleanor's three years at Allenswood would be much enhanced by her visits and travels with her Aunt Tissie.

Located in Wimbledon Park, minutes from central London by train, Allenswood was a small school dedicated to offering the daughters of Europe's liberal aristocracy, and America's leadership class, a wide-ranging education that emphasized responsibility in society and personal independence, within or without marriage.

Allenswood was not an ordinary finishing school for the *fin de siècle* smart set but, rather, a collegiate environment that took the education of women seriously, at a time when they were denied access to the great halls of learning. Feminist and progressive, Allenswood and its predecessor, Les Ruches, were responsible for the education of several generations of outstanding and notable women.

Both schools had been founded by Marie Souvestre, daughter of the esteemed French philosopher and novelist Emile Souvestre. Well connected and highly regarded throughout liberal intellectual circles, she was an integral part of that community of radical thinkers associated with John Morley, Joseph Chamberlain, Leslie Stephen, and Jane Maria Grant (Lady Strachey). Of this circle, only Leslie Stephen failed to send his daughters, Vanessa (Bell) and Virginia (Woolf), to her school. Such affluent and privileged Americans as railroad heiresses Natalie Barney and her sister Laura attended Les Ruches, and Henry James urged his brother William to send his daughter to Allenswood.

Lady Strachey spent considerable time with Marie Souvestre in Italy during the winter of 1870–71, after she had to close Les Ruches when the Germans invaded Paris during the Franco-Prussian War, and they remained personally close until Souvestre's death in 1905. Lady Strachey sent her older daughters, Elinor and Dorothy, to Les Ruches and her younger daughters, Joan Pernel and Marjorie, to Allenswood. Indeed, Lady Strachey was largely responsible for Marie Souvestre's ability to transfer her school to England, and then saw to it that the children in her extended Anglo-Indian family circle, including the Ritchies, Thackerays, Pattles, and Tennysons, all went there.

The Stracheys went on to distinguish themselves in many ways that showed the influence of Marie Souvestre. Dorothy Strachey attended Les Ruches, taught Shakespeare at Allenswood, married a French painter named Simon Bussy, engaged in heroic underground work against the fascists during World War II, and became noted as the translator of her great friend André Gide. She also wrote *Olivia,* an ardent novel that remains to date the only portrait of Marie Souvestre. Joan Pernel Strachey became principal of Newnham College, Cambridge. Philippa Strachey, profoundly affected by the feminist ideas of Marie Souvestre, became secretary to the London National Society for Women's Service, from 1914 to 1951. Marjorie Strachey, a teacher and writer whose novel about Bloomsbury, *The Counterfeits,* created quite a stir, was never given proper credit for the work she co-authored with her brother Lytton.

The Strachey sons were also embraced by Marie Souvestre. Frequent dinners, and Christmas holidays brought the entire family to Allenswood for occasions of stirring conviviality. Over the years, Lytton Strachey especially was drawn by Mademoiselle Souvestre's magnetism. According to his biographer Michael Holroyd, "In the grace, the quick and witty brilliance of his literary style can be seen some reflection of her own peculiar charm and mental agility." With her, "Lytton for the first time became . . . aware . . . that there existed . . . an entirely different environment, far more congenial to his nature." In fact, Marie Souvestre's "spirit and personality permeated the whole family." Her magnificent intensity "recharged the core" of their "literary enthralment," as it marked forever the course of the passionately committed lives of her students.

Marie Souvestre's international school thrived at the height of and in the heart of patriarchal Victorian society, in a time when education was, in more mundane circles, considered dangerous to a woman's mental health, the pathway to madness and sterility. Independent and creative education for women was also thought to be dangerous to society. It would lead to votes for women, public activity, socialism, agnosticism, utopianism, opposition to war, the dissolution of empire. It was positively subversive. Marie Souvestre entertained it all. Her ideas were dangerous.

A feminist of bold conviction, she disdained the patriarchal mind— the withering looks and cruel criticisms of male disapproval—which devoured with such ease the spirits of young women struggling to learn and to grow. Like Virginia Woolf, she condemned the giant cucumbers in the garden that spread themselves all over the roses, fed off their strength, and choked them to death. She believed that only by developing an independent vision, and by developing the means to fight and defend that vision, could young women of purpose survive.

If her methods seemed harsh to some of her students, who stood before her with palpitating, fearful hearts, clammy hands, and silent, dry throats, others thrilled to her challenge and were beckoned by her purpose. They understood her message: To achieve and to survive in the realms ordinarily denied them, women had to learn to argue, to resist, and to be forceful themselves.

Beatrice Webb, the British Fabian theorist, considered her a "remarkable woman," whose intellectual rigor helped to forge the future. Her students "felt that every idea is brought under a sort of hammering logic, and broken into pieces unless it be of very sound metal."

A passionate humanist committed to social justice, Marie Souvestre inspired young women to think about leadership, to think for themselves, and above all to think about a nobler, more decent future. To her mind, nothing was dull, no subject irrelevant. Everything creative and imaginative was encouraged. She would not, however, abide dull thoughts, dull thinkers, lazy or boorish girls who wasted their talents and abused their charms.

Dorothy Strachey Bussy described Marie Souvestre in action:

Her brilliant speech darted here and there with the agility and grace of a hummingbird. Sharp and pointed, it would sometimes transfix a victim cruelly. No one was safe, and if one laughed with her, one was liable the next minute to be pierced oneself with a shaft of irony. But she tossed her epigrams with such evident enjoyment, that if one had the smallest sense of fun, one enjoyed them too. . . . But her talk was not all epigrams. One felt it informed by that infectious ardor, that enlivening zest, which were the secret of her success as a schoolmistress. There was nothing into which she could not infuse them. Every subject, however dull it had seemed in the hands of others, became animated in hers. . . . The dullest of her girls were stirred into some sort of life in her presence; to the intelligent, she communicated a Promethean fire which warmed and coloured their whole lives. To sit at table at her right hand was an education itself.

Though Eleanor was exposed to several gifted and learned teachers at Allenswood, Marie Souvestre was "far and away the most impressive and fascinating person." Physically she was "short and rather stout, and had snow-white hair. Her head was beautiful, with clear-cut, strong features, a very strong face and broad forehead." Her hair fell back in "natural waves to a twist at the back of her head. Her eyes looked through you, and she always knew more than she was told." For Eleanor, Allenswood was Marie Souvestre. And the best part of Allenswood were the moments spent informally in her company.

Like her Aunt Bye, ER became one of Marie Souvestre's intimate favorites. Perhaps it was, as Eleanor thought, because of Mademoiselle Souvestre's romance with America and Americans; or perhaps it was her keen ability to sense Eleanor's specialness. Whatever the reason, there was no doubt that, from her first week at Allenswood, she joined the innermost ring of Marie Souvestre's personal orbit. It was a place of unique privileges, and required special obligations. Eleanor Roosevelt delighted in every one.

Entirely bilingual, Eleanor was well prepared for the French-speaking school. At an advantage for the first time in her life, she thoroughly impressed her English schoolmates. One classmate, Helen Gifford, described Eleanor's first day during an interview with the London *Daily Mail* in 1942, when ER visited England: "I remember the day she arrived at the school, she was so very much more grown up than we were, and at her first meal, when we hardly dared open our mouths, she sat opposite Mlle. Souvestre, chatting away in French. . . ."

At Allenswood, ER became confident in her abilities, and her personality flourished. A new maturity was reflected in her appearance. It was not just that she finally stood straighter. Now she claimed her full six-foot height, and walked tall with easy grace and pride. Mademoiselle Souvestre disliked Eleanor's hand-me-down and unflattering clothes, and told her so. She encouraged Eleanor to use her allowance to have a long, really glamorous deep-red dress made by a Paris couturier. ER wore that dress with great pleasure every Sunday, and regularly for parties and school dances. No dress would ever satisfy her more. The tallest girl in her class, she was no longer gawky or ill-clad. And on a daily basis she looked very smart in the school's dapper uniform of long dark skirts, high-collared and occasionally ruffled shirts, striped ties, blazers, and boaters.

Her usual place at dinner beside Mademoiselle Souvestre had several advantages, among them the chance to share special dishes prepared for the headmistress and her party, and the chance to share in the exciting conversation that sparkled about her. There was an urgency to appear to know more than she in fact did, which she achieved by listening keenly to other people's clever words, and appropriating them. But she lived in dread of being discovered, and continually made it her business to know more.

Eleanor had never before experienced female authority as a freeing rather than a constraining force. At Allenswood she was finally given permission to be herself, to act in behalf of her own needs and wants. Unlike her mother and her grandmother, Marie Souvestre encouraged direct inquiry, admired a free-ranging probing intelligence. Mannerly obedience, form without substance, mindless docility meant little, but rigorous thought was immediately rewarded, which meant that Eleanor was able to shine, to be noticed and admired. She was also given the opportunity to explore and express her own feelings. She was even allowed to cry in public, and she felt secure enough to have her very first temper tantrum. That was the greatest gift Marie Souvestre gave to Eleanor Roosevelt, the chance really to know herself—and her deepest emotions.

Physically, Eleanor was invigorated. Her chronic colds and coughs evaporated. Her frequent headaches disappeared. She began to sleep well, eat regularly with good appetite, and feel robust. Despite the cold damp English climate, ER wanted "to bear witness to the fact that I never spent healthier years. I cannot remember being ill for a day."

She played games and danced, enjoyed sports and competition. "One of the proudest moments of my life," she wrote, was the day she "made the first team" in field hockey. "I liked playing with a team and winning their approbation. It was a rough enough game, with many hard knocks." When ER made the first team and was cheered, she understood for the first time pure joy measured by personal success.

Eleanor Roosevelt was held in high esteem at Allenswood. Her presence and her opinions were sought after. She became, in fact, almost immediately the school's primary leader. Above all, she quickly created a circle of intimate friends who were among the brightest and boldest in her class, and who were acknowledged as Mademoiselle Souvestre's favorites.

Carola de Passavant, "a beautiful girl with a lovely character and real capacity," was ER's special friend and occasional roommate. Because she was from Germany, Carola was shunned by many of the English girls, but ER quickly reached out to her. She was also close to Avice Horn, sent home from Australia to be properly educated; Leonie and her sister Helen Gifford, "an extraordinarily brilliant child" whose "spectacles seemed bigger than she was," and who subsequently headed another school on Allenswood principles; Hilda Burkinshaw ("Burky"), sent home from India at the age of five, seemingly a permanent scholar at Allenswood; and Marjorie Bennett, always called Bennett, ER's first roommate, "a very shy, gentle girl" who remained ER's friend until her death.

Bennett first explained Allenswood's many rules to Eleanor, some of which she considered absurd. That only three baths a week were allowed, and none longer than ten minutes, positively appalled the daily-bathing American. The rule that required one to confess upon entering the dining room if one had used an English word at any time that day seemed "ridiculous" to Eleanor. Other rules struck her as capricious, the punishments excessive. Bed-stripping, or having the contents of one's bureau drawers and closets dumped on one's bed when disorderly, seemed rude. Whether Eleanor herself suffered such punishments is uncertain, but she was protective of others who did, particularly her best friend during her first year, "Jane," who became the subject of Eleanor's first demonstration of anguish and temper.

ER considered the girl she referred to anonymously as "Jane" "fascinating . . . brilliant and a real personality." She "had the most violent temper I have almost ever seen, and I doubt if anyone ever tried to discipline her, but she had a fine mind and a very warm heart." Jane and ER studied history with Marie Souvestre. "There were perhaps eight other girls in our class, but as far as I was concerned there was no one but Jane. This impression of mine was helped considerably by the fact that Mlle Souvestre seemed to feel there were only two members of her class—Jane and myself."

The daughter of great landed wealth in Texas and Ireland, Jane, like ER, was selected by Marie Souvestre for special consideration: evenings of poetry reading in her library; classes in which she was singled out for attention and praised for her thoughtful essays. Because Jane was "insubordinate" in the regular German class, Mademoiselle Souvestre arranged for her and ER (called "Totty" by all at Allenswood) to study German privately together. Far more obedient, Eleanor was "considered a good influence for Jane." Their private tutorial worked well until Jane threw an ink bottle at the German teacher.

Eleanor was furious when she learned that Jane was to be expelled. She appealed to Mademoiselle Souvestre. She understood that the offense was "unpardonable," but considered the punishment extreme, unnecessary, and horrid. She cried and shouted, cajoled and pleaded, wept bitterly and at length. But Mademoiselle Souvestre was adamant. "I was heartbroken," ER wrote in 1937. She had been summarily torn away from yet another passionate and undisciplined person to whom she had given her affections. For "many years" they corresponded, but, ER wrote, "after a time we lost track of each other. . . . Her glamour however is still with me, so that I would give much to see her walk into my room today."

Although firm in her refusal to reconsider the expulsion, Marie Souvestre honored ER's passionate attempt to protect her friend. She never said, as Eleanor's grandmother had, If you have to cry, cry alone. Friendship, independence, spirited and forthright behavior were encouraged. During ER's first year at Allenswood, Marie Souvestre wrote Mrs. Hall:

> All that you said when she came here of the purity of her heart, the nobleness of her thought has been verified by her conduct among people who were at first perfect strangers to her. . . . I often found that she influenced others in the right direction. She is full of sym-

pathy for all those who live with her and shows an intelligent interest in everything she comes in contact with.

As a pupil she is very satisfactory, but even that is of small account when you compare it with the perfect quality of her soul.

Throughout her three years at Allenswood, ER's scholarship ranged from good to excellent. Judging from her notebooks, however, she worked haphazardly on those subjects not taught by Marie Souvestre. Indeed, some of her notebooks are almost blank, except for a few scattered notes. In algebra, her grades were consistently "very good"; at the piano she was an "excellent worker"; on the violin she "made very rapid progress" and was "very good indeed." At painting she consistently "improved, takes pains." But Eleanor's real strengths involved language and literature.

Her teachers were not all immediately enthusiastic about her work. At first Dorothy Strachey seemed rather grudging: "Intelligent as far as can be seen in the few lessons she has had"; "spelling needs improving." But over the years she warmed to Eleanor's efforts: "Very good. Her progress has been very marked this term." Allenswood's Italian teacher, and second in command, Mademoiselle Samaia, was very impressed with Eleanor's abilities: "She works with zeal and great intelligence." "She speaks and writes Italian with ease." In French and German her work was consistently "excellent." In general, Marie Souvestre noted at the end of her first year: "Excellent. She is the most amiable girl I have ever met; she is nice to everybody, very eager to learn and highly interested in all her work."

However diligently Eleanor studied, or seemed to, she was really only involved with Marie Souvestre. She hardly remembered or considered her other teachers, except for Mademoiselle Samaia: "a very tiny and dynamic little woman who adored Mlle Souvestre and waited on her hand and foot, ran all the business end of the school, and gave our Italian lessons." ER wrote that many students worked diligently to get into her good graces, but in order to do that "you had to show practical qualities." Since ER considered herself "a dreamer," she assumed she never entered her good graces. It is clear she did not try very hard or care very much. In any case her time was fully occupied.

Classes were compulsory, and every hour was to be accounted for. There were "hours for practice, time for preparation—no idle moments were left to anyone." Exercise was also compulsory. A serious walk about the common after breakfast, in all weather—even when "the fog rose from the ground and penetrated the very marrow of your bones— but still we walked!" Although Mademoiselle Souvestre hated sports and could never understand "how girls could make such sights of them- selves for a game of hockey," she required two hours of exercise after lunch every day. Then there was a four o'clock snack: "big slices of bread about half an inch thick, sometimes spread with raspberry jam, more often with plain butter." Then a study hour; then fifteen minutes in which to change for dinner.

Dinner at Allenswood was a formal affair. But in the evenings, "we worked again." Occasionally, however, "we were allowed to go down to the gym and dance." One afternoon a week was set aside for super- vised mending, and there were occasional parties and outings. But for Eleanor the high points, the "red letter days," were those occasions when Mademoiselle Souvestre invited ER and her friends to her study in the evening to read and talk.

Mademoiselle Souvestre's library, where she also held her classes, was a "very charming and comfortable room lined with books and filled with flowers." It looked out over "a wide expanse of lawn, where really beautiful trees gave shade in summer, and formed good perches for the rooks and crows in winter." Filled with artworks—including the nudes of Puvis de Chavannes, which initially startled several of her students— Mademoiselle Souvestre's library was the site of ER's most splendid hours.

On most occasions, Mademoiselle Souvestre read aloud. ER recalled that she "had a great gift for reading aloud and she read to us, always in French, poems, plays or stories." Her voice was "like Cordelia's," pitched "soft, gentle, and low." She might read a favorite poem two or three times and then "demanded that we recite them to her in turn." For ER that was a pleasure, since her memory was well trained. But "others suffered to such an extent" that they froze, trembled, and "could hardly speak."

On other occasions, Mademoiselle Souvestre invited her favorite students to her study to proffer honors, or impart her views—messages she considered essential for this group of daughters of the leadership classes. She asked probing questions, exacted precise and thoughtful commentary, and evoked the best from those young women she judged special.

Mademoiselle Souvestre's library was the vital center for all the students of Allenswood. Every evening, they assembled there before going to bed. Mail was distributed, the roll was called, announcements were made. Then the students "passed before Mlle Souvestre and wished her good night." She had a word for each student, to encourage or to chastise. She either kissed you good night, or took your hand. And, according to ER, her judgments were generally correct. "She had an eagle eye which penetrated right through to your backbone and she took in everything about you."

Marie Souvestre's legacy to her students was her own power—her clarity of vision, her personal vigor, and her deep learning. She demanded that her students take themselves seriously. She was often impatient, and she could be cruel. But she reserved her cruelty for students who failed to think, to apply their own understanding, convictions, and ideals to her lessons. A paper without reflection or independent thought might be torn apart in public.

ER excelled at writing papers. We "were expected to do a good deal of independent reading and research . . . and I labored hard over those papers." When she handed in slipshod work, it never went unnoticed. If criticized, she worked harder—rewrote, reconsidered, reflected more deeply. Eleanor enjoyed the process, and her work was generally acclaimed. Some of the others did not fare so well. Workaday efforts enraged Mademoiselle Souvestre. ER noted, "I have seen her take a girl's paper and tear it in half in her disgust and anger at poor or shoddy work."

Mademoiselle Souvestre's explosive moods did not trouble Eleanor, whose years at Allenswood were entirely fearless: "For the first time in all my life all my fears left me." However, Mademoiselle Souvestre's displeasure was a hideous ordeal for many—not only its specific victims, but all who were stifled by her dramatic displays. ER's cousin Corinne Robinson, whose first term at Allenswood coincided with Eleanor's last, was horrified by her temper. She wrote her mother: "The classes with Mlle Souvestre are very interesting, but sometimes she gets terribly mad, and then I do pity the poor girl she is mad with. She pushes her round and screams and yells. . . . I like her much better when not at lessons. . . ."

Reading through ER's notebooks, one is surprised at how classical and traditional her studies were, though under the direction of one of the most liberal academic women in all of Europe. With emphasis on high culture, literature, and the arts, scarcely a class hour seems to have been devoted to economics, science, or that study of humanity and society that we now call the natural and social sciences then emerging in England and the United States. History, which Eleanor studied with Marie Souvestre, was essentially literary and cultural history, and the celebration of heroes.

Heroines were few. There is one page in Eleanor's notebook on a minor female saint, Sainte Eulalie, a French virgin who was martyred at the age of twelve. But the only important deviation from the celebration of classic male texts was the inclusion of Christine de Pisan's critical analysis of the utterly misogynist *Roman de la Rose.* Since Christine de Pisan, the great fifteenth-century champion of education for women, was virtually lost in the several student generations between ER's schooldays and the 1970s, her appearance at Allenswood is worth noting. Married at fifteen, widowed at twenty-five, the mother of three, Christine de Pisan earned her living by her pen. Europe's first "bluestocking," she was called the first woman "who was a man of letters." As a poet and an essayist, she was honored by her contemporaries for her brilliance and her strength of conviction. With a small number of male allies, she created an order for the defense of women, called the Court Amoureuse, inaugurated on Saint Valentine's Day 1400 to honor women and to pursue poetry. Her essays, "The City of Women" and the "Book of Three Virtues," described how a perfect lady ought to behave under every circumstance, and many of her teachings on the subject were timeless.

Despite the lack of classroom time devoted to the subject, politics, the controversies that divided Europe on the eve of the twentieth century, were discussed with passion in Marie Souvestre's informal library sessions. She was a Dreyfusard, and condemned anti-Semitism. She was opposed to the Boer War, then raging in South Africa. Although the English girls were free to celebrate their victories, she would sit in her library with the girls from North and South America, Sweden, Russia, the Netherlands, Germany, Italy, Spain, and France and question the implications of empire, the edicts of colonialism. Her heretical ideas startled many of her listeners, but they were free to reject them. She encouraged all of the girls to become politically engaged.

Marie Souvestre expected to be challenged, and she believed in controversy, the fact of it as well as the exercise of it. She selected her favorites on the basis of their ability to interest and engage her. For three years ER was her favorite of favorites. When her cousin Corinne entered Allenswood, she noted that ER was Mademoiselle Souvestre's "supreme favorite and what was remarkable was that she had made no enemies through this favoritism."

Eleanor was selected to sit beside her at dinner, and to travel with her during several holidays. In her memoirs, ER described her travels with Marie Souvestre. During her first Christmas holiday, they went to Paris together. One Easter, they journeyed to Marseilles, then down the Mediterranean coast, and spent time in Pisa and Florence. During another Christmas holiday, they visited Rome. Mademoiselle Souvestre introduced her to local cuisine, *vin du pays,* variety, experiment, adventure. She was an impulsive traveler who dashed off the train spontaneously to visit a friend and walk on the beach in the moonlight.

At Alassio, "Mlle Souvestre was galvanized into action": We are going to get off, she announced. "I was aghast, for my grandmother, who was far from Mlle Souvestre's seventy years . . . would never have thought of changing plans once she was on the train."

But Mademoiselle Souvestre's friend Mrs. Humphry Ward* lived there, and, she explained, "the Mediterranean is a very lovely blue at night and the sky with the stars coming out is nice to watch from the

---

* Mary Augusta Arnold Ward, a learned historian and British philanthropist, long identified with Oxford, the education of women, and modern ideas, became a best-selling novelist and memoirist. She is best remembered for her efforts to modernize religion, and her curious role as the head of the Anti-Suffrage League. She was so eager to educate women that few could fathom her opposition to their political empowerment. See notes, page 516.

beach." ER was "thrilled" by her spontaneity. Marie Souvestre taught ER "how to enjoy traveling. She liked to be comfortable, she enjoyed good food. . . . She always ate native dishes and drank native wines. I think she felt that it was just as important to enjoy good Italian food as it was to enjoy good Italian art, and it all served to make you a citizen of the world, at home wherever you might go. . . ." ER considered her travels with Marie Souvestre "one of the most momentous things that happened in my education."

ER was given all the responsibilities for arrangements, packing and unpacking, planning the train schedules, and buying the tickets. Her travels with Marie Souvestre changed her life. "Never again would I be the rigid little person I had been theretofore." In Florence and Paris, she toured alone with her Baedeker. Later she wrote: "I really marvel now at myself—confidence and independence, for I was totally without fear in this new phase of my life." But this phase was to come to an abrupt end the day her Tivoli neighbors, the Thomas Newbold family, saw her sightseeing alone, and wrote home to her grandmother that she "was unchaperoned in Paris!"

This letter caused Grandmother Hall to demand Eleanor's return home after her second year. Marie Souvestre was displeased by Mrs. Hall's decision, but if she made any effort to change her mind the letter is lost. As Eleanor prepared to leave, Mademoiselle Souvestre wrote her grandmother: "Eleanor has had the most admirable influence on the school and gained the affection of many and the respect of all. To me personally I feel I lose a dear friend in her."

Eleanor hated to leave, but could not refuse her grandmother's orders. The most devastating experience of that summer back home was an encounter with her Aunt Pussie, whose string of unsuccessful love affairs had made her moody and unpredictable. One day, presumably troubled by yet another romantic disaster of her own, she turned on her niece and blurted that Eleanor "would probably never have the beaux that the rest of the women in the family had had, because I was the ugly duckling." Quite out of control, she then disclosed "the painful and distressing facts about my father's last years." If Eleanor tended to dismiss her aunt's outburst as yet another instance of her overwrought behavior, when she asked her godmother, Cousin Susie Parish, and her grandmother for the truth, they offered no comfort. And she understood for the first time the mysteries of her childhood. It was a brutal summer. She was inconsolable for weeks, and "wanted just one thing, to get back to England to school and more traveling in Europe." She was in such a state that she was able to convince her grandmother that it would indeed be best for her to return to Allenswood for one more year.

In 1901, her Aunt Tissie was not available to accompany her. Since her grandmother insisted that she be fully chaperoned, and had only reluctantly agreed to her return "after much begging and insistence," Eleanor went to New York City and hired an Episcopalian deaconess as a shipboard companion. "It was one of the funniest and craziest things I ever did." "She looked respectable enough . . . , but I never saw her until the day we landed."

Her last year at Allenswood was a heady, happy time—incomparable, unique. ER was now seventeen, Marie Souvestre seventy. Eleanor was the chosen daughter, the preferred companion. That Christmas, Mademoiselle Souvestre took ER and Burky to Rome, where, at midnight mass at Saint Peter's, ER concluded, with considerable relief, that "Mlle Souvestre was not an atheist at heart for she was as much moved as we were by the music and the lights!" At Easter, she traveled alone with Mademoiselle Souvestre to France, Belgium, and Germany.

It was their last trip together, and Marie Souvestre wrote Mrs. Hall: "It is impossible to wish for oneself a more delightful companion in travelling. She is never tired, never out of sorts, never without a keen interest in all that she sees; the more I know her, the more I see what a helpful and devoted grandchild she will be to you. Ah! to me! What a blank her going away must leave in my life!"

It would leave an empty space in Eleanor's life as well: Corinne Robinson wrote in her unpublished memoirs that when she herself arrived at Allenswood ER was "everything." "She was beloved by everybody. Saturdays we were allowed a sortie into Putney which had stores where you could buy books, flowers. Young girls have crushes and you bought violets or a book and left them in the room of the girl you were idolizing. Eleanor's room every Saturday would be full of flowers because she was so admired."

In 1933, Dorothy Strachey Bussy wrote *Olivia*, a *roman à clef* of Les

Ruches and Allenswood. Like Eleanor, the character of Laura is the model of "every kind of excellence." Her *devoirs,* or papers, "were always the best; they used to be read aloud as examples of what a *devoir* might be, ought to be." The narrator, entirely in love with Mademoiselle Julie (the novel's Marie Souvestre), planned to hate Laura, to be jealous of this "altogether too perfect" paragon. But when they meet:

> we were both shy and awkward, but Laura more awkward than I, and I soon realized that, instead of feeling herself superior, on the contrary, she was curiously conscious of her deficiencies. She knew that, in spite of her efforts, she was badly dressed and clumsy. . . . that she had nothing, in fact, to atone for her intellectual superiority, while at the same time she had an uneasy feeling that that superiority ought somehow to be atoned for. Not that this want of confidence in her powers of attraction made her self-conscious. No, I have never seen anyone devote herself to others with such manifest gladness. And yet, with all her altruism, one could never think of her as self-sacrificing. She never did sacrifice herself. . . . Her face was one of the most radiant I have ever seen; grave sometimes, but never moody, never despondent. Her clear, untroubled eyes looked at one with such frank, joyful affection that for the moment she banished moodiness and despondency. . . . She was an invigorating companion. . . .

Unlike Laura, Olivia is devastated by her ardent longing for Mademoiselle Julie. One day she asks Laura, "do you love her?"

> "Oh," said Laura, "you know I do. She has been the best part of my life. . . . She has opened my eyes to all I like best in the world, showered me with innumerable treasures."
>
> "And tell me this, Laura. Does your heart beat when you go into the room where she is? Does it stand still when you touch her hand? Does your voice dry up in your throat when you speak to her? Do you hardly dare raise your eyes to look at her, and yet not succeed in turning them away?"
>
> "No," said Laura. "None of that."

"What then?" I insisted.

"Why," said Laura, looking at me with her clear, untroubled eyes, which had a kind of wonder and a kind of recoil in them: "there's nothing else. I just love her."

Writing during her sixty-eighth year, Dorothy Strachey Bussy sought to describe the awakening of the incomparable sensations aroused in her when she was sixteen and first heard Marie Souvestre read from Racine's *Andromaque:*

> I looked at her for the first time as I listened. I don't know which I did more thirstily—looked or listened. It suddenly dawned upon me that this was beauty—great beauty . . . physical beauty. I was never blind to it again. . . . And then there were the sonorous vowels, the majestic periods, the tremendous names sweep on; one is borne upon a tide of music and greatness. . . . One follows breathlessly . . . leaving at the end a child's soul shaken and exhausted.

As for her lessons, Olivia now approached them "with a renovated ardor." Every page of every lesson now held a new mystery, "some passionate secret which must be mined or I should die! Words! How astonishing they were. . . ."

Every moment in the company of Mademoiselle Julie is now filled with a new level of excitement, of enchantment. "Had I never looked at a face before?" Every detail, every smile, or scowl is devoured. She gives way to languor. Her longing for a moment alone with Mademoiselle Julie became unbearable. She sits for hours plunged in gloom, her head on the table, "in a kind of coma." She becomes "a mass of physical sensations which bewildered me, which made me feel positively sick. My heart beat violently, my breath came fast. . . . At the opening of every door, at the sound of the most casual footstep, my solar plexus shot the wildest stabs through every portion of my body. . . ."

Written fifteen years earlier, *Olivia* was published anonymously in London by Leonard and Virginia Woolf's Hogarth Press in 1948. It became an immediate best-seller and went into twenty printings within weeks. Dedicating her book "To the beloved memory of V.W.," Bussy (then over eighty) wrote in the introduction: "I have occupied this idle, empty winter with writing a story. It has been written to please myself, . . . without regard for other people's feelings, without considering whether I shock or hurt the living, without scrupling to speak of the dead."

Dorothy Strachey Bussy explained that her effort to recapture the feelings of that year when she was sixteen had been one of the most difficult tasks of her life. She had first of all to confront a variety of known and unknown enemies. It had been necessary to overthrow "the psychologists, the psychoanalysts, the Prousts and the Freuds"—all of whom had lain "in ambush" to "poison the sources of emotion," "to give it its name," and to apply their "poisonous antidotes" to the romantic realities of life. "Love has always been the chief business of my life," she wrote, "and I don't pretend that this experience was not succeeded by others." But now she had "felt the urgency of confession," the need to stand up to and assail those elements of her culture that had caused her to hide, to experience her first passion in dread and pain. "Really no one had ever heard of such a thing, except as a joke. Yes, people used to make joking allusions to 'school-girl crushes.' But I knew well enough that my 'crush' was not a joke. And yet I had an uneasy feeling that, if not a joke, it was something to be ashamed of, something to hide desperately."

Decades of biographical denial have attempted to persuade us that Eleanor Roosevelt knew nothing of "the meaning," the true meaning of *Olivia*. But *Olivia* is not a coded or esoteric book. It is a very simple love story of young, uncontrollable romance. A lesbian romance. The passions that devastated Olivia did not devastate Eleanor. But she understood the book, and she was grateful to receive it.*

Her classmate Marjorie Bennett Vaughn sent her the book, with the details of its publication. "I have ordered a little book to be sent to you which I think may be of interest. . . ." "Leonie [Gifford] and I have both liked it very much, and thought you might. It is quite short and so would not take up much of your valuable time."

* See notes, page 517.

Bennett's next letter thanks ER for her "nice little note." "I am glad you liked *Olivia*. It seemed to take me back so far! . . ."

Eleanor Roosevelt was very specific about her own feelings toward Marie Souvestre. She was her teacher, the most important person in her life after her father. She was the first woman who encouraged Eleanor to explore her heart, discover and develop her capacities. Increasingly, "day by day I found myself more interested in her. This grew into a warm affection that lasted until her death."

When Eleanor was faced with the ordeal of having to leave Allenswood at eighteen in order to make her debut into society, she was bereft. "Mlle Souvestre had become one of the people whom I cared most for in the world, and the long separation seemed hard to bear. I would have given a good deal to have spent another year on my education." But when Eleanor left Allenswood she "felt quite sure" she would return before long, to teach. She never considered not seeing Marie Souvestre again. "She wrote me lovely letters, which I still cherish," ER wrote in 1960.

Many of these letters, like so many others of key importance to ER, have disappeared. Yet the ones that survive reveal clearly that a regular correspondence existed.

On 7 July 1902, Mademoiselle Souvestre wrote:

> My dear little girl, See how little luck I have with you? The day you left I wired you a single word which expressed all my hope and all my desire, 'au revoir'. The telegram was returned to me . . . and, once more, this very warm remembrance of my friendship for you, of my regrets, did not reach you.
>
> However the letter which you sent me when you were about to leave the steamer reached me and caused me all the pleasure you intended it to do.

From Geneva, Marie Souvestre wrote:

> I am happy in the thought that these three years of such sustained and productive work on your part have also been a period of joy and rest for you and that they will, at the end of your adolescence

and at the beginning of your youth, be a period you will look back to for a long time with satisfaction and serenity.

But she worried about ER's entrance into society, lest her three years' work disappear

quickly into the mist of the past. From this very minute, when I am writing to you, life, your life, which is entirely new and entirely different, and in several respects entirely contradictory, is going to take you and drag you into its turmoil. Protect yourself to some extent against it, my dear child, protect yourself above all from the standpoint of your health. . . . Give some of your energy, but not all, to worldly pleasures which are going to beckon you. And even when success comes, as I am sure it will, bear in mind that there are more quiet and enviable joys than to be among the most sought-after women at a ball. . . .

Tell me how you have found your grandmother and little brother. He does not yet know the value of your warm sisterly tenderness; but he will . . . and you will become for him what you desire to be. . . .

Goodbye, dear child, I must get dressed; I miss you during our voyages. . . .

A thousand and a thousand tendernesses to my Totty whom I shall always love.

M. Souvestre

On 17 August 1902, Marie Souvestre wrote,

Dear Child, Although I wrote to you just a few days ago, the letter, dated from the third, which I received from you today, seems to require an answer for which I do not want you to wait.

First, about my portrait. Why didn't you ask for it? I would have given it to you immediately, and with such pleasure! But I never offer to give one. You might say it is a principle. People's impressions are variable. Some prefer the ever-changing and diverse image of a loved face which their memory shows them, to the stilted expression on a photograph or a portrait. Often one asks for a photograph more to please. . . . And I want it understood between my friends and me that I am insensitive to this small flattery. But as I believe that it is indeed for yourself you ask my photograph, you shall receive it. . . .

I am in Switzerland, at Cluny, delighted, when the weather is nice, to live in the sky, annoyed when it is bad, to live only in clouds. I would like to have you with me. I miss you every day of my life, but it is a selfish regret for which I reprove myself. You fulfill your destiny more where you are, than you would near me. Mlle Samaia is at Chaxlin with her sister, 4 or 5 kms from me.

Till soon, dear child. I love you and kiss you.

The last letter that survives from Marie Souvestre is dated 5 October 1902, from Allenswood.

Dear Child, . . . Yesterday quantities of letters from you arrived at Allenswood. There were none for me among the ones I distributed, but I hope I shall be luckier next week. Leonie's letter to Mlle Samaia written from your home, was of much interest to me also, since it portrays you, in your surroundings, as you wouldn't present yourself. I am happy to see that your brother is becoming more and more attached to you. I can understand how your aunt's regrets, seeing the preferences of such a dearly loved nephew pass from herself to you, are a source of sorrow to you. But as it is, after all, the direction his affection should take, your aunt will finally accept what is legitimate. Moreover, it seems to me your aunts are carried away in a whirl of exciting social activities which protects them against lasting regret of a sentimental nature.

Dear child, my mind is so divided in respect to you. I should like to know that you are happy, and yet how I fear to hear that you have been unable to defend yourself against all the temptations which surround you; evenings out, pleasure, flirtations. How all this will estrange you from all that I knew you to be! Mrs. Robinson assured me that she would take you with her as often as possible, and that Mrs. Cowles would do the same. . . .

Please tell me when the big season of social dissipations starts in New York? When does it end? Is it immediately after the carnival season, and is it true that we shall see you here in the spring? . . .

Ah! how we miss you here, my dear child. There are many new girls and, as is their habit, the English girls do not know how to welcome them, and leave them in the corner. You would have known how to make them feel rapidly at ease, and happy in circumstances so different from their usual lives; for some are German, others French, another one, coming from Algeria and born of English parents. . . . There is a new English girl, very bright and lively, and another one, quite stupid. Finally your fellow Americans are going to present quite a respectable front. . . . Bennett came for the opening of school. I wish she were here much more often, for she has the best influence on the girls, and they love her. However, I don't believe that her mother feels much pleasure at seeing her take such an absorbing interest in her former school, and I do not call on her as frequently as I would wish.

Please convey my best compliments to your grandmother, and my thanks for the letter she sent me. I shall answer it soon, and send her your last papers, which Mlle Samaia had given me, and which stayed in my desk.

You never told me how your money problems were resolved. Have you the control of a definite sum . . . as long as you are a minor, or does someone simply pay your expenses. . . .

Till soon, my good child. Winter is coming, the flowers are dying in the garden, the horizon is hidden behind a heavy, motionless curtain of gray mists, the sad days are beginning in this country where they are sadder than anywhere else. I wish you what we lack: light and sun.

For the rest of her life, ER always kept Marie Souvestre's portrait on her desk. In her memoirs, she noted that she cherished her teacher's letters and, like those her father had written, carried them with her all her life. In the summer of 1905, ER visited Allenswood while on her honeymoon. But Marie Souvestre had died of cancer on 30 March. She had, however, sent a one-word telegram that arrived the morning of

ER's wedding, on 17 March: "BONHEUR!" ER noted in her letter home that she "saw Mlle Samaia, but it was dreadful without Mlle Souvestre."

In October 1905, ER was part of a "Marie Souvestre Memorial" Committee, which included Anna Roosevelt Cowles, Beatrice Chamberlain, John Morley, Mrs. Humphry Ward, Alexander Ribot, Frau Dr. von Siemens, Sidney and Beatrice Webb, and the Stracheys.

The great teacher was mourned by many, and her obituary in the London *Times* testified to her extraordinary life:

> . . . She will be mourned by a large number of pupils and friends in Europe and in America, and by many in the world of literature, art, and politics. Her strong individuality, her rare eloquence, and wide learning exerted a lasting influence over all who came in contact with her. . . . The intense enthusiasm she could inspire in the young for things of the mind, for courageous judgment, and for a deep sense of public duty was the special gift by which her personality impressed itself on all around her. . . . Her lectures on history and on the great social movements of the past, rich with the fire of a French *causeur* and full of original thought, will long be remembered. . . . A zealous politician, a convinced Liberal, and a passionate friend of all great problems of nationality, she ever held up a high ideal of public honour and patriotism. Nor was she less striking in all her judgments about literature and art. . . . She will long be remembered as having brought into English society . . . some of the finest traditions of Parisian culture and not a few of the noblest gifts of the French genius.

Eleanor Roosevelt never turned away from the memory of Marie Souvestre. Her influence and spirit burned deeply within ER, and her teachings continually pointed in the direction of what was possible by way of independence, self-fulfillment, public activity, and human understanding.

6. Coming Out and Courting

"PROTECT YOURSELF." "PROTECT YOURSELF, MY DEAR child," from the turmoil, contradictions, and expectations of society's demands. "Give some of your energy, but not all, to worldly pleasures. . . . And even when success comes, as I am sure it will, bear in mind that there are more quiet and enviable joys than to be among the most sought-after women at a ball or . . . at the various fashionable affairs."

In New York and Tivoli, Eleanor reread Marie Souvestre's concerned letters many times, but they could do nothing to protect her from her sense of duty to society's demands. Social rituals were specific, rigid, ordered—and quite simple, really. At eighteen, Eleanor Roosevelt—a Livingston-Ludlow-Hall Roosevelt, the niece of the president of the United States—was supposed to emerge as from a chrysalis, full-blown and decorous, carefree and charming. She was to be a belle, an eligible mate for a suitable swain.

That she might have had contrary ideas, or feelings of terror; that her family situation alternated between disagreeable and painful, were all obscured by one reality: Eleanor was to enter society through a series of parties and balls in which she was meant to reaffirm the continued reign of the women of her line.

But Eleanor Roosevelt was no ordinary belle. And her situation did not encourage carefree joy. Her brother was now an adolescent for whom she had primary responsibility. Her uncles were no longer sober, even on occasion. At some point, three strong, very protective locks were installed on the door of her room at Tivoli. Was she ever hurt or abused? Did Uncle Vallie or Uncle Eddie ever actually get into her room? What kind of battle ensued? Three locks appeared; and nobody ever referred to their presence. Life in the house at Tivoli was now more unpredictable and gloomy than ever.

During her first summer at home, before the social season started, Eleanor lived entirely at Tivoli. Those months were marked by family disintegration, and social obligations that neither amused nor interested her. Pussie, still unmarried at thirty-two, was away most of that summer; Maude, her youngest aunt, was now married to polo player Larry Waterbury—a sportsman and gambler, often in debt and generally high-spirited. Her Uncle Eddie was then married to glamorous Josie Zabriskie, but he too had become alcoholic and querulous. The focal point of pain, however, was Uncle Vallie—the best-beloved, most irresponsible son who was now quite out of control. "My grandmother would never believe that he was not going to give it up as he promised after each spree," but all the rest of the family understood, and daily life had been rendered "distinctly difficult."

Unable even in retrospect to acknowledge the similarities to her father's ordeal, Eleanor wrote that she considered this her

> first real contact with anyone who had completely lost the power of self-control, and I think it began to develop in me an almost exaggerated idea of the necessity of keeping all of one's desires under complete subjugation.
>
> I had been a solemn little girl, my years in England had given me my first real taste of being carefree and irresponsible, but my return home . . . accentuated almost immediately the serious side of life, and that first summer was not very good preparation for being a gay and joyous debutante.

Eleanor had invited her Allenswood classmate Leonie Gifford, who had recently lost her mother, to spend part of the summer with her.

But Vallie's behavior was so unpredictable, every moment was an agony of insecurity. He shot his rifle out the window at strolling guests. Full of braggadocio, he said amazing, unbearable things. Eleanor held her breath during Leonie's entire visit, and never invited another woman friend to Tivoli. "After that I would occasionally invite a man, but never felt free to do so unless I knew him well enough to tell him that he might have an uncomfortable time."

In September, Eleanor and her grandmother accompanied Hall to Groton. That trip marked the beginning of Eleanor's primary responsibility for her brother's well-being. Though not old, her grandmother, not yet sixty, seemed now exhausted, beaten down by her own children. During the trip to Groton, Eleanor noticed that her grandmother seemed rather vague and unsettled. Responsibility for Hall slipped "rapidly from her hands into mine. She never again went to see him at school and I began to go up every term for a weekend, which was what all good parents were expected to do." For the next six years, Eleanor wrote Hall virtually every day, so that he would never forget that he belonged to somebody. She took him on trips, arranged parties for him, and in every way served as his maternal parent and confidante until his early death from alcoholism in 1941.

During that first autumn, Eleanor spent many days virtually alone in New York City. Her grandmother rarely went to town, and lived almost entirely at Tivoli, "in a vain attempt to keep Vallie there and keep him sober as much as possible." Occasionally Pussie joined Eleanor at the 37th Street house, but it was even worse when she was there. With "several love affairs always devastating her emotions," Pussie continued to go the rounds of "dinners and dances as hard as any debutante." Indeed, at the parties and cotillions Pussie remained, at thirty-two, quite the successful belle. But she was never content. Frequently she locked herself in her room, and refused to eat. Given over to rages and tantrums, vapors and melancholy, Pussie had become "even more temperamental than she had been as a young girl." To add to Eleanor's domestic stress, Uncle Vallie also appeared on occasion at 37th Street, "for one purpose and one alone: to go on a real spree."

Eleanor ran the house, "as far as it was run by anyone," and discovered within herself "a certain kind of strength and determination which underlay my timidity." With her newfound strength, she handled efficiently and tactfully the many and extraordinary "difficulties that arose during this strange winter" of her coming out—when all society expected her to do was be joyful and dance until dawn.

Then her grandmother decided to close down the New York town house. It was too little used, required too many servants, and money had become a serious issue. Although her godmother, Cousin Susie Parish, took Eleanor in and her town house at 8 East 76th Street was a comfortable place, Eleanor felt again that she had no home she could call her own. Still, even by Eleanor Roosevelt's own account, "a number of pleasant things" happened that winter. Ever since Marie Souvestre had encouraged her to discard unflattering clothes, she had enjoyed dressing well for formal occasions. Now her Aunt Tissie sent her Paris designs from the finest houses. She was at ease in conversation, especially with older people, and quickly achieved a reputation for bringing out the best in serious company. She often found herself seated next to the host, or the most esteemed gentleman in the room. Just as often he was fascinated by her sophisticated and learned conversation. She appeared to be years older than her contemporaries, and her letters during this period seem astounding when one remembers that they were written by a woman of eighteen, not twenty-five—as many people then assumed her to be. But for Eleanor these were all dubious distinctions; sophistication did not render her a belle, and there were many situations in which she felt awkward.

Nevertheless, her cousin Alice, Uncle Theodore's daughter, now known as "Princess Alice," was jealous of Eleanor. "Odious comparisons," and the idea that Eleanor was considered by many to be "more like my father's daughter than I was," and the only member of the family who truly took after him, "added nothing to family solidarity," she later explained.

Alice Roosevelt always insisted that stories about Eleanor's clumsy lurch into society were ER's own invention: "She was always making herself out to be an ugly duckling but she was really rather attractive. Tall, rather coltish-looking, with masses of pale, gold hair rippling to below her waist, and really lovely blue eyes. It's true that her chin went in a bit, which wouldn't have been so noticeable if only her hateful grandmother had fixed her teeth."

At eighteen, Eleanor Roosevelt was cautious and judgmental. Having learned from Marie Souvestre to discriminate, and to choose experiences that pleased her, she refused to suffer fools, and loathed arrogance and pomposity. She could be cold, stubborn, and haughty as well as warm and tender. She hated deceit, and feared youthful alcoholic silliness. Though she would indeed rush off from a dull dance, when the company was interesting, the conversation unusual, witty, or original, she felt free to stay and enjoy herself well into the morning.

~

DURING THESE ARDUOUS SOCIAL MONTHS, ELEANOR WAS PAR-ticularly happy to spend time with Bob Ferguson, the much-beloved family friend who had waited so tenderly upon her mother as she lay dying. The younger brother of Ronald, Lord Novar—whose Scottish lands included the magnificent Novar and Raith, on the Firth of Forth—Robert Munro Ferguson was a former Rough Rider and had once been Auntie Bye's attentive young squire. He had remained an eligible bachelor whose wide-ranging interests and bohemian friends made his company particularly appealing to Eleanor. With him, Eleanor was relieved of the burden of being chaperoned about New York by her waiting maid. And with him she met people she otherwise might not have known. Eleanor particularly liked the artists and writers who attended parties in Bay Emmet's studio in Greenwich Village.

A portrait painter of distinction, descended from a family of revolutionary Irish heroes, Ellen ("Bay") Emmet became one of Eleanor's lifelong friends. She was hardworking, robust, with masses of bright red hair, profoundly political, unpretentious, and vigorously cheerful. Like her older cousins, the equally renowned artists Rosina Emmet Sherwood (Robert Sherwood's mother) and Lydia Field Emmet, Bay Emmet studied in Boston, New York (at the Art Students' League), and in Europe, particularly in Paris, with the famed sculptor Frederick MacMonnies. By the time she returned to New York, in 1900, she was considered by many, including her cousin Henry James, "a *pure* painter, a real one, a good one."

In 1902, when she and Eleanor first met, she had her first one-woman exhibition at the Durand-Ruel Galleries in New York. She was virtually the sole support of a very large family, including her widowed mother, three sisters, and young brother. Ten years older than Eleanor, Bay's zest for life and joy in work, as well as her bohemian circle, were refreshing to the uptown debutante. Eleanor vastly preferred the many hours she spent in Bay's studio to all the "dinners and dances I was struggling through in formal society each night, and yet I would not have wanted at that age to be left out, for I was still haunted by my upbringing and believed that what was known as New York Society was really important."

~

IN OCTOBER, MARIE SOUVESTRE WROTE: "PLEASE TELL ME when the big season of social dissipations starts in New York?" The answer was actually a bit vague: there were dances and dinners, cotillions and theatre parties in the early autumn; but with the shorter, colder, grayer days of November, New York society announced its return to town by attending the great horse show at Madison Square Garden.

The New York *Herald* noted Eleanor's presence in a box full of Roosevelt-Roosevelts. (Indeed, it has been said that Roosevelts so often married Roosevelts because they never met anybody else.) The box belonged to her distant cousin, the dapper sportsman addicted to magnificent coaches and superior carriages, James Roosevelt Roosevelt. "Rosy" Roosevelt was generous and fun-loving. His marriage to Helen Astor, the second-oldest daughter of *the* Mrs. Astor (Caroline Schermerhorn Astor), and his years in England while first secretary at the Court of Saint James had rendered him mannered beyond belief. But his younger half-brother, Franklin Delano Roosevelt; his daughter, Helen, now engaged to Eleanor's cousin Theodore Douglas Robinson (Aunt Corinne's son); and most of the younger generation were generally enthralled by his witty extravagance. He had invited them all to the horse show that evening. Eleanor Roosevelt's presence was featured not only in the *Herald* but in *Town Topics,* society's gossip sheet. Franklin's presence in his half-brother's box was overlooked.

Franklin, a Harvard junior, recorded in his diary: "Dinner with

James Roosevelt Roosevelt, Helen [Astor] Roosevelt Roosevelt, Mary Newbold and Eleanor Roosevelt at Sherry's and horse show." Franklin's diary entry for 17 November 1902 was his first mention of Cousin Eleanor. There was no similar reference to this meeting, or this event, on Eleanor's part.

For all her very real successes as she entered society, Eleanor Roosevelt was haunted by one fact: She was not the belle her mother and her aunts had been. Her feelings and her fears intensified when she read nostalgic allusions to her relatives in New York's leading papers. The week before the great Assembly Ball, held on 11 December, *Town Topics* broadcast Eleanor's coming out by recalling her mother's rapturous social leadership.

For Eleanor, that Assembly was "utter agony." If she had known how awful it could be, she "would never have had the courage to go." There was, to begin with, the indignity of those blank lines on the dance card tied to her wrist. At each cotillion a suitable swain would, or would not, put his name on one's card—for the first dance, the dinner dance, the ninth dance, the last dance, and then the added and special dances. It was a slow process, a grueling mortification. Taller than most of the young men, unused to their company, Eleanor found the space between dances an agony of dread. Would she be chosen? Would she be a wallflower? Would an older relative ask her to dance out of charity or duty? Although Eleanor danced with Forbes Morgan, Pussie's most ardent escort and the man she was to marry, and with Bob Ferguson, who introduced her to Nick Biddle, Duncan Harris, and Pendleton Rogers, "by no stretch of the imagination could I fool myself into thinking that I was a popular debutante."

However differently others may have remembered Eleanor that evening, she remembered only that she left early, "thankful to get away, having learned that before I went to any party or to any dance I should have two partners, one for supper and one for the cotillion. . . . But you must also be chosen to dance every figure in the cotillion, and your popularity was gauged by the numbers of favors you took home. Pussie always had far more than I had! I knew I was the first girl in my mother's family who was not a belle, and . . . I was deeply ashamed." When combined with the emotional extravagances of her family situation, that first winter brought Eleanor to the verge "of nervous collapse."*

By Christmas, however, the ordeal of her debutante season was over. In December, there began to appear a particular young man at parties and dances who genuinely sought her company. They danced, they talked, they read poetry together. And there was that physical sense of heightened intensity that happens when the chemistry is right. He thought her willowy (everyone called her willowy), elegant, lithe. He considered her eyes and hair particularly lovely. In a secret code, he noted in his journal: "E is an Angel." He was as tall as she, and very much like her father: endlessly charming, always enthusiastic. When he looked at her, he looked at her deeply. He seemed to see her, and to care. He was attentive and ardent and complimentary. When they danced, they were striking. They made each other laugh, often and with gusto. They shared a world of interests, and of dreams. Franklin felt inspired. Eleanor felt hopeful.

Eleanor and Franklin had not seen each other since she was fourteen, and they had danced at Aunt Corinne's Christmas party. Franklin had told his mother after that party that he thought Cousin Eleanor had a fine mind, but they had not corresponded while she was at Allenswood. When they met again after four years, on a New York Central train going up the Hudson during her first summer home in 1902, an easy intimacy marked their conversation. Eleanor had been sitting in a coach, reading, when Franklin walked by and saw her. They talked for almost two hours, and as they neared Poughkeepsie he suggested they go to the parlor car so that she might greet his mother. Eleanor had always been partial to Cousin Sally, who had loved Eleanor's father and named him Franklin's godfather. Now she was stunned by Sara Delano Roosevelt's austere beauty. Considered queenly by many, her manner appeared even more regal because of the severe black mourning veils she still wore in remembrance of her husband's death two years before.

---

* When Duncan Harris read ER's version of her "ordeal," he wrote her a gentlemanly note of disagreement: "I hasten to tell you that you are far too modest about your appeal to the gilded youth of 1902. Bob Ferguson, Nick Biddle and I were not doing heavy duty at parties, and I remember well that when we asked you to dance it was because we wanted to, and contrary to your story, the spirit of competition was distinctly present."

That chance meeting was for Eleanor and Franklin the beginning of a year of frequent encounters at parties and dances, culminating in the summer and autumn of 1903, when they were both guests at several country houses and she was invited to his family home, Springwood in Hyde Park. Eleanor's memories of those early days with Franklin focused primarily on his mother: She "was sorry for me, I think." Sara Delano Roosevelt was never notably delighted when Franklin wanted to invite girls home, but Eleanor was kin, and Sara was always gracious. On the other hand, she took the opportunity of Eleanor's first party weekend at Hyde Park to remind Eleanor that her mother had publicly humiliated her when she was two years old—during her very first visit to Springwood:

Cousin Sally told Eleanor that she remembered "my standing in the door with my finger in my mouth and being addressed as 'Granny' by my mother, and that Franklin rode me around the nursery on his back. This visit, however, is purely a matter of hearsay to me."

For many months, Eleanor and Franklin saw each other only in stolen bits of time. Before Christmas, there were several lunches and teas, but only when Franklin could escape his mother—who kept a very close watch on her boy, and was entirely unready to imagine that he might have a special friend. Nevertheless, they spent New Year's together at the White House. The dinner was sumptuous, the theatre party delightful, and Franklin noted in his diary: "sat near Eleanor. Very interesting day."

On 30 January 1903, Rosy gave a "very jolly!" dinner party for FDR's twenty-first birthday, which for Franklin was highlighted by Eleanor's presence. Franklin hesitated to say anything about her to his mother, however, perhaps because Sara had become so dependent on his solace and companionship after his father died. Recently her loneliness had intensified so much that she had taken an apartment in Boston, in order to be closer to Franklin while he was at Harvard.

Franklin had been similarly discreet about his romance the previous year with seventeen-year-old Alice Sohier. Franklin, then twenty, evidently seemed to her parents too intent on a serious relationship, and they sent her off on a grand tour of Europe and the Middle East. Alice Sohier remembered that she accepted her family's offer of a grand tour with alacrity after Franklin confided to her that his lonely childhood had created a great desire to have a large brood of children, six at least. Years later, she told a friend that she had decided not to marry FDR because she "did not wish to be a cow."

Although Franklin had proposed to Alice Sohier, he never mentioned her to his mother—just as he now failed to mention Eleanor's new presence in his life, which began to be of real interest to him at that November 1902 horse show, less than two months after Alice Sohier sailed for Europe. The following summer and autumn were largely devoted to Eleanor, but he continued to be silent on the subject of their relationship, never referring to her in either correspondence or conversation with his mother.

For her part, Eleanor actively sought a variety of other interests. She had now, she acknowledged, "made many friends." She mentioned Harry Hooker, who was to remain her adviser and attorney, Isabella Selmes, who would soon marry Bob Ferguson, and her mother, Martha Flandreau Selmes, who was Cousin Susie Parish's particular friend.

Many of Eleanor's most gratifying hours during this period were spent in volunteer work. In 1900, while still freshmen at Barnard, Mary Harriman (daughter of railroad builder Edward Henry Harriman and philanthropist Mary Williamson Averell Harriman), Nathalie Henderson, Jean Reid (daughter of Elizabeth Mills Reid and Whitelaw Reid), Gwendolyn Burden, and others had been moved to action by the dreadful crowding, lack of sanitation, cruel working conditions, frequent epidemics, and general misery that faced New York's poor and immigrant population. They decided to join their middle-class sisters in an effort to create centers for social reform. Inspired by Jane Addams, who founded Hull House in Chicago; Lillian Wald, who founded the Henry Street Settlement in New York; and the university-educated radicals who built Toynbee Hall in London, these debutantes founded the Junior League for the Promotion of Settlement Movements, and its affiliated organizations—notably the University Settlement. According to Gladys Vanderbilt (Countess Széchényi), the members of the Junior League were admired, fashionable, beyond mockery: "They were smart, and they made it smart." Several of these women, although two years older than Eleanor, had been among her closest friends and Roser school-mates, and in 1903 she decided to participate actively in the work of the League: "There was no clubhouse; we were just a group of girls anxious to do something helpful in the city where we lived."

Specifically, she agreed to teach calisthenics and fancy dancing to classes of children at the College Settlement on Rivington Street, in New York's Lower East Side. While Eleanor taught the young girls every exercise and dance step she had ever learned, Jean Reid played the piano. Jean frequently arrived "in her carriage," but Eleanor decided to make the trip downtown by public transportation. Whether she took the elevated train or the Fourth Avenue streetcar, she had to walk across the Bowery—which "filled me with a certain amount of terror and I often waited on a corner for a car, watching, with a great deal of trepidation, men come out of the saloons or shabby hotels nearby, but the children interested me enormously."

Eleanor Roosevelt never compromised her decision to take public transportation. Even in the evenings, no matter how cold and dark, she refused Jean Reid's offer of a ride home. She preferred to walk through the streets and to observe the Bowery's lost and lonely men, generally drunk if not particularly threatening. They gave the concerned debutante yet another level of insight into the ravages of alcoholism, and the costs to the children who moved her so deeply.

Eleanor wrote Franklin that she found her hours at the settlement always the "nicest part of the day." She liked the children who took her classes. She enjoyed their spirit, and admired their ability to learn and to play even after twelve to sixteen hours of toil, whether in factories or doing piecework at home. On occasion they were too spirited, and once she "had to send two children home which I hated doing." Generally, however, her classes were harmonious, and her students eager to please. "I still remember," she wrote in 1937, "the glow of pride that ran through me when one of the little girls said her father wanted me to come home with her, as he wanted to give me something because she enjoyed her classes so much."

She also joined the Consumers' League in 1903, and investigated working conditions in garment factories and department stores. The Consumers' League, then headed by Maud Nathan, sought through exposure and publicity, through political lobbying and direct action, to improve the most dreadful places. It worked for better lighting, hygiene, toilet and restroom facilities. As Eleanor Roosevelt, always accompanied by "an experienced, older woman," witnessed the actual working conditions under which so many young girls and women toiled, she gained a "great deal of knowledge of some of the less attractive and less agreeable sides of life."

Her family was somewhat appalled by her good works, and continually pressured her to leave it all behind "for a summer of idleness and recreation." Cousin Susie in particular urged her to quit all her settlement work and join her in Newport. She feared that Eleanor would bring home an immigrant's disease, or be in some way harmed. Moreover, Cousin Susie could see no reason for or benefit from Eleanor's efforts.

But Eleanor considered her work valuable, because it was the first work she did in order to improve the lives of others—a theme that would become a hallmark of her vision. And working on New York's Lower East Side with poor children made her feel connected to her father. She had, from the age of six, helped him serve Thanksgiving dinners to the Newsboys, and had accompanied him to the Children's Aid Society. She decided to continue her work—even if her family and her friends, including Franklin, might not understand. Moreover, while believing in the charitable responsibilities of her class, she also began to understand the need for real economic and political change, and was eager to learn more about what could be done.

On 6 January 1904, Eleanor wrote Franklin that she had spent the morning "at a most interesting class on practical Sociology! Now, don't laugh, it *was* interesting and very practical and if we are going down to the Settlement we ought to know something—I know you are laughing at this and if you were only here to take up all my time I would not be going I'm afraid but one must do something or not having the one person who is all the world to one, would be unbearable. . . ."

Eleanor at nineteen was deeply moved by the sight of a society undergoing fundamental transformations on every level. As new work, new visions, new expectations for young women unfolded, Eleanor felt torn between the traditions of her mother and her aunts, and her own inclinations—as awakened by her father and Marie Souvestre, and as now supported by the small group of unconventional debutantes led by Mary Harriman and Jean Reid.

Eleanor was also inspired by her Aunt Bye, who during TR's presidency (1901–09) became a publicly admired intellectual and salonist. Her Washington home was now known as "the little White House," and few decisions of any importance were made without her guidance. Eleanor spent part of each winter in Washington with Bye, who introduced her to all the most interesting and influential young women in town—Marjorie Nott, Cissy Patterson (subsequently the owner and publisher of the Washington *Times-Herald*), Harriet and Mary Winslow, Catherine Adams (daughter of Charles Francis Adams), and Margaretta MacVeagh, among many others. Eleanor accompanied Aunt Bye, whose husband had recently been promoted to admiral, on her daily rounds of card-bearing calls, which at the time seemed to her "most entertaining" rather than tedious; and was taken to "exciting" dinners, luncheons, and teas marked by "people of importance, with charm and wit and *savoir faire.*"

At Aunt Bye's, Eleanor Roosevelt acquired still another level of "social ease" and an understanding of Washington and the political world. Until the winters of 1903 and 1904, she had not thought much about politics, or the men who shaped them. She did not connect the poverty she witnessed daily at Rivington Street with the kind of movements for social change that created anarchists and revolutionaries. Actually, she never thought much about Uncle Theodore's election, or his elevation to the presidency after William McKinley had been assassinated by an anarchist. She never discussed his vision of empire, his Rough Rider heroics during the Spanish-American War, or even his progressive support for the work of settlement pioneers, who championed a Children's Bureau and better conditions for America's poor—as she herself was then doing.

Uncle Ted's campaign and reelection had meant very little to me. . . . I lived in a totally nonpolitical atmosphere. In Washington, however, I gradually acquired a faint conception of the political world, very different from my New York world. I also acquired little by little the social ease which I sorely needed.

Because of Aunt Bye's influence, Eleanor Roosevelt came to believe that, though women might not have the vote, they could be influential—perhaps even powerful. She realized too that Washington was a city with a different rhythm, a different purpose. New York society tended to frown on public life, and scorn publicly engaged citizens—men and women. Eleanor felt oddly at home in Washington. "The talk was always lively," there was excitement, and a passion for things beyond petty personal concerns. Moreover, she found great comfort in Bye's generous warmth and hospitality; the "unexpected guest was always welcome, and, young or old, you really felt Aunt Bye's interest in you." "I loved to be with her."

During their courtship Franklin supported Eleanor's interests. Though he may have laughed, he never suggested that she abandon her work at Rivington Street. When they met after her classes, he was greatly moved both by the poverty of the neighborhood and the enduring enthusiasm of her young students, who called him her "feller." On one of his visits, he accompanied Eleanor and a young student who had fallen ill to the girl's home. Although he had occasionally volunteered to teach at a boys' club in Boston, he had never seen such tenement conditions. He kept repeating that he "simply could not believe human beings lived that way." Eleanor Roosevelt always believed that those early visits to Rivington Street had a lasting and powerful impact on him.

For all her interests, Eleanor at nineteen was above all in love. She spent her days in a variety of ways—she did good works, she attended German classes and literature classes, she danced and partied, she went to the opera and the theatre—but every night she wrote to her secret love, her fiancé, now a junior at Harvard. Nobody knew. It was their secret. Eleanor did not really approve of secrets, however, and she waited for him to tell his mother. Nonetheless, romance flourishes in secret, and Eleanor was very happy.

I had a great curiosity about life and a desire to participate in every experience that might be the lot of a woman. There seemed to be a necessity for hurry; . . . and so in the autumn of 1903, when Franklin Roosevelt . . . asked me to marry him, though I was only 19, it seemed an entirely natural thing and I never even thought that we were both young and inexperienced. . . . I know now that it was years later before I understood what being in love or what loving really meant.

Whatever that last phrase meant to Eleanor Roosevelt so many decades later, her letters to Franklin between 1903 and 1905 were as full of love as any letters she would ever write. On 6 January 1904, she wrote:

Oh! darling I miss you so and I long for the happy hours which we have together and I think of the many which we have had these last two weeks constantly—I am so happy. So *very* happy in your love dearest, that all the world has changed for me. If only I can bring to you all that you have brought to me all my dearest wishes will be fulfilled and I shall know that you too will always be happy—

Goodbye dearest Boy, take care of yourself in this cold weather and think always of

> Your devoted
> "Little Nell"

Signing herself "Little Nell," the term of endearment her father had used, indicates the new level of intimacy and trust that had been reached during the holiday season of 1903. After almost a year of casual correspondence, everything changed over the pre-Thanksgiving November weekend when Eleanor visited Franklin in Cambridge for the Harvard-Yale game—well chaperoned by Cousin Muriel Robbins and her mother, Aunt Kassie. After the game (Franklin led the cheers but Yale won), he showed Eleanor his room, and she left for Groton to spend the rest of the weekend with her brother. The next day, Franklin joined her there, and they spent that Sunday, 22 November 1903, together—somehow finding sufficient time alone, without Hall, for Franklin to propose. That evening, in his secret code, he noted in his diary: "After lunch I have a never to be forgotten walk to the river with my darling."

The next week was hard for Eleanor. The day after she had accepted Franklin's proposal, her Great-Uncle James King Gracie died. She wanted her first letter to her new fiancé to be "cheerier and more coherent," and in spite "of it all I am very happy." But her great-uncle's death was a terrific blow, and "I am more sorry than I can say for he has always been very kind and dear to us," and because he and Aunt Annie (her father's favorite aunt) "both loved my Father very dearly so it is just another link gone." Eleanor spent the day with her Aunt Corinne, who was devastated and looked "so worn & I wish I could do something more to help her." The funeral was planned for the Friday after Thanksgiving, and Eleanor dreaded it: "I know I ought not to feel as I do or even to think of myself but I have not been to a funeral in ten years and it makes me shudder to think of it."

Eleanor wrote to Franklin twice on the 24th. The second letter, written late at night after a "very trying" day of grief and mourning, was in reply to his pleasing letter from Fairhaven: "I wanted to tell you that I *did* understand & that I don't know what I should have done all day if your letter had not come." His words encouraged her to spend part of that day searching for Elizabeth Barrett Browning's "A Woman's Shortcomings," which she had "tried to recite" on Sunday.

I am going to write it out for you, because it is in part what it all means to me:

> *Unless you can think when the song is done,*
> *No other is left in the rhythm;*
> *Unless you can feel, when left by one,*
> *That all men else go with him;*
> *Unless you can know, when upraised by his breath,*
> *That your beauty itself wants proving;*
> *Unless you can swear, "For life for death!"*
> *Oh, fear to call it loving! . . .*

Anna Livingston Ludlow Hall, 1890. "My mother was one of the most beautiful women I have ever seen."

Elliott Roosevelt. Father was "charming, good-looking, loved by all. With him I was perfectly happy."

But as a child, "I never smiled."
Left: Eleanor Roosevelt, 1888.

Right: ER with her father, April 1889.

Below: ER with brothers Elliott, Jr., and Gracie Hall, and Father, 1891.

After her parents died, Eleanor lived at Tivoli with her grandmother, uncles, and aunts, who taught her to ride and jump, to play tennis and bicycle.

Eleanor at Oak Terrace, in Tivoli, with her horse, 1894.

Below, left to right: Grandmother Hall, ER's daughter Anna Eleanor, ER (standing), and Aunt Tissie, c. 1912.

Above: Aunt Tissie (Elizabeth Livingston Hall Mortimer), 1910. Of the four sisters, she was closest to ER's mother. Eleanor traveled with her in Europe and England, where Aunt Tissie lived for many years: She was "one of the people that the word 'exquisite' describes best."

At Allenswood, Marie Souvestre's school in South Fields, near Wimbledon Common, in England, ER spent "the happiest years" of her life. Shown here during the summer of 1900, she is standing to the right of the doorway, wearing a hat and large black bowtie.

Marie Souvestre. Eleanor was devoted to her teacher. "Her head was beautiful. . . . Her eyes looked through you, and she always knew more than she was told." After leaving Allenswood, ER requested Marie Souvestre's portrait—which ER kept with her always.

During her years at Allenswood, ER was encouraged by Marie Souvestre and Aunt Tissie to spend her money on fashionable clothes, which she did. When ER returned to New York, Aunt Tissie sent her costumes made by Europe's most stylish couturiers.

Left: ER in New York, c. summer 1899.

Above: ER in a new suit during a visit with Aunt Tissie and Uncle Stanley Mortimer, in Saint-Moritz, Switzerland, summer 1900.

Right: ER in hat.

Although she agonized that she was not the belle her mother had been, in most company ER was self-assured and happy the year that she came out. And then she became secretly engaged to FDR, her fifth cousin once removed. Here she is with other cousins, Muriel Robbins and Helen Astor Roosevelt Roosevelt, at Hyde Park, in June 1903.

In the company of Sara Delano Roosevelt, shown here during ER's first visit to Campobello, her confidence withered. ER hoped that she might win a corner of her future mother-in-law's heart: "I do so want you to learn to love me a little."

ER's wedding portrait was taken in a studio on 20 January 1905. There are no pictures of ER's wedding, and evidently no photographer was hired for the occasion.

Theodore Roosevelt's family, Alice in the center, August 1905.

Uncle Theodore gave the bride away. The President had offered the first White House wedding to Eleanor, but she preferred to be married in the home of her godmother, Cousin Susie Parish. Although Edith Roosevelt had discouraged any friendship between Eleanor and Alice while they were children, Alice was delighted to be a bridesmaid at Eleanor's wedding.

ER particularly cherished Ellen ("Bay") Emmet's wedding present, this portrait of Eleanor's Aunt Bye, Anna Roosevelt Cowles. During the years between Allenswood and her marriage, ER preferred the time she spent at Bay Emmet's Greenwich Village studio, with her bohemian friends, to any society event she felt she had to endure.

I wondered if it meant "for life, for death" to you at first but I know it does now. I do not know what to write. I cannot write what I want. I can only wait and long for Sunday when I shall tell you all I feel. . . .

Their plan to see each other that Sunday was a subject of tension. Franklin had planned to lie to his mother, and tell her that he would be in New York to visit "Mr. Marvin." Eleanor wanted him to tell his mother the truth, "because I never want her to feel that she has been deceived. . . . Don't be angry with me Franklin for saying this and of course you must do as you think best."

Evidently Franklin did tell his mother the truth. At some point during the Delano Thanksgiving party at Fairhaven, he asked to see her quietly, alone; Sara Delano Roosevelt wrote in her journal: "Franklin gave me quite a startling announcement." She was staggered. It was all so sudden and unexpected. They were too young and ill-prepared. It was impossible. They simply must wait—a year at least. And nobody need know.

Franklin spent Sunday and Monday in New York. Afterwards, Eleanor wrote: "It is impossible to tell you what these last two days have been to me, but I know they have meant the same to you so that you will understand that I love you dearest and I hope that I shall always prove worthy of the love which you have given me. I have never known before what it was to be absolutely happy, nor have I ever longed for just one glimpse of a pair of eyes. . . ."

She wrote to him late at night, and then again on rising:

Dearest Franklin,

Though I only wrote last night I must write you just a line this morning to tell you that I miss you every moment & that you are never out of my thought dear for one moment. I was thinking last night of the difference which one short week can make in one's life. Everything is changed for me now. I am so happy. Oh! so happy & I love you *so* dearly. I cannot begin to write you all I should like to say, but you know it all I am sure & I hope that you too dearest

are very, very happy. I am counting the days to the 12th & the days
in between seem so *very* long.

But the weekend of 12 December 1903 was to become an embattled
one. During the week that followed Eleanor's letter to Franklin, Sara
Delano Roosevelt met with her to issue several decrees. Eleanor wrote
Franklin:

"Boy darling, I have rather a hard letter to write to you tonight and
I don't quite know how to say what I must say and I am afraid I am
going to give you some trouble, however I don't see how I can help
it. . . ." Cousin Sally was not pleased. She did not want Franklin to stay
with Eleanor in New York for the two days they had planned, however
well chaperoned. They would be seen in church, and people were beginning to notice them together. Sara wanted him to spend Sunday in
Hyde Park. "She asked me to write you and I tell you all this dear
because I think it only fair. Of course it will be a terrible disappointment
to me not to have you on Sunday as I have been looking forward to it
and every moment with you is very, very precious as we have so little
of each other but I don't want you to stay if you feel it is your duty to
go up and I shall understand of course."

Also, his mother had told Eleanor of the house she rented in Boston.
She intended to invite Eleanor up only "once or twice," and she did
not want Franklin to "be coming to New York." Eleanor could understand "how she feels but I am afraid I can't promise not to want
you more than twice in all that time, however I think that you and she
will have to talk it over. . . ."

Eleanor left it up to Franklin to decide: "You mustn't let what I
want interfere with what you feel to be right dearest. . . ." Nonetheless,
she appeared certain she would see Franklin as planned, for she urged
him "to get a little rest sometime, for I don't want to receive a wreck
next Saturday." As for herself, his concerns were unfounded: "I am
very good about resting and you must not worry about me dear. I take
great care of myself and I assure you that I never will tire myself through
my unselfishness."

Sara was equally certain that Franklin would in fact be in Hyde Park
on the contested Sunday, and Eleanor noted: "You see it is hard for

her to realize that any one can want you or need you more than she does. So I suppose I ought not to mind, only I do mind terribly, as you can understand dear, however I mustn't complain, must I?"

Although all evidence suggests that the young couple won this particular battle and spent the whole weekend together, Eleanor began to feel that it was all going to be more difficult than she had imagined. At first she felt stoical, resigned. Franklin reassured her. He seemed so confident, and untroubled. Still, familiar sensations, old feelings of self-doubt, began to gnaw their way into her newfound happiness. She had no doubts about Franklin; she trusted his love, and believed in his enthusiasm. But his mother could be so cold, so disapproving. There were moments, especially when the two women were alone with each other, when Sara's firm jaw and direct gaze seemed hard to endure.

Franklin Delano Roosevelt was the only child of Sara Delano and "Squire James" Roosevelt. When James met Sara, at the home of Eleanor's paternal grandmother, Mittie Bulloch Roosevelt, he was a fifty-two-year-old widower, who sported lush muttonchop whiskers and rode about his estate in full and formal English country attire. His first wife, Rebecca Howland, had died three years before, in 1876, shortly after their son, James Roosevelt (Rosy) Roosevelt married Helen Schermerhorn Astor. Widely traveled, well educated, and classically beautiful, with great masses of auburn hair worn high, Sara had had many suitors by the time she met James, but her father, Warren Delano, had vetoed them all as unworthy (including the architect Stanford White, said to be the great love of Sara's youth). At twenty-six (the same age as James's son Rosy), she believed herself committed to "spinsterhood."

Squire James, who had graduated from Harvard Law School in 1851, owed his wealth to anthracite coal, steamships, railroads, and considerable real estate. Although he lost several big financial gambles, including a plan to build an interocean canal through Nicaragua, which failed during the depression of 1893 (and was finally scuttled when TR decided to construct the Panama Canal), his holdings were sufficient to please his business associate Warren Delano, who objected only momentarily to his advanced age.

The Delanos were very proud of their lineage, which Sara could—and did, repeatedly—recite, back to William the Conqueror. The first

American de la Noye, a Huguenot, settled in Plymouth in 1621. For generations the Delanos circled the world as fortune-hunting merchants and seamen. Both Warren Delanos, Sara's father and grandfather, met with particular success in China—notably in the opium trade. And on 21 September 1854, Sara Delano was born (the seventh of eleven children) to Catherine Lyman, daughter of an equally prominent family of Massachusetts jurists and financiers, and Warren Delano at Algonac— a splendid villa across the Hudson River, and twenty miles south of Springwood.

Educated by tutors in Europe—especially Paris, where the family lived for many years—Sara Delano Roosevelt was a prominent member of society in New York, Boston, Paris, and London. She loved to travel and had a wide range of interests. She was rigid in her views, and opinionated on all matters. She hated, with considerable verve and in no particular order, ostentation, vulgarity, shabby politicians, the new resorts of the new rich, and virtually all races, nationalities, and families other than her own.

Although known for his good humor, Squire James was equally opinionated, and shared many of Sara's social views. In some ways he was more rigid. Once, in Germany, when she met an old girlhood friend, he forbade their planned luncheon because the friend had been divorced. Later, when their new neighbors, the Vanderbilts, invited them to their grand and garish manor for dinner, Sara was curious and intended to go. But Squire James was appalled: "If we accept, we shall have to have these people to our home." Profound snob that he was, he was nevertheless in some ways more liberal than his wife. While idealizing work and thrift, he specifically scorned the Social Darwinist survival-of-the-fittest notions that had been vigorously embraced by most of the gentry and had become the new religion of the new rich of his generation. He believed that spirituality required social responsibility, and near the end of his life he delivered a passionate oration, at a guild meeting of the Saint James Church in Hyde Park, on the perils of extravagance and the sin of human carelessness within the human community.

In London, New York, and Paris, he said, he had witnessed the desperation of poverty; he had seen the hovels and the squalor; the overworked children, naked, bony, and filthy; the sick and dying mothers, abandoned to poverty and disease. "In all countries and all ages there have been more workers than work." He had seen the dreadful place of a family in London, into whose home one descended by ladder, "several feet below the sewage and gas pipes." There was never any daylight or breathable air; pests abounded. "Help the Helpless!" Squire James demanded. "Help the poor, the widow, the orphan; help the sick, the fallen man or woman, for the sake of our common humanity. Help all who are suffering. . . . Work for humanity. Work for your Lord. . . ." It was for "that single cause that we have, all of us, one human heart."

Such views were irrelevant to Sara, but they were part of James's legacy to his son Franklin—and thus familiar and congenial when Franklin met with them again in Eleanor Roosevelt.

Although Sara was devoted to her husband, she repeated frequently over the years her most profound conviction: "My son Franklin is a Delano, not a Roosevelt at all." Perhaps she referred to what she perceived as hereditary flaws among the Roosevelts. Had she wanted Franklin to marry into a family with better genes, better bones, less alcoholic blood? Was there among America's aristocracy at the *fin de siècle* such a family? Perhaps she would have preferred that he be involved with a less political family, one less engaged in public life, committed to social responsibility. Certainly, over time, Eleanor Roosevelt Roosevelt and Franklin Delano Roosevelt were in combination more Roosevelt than she approved of; and in the beginning she never missed an opportunity to keep them apart.

Born on 30 January 1882 into the comfort and security of Springwood on the Hudson, FDR loved his home, which then included thirteen hundred acres of rolling meadows and dense virgin woodlands. There were vineyards and orchards, fields of grain, gardens dedicated to roses, greenhouse, icehouse, servants galore, and very serious stables.*

---

* Springwood stables were noted for very fine and fast racing trotters. James Roosevelt bred Gloster, for example, the first trotter to do a mile under 2:20. But Squire James agreed to sell Gloster for the heady sum of $15,000 to California's Leland Stanford. Before he could race again, Gloster was killed in a railroad accident. His attendant returned Gloster's tail to FDR years later, and he kept it on his bedroom wall, both in Albany and at the White House.

From the beginning, Franklin was above all Sara's very own little darling. She kept him attached to her physically for as long as it was humanly possible. (Rumors that he was breast-fed until he was three, six, or even eight persisted for decades.) For many years, his hair, meticulously curled and fluffed, went uncut. He wore long blond curls and dresses until he was five. From five to eight, he wore either kilts or Lord Fauntleroy suits—costumes of considerable derision among his Oyster Bay cousins. Alice Roosevelt Longworth commented that she wasn't even allowed to read *Little Lord Fauntleroy* "because it was so dreadful. That awful child being frightfully condescending to everyone including Grandfather Dear, ugh!" But Franklin, with his cultivated English accent and smug manner, "*was encouraged to read Little Lord Fauntleroy.*" When he was eight, Franklin persuaded his parents to dress him in English sailor suits. He was almost nine when he wrote his father: "Mama left this morning and I am going to take my bath alone."

However protected, Franklin was not brought up to be Caspar Milquetoast. His father taught him to swim, to fish, to sail, to hunt, to ride, to golf, to skate, to iceboat, and in general to become a self-reliant, fun-loving, and capable youth. He shot birds and had them stuffed. He collected old prints, great books, and mountains of stamps. His parents indulged his every whim, and delighted in his every word. They simply could not bear to part with him until he was fourteen, and so he failed to enter Groton with his form. When he arrived there, he was plunged into a society of 110 boys who by then had had two years in which to settle themselves into their various teams, clubs, and cliques.

Congenial and self-assured among adults, Franklin Delano Roosevelt had never been among many boys before. Their mores, manners, and attitudes were as strange to him as his were to them. The new boy on campus had an odd manner, and his speech was aggressively haughty—the influence of European nannies, exclusively adult company, and studies abroad. He preened, and was unused to various merriments. Although he had a ready, hearty, and engaging smile, he was frequently arrogant. Rather spindly, he was lackluster at team sports, despite his best efforts and sincere enthusiasm. He was far more popular with his teachers than with his peers, and certainly his awards for punctuality did nothing to win him any friends.

Franklin was also mocked as the younger "uncle" of a high-spirited and independent youth in the class ahead of him, and a perpetual outsider. At Groton, Franklin considered James Roosevelt Roosevelt, Jr.—Rosy's son, known as "Taddie"—a "queer sort of boy." Later, at Harvard, Taddie became a decided embarrassment. In 1900, he eloped with a hardworking woman of the night called Dutch Sadie. Stories conflict as to whether Sadie Meisinger and Taddie lived happily ever after or bitterly until her death in 1940. They lived, however, in familial isolation in a small apartment above a garage in Queens where Taddie worked as an auto mechanic. He remained a recluse until his death in 1958, and never touched his inheritance. He left his entire and considerable Astor fortune to the Salvation Army.

The Astors and the Roosevelts were scandalized by Taddie, whose elopement with Dutch Sadie made newspaper headlines and became the butt of society jokes for weeks. His father, Rosy, rushed back from England to have the marriage annulled; his maternal grandmother, Mrs. Astor, went into hiding; and two days after the story broke, his paternal grandfather, Squire James, suffered the first of the heart attacks that would later kill him. Young Franklin worried about his father, whose condition rapidly declined, and he personally blamed Taddie. On 23 October 1900, he wrote that "the disgusting thing about Taddy did not come as a very great surprise"; but "the disgrace to the name has been the worst part of the affair [and] one can never again consider him a true Roosevelt. It will be well for him not only to go to parts unknown but to stay there and begin life anew."

Franklin's own inclinations at Groton and Harvard tilted toward conformity, acceptance, and well-rounded if limited achievement. He adored Groton and its headmaster, Endicott Peabody. A Cheltenham- and Cambridge-educated Anglican minister, Dr. Peabody intended to re-create Britain's public (private, in U.S. parlance) school tradition. Groton was conceived to serve as an academy for the preparation of America's leadership class. In order to produce proper Christian gentlemen with ideals and manners, six years of Latin, Greek, history, literature, and science were secondary to six years of Christian principles and ethics, vigorous sports, clean and Spartan living, and class-conscious comradeship. Sara Delano Roosevelt enrolled her son into this extended-family environment as soon as she met Dr. Peabody in 1884, the year he founded Groton.*

FDR considered himself a model Grotonian and a champion of its precepts. Dr. Peabody's goal had been, after all, to raise a new class of gentlemen who would rule with a patrician sense of service to God, country, and humanity. However romantically FDR came to regard Groton, he had been in fact an ordinary if not indifferent student, although he debated with gusto, sang in the choir, and excelled in Latin. Tall and gawky, he was burdened at Groton by glasses on his nose and braces on his teeth; for glasses he affected Cousin Teddy's pince-nez, which made him look just a wee bit silly.

As a youth, Franklin was something of an outsider along society's fast track. According to Eleanor's cousin Joseph Alsop (Corinne Roosevelt Robinson's grandson), Franklin was not popular. Though never specifically "disliked," he was not taken very seriously. The girls in his circle said "F. D." stood for "feather duster." Franklin was seen as a spoiled and smug "mama's boy." Never dashing, he was too pretty to be handsome; some said he resembled the faces painted on "presentation handkerchief boxes." Throughout his Groton years, to judge from Franklin's words, the feelings were mutual. His utter devotion to his mother was matched only by the disdain he felt for the girls he knew. Even when he had to select a partner, he asked his mother to do it for him,—and to be sure he was not stuck with an "ice-cart," a "brat," a "pill," or anything "elephantine." During one Christmas season, Sara planned to have some of his young cousins stay over for the holidays, to Franklin's chagrin: "It will be a horrible nuisance having those *squaws*

---

* Although a conservative Republican, Endicott Peabody remained amazingly loyal to Franklin Delano Roosevelt. During the first years of the New Deal, anti-Roosevelt antagonism ran so high among Groton boys that Peabody warned all alumni who cared to participate in the fiftieth homecoming celebrations that they should not do so unless they were "prepared to be polite to the President and Mrs. R." On another occasion, at New York's Union Club, Peabody spoke directly of the tensions among his boys and announced: "I believe Franklin Roosevelt to be a gallant gentleman. I am happy to count him as my friend." Stony silence greeted his words.

on our hands for such a long time." But while he was a junior at Groton, after the party at Aunt Corinne's where he had recently encountered Eleanor, Franklin wrote his mother: "I cannot think of anyone to get up here, as most of the boys are already engaged that I would like to have, so I hope you will be able to find someone else. How about Teddy Robinson [Aunt Corinne's son] and Eleanor Roosevelt? They would go well and help to fill out chinks."

If the girls he knew called him "feather duster," the boys simply declined to admit him into their company. His social failures continued during his first years at Harvard, the cruelest and most lasting blow of all being his exclusion from the Porcellian, the club to which his own father and Theodore Roosevelt had both belonged. In 1918, FDR told Aunt Bye's son, William Sheffield Cowles, Jr., that his failure to make Porcellian was the worst disappointment of his life.

FDR recovered from these defeats by becoming more politically aware, by being a devoted member of the clubs to which he did belong—Hasty Pudding and Alpha Delta Phi (the Fly)—and by contributing most of his time to the student newspaper. Eleanor's influence was to be a key factor in his new successes. At the beginning of their courtship, she encouraged him to run for class office, to do better work, and to take himself, his concerns, and his talents more seriously. Her letters to him are full of advice and enthusiasm for his work and his ideas. In his junior year, he was elected president and editor-in-chief of the *Harvard Crimson,* to which he devoted his entire senior year, having actually completed his courses after three years.

Eleanor's good influence notwithstanding, Sara Delano Roosevelt determined to separate the couple as soon as Franklin revealed their secret to her on Thanksgiving Day 1903. They were children, with neither the emotional moorings nor the financial security to begin an independent household. Their irrepressible enthusiasm and unqualified happiness galled her. She tried patience and subterfuge, seduction and spite. And they responded with equal cunning, equal determination.

~

BECAUSE ELEANOR ROOSEVELT DESTROYED ALL OF FDR'S courtship letters, we have only a few letters from Franklin to his mother

to suggest the happiness that his love for Eleanor had aroused in him.
On 4 December 1903, Franklin wrote:

Dearest Mama—I know what pain I must have caused you and you
know I wouldn't do it if I really could have helped it—mais tu sais,
me voilà! That's all that could be said—I know my mind, have
known it for a long time, and know that I could never think
otherwise:

Result: I am the happiest man just now in the world; likewise
the luckiest—And for you, dear Mummy, you know that nothing
can ever change what we have always been and always will be to
each other—only now you have two children to love & to love
you—and Eleanor as you know will always be a daughter to you
in every true way. . . .

Eleanor Roosevelt wrote to "Dearest Cousin Sally" in much the
same spirit on 2 December:

I must write you & thank you for being so good to me yesterday.
I know just how you feel and how hard it must be, but I do so
want you to learn to love me a little. You must know that I will
always try to do what you wish for I have grown to love you very
dearly during the past summer. It is impossible for me to tell you
how I feel toward Franklin, I can only say that my one great wish
is always to prove worthy of him. . . .

> With much love dear Cousin Sally,
> Always devotedly
> Eleanor

Cousin Sally was not so easily charmed. Having gotten their agreement to postpone any announcement for a year at least, she arranged
a leisurely six-week Caribbean cruise for February and March 1904, to
fill Franklin's mind with other interests. His roommate, Lathrop Brown,
accompanied them aboard the luxurious Hamburg-American liner *Prin-
zessin Victoria Luise,* which took them to Saint Thomas, Puerto Rico,
Jamaica, Cuba, Martinique, Trinidad, Venezuela, and Curaçao. When

that ploy failed—despite FDR's shipboard flirtations with several considerably older women, which also annoyed his mother—she encouraged her friend Joseph Choate, then U.S. ambassador to the Court of Saint James, to name Franklin his secretary and remove him to London. But Choate refused; he already had a secretary.

Although Eleanor resented Cousin Sally's dominating interference, she seemed to have embarked on this struggle of wills with a remarkable sense of security. She kept her feelings of frustration and anger in check, and set about to court her future mother-in-law. She did this not just because of her love for Franklin, but because she craved his mother's love as well, and longed to be accepted as part of Sara's family. Eleanor wanted desperately to belong to this family that seemed so different from her own, its members closely united by great quantities of generous and devoted support for each other.

When she was first invited to meet the Delano "clan," at Fairhaven, Massachusetts, she was struck above all by "a sense of security which I never had known before." There were among the Delanos many differences and many disagreements, but there was also the most remarkable sense of unity and connectedness, which to Eleanor was "something of a revelation" and "relief." There had always been such a "feeling of insecurity in most of the relationships of my Hall family." There had also been an obsession with money, and what Eleanor had come to consider rather meaningless display, which led to many problems, since there was somehow never enough money to go around. ER's grandmother, left without a will, had nothing but her "dower right in her husband's estate," with which to meet her expenses and help her "extravagant children." When, for example, her Aunt Maude and husband, Larry Waterbury, had visited her in England, she had watched them "with awe and envy." There were so many magnificent costumes, so much polo, endless gaiety. "Theirs was a world where pleasure dominated." But they gambled and were frequently in debt. Both Eddie and Vallie needed help, for they "had squandered what money was left to them." And part of Pussie's perpetual angst was due to the fact that she had handed over her investments to various men "with good intentions" and dreadful "business judgment." Only Aunt Tissie, who had married Stanley Mortimer, was financially secure, and for years

"Tissie spent practically every penny she had" bailing out members of her family. The financial and emotional strains involved in trying to "keep up with the Joneses" had come to seem a disagreeable, joyless enterprise to Eleanor.

The Delanos were not only financially secure, they "watched their pennies, which I had always seen squandered." They could afford, therefore, to be "generous in big things, because so little was ever wasted or spent in inconsequential ways." But, more than that, they "were a clan, and if misfortune befell one of them, the others rallied at once. My Hall family would have rallied, too, but they had so much less to rally with." They might criticize one another, but if an outsider so much as looked askance at a Delano, "the clan was ready to tear him limb from limb!"

Eleanor Roosevelt's profound longing for familial unity in the face of criticism, opposition, and hard times came from the very core of her childhood experience. To be made to feel welcomed by the Delanos— to be embraced by Sara's eldest brother, Warren Delano, now head of the tribe, and his wife, who "were always kindness itself to me," and by Franklin's aunts, Dora Delano Forbes, Annie Delano Hitch ("the most philanthropic and civic-minded"), Kassie Delano Price Collier, and his Uncle Frederic Delano, who remained her close friend and ally over the years—added what seemed a particularly satisfying dimension to her life as she embarked upon that great unknown, marriage and motherhood.

When Eleanor agreed to become engaged to Franklin, she was being courted quite vigorously by several other suitors, particularly Nicholas Biddle, Lyman Delano, and Howard Cary—one of Franklin's Harvard classmates, her most insistent admirer of all. Years later, Eleanor Roosevelt described Cary as "a charming man with a really lovely spirit, [who] wrote me occasionally about books, for we had a mutual interest in literature. His letters were charming, but formal and even stiff when they touched on anything but books. . . ." She failed to note that he pursued her with ardor and repeatedly in New York and Dark Harbor, Maine, during the summer of 1904, while she was visiting Aunt Corinne. He invited her to dinner, tea, lunch; to go climbing; to explore the island; to spend more time with him on a regular basis. When her engagement was finally announced in November 1904, Howard Cary's mother wrote Eleanor: "and so you are not going to be my daughter-in-law after all"; and Howard wrote Franklin: "You are mighty lucky. Your future wife is such as it is the privilege of few men to have."*

Nicholas Biddle did not manage his disappointment so gracefully: after three disastrous efforts, he finally was able to write a barely satisfactory letter to Franklin. Cousin Lyman Delano (Warren's son) was more effusive: "I have more respect and admiration for Eleanor than any girl I have ever met, and have always thought that the man who would have her for a wife would be very lucky." To Eleanor he wrote: "I never saw the family so enthusiastic in my life and I am sure your ears would have burned if you could have heard some of the compliments paid you."

Although all letters to Eleanor rhapsodized over her good news, many of them conveyed sentiments of loss that reflected Eleanor's impact, even as a young woman, upon everyone graced by her presence. Aunt Maude wrote: "Do be good to Grandma I think she will miss you frightfully." Uncle Henry Parish, who taught Eleanor how to keep accounts, deal with her bills, and balance her checkbooks, and whom she considered "the kindest person I have ever known," feared that his wife, Eleanor's Cousin Susie, would feel bereft without her presence: "Much as I am to Susie, you are more and I pray that you always will be." And her colleagues at the Junior League threatened to hold a "grudge" against Franklin if her engagement deprived the League of its "most efficient member."

Over the years, FDR altered the custom of congratulating the groom, while giving best wishes to the bride, by always congratulating the bride as well. When his secretary Grace Tully asked him why he did that, he replied that, when his engagement to Eleanor had been announced, he was drowned by such effusive congratulations for his great good fortune in winning her that he always felt miffed at the fact that no one had

---

* After Eleanor, Cary turned his attentions to Dorothy Payne Whitney, who evidently also rejected him, and he died on 5 May 1905, of what appeared to be suicide. Still in evening clothes, holding a gun in his right hand, he was found dead with a bullet in his right temple. He was visiting his cousin Lord Fairfax (the only American-born British baron), seemed to be having a pleasant time, and left no note. His death remained a puzzling tragedy among the gilded youth of the *fin de siècle*.

acknowledged that she too might have been congratulated on her luck.

Why in fact did Eleanor choose Franklin, considered by so many a lightweight and a mama's boy? A middling scholar and a middling swain, he had little really to recommend him over her other suitors. He was less serious than many; not as rich as others; was considered by some frivolous and frothy, and by others arrogant and deceitful. He was known to be a womanizer, a tippler, and a careless flirt. According to Joseph Alsop, Alsop's mother, Corinne Robinson Alsop—who knew Eleanor better than most and had witnessed her triumphs at Allenswood—was adamant in her feeling that Franklin was unworthy, and confided in her diary that he was "by no means good enough for her."

But Eleanor Roosevelt, who had a gift for bringing out the best in people, saw special qualities in Franklin. To her he was tender, considerate, attentive. She felt that he admired her intelligence, and relied on her advice. Above all, she perceived that he needed her, and in many ways Franklin resembled Eleanor's romantic image of her father—that debonair man who had been the first to call her Little Nell.

Franklin was ardent, affectionate, flamboyant. He sent her poetry and "a gift from the sea," which she cherished. He brought her flowers and books. They shared a sense of awe about the mysteries of love; and they courted the highest idealism. In the beginning, Franklin seemed even more romantic than Eleanor. In response to one of his first letters after they became secretly engaged, she wrote that she considered a poem he had sent her "splendid, but what ideals you have to live up to. I like 'Fear nothing and be faithful unto death' but I must say I wonder how many of 'we poor mortals' could act up to that!" A month later, he sent her Elizabeth Barrett Browning's *Sonnets from the Portuguese,* which, she wrote, "is an old friend of mine and queerly enough I read it over the other evening also and thought how beautiful and expressive it was."

Their affinity was chemical, intellectual, total. Together, they might reach beyond their family constraints. With Eleanor, Franklin might limit his mother's imperious domain; and the announcement of his engagement constituted a first and successful beginning. With Franklin, Eleanor might have security and a home of her own. Her great capacity to give and to love, cut off so abruptly when her father died, was now once again focused on one person, who seemed to love her with equal ardor, and entirely for herself.

From the beginning, however, they sailed on rough seas. Sara Delano Roosevelt was uncertain of her new position, but she intended to retain a central position in the life of her boy, and did everything she could to undermine the young couple's affection for each other. Franklin distanced himself from any possible conflict between his mother and fiancée. For her part, Eleanor made every effort to accommodate Sara's needs and wants: She urged Franklin to be patient with his mother, as she intended to be, and to realize "how hard it is for her and we must both try always to make her happy and I do hope someday she will learn to love me."

While Eleanor did consent to keep their engagement secret for a year, as Sara wished, she nevertheless consulted Cousin Susie, who "felt as I do that your Mother's feelings ought to be considered first of all." She also spoke with her grandmother, who asked only if Eleanor were "sure that she was in love," and encouraged her to feel that everything would follow in due course from that assurance. Eleanor was sure, and pleased with her grandmother's reaction: She was "very quiet and wise about it and never asked any questions." However aware, steady, and poised Eleanor had become, Sara's cold opposition to her very presence recalled childhood feelings. However unconscious they were as memory, they began to erupt in old patterns, old insecurities, old hurts.

Two themes now began to recur in Eleanor's daily letters to Franklin, letters that were generally between four and nine pages: her growing dependency on his presence in her life, and her increasing commitment to his career. Indeed, her first serious letter to him, written even before he invited her to the Harvard-Yale game, was one of vigorous encouragement regarding his decision to spend his senior year taking courses for a master's degree: "You know quite well you need not apologize for writing about yourself—I should think history and political economy would be most interesting and much the most useful for you in the future and *of course* you are going to get an AM. . . ."

She promoted all his activities, and congratulated his every success. "My own dearest Boy, I cannot tell you how glad I am you got on the

Class committee for I know how much it means to you and I always want you to succeed. Dearest, if you only knew how happy it makes me to think that your love for me is making you try all the harder to do well and oh! I hope so much that someday I will be more of a help to you. . . ."

But a third theme also began to appear in Eleanor's letters, a virtual litany of self-deprecation and apology. "Why do you read over my old letters dearest, they really are not worth it—However I don't suppose I ought to talk as I have kept all yours and probably read them far oftener than you read mine, but you write nice letters and I love them and mine are often very dull I fear. . . ." It was as if to be fully herself was not enough, or too much, and so she felt a need to make herself appear less than she was, and repeatedly to apologize for being precisely herself. There is almost a geometric symmetry to her letters. As she reassures him, bolsters his spirits and self-image, cares for his future, worries over his health, and actually instructs him, she demeans herself, apologizes for her care, her worry, and all of her "woman's shortcomings."

One must pause here to consider her conception of her role: to make him, and all those she loved, happy; to secure harmony; to remain patient and calm through all adversity and under any assault. Their roles were different, and predetermined. He was being educated to lead, to command, to take his place at the helm. She wished only to encourage, to guide, to help him take over. If he laughed at her decision to take a course in political economy or sociology, which would be so useful at Rivington Street, she laughingly apologized for taking it. What would he have thought had she joined Jean Reid and Mary Harriman at Barnard? They seemed never to have discussed the possibility, and Eleanor later regretted her inability to defy her relatives who scorned a college education for women.

At nineteen, she had accepted her prescribed role in life: to grow while never allowing herself to appear taller, to be worldly but always supportive, sophisticated but always secondary. She must never, under any circumstances, appear competitive. To play the role well, she swallowed her ambition, and her words. Over time, it sapped her strength, but as she looked forward to her new life, she understood the function that limits serve: "Perhaps it is just as well we haven't the power of fulfilling our desires for we would do so many things which we ought not to do."

In considering Eleanor's understanding of her range of choices during her year of coming out and courting, one might recall Virginia Woolf's observations regarding the cost to women of a life devoted exclusively to service:

> Women have served all these centuries as looking-glasses possessing the magic and delicious power of reflecting the figure of man at twice its natural size. . . . Whatever may be their use in civilised societies, mirrors are essential to all violent and heroic action. That is why Napoleon and Mussolini both insist so emphatically upon the inferiority of women, for if they were not inferior, they would cease to enlarge. . . .

As the days between her secret engagement and her marriage—days whose limits were largely imposed by her future mother-in-law—dragged on, Eleanor Roosevelt became increasingly irritable and weary. On those occasions when her energies were exhausted and she expressed herself directly, with anger or impatience, she was overcome with remorse. "I've come to the conclusion that I need someone to watch over my temper, it makes me so cross with myself to lose it and yet I am forever doing it." But "the thought of you makes me happy and I only hope that I shall bring you happiness. I don't seem to succeed in bringing it to most people, however, do I?" When, on occasion, a day passed without a letter from Franklin, she felt "absolutely lost." "I really am afraid sometimes when I think of what an hour with you means to me." And when he left for the Caribbean, she missed him each day: "I miss you so much dear, it really frightens me to see how dependent I am growing and how the whole world turns for me around one person. . . ." During those five weeks of separation, she wrote him daily, five-to-ten-page letters, and occasionally cabled:

> I think of you all the time dear and try to imagine what you and your mother and Mr. Brown are doing.

I cannot tell you the awful fear which came over me, when no letter came. I suppose women are always fools about the people they love and I know you will laugh at me for worrying so. . . .

I feel lost without you somewhere near. I used to think myself so self-sufficient but I'm learning too quickly how much of my happiness lies in someone else's hands—Well, honey, when this is over you won't leave me again will you dear? I know I'm selfish but I cannot help it and if you only knew how much more I would like to ask and do not I think you would forgive me this. . . .

Please give your mother my love and tell her I hope it has been very smooth and that she is having a lovely trip. . . .

Still, some moments away from Franklin were diverting, even entertaining. She enjoyed the exclusive Tuxedo Ball more than she might have imagined. There was a party at Jean Reid's parents' Madison Avenue town house (which resembled a Florentine villa and featured a dinner table for eighty) that was so agreeable she stayed until almost four in the morning. She also spent a weekend at the Whitelaw Reids' eight-hundred-acre estate, Ophir Hall, in Purchase, New York, which was thoroughly delightful; she attended the Bible classes of Barnard-trained theology scholar Janet McCook; and she read with ardor, sometimes three books a weekend, some so wonderful she hoped she and Franklin might reread them together some day—especially, for example, *Sesame and Lilies,* John Ruskin's passionate protest against injustice and war, and for the increased participation of women in political affairs.

Most significantly, she saw George Bernard Shaw's play *Candida* at least three times. A class-conscious comedy about love and marriage, *Candida* opened in 1897 and was taken on a "propagandist tour" on the Woman Question with Ibsen's *A Doll's House. Candida* explored many themes that were later to become significant in Eleanor Roosevelt's life: love between people of different generations, unrequited love, loyalty in marriage, a woman's right to her own unfettered spirit, and especially Candida's decision to give her heart to the one who needs her most, the one who cannot function successfully without her.

Candida, the enchanting wife of a highly regarded and popular

Christian Socialist minister, James Morell, who takes her and her generous deeds entirely for granted, becomes interested in her husband's protégé, a callow youth and inflamed poet of eighteen, Eugene Marchbanks. He is devastated by his love for the lady, and tries to persuade her that her husband does not appreciate her: Love will be served only if she chooses *him:*

> "We all go about longing for love: it is the first need of our natures, the first prayer of our hearts; but we dare not utter our longing: we are too shy. . . . I go about in search of love. . . . And I see the affection I am longing for given to dogs and cats and pet birds, because they come and ask for it. It must be asked for: it is like a ghost: it cannot speak unless it is first spoken to. All the love in the world is longing to speak; only it dare not, because it is shy! shy! shy! That is the world's tragedy."

Though Candida is stirred by the young man's passion, he has mistaken his own intensity for shared desire. She cannot be taken for granted; she "belongs to herself," and will choose the weaker, the more dependent, of the two. She will stay with her husband—if only he will acknowledge his need for her, and the real role she plays in his life. "Quite overcome," Morell embraces his wife: "It's all true, every word. What I am you have made me with the labor of your hands and the love of your heart. You are my wife, my mother, my sisters: you are the sum of all loving care to me." Exit Marchbanks.

Throughout the winter of 1904, stimulated by romance and anticipation, Eleanor Roosevelt longed for an end to the silence of her engagement, the ordeal of the year of waiting imposed by Sara. Nevertheless, she continued to work with delicacy to win a corner of Sara's heart.

Eleanor was ready to compromise in many ways. She understood Sara, and wrote Franklin after they returned from the Caribbean: "Don't let her feel that the last trip with you is over. We three must take them together in the future . . . and though I know three will never be the same to her still someday I hope that she will really love me and I would be very glad if I thought she was even the least bit reconciled to me now. I will try to see her whenever she comes to town if she lets me know."

Sara and Eleanor did spend more time together. They lunched, dined, went to the theatre, walked in the park. Even before her outings with Eleanor, Sara made an effort to accept the inevitable with good grace. Shortly before Christmas 1903 she wrote her son: "I am so glad to think of my precious son so perfectly happy. You *know* that I try not to think of myself. I know that in the future I shall be glad & I shall love Eleanor & adopt her *fully* when the right time comes. Only have patience, dear Franklin, don't let this new happiness make you lose interest in work or home. . . ."

Finally, after their return from the Caribbean, Sara seemed resigned: "I am feeling pretty blue. You are gone. The journey is over & I feel as if the time were not likely to come again when I shall take a trip with my dear boy . . . , but I must try to be unselfish & of course dear child I *do* rejoice in your happiness & shall not put any stones or straws even in the way of it. . . ."

For her part, alone at Tivoli that spring, Eleanor wrote that she realized every day "more and more how much fuller my life had become . . . and I lay and wondered this afternoon how life could have seemed worth living before I knew what 'love' and 'happiness' really meant. . . ."

There were momentous times spent together during the spring and summer of 1904. On 18 June, Helen Astor Roosevelt married Teddy Roosevelt Robinson at Hyde Park. Franklin was an usher, Eleanor a bridesmaid, and the weekend was jolly. On 24 June, Eleanor and Sara attended Franklin's graduation from Harvard. Eleanor spent a magical August with Franklin and his mother at their summer home on the rocky Canadian shore at Campobello. When she left, Mrs. Hartman Kuhn, a friend and next-door neighbor who appreciated the ardor the young couple did so much to hide, wrote Eleanor: "I wish you could have seen Franklin's face the night you left Campo. He looked so tired and I felt everybody bored him."

But the rest of the summer and autumn were tedious. Eleanor spent a good deal of her time going from one great house to another, visiting friends and members of her family, but feeling trapped, and longing for Franklin. From Cousin Susie Parish's Long Island home she wrote that she had a "feeling that doing one's duty isn't all that it's cracked up to be and I very much wish I wasn't doing it now! One thing I am glad of every minute I stay here and that is that we won't ever have a house half so beautiful or half so overwhelming! I'm afraid I wasn't born to be a high life lady, dear, so you'll just have to be content with a simple existence, unless you teach me how to change!"

There would be many changes over time for both members of one of America's unique and abiding partnerships. Though Eleanor declined the life of "a high life lady," in the grand manorial style, there was to be nothing simple about her future with Franklin.

7. Franklin and Me, and Sara Makes Three

ANNA ELEANOR ROOSEVELT AND FRANKLIN DELANO Roosevelt were married on 17 March 1905. It was, coincidentally, the anniversary of Anna Hall Roosevelt's birth, but the date had not been selected to honor Eleanor's mother. It had been selected to accommodate President Theodore Roosevelt, who was scheduled to be in New York City for the Saint Patrick's Day parade. Uncle Ted and Aunt Edith had offered Eleanor a White House wedding, but she preferred to be married from Cousin Susie Parish's home—actually the twin homes of Cousin Susie and her mother, Elizabeth Livingston Ludlow—at 6–8 East 76th Street.

Eleanor looked "beautiful," "regal," "magnificent" on her wedding day. As she walked slowly down the aisle on the arm of her Uncle Theodore, people whispered to each other. For the first time, she seemed to resemble her mother, in the grace and dignity of perfect bearing—justifying all those years of practice up and down the River Road. Her thick golden hair was swept high, her blue eyes luminous, her gaze steady, focused on the future, and the present, and the past. In long-sleeved heavy satin, with shirred tulle at the neck, Eleanor wore the same lace veil and long train her mother had worn at her own wedding—Grandmother Hall's rosepoint Brussels lace, which covered her dress—and "was festooned with natural orange blossoms." Her mother's diamond crescent fastened her veil. She also wore a dog collar of pearls and diamond bars given to her by Sara that made her feel "decked out beyond description." Would her mother have thought her beautiful? Would she have been pleased? How different would it have been had her father led her to this altar adorned with palm, roses, and ferns in front of the fireplace?

There were over two hundred guests, a great union of families, of generations connected in complicated ways. The room seemed filled with ghosts and shadows. Grandmother Hall, in black velvet, sat in front, in her sister's home, surrounded by Halls and Roosevelts, Livingstons and Ludlows, her remaining sons and daughters. Close beside her sat Sara Delano Roosevelt, in white silk covered with her own mother's black lace. Nearby sat Aunt Bye and her husband, Admiral Will Cowles. Aunt Bye had introduced Sara to Squire James. He had courted the one, married the other, named Bye's brother Elliott the godfather of his son. And now, joined in holy matrimony, the circle was unbroken.

Aunt Pussie, married the year before in the same room, had given Eleanor a note of advice (drink strong tea shortly before the wedding march, to heighten your color and make you glow; no milk or sugar) and three kisses: "for Father & Mother & Ellie." Aunt Maude gave her a note of great loving affection: Let us always be as sisters. And as she was dressing, a telegram arrived from Marie Souvestre: "BONHEUR!" Eleanor knew that cancer was about to claim her great friend and teacher; she died two days later.

Now, in the attached brownstones of her godmother and great-aunt, surrounded by white and lavender lilacs, and large lilies in great profusion, standing in a bower of roses and palm, carrying a bouquet of her very favorite lilies of the valley, Eleanor was flushed with excitement. Nothing should have been able to mar the happiness of that day; but the day was marred.

It had seemed to take so long to get to this room. On 11 October 1904, Franklin had given Eleanor a secret gift for her twentieth birthday. With consideration for what might truly please her, "after much inspection and deliberation" at Tiffany's, he had chosen her engagement ring. It was just right: "You could not have found a ring I would have liked better," she wrote. "I love it so I know I shall find it hard to keep from wearing it!" After almost a year of hiding and dissembling, there were still weeks of silence to endure. At least they were now geographically closer. Franklin had entered Columbia Law School, and lived with his mother in a newly rented house at 200 Madison Avenue.

Finally, on 1 December, their engagement was officially announced. New York's society sheets featured the engagement and celebrated Eleanor. According to *Town Topics,* Eleanor Roosevelt had "more claim to good looks than any of the Roosevelt cousins. . . ." She was "attractive . . . unusually tall and fair," with "a charming grace of manner that has made her a favorite since her debut."

Now Eleanor was free to write her closest relatives the truth. Aunt Bye replied: "My own darling soft-eyed child, your letter has given me great joy. I love Franklin as you know on his own personal account because he is so attractive & also because I believe his character is like his Father's whom Uncle Will & I always feel was the most *absolutely* honorable upright gentleman (the last in the highest sense) that we ever knew." Clearly, for Aunt Bye, Franklin was a Roosevelt—and not a Delano at all.

Theodore Roosevelt wrote Franklin a letter of congratulations:

We are greatly rejoiced over the good news. I am as fond of Eleanor as if she were my daughter, and I like you, and trust you, and believe in you. No other success in life—not the Presidency or anything else—begins to compare with the joy and happiness that come in and from the love of the true man and the true woman. . . . You and Eleanor are true and brave, and I believe you love each other unselfishly. . . . May all good fortune attend you both, ever.

Although TR loved his niece, and felt responsible for her well-being, Aunt Edith had never cast any noticeable warmth in Eleanor's direction. She invited Eleanor to White House festivities, including all the most intimate family parties that attended TR's inauguration on 4 March, but she retained a cold edge, a frosty formality, that rendered Eleanor distinctly uncomfortable in her presence. Even when specifically invited to stay at the White House, Eleanor preferred to stay at Aunt Bye's. Nevertheless, Aunt Edith wrote Eleanor:

Your Uncle and I have thought and talked so much of your wedding and he feels that on that day he stands in your father's place and would like to have your marriage under his roof and make all the arrangements for it. . . . Of course dear Eleanor your Uncle and I will understand if you prefer to have your wedding in New York as you have planned, but we wish you to know how very glad we shall be to do for you as we should for Alice. . . .

Eleanor did not even consider a change in plans. Her grandmother sent out the invitations; Cousin Susie made all the preparations, and together they shopped for her trousseau. Except for Isabella Selmes and Helen Cutting, Eleanor's six bridesmaids were chosen from the extended family circle: Corinne Robinson, Ellen Delano, Muriel Delano Robbins, and Alice Roosevelt. Alice, always wild and beyond control, was now frequently in the headlines for her outrageous behavior. Her father's remote attitude toward his firstborn child, his seeming lack of concern as to her whereabouts for months at a time, his willingness to have her live elsewhere as often as possible, caused Alice to resent her cousin out of all proportion to TR's alleged favoritism for Eleanor. Over time, Alice's resentment would surface in specifically nasty ways. But on this occasion, any jealousy she may have felt because her father had offered the first White House wedding to her cousin, who had actually beaten her to the altar, was veiled by a letter of unbridled gratitude: "You angel, to ask me to be your bridesmaid. I should love to above anything. . . . Really you are a saint to ask me. . . ."

By this time, Eleanor's own feelings toward her cousin had become frayed. She had heard many of the cruel things Alice had said about her (the boring, dowdy, somber thing); and about Franklin (Alice had called him a prissy, fluttering boy who might be "invited to the dance, but not the dinner"). And Eleanor in turn was critical of Alice's behavior. Once she spotted Alice in New York, "looking well but crazier than ever. I saw her this morning," she wrote Franklin, "in Bobbie Goelet's auto, quite alone with three other men! I wonder how you would like my tearing round like that! . . ."

Eleanor's feelings for her other bridesmaids were far more harmonious, as were theirs for her. Her good friend Isabella Selmes seemed entirely to identify with Eleanor. As she helped her with the thank-you notes for the 340 presents that arrived, she wrote, "Franklin and I are so pleased with your gift," etc., and signed her own name.

Franklin had as his ushers Nicholas Biddle, Owen Winston, Lyman Delano, Charles Bradley, Thomas Beal, Warren Robbins, and Lathrop Brown, who (because Rosy was ill in Florida) served as his best man. All wore tie pins, which FDR had designed, with three feathers in diamonds. Indeed, the Roosevelt family insignia was much in evidence. The bridesmaids, in white silk, with sleeves embroidered with silver roses, wore white "demi-veils of tulle fastened with three white feathers tipped with silver" in their hair. In addition, Franklin had given Eleanor a gold watch-pin, which he had designed with her initials, ER, in diamonds attached to a three-feathered pin. Eleanor was moved by Franklin's thoughtful design, and she wore it throughout her life. Franklin was as serious about the family insignia (three feathers above a cluster of roses) as his mother was about the family tree. There were roses in bookplates and crested rings. He later incorporated the family symbol into the White House china.

Theodore Roosevelt arrived at three-thirty to "give the bride away." He had "scuttled" into New York, he wrote his son, to review the Saint Patrick's Day parade, make two speeches, and, in between, perform his familial duty. The Saint Patrick's Day parade continued up the avenue as the president detoured to his niece's wedding; it blocked both avenues (Fifth and Madison) leading to the Parish-Ludlow entrances. There was so much police protection for the president, and so much fanfare and hoopla as he arrived, that many wedding guests were detained. To Eleanor's dismay, some "irate guests could not get into the house until after the ceremony was over!"

The ceremony itself was practically drowned out by the Ancient Order of Hibernians, who passed below the windows singing "The Wearing of the Green" as the vows were exchanged. Perhaps because he was afraid he might not be heard, when the Reverend Endicott Peabody asked, "Who giveth this woman in marriage?," TR declaimed in what seemed to some his most inappropriate "loud emphatic tones, *I* do!" Then, after Eleanor and Franklin exchanged vows and rings and kissed each other, the president, reaching up to kiss the bride, exclaimed: "Well, Franklin, there's nothing like keeping the name in the family."

On that note, according to Eleanor Roosevelt Roosevelt, her uncle spun about and headed directly into the library for the refreshments, leaving the young couple standing alone at the altar waiting "to receive congratulations from the various members of our families and our friends." But "the great majority" had followed Uncle Theodore. Decades later, Eleanor recalled that "Those closest to us did take time to wish us well." But most of "the guests were far more interested in the thought of being able to see and listen to the President—and in a very short time" the newly married couple "were standing alone!" Even at the cake-cutting they were left all but unattended.

Eleanor Roosevelt never criticized her uncle. When writing about the one day that might have been, above all, her day, she recalled the facts with wry detachment—leaving the rest of us to imagine the pain beneath the words. TR had upstaged the putative stars and stolen the show's entire audience of Roosevelts, Halls, Delanos, Ludlows, Vanderbilts, Belmonts, Sloans, Winthrops, Van Rensselaers, Mortimers, and Burdens. He held forth for the next hour and half with his "stories which were always amusing. I do not remember being particularly surprised by this, and I cannot remember that even Franklin seemed to mind. We simply followed the crowd and listened with the rest" until "the lion of the afternoon had left!" As his daughter Alice understood: "Father always wanted to be the bride at every wedding and the corpse at every funeral."

Eleanor Roosevelt at twenty had a very specific understanding of the whims and vagaries of life. In her experience, death always flew after the heels of life; sadness was frequently trapped in the heart of joy. The choreography of the entire ceremony served well as metaphor for the early years of Eleanor's marriage—which were for her primarily years of struggle to establish a place for herself.

During the early years of her marriage Eleanor Roosevelt faded into the demands of a home life that was orchestrated by her mother-in-law, and that she could not claim as her own. For the first time since her own mother had died, she was faced with a situation in which she simply could not please the woman of the house. Where Grandmother Hall and Marie Souvestre had both appreciated Eleanor's special gifts, the rare nature of her heart, and the "purity of her soul," Sara Delano Roosevelt was more like Anna: careless of Eleanor's presence, oblivious to her pain, focused elsewhere—on her son, and her own need for his devotion. She was not crude or cruel, merely distant, and implacable. Sara Delano Roosevelt knew best; the young couple could not possibly do for themselves what she could do for them. They were so inexperienced; they needed her money, her help, her presence, her advice—about everything, and at all times. Sara's imperious, cold manner plunged Eleanor back into the hurt and sullenness she seemed for several years to have left behind her.

Eleanor Roosevelt never used the word "depression"; but during these years she never missed an opportunity to mock her own ignorance, her clumsiness, her many and various inadequacies as a young wife. She never blamed Franklin, or her mother-in-law, or the strange arrangements they chose—which always involved Sara's preferences, Sara's generosity, Sara's control.

Their immediate honeymoon was a week in Hyde Park, which Sara allowed them to have alone, supervised only by Elspeth McEachern ("Elespie"), the Scottish "caretaker" who had presided over Spring-wood and attended to the needs of its mistresses since the days of Rebecca Howland. She had lighted all the candles in the windows, and the house was aglow as Eleanor and Franklin's carriage drove up the long tree-framed entrance. She was at the open door to greet the young couple when they arrived. What Eleanor may have thought of the dour critic, so important to Franklin and his mother, she never said. But, she noted, Elespie "looked me over critically and appraisingly, wondering if I could come up to her expectations as the wife of 'her boy.'"

The next day, at her sister Kassie's in Tuxedo Park, Sara wrote: "My precious Franklin & Eleanor." "It is a delight to write to you together & to think of you happy at dear Hyde Park, just where my great happiness began. You have a real spring day and I can just see the sun . . . and feel how you two are resting and reveling in your quiet time together."

Whatever she really thought of the wedding, she wrote the newlyweds with pride:* "Everyone says it was the most perfect wedding so simple and yet so elegant and so refined. . . . Eleanor dear you were a perfect bride and I was very proud of both my dear children." Still, when she wrote *My Boy Franklin,* a memoir of her son, she relished the memory that he was not "so deeply engrossed" in his bride to have heard his cue. Franklin had been reminiscing about Groton with Dr. Peabody and Lathrop Brown, and they all evidently failed to hear the wedding march. They had to scurry to meet Eleanor at the altar after the procession was actually under way.

After their honeymoon, Eleanor and Franklin returned to New York City, where Franklin's primary task was to pass his law-school courses at Columbia (he failed two), and Eleanor's primary task was to make life comfortable for her new husband, his mother (who accompanied them frequently), and her brother, Hall, who immediately moved in with them for Easter vacation and made many subsequent visits from Groton. He "seemed to fill the entire apartment," which was a very modest one in the old Hotel Webster.

As soon as Columbia's semester ended, they embarked on a three-month European honeymoon. The trip over was calm, and Eleanor's fear of the sea abated. She was not sick once. Relieved, Franklin reported to his mother: "Eleanor has been a *wonderful* sailor and hasn't missed a single meal or *lost* any either." Unlike her previous ocean voyages with aunts who insisted that the only comfortable place to be was in one's cabin, under the covers, Eleanor thoroughly enjoyed this crossing. She felt loved, and protected: "Franklin has been a wonderful maid & I've never been so well looked after." They walked on deck; they danced; they had interesting talks with interesting people; they went with the captain on a tour of the ship, in the course of which Eleanor saw—and was horrified by—the conditions the steerage passengers had to endure; and they played endless games of cards—mostly piquet, which Franklin always won, "all due to skill!" he claimed, though she suspected he cheated, and was willing only to credit him with luck.

For all his outward confidence, Franklin had nightmares and began

---

* *Town Topics* had criticized the wedding for the Ludlow-Parish-Hall frugality. The food was too ordinary; the orchestra lackluster; and they had failed to use a first-rate florist. See notes, pages 522–23.

to sleepwalk during his honeymoon. On the steamer, he walked out of the cabin. "He was very docile, however, when asleep," Eleanor noted, and simply returned to bed at her suggestion. On another occasion, she awakened to "wild shrieks" as he battled against an imaginary "revolving beam." She assured him there was no beam. Another night, he stood at the foot of the bed, cranking away at the air as fast as possible, muttering: "The damn thing won't start." She said: "Franklin, if you get into the car I'll help you to start it." He returned to bed and held an imaginary steering wheel while she pretended to do the cranking, until he went back to sleep. There were other moments of somnambulism, outbursts of sleep-time distress, anxiety, anguish. There were also daytime moments when Eleanor noticed a pattern of casual flirtation and occasional overindulgence that disturbed her. But on the whole, their three-month honeymoon was tranquil and pleasurable.

In Europe, for "the first time we did things that I had always longed to do." They spent weeks in Britain, France, Italy, and Germany. They visited relatives and friends of relatives. They saw Eleanor's Great-Aunt Annie Bulloch in Liverpool, who wept at the sight of her newlywed niece and spoke only with kindness of her beloved Ellie-Boy. They spent a week in London, which was Franklin's favorite city, and which Eleanor grew to enjoy as never before. They shopped and shopped, for clothes, books, and prints. They were identified with Uncle Ted and given the royal suite at Brown's Hotel, which they could neither afford nor leave graciously. The sitting room was so large, Eleanor complained, "I could not find anything that I put down." They lunched at the embassy with the Whitelaw Reids, and Eleanor was seated beside the ambassador. Alone, Eleanor went out to Allenswood to visit, but it was desolate without Marie Souvestre.

When they crossed the Channel Eleanor became "really excited." In Paris they "dined in strange places," always ordering the *spécialités de la maison,* and had a festive time. Again they shopped for clothes, books, and prints, and, Franklin noted, "ordered thousands of dollars worth of linen." However exaggerated his claim, their primary joy for weeks seemed making rather lavish purchases—including "such lovely furs," which Franklin insisted she have: "I don't think he ought to give them to me but they are wonderful and of course I am delighted with them."

For Eleanor, Italy was magical. Rome, Florence, and Venice recalled her happiest memories—memories of good times with her father, of splendid days with Marie Souvestre. Nothing, she believed, "could be quite so lovely as Venice" in July. They walked in leisure all day; spent endless idle hours feeding the pigeons on the Piazza San Marco, "as I remembered doing as a little girl"; and spent many of the warm nights on the canals with "a delightful gondolier who looked like a benevolent bandit" and sang much as she remembered her father had sung. Eleanor had a chance to practice her excellent Italian, and evidently her conversation so charmed the gondolier that he gave her a volume of sixteenth-century poetry by Torquato Tasso, that she might always remember him.

The spell of Venice was intensified by the presence of Charles Stuart Forbes, Franklin's cousin, a Venetian resident and painter who had given them one of his paintings as a wedding present. He loved the city and its people; he knew everybody and took the young couple everywhere. They ate sumptuously where few tourists knew to go, followed canals right into the heart of luxurious homes and secret gardens, visited artists and art galleries, churches, museums, and palaces. They also toured the island of Murano and ordered Venetian glasses adorned with the Roosevelt crest, and glass dolphins for table decorations. In Venice, Eleanor bought yards of very old and "very beautiful red damask," which she always cherished; some of it was made into curtains, some used for an evening coat. There was not only beauty, but harmony and friendship associated with each day spent in Venice.

From Venice, the Roosevelts traveled north to the Dolomites. "It was a beautiful trip to Cortina," where they remained for several days. In the foothills of those lovely mountains, Eleanor experienced her first moment of pain and fierce resentment as a wife. For no apparent reason, Eleanor believed that the rather modest four-hour hike up the Faloria was beyond her endurance. The woman who would later climb thousands of feet up the High Sierras, leaving her companions exhausted in their efforts to match her pace, evidently wanted to be encouraged by her young husband. But he never did encourage her, not at climbing, golf, sailing, or even tennis—which he played so poorly he was known as "Miss Nancy" on the courts. Pausing neither to give her any good reasons to accompany him nor to persuade her of the ease of the walk, he took off accompanied by the somewhat older and very stylish Kitty Gandy—a hard-smoking New York milliner who had been flirting with him since their arrival in Cortina. After dinner, as they all played cards, she puffed his best cigarettes and promised him a fine autumn hat with a plume. While they climbed, Eleanor fretted. After waiting several hours, she set out on the trail with two sisters (the Van Bibbers), but failed to find Franklin, who did not return with the "charming lady," until after dark. Subsequently, Kitty Gandy and Eleanor Roosevelt became "very good friends"; but that day she felt abandoned, and betrayed. Although "I never said a word I was jealous beyond description."

She did not feel better until they drove toward Germany, where they visited Augsburg and Ulm, and Franklin impulsively stopped to pick a beautiful bouquet of wildflowers for his wife: the wild jasmine were "sweeter than anything I ever had." They drove through the Alps and on to Saint-Moritz, to visit the Mortimers. Switzerland's prices appalled them, and they were pleased to return to the relatively inexpensive splendors of Paris.

Eleanor and Franklin stayed at the Imperial Hotel in Paris, but Sara's sister, Aunt "Doe" (Deborah Perry Delano Forbes, also called Aunt Dora), opened her apartment "which became the most hospitable home to us." Aunt Dora entertained them lavishly. Eleanor was vastly impressed by Franklin's aunt, with whom she spent many days touring museums and shops. They also played cards during several evenings when Franklin cavorted with an array of visiting Harvard friends and cousins and went "on a prolonged bat."

One evening FDR and his friends thought it would be naughty and amusing to take Eleanor and Aunt Dora to "an extremely 'French play.'" Eleanor praised Aunt Dora's reaction to the risqué: She "had lived many years in Paris and did not give them the satisfaction of turning a hair!" Although ER later noted in her memoirs that the evening "strained" her "Anglo-Saxon sense of humor," at the time she wrote Sara: "We all went to the Français to see 'Le Depit Amoureux' and

'Andromaque,' both well given and the latter quite marvellous. There is really nothing like an old classic and the French language to bring one to the highest pitch of excitement, is there?"

Before they sailed home, they returned to Britain, where Eleanor felt particularly conscious of the reality of Marie Souvestre's passing. She spent time with Marjorie Bennett, her great Allenswood friend, and became aware during this trip that she had not had time to mourn her teacher's death. It "had been a great sorrow to me," coming as it did immediately after her wedding, when "life was so full I had little time for repining." But her trip to so many places they had been to before "brought home the loss, and made me long for her more than once."

In Scotland, Eleanor and Franklin visited with her friends the Fergusons, who had been connected in so many complicated ways to so many Roosevelts. Their family seat at Raith, near Kirkcaldy, north of the Firth of Forth, was a center of Liberal Party politics and great activity, and their country seat at Novar had been Auntie Bye's second home whenever she was nearby. In the beginning, Robert H. Munro Ferguson, fourteen years younger than Bye, had been her particular friend; more recently, his charming, affectionate presence had enabled Eleanor to endure the agony of her coming-out year with far more happiness and many more interests than would otherwise have been possible. Now, while on her honeymoon, Eleanor received a surprising telegram about Bob Ferguson and her dear friend Isabella Selmes from Isabella's mother: They had suddenly, and with little notice, married, and were also in Scotland. He was eighteen years older than Isabella, and although it seemed to Eleanor "an incongruous marriage," it was born of the deepest love. ER visited with them and wrote Sara that they were unimaginably "sweet . . . together." Bob Ferguson had "become demonstrative if you can believe it and they play together like two children."

For a time, Eleanor and Franklin stayed with the senior Fergusons at Novar, and Eleanor spent many hours with Emma Munro Ferguson, the family matriarch, and Bob's sister Edith Ferguson, who was a great friend of Aunt Bye's. Both women were as interested as the Ferguson men in all things political, and Eleanor realized in their company that she had allowed herself to remain unacceptably ignorant. She resolved to change her own attitude toward politics. But when they invited her to give a talk to open the local fair, she at first felt undone, "quite certain that I could never utter a word aloud in a public place." By contrast, the women of the Novar were routinely expected to speak in public, and for years they served for Eleanor as models of how to be in society, and in any company.

From Novar, Eleanor and Franklin went to Raith—a "beautiful place, with wonderful woods and rhododendrons," and extraordinary plantings everywhere—to spend a week with the eldest brother and head of the clan, Sir Ronald ("The Novar") Ferguson and his wife, Lady Helen. Eleanor felt entirely comfortable until one afternoon at tea when Lady Helen "suddenly asked me a devastating question." It was an ordinary question, really, about the differences between national, state, and local government in the United States. But ER was uninformed. She knew vaguely that Uncle Theodore had been involved with New York City offices, had been governor, and was now president, but she had never concerned herself with government: "My heart sank, and I wished that the ground would open up and swallow me." She was spared by Franklin's reappearance. His answer "was adequate," and Eleanor vowed anew that she would study her own government, and never be unprepared or seem ignorant again. She left the Fergusons determined to change, to learn more, and to do more.

On her return, however, her resolve was initially derailed by the daily necessities of matronly existence. She was, to begin with, pregnant. The voyage home had been an agony of seasickness, in no way made easier when she realized that its true cause was morning-sickness. Nor did her spirits lift when she realized, upon landing, that in their absence Sara Delano Roosevelt had not only rented a house for them, as they had agreed, three blocks from her own, at 125 East 36th Street, but had also furnished it herself and engaged their servants. There was nothing for Eleanor to do. Everything was arranged and in order. And until the last finishing touches were applied, they were to live with her mother-in-law, in New York and at Hyde Park.

Eleanor Roosevelt had wanted, above all, a home and a family of her own. Her husband, however, considered Hyde Park his family home and was content there. But it belonged to Sara, and she presided over the dining-room table. It was her table, at either end of which she and Franklin sat. Eleanor, and later the children, sat along the sides. There were no spaces at Hyde Park dedicated to making Eleanor feel welcome, and she had no study. There was a particularly small and cozy reading room she might have liked, but it was Sara's "snuggery." There were two comfortable wing-backed chairs on either side of the fireplace, FDR's and SDR's. No one thought to buy a third. Eleanor generally sat on the floor, occasionally on the sofa, or just anywhere. At Hyde Park the family geography was rigidly determined. All her life an outsider in the homes of others, Eleanor was once again on the periphery, and could not imagine claiming a place at the family hearth. Though she sought Sara's advice on "almost every subject," she never asked her "for anything that I thought would not meet with her approval."

Eleanor Roosevelt's initial efforts to please her mother-in-law were monumental. Her honeymoon letters to Sara had been full of love and longing. On 7 June 1905, the first day out aboard the RMS *Oceanic,* she wrote: "Dearest Mama, I am all unpacked and settled and F is now getting his things in order. . . . Thank you so much dear for everything you did for us. You are always just the sweetest, dearest Mama to your children and I shall look forward to our next long evening together, when I shall want to be kissed all the time!"

Her daily letters to Sara contained full reports concerning parties and social events, servants and the problems of servants, the many tedious details of dining and travel. She asked Sara to send *all* the news and family gossip, and she longed for Sara's advice and wisdom. Eleanor wanted Sara's approval and love so much that she temporarily abandoned her liberal inclinations and parroted Sara's narrow views, her rigid ethnic stereotypes, her likes and dislikes.

To appreciate the young wife Eleanor, who tried so hard to fit into a family run by a powerful matriarch for the exclusive benefit of her only son, one has to keep in mind Eleanor's childhood. She had no experience of belonging, no idea what a mature, loving mother-daughter relationship might look like, unless one counts what she had learned from Marie Souvestre—her tutor, her mentor, her friend. But that relationship occurred outside the confines of the family and was informed by values that seemed irrelevant to the present situation—freedom, independence, equality. Eleanor had no idea how to achieve what she wanted in her relationship with Sara, nor any sense that the cost of achieving it would be higher than any she ought to pay. And so, for over a decade, she submerged and distorted her own needs and convictions. Comparing the first years of her marriage with her school years at Allenswood, she noted that in marriage she had allowed herself to become entirely dependent and servile, whereas with Marie Souvestre, she had risen to the challenge of the great responsibilities thrust upon her. When they traveled, she did the "packing and unpacking," looked up the train schedules, mapped the route, made all the arrangements. She was an entirely competent sixteen-year-old. But she lost her "self-confidence and ability to look after myself in the early days of my marriage." There were "no tickets to buy, no plans to make." Instead, there was always someone "to decide everything for me." At first it seemed a "pleasant contrast to my former life, and I slipped into it with the greatest of ease." Within months, Eleanor Roosevelt fit very well "into the pattern of a fairly conventional, quiet, young society matron."

Initially she believed that she could establish a relationship with her mother-in-law similar to the one she had had with her beloved friend and teacher. Both were strong and elegant women, resourceful, independent, vigorously opinionated. But Marie Souvestre encouraged Eleanor Roosevelt to grow according to her own inner vision, to be critical about the world—its shibboleths and rigidities. Sara Delano Roosevelt liked the world the way it was. She believed it had been created by her and her class, for her and her class. She wanted those around her to think precisely as she did, to share her concerns and her priorities. Indeed, she believed that those around her did believe as she did. To be loved freely by Sara meant to become fully like Sara. To be loved by Marie Souvestre had meant to display an independent spirit with individual flair, and a playful imagination. Marie Souvestre cared mostly for young people with intelligence and daring, who were willing to challenge her authority and to become skeptical of all authority. Sara Delano Roosevelt insisted that her convictions were correct, and they would do for the entire family. Since Sara now represented her only chance for maternal love and affection, Eleanor capitulated to her.

Capitulation meant imitation. For over a decade, Eleanor Roosevelt's letters to her mother-in-law reflected precisely her mother-in-law's views. During the first years of her marriage, Eleanor moved away from Souvestre's example and buried herself in the details of childrearing, homemaking, seasonal travel, and lavish entertainment. Her letters are dominated by purchases, servant problems, parties, and children. They are also full of observations intended to please Sara, who loathed politics and political people, especially political women. One is continually surprised to read sentences in this correspondence of flip, class-bound arrogance and egregious racism.

Eleanor's growing suspicion that nothing she could do or write or say would ever fully satisfy Sara Delano Roosevelt was correct. Nevertheless, she continued to make every effort to be a pleasing daughter-in-law, a dutiful wife and mother. Of this time she wrote: "For ten years I was always just getting over having a baby or about to have one, and so my occupations were considerably restricted."

Although the needs and wants of young children might have made a satisfying claim on her time and energy, her mother-in-law ran the Roosevelt household, managed the staff, and in every significant way dominated the only sphere Eleanor then occupied. It seemed never to have occurred to Franklin to live for any time on the combined trust income he and Eleanor then received. Together, their annual earnings (Eleanor's was more than $7,500 and Franklin's was $5,000) would have insured a comfortable, although different, standard of living away from Sara's authority. ER often referred to her unsuccessful effort to persuade Franklin of this option, which would have allowed their marriage to develop its own rhythms and chemistry. Denied that opportunity, Eleanor grew passive and silent. While she continued to encourage Franklin to study hard and excel in law school, she submerged her abilities and repressed her feelings. Things began to taste bitter; plants began to wilt; her dutiful daily walks through the park with Mama failed to renew her spirit. Trapped in a situation that she could neither move out of nor grow within, she began to lose her sense of purpose. As fewer and fewer responsibilities were left in her hands, her usual delight in service and helpfulness was momentarily forgotten. Even the tasks of motherhood were performed by others, and pregnancy kept her literally confined.

Bound by custom and convention, Eleanor was not to be seen in public while pregnant. As a result, on 17 February 1906, Franklin attended Alice Roosevelt's White House wedding with his mother, leaving Eleanor behind though she was only in her sixth month. The festivities were elaborate, but Alice chose to have no bridesmaids. Like Eleanor, she wore white satin trimmed with point lace that had been worn by her deceased mother, Alice Lee, and grandmother. When the bishop of Washington asked, "Who giveth this woman to be married to this man?," TR placed his daughter's hand into that of the congressman from Cincinnati, Nicholas Longworth, and uncharacteristically said not one audible word. The press reported that throughout the ceremony the president looked glum and his wife (in brown brocade which "accentuated her tired pallor") looked impassive, fulfilling her reputation as a storybook Mean Stepmother. To Alice's spontaneous outburst of gratitude for her beautiful wedding, Edith Carow Roosevelt replied: "I want you to know that I'm glad to see you go. You've never been anything but trouble."

Alice's wedding, like Eleanor's, was a metaphor for her marriage. In Alice's show, she was the star and sole performer. Eleanor was often in the shadows, on a very crowded stage.

All preparations for Eleanor's first child, Anna Eleanor Roosevelt, born on 3 May 1906, were made by Sara. Although she had entirely controlled Franklin's infancy, and fired any servants who challenged her dominion, it never occurred to her to encourage Eleanor to follow her example. On the contrary, she encouraged her daughter-in-law's sense of inadequacy, and usurped her role. Eleanor blamed herself: "I had never had any interest in dolls or in little children, and I knew absolutely nothing about handling or feeding a baby." The fact is, nobody cared to teach her, and her every effort was sabotaged.

Except for a trained nurse, Blanche Spring, who attended her children during infancy and became personally close to and supportive of Eleanor, most of the nursery staff tyrannized her. Blanche Spring had suggested that ER raise her children by herself, but her mother-in-law and Cousin Susie so vigorously opposed the idea, she hardly considered it.*

Trapped by the dictates of her class and culture, Eleanor allowed a series of strict, occasionally cruel British martinets to dominate the nursery. In addition, she had some strange ideas about how to be a modern mother. Fanatical about fresh air, she left Anna Eleanor outside a window in a wire box every morning for her nap. But she placed the box on the dark and cold side of the house, and little Anna screamed so long and loud, the neighbors were aghast. They threatened to call the Society for the Prevention of Cruelty to Children to report that Eleanor Roosevelt treated her child "inhumanly." ER was shocked: She had read that "you should not pick up a baby when it cried," and she had not thought much about warmth and sun.

Later, ER tied little Anna's hands above her head to the bedposts so that she could not masturbate. Later still, one of her sons found his thumbs enmeshed in wire to discourage his thumb-sucking habit. Generally, she left the children to the exclusive care of whichever tyrant she had hired, until the children's complaints were substantiated. One particularly sadistic nanny was promptly fired when liquor bottles were found in her closet.

The destructiveness of the household dynamic was compounded by Franklin's refusal to participate in domestic matters. As primary provider, Sara Delano Roosevelt went to great material lengths to seduce and captivate her grandchildren. So eager to be regarded as the essential parent, she repeatedly asserted: "I was your real mother, Eleanor merely bore you."

Increasingly afloat in a sea upon which she never got to chart the course, never fully understood the tides, and could not quite count on her mate for support in a storm, Eleanor found the early years of her marriage to be the loneliest of her adult life.

Denied control and authority, Eleanor became ever more depressed and withdrawn. Her childhood willingness to go to great lengths to avoid a scolding "developed now into a dislike for any kind of discus-

* Decades later, she believed that, had she decided to explore and discover the mysteries of child-raising for herself, or at least paid more and closer attention, "my subsequent troubles would have been avoided and my children would have had far happier lives."

sion." She offered few opinions, never disagreed, rarely indicated her true feelings about anything. But she was often miserable. Whenever she was hurt, disappointed, or angry, she shut up "like a clam," became long-suffering, "humble and meek," felt "like a martyr," and acted like one. Although she may have deluded herself into thinking that she suffered in silence, her anguish was hardly a secret. Everyone around her during those years felt the chill of what she called her "Griselda" moods.*

Although she spent much of her time with Isabella Selmes Ferguson and her former Roser classmates, who were also in the process of becoming society's perfect matrons, she did not feel she could confide in them. In 1933, looking back on this period, ER wrote: "I never talked to anyone. That was why it all ate into my soul. . . . In other words, I was a morbid idiot for many years! Only in the last ten years or so have I made friends to whom I have talked."

Her husband in particular had no interest in intimate talk. He turned aside serious household problems with a shrug, or with a kind of careless gaiety that Eleanor could not share. Franklin wanted no part of the growing tensions between his wife and his mother. Their disagreements, he firmly maintained, were their business. ER later understood FDR's lifelong ability to ignore anything difficult or painful. She even came to marvel at his patience while he waited for all unpleasantness to wither with neglect. But these skills, when applied to her and to his home

---

* The medieval metaphor "Patient Griselda"—the heroine of a tale told by Petrarch, Chaucer, and others—is a monster of passivity. From the fourteenth to the twentieth century, men have romanticized her "sweet servility." There are hundreds of versions, over forty in English, and a simple plot: Walter, the marquis of Saluzzo, seeks a wife to bear his heirs. He selects an attractive peasant girl and offers her title and comfort if she will be uncomplainingly and absolutely obedient. She promises to do so. All goes well until she has a daughter; the marquis decides he will not accept a peasant heir, so the child must be killed. Griselda uncomplainingly hands the infant to her husband. A son is born; the ritual is repeated. Then the marquis decides to return Griselda to her father. She is banished in tatters, and with nothing, exiled for over fifteen years. At that point, the marquis sends word that he plans to marry a beautiful young bride, and asks Griselda to come prepare the feast. She returns, scrubs, and cooks. He calls her before the assembled guests, in her tattered rags, and asks what she thinks of the bride. Griselda finds her lovely and praises her generously. The marquis announces that the bride and her brother are Griselda's children, and he at last is satisfied with her obedience. All are united; jubilation and rejoicing are her reward. Did ER find her situation so noxious she could compare Griselda's trials to her own? Or did she identify only with the extremism of her self-imposed and ever-patient silence?

during their first years together, made her feel betrayed, meanly abandoned.

Eleanor did try to glean moments of pleasure out of each day. She loved the theatre; enjoyed concerts and classes; and looked forward to the many lectures, social obligations, family gatherings, holidays, and other rituals around which her days were carefully planned. She even had good times with Sara. She lunched with Sara; they shopped and took classes together; they dined together and played cards. There were happy times with Franklin too. She and Franklin moved with the seasons from the city to Hyde Park to Campobello.

But to glean is not to reap. Both Eleanor's husband and her mother-in-law discouraged her from enjoying some of the most ordinary pleasures. She had always liked to ride horses: "as a girl I had ridden all the time." She had her favorite saddle and harness sent down from Tivoli to Hyde Park. But only one horse remained in the Springwood stable, Bobby. And FDR had trained him to trot when he reached one crossroad, canter when he got to a particular post, and then gallop until he reached the last marker. Bobby followed his ritual, no matter who rode him or what alternative orders he received. Unable to ride at her own pace, or ever to ride with Franklin, ER wanted to buy another horse. But Sara refused: It was a waste of money to keep two horses for such infrequent use. Since FDR did not support his wife's request, she temporarily gave up riding altogether.

During the summer of 1908, with their infant son, James, recovering from pneumonia, they decided to rent a house at Sea Bright, New Jersey, on the boardwalk. Born in the early morning hours of 23 December 1907, James had required medical care. Eleanor spent much of that summer alone with her two children and three servants in a state of high anxiety. She had never had neighbors close by before, and they were noisy. The boardwalk was dangerous and, one day, Anna toppled her brother's baby carriage onto the sand. Weekends, when houseguests and Franklin and Hall arrived, Eleanor was more relaxed, and the endless hours on the beach were wonderful for the children. But she was generally distraught. She even gave up driving before she began. One weekend Franklin bought a little Ford car, and Hall and his friend Julia Newbold encouraged Eleanor to drive. After a happy few moments at the wheel, she turned into the driveway and ran into a post, causing minor damage. Instead of encouraging her to get back behind the wheel immediately, Franklin allowed her to feel guilty beyond endurance, and she refused to learn to drive for years. Toward the end of August, Franklin and Hall left for a hunting trip to Newfoundland, and she was left alone with her two children: "I played no games, I could not swim, I was feeling miserable."

The next summer, because Franklin liked the game, Eleanor secretly took lessons in golf. She practiced every day for weeks. Then, one day, they went out together. After several minutes, Franklin smugly suggested she just not bother. "My old sensitiveness about my inability to play games made me give it up then and there! I never again attempted anything but walking with my husband for many years to come." Instead, she did what a proper matron was supposed to do. She took classes to keep up her French, Italian, German. She knitted and embroidered, walked and wove fantasies.

Her one consolation during this period was the pleasure she found on Campobello Island in New Brunswick, Canada, the first real home of her own. Her romance with its rugged rocky shores, its intense mists and chill grey days, had much to do with the fact that on Campobello she and Franklin lived in a cottage that was well separated from Sara's by plantings and privets.

Sara's neighbor Mrs. Hartman Kuhn, who had met Eleanor during her first trip to the island in August of 1904, had been one of the few to notice the love that radiated between Franklin and his then secret fiancée, and had entertained warm feelings for them ever since. In her will she gave Sara first refusal on the purchase of her home for the minimal price of $5,000, if she would buy it for her children, which Sara did upon Mrs. Kuhn's death in 1908. Eleanor never tired of this place. She never apologized to guests for the endless fogs; they comforted her. She never tired of the howling winds; they made her feel serene. And when the sun shone, Campobello's lush and vivid green-and-blue splendor was unrivaled. Here she enjoyed long, leisurely evenings reading aloud beside the fire—books of her own choosing, in a chair of her own choosing. Though Mrs. Kuhn had left all the furniture, linen, crystal, and silver, ER spent weeks rearranging the furniture, and used only what pleased her. She was mistress of this home; she invited her own guests, employed her own servants, and imposed her own order on the day.

The situation was vastly different in the Siamese-twin town houses the Roosevelts also moved into in 1908: 47–49 East 65th Street, designed by Charles A. Platt under Sara Delano Roosevelt's direction. On each floor, sliding doors gave Sara full reign of both houses. On the parlor floor, the dining rooms and drawing rooms could be opened onto each other to create a spacious party environment. On the bedroom floor, the children's floor, and the servants' floor, there were connecting passageways. The house was designed so that Sara could at any time intrude herself on every level into her children's lives. One never knew, ER wrote, "when she would appear, day or night."

Shortly after they moved into the new six-story town house, Eleanor sat in front of her dressing table, looked into the mirror, and wept. She cried and cried, until Franklin appeared to find out what was delaying her for dinner. "I said I did not like to live in a house which was not in any way mine, one that I had done nothing about and which did not represent the way I wanted to live." Franklin made no effort to console his wife or comprehend her pain. He announced that he thought her "quite mad," and assured her she would "feel differently" as soon as she became "calmer."

Five children were raised in that house. James, the firstborn son, was named after Franklin's father. Then came Franklin, born on 18 March 1909. At eleven pounds, he was "the biggest and most beautiful of all the babies." But he was not robust. There was something wrong with his heart, and after a bout of influenza, he died, seven months and fourteen days old, on 1 November. Eleanor was devastated by his death. Sara wrote in her journal, "my heart aches for Eleanor." He was buried in the Saint James Church at Hyde Park on 7 November. Sara noted, "E. brave and lovely," but Eleanor Roosevelt blamed herself for her baby's death, and remained melancholic for months. "To this day," she wrote decades later, "I can stand by his tiny stone in the churchyard and see the little group of people gathered around his tiny coffin, and remember how cruel it seemed to leave him out there alone in the cold."

During that year of intense mourning, she carried Elliott, who was born on 23 September 1910. She spent much of that summer alone with the children at Campobello. Although she was happiest there, she wrote Franklin: "I miss you dreadfully and feel very lonely, but please don't think it is because I am alone, having other people wouldn't do any good for I just want you!"

Eleanor's depression was intensified by Franklin's habits. Like her father, he had started to stay out late at night. Frequently he returned close to dawn, after poker games at the Knickerbocker Club, or dinner at the Harvard Club, or some allegedly urgent meeting related to his lackluster legal business. When her high spirited, happy husband came back from wherever he had been, he generally found a very somber wife—who sulked and said nothing. Silently she nursed her fears, and her romantic ideals of "goodness," which she fully expected Franklin to share. What a "tragedy it was if in any way my husband offended against these ideals of mine—and, amusingly enough, I do not think I ever told him what I expected!"

Immediately after law school, FDR had been hired by Carter, Ledyard and Milburn, a commercial firm that represented such corporations as Standard Oil of New Jersey and the American Tobacco Company when TR's antitrust lawyers targeted them. But FDR did little if anything significant for them, and was exceedingly bored. Basically, he spent these early years waiting for something more interesting to turn up.

In 1910, the year of Eleanor's most severe depression, opportunity not only knocked—it came a-courting, hat in hand. Reform Democrats led by Thomas Mott Osborne, the wealthy independent mayor of Auburn, New York, wanted to end the rule of political boss Charles Francis Murphy, who had had the audacity to support the unscrupulous father of "yellow journalism" and "jingo imperialism," William Randolph Hearst, for governor. The upstate Democrats needed new faces, and the 26th State Senate district, comprising Putnam, Columbia, and Dutchess counties, was up for grabs. They offered the race to the twenty-eight-year-old, relatively unknown but affluent Franklin Roosevelt, with their full and enthusiastic support. Several of FDR's neighbors, allied with Osborne—notably John Mack, an attorney and Dutchess County farmer, and Ed Perkins, president of the First National Bank of Poughkeepsie and Democratic county chairman—had been watching the squire's son, and found him pleasing.

Although FDR had never thought much about politics or party, both his father and Rosy were Grover Cleveland Democrats identified with reform. They were Democrats in a Republican family, Democrats in a Republican district. FDR himself was no party regular—he had paraded around Harvard in Republican rallies, and had cast his first vote for Eleanor's Republican Uncle Ted—but he was at least vaguely a Democrat, and he was positively intrigued by the new anti-Tammany movement, which opposed boss rule in New York's Democratic Party. When Ed Perkins appeared at his office one Friday with the proposal—and incidentally, the offer of a ride up to Hyde Park—FDR at first replied that he had to discuss it with his mother. But as they drove up to the door of the Poughkeepsie bank to meet his supporters, Perkins said: "Frank, the men that are looking out of that window are waiting for your answer. They won't like to hear that you had to ask your mother." FDR answered with finality: "I'll take it."

His mother would have discouraged him, had he asked. She thought politics messy, and considered politicians ruffians. But Eleanor was delighted. Throughout the summer of 1910, the summer she spent alone, pregnant with Elliott, at Campobello, while he met with Democratic leaders to plan strategy and the future, she wrote letters of encouragement and asked to be kept informed of every step, every detail, every decision.

In October 1910, a week after Elliott's birth, FDR embarked on his first political campaign. Eleanor wrote from home that she wished she could be with him, and sent notes conveying deepest love and endless luck. He spoke in every village and hamlet; he spoke in taverns and train stations; he spoke to people who despised the wealthy River Road families, and he asked for their votes—promising to represent them and their interests, directly and full-time. He bought a bright-red open Maxwell touring car, and bumped along two thousand miles of rugged country roads with his new political tutor, the congressional candidate and flamboyant orator Richard Connell. They got soaked; the car broke down; they hit a farmer's favorite dog; they went deep into ravines and muddy ditches. But Franklin was a winner. Connell told him to take off his pince-nez, which made his eyes look mean and exaggerated his haughtiness. Connell told him to be plain, and direct, and roll up his sleeves. He began each speech: "My Friends!" He promised nothing, sidestepped all issues, and was entirely superficial. But he was charming and enthusiastic; he stood as an independent and a progressive; he deplored "rotten corruption"; he praised the popular former governor, Charles Evans Hughes, and identified himself with his cousin the former president (both progressive Republicans).

FDR spent more than five times as much on his campaign as any other candidate in the district. But it was his ability to spar with the crowd and entertain the hecklers, to think fast and speak earnestly, that accounted for his unprecedented majority in Republican territory, and he ran far ahead of the state ticket in Dutchess County. The Democrats won statewide for the first time in eighteen years, and FDR's 26th Senate district was Democratic for the first time since his neighbor Thomas Jefferson Newbold had won in 1878.

The year 1910 changed everything.

8. Eleanor Roosevelt, Political Wife

A FTER THE ELECTION, ELEANOR AND FRANKLIN WENT together to Albany to choose a congenial house. At 248 State Street they found a sunny, spacious, three-story place, with wide rooms, and so many of them that Eleanor decided to use only two floors. It was the first home they had to which Sara Delano Roosevelt came only as a guest, and she came infrequently. ER unpacked, established order and comfort, did her own marketing, and managed her own family entirely by herself. Neither Cousin Susie nor her mother-in-law was nearby to question her purchases or influence her routine.

ER's new freedom was as profound a change as FDR's decision to plunge into politics, and both involved her in an immediate choice: She could emerge from her depression and fulfill her lifelong wish to be really useful to someone she loved, or remain withdrawn and morose and be a terrible liability to her husband's new career. Her personal transformation into a woman of public affairs had begun that summer, as she contemplated and encouraged FDR's campaign from the isolation of Campobello. Geographically distant, she was enthusiastically involved in this new phase of her husband's life.

She experimented on every level, even before the move to Albany. Although she had breast-fed her other children, she now hired a wet nurse for Elliott, in the belief that baby Franklin might have lived had she been able to nurse him longer. ER's relationship with the wet nurse, a woman from Central Europe "who spoke no language known to us," reintroduced her to the ravages of poverty. ER felt "a great responsibility" toward the woman's own baby, visited the New York City tenement where she was boarded, and suffered "agonies" when she contemplated removing the infant's mother to Albany. Ultimately she could not do it: The mother's suffering was unbearable. ER left the wet nurse behind, opened a bank account for her baby, and "kept in touch" for many years, until she disappeared. ER's ability to identify with that temporarily abandoned baby, and her mother—who "always seemed to me a defenseless person"—informed her perspective as she assumed her new role as a New York State politician's wife: "My conscience was very active in these days." She became immediately absorbed by the issues around her, as she recognized how deeply something within her "craved to be an individual. What kind of individual was still in the lap of the gods!"

For the new house in Albany, ER hired an entirely new staff. She dismissed the French nurse the children hated and replaced her with an English governess for Anna and James, and three efficient servants. Within twenty-four hours of her arrival on 1 January 1911, ER had the house settled; she also orchestrated and catered an Inaugural Day "open house" for as many of FDR's supporters, colleagues, friends, and constituents as cared to attend. For three hours on 2 January, the house was filled with revelers. And then it was cleaned. And then she unpacked, hung her photographs, and arranged all her ornaments. "I think it was my early training which made me painfully tidy. I want everything around me in its place. Dirt or disorder makes me positively uncomfortable!" After all that, she went to a dance at the home of the new Democratic governor, John Alden Dix.

The very next morning, she did all her marketing and began to meet her neighbors. Like Washington, Albany was a small, almost intimate political town. Everybody knew everybody; cautious friendliness was a way of life. Business was done everywhere—in the market, on the street, at meals, and over coffee. It was the kind of life ER enjoyed, the kind of politics that came naturally to her. Within weeks, she had won the heart of virtually every political notable in town. She met their wives, talked with them easily, directly, and at length. She wrote Isabella: "We had 250 constituents to lunch on inauguration day . . . [and] since then I have met so many people that I feel quite bewildered and I pay calls in every spare moment!" She had an amazing capacity to listen, to understand, and to care deeply. Even Tammanyites who considered Franklin a disloyal and stuffy prig quickly came to admire and like Eleanor. "I was to be very, very busy that year."

Eleanor Roosevelt would never be a society matron again. However proper and correct she might continue to appear when with Cousin Susie or her mother-in-law, or as other circumstances occasionally demanded, ER was now a political wife. She was involved in every step of the political game. People asked her why she did so much, and she said she did it all for Franklin. Nobody ever asked her if she enjoyed it. The fact is, from her first day in Albany she loved every minute of it.

Her renewed enthusiasm reinvigorated their marriage. From the beginning, ER had encouraged FDR's political ambitions. Unlike his mother, she understood that he would not have been satisfied with his father's country-squire routine; she knew that he deplored his days as a junior partner in a law firm, however prestigious. His entrance into politics saved them both from the kind of ordinary upper-class life, vapid and fatuous, that ER associated with society—at least that part of society where she had never felt welcome, comfortable, or understood.

Franklin's entrance into politics changed the family dynamics. Sara Delano Roosevelt's previously unchallenged power over her son and daughter-in-law began to be eclipsed. Their new concerns, those related to local and progressive politics, neither required nor interested her, and she rarely visited. Now that Sara was no longer so centrally involved in their lives, Eleanor began to take over those maternal duties that had been arrogated by Sara. Every afternoon was devoted to her children, ending with a children's tea before dinner, when she generally read to them, and she played with them after dinner.

ER patterned her entrance into the political arena on the example of her Aunt Bye. She met with people in their homes, and lobbied for causes. She encouraged debate and never avoided disagreement. Listening to all those conversations between her aunt and Uncle Theodore, ER had absorbed information, and style. FDR appreciated ER's opin-

ions. He listened to her ideas, and trusted her insights about his colleagues. He appreciated from the first that she was one of his biggest
political assets. She built bridges, even over the most treacherous terrain;
she made what might have seemed impossible alliances.

Although ER dreaded speaking in public, she wanted FDR to become an appealing orator. She criticized his first efforts, which were
slow and hesitant. He needed to sound both more assured and less
arrogant. He needed to be more precise with facts, and more concerned
about the real needs and wants of his constituents. FDR listened to his
profoundly political wife as he listened to few others. It was she who
went around and found out what his colleagues, and their wives, really
thought. She went out among his constituents and talked with them,
she attended Senate and Assembly debates regularly, and she reported
on the subtleties and tricks lodged in every issue.

Within his first year as state senator, FDR became the leader of the
anti-Tammany "Insurgents." The controversial Insurgency generated
much attention, but it was a crusade that lacked substance, and it led
nowhere. The Tammanyites included Boss Murphy's hand-picked
rising stars (who were, incidentally, real reformers) Robert Wagner and
Alfred E. Smith. The Insurgent group included anti-Tammany upstaters,
some of whom genuinely supported reform, but some of whom were
opportunists all too vulnerable to the charge of being anti-Irish and
anti-Catholic. They were generally considered anti-big-city elitists.

The first real battle involved the Democratic nominee to the U.S.
Senate. Until 1913, when the Seventeenth Amendment guaranteed the
voters direct election of senators, senators were selected by state leg-
islatures. Tammany supported "Blue-eyed-Billy" Sheehan, a symbol of
city corruption. The Insurgents supported Brooklyn's mayor, Edward
Shepard, a friend of J. P. Morgan and William C. Whitney. William
Randolph Hearst, and his enemies Ralph Pulitzer and Oswald Garrison
Villard (owner of *The Nation*), allied with Shepard against Tammany.
It was an old battle, within a narrow frame: power, not real political
change, was the issue. FDR agreed with the contours of the struggle:
"Most of us want" the right kind of man—"conservative in regard to
business interests and yet a man whose position can never be questioned

by the radical element of society. . . ." Within days, FDR was called the "Galahad of the Insurgency."

There were thirty Insurgents, and they met every evening for drinks and dessert at the Roosevelts'. They shouted and smoked so much the children complained, the nurses were horrified, and ER emptied out the room above the Insurgents' quarters, moving the children and their nurses to the third floor so that they might breathe, and sleep, again.

For months FDR heaped ridicule upon Tammany bosses. He made headlines regularly. Before he had even cast his first vote in the State Senate, FDR had become one of New York's most famous politicians. When Tammany finally offered an acceptable compromise candidate for the U.S. Senate, Judge James O'Gorman, and FDR, one of the last holdouts against the appointment, finally agreed to it, he was denounced with a flamboyance equal to his own. Democratic newspapers attacked him as a traitor, "fop," and fool. But he could never be ignored again. His crusade against "these political manchus who now control the party" was nationally acclaimed. And he had learned some hard lessons: In politics, "self-righteousness is not enough"; party regularity and loyalty were needed for survival. In 1911, ten Insurgents lost their Assembly seats; within two years, most of the others were finished. FDR parried and compromised; he learned to work and play well with Tammany— and in 1912 was re-elected.

During the winter of 1911, Eleanor sat with the Insurgents every evening: listening, observing. She entertained them, prepared their drinks and snacks, and learned "that the first requisite of a politician's wife is always to be able to manage anything." She also learned "how to get on with people of varying backgrounds." She entertained Tammanyites and anti-Tammanyites with equal consideration. She enjoyed the company of many of these hard-drinking, hard-smoking politicians, and forged some unlikely friendships. Brooklyn Assemblyman Ed Terry brought his poetry, and they read to each other for hours.

Her understanding of the personal aspect of politics seemed almost instinctive. Although she abhorred the "grimmer side of machine politics," her interest in people as people crossed partisan lines. Tammanyites, who hated her husband, admired her; and she judged them on the basis of their political views and their oratory, quite apart from their Tammany affiliations. The list of the politicians who immediately interested her when she heard them speak was a curious mix: Bob Wagner, Al Smith, "Big Tim" Sullivan (the "Boss of the Bowery"), and his cousin Christy Sullivan. She was particularly charmed by State Senator Tom Grady: He "could make a better speech than many people who are considered great orators today," she said years later. She was charmed by him, even though she acknowledged that he was rarely sober. And the feeling was entirely mutual: Tom Grady wrote ER on Saint Patrick's Day: "Be with the insurgents, and if needs be with your husband every day in the year but this—to-day be 'wid us.' "

ER was largely responsible for smoothing FDR's path to better relations with the Tammany reformers; men like Al Smith and Robert Wagner quickly appreciated the sincerity of her reform instincts. Although ER had withdrawn from doing settlement-house work when she married, she continued to support the emerging institutions and networks that advocated change and remained active in their behalf. Among FDR's few surviving letters to her is a curious one that indicates Franklin's attitude toward Eleanor's earnest fund-raising activities for the benefit of poor Jewish children.

Dear Lady—

Your beauteous bounty requires more than a merely verbal display of homage and praise, hence this.

The honored draft for fifty plunks has gone the way of all . . . and you can pat your little back about fifty times and with eyes raised Heavenward exclaim in accents of deep content "Yea! I have saved the lives of a score of blessed little ones of the Chosen Race!" Truly, "this is no joking matter."

All the same thanks again . . .
Your slave
FDR

After 1910, issues of reform, education, the eradication of poverty, and better working conditions involved her directly once again. But her first concern was always for the people she met and worked with. Once established in Albany, she felt "responsible" for the wives of newly elected officials; she was also concerned about the lonely hours newspaper wives endured. "I religiously called on them," and she invited them to her home. "I was not a snob, largely because I never really thought about the question of why you asked people to your house or claimed them as friends. Anyone who came was grist to my mill . . . and I found that almost everyone had something interesting to contribute to my education."

With FDR's entrance into politics, ER began her public career. Although FDR remained aloof from most of the immediate reform issues on the agenda in 1911, ER was galvanized by the debates as she watched them from the gallery. But her memories of these years contain an element of self-deprecation that is so pervasive, one must pause to wonder at its origins. She did what she did, she wrote over and over again, out of her duty to be interested in her husband's interests, whatever they were—be it his favorite dessert or a piece of legislation. The fact is that Eleanor Roosevelt was personally ambitious in an era that denied ambition and self-fulfillment to women. In these presuffrage years, she did not yet see a political role for herself beyond helpmate and hostess.

But ER quickly became aware of potential allies in the cause of reform, and gravitated to them. Ironically, the very people ER named as of particular interest to *her* found FDR noxious in 1911. Big Tim Sullivan, Christy Sullivan, Thomas Grady, Al Smith, and Robert Wagner were associated with Tammany and were also ardent reformers, who knew the tall and pompous young man with the pince-nez to be disinterested in their issues. Al Smith distinguished between upstate Democrats like FDR, whose interests were limited to good government and civil-service reform, and his own allies among big-city reformers, who championed social legislation to "benefit the common people." Smith considered FDR a "damn fool" who had an unfortunate habit of throwing his head back, which made him seem perpetually to look down his nose at people. Tim Sullivan dismissed him as "an awful arrogant fellow."

In 1911, Franklin was not the reformer he claimed to be. After the infamous Triangle Shirtwaist Company fire of 25 March 1911, in which

147 women died, trapped at their sewing machines or forced to jump to their deaths because the Manhattan sweatshop doors were locked, a New York State Factory Commission was created to avoid such disasters in the future and begin to regulate the dreadful labor conditions under which women toiled. The commission was chaired by Robert Wagner, with Al Smith as vice-chair and Frances Perkins as chief investigator.

A Mount Holyoke–educated social reformer, Perkins had been secretary of the Consumers' League, and its main Albany lobbyist, since 1910. She was also executive secretary of the Committee on Safety for New York City, specifically charged with the inspection of all dwellings and public buildings for the purpose of enforcing safety and fire-prevention needs. FDR had nothing to do with the efforts of the commission, and his name appeared nowhere in debate or support. Years later, however, FDR took public credit for the success of the fifty-four-hour week for women and children passed in 1912, and for all of the thirty-two labor reform acts that were passed because of the Wagner-Smith-Perkins investigative team. Though he may have voted for some of the bills, he was not instrumental in their passage. Perkins was in fact offended by his offhand disregard of her efforts: "I remember it clearly because I took it hard that a young man who had so much spirit did not do so well" in this area, which she considered "a test" of "progressive convictions." FDR explained, when pressed, that he did not represent a labor constituency, and he was very, very busy.

FDR's constituents were rural farmers and his work as chair of the Agriculture Committee, and on the Forest, Fish and Game Committee, helped broaden his view of progressive causes. He became a leading conservationist, particularly identified with reforestation, and over time his commitment to conservation led him to a more liberal progressivism. Eventually he believed that just as government intervention was needed to protect and restore America's natural resources, so was government intervention needed to protect American citizens. Laissez-faire capitalism, unconfined and unregulated, endangered the future—the survival of resources, and the health of citizens. But as state senator his reform efforts concentrated on restraining the lumber interests, and he vigorously scorned their careless plunder. He invited Gifford Pinchot, the United States' chief forester, to lecture to New York's legislators. Pinchot showed slides of a Chinese valley, green and verdant in 1500; a parched, desertified wasteland in 1900: the result of careless lumbering. FDR observed: "It is an extraordinary thing to me that people who are financially interested should not be able to see more than about six inches in front of their noses."

Of those first years in Albany, ER remembered "little of what my husband did in the legislature, except that he came out for woman suffrage." He always claimed that he supported votes for women after Inez Milholland visited him, sat upon his desk, and persuaded him that it was the only chivalric position for a decent man to hold. But ER wanted it clear that the tall glamorous suffragist known as "the Amazon" had not dazzled him with her Vassar wiles and attorney's arguments: "As a matter of fact he came out for it two months before that memorable visit."

In 1911, FDR's suffrage conversion left ER "somewhat shocked, as I had never given the question serious thought." She "took it for granted that men were superior creatures and still knew more about politics than women." After his announcement, "I realized that if my husband were a suffragist I probably must be, too." Still, she could not "claim to have been a feminist in those early days." She was not yet a member of the Women's Trade Union League, did not actively support the Woman Suffrage Party or subscribe to *The Woman Voter*. She was not, on the other hand, "an anti-suffragette [a word she never used], and vigorously so," as has been repeated so often.

ER never had anything to do with the New York State Association Opposed to Woman Suffrage, nor did she support Ida Tarbell's crusade against the vote. She never uttered a public word in opposition to the vote. And after 1911 she counted herself a suffragist. Still, her belated and vague support for suffrage set her apart from the ardent activities of so many of her future allies and friends, Carrie Chapman Catt and Jane Addams particularly.

In 1912, Jane Addams campaigned throughout the country for Theodore Roosevelt's new Progressive Party's "Bull Moose" platform, on which he was trying to make his political comeback after his handpicked successor to the White House, William Howard Taft, backed away from reform politics. The Bull Moose movement emphasized votes for women, an eight-hour workday, and protective labor legislation. Although she "found it very difficult to swallow" TR's militarist ambitions, and his promise to build two new battleships a year, Jane Addams seconded TR's nomination with a speech so rhetorically useful to him that he had it reprinted and widely distributed:

> A great party has pledged itself to the protection of children, to the care of the aged, to the relief of overworked girls, to the safeguarding of burdened men. Committed to these human undertakings, it is inevitable that such a party should appeal to women. . . .
>
> I second the nomination of Theodore Roosevelt because he is one of the few men in our public life who has been responsive to the social appeal and who has caught the significance of the modern movement.

TR's 1912 third-party platform, Jane Addams noted, "contained all the things I have been fighting for for more than a decade." Drafted by a committee of social reformers almost all of whom later became ER's closest allies, the platform included regulations to guarantee decent housing; a law to end child labor; protection for women workers; a national system of accident, old-age, and unemployment insurance; and "equal suffrage." The Progressive Party platform affirmed: "No people can justly claim to be a true democracy which denies political rights on the account of sex." TR assured Jane Addams personally that he was "without qualification or equivocation" for votes for women.

Ironically, ER refrained from any public support of her uncle's efforts, for her husband had become New York's leading supporter of Governor Woodrow Wilson of New Jersey, having decided that he was a kindred spirit, and a winner. Wilson, trained as an historian, formerly president of Princeton University, seemed to some an arrogant, rigid, Southern Presbyterian aristocrat, to others the very model of moral rectitude in the service of progressive ideals. He had rid New Jersey of bossism, and was beholden to no one. FDR considered him the perfect candidate. Putting family loyalties aside, and considering all the angles, FDR believed that the Bull Moose movement was doomed to failure, and worked vigorously for Wilson. ER joined her husband in his defection with only quiet misgivings. She wrote her closest friends, Isabella and Bob Ferguson, who worked vigorously for her Uncle Ted, "F is of course well satisfied with Mr. Wilson's nomination as he has been working hard for him. . . ." But, she added, "I wish Franklin could be fighting now for Uncle Ted, for I feel he is in the Party of the Future."

The year 1912 was a watershed time in ER's private as well as political life. Her brother, Hall, brilliant and beloved at Groton and Harvard, Phi Beta Kappa, and senior prefect, was twenty. From the moment of her mother's death, when her father had visited her at 37th Street and made all those promises to her about their future together, she had felt responsible for her younger brothers. After Ellie died, there was only Hall. "I loved him deeply and longed to mean a great deal in his life." Popular and charming, Hall had grown up to be much like their father—he drank too hard and partied too frequently—and since he was always surrounded by adoring young women, there were countless jokes about Hall's harems. But he also worked hard to develop his considerable talents, and earned an advanced engineering degree on his graduation from Harvard. Like ER, he was in a great hurry to have a home of his own, and he decided to get married before he was twenty-one. His wedding to the beautiful Margaret Richardson of Boston closed a chapter in ER's life: She felt as if "my own son and not my brother was being married." But she remained Hall's mother-surrogate, and rushed to Cambridge during the first year of his marriage to be with Margaret when their baby died at the age of only a few weeks, while Hall was in the hospital with appendicitis.

During the Albany years, ER and FDR were separated frequently, but they wrote daily and devotedly. In April 1912, FDR and Hall went on a vacation together aboard the United Fruit Company's SS *Carillo* to Panama, to visit the new canal. FDR had wanted his wife's company, but she was faced with the task of closing their Albany house, and agreed to meet them after their cruise. Whereas in the first years of her marriage this separation might have been the occasion for hurt feelings, it seemed now to have deepened their affection. They planned the itinerary together, and agreed to meet in New Orleans for the train to

New Mexico to visit the Fergusons, who had moved there after Bob was diagnosed with tuberculosis.

On 14 April, as FDR sailed out beyond the Bahamas, he wrote:

> I do wish you were here—it is hard enough to be away from the chicks, but with you away from me I feel too very much alone and lost. I hereby solemnly declare that I *refuse* to go away the next time without you. . . . I can't tell you how I long to see you again. . . . Give a great deal of love & kisses to sister & Brud and Snookums—I am just so crazy to see my four precious ones again that I am almost tempted to turn around in Kingston and sail straight back. Take good care of yourself dearest, and please don't overdo it in moving.

Toward the end of June, ER and FDR went to Baltimore for their first national political convention. It was hot and disagreeable—noisy, crowded, smoky, raucous, and stifling in many ways. FDR had failed even to be nominated as an alternate delegate—he had no particular role and could not even get on the floor—but he worked the crowd with enthusiasm, and made several new friends who would later be important to him, notably Cordell Hull, member of Congress from Tennessee, and North Carolina newspaper editor Josephus Daniels. Daniels was immediately attracted to the tall, dashing thirty-year-old independent upstart: It was "love at first sight," Daniels recalled.

With nothing to do, virtually nobody to talk to, bored and uncomfortable, ER decided to leave the heat and histrionics of her first convention and go to Campobello. On 2 July, after the forty-sixth ballot, FDR telegraphed her in ecstasy: "Wilson nominated this afternoon. All my plans vague. Splendid triumph." The next day, he went to New Jersey to plan New York State campaign strategy, and establish his credentials as New York's most ardent Wilsonian booster. Then Franklin rejoined Eleanor at Campobello, and together they boarded a ship for an early return to New York City, where they could work on FDR's re-election campaign for the State Senate.

Neither ER nor FDR thought very much about the fact that they had brushed their teeth with the water in their stateroom pitcher during their voyage home. They had planned to spend one night in the city, but FDR felt feverish and took to his bed. ER went out that night with Ronald Ferguson, who was visiting from Scotland. The next day, FDR felt worse, and though ER also felt "peculiar," she went on about her business, ran up and down the stairs with FDR's medicines, and generally took care of things, nobody quite knowing what was wrong. Eleanor continued to ignore her own discomfort until, after ten days of uncertainty, Sara Delano Roosevelt arrived, and upon kissing her good night, exclaimed, "You must have a fever!," and insisted she take her temperature. It was over 102 degrees. Finally, tests were taken. They both had typhoid fever, remained in bed for weeks, and faced a lengthy recovery.

Fearing his campaign was doomed, FDR appealed in desperation to Louis McHenry Howe, a brilliant strategist and propagandist, who was a political reporter and all-purpose manipulator for Thomas Mott Osborne's upstate Democratic leadership. Witty and artistic, Howe possessed an odd and eclectic assortment of talents. But he was a physical wreck. He claimed to be dying for decades; and for decades he hacked and wheezed with asthma, heart problems, and emphysema. Scrawny, unkempt, and ugly (he boasted that he was one of the four ugliest men in the state), he weighed less than a hundred pounds, and had pitted and scarred his face in a horrible childhood accident. He "looked like a troll out of a Catskill cave." He rarely changed his suit, hardly changed his socks, and regularly covered himself with the ashes from his endless and malodorous Sweet Caporal cigarettes.

Howe had sought to attach himself to FDR immediately after Wilson's nomination, and sent him a letter of congratulations with an invitation to visit him at Marblehead, Massachusetts, for "some swimming" and plotting. Howe addressed his July 1912 letter: "Beloved and Revered Future President." ER was not immediately charmed by Howe. She appreciated his innovative advertisements and admired his wit; but his smelly cigarettes fouled the air around her sick husband. "I was very disapproving" and "simply made a nuisance of myself," she said. It would be years before ER and Howe became friends.

Howe did, however, engineer her husband's re-election, and Wilson won the presidency as well. On 4 March 1913, Eleanor and Franklin attended Woodrow Wilson's inauguration. FDR arrived three days early to negotiate his future, and was not disappointed. Wilson's future son-in-law, William Gibbs McAdoo, designated Secretary of the Treasury, offered him alternatives: Assistant Secretary of the Treasury, or collector of the Port of New York—a lucrative plum. But Josephus Daniels, named Navy Secretary, offered him what he longed for: Assistant Secretary of the Navy. Following in TR's wake, he answered in TR's language: "I'd like it bully well. It would please me better than anything in the world."

Daniels checked FDR out with his New York colleagues. Senator O'Gorman reservedly considered him "acceptable." TR's former Secretary of State, now New York's Republican Senator Elihu Root, replied: "You know the Roosevelts, don't you? Whenever a Roosevelt rides, he rides in front." Undisturbed, Daniels wrote in his journal: "His distinguished cousin TR went from that place to the Presidency. May history repeat itself."

During the inauguration ER remained a silent and bemused witness to the largest and most elaborate suffrage parade in United States history. She wrote Isabella: "The suffrage parade was too funny and nice fat ladies with bare legs and feet posed in tableaux on the Treasury steps!"* The President was "dignified," ER observed, but "has none of Uncle Ted's magnetism and really exudes little enthusiasm in a crowd. So if he becomes popular it will be entirely due to things done." She was even less impressed by Mrs. Wilson, who "seemed a nice intelligent woman but not overburdened with charm."

After the inauguration, ER "dashed" to Oldgate, Aunt Bye's home in Farmington, Connecticut, for information and advice on how to be an effective partner in official Washington. An eager political wife and the mother of three children who ranged in age from six to two, ER was determined to excel in her new position, but she could not yet imagine being both a political wife and a political activist.

* See notes, pages 528–29.

9. The Roosevelts in Wilson's Washington

O N 17 MARCH 1913, THE EIGHTH ANNIVERSARY OF THEIR wedding, Franklin Delano Roosevelt took the oath of office as Assistant Secretary of the Navy. Eleanor was not with him. After the brief ceremony, he wrote his first letter on his new and impressive letterhead, embossed with four stars circling an anchor, to his wife:

> My own dear Babbie, I didn't know till I sat down at this desk that this is the 17th of happy memory. In fact with all the subdued excitement of getting confirmed and taking the oath of office, the delightful significance of it all is only beginning to dawn on me. My only regret is that you could not have been here with me, but I am thinking of you a great deal. . . .

This was the first time they had been separated on their anniversary, and ER wired her congratulations: "I ordered your 17th of March present as we couldn't do anything else together!"

His second letter was to his mother: "I am baptized, confirmed, sworn in vaccinated—and somewhat at sea! For over an hour I have been signing papers which had to be accepted on faith. . . ."

His mother was delighted that his "was a *very* big job," and advised him: "Try not to write your signature too small." Big people should cultivate big, distinct signatures: Avoid "a cramped look."

ER spent the summer of 1913 with the children, and assorted guests, at Campobello, busy and content, and very involved with the needs of her extended family. Her grandmother was increasingly depressed over her children's dire problems. Uncle Eddie Hall (whose wife, Josie Zabriskie, had died after a long illness) was on an alcoholic binge, and ER feared for his daughters: "I feel after this he should not dream of taking the children to his own house." Although she had never acknowledged the reasonableness of her own separation from her father, she now hoped these virtually orphaned young girls would be able to stay with their maternal grandparents.

At Campobello, her mother-in-law was stunned when Harry Hooker arrived to visit Eleanor in Franklin's absence, and never left them alone: "Mama has chaperoned us pretty carefully." She was even more annoyed when Aunt Maude, recently divorced from Larry Waterbury, arrived with her new companion: a dapper, entertaining, and creative writer, David Gray. SDR "fairly snorted" when ER tried to discuss David with her; and ER knew that "all her outraged feelings in regards to Maude, David and me" would result in a "grand scene with Mama and tears one of these days." But ER liked David. His love for poetry and literature, and his serious interests and idealism, seemed to her to outweigh his reputation as a society reveler. She enjoyed his company, considered him talented, and altogether hoped Maude would marry him.

~

WHEN THE ROOSEVELTS MOVED TO WASHINGTON IN THE AUtumn of 1913, they were as close as they had ever been. The years in Albany had been good for their marriage, and good for them individually. ER recognized that she had administrative and executive talents, took pride in all that she managed to get done, and appreciated particularly her new independence from her mother-in-law. Most of the time, she did as she pleased; she came and went according to her own schedule; she no longer asked for advice, and never suspended her judgment in fear or compromise. There were arguments, and occasional confrontations, but few moments of serious difficulty. Between ER and FDR there seemed to be real understanding, a sense of union and common purpose. They were allied, tender, generous, and loving with each other, expectant and happy.

Two more children were born during the Washington years, and they were raised very differently from their older siblings. On 17 August 1914 the second Franklin Delano Roosevelt, Jr., was born at Campobello, the first child she successfully breast-fed ("I have a little more milk"). ER was finally in charge, no longer fearful, or uninformed, or intimidated by nurses and governesses—or anybody at all. On 13 March 1916, John Aspinwall Roosevelt was born. His arrival, in Washington, had been awaited almost casually. Long past were the days when ER could not be seen in public while pregnant. She gave a party for 225 naval and diplomatic dignitaries the month before his birth, and dined with Caroline Phillips until 10:00 P.M. the night of his birth.

The Roosevelts were prepared to take Washington by storm; and they did. At twenty-nine, ER felt healthy and robust; she was eager to greet each day, ready for every challenge. The new costumes of the second decade of the twentieth century seemed created with her in mind. At dinner parties she seemed the perfect "Gibson girl." Tall and reed-thin, with her magnificent hair put up, she looked so attractive during this time that even her mother-in-law noticed. Politics offered her a new and exciting setting within which to flourish. Old Washington embraced and welcomed her as one of their own; new Washington was enchanted.

President Wilson's entourage was a dramatic mixture of the old and the new. The Democrats had returned from a sixteen-year political exile in a forward-looking and experimental mood—except on the issue of race. Woodrow Wilson was the first Southern president since Andrew Johnson, and he segregated government facilities and the civil service. In government offices, including the Navy Department, physical barriers were erected to separate federal workers by race for the first time.

Wilson's most radical allies, Secretary of State William Jennings Bryan and Josephus Daniels, were Christian fundamentalists, and Daniels (FDR's boss) was a bone-deep Southern racist. They represented the essence of America's contradictory themes. Hated by the trusts and vested interests, the Northeastern establishment, and the planting-mining Southern aristocracy, they opposed robber barons, corruption, and vice. They represented the "little people"—workers, tenants, and farmers—so long as they were white.

Only a month before Wilson's election, Josephus Daniels editorialized in his Raleigh newspaper, *News and Observer* (called by conservatives "The Nuisance and Disturber"): "The subjection of the negro, politically, and the separation of the negro, socially, are paramount to all other considerations in the South short of the preservation of the Republic itself. And we shall recognize no emancipation, nor shall we proclaim any deliverer, that falls short of these essentials to the peace and the welfare of our part of the country."

Wilson was the darling of what would later be called the Dixiecrats. But Northern progressives like FDR rallied to him with equal fervor. For them, race was simply not an issue. Indeed, among whites race had become an issue only for the very few progressives who had founded the National Association for the Advancement of Colored People in 1909, led by W. E. B. Du Bois, Mary White Ovington, Jane Addams, Oswald Garrison Villard, and others—most of whom were associated with TR's third party. But even Theodore Roosevelt had refused to seat at his convention black delegates from Florida and Mississippi, and refused to include a plank on Negro rights, despite Jane Addams's vigorous protests.

Among Washingtonians, the subject of race was rarely discussed. There was one tense moment when Josephus Daniels expressed horror that Eleanor Roosevelt brought four white servants, and a nurse and governess, to Washington. He practically ordered her to fire them: Only Negroes, he felt, should do servile work. She was stunned by what she considered the "brutality" of his prejudice, and subsequently referred to it as a "shocking" moment.

At the time, however, ER was largely undisturbed by the racism of prewar Washington. She failed even to support First Lady Ellen Axson Wilson's crusade against the vile housing conditions endured by Washington's black population, conditions that demeaned both the city and the entire idea of progress. Mrs. Wilson's activities were mocked and reviled in the local newspapers, but she worked on tirelessly, with Mrs.

Josephus Daniels and others, including one of Washington's most active aristocrats, Mrs. Archibald (Charlotte Everett) Hopkins. As First Lady, Ellen Wilson made it clear that "Good works" were not comic subjects "to all nice people, even in those days." When she lay dying of Bright's disease in 1914, her final request was that Congress pass the legislation she had worked so hard for: to prohibit back-alley slum housing by 1918. The Senate passed the bill, and she was told on the day she died, 6 August 1914, that the House votes were assured. But wartime crowding ended all efforts to enforce the law, and a district court ruled it unconstitutional.

Twenty years later, Eleanor Roosevelt's first public act as First Lady was to accompany Charlotte Everett Hopkins on a tour of the back-alley slums; she continued Ellen Wilson's crusade for twelve years. But at this time, ER remained aloof from many of the social issues that later absorbed her. Still, she was now convinced, she wrote her Aunt Maude, "If we are not going to find remedies in Progressivism then I feel sure the next step will be Socialism."

For most progressives, Wilson's Washington seemed full of hope and promise. If these were not quite the days of Andrew Jackson, at least some country folk—pacifists, and radical populists like William Jennings Bryan (Secretary of State), and his great friend Josephus Daniels (Secretary of the Navy)—had returned in positions of power. In 1896, Bryan and Daniels had joined forces to declare war on robber barons and big-city bandits; they were now willing to work with any allies they might have along the Groton-Harvard-Princeton axis. The young Roosevelts were at the very heart of the new alliance.

They rented Aunt Bye's house at 1733 N Street (Aunt Bye now lived in Connecticut), and plunged into the rituals and rondelays of Washington life. Wilsonian Washington was alternately formal and staid, rambunctious and carefree. Wilson shocked everybody by canceling the Inaugural Ball. But there was promise of ongoing merriment. Formal dinners, champagne balls, and old school ties represented the other side of Wilsonian Washington, which quickly embraced the Roosevelts. Politically, Josephus Daniels championed FDR, who seemed to him to represent independence, defiance, progressivism. FDR was, as Daniels told Wilson, "our kind of Democrat." His "love at first sight" for the attractive young "Gibson boy" would survive many disagreements and disappointments.

ER's personal politics and her respect for Mrs. Daniels served to mitigate the tense relationship between the two men. ER considered Addie Bagley Daniels, a Colonial Dame and a Daughter of the Confederacy, "a dear." A socially concerned aristocrat, generous and compassionate, Addie Daniels appealed to Eleanor on both political and temperamental grounds. According to her son, Jonathan Daniels: "Not even the cow in the crystal could disturb a lady who, as a combative editor's wife, sometimes put on her hat and walked up town to see who was still speaking to her."

Well connected and well received, the Roosevelts embarked on a social life in Washington that featured bipartisan privileges. Evidently unruffled by the 1912 breach in family solidarity, TR wrote FDR on 18 March: "It is interesting to see that you are in another place which I myself once held. I am sure you will enjoy yourself to the full . . . , and that you will do capital work. When I see Eleanor I shall say to her that I do hope she will be particularly nice to the naval officers' wives. They have a pretty hard time, with very little money to get along on, and yet a position to keep up, and everything that can properly be done to make things pleasant for them should be done. . . ."

With TR's blessing, in Aunt Bye's home, the young Roosevelts inherited neighbors and family friends that kept them busy, informed, and at the center of political intrigue. Senator Henry Cabot Lodge and Nannie Lodge, who ER considered "one of the loveliest women I have ever known," England's Ambassador Sir Cecil and Lady Spring-Rice, members of the French Embassy—Marie and Lefebvre de Laboulaye, and M. Jules Jusserand and his wife, Eliza Richards, all once so close to Uncle Theodore—now opened their doors to the attractive couple. ER and Marie de Laboulaye particularly "became great friends." Similar in background and interests, they shared an abiding sense of social responsibility. ER described Marie de Laboulaye as "one of the finest characters it has ever been my good fortune to know."

Even the seventy-five-year-old curmudgeon Henry Adams was warm and cordial to the young Roosevelts. He would drive by Aunt Bye's house on N Street in his antique victoria, drawn by his ancient horse, and offer the Roosevelt children his company. They all piled in, including their little Scottie dog, and played and laughed for hours. ER never considered Adams so awesome once she had seen him with her children. Also close to Aileen Tone, who was Henry Adams's friend and secretary, ER frequently stopped at "Uncle Henry's" for tea during a day's calling. He found her openhearted warmth appealing, and enjoyed her company. The Roosevelts were often invited for luncheon and dinner at this center of worldly gossip where the old surveyed the new with a highly critical eye. Henry Adams made "a great impression," but his pessimism appalled ER. Although she did not go so far in her criticism as Justice Oliver Wendell Holmes, who bemoaned Adams's effort to turn "everything to dust and ashes," she believed that he "loved to shock his hearers" with his petulant cynicism. She considered it "an old man's defense against his own urge to be an active factor." Having rejected activism "in his youth," he spent the rest of his life in a fit of disdain for all those who made any effort to improve things. ER wrote SDR while reading *The Education of Henry Adams:* "very interesting but sad to have had so much and yet find it so little."

During ER's first years in Washington, she devoted almost every afternoon to the tedious tradition of "calling." She left her calling cards at the door or in the hands of Cabinet wives, Supreme Court wives, congressional wives. There was not a notable wife she missed. She called on ten to thirty wives a day, never staying longer than six minutes at one place. Aunt Bye said she should, and she did. It was exhausting, and only marginally useful, but she met everybody, looked for potential friends and allies, kept a detailed record in a calling journal, and reported it all to FDR.

Several women in Washington had actually dispensed with this time-consuming chore, among them Alice Roosevelt Longworth. But ER was not impressed by Alice's flamboyant independence. In 1916 she wrote Isabella: "now that I am older and have my own values fixed a little," Alice's life seems one of "dreariness and waste":

> Her house is charming, her entertainments delightful. She's a born hostess and has an extraordinary mind but as for real friendship

and what it means she hasn't a conception of any depth in any feeling or so at least it seems. Life seems to be one long pursuit of pleasure and excitement and rather little real happiness either given, or taken on the way, the "Blue Bird" is always to be searched for in some new and novel way.

I sometimes think that the lives of many burdens are not really to be pitied for at least they live deeply and from their sorrows spring up flowers but an empty life is really dreadful!

And so ER dutifully, even contentedly, fulfilled her obligations as a Washington wife. Each evening, there was a formal dinner, sometimes a dance. Her diary entries for these years were almost exclusively devoted to menus and seating plans for dinners of ten to forty guests that she agonized over, at least once a week.

Two Sundays a month were reserved for quiet dinner parties of eight to ten intimate friends who remained political allies over the years: William Phillips, a career diplomat later appointed undersecretary of State in 1933 and ambassador to Italy in 1936; his wife, Caroline Astor Drayton Phillips, first cousin to Helen Astor Roosevelt Robinson; Anne and Franklin K. Lane, Secretary of the Interior; and their friends from California Adolph Miller (Lane's assistant secretary, and later a member of the Federal Reserve Board) and Mary Sprague Miller. They called themselves "The Club," and had scintillating and serious conversations over salad and scrambled eggs that ER prepared in a silver chafing dish at the table. Some commented on the indifferent fare and mediocre wines, but all agreed theirs was a very special, intimate group.

FDR's Harvard roommate, Lathrop Brown, was elected to Congress in 1912, and together they frequented the Metropolitan and Chevy Chase country clubs. ER was especially fond of Mrs. James Leavitt, "a most enchanting, white-haired lady," who had been a friend of her grandmother Mittie Roosevelt. Visits with Mrs. Leavitt, who taught her "many a lesson," were ER's "greatest joy." Isabella Ferguson envied ER's situation: "It must be nice to live where, when you want to see an angel, you can call on Mrs. Leavitt."

ER was also keenly attracted by the integrity of Interior Secretary Franklin K. Lane, one of the members of "The Club." He looked to some like Humpty-Dumpty but was always generous and courtly, and he had a code of ethics ER admired. She believed that if anything decent needed to be done, and Lane could do it, it would be done immediately. During the war, when she first toured Washington's miserably under-funded mental hospital, Saint Elizabeths, she was offended by the conditions allowed. She knew that the hospital was under the jurisdiction of the Secretary of the Interior, and went directly to him to demand an investigation. He quickly organized an investigative team; they wrote a blistering report, which they presented before a congressional hearing, and the hospital's budget was significantly increased.

ER's feelings toward Lane were reciprocated. On an official cross-country tour they made together, she was awakened as they entered his home state of California by a train conductor who presented her with a most beautiful bouquet of local flowers and Lane's moving note of welcome. In 1920, when he went in for surgery at the Mayo Clinic, Franklin K. Lane sent one of his last letters to ER:

> Just because I like you very much, and being a very old man dare to say so, I am sending this line—which has no excuse in its news, philosophy or advice;—has no excuse in fact except what might be called affection, but of course this being way past the Victorian era no one admits to affections. I will not belittle my own feeling by saying that I have a wife who thinks you the best Eastern product—and probably she'd move to strike out the word Eastern. At any rate I think I should tell you that I am to be operated on tomorrow. . . . I'd love to see you and the gay cavalier—but let us hope it won't be long till we meet! Au revoir.

For FDR Lane served more as a mentor. When, for example, he overheard FDR mimicking his boss, whom he called a funny-looking "hillbilly," Lane told FDR that he should be "ashamed." He had an obligation to show Daniels loyalty, or he should resign. Over time, despite his arrogance and his sense of superior knowledge regarding all things nautical, FDR did grow to respect Daniels, and to depend on his political skills and friendships. On issues that concerned them most directly, they were in considerable agreement. FDR's particular job was to order naval stores—steel, oil, and every necessity—at the lowest possible prices. They both agreed that profiteers were unpatriotic. Their experiences confirmed Daniels's long-standing political outrage against the trusts—collusions of businessmen who jacked up prices in their own interests, the national interest be damned. FDR scouted the planet for bargains, and, with the help of Louis Howe's aggressive work among the lobbyists, began to receive competitive domestic bids.

Louis Howe, hired to be FDR's assistant, played a dual role during these years: He worked vigorously to keep the profiteers at bay and save the navy money, but he also promoted FDR's political reputation whenever and wherever possible. Unfortunately, that led to a campaign to diminish Daniels's reputation, by suggesting falsely that anything of interest and importance done by the Department of the Navy was done by FDR. In the face of the Roosevelt-Howe braggadocio, which on occasion involved mendacity and insubordination, Daniels's ongoing support for his assistant was remarkable.

Through all the tensions and changes of prewar Washington, Eleanor and Franklin appeared to be a uniquely devoted and hardworking couple. Their intimate Sunday evenings at home, their conscientious and occasionally fabulous dinners, their open-house luncheons (FDR liked to lunch at home, and ER never knew whom or how many he would bring), and her arduous calling rendered them a very visible and agreeable pair. At diplomatic dinners, ER was frequently the only person present who could converse with everybody, and translate for everybody. ER herself considered her achievements in Washington society extraordinary, although she later wondered at the "compulsion" with which she had done it all.

Hardly anybody knew that she did much of it beneath the cloud of painful migraines; people only noticed that she did it all so efficiently and so well. For years husbands in Washington held her up to their wives as an example. Any time a political wife demurred from making the all-out effort her husband expected of her, she was likely to be told to think about Eleanor Roosevelt. *She* moved an army of five children, assorted servants, and various pet dogs and birds six times a year, alone and without complaint. Society reporters also celebrated her skills. During the war, she single-handedly rescued the "little season" by planning a Halloween dance at Rauscher's to benefit the American Hospital at Neuilly. Mrs. Franklin Lane helped, "but all the arrangement is in the capable hands of the wife of the Assistant Secretary of the Navy." In addition, she continued her efforts to inform herself politically, and voraciously read books on the history, economics, and intrigues of nations. FDR was grateful and wrote to her Aunt Maude, now married to David Gray, of "her really brilliant mind and spirit."

When Europe exploded into war, on 7 August 1914, the United States was torn apart by confusion. Many progressives had become convinced that the wild savagery of international war had, like slavery, become outmoded by civilization. There were navies and empires, of course, and competition. But there had been the illusion that gentlemen would now solve their differences in board rooms and, if necessary, the back rooms of banks. During the first month of the war, a hundred thousand French boys died on the fields of Flanders. Wilson, Bryan, and Daniels called for neutrality, and prayed for peace. TR roared for troops, action, battle.

From the beginning of the war, ER wrote, the United States became "the battleground of opposing ideas, and our family was being torn by the differences between Theodore Roosevelt's philosophy and that of President Wilson and his Administration in general. I had a tremendous respect for this uncle of mine, and for all his opinions. I knew that he felt we should take sides in the European war. He was such a definite person that he could not understand how one could sit by. . . ." She recognized that her husband shared her uncle's Big-Navy and Big-Empire views, rooted in the teachings of Admiral Alfred Thayer Mahan. FDR shared TR's impatience and marched in the direction of his bellicosity. ER, however, had an "instinctive belief" in William Jennings Bryan's "stand on peace." When he forged miniature plowshares out of old sabers and gave them to his friends and colleagues, many people ridiculed his gesture: "But to me they were not in the least ridiculous. I thought them an excellent reminder that our swords should be made into plowshares."

Nonetheless, ER did not become involved in the peace crusade that engaged so many Americans. She did not join the many women and men who later became her closest allies as they organized the Woman's Peace Party and the American Union Against Militarism. While Lillian Wald, Jane Addams, Crystal Eastman, Oswald Garrison Villard, Roger Baldwin, Amos Pinchot, John Haynes Holmes, and so many others opposed preparedness, ER's husband immediately took charge of the Big-Navy crusade, which parroted TR's wail—however untrue—that the United States had "a puny little egg-shell of a navy." And whatever her private hesitations about the future direction of America's foreign policy, Eleanor supported her husband publicly.

On 7 August 1914, ER wrote FDR: "All one's thoughts these days are on war. . . . Isn't it extraordinary how quickly it happened? . . . Life must be exciting for you and I can see you managing everything while Josephus Daniels wrings his hands in horror!"

FDR was astonished that nobody in the navy, except himself, cared to plan for the future. Nobody even "seemed the least bit excited." Josephus Daniels went about sighing and moaning, "feeling chiefly very sad that his faith in human nature and civilization and other idealistic nonsense was receiving a rude shock." Only Franklin—single-handedly, he wrote ER—worked all day to get things moving; and he did actually succeed one day "in getting one ship north from Mexico."

And then there was Mexico, and Haiti. In 1914, the United States almost went to war with Mexico to protect its oil interests against Mexican revolutionaries, then called "bandits." Although military action against Mexico was ultimately averted, military rule was imposed on Haiti. Also in 1914, the United States invoked the Monroe Doctrine to settle European business claims in Haiti. Allegedly to prevent Haiti from becoming a German naval base, the United States offered to take over the country's finances and resources. When Haiti, the only independent black republic in the world besides Abyssinia, refused to sign a treaty of domination, Marines were sent to establish "law and order." At the same time, Marines were also sent to impose a military government on Santo Domingo, to quiet the "unrest." In 1916, FDR accompanied the Marines to Haiti to pacify the island, and subsequently claimed he wrote the new Haitian constitution himself. Josephus Daniels pursued these colonial actions with vigor, while he continued to hope for neutrality regarding Europe.*

However ambivalent ER felt about war, her letters to her husband were full of sympathy for the ordeal he faced trying to convince his superiors to act boldly regarding Europe. She, too, came to consider Bryan and Daniels unschooled regarding the nature of the real world; and she was an Anglophile who hoped especially for Britain's quick "and decisive victory at sea."

During the early months of the war, she wrote with dismay: "I am not surprised at what you say about JD [Josephus Daniels] or WJB [William Jennings Bryan] for one could expect little else. To understand the present gigantic conflict one must at least have a glimmering of understanding of foreign nations and their histories. I hope you will succeed in getting the Navy together and up to the mark. . . ." "The situation in Washington must be intense and I should think we'd have to wake up when a German liner gets out of the port of New York with coal and supplies, otherwise we'll soon be in trouble!"

William Jennings Bryan resigned as Secretary of State to lead a peace crusade on 8 June 1915, after the passenger liner *Lusitania,* which he knew was carrying munitions to Britain, was torpedoed and more than a thousand passengers were killed, including 118 Americans. ER wrote: "I'm glad Bryan is out but I can't help admiring his sticking to his principles." ER continued: "How about JD? I wonder how would his resignation affect you!" Josephus Daniels did not resign, to FDR's temporary "disgust." He did, however, change his views, and by 1916 was in full agreement with FDR's commitment to preparedness. While Wilson campaigned as the president who "kept us out of war," his administration prepared for combat.

World War I destroyed the progressive alliance. The progressive-suffragist coalition was the first damaged, as the suffragists themselves split into different camps. In the presidential election campaign of 1916, Jane Addams, Lillian Wald, and Crystal Eastman opted for a peace-first strategy and supported Wilson, even though he opposed suffrage.

* FDR never referred to the forced-labor policies initiated to "modernize" Haiti and build roads; or the three thousand deaths reported during the first years of occupation, although the island was governed officially by the U.S. Navy. See notes, page 532.

Others supported Republican candidate Charles Evans Hughes, who stepped down from the Supreme Court to campaign, on a platform of suffrage and war. One of the suffragists who joined his campaign was Inez Milholland, who had so intrigued FDR when she visited his office in 1911. In 1917, at the age of only thirty, she died suddenly while lecturing in behalf of votes for women. TR now attacked all his former progressive allies who wavered on the war. He called them "silly and base," and particularly scorned "poor bleeding Jane," a veritable "Bull Mouse." Addams, however, became the spirited leader of the Woman's Peace Party, which influenced Wilson's "Fourteen Points" peace proposal.

TR was desperate to get the United States into action, and to lead the bully bloody fray himself. Almost sixty and rotund, he campaigned to resurrect the Rough Riders. FDR tried to get him an audience with Wilson, but they were both cautious: TR wrote his niece early in 1915: "I am very anxious to see you and Franklin, whenever the chance offers; but I do not want to compromise Franklin by being with him just at this time. I wish you would tell him that from all quarters I hear praise of the admirable work he has done for the Navy, under very difficult conditions. With love, Your affectionate Uncle."

Wilson finally agreed to see TR, but was cold and uninterested. TR could play no role; there was no place for him. He was shattered, and called Wilson a "skunk in the White House." ER "hated to have him so disappointed and yet I was loyal to President Wilson." She was much relieved when familial pressure succeeded in forwarding TR's appeal through channels and on to General Pershing; but the War Department also rejected his offers. ER thought it "was a bitter blow from which he never quite recovered."

On 2 April 1917, Woodrow Wilson addressed Congress to ask for a declaration of war. ER wanted very much to attend, and FDR had to comb Washington for a ticket for his wife. ER "listened breathlessly and returned home still half dazed by the sense of impending change." After his thirty-six-minute "message of death" one could actually "feel the world rocking all around us."

ER's brother Hall joined the one service that would consider a father of two: On 14 July, Hall and his cousin, TR's son Quentin, went together to enlist as aviators, after having memorized the eye chart in order to pass their physicals. Grandmother Hall was aghast, and asked ER why her brother, as a substantial gentleman with responsibilities, did not hire a substitute. ER had never heard of such a thing; she did not know that both her grandfathers had done just that during the Civil War, and in her "first really outspoken declaration against the accepted standards" of her grandmother and her society, ER "hotly responded that a gentleman was no different from any other kind of citizen in the United States, and that it would be a disgrace to pay anyone to risk his life for you, particularly when Hall could leave his wife and children with the assurance that at least they would have money enough to live on." ER wrote proudly of that confrontation, and her "increasing ability to think for myself" and assert "my changing point of view."

In many ways, the twentieth century began with World War I. Nothing remained the same. Traditions were smashed; empires were sunk; understanding was transformed; everything not destroyed was shifted about. Modernity arrived with uniforms and guns, born of ashes and blood. The war spawned revolution and counterrevolution; contradictory theories and violent heroics; endless and shifting political alliances.

For ER the war meant new work: "The women in Washington paid no more calls." Mrs. J. Borden (Daisy) Harriman organized a Red Cross motor corps. ER would need to learn to drive, and did so within the year. But first she organized the Red Cross canteen, and with Addie Daniels organized the Navy Red Cross. She knitted and distributed free wool to the Navy League, entertained troops in and out of Washington's Union Station, and made coffee and sandwiches. ER visited sailors in hospitals and homes for the wounded and shell-shocked; she organized and worked from nine in the morning until long past midnight. ER knew the world had changed, as she felt her own world transformed.

The tensions of Washington, its interminable gaiety, its illusions and temptations, intruded a new factor into the Roosevelt marriage: FDR began to stay later and later at parties, and ER began to leave earlier and earlier. This pattern had begun in 1909, when ER made it clear that, although she did not want to interfere with her husband's seemingly insatiable need for frolic, certain frolics bored, annoyed, and even pained her. In Albany, they had come to an agreement: He might do precisely as he liked, as long as she did not have to endure frivolous, and frequently alcoholic, evenings with him.

But in Washington, as in Albany, there was more to a long night on the town than idle conversation: Work was done, deals were made, liaisons were forged. And ER enjoyed many aspects of Washington's night life. She liked to dance, and found diplomatic receptions and balls particularly congenial. She missed the "gay side" of French and British entertainments when they ended during the war, she confided to Bob Ferguson, and always found Washington the most "interesting place to be."

By 1917, however, ER's and FDR's social interests began to diverge. FDR seemed increasingly more comfortable in company that ER did not care for. That year, he invited his Harvard classmate Livy (Livingston) Davis to join him as special assistant to the assistant secretary. An especially flamboyant bon vivant who imbibed all day and partied all night, he was a new influence on her husband. ER judged Livy Davis "lazy, selfish, and self-seeking to an extraordinary degree." From her point of view, he was duplicitous and dangerous.

Wartime Washington was for Livy Davis "gay and glamorous." FDR spent more and more time with him in the palatial homes of their old Harvard Gold Coast pals. In addition, there were the Army, Navy, and Racquet clubs; there was the Chevy Chase Club, golf, poker, stag dinners, and occasional flirtations. ER knew it all, or all she could bear to know. Her thirty-five-year-old husband was high-spirited, handsome, energetic, dashing. Women flocked to him. She was determined not to become like her mother, distanced and cold, closing off the very source of comfort that might make one want to return home. She knew it was possible to freeze the heart away. She tried to say little, generally looked the other way, occasionally plunged into a Griselda mood, and tried to be gallant.

From 1913 to 1917, Franklin spent less and less time at Campobello with ER and their children, family, and friends. Eleanor understood the demands and constraints of his job, but she wondered at FDR's failure to spend any significant time with her. She became suspicious. Flirtations were one thing; a serious romantic affair was another.

In 1914, ER had hired as her social secretary a young, attractive society belle, whose father had died poor and whose hardworking mother had trained her to be self-sufficient. Lucy Page Mercer was warm, charming, and efficient. She served easily as the "extra" woman whenever needed at dinner parties. She was wonderful with the children, who adored her. She did everything before she was asked, never looked at the clock, and was always cheerful. ER considered her a reliable friend.

ER's first querulous mention of Lucy Mercer was written at Campobello on 23 July 1916: "Dearest Honey, Your letter of Thursday is here and one from Miss Mercer. Why did you make her waste all that time [answering my] fool notes. I tore them and [Lucy Mercer's answers] up and please tear any other results of my idiocy up at once. She tells me you are going off for Tuesday and I hope you all had a pleasant trip but I'm so glad I've been here and not on the Potomac!" Campobello was tranquil; "the fog is never far out," the breeze cool, and it was "lovely all day and really I don't think I ever want to take the trip down!" On the other hand, "if we stay here long you will be ruined, labor is terribly high," and food prices soared: "lamb is 33 cts a lb., when bought by the side!"

That summer and autumn, because of a polio epidemic that raged through the Northeast and as far south as Washington, ER stayed with the children at Campobello until October. But during the winter and spring of 1917, she saw enough and sensed enough to make her extremely reluctant to leave her husband alone with his new friends. They had words; she hesitated; but in July she packed up her army and went off to Campobello. FDR wrote her en route that he had a cold, and "a perfectly vile day" as soon as she left:

> I really can't stand that house all alone without you, and you were a goosy girl to think or even pretend to think that I don't want you here *all* the summer, because you know I do! But honestly *you* ought to have six weeks straight at Campo, just as *I* ought to, only you can and I can't! I *know* what a whole summer here does to people's nerves and at the end of this summer I will be like a

bear with a sore head. . . . as you know I am unreasonable and touchy now—but I shall try to improve.

They had both become unreasonable and touchy. There were arguments and upsets, but it was all vague: No words were spoken directly. ER returned to familiar habits: silence and solitude. It was impossible not to feel resentful when left alone by the "gay cavalier," whose every word was filled with mirth and seemed mired by falsehood. FDR told his wife of each jolly day, about the lunches, dinners, cards at the country club, wonderful sails with "The Charlie Munns, the Cary Graysons, Lucy Mercer and Nigel Law." Nigel Law, a dapper fellow closer to Lucy's age of twenty-five, frequently squired ER's social secretary about. FDR was generally with them, but *Town Topics* rarely reported that. Law was one cover, Livy Davis another. They were often together, and there was always an official purpose. On one occasion, they sailed down the Potomac to visit the fleet. FDR rhapsodized to ER: "Such a funny party, but it worked out *wonderfully!*"

In the course of going about her own business on the home front, ER gave an interview to *The New York Times,* which appeared on 17 July and caused her immense embarrassment.

> The food-saving program adopted at the home of Franklin D. Roosevelt . . . has been selected by the conservation section of the Food Administration as a model for other large households. Mrs. Roosevelt on her pledge card said that there were seven in the family, and that ten servants were employed. Each servant has signed a pledge card, and there are daily conferences.
>
> Mrs. Roosevelt does the buying, the cooks see that there is no food wasted, the laundress is sparing in her use of soap, each servant has a watchful eye for evidence of shortcomings on the part of the others. . . .
>
> No bacon is used . . . ; corn bread is served once a day. . . . Meat is served but once daily, and all "left overs" are utilized. . . . Everybody eats fish at least once a week.
>
> "Making the ten servants help me do my saving has not only been possible but highly profitable," said Mrs. Roosevelt today.

FDR wrote his wife the next day that her "newspaper campaign" was a "corker":

> I am proud to be the husband of the Originator, Discoverer and Inventor of the New Household Economy for Millionaires! Please have a photo taken showing the family, the ten cooperating servants, the scraps saved from the table. . . . I will have it published in the Sunday Times.
>
> Honestly you have leaped into public fame, all Washington is talking . . . and I begin to get telegrams of congratulations and requests for further details from Pittsburgh, New Orleans, San Francisco. . . .

FDR did not write of his mother's response, but he did note that Uncle Fred Delano thought it would all pass quickly; "but Gee how mad Eleanor will be!"

ER was in fact mortified: "I do think it was horrid of that woman to use my name in that way. . . . So much is not true and yet some of it I did say. I never will be caught again that's sure and I'd like to crawl away for shame." It was her first learning experience at the hands of the press: ER had had no idea how her candor and innocence could be used against her. She never did get "caught again" in that way, and she never again referred publicly even to the existence of her household staff.

This public relations disaster only momentarily distracted her from a much more serious source of pain. ER's lifelong fear of abandonment was not relieved by FDR's breezy letters, and the summer of 1917 seemed the longest summer of her life: "I don't think you read my letters for you never answer a question and nothing I ask for appears!"

Then, at the beginning of August, FDR was hospitalized for a serious throat infection, and requested her company. ER left Campobello instantly to nurse him. They were together for almost two weeks, and they had a serious talk. On 15 August, ER wrote: "I hated to leave you yesterday. Please go to the doctor twice a week, eat well and sleep well and remember I *count* on seeing you the 26th. My threat was no idle one."

As soon as he recovered, FDR was out and about. On 20 August, FDR wrote of another jolly outing to Harpers Ferry, with the Graysons and Lucy Mercer. One day, Alice Roosevelt Longworth telephoned FDR: "I saw you 20 miles out in the country. You didn't see me. Your hands were on the wheel, but your eyes were on the perfectly lovely lady." Franklin replied, "Isn't she perfectly lovely." Alice invited FDR and Lucy Mercer to her famous and fabulous dinners, and they went.

Alice reveled in the gossip about FDR and Lucy Mercer, and promoted the romance. The woman who became famous for her barbed tongue and a needlepoint cushion that directed guests to the honored place upon her sofa—"If you haven't got anything good to say about anyone come and sit by me"—now struck out cruelly at her cousin. She loved to tell the story of an evening witnessed by Irene and Warren Delano Robbins that dramatized ER's Griselda mode. ER had left a particularly merry party at ten, reportedly because Lucy Mercer was there and FDR could hardly bear to be away from her side. FDR and the others returned home at 4:00 A.M., in very high spirits, to be greeted by the grim reality of ER rising from the doormat, "looking like a string bean that had been raised in a cellar." She explained to the merry trio that she had forgotten her key and preferred not to disturb the servants, or disturb the group by returning to the Club since "I knew you were all having such a glorious time, and I didn't want to spoil the fun."

Alice's incipient cruelty toward ER, a wee festering sore since childhood, turned gangrenous as her own marriage disintegrated.

Nicholas Longworth was an ardent politician, a dandy, a superb violinist, and a notorious drunk. He made no effort to hide his affairs, his gambling, or his drunkenness from his wife, who sought to outdo him by behaving as outrageously, if in different ways. But even Alice had limits. They were reached when Nick focused his attentions upon Cissy Patterson, Aunt Bye's young friend during TR's presidency and then much in the company of both Bye's nieces.

No stranger to bitter familial rivalry, Eleanor Medill Patterson was one of the four grandchildren of Joseph Medill, who had founded the Chicago *Tribune*. As the only girl-child in the Medill-Patterson-McCormick clan, she had money and privilege but nothing specifically to do with her energy or her brilliance. The boys (Colonel Robert Rutherford McCormick, Senator J. Medill McCormick, and her beloved brother, Joseph Medill Patterson, who subsequently founded the New York *Daily News*) ran the family businesses. After a disastrous marriage to a scoundrel Polish Count, Josef Gizycka, who beat and abused her, she returned to Washington. Discontented and adventurous, she spent several months each year hunting and living in Wyoming, but with the snows always returned to Washington in search of diversion. Eventually she allied herself with William Randolph Hearst and became one of the most powerful women in American public life, as editor and publisher of Washington's *Times-Herald.*

But during the war years, the Countess Gizycka was most notable as one of the wildest women in wicked Washington. At one party in her own home, Alice Longworth discovered her husband and her great friend Cissy in the bathroom: with the door unlocked and the light on, having sex on the floor. Alice countered by having a torrid and long-lived affair with Idaho Senator William E. Borah. Much like her father, Borah was rotund, opinionated, powerful, insufferable. Politics consumed him. And Alice adored him. His wife left town, and Borah enhanced his reputation as the "stallion of Idaho." Alice Longworth became widely known throughout Washington as "Aurora Borah Alice." Best of all, she beat Cissy Patterson in the race for Borah's affections.

There seemed to be a specific pattern to their rivalry: Cissy Patterson would pursue Alice's husband and lovers at parties in Alice's home. One evening, Cissy disappeared with Borah. The next morning, a maid found her hairpins in the library. Alice sent them with a note: "I believe they are yours." Cissy replied: "And if you look up in the chandelier, you might find my panties." But Borah disliked Cissy's gloating, and her writing of him indiscriminately in one of her columns. He chose Alice. (Cissy Patterson got even: She killed him off in her novel, *Glass Houses,* which she wrote during the 1920s, when she lived in Paris.)

By 1920, Alice and Borah had become inseparable, and in 1925, at the age of forty-five, Alice had a daughter. She looked just like Borah, and Alice intended to name her Deborah. Nick could not abide that—

De-Borah, indeed—and Alice reluctantly agreed to name her daughter Paulina.

For all her own flamboyance, Cissy Patterson never demeaned or criticized Eleanor Roosevelt. Even later, when their political differences became profound, she would never allow anybody to ridicule ER in her company. Although Cissy Patterson frequently referred to herself proudly as "just a plain old vindictive shanty Irish bitch," her biographer believed that "she wanted to be Eleanor Roosevelt." Cissy Patterson admired ER and called her "the noblest woman I have ever known. I adore her above all women."

Nicholas Longworth was one of the most popular men in Washington, and the most beloved Speaker of the House. He was also a playful and contented father. However, there was nothing but venom between him and his wife. By the time he died in 1931, Alice hated him so thoroughly that she burned virtually all his papers and treasures, including his Stradivarius violin—an act of wanton destruction for a financially troubled widow, since that 1690 violin (one of only twelve hundred that Antonio Stradivari made) might have saved her considerable hardship. Clearly, Alice's bilious attitude toward ER had more to do with her own life than with her frequently repeated gibe that Franklin "deserved a good time. He was married to Eleanor."

Alice Longworth and FDR became closer during the summer of 1917 than ever before. Their new attachment was forged as they created a dirty little scheme to spy on another Washington romance, in the name of patriotism. Bernard Baruch, chairman of the War Industries Board and the personal financier of America's early efforts at large-scale economic warfare, was having an affair with a Roosevelt family friend, May Ladenburg. Subsequently the wife of Preston Davie (a ferocious Republican enemy of Roosevelt's New Deal), she was the beautiful daughter of the senior partner in a German-American banking house, Ladenburg, Thalmann and Co. Her home was one of Washington's most congenial social centers, and Alice knew her house, gardens, and stables well. She and FDR went about with military agents, bugging the place; and together they listened above a horse stall as Baruch and May Ladenburg made love and talked in her adjoining studio: "We did hear her ask Bernie how many locomotives were being sent to Rumania. . . .

In between the sounds of kissing . . ." It was a "most disgraceful" thing to do, "of course," Alice Roosevelt Longworth acknowledged; "but it was sheer rapture!" ER considered it a vile caper, and "most unjust to poor May Ladenburg."

FDR managed to tear himself away from his summer activities to come to Campobello the last week of August, as promised, and he left with the family on 2 September for Hyde Park, although he left New York almost immediately for Washington. ER remained at Hyde Park until November, for the first time finding respite and comfort in her mother-in-law's home. ER expected FDR to return the first week of November, to visit and to help the family move back for the winter season in Washington. But on 5 November, ER wrote: "We are terribly disappointed and I am very cross for I would have left here with the babies today if I had known even yesterday. . . ." His wire arrived too late, but all the chicks "sent love and were so sorry you could not come." Unable to acknowledge the depth of her anger, ER effused gratitude instead: FDR had "been a marvelous correspondent and it has been such a pleasure to see your handwriting daily!"

When ER returned to Washington, she resumed her canteen work and spent many hours listening to the intensifying debates in Congress. There she had an unpleasant encounter with her busybody cousin Alice while FDR, his mother, and several of their children went on a brief excursion to pin medals on heroes:

Dearest Honey,

All is quiet here and I hope you and Mama have had good weather and a fine "Welcome Home." I wish I could have been there to have seen you give the medals and I hope F Jr and John saw and heard everything for they should remember some of it. . . .

This afternoon I went to the Capitol about 4. . . . On the way out I parted with Alice at the door not having allowed her to tell me any secrets. She inquired if you had told me and I said no and that I did not believe in knowing things which your husband did not wish you to know so I think I will be spared any further mysterious secrets! . . .

I am very lonely without you and shall be very glad to see you on Monday. Much love from the chicks, Devotedly Always,

E.R.

Whether ER was consciously aware at this time that FDR spent as many hours as possible with Lucy Mercer, or that members of her own family, many of her canteen and Red Cross co-workers, and almost everybody else of importance in Washington knew that Franklin and Lucy were sweethearts, we will never learn. Certainly on some level she knew it all, the way lovers always know, unconsciously and through every cell of their being, when somebody else has pre-empted some big or little piece of their beloved's heart. But denial ("I did not believe in knowing things . . .") is inevitable, until it becomes unbearable.

It is clear that FDR did very little to protect his wife from gossip, did nothing significant to hide his affair, and went so far as to enlist many of their mutual friends in his relationship. His willingness to dine with Lucy Mercer in public and at the home of Cousin Alice, already established as one of Eleanor's cruelest detractors, was certainly among his boldest acts of betrayal. Although ER might choose to ignore her rapacious cousin, she could not ignore material evidence when she held it in her hands.

During the winter and spring of 1917–18, ER and FDR saw little of each other. She devoted every day to war work, and he was elsewhere. That summer, she decided to stay in Washington, and sent the children and most of the servants off to her mother-in-law at Hyde Park. In July, alone with one maid in Washington, ER made her daily rounds in her Red Cross uniform, comfortable despite the heat. "I loved it. I simply ate it up"—in part because it left her no idle moments during which to think. On 9 July, FDR sailed for Europe to inspect the fleet. On 20 July 1918, she wrote her husband: "They have asked me to go . . . with a unit of five to start a canteen in England. It is quite a temptation." Eager to go to the front, be at the center of activity, and remove herself from the tensions around her, ER seriously considered this offer, but reluctantly declined because of her children.

Eleanor Roosevelt was the mother of five children between the ages of two and twelve. She had money, and she knew she could do good work. She liked to work, and she worked well under the most arduous circumstances. She worked through the steamiest heat wave in a tin-roofed canteen; she worked after she had cut her finger to the bone on the new bread-cutting machine. She wrapped handkerchiefs around that finger all day, and bore the scar forever; but she was so busy trying to prepare for the several troop trains scheduled to arrive that day she had not even felt the pain.

During the war, ER's personal interest in the wounded sailors and their families she visited was profound. She brought fresh flowers, candy, newspapers, and always genuine compassion; she took time and noticed details. She received several letters of gratitude like the following: "I want to thank you as the mother of one of the boys who was in the Naval Hospital . . . for the kind words—the little favors—the interest you took in my son. . . . He always loved to see you come in. You always brought a ray of sunshine with you, always had something to say to him. . . ."

And then there was her amazing capacity to raise money from various and unlikely sources. When she wanted to see a recreational center built for wounded men who needed physical therapy, she went to the Colonial Dames, and "in a short time" the center was not only built but self-supporting. She raised money for crippled Southern boys through the Daughters of the Confederacy, by going directly to the personal friends and endless associates who rarely said no to her. Her effectiveness was widely recognized. In July 1918, Theodore Roosevelt decided to divide the Nobel Peace Prize money he had not spent among those best aiding the war effort. He gave the largest sums to the Red Cross ($6,900), his niece Eleanor ($5,000), and the Jewish Welfare Board ($4,000).

ER had also learned to drive that July. Huckins, the family chauffeur, taught her in the Stutz, and then in the Buick. He praised her efforts, and she did "finely." ER loved to drive, and after that summer she drove all the time—occasionally so fast that her best friends thought her reckless. And she finally learned to swim that summer. She took lessons; she practiced; she persevered; she swam. She felt safe and comfortable now in any water, and no longer nervous about the children. Trifles, minor mishaps, inconsequentials no longer unnerved her.

Over the years ER had grown accustomed to spending weeks alone with her children, and gradually her relations with them had become easier, and for Eleanor more contented. As early as 1912, ER's brother Hall wrote to her: "Is F paying any attention to his family this summer or is the bee buzzing as hard as ever?" Hall suggested that his sister "build a little cell for him at Campo and tie him down." Five years later, ER wrote her friend Isabella: "I've had many quiet evenings this summer and since infantile paralysis kept us a month later than we expected at Campo I really did much reading and worked hard over the chicks all day. Anna is going to be capable and dependable I think and James already devours books and I think will have a quick and interesting mind. Elliott is just very lovable and sensitive and stormy and the two babies very soft and adorable." By the autumn of 1918, ER believed she could in fact do anything she had to do.

During August and September of 1918 ER made frequent trips to be with her children and mother-in-law at Hyde Park. It was an odd choice for a port in the storm, but usable. Indeed, during this year ER's relations with her mother-in-law were the warmest they had ever been, or were to be. Sara was solid, direct, without artifice, dependable. She was aggressive and demanding, and her bluntness lacked charm, but there were no tricks, no devious games. Her insistence on the primacy and sanctity of family and tradition was particularly congenial to ER that year, though at other times it had caused friction, even acrimony.

For years ER had struggled to work herself free of some of her mother-in-law's less appealing convictions, and by 1917 both ER and FDR had started moving away from Sara Delano Roosevelt's dearly held ideas about the role America's aristocracy must continue to play. One Sunday evening, after a long and discordant weekend, SDR wrote to "Dearest Franklin and Dearest Eleanor" about her views regarding "noblesse oblige" and "honneur oblige." She was sorry they disagreed, "sorry to feel that my views are not [yours]." But she wanted to explain herself:

> One can be democratic as one likes, but if we love our own, and if we love our neighbor, we owe a great example. . . .
> After I got home, I sat in the library for nearly an hour reading, and as I put down my book and left the delightful room and the

two fine portraits, I thought: after all, would it not be better just to spend all one has at once in this time of suffering and need, and not think of the future; for with the *trend* to "shirt sleeves," [and the abandonment of] the old fashioned traditions of family life, simple home pleasures and refinements, and the traditions some of us love best, of what use is it to *keep up* things, to hold on to dignity and all I stood up for this evening. Do not say I *misunderstood*. I understood perfectly. But I cannot believe that my precious Franklin really feels as he expressed himself.

Well, I hope that while I live I may keep my "old fashioned" theories and that *at least* in my own family I may continue to feel that *home* is the best and happiest place and that my son and daughter and their children will live in peace and keep from the tarnish which seems to affect so many. . . .

During that time, when ER felt most adrift, she turned to her mother-in-law for a sense of security. Sara Delano Roosevelt's verities were familiar, comforting; and she welcomed and embraced her daughter-in-law. On 22 January 1918, ER had written SDR that over the years she had come to "realize how lucky we are to have you and I wish we could always be together. Very few mothers I know mean as much to their daughters as you do to me." Her letters frequently told of her need to confide, to talk intimately; she considered "running away" from Washington several times "to see you." On her thirteenth wedding anniversary, ER had written a letter of gratitude to Sara: "I often think of what an interesting, happy life Franklin has given me and how much you have done to make our life what it is. As I have grown older I have realized better all you do for us and all you mean to me and the children especially and you will never know how grateful I am nor how much I love you dear."

Eleanor was at Hyde Park with her mother-in-law when, on 12 September, they received a telegram: They were to meet FDR's ship in New York with an ambulance and a physician. He had double pneumonia and influenza, as did most of the men on that ship—and many crew and officers had been buried at sea. It was a worrisome time: The deadly flu epidemic of 1918 raged throughout the country, and within weeks ER's entire household would be in bed. But FDR's health turned out not to be the main issue. The night she unpacked FDR's baggage, the "bottom dropped out" of ER's world.

As she sorted his mail and ordered his papers, she found a neat and hefty packet of Lucy Mercer's letters. Did she read every letter? Did she merely note the salutations and the signature? With what words did she arouse FDR from his deep-fevered sleep? We know only that she offered him "his freedom." For Eleanor, the prospect of a life alone must have been easier to imagine than that of facing one moment longer in a home where she was not wanted. There had been so many homes in which she was an outsider, a guest—where she felt tolerated and only marginally loved. Her Aunt Maude had recently divorced and remarried. Divorce was certainly preferable to the cruel alternatives she had witnessed throughout her childhood.

Sara Delano Roosevelt, however, was aghast at the prospect. She would not abide it. If her son abandoned his wife and her grandchildren for that woman, she would cut him off without another cent. She would not hear of it. There was nothing to discuss. FDR had to choose. That woman; or his wife and family and the money he needed for his career.

Divorce would have ended FDR's political career. His boss, Josephus Daniels, would certainly have fired him. Daniels, a fundamentalist Christian, was the man who brought morality to the navy. He banned the condom packet sailors once received, since he believed in virginity before marriage and in abstinence outside of marriage; he ended the sailors' wine-and-beer mess before Prohibition; he condemned divorce and fired his own brother-in-law from his newspaper when his marriage ended. And then there were the voters. Divorce was an unacceptable public scandal. Moreover, without his mother's financial support, FDR could not afford politics. Nor could he pay for his customary life-style, which then included his share of three houses, servants, membership in every major club in New York and Washington, not to mention his book, stamp, print, model ship, button, and various other collections. It was impossible.

There was also the question of Lucy Mercer's Catholicism. Would she have married a divorced man? What were all that passion and all that pain about? Undoubtedly too much has been made of the chilling effect of Lucy Mercer's Catholicism, since FDR was in fact the love of her life, and FDR had risked everything for that love. One may assume that, had FDR taken his freedom, she would have married him. But he evidently told Lucy Mercer that he could not get free, that ER would not give him a divorce. This was not his final lie.

On 14 February 1920, ER wrote SDR a postscript to a long and otherwise detailed letter: "Did you know Lucy Mercer married Mr. Wintie Rutherford two days ago?" Winthrop Rutherford, a widower with five children, was fifty-six, more than twice Lucy Mercer's age, and one of the richest and most attractive men in society circles.* His wife, Alice Morton (Levi Morton's eldest daughter), always close to the Roosevelts, had died in 1917. FDR was stunned by the news of Lucy's marriage, which he overheard at a party. Although he had agreed never to see Lucy Mercer again, Lucy and FDR did see each other, even before Winthrop Rutherford's death in 1941. FDR arranged to have her present at his first inaugural and saw her whenever she visited her mother in Washington. Subsequently, he visited her near her estate in Aiken, South Carolina, with the help of Bernard Baruch, who arranged several meetings. There is the famous story of FDR's railroad car being taken off to a siding near the Rutherford place at Allamuchy in New Jersey; and the fact that, when ER was away and her daughter, Anna, presided over White House social evenings, she occasionally invited Lucy Mercer. Finally, Lucy Mercer was with FDR when he died at Warm Springs, while he was having his portrait painted by her friend Elizabeth Shoumatoff, as a gift for Lucy Mercer Rutherford's daughter Barbara.

ER suffered the Lucy Mercer affair on several levels. Franklin had not only betrayed her; he had betrayed her in the company of many others. He had humiliated her, and connived with Alice. Did FDR want ER to know? Did he resent her removal to Campobello, her refusal to be baited, her failure to ask questions? He was used to his mother's firm and tight rein. His wife, in contrast, had set no limits. FDR did not destroy or hide Lucy Mercer's letters. Had he forgotten them? Was

---

* Indeed, in 1896, Alva Erskine Smith Vanderbilt Belmont (Mrs. O. H. P. Belmont) earned her reputation as America's meanest mother when she forced her seventeen-year-old daughter Consuelo Vanderbilt to leave the country after she became secretly engaged to Winthrop Rutherford, then thirty. See notes, pages 535–36.

he too sick to remove them from his luggage? Curiously, the only point ER made in her memoirs concerning that dreadful moment of discovery was that, when they boarded FDR's homecoming ship, with so many truly sick and dying men, "My husband did not seem to me so seriously ill as the doctors implied."

ER wrote of that time only obliquely, and in code. She never referred to Lucy Mercer or her pain. But she did write of the "liberal education" she received in wartime:

> I think I learned then that practically no one in the world is entirely bad or entirely good, and that motives are often more important than actions. I had spent most of my life in an atmosphere where everyone was sure of what was right and what was wrong, and as life progressed I have gradually come to believe that human beings who try to judge other human beings are undertaking a somewhat difficult job. . . .
>
> . . . during the war I became a more tolerant person, far less sure of my own beliefs and methods of action, but I think more determined to try for certain ultimate objectives. . . . I knew more about the human heart, which had been somewhat veiled in mystery. . . .

In September 1918, ER began a long process of introspection and change. Her life seemed suspended, awash in bitterness, and it would take years for her to regain the self-confidence that she felt she had lost overnight. Still, her quest for understanding began immediately, and it occupied her entire soul. Eleanor Roosevelt had married a man who was not unlike her father. But ER had never lost her romantic feelings for her dashing, womanizing, undependable, mercurial father. She had always blamed her cold and judgmental mother for the tragedy of their lives. It was inconceivable that she would react to *her* husband's behavior as her Uncle Theodore had successfully persuaded her mother to do: to leave him, abandon him—whatever his protest or explanation, whatever his preference or primary commitment. As an adult, ER became convinced that greater tenderness and empathy on her mother's part might have averted the great failure of her parents' lives, and their early deaths.

Now, at thirty-four, the age at which her father died, ER sought to avoid what she considered her mother's mistakes. As ER scanned her memory, her heart, literature, all she then understood about life and love, she paused at the world of passion and intensity mandated by individual needs in the teachings of Marie Souvestre. ER considered the realities, the romantic myths, the unexpected foibles, the surprising lusts, the mysteries. She feared rigidities; despised cold, judgmental abstractions. She trusted the heart to be tender.

First Eleanor offered Franklin "his freedom." If he loved Lucy Mercer enough to marry her, she wanted him to be free. But FDR turned down her offer of divorce. He made promises, provided explanations. This "golden boy," this vibrant "apollo" who charmed everyone he met, now directed all his influence and charm toward his wife. He would never see Lucy Mercer again. Did he apologize? Did he explain? Had he been engaged in a long-overdue emotional rebellion—against being a mama's boy who always did the right and proper thing; who condemned all departures from the proprieties of his class and culture; who had mocked his half-brother's son's love for a socially unacceptable woman and blamed Taddie for his father's death; who at the young age of twenty-three had taken on the responsibilities of a wife and home? Well, he had erred. Washington was so full of temptations; he had been trying out his new power, his new independence, for the first time in his life. It was a flamboyant, fatuous time. And it was over. He cared about his wife; he loved her. He was sorry he had hurt her. There was so much at stake—so much to do, and to do together.

Louis Howe played a significant role in their discussions. He persuaded FDR that his career and all his political dreams would end with divorce, and that he needed his wife, whose skills were special; and he persuaded ER that FDR could not go on successfully without her. If he wanted her, ER had no intention of destroying his career or discouraging his future. And then there were five young children, and Mama, and their lives together.

Was there anything left between them? Was there love? Could there be trust? Could they start over? Was all passion spent, or forever re-routed? Might they even try?

They did try. History confirms some details: FDR took care to protect his wife's feelings, and allowed nobody to criticize her in his presence. Indeed, they both protected and defended each other with the vigor and strength of a bond sealed by the deepest pain. If there had been too much pain for their relationship to become an unselfish love, it became a most unselfish partnership.

Our common understanding is that Eleanor and Franklin never again resumed a sexual relationship. The source for that understanding is exclusively the testimony of the Roosevelt children who knew at the time nothing of their parents' struggle. According to them: Mother never slept with Father again (James and Elliott); Mother considered sex an ordeal to be borne (Anna). But children are unreliable sources concerning their parents' sexuality, and are particularly vulnerable to the historical stereotype that conjures up the frigid mother and the deprived father.

~

WHATEVER THE WORDS SPOKEN, WHATEVER THE AGREEMENT forged in that time of highest tension and most bitter feeling, ER and FDR subsequently made every effort to recover the joy between them that they had allowed to evaporate. ER went to and determinedly enjoyed more parties. FDR spent more time with the children and doing other things he knew would please ER. He gave up golf on Sunday mornings to go to church; he bought her thoughtful presents, and persuaded Josephus Daniels to allow ER to accompany him on his European tour of January 1919, during which he presided over the liquidation and distribution of America's vast military stores. That trip served as a second honeymoon. On the way over, however, ER was shocked to hear of the sudden death of her Uncle Theodore Roosevelt, on the morning of 7 January 1919. The old warrior had died unexpectedly and peacefully in his sleep. ER's thoughts turned immediately to "Aunt Edith for it will leave her very much alone." There was no suggestion of personal sorrow, but ER did grieve for the country: "Another big figure gone from our nation and I fear the last years were for him full of disappointment."

Postwar Paris was for the Roosevelt circle something of a carnival. All of their friends and relatives were there. ER and FDR had never seemed so gay together. And ER participated in all discussions with a new vigor. She made suggestions and connections. She toured hospitals and battlefields.

It was a transforming experience. She wrote Isabella: "We were able to motor from Paris to Boulogne through the northern part of France over which the British and French had fought for years and I do not think one can quite realize without seeing— Boulogne Wood with its few bare sticks to mark what once had been . . . gave one an even more ghastly feeling than the shelled and ruined towns. . . . What the men who fought there lived through is inconceivable. . . ."

Astounded by the devastation of war—the millions of dead after four years of carnage, which left "every other woman in a black veil to her knees"—ER became committed to Wilson's postwar vision as expressed in his most generous rhetoric; and she dedicated herself to the fight for the League of Nations.

During this trip, ER explored the new boundaries of her own independence, and together she and Franklin explored the contours of their new relationship. Understandings were reached, and renegotiated. There were moments of disappointment, occasional lapses. But these were no longer ignored, denied, dusted away, or hidden behind a sullen front. On 31 January, ER wrote SDR that she was grieved not to be with FDR on his tour of Brussels, Cologne, and Coblenz. Her husband had decreed: "it was easier for everyone concerned not to have women along." ER was disappointed, as she had been when she wrote FDR on 1 August 1918, while he was in the Azores: "It was wonderful to hear only I hate not being with you and seeing it all! Isn't that horrid of me!" But now ER no longer thought it horrid or even unreasonable to resent the notion that woman's place was on the sidelines, while the hunters and heroes went off for adventure and fun. She resented it and said so—loudly and often.

ER now resolved to speak, and act, whenever she was displeased.

She wrote Sara: "We had a most interesting dinner . . . and I dragged F home with difficulty at 11 o'clock he was so fascinated by Lady Scott." She would no longer stand idly by while FDR fluttered and courted: When a flirtation arose, they would now leave together, early.

Paris was dramatically changed. ER decided it was not for the squeamish or the young. And "the scandals" that involved many of the officers "would make many a woman at home unhappy." On the other hand, ER understood why everyone drank wine with meals: "The cheer would certainly be too cold without it. . . . Decidedly we are growing effete at home from too much comfort & I always thought myself something of a Spartan!"

Spartan, Puritan, and Prude were names that ER had routinely assigned to herself. Slowly, deliberately, she began to discard the heavy weight of these affects. Gradually personal freedom, emotional liberty, happiness became once again important to her. This postwar trip to Europe helped point the way.

For many years, nobody referred to the Lucy Mercer affair, including Eleanor, who wrote to her friend Isabella on 11 July 1919: "This past year has rather got the better of me it has been so full of all kinds of things that I still have a breathless, hunted feeling about it though for the moment I am leading an idle if at times a somewhat trying life!" But she referred specifically only to Franklin's pneumonia and the children's bout with flu.

The first major storm that confronted the Roosevelts, it challenged more fundamentally than any subsequent upheaval their ability to keep their two ships sailing along a parallel and connected course. For all of ER's autobiographical candor, she does not refer to her most painful marital moment—the moment that most profoundly changed her life. If she grew to tolerate FDR's continued reputation as a flirt, a bottom-pincher, and a knee-holder—a reputation that increased with age and was considered part of his congenial, innocent, and charming style—that tolerance was rendered possible by the critical years of reassessment and reconsideration between 1918 and 1920. During those years, ER resolved to design for herself an independent life that freed them both to live according to the rhythms of their individual needs and wants.

Her decisions were not made with ease, and her days were not without heartache. During these years, ER lost her appetite; when she did eat, she frequently could not keep her food down. In May 1919, for example, ER noted that she had had a quiet dinner with Mama, "but I might as well not have eaten it for I promptly parted with it all!" Photographs of this period portray an underweight, dejected woman whose face is averted. Few pictures from these years, pictures of the entire family and Mama, show ER with her face to the camera. She rarely smiled; she was depressed; and today we would call her loss of appetite, which continued for years, "anorexia." We now know that one of the results of frequent vomiting is a deterioration of the teeth and gums. During this period, ER's teeth loosened, spread, and protruded more than ever. She felt profoundly tired, suffered headaches, and had days when she wondered about her will to live.

ER spent several days each week, in the months before she left Washington for Europe, at Rock Creek Cemetery. She drove herself many miles out of the center of town to sit alone in the quiet and regard the statue Henry Adams had commissioned Augustus Saint-Gaudens to sculpt in his wife's memory. Marian Hooper Adams was a pioneer woman photographer, a learned "bluestocking" and linguist whose translations and research Henry Adams had found indispensable for his early histories. A witty, gracious hostess, much beloved by old Washington's inner core, she was one of the famed "five of hearts"—that collection of earnest eccentrics consisting of Clover (as she was known) and Henry Adams, Clara and John Hay, and pioneering geologist Clarence King.

Clover Adams committed suicide by drinking photographic acid, evidently when she heard of her husband's affair with Elizabeth Cameron. Adams had the monument and garden built, and then erased all evidence of Clover's existence. Erected without a name, or designation of any kind, the statue was more a monument to his loss than to her memory. He called the statue *Peace of God;* a peace "beyond pain and beyond joy," Saint-Gaudens noted. Most people, including ER, called the statue *Grief.*

ER found comfort in that sheltered green holly grove, with its curved stone benches facing a hooded, robed figure of timeless beauty and endurance. There it was easy to contemplate the lives of women, and commune with the spirit of one particular woman who had given in to pain but now seemed impassive, perhaps victorious, and filled with determined strength. ER always kept a copy of the poem Cecil Spring-Rice had written about the bronze statue she would visit so many times over the years. It was among her bedside papers at her death:

> *O steadfast, deep, inexorable eyes*
> *Set look inscrutable, nor smile nor frown!*
> *O tranquil eyes that look so calmly down*
> *Upon a world of passion and of lies! . . .*

For ER, the Lucy Mercer affair involved an agonizing struggle to recover her self-esteem. In the process, she enlarged her ability to love and trust, and found new paths to happiness and fulfillment.

10. 1919–20: Race Riots and Red Scare, Grief and Renewal

THE YEARS 1919–20 WERE FULL OF TUMULTUOUS UP-
heaval, not only for Eleanor Roosevelt personally but for the
world. With the war in Europe over, the battle for the future
began. Everywhere profound changes in politics, culture, and understanding were under way. Anticolonial movements flourished. The
Russian Revolution was greeted with "mad, glad joy"—and unbridled
horror.

The map of the world was being redrawn with abandon. National
groups that had histories of the most bitter hatred were herded together
into newly created countries with no cultural affinity or political unity.
The great and divisive schisms of the twentieth century were being
forged by the contradictory visions that emerged at the end of World
War I.

Nothing was stable; nothing was certain. German soldiers in uniform
marched beneath the Red flag and sang the "Internationale." British
miners went on strike to demonstrate their solidarity with the workers
of the world. In the United States, more than four million workers
participated in 2,665 strikes.

Women demanded the vote, power, a real voice in society. For fifty
years, in England and the United States, they had picketed, marched,
petitioned, demonstrated. They had been arrested, brutalized, and,
when they conducted hunger strikes in prison, force-fed. English and

American women thrilled to the rallying cry of Emmeline Pethick-Lawrence: "There is no life worth living except a fighting life." But during the war they had suspended their militancy to support the troops, and expected now to be vindicated and rewarded.

In every area, long-overdue accounts were to be redeemed, as sacred myths about authority and control met the wrecker. Children of workers, serfs, and slaves demanded education, economic security, political rights, equality—and dignity. The colonized sought independence. Nationalists wanted new boundaries. Racial and religious minorities called for an end to violent repression. Workers organized unions. Everybody wanted freedom, security, and self-respect. As feudalism in Europe ended, the titled nobility and the ruling classes lost their prerogatives and prestige, if not yet many of their crown jewels. The Hapsburg, Hohenzollern, Romanov, and Ottoman Empires were smashed. The wealth of the resource-rich world, including vast Arab oil fields, was once again up for grabs.

Woodrow Wilson's sonorous phrases about peace with justice, and open treaties openly arrived at, masked secret treaties secretly arrived at. The Treaty of Versailles was punitive and imperial, and mocked every one of Wilson's Fourteen Points. ER wrote Bob Ferguson: "I think the terms must please you, they certainly could not be more drastic and all the English and French here seem well pleased." ER, who doubted that the treaty was in the United States' best interests, was more appreciative of Wilson's Fourteen Points, which had included self-determination for all peoples, freedom of the seas, the removal of trade barriers to international commerce, and a League of Nations to guarantee the independence of nations, great and small. From the beginning, the new Soviet government was excluded from the League, and greeted with a blockade of food and industrial products that completely contradicted the words and purpose of the peace. Indeed, before the treaty was completed, the world was again at war.

Revolution was met by counterrevolution and reaction. Repression greeted every movement for social change. In the United States, a year of tyranny and violence, of Red Scare and race riots, called America's constitutional precepts into question. Freedom of speech, press, and assembly was buried in an avalanche of superpatriotism led by vigilante missionaries of a new "Americanism." The war to make the world safe for democracy ended with the secret Allied Intervention against the Soviet Union and bloodshed in streets throughout America, as Wilsonian crusaders declared war against Bolsheviks and all their soft-minded liberal friends. The Red Scare carved the heart out of American liberalism, and charted the course of twentieth-century politics.

After 1919, most of the promises of women's suffrage and progressive reform fell victim to the repressive crusade. At the direction of Attorney General A. Mitchell Palmer, all opponents of World War I— all pacifists, anarchists, socialists, and political dissenters—became the target of a massive campaign of arrests and reprisals. Thousands of foreign-born women and men, as well as American-born unionists and thousands of other perfectly innocent people who just happened to be in the path of Palmer's dragnets, were arrested on no evidence of wrongdoing, without warrants or due process.

Bolstered by the Espionage Act of 15 June 1917 and the Sedition Act of 16 May 1918, Palmer's agents were free to arrest all who gave aid or comfort to the enemy; all who seemed disloyal in word or deed or attitude; all who opposed the draft or who spoke ill of the president, his advisers, the government, or the military. "Scurrilous" or "abusive" newspapers or journals were denied U.S. mailing privileges. People were arrested for "suspicious" postures, "disloyal thoughts," displeasing "foreign" accents.

Secret agents infiltrated union meetings, attended political rallies. The new twentieth-century sleuth, with his eye in the keyhole and his ear at the door, took copious notes, as if all political interests and public demonstrations were sly, un-American secrets. From these meetings records were compiled relating to all the supposedly dangerous and disorderly elements in America, forming the basis of John Edgar Hoover's famous index-card files of revolutionary Reds. Hundreds of people were imprisoned under the Espionage Act, and Hoover kept files on the activities of thousands of Americans in every village and town. Activists as diverse as Jane Addams and Eugene Debs, Carrie Chapman Catt and Margaret Dreier Robins, Lillian Wald and Eleanor Roosevelt—all the twentieth-century visionaries who imagined there might be political, economic, and social change in the United States in their lifetime—were monitored, spied upon, and often hounded and harassed by state-sponsored officials and self-appointed patriots. They were transformed from the conscience of America into the enemies of America.

Joining the new crusade, on the eve of the women's-suffrage victory, the National Association Opposed to Woman Suffrage, still chaired by Alice Hay (Mrs. James) Wadsworth, changed the name of its journal from *Woman's Protest* to *Woman Patriot,* asserting that suffragism and socialism were the same and indivisible. And in 1920, the NAOWS became the Woman Patriot Corporation, which over the years targeted and red-baited such social feminists as Jane Addams and Eleanor Roosevelt.

Ironically, Alice Wadsworth and Eleanor Roosevelt lunched together one afternoon on the New York–to–Washington train, just before the suffrage amendment became law. According to ER, Alice Wadsworth spent the entire time "trying to persuade me to come out against ratification. I was very noncommittal." Although ER "considered any stand at that time quite outside my field of work," she sidestepped Wadsworth's efforts and urged her mother-in-law to do the same.

The Red Scare went beyond patriotic harassment of suffragists, socialists, and reformers. From 7 November 1919 to the spring of 1920, in what were called the "Palmer Raids," federal agents invaded "gathering places" of alleged Reds in eighteen cities; they "broke up meetings, seized tons of literature, and herded . . . foreign men and women into various offices for examination." On 9 November, *The New York Times* reported that "Thirty-three men, most of them with bandaged heads, black eyes or other marks of rough handling," were removed to Ellis Island, while of the 150 who were set free, most of them "also had blackened eyes and lacerated scalps as souvenirs of the new attitude of aggressiveness which has been assumed by the Federal agents against Reds and suspected Reds."

On 21 December 1919, the first "Red Ark"—the *Buford*—sailed for Russia with 249 women and men aboard, including the famous anarchists Emma Goldman and Alexander Berkman. But they were practically the only anarchists on the ship. Of the deportees only four were known anarchists. The *Buford* seemed to sail with America's most fundamental principles in its hold: freedom of speech and opinion; due process of law; a fair judicial trial. Max Eastman and his sister Crystal Eastman, then co-publishers of *The Liberator,* printed an angry protest: The deportations rendered the United States' "boast of a superior liberty and regard for human rights hollow and absurd."

On 5 January 1920, *The New York Times* ran an approving headline—" 'RED' CONCENTRATION CAMPS HERE URGED"—and in an editorial entitled "REDS BY THE THOUSAND" praised the "shrewdness" and "large wisdom" of the Department of Justice, and prophesied that these raids were "only a beginning": "Without notice and without interruption the department will pursue and seize the conspirators against our Government. Some 60,000 Bolshevists' names are recorded in the department. Its future activities should be far-reaching and beneficent. . . ."

Palmer's descriptions of radicals and the foreign-born encouraged the crudest racism and xenophobia: Just gaze into the face of an alien and see the criminal, the thief, and the murderer. In article after article, A. Mitchell Palmer spread his venom: "Out of the sly and crafty eyes of many of them leap cupidity, cruelty, insanity and crime; from their lopsided faces, sloping brows, and misshapen features may be recognized the unmistakable criminal type." They represented evil, and the "chief evil of the Red movement, both here and abroad, consists in the . . . constant spread of a disease of evil thinking."

In February 1920, Palmer warned the readers of *The Forum* to guard against the Reds: "Like a prairie-fire, the blaze of revolution" would devour "every American institution." "It was eating its way into the homes of the American workman, its sharp tongues of revolutionary heat were licking the altars of churches, leaping into the belfry of the school bells, crawling into the sacred corners of American homes, seeking to replace marriage vows with libertine laws, burning up the foundations of society."

For a time, democracy seemed limited to American anti-radicals. In the House of Representatives, the anti-Bolshevik socialist Victor L. Berger, who had been elected by a vast majority of the people of Milwaukee, was denied his seat. Some members of Congress recognized that the very principle of representative government was at stake. But in January 1920, their second vote to reseat him was defeated, 330 to 6. That same week, the New York State Assembly refused to seat five elected socialists from New York City. When, in April, their expulsion was again debated, Eleanor's cousin Teddy, Assemblyman Theodore Roosevelt (III), was almost alone in his opposition to this unprecedented disenfranchisement of sixty thousand voters. His protest on behalf of the principle of a free and representative government was met with derision: Assembly Speaker Thaddeus C. Sweet read a passage from Theodore's father, TR, on "Americanism" and denounced his son as "painfully un-American."

Although the Palmer Raids and the Red Scare frightened many and silenced some, they did not kill the commitment to justice that had been at the heart of the bipartisan progressive movement before World War I. A core of progressives remained active, as they watched with dismay the cruel death of Wilsonian liberalism, hurled into a mass grave by Wilsonians who allowed "Americanism" to replace reform.

In 1920, Warren G. Harding, a congenial but lackluster senator from Ohio running for president on the Republican ticket, called for a "Return to Normalcy": "America's present need is not heroics but healing; not nostrums but normalcy." He believed that the number of radicals in the United States had been greatly exaggerated, and announced that "too much has been said about Bolshevism in America." Woodrow Wilson had refused to release Eugene Debs, the Socialist Party's candidate for president who received one million votes while in prison, where he was serving a ten-year sentence for having said: "Wars throughout history have been waged for conquest and plunder. . . . The master class has always declared the wars; the subject class has always fought the battles. . . ." President Harding, on the other hand, pardoned Debs in 1921—and invited him to the White House. But, despite Harding's pardon and Debs's release after thirty-two months, the Red Scare continued throughout the Harding-Coolidge-Hoover decade.

During that entire time, ER was active in many of the groups and causes Palmer and his successors opposed, including the League of

Women Voters, the Women's Trade Union League, and the Foreign Policy Association. Moreover, she publicly condemned the mean-spiritedness of the Red Scare and the excesses of many superpatriotic organizations.

As a member in good standing of the Daughters of the American Revolution, she was particularly outraged by the shift in its tone. It had been a progressive organization that supported suffrage, conservation, the League of Nations, federal aid to education, an end to child labor, and such social reforms as the Children's Bureau and the Sheppard-Towner Act (guaranteeing maternity and infant health care). During the 1920s, new leadership emerged that transformed the DAR. It abandoned its former vision, purged all opposition, called for censorship of books and teachers, and sponsored wild antiradical tracts that outdid even the Department of War's "Spider Web." The DAR's screed, "The Common Enemy," expanded to ninety the list of un-American groups caught in the Bolshevik web. In addition to all those in the original web, as mapped out in 1924 by the librarian of the Chemical Warfare branch, Lucia Maxwell, the DAR included the YWCA, WCTU, NAACP, Federal Council of Churches, and U.S. Department of Labor.

ER was appalled. In the July 1927 issue of the *Women's Democratic News,* which she edited, she suggested that "all our leaders," the leaders of the women's committee of the Democratic Party, read, circulate, and discuss an article critical of the DAR by Carrie Chapman Catt, which ER considered the most significant words written on the subject of the Red Scare.* Like Catt, ER believed that the Daughters had made a fundamental error: They had failed to recognize the real threat—all the economic and political factors that had led to the emergence of communist parties everywhere. Not until poverty and injustice were dealt with, she insisted, would the revolutionary threat disappear.

As early as 1919, ER was certain that progressive change was the answer: "Now everyone is concerned over strikes and labor questions and I realize more and more that we are entering on a new era where ideas and habits and customs are to be revolutionized if we are not to

---

* For Catt's article, see notes, page 538.

have another kind of revolution." By 1927, she was convinced "oppression and suppression and the fear of those in places of power . . . have brought revolutions in the past and will do so again. Courage, justice and fair play do not breed revolutions, let us bear that in mind."

~

OVER THE YEARS, ELEANOR ROOSEVELT BECAME IDENTIFIED with every progressive issue condemned as un-American. As a result, agents of the FBI recorded her speeches, clipped her columns, and monitored her every word in behalf of racial justice; international peace; the right to economic security and collective bargaining; the right to housing, health, and education; the hope for human rights around the globe.

But ER's hostility to Palmer and to the activities of the Red Scare had not been immediate. The Roosevelts and the Palmers had in fact been friendly colleagues and neighbors during Wilson's administration—they lived across the street from each other. On the evening of 2 June 1919, Palmer's house was dynamited. Returning home after midnight from a formal dinner party, the Roosevelts were amazed by the commotion on quiet, tree-lined R street. Glass, debris, and blood were everywhere: Their windows were blown out, and the man who had thrown the bomb had been blown up. Shards of his bones were found for days.

ER related the scene to SDR: "We certainly had an exciting night and got to bed at 2:15 A.M.! It was a wonderful escape for the Palmers, if he had not gone to bed and had still been sitting in his sitting room in his usual chair he would have been blown to bits for there is nothing left of the chair. The roof of our sun parlor & our front windows on the lower floor don't exist, all our front curtains & shades on all 3 floors were down, plaster fell promiscuously inside & out! James did not hear the explosion but heard the resulting confusion." ER told James, her only child at home at the time, of the explosion "in the most matter of fact tone as though it was a daily occurrence and he returned to bed & sleep at once." The Roosevelts offered to take the Palmers in, but they preferred to leave. "Now we are roped off and the police haven't yet allowed the gore to be wiped up on our steps and James glories in every new bone found! I only hope the victim was not a poor passerby instead of the anarchist."

~

IN 1919 AND 1920, AT A TIME WHEN MOST OF THE WOMEN AND men who were to become ER's closest friends and allies were directly engaged in the political turbulence that swirled around her, ER herself was only marginally involved in the fray. In 1919, she was still a political bystander. But her own revolution, while largely private, was well under way.

During her years in Washington, her world fell apart and was reconstituted; her heart was devastated and refurbished; her direction changed. Subsequently she told her friends that she could forgive but could never forget. Cloaked by a mantle of lonely determination that occasionally made her seem cold and detached, she moved on. She contemplated new questions, and arrived at different decisions. Eventually she could say: "There was a time when I thought happiness did not matter but I think differently today."

To reconstruct the process by which Eleanor Roosevelt transformed her life, we need to reconsider the holly grove dedicated to Clover Adams where, day after day, ER spent most of her quiet, solitary hours whenever she was in Washington during that year. It is a closed, secluded space, almost hidden, though at the center of the cemetery's meadows. Stone benches designed by Stanford White face the imposing statue, with the haunting, handsome face for which both young men and women posed. Occasionally there is the sound of the wind and the songs of birds; nothing else disturbs the solitude.

In that sanctuary ER contemplated her life, the lives of women and of wives: She was connected to generations of Washington wives, married to officials and notables, with or without talents of their own, always with expectations and dreams, always with something special to contribute; mostly overworked, frequently ignored, generally misunderstood, often betrayed, casually mistreated.

In the Lincoln era, Marian Sturgis Hooper (Clover) represented the pinnacle of modern womanhood. Although her mother had died when she was five, her father, Robert William Hooper, a prominent physician, took pains to continue his wife's commitment to the education of their daughters. Marian Hooper was educated in Greek, Latin, and the modern languages at Elizabeth Cary Agassiz's school for girls in Cambridge. During the Civil War, she worked with the U.S. Sanitary Commission, and in 1866, while on a trip to England with her father, she met Henry Adams, whom she married in 1872. In 1877, they moved to Washington, and eventually resided directly across the street from the White House. Clover Adams was known as the most considerate and brilliant hostess in town, and their Lafayette Square home quickly became the center of entertainment for political and intellectual leaders, including Eleanor's Uncle Theodore and Aunt Bye.

It was generally alleged that Marian Sturgis Hooper Adams took her own life on 6 December 1885 at the age of forty-two, while in a profound depression over her father's death. Clover Adams did indeed mourn her beloved father. Except for her sisters, who had done so much to extend education for women, and who had worked so hard to build the Harvard Annex, only he had seemed fully to understand her and to appreciate her wit and talents. But she had another cause for depression: her husband's obsession with Elizabeth Cameron.

Those who claimed to know what went on behind the privets and façades of Washington society never doubted that Clover Adams drank that bottle of photographic acid when she learned of Henry Adams's love for Elizabeth Cameron. Married to a powerful senator, William Don Cameron, and known as the "most beautiful woman in Washington," Elizabeth rivaled Clover for Henry Adams's affections. There were those who said their love was chaste; and Elizabeth explained that was out of her loyalty to that "lump of clay" she married. Chaste or lustful, their love was ardent. Henry Adams wrote Elizabeth Cameron in 1884: "I shall dedicate my next poem to you. I shall have you carved over the arch of my stone doorway. I shall publish your volume of extracts with your portrait on the title page. None of these methods can fully express the extent to which I am yours."

While Henry Adams swooned in praise of Elizabeth Cameron, he discouraged his wife's work. A diligent researcher and skilled translator, she contributed significantly to his histories. But he never acknowledged his wife, or expressed his gratitude in any public way. Rather, he wrote with horror of women's intellectual ambitions:

> Our young women are haunted by the idea that they ought to read, to draw, or to labor in some way . . . to "improve" their minds. They are utterly unconscious of the pathetic impossibility of improving those poor little hard, thin, wiry, one-stringed instruments which they call their minds, and which haven't range enough to master one big emotion much less to express it in words or figures.

Longing for her own creative work, she achieved success with her photographic studies. But when her portraits were acclaimed and sought for publication, Henry Adams prohibited their sale.

Even as late as 1885, the year of Clover's suicide, Henry Adams wrote a howling letter of protest to the American Historical Association when he found a woman historian listed in the program. How did his wife feel about his blistering contempt for educated women, including presumably all the women in her own family?*

After her death, Henry Adams never publicly referred to his wife again. He never mentioned her or even the fact of their twelve-year marriage in any of his writings. He destroyed much of her work, and burned every letter that had been sent to her, including her father's entire correspondence, as well as his own early diaries. As he erased her name, he embarked upon a romance of Womanhood, dedicated himself to the celebration of women's superior intellectual and emotional gifts, and arranged to be buried beside her upon his death.

Clover Adams took her own life a year after Eleanor Roosevelt's birth, and Eleanor had heard the stories—the whispers and mysteries persisted. ER and Clover Adams shared a set of realities: the realities of women who have been trifled with, humiliated. And they shared a quest: During a time when women were without place or honor, they

---

* For a reconsideration of the curious details of Clover Adams's suicide and the Elizabeth Cameron factor, see notes, page 539.

sought to live a generous life, to give of their talents and vision, to do significant work, to find meaningful activity. As ER contemplated the statue of *Grief* in that unmarked holly grove, she forged a healing bond with a stranger—a bond that helped to strengthen her to live the kind of life she wished to lead.

Over the years, ER brought many of her closest friends to see the statue. Those to whom she wanted to show something of her own hard-won struggles, something of her deepest feelings during those years of her greatest discontent, were generally invited to make a pilgrimage with her to *Grief* early in the days of their friendship.

It was not that ER was half in love with death. She did not romanticize suicide. Her instincts craved happiness and fulfillment. Sitting before the statue of *Grief* gave her permission to contemplate the great range of contradictory emotions she had struggled so hard to suppress. There she could cry and rage, and begin to feel the stirrings of understanding, forgiveness, hope.

~

IN 1919, ER'S LIFE SEEMED TO HANG SUSPENDED. AT THIRTY-five, she felt abandoned, and unlovely. She had felt abandoned before, but then she was young and life seemed so vast and mysterious. As an orphan of ten, she had a world of fantasies; as a Washington wife of thirty-five, she had a world of responsibilities. Her five children now ranged in age from three to thirteen. She did not want them to suffer, to experience upheaval or pain, or to wake up to the cold mornings of a house blanketed by betrayal, jealousy, and contempt. She had criticized her mother's cold embrace, and now struggled to climb out of a frozen gloom all her own.

As she contemplated Clover Adams's life, her thoughts turned to other women, other lives. Her Aunt Bye was thirty the year Clover Adams died—a dutiful daughter, a well-educated spinster. Everybody had relied on her many services and attentions, until, twelve years later, at the same age Clover Adams had ended her life, Bye married and created a new life for herself, though her family was greatly shocked and inconvenienced by her decision. Marie Souvestre created and re-created her life several times, and she always seemed entirely satisfied.

ER's mother, dead at twenty-nine, never had a chance to redefine or rebuild her life. And her grandmother, who lived a long and unhappy life, had refused every opportunity to change or enhance her circumstances.

~

ULTIMATELY, ER CONSIDERED GRANDMOTHER HALL'S UN-happiness critical to her own determination to begin again, to take charge of her life with a new authority, a bolder purpose. As ER explored the contours of her life, death was very near. On 14 August 1919, Grandmother Hall died. It was the twenty-fifth anniversary of her father's death. Mary Livingston Ludlow Hall died in her seventy-seventh year, in her home at Tivoli, where, ER wrote, "she would have wished to be." ER and Franklin journeyed from Washington to be with her family: "Her life was a sad one in many ways, and yet those who were closest to her mourned her deeply and sincerely."

ER considered her grandmother's life largely wasted: "I wondered then and I wonder now whether, if her life had been less centered in her family group, that family group might not have been a great deal better off. If she had some kind of life of her own, what would have been the result?" ER recalled that when her grandmother "was young she painted rather well. Could she have developed that talent? I know that when she was young she might have had friends of her own, might even have married again. Would she have been happier, and would her children have been better off? She was not the kind of person who would have made a career independently; she was the kind of woman who needed a man's protection. Her willingness to be subservient to her children isolated her, . . . and it might have been far better, for her boys at least, had she insisted on bringing more discipline into their lives simply by having a life of her own."

Her grandmother's unused capacity for a full life now intensified ER's intention to recast her own. "I determined that I would never be dependent on my children by allowing all my interests to center in them." Unlike her grandmother, ER would no longer allow anyone "to feel assured" of "love and unquestioned loyalty" unless it was justified by specific "behavior."

As ER waited for the warming sun to heal her heart during those days she spent at Rock Creek Cemetery, a new resolve emerged. It came in the shape of words she repeated over and over again—words that were to be the banner of her adult life, words she repeated as advice to her many friends and the young people who would from then on enter her world, a new world of action and activism: "The life you live is your own." "Life is meant to be lived."

With those words, ER determined to take charge of every aspect of her world. Nothing would remain the same. To begin with, she fired all the servants in her Washington home. Perhaps she considered them disloyal—in collusion with Lucy Mercer, or her mother-in-law, or both—but her decision was stunning. Certainly they had come to represent her mother-in-law's preferences, her mother-in-law's tastes. ER realized that Sara Delano Roosevelt, who had never given up a shred of control in her own homes, had encouraged ER to surround herself with servants who bullied her, and who recognized her mother-in-law as the final arbiter of all decisions. She had allowed herself to give up a sweeping measure of independence and control. During the spring of 1919, in open defiance of her mother-in-law, ER suddenly staffed the entire household with black servants. Indeed, her timing was stunning: ER had the audacity to hire black servants when Wilsonian Washington was in a state of racial turmoil.

As America's troops returned from Europe, those hired to replace them when they had left two years before, women and blacks particularly, were summarily fired. The intensified economic dislocation and competition added fuel to the fires of resentment that Wilson's segregationist policies had ignited. During the spring and summer of 1919, racial tensions erupted in a series of race riots and racial confrontations throughout the country. The benefits of the war to make the world safe for democracy were to be restricted to whites. As Ku Klux Klan activists marched through black neighborhoods accompanied by jeering and violent white men still wearing their uniforms, African-American veterans and their families organized to defend themselves.

It was in that tense environment that ER replaced all her servants, retaining only an English nurse and a Scottish governess. Within "a day or two I had a new cook, kitchenmaid, butler and housemaid." Steeped in the language of her class and culture, ER explained her decision in stereotypic racialist terms: Perhaps it was her Auntie Gracie's "tales of the old and much-loved colored people on the plantation," or perhaps it was "the Southern blood of my ancestors, but ever since I had been in Washington I had enjoyed my contact with such colored people as came to work for me. I have never regretted the change which I made when I completely staffed my house with colored servants. . . .

"The colored race has the gift of kindliness and a fund of humor. . . . Though their eyes may mirror the tragedies of their race, they certainly have much to teach us in the enjoyment of the simple things of life and the dignity with which they meet their problems."

ER wrote those words in 1937, when Washington was still as segregated as it had been under Wilson. During the summer of 1919, race riots transformed twenty-six U.S. cities into war zones, where black citizens, many still in uniform, were lynched with impunity and their homes were burned because they dared to organize to demand job opportunities, access to public beaches and parks, an end to discrimination. In response, throughout America, blacks armed themselves for self-defense and retaliation.

ER had decided to remain in town during part of the summer of 1919. Realizing that her traditional departures to Campobello had eased and encouraged her husband's gambols, she also hoped that spending more time with Franklin might bring them closer together. So Eleanor and Franklin remained in Washington throughout June and spent part of July at Hyde Park. FDR then returned to spend some of August alone in Washington. Their time at Hyde Park had not been pleasant. ER's new determination to do things her way led to acrimonious confrontations with her mother-in-law. There was tension between Eleanor and Sara over the children; over food, politics, money; over social attitudes and clothing styles. ER felt insulted and demeaned. Her temper flared and her disposition soured. When she left Sara and Hyde Park for the calm of the Delano family compound at Fairhaven, she was momentarily relieved to be alone again with the children. On 23 July, she wrote FDR: "I feel as though someone has taken a ton of bricks off me and I suppose she feels just the same."

Although she had planned to vacation with the children at Fairhaven for several weeks, she soon changed her mind when race riots consumed Washington. For three days, she endured nerve-racking tension when she failed to hear from Franklin. "You seem to have had pretty bad race riots in Washington," she wrote him. "Have you seen anything of them?" Then, the following day, "No word from you and I am getting very anxious on account of the riots. Do be careful not to be hit by stray bullets." And on the day after that: "Still no letter or telegram from you and I am worried to death. . . . Even if something is wrong why don't you let me know. I'd always rather know than worry. I couldn't sleep at all last night thinking of all the things which might be the matter."

ER was concerned about the riots, and she was suspicious. Was FDR alone? Was he even at home? Had he been shot, wounded, or killed? Or was he with Lucy Mercer, or another?

Their letters (which at the time took only a day to deliver) had crossed. On 22 July, he had written a glib and jaunty note:

> It is surely a rainy time. It has poured ever since I got here. . . .
> This AM I was awakened . . . by a drip, drip, drip and found your bureau afloat, rushed upstairs and found the sun parlor a lake. Worked hard for an hour in my pajamas with bath towels and tooth mugs and saved the house! Westcott will send a man.
> Do hope you had a fairly good trip. . . .
> Kiss the chicks and I miss you so much.

Always unprepared to deal directly with the tensions between his mother and his wife, FDR concluded his letter: "Wasn't it a nice 9 days at Hyde Park?"

Then, on the 23rd, he wrote again: "The riots seem to be about over today, only one man killed last night. Luckily the trouble hasn't spread to R Street and though I have troubled to keep out of harm's way I have heard occasional shots during the evening and night. It has been a nasty episode and I only wish *quicker* action had been taken to stop it." FDR ended this letter by noting: "A letter from Mama this morning. It will amuse you as she says everything is going *very smoothly!*"

The "nasty episode" swamped Washington in terror and bloodshed. One of the most violent episodes of white racism since Reconstruction ravaged the black community for days. Law-enforcement officials and the military virtually ignored the mob violence, when they did not directly exacerbate it. Homes were burned; men, women, and children were beaten.

The actual riot began when two hundred sailors and Marines attempted to find and lynch two released youths accused of "jostling" and insulting the wife of a naval officer. White sailors marched into southwestern Washington and stopped every resident on the street. Women, men, and children returning home from school and work were questioned; every instance of resistance was met with violence. If Josephus Daniels or his assistant, FDR, made any effort to curtail the situation that first night, there is no record of it.

During that night, a black citizen shot and wounded an abusive police officer in self-defense. There were many witnesses and no disagreement as to what happened. But self-defense was an unacceptable breach of race etiquette in Wilson's Washington. The next day, scores of white soldiers and sailors rampaged through the area, pulled women and men off streetcars, beat them senseless and unconscious. The violence went on for hours, and nothing was done to stop it. When the officials of the NAACP petitioned Secretary of the Navy Daniels to restrain the sailors and Marines responsible to his authority, Daniels rebuffed them without explanation; their petitions were simply ignored.

After two more nights of violence, *The Washington Post* headlined: "It was learned that a mobilization of every available serviceman . . . has been ordered for tomorrow evening. . . . The hour of assembly is 9 o'clock and the purpose is a 'clean up' that will cause the events of the last two evenings to pale into insignificance."

This public threat and call to arms, this advertisement for an officially sanctioned lynching bee, was taken seriously. Throughout Washington, black citizens armed themselves for self-defense. Rumors persisted that Howard University's ROTC prepared to distribute arms and ammunition to the attacked black community. For the next two days, attacks on black neighborhoods were resisted, and retaliatory attacks on white neighborhoods were made. Scores of people of both races were wounded and at least ten died. Seven hundred police and four hundred military officers attempted to quell the situation. But a wild mob of over a thousand white civilians stormed a cavalry cordon in an effort to destroy a black residential neighborhood. Even though homes were invaded and destroyed, blacks attempting to defend their property, themselves and their families were arrested, while the white mob rampaged through the night. In prison, those arrested were again beaten. Finally, Secretary of War Newton D. Baker and Josephus Daniels called for self-control and prepared to bring in Marines from Quantico, sailors from two ships anchored in the Potomac, and additional troops from Camp Meade. With two thousand supplementary troops, a serious (though belated) appeal for an end to the assaults, and a driving rain, the riots began to subside.

As the wounded city healed, the NAACP demanded a congressional hearing into the violence and the officially accepted practice of lynching. A. Mitchell Palmer queried the district attorney's office about the "unreasonable" bail and "extreme" sentences demanded for those blacks arrested, but refused to hold hearings. Some black organizations praised the "heroic resistance" of the community, which "defied the point of bayonets, the sting of blackjacks and the hail of bullets in defending themselves" against lynch mobs of white citizens who were never held accountable for their actions. Until people of color were actually protected by the law, and by a system of equal justice, they would have to prepare to defend themselves. One editorialist frankly concluded: "As the police have failed to protect the Negroes of the capital there is but one course open. Let every Negro arm himself and swear to die fighting in defense of his home, his rights and his person. In every place where the law will not protect their lives, Negroes should buy and hoard arms." Although official Washington paid little heed, the Washington race riots of 1919 "gave birth to the new Negro," and reignited the civil-rights crusade abandoned so quickly after Reconstruction.

A decade later, ER began to campaign for an enforceable antilynch law (which never passed), and an end to discrimination, prejudice, and segregation. But during the summer of 1919, she was concerned exclusively about her husband's safety and whereabouts. On that score, his letters were not reassuring. His plans were vague, his hours of leisure many. There were no details to indicate precisely how or with whom they were spent: "I don't know whether I shall be here Sunday or not. I have given up Norfolk. . . . I *may* go to Harrisburg to make a speech Sat. night and come back here Sunday. I long to have you back—very lonely, also hot again!"

ER planned to join him that Monday. FDR would meet the train, and they were to dine at Chevy Chase. But the party at Chevy Chase, which began as a celebratory reunion, turned into an unacceptable spree. FDR flirted and danced with others—including, evidently, Lucy Mercer—and his attentions seemed altogether elsewhere. ER left the party, insisting that FDR continue to enjoy himself. But she had forgotten her key. This was the final public episode in the Lucy Mercer story that over time gave Alice Roosevelt Longworth such pleasure in the telling. When FDR returned home toward dawn with his cousins Irene and Warren Delano Robbins, ER had been waiting, asleep, on the doormat for almost six hours. Years later, in *You Learn by Living,* ER wrote that she had made FDR "feel guilty by the mere fact of having waited" for her gay blade to come home.

However much this display might have gratified her momentarily, ER understood that she needed to care less about her husband's activities and more about her own. Neither his joy nor his guilt could satisfy her own increasing longing for some interests and some community of her own. She longed for new friends to whom she could turn for fun, companionship, diversion; confidantes with whom she could talk and share her life. All the relationships in her life were in disarray.

As ER contemplated the changed circumstances of her life, she felt a great empty space. Above all, she wanted serious work of her own. She wanted, in fact, to participate in the very aspects of life traditionally denied to women—who were, after all, supposed to find total satisfaction in their husbands and homes and the unfolding lives of their children. From 1905 to 1919, ER had imagined that she might be satisfied by her efforts to fulfill her husband's needs and promote the happiness of his hearth. Immediately after her marriage, she withdrew from her interests and many of her friends, and confided only in her baby nurse, Blanche Spring. Of that period, she wrote: "I do not remember having any other friends." "My family filled my life."

For fifteen years, she kept up with only two friends, her childhood companions Isabella Selmes and Bob Ferguson. Although they lived in New Mexico and she saw them infrequently, correspondence had, beginning with her father, "meant much" to ER: "I would often have been lonely in my life if it had not been for letters. I have always had many people about me but few close friends."

As FDR's interests expanded and included new friends concerned primarily with his well-being, his happiness, and his future, ER felt increasingly lonely and alone. While she cared for the moods and the needs of others, there was nobody in her life who cared very much about her.

She had been a model Washington wife, and she was proud of her "feats of endurance." Official trips built up her stamina, revealed many hidden reservoirs of strength and perseverance. She learned that she could be tired and go right on with her obligations. "I could never say in the morning 'I have a headache and cannot do thus and so.' Headache or no headache, thus and so had to be done, and no time could be wasted. I could not be a burden and add any care to a man who had plenty of official things to do."

During the summer and autumn of 1919, ER addressed the depth of her discontent and acknowledged her confusion. In September, she returned to Hyde Park, still unsettled in her feelings toward FDR. When he left for a short trip, she wrote: "I'm glad you enjoyed your holiday dear. & I wish we did not lead such a hectic life, a little prolonged quiet might bring us altogether & yet it might do just the opposite! I really don't know what I want or think about anything anymore!"

But she increasingly resented FDR's refusal to leave his mother's homes. As she felt more estranged from him, she grew to hate his childhood environs, his mother's daily presence, her presumptuous dominance. On 3 October, ER wrote from Hyde Park: "Mama and I have had a bad time. I should be ashamed of myself but I'm not." For over fifteen years, ER had hoped that by being the perfect wife and the perfect daughter-in-law she might win her mother-in-law's acceptance and approval, perhaps even a corner of her heart. Now, no matter how hard she tried, it felt a bottomless well of vain effort.

Even with her children she was eclipsed by SDR, entrapped by conventions, and regularly confronted by Sara's opposition and frank subversion. ER's efforts at maternal discipline and concerned love were no match for her mother-in-law's imaginative largesse and unlimited bounty. Granny pampered the children with generous gifts that devoured parental authority. Over time, SDR would replace a car smashed by an errant college boy while driving drunk, just as swiftly as she had replaced toys broken by hapless toddlers. She took two of her grandchildren on the European grand tour that ER herself had longed to make with them, and in many other ways came between Eleanor and her children. If ER complained, she was made to seem a cold, uncaring ogre.

Sara Delano Roosevelt expected her daughter-in-law to transcend it all, carry on with a cheerful demeanor: for the children, for the family, for the future. ER was not supposed to have a life of her own. With her emotional life discounted, ER felt again an outsider with no safe space for her feelings. ER and her mother-in-law quarreled; they grew cold and distant; they hurt each other.

After every argument, every scene, ER felt remorse, and more estranged. On 6 October, she wrote a letter of apology:

> I know, Mummy dear, I made you feel most unhappy the other day and I am so sorry I lost my temper and said such fool things for of course as you know I love Franklin and the children very dearly and I am deeply devoted to you. I have, however, allowed myself to be annoyed by little things which of course one should never do and I had no right to hurt you as I know I did and am truly sorry and hope you will forgive me.

On 11 October 1919, ER, alone on her birthday, wrote in her journal, "I am 35. Margaret and Hall sent me a book. Mama and Tissie and Franklin wired." Her birthday seemed no particular cause for celebration that year. She was in Washington. SDR was in Hyde Park. FDR was on his way to a hunting trip in New Brunswick with his friends. There was as yet no particular friend of her own that she might have dined with, no circle of friends who might have surprised her with a cake.

That October, however, ER made her first contact with "women's organizations interested in improving working conditions for women." From 28 October to 5 November, representatives from nineteen nations attended the International Congress of Working Women in Washington, chaired and largely financed by Margaret Dreier Robins, president of the Women's Trade Union League, which existed above all to promote the organization of women into unions. Because so many delegates could not speak English, ER and other Washington wives who spoke several languages volunteered their services. "I liked all the women very much indeed, but I had no idea how much more I was going to see of them in the future."

At the height of the Red Scare of 1919, ER joined the activist labor women who were to become her lifelong friends and allies. The U.S. delegation included union activists Rose Schneiderman, Leonora O'Reilly, Maud O'Farrell Swartz, Mary Anderson, Fannia Cohn, Julia O'Connor, Lois Rantoul, representatives of the Women's Trade Union League, International Ladies' Garment Workers' Union, Telephone Operators, the waitresses' union, various teachers' unions, boot and shoe workers, the Federal Employees Union, and many other groups then assailed as subversive, dangerous, un-American.

Margaret Dreier Robins and her husband, Raymond Robins, were progressive Republicans. Passionate about peace, full employment, union protection, and economic security for all, the Robinses had been quickly added to the long lists of subversives being compiled by John Edgar Hoover, a new bureau chief in Wilson's Justice Department. Like ER, Margaret Dreier Robins was independently wealthy, and used her inheritance to support the causes she believed in: "I never earned a dollar of it and I recognize that I hold it in trust."

Margaret Dreier Robins opened the First International Congress of Working Women in 1919 with an angry denunciation of the Treaty of Versailles, for *feminist* reasons: "Women had no direct share in the terms of the Peace Treaty. It's a man-made peace. Women have had no direct share in the labor platform with its emphasis on the protection of women in industry rather than its emphasis on the participation of women in plans to protect themselves which is significant of the attitude of men, even in the labor movement, toward women."

The Labor Platform that she now called for demanded a universal eight-hour day for workingwomen, and laws guaranteeing maternity benefits, before, during, and after childbirth. The Congress heard a petition from the two million "Negro Women Laborers of the U.S." who were not represented, and asked for cooperation "in organizing the Negro women workers of the U.S. into unions, that they may have a share in bringing about industrial democracy and social order in the world."

ER was impressed by the women who gathered for this first International Congress of Working Women. She was interested in their ideas, and invited the U.S. delegation and several others to her home for lunch. From that moment on, she supported their efforts. Over the years, she sought their advice on national policies. But in 1919, she might have been as intrigued by the unusual marital partnership between Margaret Dreier Robins and her husband as she was by her vision. Married the same year as ER, the Robinses had exchanged unusual vows: They promised each other independence and unity, the "unhampered freedom to serve." They might work together or separately, but each agreed "to work untrammeled for the growing good of the world."

Philanthropists and activists, they were long identified with the peace movement, unionism, women's rights, the Chicago settlement-house movement, and TR's Progressive Party. In 1915, Theodore Roosevelt had written to Raymond Robins that his friendship was a particular "honor of which all my life I shall be proud." A businessman and an adventurer, Robins was both practical idealist and romantic mystic. Leonard Woolf, who posthumously published Robins's sister's celebration of his adventurous years in Alaska (Elizabeth Robins's *Raymond and I*), called him a quixotic "crusader on behalf of any peoples or persons whom he thought to be despised, downtrodden, or persecuted." But in the United States in 1919, he was attacked as a Bolshevik.

He was, after all, the most outspoken opponent of the Allied Intervention against Russia. In 1917, as head of the Red Cross Commission to revolutionary Russia, Robins had established a working relationship with Lenin and counseled continued commercial relations with the new government. He argued that it was folly to attempt to destroy Bolshevism by starving the Russian people. He criticized the blockade, and when

Wilson decided, in July 1919, to join Britain, France, and Japan in the counterrevolutionary military intervention, Robins returned to the United States to protest.

At the same time, on 10 July, Wilson presented the Treaty of Versailles and his League proposals to the Senate. Ignoring all the imperial deals, border disputes, and military activities in Europe, Wilson's rhetoric focused entirely on the League, a future of democracy and self-determination: "Dare we reject it and break the heart of the world?"

For Robins, and for the thirty-nine Senate "irreconcilables" led by William E. Borah, Henry Cabot Lodge, and others particularly faithful to Theodore Roosevelt, the League now meant only entangling alliances and deadly military adventures that would devour capital and inhibit the growth of business and international commerce.

League opponents differed in tactics. Borah, an absolute "irreconcilable," opposed the League absolutely. Lodge was willing to compromise: To parallel Wilson's Fourteen Points, he introduced fourteen amendments to protect America's national sovereignty, and a fifteenth that called for the independence of Ireland.

Eleanor Roosevelt's association with her new friends put her at odds with the administration her husband served. Although ER hoped that the United States would enter the League, she agreed with the need for Lodge's amendments, and hoped particularly that Congress would retain the right to declare war anywhere and at all times.

ER never quite warmed to Woodrow Wilson. He did not evoke warmth particularly. He was rude to individuals, contemptuous of entire groups, and never notably interested in seeing or hearing very much around him. She judged him harshly for his lack of concern for people, especially young people, and his failure to read the newspapers, a fact about which he boasted. In Europe, she regretted that even on official inspection tours of hospitals and other centers of human interest he seemed uninterested: "I can't say the President looked as though he saw much!" Still, she agreed with his rhetoric concerning the League of Nations: a forum for negotiation, arbitration, and peace was "the only hope for mankind."

But almost immediately on their return from Europe, the Roosevelts were perceived as allied with Wilson's enemies. Wilson distrusted

Eleanor and Franklin Roosevelt; and he evidently told Josephus Daniels that he "hated" FDR. Above all, he despised the Roosevelt friendship with Sir Edward Grey, Britain's former foreign secretary who had returned to the United States to persuade Wilson to accept Lodge's amendments. Britain favored U.S. participation in the League on any terms.

Grey had been an intimate friend of Theodore Roosevelt, and a family friend for many years. Now old and almost blind, he had agreed to go to Washington because he believed Wilson would see him; talk with him. He had, after all, long supported the idea of a League of Nations. He had no idea, nor did anybody else, just how infirm, peevish, distrustful Wilson had become, or how intransigent. Wilson refused even to see him.

ER invited Sir Edward to dinner on several occasions. She also invited Alice Longworth, who had dedicated herself to Wilson's destruction. Alice Roosevelt Longworth had become maniacal in her hatred of Wilson and the League. She blamed him for her father's sudden death, and fervently believed that the Rough Rider would have been re-elected president in 1920. She kept a doll representing Wilson into which she regularly stuck pins. She met his train at Union Station and stood anonymously on the curbstone, fingers crossed, making the "sign of the evil eye," incanting over and over: "A murrain on him! A murrain on him!" Wilson's opponents were known as the "Battalion of Death," and she was their acknowledged "Colonel of Death." Daily, she and Ruth Hanna McCormick watched the Senate debates until 3:00 A.M. and returned at ten that same morning to cheer the most insistent irreconcilables: Ruth's husband, Medill, and her friend William Borah. But she continued to dine with Cousin Eleanor and Franklin, and was at their home to entertain Sir Edward Grey.

Moreover, ER invited Grey not only for occasional dinners but also for Christmas, an intimate family affair attended only by the Howes and their children and Sara Delano Roosevelt. The Wilsons were evidently appalled.

His mission a failure, Grey returned to London in January 1920 and wrote a letter to the London *Times* to state that in his opinion the Lodge amendments were insignificant. Tensions escalated; Wilson refused to negotiate, even after Lodge indicated that he would compromise further. The Senate refused to ratify the treaty; Wilson's diplomacy ended in disaster and ER would spend over a decade in an ardent campaign to promote America's entrance into the League and the World Court.

~

AS ER'S MOST TUMULTUOUS YEAR ENDED, SHE CAST ABOUT for a new way to be. She acknowledged her loneliness and yearning for change, looked for new alliances and new work to do. There seemed at first nobody she could turn to for advice or encouragement. Her godmother and former confidante Cousin Susie Parish was increasingly incapacitated by profound psychological maladies. ER was disturbed by her self-indulgence and distressed by her reactionary political and social views.

ER had been concerned about Cousin Susie for years. Although she was devoted to her godmother, and visited her whenever she was in New York, she confided to Isabella that "the root of all her trouble" was her addiction to prescription drugs, pain killers and antidepressants—laudanum, Eudunal, and "lately Veronal," which "undermined her health and I think her character." ER was also convinced that another part of her problem was that she never "had to consider anyone but herself." After spending "three months with Dr. Riggs [in Stockbridge]," Cousin Susie "returned to taking no interest in life, dreading the lightest care or even the thought of seeing a friend. The root of it all is that she cares for no one sufficiently to forget herself. . . . She was a spoiled child and a spoiled woman and never was forced to sink her own feelings in anyone else's good."

The Delano women, who had once seemed to ER models of generosity and familial love, now seemed to her arrogant and overbearing. One evening, after dinner with her mother-in-law and her sisters, Aunt Dora and Aunt Kassie, ER wrote Franklin: "They all in their serene assurance and absolute judgments on people and affairs going on in the world, make me want to squirm and turn bolshevik."

Her maternal aunts were also unavailable. Aunt Tissie, who wrote with frequent concern, lived largely in England; Aunt Maude was preoccupied with David Gray, her new husband, and her new home in

Portland, Maine. Aunt Pussie, always mercurial and emotionally over-wrought, had lived for some time in California, but had recently divorced her husband, Forbes Morgan, a nephew of J. P. Morgan, and returned to New York. But on 4 February 1920, she perished with her two young daughters, Barbara (fourteen) and Ellen (ten), in a mysterious and tragic fire that sent billows of smoke throughout her Greenwich Village car-riage house on 9th Street. Trapped in an upstairs bedroom, they were overcome by the smoke while neighbors tried desperately but unsuc-cessfully to rouse the fire department.

This final tragedy in the life of Edith Livingston Ludlow Hall Mor-gan, thought by many to be the model for Edith Wharton's complex and doomed Lily Bart in her 1905 novel, *The House of Mirth,* added another jolt to the course of ER's life during the first months of 1920. Alone in New York, then enveloped by one of the worst blizzards in the city's history, ER made all the funeral arrangements: "It was one of those horrors I can hardly bear to think of. . . . To this day I cannot bear any funeral parlor."

New York was at a standstill. In the solitude of her grim errands, as she walked back and forth across Central Park to complete the details, ER mourned the woman who had once "called out my deepest admi-ration and devotion." Aunt Pussie was the first to take ER to the theatre and the opera; she introduced her to the mysteries of music, the beauty and rhythm of poetry. Aunt Pussie and Aunt Maude, who was delayed by the blizzard on her journey from Maine, were ER's "early loves and few women since have seemed to me to surpass them in beauty and charm." But Pussie had never been dependable in her affections: Flam-boyantly generous, she could be cruel and petty. Her insults had dev-astated the young ER, and the harsh, careless way she told her about her father's life had been unforgivable. Now, however, ER concentrated on what she might have been. Women's abilities were never encouraged or much valued in Pussie's world; and ER mourned especially a creative life misspent: "Given greater discipline, the drive of necessity and wider opportunities, I believe that Pussie might have been an artist of real quality."

ER wrote Isabella Ferguson: "If it were not for the horror, I would feel sure that Pussie was happier than she's ever been here. She could not meet an everyday existence, [although] she had some lovely qualities and was always groping for spiritual thoughts. Forbes . . . had a deep affection for her and loved the children and often went to see them but no one could live with her. Isn't it a strange world, tragedies on every side in life and death and yet so much kindness, goodness and helpfulness that one knows it must all be for some worthwhile end."

The three bodies were buried at Tivoli, in the family vault, "where the summer before, we had laid my grandmother. I could not help being devoutly thankful that my grandmother was dead. One more tragedy in her life had been avoided."

During this ordeal, ER realized consciously for the first time in her adult life how much she needed to feel in charge, and she allowed herself to appreciate the range of her own managerial skills. Pussie's husband and her entire family welcomed her support and advice, and were grateful for her presence and direction: "It is a curious thing in human experience, but to live through a period of stress and sorrow with other human beings creates a bond which nothing seems able to break. . . . Happiness will not lead you to feel that your presence is always welcome should an emergency arise, but a period of stress lived through together will give you this assurance." With her Aunt Maude, Forbes Morgan, and William Forbes Morgan, Jr., who had been at boarding school, ER consciously experienced that assurance, and concluded that it was above all "the sense of being really needed and wanted which gives us the greatest satisfaction and creates the most lasting bond."

Months later, as ER prepared to leave Washington and the official chores of her role as wife to the Assistant Secretary of the Navy, as she packed to leave R Street and eight years of obligations and social responsibility, she understood how much she had missed that sense of being needed and wanted. Determined to embark on a new life, she broke no ties, created no public disturbances. The Roosevelt hearth seemed steady and united, a partnership of trust and mutual regard. Few recognized that its survival depended on shared political enthusiasms, and the most painfully derived understanding and respect.

11. The Campaign of 1920 and Louis Howe

ELEANOR ROOSEVELT NEVER WROTE THE TRUTH ABOUT her heart. As she erased Lucy Mercer, as she denied her husband's infidelities, so she obscured her own emotional being from the public record. Regarding her relationship with her husband after 1919, we have only her deeds—as a politician, and as a politician's primary and most devoted partner.

Ironically, during the years of her own deepest pain, ER was called upon to rally behind her husband as never before: to encourage him and support him during a series of ugly political scandals, and to stand beside him on his political rounds as Democratic vice-presidential candidate during the campaign of 1920.

Tensions over the scandals began in February 1920 when FDR shocked and dismayed Josephus Daniels by making a boastful, self-serving, and bizarre speech at the Brooklyn Academy of Music to support partisan charges against the navy, and Daniels particularly. Admiral William Sims, formerly commander of the U.S. naval forces in Europe, had returned from London to resume the presidency of the Naval War College in Newport, and began vituperative attacks against Daniels—who had prevented Sims from accepting the title of honorary sea lord from the British Admiralty. In retaliation, Sims attacked Daniels's medal and awards policies, his wartime judgment, and his early pacifistic tendencies. Republicans, eager to discredit Wilson, his entire administration, and all Democrats called for a Senate investigation into the Sims charges, especially his accusation that Daniels's inaction prolonged the war by four months, thereby causing the Allies to lose "2,500,000 tons of shipping, 500,000 lives, and $15,000,000."

Before an audience of fifteen hundred, FDR confirmed Sims's charges, and took for himself all the credit for whatever action the navy had initiated: "Two months after the war was declared, I saw that the Navy was still unprepared and I spent $40,000 for guns before Congress gave me or anyone permission to spend the money." FDR boasted further that he had "committed enough illegal acts" to be impeached and jailed had he made "wrong guesses." He even bragged that he personally chose Sims for the London post.

Although there is no record of ER's reaction to her husband's indiscretion, or to his personal disloyalty toward his boss, Livy Davis, FDR's own "jolly boy," was astonished: "What in the world is the matter with you for telling the public that you in your tenure of office committed enough illegal acts to keep you in jail for 900 years?"

Perhaps his motivations for this astounding speech were political. It was an election year, and his name was being batted about for senator; for governor; for vice-president. Presumably he intended to distance himself from Wilson and Daniels and appear as always independent, fearless, and free. Besides, he was under a lot of pressure and not in the best of health, having suffered a seemingly endless array of ailments during this period: throat infections and tonsilitis, pneumonia, "the grippe," gastrointestinal upsets, and influenza. Josephus Daniels used to say that if there were a mean bug running about Washington it would just automatically lodge in FDR's overworked body. Possibly he was depressed, a condition he never acknowledged except by seeking out still more work and distraction. There certainly were reasons for depression—in addition to Lucy Mercer, FDR was in deep financial distress. His mother had sent him a significant check for his birthday, and his gratitude was profound:

> You are not only an angel which I always knew, but the kind which comes at the critical moment in life! For the question was not one of paying Dr. Mitchell for removing James' insides [ap-

pendix], the Dr. can wait, I know he is or must be rich, but of paying the gas man and the butcher lest the infants starve to death, and your cheque which is much too much of a Birthday present will do that. It is so dear of you.

By the time he wrote that letter to his mother, on 11 February, he could report that "the office is less busy, the Sims episode being quiet for the moment and of less public interest as time goes on."

Whatever his motives, Roosevelt had played a dangerous game. It could not have served him politically to embarrass Daniels; public insubordination looks too much like treachery—and Daniels might have fired and disgraced him. As mysterious as FDR's motivations for betrayal is the history of Daniels's extraordinary generosity and paternal protectiveness toward his assistant. FDR retracted his statements, and supported Daniels with such vigor during the hearings, which lasted from March to May, that the committee chose not to have him testify. Still, Sims and his allies were not through with Daniels, or FDR. Other charges and hearings regarding immorality in the navy were under way—relating to activities FDR himself had officially authorized.

The Newport sex scandal involved "the most extensive systematic persecution" of homosexual men in American history. Although the intensity of FDR's involvement in the "clean-up" of Newport remains unclear, he signed the order that gave a team of undercover agents, agents provocateurs, and entrapment volunteers authority to go "to the limit." And he put the team directly under the authority of his personal office. When the facts emerged, he denied all responsibility for them.

World War I had transformed Newport, society's favorite resort. By 1917 it was the home of a major naval training center, and there were more than twenty-five thousand sailors in town. Town officials and Josephus Daniels protested the kind of vice associated with military centers, and every effort was made to end the drug traffic in cocaine, to close the houses of "ill fame," and to end all access to liquor. Daniels's introduction of Navy Prohibition was particularly effective. But access to prostitutes and reports of widespread homosexuality continued. Since consenting adults, and young sailors simply walking with their "buddies" two by two, were not breaking any particular law, and did what they did in private, a team of investigators decided to entrap sailors. It was a sleazy business, and the investigators used were young sailors who volunteered. They would seduce a suspect, date him, and to collect evidence go as far as necessary, or "to the limit." In the process, they entrapped a popular local chaplain, the Reverend Samuel Nash Kent. He denied all allegations against him, blew the whistle on the naval entrapment procedures, and was acquitted in two separate trials, where his bishop, fellow clerics, and scores of local dignitaries served as character witnesses.

Feelings about homosexuality in many Newport circles, and indeed throughout the navy, were still unsettled at this time. Drag shows, for example, were popular, and nobody had protested them. Indeed, ER referred to the entertainment on navy ships during her European voyage home in 1919, when they traveled with the president's party. It was the only time she saw anything of President Wilson's "understanding of young people," and she was impressed: When President Wilson "came down under pressure" to watch the drag show, he "received only perfunctory applause" when he entered and took a seat on the aisle directly in front of the ship's captain, Edward McCauley.

> At the end of one of the popular songs, the "ladies" of the chorus attired in pink tulle and pink socks in spite of hairy legs, arms and chests, still most coy, ran down into the audience. One boy, carried away by the spirit of the play apparently, as he passed the President chucked him genially under the chin. I thought Captain McCauley would have apoplexy and everyone held his breath. You almost heard the unspoken order: "Put him in irons on bread and water." When it was over and the President's party had retired, Captain McCauley received a message from the President to the effect that he hoped the young man would receive no punishment.

Similarly, Admiral Sims enjoyed the frequent drag shows navy personnel put on in Newport. After a thoroughly entertaining performance of *Jack and the Beanstalk,* in June 1919, Sims wrote: "I have never in my life seen a prettier 'girl' than 'Princess Mary.' She is the daintiest little thing I ever laid eyes on."

But at the same time, the sailors of Newport were being entrapped by a squad of sex-hunters created and trained by a physician, Dr. Erastus Hudson, and a former detective, Ervin Arnold, who claimed to be able to tell a homosexual just by looking at him. Evidently impressed by their diligence, FDR, in March, went to Attorney General A. Mitchell Palmer to have the Justice Department begin "a most searching and rigid investigation" to uproot the "conditions of vice and depravity" that existed in Newport. Palmer refused. He could not afford to take any of his investigators away from his more urgent anticommunist crusade. In May, FDR turned to Naval Intelligence, which seemed less than interested. On 11 June 1919, he took it upon himself: The entire secret sleuthing detail, its funds and personnel, was hidden in an undercover department called simply "Section A, Office of Assistant Secretary of the Navy."

In January 1920, the publicity that surrounded Reverend Kent's second acquittal resulted in blistering attacks against Daniels and Roosevelt. Local newspapers and a committee of Newport clergy were outraged. The clergy petitioned Woodrow Wilson for an immediate investigation, and included their understanding of the facts and the "vicious methods employed by the Navy Department." Under the supervision of Dr. Hudson and Ervin Arnold, a team of dozens of sailors were "instructed" in the details "of a nameless vice and sent through the community to practice the same . . . and in particular to entrap certain designated individuals." These activities persisted for months, despite the

> strong and continued protests [from many of the most] prominent citizens of Rhode Island. . . .
>
> It must be evident to every thoughtful mind, that the use of such vile methods cannot fail to undermine the character and ruin the morals of the unfortunate youths detailed for this duty, render no citizen of the community safe from suspicion and calumny, bring

the city into unwarranted reproach, shake the faith of the people in the wisdom and integrity of the naval administration.

Wilson, incapacitated by his stroke, had the petition sent to Daniels, who assigned Admiral Herbert O. Dunn to head the naval board of inquiry. It quickly became common knowledge that Dunn and FDR were personal friends: They had vacationed together in the Azores in 1918, and FDR had helped to secure an Annapolis appointment for Dunn's nephew.

FDR appeared before the Dunn Board in May. Arrogant in manner and dismissive in tone, FDR acknowledged that he had signed the order to create Section A on 11 June 1919. But he knew nothing of the details of its operations. Several times during that summer, Dr. Hudson (Lieutenant, USN) had reported to him that "the investigation was proceeding very satisfactorily." But he knew nothing else, and asked for no further information. Why did he not ask "what methods" were used?

"Because I was interested merely in getting results. . . ."

"Mr. Roosevelt, would you sanction the method of having enlisted men in the Navy submit their bodies to unnatural vices to obtain evidence?"

"As a matter of information, of course, no."

And had he known what was going on, he would have stopped it. But, the investigator asked him, how did he suppose evidence for sodomy "could be obtained?"

"As a lawyer, I had no idea. That is not within the average lawyer's education."

"Did you realize as a lawyer or as a man of intelligence that the investigation of such matters, very often has led to improper actions. . . ."

"I never had such an idea. Never entered my head. . . ."

"How did you think evidence of these things could be obtained?"

"I didn't think. If I had I would have supposed they had someone under the bed or looking over the transom."

In October, the Dunn Board presented its findings. It censured the "use of immoral methods," acknowledged that it had been "unfortunate and ill-advised" that FDR had "either directed or permitted the use of enlisted personnel to investigate perversion," and condemned Hudson, Arnold, and several others for "extremely bad judgment." No disciplinary action was recommended, FDR and Daniels were exonerated, and the enlisted investigators were immune from prosecution.

Admiral Sims—still seeking to discredit Daniels—was outraged, the clergy were outraged, the Newport press claimed a cover-up and called for a full and fair investigation by the U.S. Senate Committee on Naval Affairs. Although the Dunn Board hearings were held throughout the campaign, and the report issued less than a month before the election of 1920, the matter was never publicly discussed outside Newport and received no national news coverage. The Senate investigation did not begin until after the election. Therefore, when FDR went to the Democratic convention in June 1920, he was under no particular cloud.

~

FDR WENT TO THE CONVENTION IN SAN FRANCISCO ALONE. ER did not accompany him. With the war's end, Washington wives, like other women workers who had served the country and the administration so well, were rendered jobless and simply sent home. ER's canteens closed and her Red Cross work subsided, her last effort being "to get restrooms for the girls established in the [Navy Department] with a woman doctor in charge!" Although she continued to raise money for several causes that interested her, notably the Women's [Theodore] Roosevelt Memorial Association, for the first time in years she was without significant public activity and her future looked empty. She complained to Isabella: "Sometimes I wish I could disappear and lead a hermit's life for a year. . . ." But what she really wanted was to be invited into the political game. At San Francisco, ER had no task. No service was asked of her; and she was not encouraged to attend. She took the children to Campobello, while FDR went to the convention to second the nomination of New York's Governor Alfred E. Smith.

Initially there were three major contenders: Al Smith represented the progressives who considered reform the best guarantee against violent revolution. A. Mitchell Palmer represented the worst excesses of bigotry and reaction. William Gibbs McAdoo, Woodrow Wilson's son-in-law, was committed primarily to the League of Nations and was on all other issues profoundly vague. McAdoo was not a progressive in the manner of Smith: He was supported by and associated with the Ku Klux Klan. For forty-three ballots, the convention was deadlocked over Smith, "Ku Ku" McAdoo, and Palmer.

The Democrats were in disarray. They were regionally, ideologically, and personally divided on virtually all major issues having to do with the future direction of the party and the country. On the forty-fourth ballot, exhausted and eager to be done with it, the convention chose a relatively unknown reform governor of Ohio, James M. Cox, as their compromise candidate. Not identified with Wilson, and not known to be committed to the League of Nations, he was nevertheless intent on party harmony and suggested a Wilsonian loyalist for his running mate: Franklin Delano Roosevelt.

Earlier, FDR had not only stirred the convention with his rousing speech for Smith, he had won the approval of all Wilsonians with his display of athletic bravura during the only exciting moment of the tedious proceedings. At the opening of the convention, a tribute to Wilson and the League was followed by the unveiling of a large oil portrait of their president. This touched off a jubilant demonstration. State after state marched with wild convention fanfare, their banners flying high, behind Wilson's portrait. But the New York delegation, controlled by Tammany boss Charles Murphy, refused to join the parade. Furious, FDR leaped for the New York State banner. Murphy held it firm. They struggled until, with one final wrench, FDR lifted that banner proudly, amid great cheers, and led New Yorkers into the line of march.

On 3 July ER wrote that his heroics troubled her, and she worried about Tammany's opposition: "Mama is very proud of your recovering the state standard from them! I have a feeling you enjoyed it but won't they be very much against you in the state convention?" They were against him. But Cox had diplomatically consulted Murphy on Roosevelt's nomination. Flattered, Murphy replied that he despised FDR but would support anybody Cox wanted.

ER learned of FDR's unexpected victory when she received a telegram from his proud boss, Josephus Daniels: "IT WOULD HAVE DONE YOUR HEART GOOD TO HAVE SEEN THE SPONTANEOUS AND ENTHU-

SIASTIC TRIBUTE PAID WHEN FRANKLIN WAS NOMINATED UNANIMOUSLY
FOR VICE-PRESIDENT TODAY." FDR's achievement may have been less
a surprise to ER than the expression of Daniels's joy and support for
his assistant, which overcame months of antagonism between the two
men. ER's own initial response to her husband's nomination to the vice-
presidency was guarded and desultory: "I was glad for my husband,
but it never occurred to me to be much excited." She intended to carry
on her own life, and her children's, calmly, no matter how intense the
political climate might become. For the moment, she felt an outsider,
as if watching a new and interesting game being played while she was
left to gaze silently behind a glass partition. Until she was welcomed
into the political scene, ER "felt detached and objective, as though I
were looking at someone else's life."

Generally, ER agreed with FDR's campaign emphases on internationalism and progressivism:

> Some people have been saying of late: "We are tired of progress,
> we want to go back to where we were before . . . ; to restore "nor-
> mal" conditions. They are wrong. . . . We can never go back. . . .
> In this faith I am strengthened by the firm belief that the women
> of this nation, now about to receive the National franchise, will
> throw their weight into the scale of progress. . . . We cannot anchor
> our ship of state in this world tempest. . . . We must go forward
> or flounder. America's opportunity is at hand. We can lead the
> world by a great example. . . . The Democratic program . . . is a
> plan of hope. . . . We oppose money in politics, we oppose the
> private control of national finances . . . the treatment of human
> beings as commodities . . . the saloon-bossed city . . . [and] we
> oppose starvation wages. . . .

As FDR delivered his acceptance speech to a crowd of more than
eight thousand people from the front porch of his mother's Hyde Park
home, ER sat on the balustrade looking intent and involved. Years later,
her predominant memory about FDR's debut as a national political
candidate was a feeling of sympathy for her mother-in-law. It was the
first political rally held on SDR's lawn: That moment ended an era.

Throughout her life, Sara Delano Roosevelt had protected the sanctity and privacy of her home. She had invited few guests: "The friends were chosen with great discrimination and invitations were never lightly given." When ER saw that "lawn being trampled by hordes of people," her admiration for SDR's remarkable adjustment was boundless.

ER wrote nothing of her own adjustment, or of her feelings during the first weeks of the campaign. Her chores were to take James, now twelve, to Groton; close the house in Washington; pack and unpack; settle and rearrange. Women's work. And not very satisfying.

Occasionally she gave interviews to the press. Brought up a staunch Republican, she told the Poughkeepsie *Eagle News,* she was now a convinced Democrat, "for I believe they are the most progressive. The Republicans are,—well they are more conservative, you know, and we can't be too conservative and accomplish things." She was committed to the League of Nations because she believed it was "the only way that we can prevent war," but opposed giving up the constitutional mandate that Congress declares war. She hoped the League of Nations would be adopted with that reservation. If she was disappointed that the Democrats did not do more to encourage the new women voters, she said nothing to criticize her husband's party.

~

WOMEN WERE TO VOTE NATIONALLY FOR THE FIRST TIME IN the 1920 presidential election, but their hard-won suffrage victory was greeted with minimal enthusiasm within the Democratic Party. Although 299 women attended as delegates or alternates (only twenty-two women attended in such positions in 1916), no particular effort was made to include them in the more significant convention proceedings. The Republican Party, for so many more years the party that supported suffrage, was still the party that vigorously courted the women's vote.

On 1 October, Harding held a day for suffragists, "Respectable Women's Day," and invited an extraordinary range of women: Corinne Roosevelt Robinson and Alice Roosevelt Longworth, of course; and the wives of several progressive governors, senators, and officials—most notably Cornelia Bryce (Mrs. Gifford) Pinchot. But he also invited socialist economist Florence Kelley, journalist Mary Roberts Rinehart, and Esther Everett Lape, who was associated with the Women's Trade Union League, was one of the founders of the League of Women Voters, and was soon to become ER's closest friend.

The Republican women were angry that the Democrats had adopted twelve of the fifteen planks the League of Women Voters had introduced, while the Republicans had adopted only five. After considerable pressure by such Republican feminists as Margaret Dreier Robins (who was a member of the Women's Division of the Republican National Executive Committee), Harriet Upton, and Cornelia Bryce Pinchot, Harding made amends: He sponsored another day to woo progressive supporters, especially the women. During "Social Justice Day," he called for equal pay for equal work, an eight-hour day, the end of child labor, prevention of lynching, maternity and infancy protection, an extended Children's Bureau, appointment of women to state and federal employment boards, a minimum wage, national health-care programs, and the creation of a department of social justice. The women were astounded. Harding had adopted virtually the entire program of the League of Women Voters. As a result, the vast majority of progressive women who voted in 1920 voted for Harding.

Still, the women's vote was up for grabs, state by state. When the National American Woman Suffrage Association created the National League of Women Voters in 1919, their intention was to be nonpartisan, and to support those candidates, regardless of party, who promised further reform. Carrie Chapman Catt wanted to make it clear: The League was not a woman's party intent on sex segregation. Nor was it "a parlor uplift movement." Women intended, she declared, to join parties, to work within parties, to claim and achieve power "in the fight for women's progress." "If the League of Women Voters hasn't the power and the vision to see what is coming, and what ought to come, and to be five years ahead of the political parties, then our work is of no value."

When ER personally entered the political fray, she cast about for her own place and carefully considered the divisions within the suffrage movement. Unlike Carrie Chapman Catt and the women of the League, the women of the National Woman's Party predicted the betrayal of women in male-dominated parties. By 1925, Anne Martin, the founding

chair of the National Woman's Party and the first woman to run for
the Senate (as an Independent from Nevada in 1918), concluded that
Catt's advice to women to join the majority parties "sounded the doom
of feminism" for decades. Women needed, Martin argued, a party of
their own—a party that would select and nourish and train women for
office. She was supported by one of the most generous feminist philanthropists, Alva Erskine Smith Vanderbilt Belmont. As president of the
National Woman's Party, she considered membership in the old parties
an "indignity." "I do not want to see any woman in the Senate as a
Republican or a Democrat." The man-made world would not be re-
constructed through man-made parties. Only women, she and her allies
believed, could redeem the world.

Although ER was unimpressed by the Democrats' efforts toward
women, and was not fooled by Harding's rhetoric, she was never a
separatist, and soon gravitated to the activists of the League of Women
Voters. Over time ER became a Democratic Party loyalist, but she was
disappointed by the run of politicians she knew in 1920. "I feel rather
sad about politics," she wrote Isabella, "there are so many who are out
for themselves and not for the good of the country in both parties and
conditions are so unsettled that we need a really fine leader." Initially,
she had hoped that Herbert Hoover would declare himself a Democrat.
ER considered Hoover "the only man I know who has firsthand knowledge of European questions and great organizing ability and understands
business not only from the capitalistic point of view but also from the
worker's standpoint. . . ." But when he announced himself a Republican,
only to be overlooked by his party, as were other progressive contenders
such as Chicago reformer Harold Ickes and Senator Hiram Johnson of
California, she had no doubts about the conservative direction of her
paternal family's traditional party.

Although virtually all the women of her family stumped for Harding,
they privately considered him a scoundrel. Alice Roosevelt Longworth
reputedly made a deal with Harding, to support her brother Ted's
political career in exchange for her strenuous efforts. But she remained
aghast at Harding's private manners, his stand-up affairs (in a closet,
while his wife pounded on the door), his whiskey-filled White House
poker games, and she would decry the air of corruption that quickly

surrounded his presidency. "My God," Alice Longworth announced, "we have a president . . . who doesn't even know beds were invented—and his campaign slogan was 'Back to Normalcy!' "

His running mate, more sober by far and with no progressive pretenses, was Massachusetts's Governor Calvin Coolidge, who had achieved national prominence when he fired and blacklisted Boston's striking police force and made dire warnings about Bolsheviks in civic office.

They were an undistinguished team, surrounded by politicians who seemed cynical and craven. Progressive Republican journalist William Allen White believed that he had never before seen a convention "so completely dominated by sinister predatory economic forces." Whereas Harding's convictions were unclear, Coolidge idealized business and enshrined businessmen: "The chief business of the American people is business. . . . The man who builds a factory builds a temple. . . . The man who works there worships there."

But the Democrats offered little more by way of an alternative vision for America's future. Both Cox and FDR promised to further Wilsonian goals and were generally vague about the great and impending issues that faced the nation. Nevertheless, the campaign of 1920 forged a new political partnership between ER and FDR.

Previously Franklin had discouraged Eleanor's company. For eight years they had done most of their public work separately. Everything changed in 1920. Now FDR wanted ER with him on the campaign train. He wanted her to record the doings, to keep notes, a record, a diary. Now, as never before, she was called upon to smile and be gracious and at her husband's side from town to town across America. She agreed, and in September joined the campaign train for the second tour of the country.

The Roosevelts were widely perceived as a devoted couple, an outstanding team in Washington circles. Steady and stable, they were the envy of most political families—especially at a time when talk of divorce abounded, as it did during the campaign of 1920. When Harvard's former president Charles W. Eliot withheld his support for James M. Cox because of his divorce, FDR wrote Eliot that the Hardings were equally tainted by divorce: "Mrs. Harding was divorced by her first husband, and almost immediately afterwards married Mr. Harding. I hate, of course, to have this sort of thing enter into the campaign at all, but if the Cox divorce is made a factor . . . you may be sure that the Harding divorce will be brought out. . . ."

In July FDR had written ER: "I miss you so, so much. It is very strange not to have you with me in all these doings." But he only wanted her with him to bear witness. He was delivering from two to twenty speeches a day, and spent most evenings playing poker. There was really nothing for ER to do.

After ER publicly joined the campaign, the political and personal rift in her family deepened. FDR was frequently mistaken for Theodore Roosevelt or his son, and the Oyster Bay clan became increasingly incensed. Alice Roosevelt Longworth honored her father's memory by battling Wilsonians, including FDR. All semblances of family loyalty, all memories and pretenses of friendship, were obliterated. TR, Jr., was sent out to haunt FDR's whistle-stops and make it clear that he represented a different tribe. Cousin Ted announced in Wyoming that FDR was "a maverick—he does not have the brand of our family." Alice Longworth's husband, Ohio Congressman Nicholas Longworth, joined the family's nasty brigade by calling FDR a "denatured Roosevelt." And Edith Roosevelt, TR's widow, announced: "Franklin is nine-tenths mush and one-tenth Eleanor."

ER, always an outsider among her father's people, deeply resented their antics and public name-calling. She never forgave them, and eventually participated in increasingly imaginative political brawls of her own design. As the family feud intensified, FDR asked ER to keep "some kind of diary *please* or I know I will miss some of the things that happen!"

ER was the only woman on the four-week train trip from New York to Colorado. Surrounded by hard-drinking, continually smoking politicians, virtually ignored for hours on end and with absolutely nothing to do but look at the scenery, knit, and write letters, ER hated most of the journey. She took to her cabin for longer and longer periods, and ate many meals alone. She was bored and uncomfortable. Her only task was to appear at whistle-stops to look gracious and smile adoringly as FDR addressed the crowd. FDR had hit a new stride. Crowds loved him; they shouted and cheered. When he was asked to speak for ten minutes, he spoke for twenty. If he was scheduled for an hour, he spoke for two. His staff was amazed. He would not stop. His advisers—Louis Howe, Marvin McIntyre, Stephen Early, Tom Lynch—made faces and waved their arms, calling time. But he went on and on. ER's chief contribution was to pull his coattails with vigor. Only then might he subside.

Although Steve Early complained that FDR was largely a playboy, unprepared and casual about his commitments during this campaign, most of his speeches were earnest, if occasionally condescending. There were, however, several disturbing moments.

In Butte, Montana, before ER joined the campaign train, FDR defended the League of Nations against the complaint that Britain would have six votes, and the United States only one, with a grandiose imperial boast: "Well, I will say that the U.S. has at least twelve votes." At least twelve nations "will stick with us through thick and thin through any controversy." "Does anyone suppose that the votes of Cuba, Haiti, Santo Domingo, Panama, Nicaragua and of the other Central American States would be cast differently from the vote of the United States? We are in a very true sense the big brother of these little republics."

FDR went so far as to take personal credit for that situation. As Assistant Secretary of the Navy, he had "something to do with the running of a couple of little Republics. Until last week, I had two of these votes in my pocket. Now Secretary Daniels has them. One of them was [Santo Domingo, and the other was] Haiti. I know, for I wrote Haiti's Constitution myself, and if I do say it, I think it was a pretty good little Constitution."

FDR had in fact participated in several expeditions of gunboat diplomacy during Wilson's presidency: He helped quell revolution in Mexico, and personally applauded Marine activity in Santo Domingo and Haiti. Haiti's new constitution tied the country firmly to the United States. U.S. intervention and appropriation of Haiti was not a secret precisely, but in 1920 it seemed impolite and aggressive to boast about it on the campaign trail.

After a howl of protest greeted his words, he denied them. But he had repeated his Butte speech again in Billings, and thirty-one citizens signed a letter to local editors affirming that they heard FDR say what the Associated Press said he did. His timing was grievous. *The Nation,* a liberal journal, had just run a series of articles on the cruelties and horrors of America's naval occupation of Haiti.

The postwar climate was anti-interventionist, anti-imperialist, nationalist. Within weeks, Harding used FDR's words to full advantage: "Practically all we know is that thousands of native Haitians have been killed by American Marines, and that many of our own gallant men have sacrificed their lives at the behest of an Executive department in order to establish laws drafted by the Assistant Secretary of the Navy, to secure a vote in the League. . . ." Harding called FDR's bravura "shocking" and irresponsible, and promised: "I will not empower an Assistant Secretary of the Navy to draft a constitution for helpless neighbors in the West Indies and jam it down their throats at the point of bayonets borne by U.S. Marines."

FDR gave those Democrats who hoped that the Cox-Roosevelt team might be a departure from Wilson's legacy of Red Scare and foreign entanglements little to cheer about. Although he spoke of progressivism, he emphasized Americanism with equal ardor. In a blast at immigrants, whom Woodrow Wilson had called "hypenated Americans," FDR accused Republicans of "making special appeals to the very small but dangerous element in our country which was not loyal or was of doubtful loyalty during the war. Republican leaders are making open solicitation of the Italian-American vote. . . ." Presumably to woo the Dixiecrats and xenophobes who then dominated a large part of the Democratic Party, he exclaimed: We "want all-American votes only."

He presented his most Palmerite speech in Centralia, Washington, on 20 August, also before ER had boarded the campaign train. Centralia was the site of a bloody battle between the American Legion and lumberjack members of the Industrial Workers of the World (the IWW, or Wobblies), which resulted in one of America's most notorious lynchings. On Armistice Day, 11 November 1919, the American Legion had paraded through Centralia with rubber hoses and gas pipes, vowing to destroy every Wobbly in town. (Although most of their leaders were in jail, and their movement was shattered by 1919, remaining IWW groups were militant: "The working class and the employing class have nothing in common.")

When Centralia's vigilantes stormed Wobbly headquarters, they were shot at by defending Wobblies, all of whom were quickly arrested—except one, Wesley Everest. A veteran, Everest ran for his life, fought off the mob, fired into the crowd, only to be caught in the current of Centralia's Skookumchuck River. He was tied behind a car and dragged to town, tied up to a telephone pole, and hanged for hours. Still not dead, he was thrown into a jail cell, where that night the mob returned to cut his genitals off, hang him from a bridge, and finally throw his body into the river. Subsequently the local coroner announced that this clever Wobbly lumberjack had committed suicide by jumping off a bridge "and then shot himself full of holes." Eleven Wobblies were tried for killing a Legionnaire. Throughout America, Wobblies had been imprisoned for their antiwar views, their antidraft demonstrations, and their militancy. Most remained in jail until they were pardoned by FDR, then president, in 1933. But in 1920 the vice-presidential candidate said:

> I particularly wanted to make this visit to Centralia. I regard it as a pilgrimage to the very graves of the martyred members of the American Legion who here gave their lives in the sacred cause of Americanism. Their sacrifice challenged the attention of the Nation to the insidious danger to American institutions in our very midst. Their death was not in vain for it aroused the patriotic people of our great nation to the task of ridding this land of the alien anarchist, the criminal syndicalist and all similar anti-Americans.

During the campaign, ER monitored the press for FDR. Even his worst gaffes were treated mildly, and the Republican papers treated him generally as "an amiable, young, boy. Belittlement is the worst they can do."

Although there is no record of ER's response to any of FDR's speeches after she arrived on board, there is a consistency to her mood. She was tense, disgruntled, dissatisfied. Her effort to look generally enraptured by her husband's words, the same words or different, as they rode south and west through America, began to wear on her spirit.

His were words she never used in speeches, and her emphases were always different. If she urged him not to get so carried away by the crowds, by their enthusiasm and zeal, and to remember always his own principles; if she urged him to emphasize the League of Nations more and conquest less, and especially to stress his progressive commitments and shun xenophobic impulses; if she encouraged him to be more a statesman and less a careless politician, she never criticized him or challenged him in public.

In her stateroom for hours on end, ER was stirred by the fleeting scenery, and she read a lot, often a book a day: novels, poetry, and journals, as well as newspapers and broadsides. But she was frozen out of the political discussions and was never invited to a policy or strategy meeting. At night, after a full day's campaigning, speech-writing, and meetings, FDR drank and played poker. ER thought he should get a good night's rest and set an example to his staff. She also thought that FDR might want to spend some time with her, since he had begged her to come. It was not until Louis Howe noticed her long disappearances that ER's presence was actually taken into account.

~

LOUIS HOWE HAD BEEN FDR'S PRIMARY ASSISTANT SINCE HIS election to the New York State Senate, and had served as FDR's chief assistant and troubleshooter in Washington for eight years. Howe had believed from the first that FDR would become president of the United States, and he sacrificed his own private life to work toward that goal. He coached FDR in every way. He provided information, intelligence, bills to support, people to meet, contacts, and connections. He arranged deals, wrote speeches, made friends in business, labor, and Congress. During the war, he was known as "an ambidextrous genius" who solved the navy's labor-management problems while he continued to build Democratic party strength.

Howe packaged FDR. They were also intimate friends and spent hours of each day together, planning the day, planning the future. Howe's influence over FDR, over his vision and style, were extraordinary. ER had at first resented it. Then she ignored it. She ignored his influence and his existence for almost a decade, even though she saw him practically every day. In Washington, he arrived at her home each morning to collect her husband for their stroll to the office. More recently, the Roosevelts and the Howes and their children had spent weekends and holidays together. She was always polite and correct. She was to him as she was to a variety of servants: executive, but distracted and inattentive. ER had never imagined that Louis Howe would become her friend, or that he would be in the least interested in her views.

Moreover, she had been for many years simply revolted by his appearance. He was gaunt and unhealthy, and smoked foul Sweet Caporal cigarettes end on end. ER watched with amazement as he allowed the ashes to dribble onto his shirt, his tie, down his vest. He coughed and wheezed with an advanced case of asthma for twenty-five years. He looked and sounded as if he were about to die. ER wrote that "Louis was entirely indifferent to his appearance; he not only neglected his clothes but gave the impression at times that cleanliness was not of particular interest to him." For many years she thought nothing of his sensitive, creative mind, did not notice his "rather extraordinary eyes," and like SDR deplored his gnomelike presence. For years, in fact, their mutual dislike for Louis Howe was a primary connection between ER and her mother-in-law. But during the campaign of 1920, ER and Louis McHenry Howe developed a deep and lasting friendship. In addition to all the warmth and support they gave each other, their new unity impacted fully on the political career of FDR—refining the tone of his speeches and enlarging the direction of his vision.

~

HOWE DISSOLVED ER'S ANTAGONISM DURING THE LONG tedious train rides when he knocked on her stateroom door and asked her to review speech drafts, consider new ideas, contemplate proposals for press conferences. They talked for hours, and he persuaded Eleanor that he cared about her opinions and that her views mattered. "I was flattered and before long found myself discussing a wide range of subjects." Eventually Stephen Early, FDR's campaign advance man, also a journalist, joined their conversations.

During that trip ER and the journalists became friendly. Howe explained their behavior, and the political etiquette. They were brusque but shy; she was in charge: She had to cut the ice. ER's first face-to-face conversations with the political reporters of America were a revelation to her. She liked their hearty style; she liked their no-nonsense approach to politics and to life. And they liked and admired her.

From then to the end of her life, ER was relaxed in the company of reporters. She enjoyed their jokes, their direct manners. She felt comfortable with them, and they appreciated her unexpected warmth, generosity, and good-humored intelligence. As ER and the journalists "became more friendly, they helped me to see the humorous side" of all those daily incidents that had in the past enraged and depressed her. When countless women flirted with FDR, the newsmen stood behind her and teased. The campaign of 1920 inaugurated a new phase of ER's public life. Even on the campaign trail, she no longer felt alone, and isolated.

For ER, Niagara Falls was the highlight of this long and tumultuous journey. She had never seen the Falls, and Louis Howe persuaded her to run off with him on a day trip. They both loved the incomparable grandeur of the sight, and responded to its free-flowing energy with the kind of romantic intensity that people feel who truly love nature in its untrammeled wildness. Their excursion gave them a chance to know each other under the best possible circumstances. They thrilled to the same experiences, were moved by the same purpose.

For ER, Howe was transformed from her husband's unappealing acolyte to a friend and confidant with many and unusual talents. Louis Howe was an artist. In Washington he sang in the choir of the Saint Thomas Church. He painted landscapes and portraits, almost always in watercolor. He loved the seashore in all seasons, and was happiest in his cottage at Horseneck Beach in Massachusetts, where he and his wife, Grace, often vacationed together with their children—a daughter, Mary (a student at Vassar), and a young son, Hartley. But Howe and his family were frequently separated. And Howe never really took time off: His work went with him wherever he went. He continually wrote speeches, press releases, letters, fund-raising appeals. During the Washington years, he spent his leisure time working at his true love, the theatre. He wrote plays, acted and directed in the little-theatre movement, and was especially noted for his remarkable wit.

If Howe's motives for befriending ER on the campaign train related to his hopes for FDR's political future, their friendship as it developed over time had a life and a force all its own. They were devoted to each other. Louis Howe was the first of many intimate friends that ER grew to trust and to love, with a warmth and generosity both spontaneous and unlimited. He encouraged her political talents, and helped her express them. He understood her moods, and the reasons for them. He cared profoundly about her well-being and her happiness. He dedicated himself to bridging the emotional distances between ER and FDR. On occasion he would teeter to one side or the other. But he always managed to transcend any possible conflict, and position himself equidistant from either side. Louis Howe was important to Eleanor, and she trusted him sufficiently to be able to share him with FDR. In that regard, his friendship was unique.

Its impact was immediate. When ER and Howe returned to the train from Niagara Falls, she exhibited a new level of confidence. They were greeted with frolicsome tales of FDR's flirtatious day campaigning in Jamestown, surrounded by groups of political women who adored his company. For the first time, ER could joke about the "lovely ladies who served luncheon for my husband and who worshiped at his shrine." FDR "had to stand much teasing from the rest of the party about this particular day."

By the end of the campaign of 1920, ER seemed resigned to the antics of her womanizing husband, who was seen by many as a knight-errant and a "playboy." She even seemed resigned to the permanent presence of his new secretary, Marguerite (Missy) LeHand, who had joined his staff during the campaign.

Like Lucy Mercer, she had extraordinary blue eyes and was almost as tall as ER. Eleanor described Missy LeHand as "young and pretty but delicate, for she had had rheumatic fever as a child. While she could ride and drive and swim, the more strenuous forms of exercise were forbidden. Though she did not come to live with us until we went to Albany [in 1928], she often stayed with us in Warm Springs and in Hyde Park, and was devoted to my husband and his work." ER always

treated Missy LeHand with warmth and protective affection, and seemed
to favor her as an elder daughter or, in the manner of Asian matriarchs,
as the junior wife.

Freedom was now a cherished factor in the Roosevelts' family
arrangement—but balance, fairness, equality were still to be achieved.
FDR's freedom necessitated ER's freedom. In an undated 1920s article,
"Politics Here and Elsewhere," ER wrote: "News comes that the ladies
of Thibet find it necessary to have at least three husbands each in order
to make up between them the necessary qualifications for a model
spouse." ER considered the "Thibetan idea" "food for thought" so that
women might "get all of the qualifications we consider" needed and
desirable from "our better halves." Moreover, if men by custom and
circumstance might have many spouses in different supporting roles,
how refreshing to think that in Tibet at least so had the women.

~

THE ELECTION OF 1920 WAS A DISASTER FOR THE DEMOCRATS.
Harding and Coolidge won with 61 percent of the popular vote, and
vast majorities in thirty-seven states. The Republicans also took most of
the statehouses and Congress. In New York, Governor Al Smith was
defeated by the antisuffrage, antireform conservative Nathan L. Miller.

Despite the enormity of the defeat, FDR maintained his usual buoy-
ancy, at least on the surface. He was thirty-eight, and eager for new
battles. He joined the business-boom parade, and dedicated himself to
making serious money for the first time in his life. There were a variety
of speculative schemes—slot machines, oil refining, lobster traps, zeppelins as commuter transports. FDR was willing to gamble. Sometimes
he won; sometimes he lost. With Grenville Emmet and Langdon Marvin
he created a new law partnership. Emmet, Marvin & Roosevelt was a
Wall Street operation specializing in estates and wills—all of which
bored him to death, FDR later acknowledged. He also accepted his
Harvard friend Van Lear Black's offer of a lucrative job as vice-president
in charge of the New York office of the Fidelity & Deposit Company
of Maryland, one of the United States' most successful bonding firms.
Van Lear Black, owner of the Baltimore *Sun,* offered FDR $25,000 to
use his Washington and Albany business and labor connections to in-

crease the company's assets. Having earned no more than $5,000 in all his years in government service, and frequently forced to dip into his mother's capital, FDR and his family were delighted with the change.

While FDR returned to New York to make money and await the next election, ER returned to New York to embark on her own political career.

12. ER and the New Women of the 1920s: Esther Lape and Elizabeth Read, First Feminist Friends

ISAPPOINTED BY THE TRADITIONS AND OBLIGATIONS she had so carefully honored, ER returned to New York unwilling to be bound by convention. Within weeks she made new friends and joined political organizations—the Women's City Club, the League of Women Voters—enrolled in a secretarial course to learn shorthand and typing, and took cooking lessons. She wanted especially to remove the mystery from everyday things that had made her feel dependent, inadequate, out of control. ER liked to type, when she had to; her shorthand would forevermore be useful. She felt pride the day she actually prepared a full five-course dinner. Even though she never did it again, she was glad she knew how to do it. Little victories, but they built her confidence.

She stepped outside the magic circle of charity boards, ladies' luncheons and society teas presided over by Cousin Susie and her mother-in-law. "The war had made that seem an impossible mode of living." And so, during the 1920s, Eleanor Roosevelt joined the ranks of those she believed determined to continue the progressive struggle: ER became a social feminist (part of that network committed to women's emancipation and social reform), a political activist, a New Woman.

ER had been in New York City only a few days when Narcissa Cox Vanderlip, then chair of the New York State League of Women Voters, invited her to become an active member of the League's board. A

Republican, Narcissa Vanderlip was, like the other members of the League, committed to progressive, bipartisan, and feminist activity. Most of its active members had been radical suffragists, and were internationalists dedicated to the League of Nations. And most of them were, like ER, members of America's privileged and affluent leadership class.

ER knew and admired Narcissa Cox Vanderlip—in fact, the two women had much in common. Vanderlip was the mother of six children; she managed several households and a considerable estate, Beechwood, along the Hudson River, in Scarborough, twenty-eight miles north of New York City. During the war, she and Eleanor had both devoted many hours of each day to the war effort, and ER had been impressed by her profound love for learning and her practical political style: her executive skills, efficiency, and dash.

ER was enthusiastic about her new work with the League, and told Esther Lape that she would like to do more. Lape, perhaps the first of ER's new friends fully to appreciate the range of her abilities, recommended that Vanderlip consider ER for fund-raising purposes. Lape thought that she would be a "useful adjunct" and pleasant company on League trips: "Eleanor Roosevelt says that if you would care at all to have her go along with you . . . she would be glad to. . . . She said when speaking of the League in general that she 'liked to do things' with you. And she said it in such a nice warm way."

Attractive and athletic, Narcissa Vanderlip had a crisp and robust manner. She rode horses and played politics with equal joy and intensity. While a student at the University of Chicago, she managed the girls' basketball team. Like ER, as a young Junior Leaguer she volunteered to teach gymnastics at the University Settlement. Although she left college in her senior year to marry her earnest suitor Frank A. Vanderlip, she had relished its "feast of learning" and was always proud that she had read Socrates, Plato, Aristophanes, and Aristotle in the original. Over the years, she raised significant sums of money for the university, and in 1933 would return to receive her degree.

ER was impressed that Narcissa and Frank Vanderlip had done so much public work together, notably for women's suffrage and progressive education. In 1912, they founded the Scarborough School, and during the war they toured the country together, selling bonds and promoting postwar reconstruction. Frank Vanderlip was president of the National City Bank and founder of the American International Corporation, capitalized at $50 million. Created to finance trade, investment, and ambitious transnational engineering projects in Europe and Asia, it was America's first global development bank and construction company. A liberal Republican, Vanderlip's financial status did not protect him from the Red Scare. He was attacked as a Bolshevik—after all, international financiers believed in "foreign" trade. Indeed, Edward L. Doheny (later mired in the Teapot Dome scandal) announced on 1 February 1919 that "Vanderlip is a Bolshevist, so is Charles R. Crane. . . . Henry Ford is another and so are most of those one hundred historians Wilson took abroad with him."

ER admired the concerned and politically astute women who dedicated themselves to making their hard-won right to vote meaningful. In 1920 and 1921, the League's platform set the reform agenda far into the future: national health insurance, unemployment insurance, state and federally funded old-age pensions, expanded appropriations for the Women's Bureau and the Children's Bureau, an end to child labor, maximum-hour and minimum-wage legislation, the Sheppard-Towner Maternity and Infant Protection Act, pure-milk-and-food legislation, federal aid to education, civil-service reform, full citizenship for women (whether or not married to U.S. nationals), the participation of women at every level of national life, the promotion of international peace and membership in the League of Nations.

A. Mitchell Palmer and his successors throughout the 1920s—most notably New York's Lusk Committee—condemned the League of Women Voters, and all its works, as Bolshevism, and feared that Leaguers intended to weaken America by destroying the family. But for ER the League filled the vacuum that had existed in her life since she took off her Red Cross uniform. In January 1921, she attended the annual convention of New York's League at Albany, one of very few Democratic women present (127 of the 157 women were Republican). It was an extraordinary session. Vanderlip had invited Governor Nathan Miller to speak to the newly enfranchised women of his state. He agreed—in order to attack them: "There is no proper place for a *League of Women Voters*. . . . Any *organization* which seeks to exert political power is a *menace to our free institutions and to representative government.*" He condemned all their efforts outside the two-party system, and particularly assaulted their legislative program.

Miller's attack resulted in a vastly increased membership for the League, in part due to Carrie Chapman Catt's spontaneous reply, which received front-page headlines across the country. There remained, she stated, a minority of political men who were bitter against suffragists "because we are women." "I do not recall one time in history when a great reform was brought about by a political party," Catt said. "The League of Women Voters aspires to be a part of the big majorities which administer our government, and at the same time it wishes to be one of the minorities which agitate and educate and shape ideas today which the majority will adopt tomorrow."

Carrie Chapman Catt inspired Eleanor Roosevelt. In April 1921, ER attended the National League's convention in Cleveland, where she was particularly stirred by Carrie Chapman Catt's speech to the delegates on 11 April. As Catt strode to the podium, she tore up her prepared remarks. That day she had read Harding's first address to Congress, in which he declared that "This Republic will have no part" in a League of Nations. Catt was outraged: "The people in this room tonight could put an end to war. Everyone wants it and everyone does nothing. . . . I am for a League of Nations. . . . Let us consecrate ourselves to put war out of the world. . . . Men were born by instinct to slay. It seems to me God is giving a call to the women of the world to come forward, to stay the hand of men, to say: 'No, you shall no longer kill your fellow men!' "

That night Catt stirred the convention to a women's crusade for peace. For Eleanor Roosevelt it was an exhilarating meeting. The women she met in Cleveland, including many former suffrage militants, were different from the affluent and privileged circle around Vanderlip. ER was moving far beyond her familiar orbit. As she wrote to her husband:

> I've had a very interesting day and heard some really good women speakers.
>
> Mrs. Catt is clear, cold reason; Mrs. Larue Brown is amusing, apt, graceful; [Minnie Fisher Cunningham] from Texas is emotional

and idealistic, but she made nearly everyone cry! I listened to Child
Welfare all the morning and Direct Primaries all the afternoon,
lunched with Margaret Norrie, drove out at five . . . and called on
Mrs. [Newton D.] Baker, dined and heard some speeches on Child
Welfare and attended a NY delegates' meeting and am about to go
to bed, quite weary!

But she felt a need to reassure her husband: "Much, much love dear
and I prefer doing my politics with you."

ER would continue to do some part of her politics with her husband,
but after 1921 she was centrally engaged in every aspect of the women's
political movement. Throughout the 1920s, with Vanderlip, Esther
Lape, and Elizabeth Read, she dedicated herself to the struggle for
America's participation in the World Court, created to substitute international law for international violence. Within weeks of their meeting
in 1920, Vanderlip had persuaded ER to direct the League of Women
Voters' national-legislation committee. At first ER protested that she
was not sufficiently informed. But Narcissa Vanderlip assured her that
she would have all the assistance she needed from "an able woman
lawyer" named Elizabeth Read.

A scholar and an attorney, Elizabeth Read was an honors graduate
of Smith College and the University of Pennsylvania Law School. She
was affluent and self-assured, and her personality was flavored by a
warm and quick wit. She became one of ER's closest friends as well as
her personal attorney and financial adviser. Each week, Read went
through the Congressional Record and marked the bills of potential
interest to the League. She and ER would then meet to discuss possible
activities, after which ER prepared a monthly report with her final
recommendations. A quick study, ER soon found her activities multi-
plied. She rapidly developed her own political vision and style, but she
always credited her early work with Elizabeth Read as essential to every
new step she took in activist politics during the 1920s.

The first time she went to Elizabeth Read's office, ER "felt humble
and inadequate." But "I liked her at once and she gave me a sense of
confidence." Those weekly meetings were the beginning of a friendship
with Read and her life-partner, Esther Lape, "which was to be lasting

and warm." Their "standards of work and their interests played a great part in what might be called the 'intensive education of Eleanor Roosevelt.' "

A graduate of Wellesley, Esther Lape had taught English at Swarthmore, the University of Arizona, and Barnard. But she achieved prominence as a journalist, researcher, and publicist. ER noted that "Esther had a brilliant mind and a driving force, a kind of nervous power," which she much admired. In their company, Eleanor Roosevelt became a "New Woman," a prominent member of that diverse and diffuse group that heralded modernity. Although she lived uptown, in the house that Sara built, which she hated, ER spent several evenings each week downtown, with the women who became in 1921 her most intimate friends. They were among the first generation of college-educated women, independent and hardworking, who kept the flame of feminism alive.

Like many radical women, Lape and Read lived in Greenwich Village, which for decades had been a haven for creativity and independent politics. Although after the war many artists and radicals had gone into exile to escape what they considered years of torpor, materialism, and mediocrity, those who stayed continued to find Greenwich Village an appealing and harmonious environment. During the 1920s, rumors abounded that Greenwich Village was dead, that after the war it had become a "bogus and lewd bore," a philistine swamp filled with lesbian harems and other licentious things. Whatever the myth, the area's residents included a community of fighting political women who chose their battles and their neighborhood with great care.

~

STEREOTYPES AND FANTASIES OF THE 1920S HAVE TENDED to concentrate on flappers and speakeasies, to emphasize new styles—short hair, short skirts, and very red lipstick—and to consider smoking, drinking, and lust the essence of it all.

In reality, the "New Women" were not flappers at all. To begin with, they were too old. ER called her teen-aged daughter a "flapper." But nobody would have called ER or Esther Lape a flapper. Nor were their political opponents associated with the National Woman's Party—

Crystal Eastman, Doris Stevens, Alice Paul, or Agnes Brown Leach—flappers. Surely the president of the Woman's Party, Alva Erskine Smith Vanderbilt Belmont, who had become a separatist personally as well as politically (self-supporting women, she now maintained, needed to have nothing to do with men—neither in political parties nor in marriage), was no flapper. But they were all "New Women," as were their older colleagues in progressive reform, such as "social feminists" Jane Addams and Lillian Wald.

The ongoing stereotype of the 1920s is that postsuffrage activist women who sought emancipation and independence were politically uninvolved but sexually aggressive. The New Women, however, concentrated on political power and economic change. Some organized for social reform, and sought protective labor legislation for women and children, unions for all workers, equal pay for equal work. Others organized for constitutional equality, and paid scant attention to labor legislation. The New Women disagreed about priorities and strategy. And they disagreed among themselves: Among the equal-rights feminists of the Woman's Party, Crystal Eastman was a socialist; Alice Paul and Alva Belmont were not. Among the social feminists, ER was a Democrat; Narcissa Vanderlip a Republican. They all organized vigorously for political change and enjoyed emancipated private lives. Their sexual freedom included the freedom *not* to have "premarital" or freewheeling heterosexual sex, as well as to have it.

The New Women of the 1920s considered themselves part of a movement that was both international and inevitable. In 1919, a Russian feminist and economist, the first Soviet minister of social welfare, Alexandra Kollontai, introduced the concept of the New Woman to the new revolutionary government. The New Woman was economically independent, and sexually liberated. She "asserted her personality," and "protested the universal servitude of women to the state, the family, and society." She believed in equality of the sexes even in the sphere of physical and emotional experience. The New Woman was free, sometimes lonely, but always self-defined. She was different: "The feminine virtues on which she has been raised for centuries: passivity, devotion, submissiveness, gentleness, proved to be fully superfluous, futile and harmful," wrote Kollontai. "Harsh reality demands other characteristics from independent women: activity, resistance, determination, tough-ness, that is to say, characteristics which hitherto were viewed as the hallmark and privilege of men. . . . The woman of the past had been raised by her lord and master to adopt a negligent attitude toward herself, to accept a petty, wretched existence as a natural fate. . . ." But today the wife no longer stood beneath the shadow of her husband. Before us stood "the personality, the woman as human being."

Within two years, Kollontai's writings were condemned in Russia as bourgeois Western feminism, and after 1921 she spent most of her political life in exile. Although she was one of the very few of the first revolutionaries not killed after Lenin's death, she was silenced and her feminist works were virtually erased.

In the United States, New Women with similar views were con-demned as Bolshevist. They too were exiled, dishonored, or bitterly attacked. Wherever they were, the New Women of the 1920s continued to organize, and to write. Their ideas were in ferment all over the world. They would be embattled for the rest of the twentieth century. In the meantime, they created communities of work and friendship that enhanced their lives, empowered their work, and fueled their understanding.

Like most people ER and her new friends defied simplistic cate-gories. Nevertheless, a variety of stereotypes were applied to the polit-ically engaged New Women of the 1920s. They were, to begin with, branded "spinsters"—a new word in the vocabulary of the 1920s, which rapidly became the decade of Freudian misunderstanding. "Old maids" were dismissed as dreary, unfulfilled harpies who sublimated their long-ings in good works. "Spinsterhood" became the worst imaginable fate for young girls.

Not only were "old maids" ridiculed and reviled, however; they were diagnosed as deviants, as were all women who sought to extend their lives beyond the traditional roles of wife and mother. Under the spell of Krafft-Ebing and Freud, psychiatric handbooks began to feature the scariest deviant of all: the "Mannish Lesbian." Portrayed as a woman in tie and high collar, she was known especially to have inappropriate and selfish ambitions—for a university education and a career. Whether or not she had sex with other women mattered less to her diagnosticians than her independence and the range of her interests and concerns. In that respect the misogynists were correct. The "New Women" did indeed live "deviant" lives. They were different. Having broken free of tradition, they sought to live fully according to the dictates and rhythms of their own nature. By doing so, women like those in ER's new circle of friends began the long and ongoing process of expanding the boundaries of "normalcy."

Esther Everett Lape and Elizabeth Fisher Read lived together in a house that Esther owned at 20 East 11th Street, a quiet tree-lined street just off Fifth Avenue. Nearby lived the women with whom ER was to build Val-Kill and share many years of her life, Marion Dickerman and Nancy Cook. They lived at 171 West 12th Street, in a cooperative building filled with social feminists—virtually all of whom were to become ER's friends. Just across the hall lived Polly Porter and Molly Dewson, who would become the driving force of the women's committee of the Democratic Party. But during the first years of her emancipation, ER spent most of her time with Lape and Read.

Cultured, learned, and ambitious, Esther Lape and Elizabeth Read created an atmosphere that reminded ER of Marie Souvestre and her circle. They celebrated excellence in food and champagne, art and conversation. They were passionate about music and theatre. Cut flowers in great profusion decorated their homes in the city and in the country. Their candlelit dinners were formal, splendidly served, and spiced by controversy. After dinner Lape, Roosevelt, and Read read poetry aloud, French poetry in particular, for hours on end. The evenings were incomplete if they did not include discussions of new and imaginative political strategies, and the contents of the following week's editorials in the weekly newsletter Lape and Read published: *City, State and Nation.* That journal was addressed to women and men, politicians and voters. Lape and Read enlisted ER and their closest friends to support and write for it, and many dinners were working editorial-committee meetings with ER, Vanderlip, and Helen Rogers Reid, married to Ogden Reid, subsequently publisher of the New York *Herald Tribune.* Not since Allenswood had ER spent such stimulating, exciting, and purposeful hours—hours that engaged her talents, advanced her vision.

In the early 1920s, ER spent as much time as possible with Esther

Lape and Elizabeth Read. During the White House years, Lape suggested she rent a floor on 11th Street. It became ER's sanctuary, a hiding house from the press and the rituals of First-Ladyhood.

Like most of the New Women of the 1920s who lived in Greenwich Village, Esther Lape and Elizabeth Read were committed to personal and emotional freedom. Dedicated to public affairs, they were also devoted to each other. They sought to maintain a balanced and artful life, and lived in a world of elegance and daring. It was a world that they created; there were no blueprints or tradition. They answered to nobody, and to no established order.

Style mattered to Lape and Read. Their costumes were dashing, and they dressed for each other. Their clothes were custom-made of the finest imported fabrics. Over the years, they persuaded ER to use their favorite designer, and frequently gave her gifts of unique and dazzling fabrics. Elizabeth Read was more casual and preferred dark, basic colors, comfortably tailored suits with string ties, and sensible walking shoes. In the country, she wore working corduroys and knickerbockers, with high-laced hunting boots. Short and agile, she was proud of her athletic and powerful body. She uprooted trees and personally built the stables that housed Esther's horses. Esther Lape was more extravagant—eccentric, even. Her clothes were exquisite, and they lasted forever. Patterned silks, velvets, satins, a variety of brocades: She wore during the 1970s what she had designed during the 1920s and 1930s. She preferred white in the country and black in the city—except on Christmas, when she wore red velvet. In the country, she wore riding jodhpurs, and she never rode side-saddle. Slacks were for working in her well-considered gardens and for taking country drives. No pants ever hung in her New York City closet.

Ceremony was as important as fashion to Lape and Read. Their cats, for example, were always called Ariel and Pan. Above the door of their 147-acre Connecticut estate, Saltmeadow, Elizabeth Read carved in wood Plato's invocation to the god Pan, ruler of woods and fields: "Beloved Pan, and all ye other gods that haunt this place / give me beauty of the inward soul. . . ."

In a philosophic mood during particularly annoying negotiations in behalf of a compromise between the League of Women Voters and the

National Woman's Party, Elizabeth Read wrote Narcissa Vanderlip a letter in which she examined her feelings about balance in life. She said that they had spoken only

> about whether it was better to resign—[and] we did not get down to the real issue: Whether a cause, or one's human relationships, is the more important. EL and I were speaking of it that night. I know that for myself the human relationships are; not that selfish absorption in them can be satisfactory, for life cannot be big and sweet that way; but on the other hand causes won't make life endurable either. You could work fifty years for a cause, and find your life too dreary and barren to be endured. If a person is lucky enough to meet a human being that is worth devotion, that—in the absence of a crisis, or an all-compelling call—is the important thing—always remembering that *selfish* devotion defeats its purpose, that limiting life to the devotion eventually kills it. In other words, it is a matter of a balance that changes every day. . . .

Esther Lape shared Read's commitment to a balanced life of work and love, in unity with nature. The spirit of their lives, Esther Lape wrote in her history of Saltmeadow, which she gave to ER, was to be found "in the inscription 'toujours gai' " painted in large green letters on the double-sized "doormat of the big house." When she was over ninety years old, she asked a friend to repaint that inscription, because she hated to see it fade.

Lape and Read believed that life could be crafted, made into a work of art. Their friends were central to the world of "beauty and the gaiety of life" that they created in New York and at Saltmeadow, where ER would spend some days in each season every year. It was in fact at Saltmeadow that ER spent the last vacation weekend of her life.

ER believed that "Providence was particularly wise and farseeing when it threw these two women together, for their gifts complement each other in a most extraordinary way. From their association has come much good work which has been of real service in a good many causes."

Esther Lape and Elizabeth Read became the core of her female support network. Similar networks of shared work and friendship sustained many political women who struggled for change and equality in a world they were not supposed to inhabit, a world that continually erected barriers to their presence and all their contributions.

~

LAPE AND READ CARED ABOUT ER'S WELL-BEING, AND HER spirits. They encouraged and promoted her work and reintroduced her to a way of life she had not considered since she left Allenswood. As a student, she had always believed that she would return to England to teach. But for twenty years, that independent female world of work and community had been very remote. It seemed ages away. Within weeks, the charm and intensity of their lives restored to ER a range of possibilities she had forgotten she ever knew.

ER hated to be alone. When she discovered how much she really enjoyed people, she realized just how lonely she had been. To the end of her life, her daily calendar might have seemed to anyone less robust like a political and emotional carnival. ER's appetite for life was vast, unlimited. After 1920, she set out, consciously and with gusto, to pursue her own independent destiny. Nevertheless, she made compromises with form and tradition. She avoided scandal, broke no fundamental ties with her husband or her mother-in-law, and, where her children were concerned, allowed convention to rule.

ER was never able to prevail against the stern opposition of her mother-in-law and the passivity of her husband when it came to her children. Although she disapproved, and spoke vigorously against the tradition, all her boys went to Groton when they were twelve. And when her daughter was eighteen, she came out. Like her mother and her mother before her, the third Anna Eleanor Roosevelt was a debutante in society. She hated it and protested, but her grandmother insisted, and ER agreed: "Yes, you must." Anna never got over her outrage: "My mother *made* me . . . go to Newport for what they call 'Tennis Week.'" She was made to stay with Cousin Susie Parish, whom ER's brother, Hall, by then called a Ku Klux Klanner and whom ER herself had come to consider perfectly dreadful. But ER did not stand up for her daughter: "She didn't help me a bit."

She made me go there, and I completely abhorred this stuff. . . .
But Mother made me do this. It was Granny who took me to get
the clothes. . . .

Now, Father, you couldn't draw into this. He'd just say, 'That's
up to Granny and Mother. You settle all this with them. . . .' He
wouldn't give me the time of day."

Anna wished "Newport would blow up and bust," but in 1924 she
went, and endured the time-honored and primary rite of passage still
enjoyed by so many of the women of her class. ER, always uncomfortable
in Newport, did not join her daughter. Like many women of her generation, and later generations, ER's own removal from her family's
culture, from rituals she found suffocating, did not extend to her daughter. Badgered by her mother-in-law and her godmother, with all the
ghosts of her foremothers and all the pain of memory haunting her
decision, ER was not free to share her liberation with her daughter:
Anna must go through the form and then decide, later, for herself.

During the week, Anna's objections subsided: "This *is* a strange
place! Even more formal than I imagined." "How those dances scare
me." After several days, she felt less "belligerent to Society's claim."
"Newport seems to me a good education for a girl for one week when
she comes out. . . ."

Even regarding the issue of a college education for women, ER's
views for herself were not translated into action for her daughter. ER
had always wanted to go to college. That she did not attend Vassar or
Barnard, as so many of her contemporaries did, was one of the biggest
disappointments of her life. But her daughter recalled: "College for me
was never even discussed that I remember." She recalled vaguely that
her parents had perhaps talked of her learning "to do something," and
encouraged her to go to Cornell's School of Agriculture, at least for a
year (which she did). But she remembered vividly that her grandmother
was entirely against it, and she "was most outspoken." "Girls who went
to college were very apt to be 'old maids' and become 'bookworms' . . .
a dire threat to any girl's chance of attracting a husband!"

ER's commitment to the idea of advanced education for women was
no match for the fear of spinsterhood. There were household battles

over the subject—between Anna and ER, between ER and her mother-in-law. ER and FDR finally persuaded Anna to attend Cornell on a trial basis. But she was so angry with her mother, she refused to talk to her during the entire drive up to college. Moreover, Anna evidently hated the school, did virtually no work, spent most of her time at parties, and left to get married within a year.

From 1920 to the end of her life, ER lived in two worlds: the world she made for herself, and the social world into which she was born. ER never abandoned that familial world. But she did redefine her place in it. She had the courage to speak and to act, to bear witness, to disrupt and change it profoundly.

13. Convalescence, Marital Unity, and Separate Spheres: Polio, Val-Kill, and Warm Springs

U NTIL FDR'S STALLED POLITICAL TRAIN MOVED FOR-
ward, he was ambivalent about his wife's political career and
her emergent activist style. He joked with Josephus Daniels
about their famous headline-hunting "squaws." He and Louis Howe
called many of ER's new political friends "she-men," and worried that
Eleanor's pronouncements on various controversies might tarnish his
very polished veneer. On the other hand, he encouraged her work, and
he enjoyed the role of tutor. He helped her with legal terms when she
drew up a League plan to reorganize and democratize New York State
(a shorter ballot, a four-year term for governor to replace the two-year
term then current, an executive budget, and more efficient departmental
organization). He gave her parliamentary advice and shared the tricks
of politics that men had refined with years of practice.

During early power struggles within the League, occasional evenings
were spent at East 65th Street devoted to the collective development
of usable strategies: ER and Louis Howe worked on publicity; Elizabeth
Read and FDR considered the legal angles; hours were spent on every
detail. All crises were met by the full team. During a particularly nasty
situation when their competitors sought to introduce a damning report
to discredit Lape and Vanderlip, FDR coached ER. Arrive early; sit up

front; as the last word of the report is being read, immediately "be on your feet." You rise to have it tabled—"That motion is not debatable"—"and that should end the matter." It worked. ER—tall, regal, in a rose-colored suit, with a long fur boa about her neck (borrowed from SDR)—stunned her adversaries. Esther Lape was triumphant: "The jaws of Mary Garrett Hay and her followers dropped as they filed slowly out of the . . . University Club."

Although she remained concerned that her activities might reflect poorly on FDR's various efforts to juggle adversaries and remain above the fray, Eleanor was no longer an ornamental wife who existed to accompany her husband on his political rounds. After the campaign of 1920, she might measure her words but she would not be silenced.

She continued to work for the League of Nations and the World Court after FDR gave up the subject entirely; and she publicly opposed the excesses of the Red Scare, about which he said virtually nothing. At New York's annual League of Women Voters convention in May 1921, ER introduced a resolution to condemn Vice-President Calvin Coolidge's attack against women's colleges. Hotbeds of radicalism, Coolidge called them, filled with women mired in Bolshevik heresy.

The local press featured ER's resolution against her "Husband's Victorious Rival" with indignation. ER noted in her diary: "Foolish of me ever to do anything of the kind." But she rarely hesitated when a cause was just and compelling, and endured endless amounts of press criticism, some of it potentially harmful to FDR's interests.

Most startling was her departure from her original position on party loyalty. In one of her first editorials for the weekly *News Bulletin* of the State and City League, "Common Sense Versus Party Regularity," she argued that voters of "the modern stamp" no longer adhere slavishly to their party's candidates. Although she agreed that women should enroll in the party that best represented their principles, issues of personal integrity, vision, superior qualification should determine a person's vote: "Small minded people will tell you that but for party regularity in all things party organization would not exist, and that party government is necessary to our National institutions. This argument has . . . been refuted a thousand times." Better government depends on "individual nominees." If our partisans "appear to us unworthy, then we have an even higher duty. . . . America must come first, not party."

Tensions between the Roosevelts escalated during the spring of 1921. Although publicly FDR faced his election defeat in jolly style, and ER believed that he had never had any illusions of victory, its overwhelming nature was something of a jolt. After the campaign, FDR became involved with activities that only momentarily amused him; his new business enterprises did nothing to boost his spirits; and the navy scandal had not yet run its course. He drank more, and partied more.

During the early months of 1921, he seemed abstracted, frantic, and frivolous. In May, ER returned home from a weekend conference late one Sunday afternoon to be greeted by her maid's announcement that her husband was in bed and unwell. ER rushed up the stairs, only to find him profoundly hungover "after a wild 1904 [reunion] dinner and party." She would not abide it. Her words were harsh and bitter, her anguish profound and familiar. Then, in June, during the first family celebration with her Oyster Bay relatives since their campaign antics, FDR behaved uproariously. At Aunt Bye's home in Connecticut, during the wedding party for Margaret Krech and Bye's son, Sheffield Cowles, he became drunk, loud, and silly. His behavior in that uncongenial and treacherous company inspired their snide comparisons between "poor Eleanor's" husband and "poor Eleanor's" father. ER was humiliated.

The next week, FDR remained in New York, while ER and the children embarked alone upon the long but always healing journey to Campobello. Howe and his family would be there, and Mama would not. SDR had resumed taking her annual holidays in Europe.

The first weeks of July at Campobello restored a measure of harmony to ER's spirit. The weather was splendid, her household congenial. ER had special guests whose company she particularly enjoyed: the children's tutor, Jean Sherwood, and her mother, Mrs. Sidney Sherwood, who had become a good friend; Elizabeth Asquith Bibesco (daughter of Britain's Liberal Party leader, Herbert Asquith) and her husband, the Romanian diplomat Prince Antoine Bibesco, whose company had always delighted her in Washington. To accommodate Elizabeth Bibesco's preference for whiskey before dinner, Eleanor had to break open Franklin's locked liquor cabinet, because she could not find the key. Jefferson Newbold mixed the cocktails, and they were "very bad," but Elizabeth "was sweet and I like her better than ever." Prohibition meant very little to the Roosevelts. Even ER, whose lifelong dread of alcoholism dominated her response to people and situations, never considered Prohibition a usable deterrent. She momentarily supported the law, but preferred moderation to an actual ban, never imposed Prohibition on her guests, and would herself have an occasional glass of sherry or champagne.

With several servants, tutors, children, and guests, virtually every one of the eighteen bedrooms at Campobello was filled. ER managed the days with her usual efficiency, packed elaborate lunches, orchestrated picnics, dinners, and excursions, and prepared for FDR's arrival. But FDR received an urgent telegram from Josephus Daniels. The Senate Committee on Newport had completed its investigation: "LIBELLOUS REPORT. CAN YOU GO TO WASHINGTON AT ONCE."

The Senate committee's report on the navy's crusade against homosexuals targeted FDR, called the Dunn Board a cover-up, and FDR's testimony before it "unbelievable." The committee concluded that, since FDR "was a man of unusual intelligence and attainments," he "must have known" in what activities his own operators were engaged. Therefore, the Senate committee charged, "Secretary Daniels and Assistant Secretary Franklin D. Roosevelt showed an utter lack of moral perspective." FDR's willingness to allow young officers to be used to investigate perversion "is thoroughly condemned as immoral and an abuse of the authority of his high office."

The committee denied FDR's request to testify; they gave him their 625-page report and over six thousand single-spaced pages of testimony at 10:00 A.M. and gave him until 8:00 P.M. that day to respond. Then, at four in the afternoon, he was told by newsroom friends that the report had been released to "all the papers" without his being given any opportunity to "amend it." Nevertheless, he appeared at eight that night as scheduled and presented his statement, in which he demanded an open hearing before the entire Naval Affairs Committee, certain it would be denied. With the exception of *The New York Times,* the newspapers generally reported his "complete denials fairly well." On 23 July, the front-page *Times* headline announced:

LAY NAVY SCANDAL

TO F. D. ROOSEVELT

***

DETAILS ARE UNPRINTABLE

ER wrote her husband, who had never before been under such extreme attack: "It must be dreadfully disagreeable for you and I know it worries you though you wouldn't own it." ER gave him the words of encouragement her Aunt Bye had given her so long ago: "But it has always seemed to me that the chance of just such attacks as this was a risk one had to take with our form of government and if one felt clear oneself, the rest did not really matter." The press accounts were dreadful, "but one should not be ruffled by such things. Bless you dear and love always."

FDR did not go immediately to Campobello. He wanted to prepare a full statement, consider publication of his version of the facts, discuss his options. "I have talked to a good many people today and lots of them want to rush into print. But in view of the fact that no papers have taken it up it may seem best to drop the whole thing. . . ." He was eager to get to Campobello:

> Tell Louis I expect those boats to be all rigged and ready when I get up there and I am very greatly put out not to be there now.
> Kiss all the chicks and many many for you
>
> Your devoted F.

Franklin returned to New York to find his desk cluttered with mail; he spent two weeks plunged in work, desperately trying to avoid his feelings, terrified that his political future was grounded. To distract him there were parties and sails; a Boy Scout outing; and the offer of Van Lear Black's yacht, the *Sabalo,* for a cruise party to Campobello if he could leave on Friday, 5 August.

First, however, FDR had to work on his reply to the Senate committee. Angry and anxious, his career besmirched, FDR took the offensive and denounced the report as "mistaken," "premeditated," "unfair," "partisan."

> None of this worries me, nor does the report itself worry me personally. . . . As an American . . . one hates to see the United States Navy, an organization of the nation, not of party, used as the vehicle for cheap ward politics. It rather amuses me to know that these Republican Senators consider me worthwhile attacking so maliciously and savagely. Perhaps they may later on learn what a boomerang is. . . .

FDR denied any supervisory role: "A Secretary or an Assistant Secretary has plenty to do in the general management of a navy of hundreds of ships and hundreds of thousands of men without attempting to manage the details of an investigation of one small place by a dozen or so navy men." Moreover, in September 1919, as soon as he learned of the "highly improper and revolting methods" used to get evidence,

> immediate orders went out from me . . . that day to stop it. . . .
> That is all there is to the Senator's unwarranted deductions.
> Their insinuations that I must have known, that I supervised the operations, that I was morally responsible, that I committed all sorts of high crimes and misdemeanors, are nowhere supported by the evidence. . . .
> I accuse them of deliberate falsification of evidence, of perversion of facts, of misstatements of the record, and of a deliberate attempt to deceive.

Privately, Missy LeHand wrote ER on 5 August: "I thought he looked tired when he left." They both hoped he would have a happy time on Van Lear Black's *Sabalo,* and a carefree vacation.

~

FDR ARRIVED IN CAMPOBELLO WEARY BUT DETERMINED TO drown all his feelings in frivolity. The trip up had been arduous and stormy, and he had spent many unexpectedly tense hours at the helm, engulfed by a great fog. In his effort to shake exhaustion and depression FDR had arrived "bringing quite a party with him," and for several days, ER noted, he made a nonstop effort to keep everybody entertained.

Early-morning sails, deep-sea fishing in the Bay of Fundy on the *Sabalo,* late-night conversation: There was endless recreation, but very little rest. After Van Lear Black left, ER and the children enjoyed more tranquil sails in FDR's new boat, the "little *Vireo.*"

On 10 August, they spotted a forest fire while sailing. They all worked to stamp out the fire and then returned home "around four o'clock." "My husband, who had been complaining of feeling logy and tired for several days, decided it would do him good to go in for a dip in a land-locked lake called Lake Glen Severn, inside the beach on the other side of the island. The children were delighted and they started away." It was a jog of about two miles, after which FDR decided to cool off with another swim, this time in the frigid waters of the Bay of Fundy. After the run home, FDR ended the afternoon by reading his mail in his wet bathing suit on the windswept porch. "In a little while he began to complain that he felt a chill and decided he would not eat supper with us."

Feeling unusually lethargic, FDR climbed the stairs to bed and got under the great comforter, hoping to avoid a cold. "In retrospect," ER wrote later, "I realize that he had no real rest since the war." She said nothing of his anguish over the Senate committee's attack. Today, we know far more about the effects of depression and stress on the immune system, but then ER only noted that ever since the Armistice "he had probably been going on his nerves."

The next day, Franklin came down with a mysterious fever. On 14 August, the anniversary of her father's death, ER wrote the first letter about his still-undiagnosed condition to FDR's half-brother, Rosy: "We have had a very anxious few days as on Wed. evening Franklin was taken ill. It seemed a chill but Thursday he had so much pain in his back and legs that I sent for the doctor, by Friday evening he lost the ability to walk or move his legs." Louis Howe, "who, thank heavens, is here, for he has been the greatest help," went in search of a specialist at all the nearby resorts, hoping to find somebody knowledgeable on vacation. He found a famous diagnostician, who spent several minutes, decided that FDR had a blood clot, prescribed frequent massages, and sent a bill for the astonishing amount of $600.

Daily FDR's condition worsened. Temporarily, his hands and arms were paralyzed as well as his legs; he lost control over his vital functions; and his intermittently high fever resulted in delirium and many sleepless nights. For a short time, his eyesight seemed threatened, and his pain was everywhere and unrelenting. Eleanor slept on a couch in his room and, with Louis Howe or alone, managed to move him, bathe him, and turn him over at regular intervals. She administered catheters and enemas, massaged his back and his limbs, brushed his teeth, shaved his face, waited on his every need day and night for three weeks. "It required a certain amount of skilled nursing and I was very thankful for every bit of training which Miss Spring [the children's baby nurse] had given me." FDR was thankful too, and together they rallied for that extra effort to reassure each other: They bantered, laughed, and sought to conquer their gravest fears.

In those days of devotion and struggle, FDR's trust and respect for his wife were expressed as rarely before; their lifelong union, for so long in disarray, was refortified as neither ER nor FDR would have imagined possible under any other circumstances.

During those first weeks, other specialists were brought in. Dr. William Keen arrived from Bar Harbor and suspected some kind of paralysis. He considered ER's endless ministrations exceptional, heroic; and worried about her own health: "You have been a rare wife. . . . You will surely break down if you too do not have immediate relief." But, ER recalled, it "was hard to get" anybody up from New York; when a trained nurse, Edna Rockey, did arrive, FDR wanted ER to continue many of the nursing duties. She did so until his condition stabilized.

Not until 25 August, when Uncle Frederic Delano arranged a consultation with a Boston specialist, Dr. Robert W. Lovett, was infantile paralysis—commonly called polio—diagnosed. Frequent massages, which had been incorrectly prescribed and actually increased the pain, were immediately discontinued. But there was no alternative treatment, nothing really to prescribe beyond hot baths, which might relax and encourage the patient.

~

SARA DELANO ROOSEVELT, UNAWARE OF HER SON'S CONDI-tion, returned from Europe during the first weeks of this ordeal. FDR generally met his mother's ship whenever she returned from abroad. Now ER arranged to have Sara's brother and sister meet her. On 27 August, Eleanor wrote her mother-in-law: "Dearest Mama, Franklin has been quite ill and so can't go down to meet you on Tuesday to his great regret, but Uncle Fred and Aunt Kassie both write they will be there so it will not be a lonely homecoming. We are all so happy to have you home again dear, you don't know what it means to feel you near again."

From the beginning, ER and FDR chose to appear cheerful and optimistic as they faced the unknown together. During SDR's first visit to them at Campobello after her return, she was amazed by their buoy-ancy and determined to follow "their glorious example." She wrote her brother Fred that "the atmosphere of the house is all happiness" and there was much laughter, "Eleanor in the lead."

In addition to her nursing duties, Eleanor served temporarily as secretary and social organizer. She encouraged FDR's friends to write jolly letters, and wrote notes of thanks to those who did. She was particularly grateful to Missy LeHand: "Your letters have amused him and helped to keep him cheerful."

Louis Howe, ever mindful of FDR's public career, dedicated himself to keeping all news concerning FDR's illness out of the press. In mid-September, great care was taken to move Franklin in secrecy from Campobello to Presbyterian Hospital in New York City, on a private train arranged by Uncle Fred. In the months that followed, FDR rarely complained about the extreme pain he was in, and never lost his de-termination to triumph and prevail. Everybody around him, including his mother, maintained a cheerful confidence. Eleanor wrote that SDR was "really very remarkable. . . . I am sure, out of sight, she wept many hours, but with all of us she was very cheerful."

Eleanor had been taught by her grandmother: "Never to cry where people are; cry by yourself." Certainly she too, out of sight, must have wept many hours after her exhausting, terrifying days. Franklin remained in New York's Presbyterian Hospital until shortly before Christmas. Although there was little actual improvement, she continued to believe that he would recover—but only if his attitude remained buoyant.

Because of her belief that only his spirit would enable him to triumph over his disability, Eleanor committed herself to doing whatever it would take to make him happy and contented. His very life depended, she believed, on his ability to remain active, interested, and ambitious in public life. And so, for months—for years, actually, but especially in those first months, when she was always at his side—she worked tirelessly in his behalf. ER brought friends and political associates to his bedroom to keep him informed and entertained. She clipped newspaper items for him, marked editorials he would either enjoy or abhor. She insisted, during the days of dread and despair, when he struggled without success to move his limbs or even his toes, that he continue to take a vital interest in the political world. In concert with Louis Howe, she kept up a running commentary on the current political scene—on who among FDR's associates was feuding with whom on any given day, what deals were being made, with and without his approval, for or against his interests.

But ER's battle to keep FDR's spirit alive was continually in conflict with Sara's plans, for Sara took the very opposite approach, out of her no less passionate belief that his improvement depended on his retirement from public life. SDR wanted her son to assume his proper role as the squire of Springwood. That quiet, healing place that had so well served her "beloved invalid" husband would now be best for her beloved invalid son.

Sincere on both sides and impossible to compromise, the battle raged daily, but always in tones that were muted and acts of spite that were hushed—so as not to disturb the patient. For a time, Sara sabotaged every effort Eleanor and Howe made to enliven Franklin's spirits. She opposed Howe's presence in the 65th Street house and worked to turn the children against his and Eleanor's plans and against Howe personally. When ER moved her daughter, Anna, out of her large sunny room on the second floor to give it to Howe, Sara persuaded Anna to resist:

She need not move into a small dark room—without her own bath, on the third floor in the back of the house—for that "ugly, dirty little" intruder.

The house on 65th Street was in fact very crowded once a live-in nurse and Howe were added. Howe, who spent his days downtown in FDR's office, shared his—Anna's—room with the day nurse; ER gave up her room altogether for the live-in nurse. She slept on a bed in one of the boys' rooms, dressed in her husband's bathroom, and during the day "was too busy to need a room."

For Eleanor, the winter of 1921 was "the most trying winter of my entire life." Her mother-in-law's criticisms, asides, and admonitions tore away at her spirit. But Sara's manipulation of Anna's adolescent needs was particularly demoralizing. In ER's view, Anna "felt that I did not care for her and I was not giving her any consideration. It never occurred to her that I had far less than she had." During these painful moments, ER behaved with her own daughter much as her own mother had with her: She became cold, and distanced; she "shut up like a clam" and refused to speak with Anna about any of the several issues that devastated her heart.

Anna was fifteen that autumn, the age ER had been when she left for Allenswood, and ER enrolled her daughter in Miss Chapin's school. She hoped that "the same relationship would grow up between Anna and Miss Chapin as I had with Mlle Souvestre." But Eleanor had not realized that New York schools were so "set and rigid." Anna at fifteen hated Miss Chapin and everything about her school. Tall, sophisticated for an adolescent, but frozen out of all family conversations and treated like a child, she was sent into a school where the cliques were well established. Her eight years in Washington had made her an outsider to her New York schoolmates. Anna felt rejected at school, mistreated and misunderstood at home.

Not until ER broke down one afternoon in April 1922, while reading to her youngest sons—five-year-old Johnnie and seven-year-old Franklin, Jr.—did her children begin to sense the enormity of the family's situation and the depth of their mother's sorrows. Once she began to sob, she simply could not stop. When Elliott, now eleven, returned from school and saw his mother in that rare state, he simply fled. The two little boys also ran from the room. Louis Howe came in at one point, made an earnest effort to comfort her, but soon "gave it up as a bad job." The evening wore on and on. ER was inconsolable. For hours she sat on the sofa and "sobbed and sobbed." SDR was in the country, and finally ER found an empty room on *her* side of the house, locked the door, and composed herself. "Eventually I pulled myself together, for it requires an audience, as a rule, to keep on these emotional jags." It was "the one and only time" ER went "to pieces" in that particular manner in her entire life.

It seemed, however, a fitting climax to an era of unhappiness and anxiety. And it served several purposes, not least of which was to pave the way to a new relationship with her children, and especially Anna, who now realized something of the pain and anguish her mother had endured so stoically. But not until Anna's coming-out week in Newport, where "gossipy old Cousin Susie" revealed the details of her father's "escapade" with Lucy Mercer, did Anna understand more fully the origins of her mother's erratic moods, the nature of her parents' complex relationship. For the present, she went to her mother, who "poured some of her troubles out and told me she knew she had been wrong and that I did love her." Increasingly, if hesitantly, Eleanor took her daughter into her confidence. She took her to the theatre, and to *Tosca,* her first opera; she invited her to political activities, which they both enjoyed.

~

OUT OF THE CRUCIBLE OF FDR'S ILLNESS, THE ROOSEVELTS' lives were transformed once again. Eleanor considered Franklin's triumph over his disability "a blessing in disguise." Although many believe that his strength of character predated his bout with polio, and served to help him transcend his cruel circumstances, ER believed that his struggle "gave him strength and courage he had not had before. He had to think out the fundamentals of living and learn the greatest of all lessons—infinite patience and never-ending persistence." She believed that during these grueling months and years of recovery he developed a new seriousness about himself, and a deeper empathy for other people.

His disability also caused ER to reconsider her own skills. She had, for example, never played with her children. That had always been her husband's domain. Now she realized that, if her youngest boys were "going to have a normal existence without a father to do these things with them, I would have to become a good deal more companionable and more of an all-around person than I had ever been before."

Now, inspired by her new friends, virtually all of whom knew far more than she did about games and diversions, Eleanor became a willing sport. She again took swimming lessons so she could get into the water with her boys; and began to hike, and camp, and run, and romp. She drove her own car, played cards, sailed, and became altogether a more adventurous, as well as a more considerate, person.

~

AFTER 1922, FDR SPENT MOST OF HIS TIME FISHING, RELAX-ing, and recuperating in warm waters off the coast of Florida. Although months of prescribed exercise and treatment had done little to improve his condition, he remained undaunted. He believed he needed new arrangements, pleasurable time where exercise combined with fun would change his prospects. In 1923, he rented a houseboat, *Weona II*. In 1924, he and his Harvard friend John Lawrence bought a houseboat, the *Larooco* (Lawrence, Roosevelt & Co.) for purposes of deep-sea-fishing expeditions—and general merriment.

On these ventures, aboard the *Weona* and the *Larooco*, and later in Warm Springs, Georgia, Missy LeHand was FDR's primary companion. Warm Springs was her domain. There she was hostess: She wrote the letters to invite the guests, she organized the day, supervised the menus, and presided over the dinner table, regardless of the company. When ER visited, she was a guest—an honored, respected, and welcomed guest, but always a guest. FDR's Florida jaunts and his stays at Warm Springs were always full of good friends, good cheer, and various high jinks. On his houseboat in Florida, FDR's most regular companions included Lewis Cass Ledyard, Jr., Henry de Rham, and his wife, Frances Dana de Rham. FDR had courted Frances Dana, the granddaughter of Henry Wadsworth Longfellow and Richard Henry Dana, while at Harvard, and they had remained good friends. FDR wrote his mother on

5 March 1923: "I have been in swimming four times and it goes better and better. I'm sure this warmth and exercise is doing lots of good. . . . Cass and Ruth and Henry and Frances have been dear and look after me all the time. They are great fun to have on board in this somewhat negligee existence. All wander round in pajamas, nighties and bathing suits!" FDR noted that he was writing Eleanor more "fully and I know she will read it to you." But ER did not save his letters during this period.

It was precisely the kind of environment that ER hated, and she avoided it as much as possible. She disliked the fact of free-flowing rum, and she never enjoyed the climate. On the boat, when they were anchored at night, the wind howled and the chill came up "colder and more uncomfortable than tales of the sunny south led me to believe was possible," and she felt unprotected: "It all seemed eerie and menacing to me." On calm and balmy nights, she hated it quite as much. Since she was claustrophobic and feared seasickness, Eleanor refused to sleep below deck or under covers. When the wind was listless, as it often was, Florida's mosquitoes all seemed to converge to torment her. Despite endless quantities of citronella, she always wound up with enough bites to look like an advanced case of smallpox.

Nevertheless, whenever she did go she made every effort to enjoy herself. On her first trip aboard *Weona II,* she brought along Esther Lape, who wrote to Narcissa Vanderlip on 1 March 1923: "I was happy to be with Eleanor Roosevelt when there was nothing for either of us to do. She is an utterly splendid person." Inviting her own friends to accompany her, as she generally did on these trips, gave ER a new emotional security, which enabled her to encourage FDR's pleasures, and to be glad that he had such attentive friends and companions of his own. Even Livy Davis, whose antics had in the past seemed to her both selfish and reckless, now won her admiration: Livy Davis had been among the few intimate friends who met FDR's train from Campobello at the New York station. "In the next few years Livy was always most attentive and thoughtful, always doing the things you would not expect a man to think of doing."

With Livingston Davis, Missy LeHand, and FDR's sturdy valet,

LeRoy Jones, to accompany him and take care of his most basic needs, ER knew that her husband was well attended, and joined him now only on special occasions.

In fact, Eleanor and Franklin were infrequently together after 1923. Although in almost every letter ER wrote to her "Dearest Honey," she told him "We all miss you dreadfully"; and although she always signed her letters "Ever lovingly," neither partner had or made any substantial time for the other. Their lives simply went in different directions. They were pulled by different interests, attracted by different people.

Their marriage became only one of several vital centers in their lives. With all the independence and protection that wealth and prestige can secure, they shielded the many dimensions of their lives behind a tapestry of genuine devotion and family ritual. Birthdays, Thanksgiving, Christmas, and anniversary celebrations became great public feasts at which his closest friends and her closest friends shared the table. During the 1920s, it became traditional to spend Thanksgiving at Warm Springs, Christmas at Hyde Park, and their March anniversary off the Florida coast. Though ER's birthday generally passed without notable celebration (throughout their marriage, FDR seemed to be traveling, on a hunting, fishing, or sailing trip, during the week of 11 October), ER organized elaborate birthday revels for FDR in January, usually in New York. The core revelers were members of the "cuff-links club" he had created after the 1920 election, when he presented initialed cuff links to his closest staff, and they in turn gave a pin to ER. The club was continually enlarged as new friends entered the company, and over time included several of ER's closest friends as well.

FDR counted on ER to protect his privacy, as she could increasingly count on him. They depended on each other for protection from the prying eyes of SDR, and any of their acquaintances who might not approve or understand their compatible if unique arrangements.

On 24 February 1924, for example, when Missy LeHand returned to the *Larooco* after attending her father's funeral, ER wrote FDR: "I haven't told Mama that Missy is back because I think she has more peace of mind when she doesn't know things!" If ER ever resented FDR's long absences, she never said so. On occasion she missed him; on less frequent occasion she joined him: "I miss you very much and want your advice so often but I imagine it is as well you are far away from all entanglements. . . ."

They had few, if any, secrets from each other. FDR always knew where and with whom ER was. Her daily letters were full and detailed. On 1 March 1924, for example, she spoke at Skidmore on the World Court and the League of Nations; lunched with the dean of Bryn Mawr's Summer School for Women Workers; read at the Women's Trade Union League in the evening; and "Nan spent the night following dinner, as Marion was away." Similarly, ER knew FDR's whereabouts and the details of his company. Concerning Missy LeHand, ER was routinely supportive and solicitous.

~

THE MAJOR SOURCE OF TENSION BETWEEN ER AND FDR DUR-ing the 1920s was financial. Their political contributions and FDR's Southern vacations had become costly. FDR's business instincts were often unsound, and many of his riskier investments failed to return profits. He lost money on everything from oil wells to lobsters to a fantasy of transforming zeppelins into a commuter transport service. He made money, however, in a slot-machine business and as president of a Canadian corporation, United European Investors, that bought up devalued deutsche marks to invest in booming Weimar industries. He was also guaranteed an additional $10,000 annually when, on 1 January 1925, he formed a new law partnership with Basil O'Connor—which, because of FDR's political connections, was assured of acquiring a large number of municipal contracts. During this time, FDR's civic activities proliferated. He became chairman of the Boy Scouts of Greater New York, was the national director of the $10-million fund drive to complete New York's Episcopal Cathedral of Saint John the Divine, and committed himself to his most personal concern, the Georgia Warm Springs Foundation for Infantile Paralysis.

Despite her own trust income, ER depended on FDR to pay the family expenses. He controlled the purse strings, but frequently he went to his mother for all the bills neither of them could afford. During the months of his illness, and the years of his effort to recover his health by extended trips in warm-water resorts, unpaid bills remained unpaid for weeks, even months, while ER's insistent letters of reproach were met with forgetful silence. It was untenable. Eventually she set out to earn her own money from lectures, magazine articles, and guest appearances on radio shows. During the 1920s, financial independence enabled ER to pursue the interests and causes she believed in, and to manage her own life.

This independence incensed her mother-in-law: According to ER, although her mother-in-law believed in a vague sort of way that her children and their children should work, "she wanted them all at home under her supervision and guidance, for she had a strong feeling about holding the family together in almost matriarchal style." Sara Delano Roosevelt "always regretted that my husband had money of his own from his father and that I had a small income of my own; and when I began to earn money it was a real grief to her."

In March 1925, ER joined FDR in Florida, to celebrate their twentieth anniversary. On the train ride down, she read Margaret Kennedy's *The Constant Nymph.* Published in 1924 and now a feminist classic, it is a romantic tale of cross-generational love between an intense and passionate fifteen-year-old girl and her gifted composer father's even more gifted protégé. The father dies; the lover marries another; the girl is exiled to a boarding school; their love is haunting, compelling, forever. Filled with unrequited and requited love, poverty, greed, and familial heroism and scandal, the book appealed to ER. As she read it, she noted in her journal: "No form of love is to be despised."

ER's words were a variation of a conversation in the book, where love is celebrated for all its faults: "No sort of love ought to be despised, since, in spite of its rude beginnings, it is the first source of civility." As ER traveled to meet FDR and their friends for an anniversary feast, her mind was elsewhere. In particular it was on a new cottage that she was planning to build with Nancy Cook and Marion Dickerman.

ER had left New York reluctantly and somewhat fatigued. She had in fact spent several days in the hospital alone, and was hurt that FDR had failed even to respond to her letter. He sent no flowers, no note of greeting; he completely ignored her stay in the hospital. Although her gynecological procedure was not serious, she was puzzled, and tired, and indirect:

> Dearest Honey, I don't know whether my handwriting has really become so bad that you can't read it or whether you missed a letter. But I wrote you from the hospital that Dr. Ely decided it would be wise to curet. . . . I was only there a few days but the rest was rather nice . . . though the boys wrote Granny that they were very lonely as ever since you went away I was always on the go!

As soon as she left the hospital she resumed her activities: Thursday, she went with Elinor Morgenthau to Albany; Friday she visited Aunt Tissie and Cousin Susie; Saturday she went with the boys, Nan, and Marion to Caroline O'Day's for the weekend, and stayed until Monday night. Tuesday she went with Nan to Albany for the Child Labor hearing, followed on Wednesday by the forty-eight-hour hearing. On her return to New York City she went with Nan, Marion, and Louis "to dine near the Neighborhood Playhouse on Grand Street" before they "saw James Joyce's *Exiles,* which I hated." She then took the midnight train to Syracuse University, where she was scheduled to give a speech, lunch with the staff, and dine "at a sorority with the president of the Girls' Congress." The next day she visited her sons at Groton, and made plans to be with FDR: She left on the sixth to reach Long Key on 8 March.

During the ten days ER spent aboard the *Larooco,* she experienced some lovely moments, and was particularly moved by the speech that Henry Morgenthau made to toast the Roosevelts. She played endless games of whist with Louis Howe and enjoyed several sparkling conversations filled with long-range political strategies.

ER left on the eighteenth and wrote FDR: "I think you must have had a touch of that sadness which in spite of all its sunshine the Florida landscape always gives me! It is a bit dreary as a country, but I liked the life better this time than ever before." She noted in her journal that during this cruise she had a very "satisfactory talk with F about cottage affairs."

~

ER FIRST MET NANCY COOK, WHO WAS THEN ASSISTANT TO Harriet May Mills, first director of the Women's Division of the New York State Democratic Committee, in June 1922. Nancy Cook needed a "name" speaker to chair a fund-raising luncheon for activist women Democrats, and she telephoned ER. Her timing was perfect. Although ER was fully involved with the bipartisan League of Women Voters, she was frequently badgered by Louis Howe to get into mainstream Democratic Party politics. But until Nancy Cook's call ER had repeatedly refused. Although there is no record of their discussions, they had several long conversations on the telephone before they met, which created a stimulating, oddly stirring expectancy between ER and Nancy Cook. Whether or not the friendship that developed between them embraced amorosity, from their very first meeting their relationship was marked by an element of romance.

Eleanor arrived at the luncheon with a bouquet of violets for Nancy Cook. Marion Dickerman recalled that she strode into the banquet room, looked around, said only, "Where is Miss Cook?" and, immediately "presented the violets to Nancy—a gesture of poignant sweetness for the younger woman." Between women, gifts of violets were quite the rage during the 1920s—they appear again and again in feminist literature as an international symbol of affection.

Shortly after that luncheon, ER invited Nancy Cook to spend a weekend with her at Hyde Park, and they quickly discovered they shared many interests, as well as a chemical and vibrant connection of rare intensity. ER described her as "an attractive woman who had distinct artistic ability and could do almost anything with her hands." Nancy Cook was a potter, a jeweler, a photographer, and a carpenter.

Strong and athletic-looking, with penetrating brown eyes and short-bobbed curly hair, Nancy Cook looked boyish. She was dashing and roguish, flirtatious and irreverent. A capable administrator, she was an imaginative and efficient political organizer. They had fun together, and in her company ER did things she had never done before. On one occasion, she horrified her family by appearing with Nancy in identical brown-tweed knickerbocker outfits—evidently very British, with vest and jacket—that ER had ordered made.

However much time ER and Nancy Cook spent together, the dynamic of their friendship always included Cook's lifelong partner, Marion Dickerman. Nancy Cook and Marion Dickerman had lived together since 1909, when they were graduate students at Syracuse University.

Although Cook was seven years older than Dickerman, and emotionally they were very different in style and temperament, they were drawn "together forever by ties of mutual inward need." According to Dickerman, Cook lived at a faster pace, on a more energetic frequency, which she found refreshing and stimulating. Cook in turn was attracted by Dickerman's calm steadiness and "rhythmic regularity." Ardent suffragists and pacifists, during the war they went as Red Cross volunteers to London. They worked at the Endell Street Hospital, which was a woman-centered institution created by two women physicians and staffed almost entirely by women physicians, nurses, and practitioners. There, Nancy Cook's notable woodworking talents were put to use making artificial limbs.

When they returned to New York in August 1919, Marion Dickerman was greeted at the dock by her brother with the news that she had been selected to run for the New York State Assembly against the reactionary Assembly speaker, Thaddeus Sweet, a Republican who had opposed every piece of social justice legislation introduced by the Women's Joint Legislative Conference, formed in 1918 by Mary Elizabeth Dreier, Margaret Dreier Robins's sister and closest ally.

The Women's Joint Legislative Conference, an organization that particularly engaged ER's time, consisted of post-suffrage feminists who were now active in the League of Women Voters, the Women's Trade Union League, the Young Women's Christian Association, and the Consumers' League. Florence Kelley, Maud Swartz, Margaret Norrie, Nelle Swartz, and Mrs. James Lees Laidlaw, among others, joined Mary Elizabeth Dreier to campaign for a minimum-wage law, the eight-hour day, compulsory health insurance, improved schools and educational facilities, and health and leisure standards for working women. "Having fought for democracy abroad," they announced, "let us seek to establish it on a sounder basis at home."

They determined that Speaker Thaddeus C. Sweet was their primary enemy, and Marion Dickerman—well born, well educated, attractive, dignified, eloquent, and well known in Oswego—could defeat him. She was endorsed by the state Federation of Labor, Prohibitionists, Democrats, and Socialists. But as soon as her candidacy was perceived as a serious threat to Sweet, she was personally vilified and Red-baited.

Because she had no time to have a campaign photograph taken, the first press photos showed her still in her wartime uniform. The opposition press ridiculed her as an "Escaped Nun." Her tires were slashed during campaign meetings; she was denied rental spaces in local theatres; lights were turned off as she spoke. Armed with an electric torch, she announced: "After their darkness, came our light."

Running for New York State office during the height of the Red Scare, Dickerman was accused of responsibility for the race riots in Chicago, the police strike in Boston, and the coming "nationalization of women," allegedly Kollontai's primary threat and Revolutionary Russia's chief export. Sweet's good friend, New York State Senator Clayton R. Lusk, the author of the infamous Lusk Report on Revolutionary Radicals, was brought in to campaign against Dickerman: "This country is face to face with organized treason heavily financed from abroad and drastic measures will be necessary to put down this menace."

Despite this antiwoman, antireform, anti-Bolshevik propaganda barrage, Marion Dickerman—with the help of Mary Elizabeth Dreier and Nancy Cook, who served as her campaign manager—lost by a sufficiently small margin (seventeen thousand to ten thousand votes) to destroy Sweet's gubernatorial ambitions.

After the election, Dickerman temporarily removed herself from the political fray to accept a position as dean at the New Jersey State College in Trenton, and spent the summers teaching English at Bryn Mawr's Summer School for Women Workers. Nancy Cook was invited by Harriet May Mills to help organize the new Women's Division of the Democratic Committee in 1920. While Nancy Cook remained in New York and Marion Dickerman went where her career as an educator led her until 1923, they continued to live and work together whenever possible, and to share their cooperative apartment in Greenwich Village.

ER's friendship with Nancy Cook and Marion Dickerman evolved into an intimate association that lasted for over fifteen years. Although the three friends seemed during this time inseparable, Dickerman recalled that ER was closer, more attracted, and more devoted to Nancy Cook. She "loved Nan much more than she did me." But Marion Dickerman denied that she was ever "jealous," a minor emotion she discounted—both for herself and for those she admired. Because almost all the letters between Nancy Cook and Marion Dickerman, as well as between Cook, Dickerman, and ER, have disappeared, it is impossible to recapture either the tone or the precise geometry of their friendship. The letters that have survived indicate that ER wrote to Nancy Cook and Marion Dickerman often and at length, as was her lifelong habit with people close to her. ER missed them profoundly when they were separated, and in 1925 no other friends filled the space that they did at the core of her heart: "I feel I'd like to go off with you and forget the rest of the world existed."

During the 1920s, whenever she traveled without Marion or Nancy she longed for their company, no matter whom else she might be with. In February 1926, aboard the *Larooco,* ER wrote:

> Florida is queerer each year and the people make me want to know why they are here. We have a mechanic on the boat today who brought his wife because they're living in a tent and I suspect she wouldn't be left alone. Well, she's a little German dressmaker and the most unhappy, out of place person. What is she doing here? . . .
>
> I wish you were here. It would do you good and I should enjoy it. . . . Much love to Nan and to you, life is quite empty without your dear presence.

That spring, while touring the Massachusetts countryside with her boys and on her way to visit Franklin at Louis Howe's for a day, Eleanor wrote, "I wish you were coming with Nan to-morrow, it doesn't seem quite right to be seeing things without you."

After 1925, ER, Nancy Cook, Marion Dickerman, and also Caroline O'Day created the Val-Kill partnership—which eventually included the *Women's Democratic News,* which ER edited, the Todhunter School, where Marion Dickerman was principal, and the Val-Kill furniture factory, which opened in 1927, over which Nancy Cook presided. Although Caroline O'Day's precise role in these enterprises remains unclear, and she never lived at the cottage, she was associated with and financially contributed to every aspect of the partnership, and was personally closest to Marion Dickerman.

A wealthy suffragist and pacifist, Caroline O'Day had been associated with Lillian Wald's Henry Street Settlement. After suffrage, she became co-chair of the Democratic State Committee and head of its Women's Division. She was one of the most active women in the Democratic Party after 1925; from 1935 to 1943, she would be New York State's member of Congress at large, a position that no longer exists but was tantamount to Senator.

Born Caroline Love Goodwin, she was the daughter of a prosperous and landed Savannah family. Brilliant and artistic, she graduated from the Lucy Cobb Institute in Athens, Georgia, and was sent to Paris to study with Whistler. She also studied in Munich, in the Netherlands, and at Cooper Union in New York City. Her paintings were exhibited at the Paris Salon in 1899 and 1900, where they won honors. She married Daniel O'Day, a vice-president of John D. Rockefeller's Standard Oil Company, whom she met during a blind date in Amsterdam. O'Day encouraged and supported his wife's suffrage and pacifist activities, and after he died suddenly in 1916, she devoted the rest of her life to social reform and progressive politics.

With so many gaps in the documentary record, the intensity and the nature of the emotional dyads and triangles within the rectangle are lost. Nevertheless, the first public mention of "The Cottage" on the Val-Kill was written by Caroline O'Day in November 1925, in the *Women's Democratic News:* "We will let you in to the secret of The Cottage. When politics is through with us we are retiring to this charming retreat that is now rearing its stone walls against the beautiful cedars of a Dutchess County hillside. Here we mean to embark on an absolutely new enterprise. . . ."*

---

* When I asked Caroline O'Day's son, Daniel O'Day, about his mother's intention of living at Val-Kill, he seemed amazed, and responded: "Goodness, no. Why should she? She had her own entirely comfortable place in Rye, and she lived with Frances Perkins." To my understanding that Perkins lived with Mary Harriman Rumsey until her death in 1935 and after that shared a home in Washington with his mother, Daniel O'Day (who was nineteen in 1925) was adamant: He said he was in a position to know, since he and his older sister, Elia, and his younger brother, Charles, lived with his mother, and he at least hated Frances Perkins. All of Caroline O'Day's papers have been lost; nor is she mentioned in any personal way in Perkins's writings, or in her oral histories.—B.W.C.

Val-Kill, their new "cottage," was two miles away from Springwood, on the eastern side of FDR's sprawling property, set apart by the Val-Kill stream, which served almost as a moat. A noisy rolling-logged bridge was built over the stream, presumably to discourage animals; it enabled cars to travel to the door but only after creating an unusual wood-on-wood racket—to announce visitors and interlopers alike.

According to Marion Dickerman, it was FDR who originated the idea of their home on the Val-Kill. One afternoon, ER "remarked rather wistfully" that their picnic on the banks of that rocky stream was likely to be the last of the season, because SDR planned to close the Big House. FDR protested: "But aren't you girls silly? This isn't Mother's land. I bought this acreage myself. And why shouldn't you three have a cottage here of your own, so you could come and go as you please?"

He donated the property, and offered to build the swimming pool for use by all their friends and family. Almost immediately, on 5 August 1924, he wrote his contractor friend Elliott Brown: "My missus and some of her female political friends want to build a shack on a stream in the back woods and want, instead of a beautiful marble bath, to have the stream dug out so as to form an old-fashioned swimming hole."

Val-Kill had touches of romance that fully justified FDR's sobriquet: "The Honeymoon Cottage." Much of the furniture, made by Nancy Cook and her assistants in their own factory, bore the initials E.M.N. ER embroidered towels, dressing-table covers, and linens E.M.N. And the three women received presents of silver, crystal, pewter, and porcelain engraved with their initials. FDR frequently gave ER and her friends gifts for the cottage, especially plantings and picnic accessories. He inscribed a book, *Little Marion's Pilgrimage,* to Dickerman: "To my little pilgrim, whose progress is always upward and onward, to the things of beauty and the thoughts of love, and the like—From her affectionate Uncle Franklin, on the occasion of the opening of the love nest on the Val-Kill." He autographed a favorite speech: "Another first edition for the library of the Three Graces of the Val-Kill." Sara Delano Roosevelt, on the other hand, detested Val-Kill and disapproved of ER's new friends, who smoked, wore neckties, and were entirely independent. She could never understand how or why ER preferred to live with that couple in "that hovel" rather than with her, in comfort, and with the appropriate number of servants.

Just as ER behaved toward Missy LeHand as first wife and was always gracious and solicitous, so FDR assumed the role of concerned and generous paterfamilias in relation to Nancy Cook and Marion Dickerman. He called them "the girls," and acted as if they were his charges—occasionally uncontrollable, to be sure—but fully his to guide and instruct. They, in turn, were entirely devoted to the promotion of his career, and if he felt condescending toward "the girls," it was all disguised behind genuine bonds of friendship and political loyalty, as well as considerable quantities of shared merriment.

On one occasion, for example, Marion Dickerman—believing that FDR had changed his mind about paying for the swimming pool—offered to terminate their entire agreement and abandon Val-Kill. The truth was, he responded, ER had told him to pay the contractor nothing without checking with her, since she believed the contractor was double-billing them. He continued:

> So what is it all about? Why the injured tone . . . Oh ye of little faith! Don't you poor idiots realize how much I care for you both and love having you at Val-Kill! . . .
>
> Think it over, my dears, stop talking about "cheapening our relations," stop listening to fairy stories, . . . get your feet on earth and be your own dear straight forward nice selves. . . . If I had you here I would spank you both and then kiss you.

FDR presided over every plan for Val-Kill. When ER and her friends decided to depart from his advice regarding the placement of one window, he wrote an irate letter: "*If* you build it that way, I'll *never* come to visit you."

In the same letter "To Dear Nan—also Marion," FDR wrote that ER was to arrive at Warm Springs shortly, but only for ten days: He wished that she would stay longer.

She will certainly get lots of sleep and reading down here. There is no possibility of keeping her from getting tired in New York. The only way is to plan to get her away from N.Y. and when the cottage is built that will be one means toward the end.

A great deal of love to you both. I wish you could be here too. Perhaps next year we can make it a real family party.

The letter was also signed by Missy LeHand, who wrote a postscript: "Dear Nan & Marion: I just want to send my love to you both, also. I wish you were both coming. It will be nice to have Mrs. Roosevelt."

Throughout the Val-Kill construction process, tensions over authority divided ER and FDR. Increasingly Eleanor fought for a controlling influence on all issues that concerned her. But she was continually eclipsed by Franklin's male authority in the world of blueprints and business. Husbands were supposed to bid and to bargain with contractors and construction crews. Women were not, after all, supposed to build houses for themselves.

FDR hired Henry Toombs, his friend and Caroline O'Day's cousin, to serve as architect on the project. When ER, Dickerman, and Cook indicated a willingness to pay more money to get their home built faster, FDR countered: "If you three girls will just go away and leave us alone, Henry and I will build the cottage" for much less money.

To remove themselves, they agreed to go on a camping trip to Campobello with the boys—ER's two sons FDR, Jr., and John, her nephew Henry, and young George Draper, the son of FDR's classmate and physician—and leave matters to FDR. It was a curious summer. ER would have preferred to supervise the building of her own home. She would also have preferred to be with Anna and James during their tour of Europe that summer. Because her own European tour with Marie Souvestre had meant so much to her, she had always been eager to introduce her children, and later her grandchildren, to that experience. But Sara had pre-empted her in that, as in so many other things, by inviting James and Anna to accompany her—without even consulting ER on the subject. When ER learned of the trip, according to Anna, "Suddenly to my horror Mother burst into tears. . . . She had always looked forward herself to taking Jimmy and me to Europe, but she did not have the money to do so. So Granny [did.]"

ER's camping trip, with two tents and cooking gear (including a stove upon which Nancy Cook "produced some very good meals"), was for her a first, and by no means unpleasant, experience. Still, there were accidents and tensions: The boys fought; they disappeared; Junior cut his leg with an ax; and there was a surprising animosity toward three women traveling "alone." On one occasion, a farmer refused them space to camp after he asked "Where are your husbands?" When ER replied, "Mine is not with me and the others don't have husbands," he declared that he did not "want women of that kind" camping on his fields and sent them off into the night.

The entire trip was an adventure. They went north to Ausable Chasm, then on to Montreal and Quebec, over to the White Mountains, up Mount Washington by the "little cog railway," and across another mountain on burros, which ER found "great fun," and on to Castine, Maine, to visit Molly Dewson and Polly Porter; ER and the boys stayed in a guest cottage "down by the water." From Maine, they went on to Campobello, which ER had avoided since the summer FDR was stricken. To her relief, she found it "still serene, beautiful and enjoyable."

While they camped, FDR purchased lumber and fieldstone, trim and doors, grass seed and gravel for much less than they had previously arranged. He sent them weekly bulletins: The swimming pool was completed; the ground was graded; the new road was laid out; the grass seed went in. He contracted the stone workers, carpenters, and plumbers; and agreed on all the needed materials. "In closing, I can only suggest that hereafter you call Father the 'Cascaret'—he works while you sleep."

ER was not amused: "Dearest Honey! I don't like your suggested new name though you certainly do work—But we don't sleep. I won't be slandered! If you lived with four small boys you would feel *very* active."

FDR acknowledged that the boys were a handful and were "made of steel and rubber." He did not mean to minimize ER's frequently lonely effort to keep the family on an even course. And he apologized:

He appreciated ER's ability to keep the family united, the children active and entertained.

The shared intimacy of Eleanor's court and Franklin's court stretched the limits of a delicate balance. There were occasional errors and misperceptions; then there were hurt feelings, moments of confusion and remorse. ER resented not being consulted on significant family decisions, such as her children's college intentions. She had, for example, many conversations with her son Elliott regarding his poor grades at Groton, his general lack of interest in school, and his unwillingness to go to Harvard. She agreed that he probably needed to be free of the shadow of his older brother, James. He wanted at first to go to Princeton, and then he threatened to run away out west, an idea ER never opposed. She was surprised, therefore, in the autumn of 1926 to learn that her husband, without consulting her, had made other plans. She wrote to FDR: "Elliott tells me you and James decided he would go to Harvard next year. I am sorry but I suppose you had a good reason. Write me of your talk with the boys. . . ."

Elliott never did go to Harvard, but ER was not involved in his decision, and she resented, above all, not being taken quite seriously by her sons and the male part of the world she inhabited. During the summer of 1925, when Women's Trade Union League leaders Rose Schneiderman and Maud Swartz visited at Campobello, ER's sons listened with rude amusement while their mother and her guests discussed the intolerable condition of women workers and the need for trade unions and industrial protection. ER wrote Marion Dickerman: "At lunch we had a discussion on trade unions I was left as I always am with the boys, feeling quite impotent to make a dent. . . . [They] regard me as a woman to be dutifully and affectionately thought of because I am their mother but . . . I hold queer opinions [that] can't be considered seriously as against those of their usual male environment!"

While the older boys were at Groton, the younger boys were at the Buckley School in New York, and also in dancing school, where the Roosevelts' class traditions persisted: "The little boys have their last dancing class tomorrow afternoon and are doing a minuet in costume with wigs," wrote ER. "They are so sweet!"

By the mid-twenties, ER was concerned especially about her older children. Anna was eighteen, unhappy at Cornell, where she never wanted to be, and still more unhappy at home, with all its tensions and undercurrents, particularly between her mother and grandmother. She wanted "to get out," and became engaged to Curtis Dall, a rather conventional and balding financier associated with Lehman Brothers. Then thirty, he seemed appealing to Anna above all for his apparent stability; but Eleanor was not sure. "I don't think she even thinks she's serious but he is and I'm not sure she didn't let herself get a bit further than she meant to be!" They were married in June 1926.

James was now at Harvard and attended all the appropriate club initiations and parties, but ER was dismayed by his correspondence: "I can't say that three nights drunk fills me with anything but disgust!" "Elliott as usual thinks I'm hard on him because he won't work really hard and I injured his feelings in public by making some remark about a gentleman who didn't bathe for a week!" "The trials of a large family!"

Through virtually all of her children's ordeals, her husband was away and ER was the responsible parent. She rarely complained, and more rarely still was she credited for her efforts. Rather, she was generally dismissed as a nag—and continually interfered with by her mother-in-law. SDR remained adept at salting old wounds and exacerbating their tensions about money. She succeeded especially in creating something of a stir when Anna married Curtis Dall.

SDR decided, without consulting Eleanor or Franklin, to present the young couple with an expensive cooperative apartment. She enraged ER by telling Anna to keep it a secret from her parents. When they learned of her intentions and opposed the gift because they believed the Dalls neither wanted nor could then afford to maintain it, she threatened to cancel it.

On 31 March 1927, ER wrote FDR that she had "a run in with Mama about getting a little more coal," and then a real "bust" over the apartment. SDR wrote a rare letter of apology:

> Eleanor dear, I am very very sorry that I hurt you—*twice,* first by not letting Anna tell you before it was decided & then by saying I would not give it to them. I certainly am old enough not to make

mistakes & I can only say how much I regret it—I did not think I
could be nasty *or* mean, & I fear I had too good an opinion of
myself—Also I love you dear too much to ever want to hurt you.
I *was hasty,* & of course I shall give them the apartment. I only
wanted them to decide for *themselves* & surprise you & Franklin—
No doubt he will also be angry with me—Well, I must just bear it—

Devotedly, Mama

ER wrote FDR that she had answered quite politely and apologized
as well. But "[I] told her you never demeaned yourself by getting angry
over little things. So you see I've been thoroughly nasty but I'll try to
behave again now for a time. . . ."

Throughout this period, ER's letters are laced with frustration—
bills to be paid, forgotten allowances to be sent. It was annoying, and
ER resented having to ask FDR for money. In the autumn of 1927, she
wrote: "Please answer all the questions in my last letter & send me
money. . . . How about Anna's September 1st allowance, did you remember it? My love to Missy and much love to you dear. I do wish
you were here these lovely October days."

On 25 October, she wrote again: "I wired you for Anna's September
allowance because she asked me this AM if you were giving her an
allowance. Now, was when she needed it as she was moving in & they
had $500 extra expenses. . . . I must have my money too dear. I know
you hate to be bothered but these things must be."

The more their lives diverged, the more their interests varied, the
more ER needed an income of her own. She raised all the money for
the political journal, the *Women's Democratic News,* and was proud of
her resourcefulness.

She wrote to FDR on 10 April 1926: "This has been a hectic week!
I am learning the advertising business!" After endless phone calls, ER
got enough ads for the journal to be self-sufficient. "So you see," she
wrote proudly, "this Bulletin is going to be a real business proposition."

The first issue of the monthly appeared in May 1925 with features
by prominent Democrats, legislative reports and proposals, news anal-
yses, and sufficient advertising to pay all costs. ER was editor and
treasurer; Caroline O'Day was president; Elinor Morgenthau was vice-

president; Nancy Cook was business manager; and Marion Dickerman was secretary.

~

IN 1926, ELEANOR, NANCY COOK, AND MARION DICKERMAN bought the Todhunter School, a girls' school in New York City, where ER also taught. In addition, she worked hard to sell the furniture reproductions that Nancy Cook made at their Val-Kill factory, opened in 1927. ER held showings in her East 65th Street house and at Hyde Park which brought in significant funds. They sold to Vassar, and to Sloane's Department Store. They sold to FDR for Warm Springs, and ER bought Val-Kill furniture for all of her friends and most of her relatives. Still, however much ER may have contributed to the family purse, her finances remained connected to Franklin's, and he controlled the purse strings: "Please send Nan a check if you haven't and please send me one for I am broke and so is the shop!" she wrote him on 8 February 1928.

By 1928, however, ER had decided to become personally independent and financially solvent. Within two years, she earned thousands of dollars writing articles for popular magazines, including *McCall's* and *Redbook.* Although her sons frequently mocked her efforts, she was delighted to be able to reach a wide and popular audience on a variety of subjects concerning women in politics, and relieved finally to be earning her own money. She wrote FDR, when she was offered $500 for "only 2500 words," that she supposed "James will tell me he would not write for such a magazine, as he did about the *Redbook.* But I am glad of the chance!"

ER generally minimized her own contributions and her own achievements. In retrospect, her attitude seems more a defense against being unappreciated, against seeing her work and her efforts go unacknowledged, than an accurate measure of her real sense of self-worth. Many of her letters indicate that her feelings were hurt because her work was overlooked, her contributions taken for granted—especially by FDR and the members of her own immediate household. But she did seem more and more able to appreciate herself, even when those around her did not.

Moreover, ER gradually learned during this period of her life to be direct about her feelings, to acknowledge when she was displeased, angry, or in some way wounded. Griselda no longer sulked in dreary self-righteous silence. Rifts were healed with a new honesty and forthrightness. Part of the reason for this was that for the first time she had friends who actually noticed her moods, and cared about them.

On 18 May 1926, ER wrote to Marion Dickerman: "I have just a minute and want to send you a line. I hate to think that you've been unhappy dear; it is new for me to have anyone know when I have 'moods' much less have it make any real difference & if you'll try not to take them too seriously I'll try not to let myself have them!"

Marion Dickerman remembered the 1920s as the "Invincible Summer" of their lives. During this time, ER relinquished the old "puritan" habits of social duty that had prevented her from enjoying spontaneous fun and the most casual pleasures. She embraced the countryside she loved in a new and athletic way. Her old fear of mountain climbing evaporated. ER hiked everywhere, covering great distances with an incomparably long and steady stride. She could outwalk anybody. She enjoyed swimming and riding. She loved to drive, and she drove fast. She wanted to fly, and she did fly with Amelia Earhart. ER became one of the first women to promote flying as a hobby, for the thrill of it. Her headaches and routine winter colds disappeared. She began to enjoy good food, different foods, and put on weight for the first time in her adult life.

SDR, who had an amazing capacity to reconcile herself to virtually all situations, wrote her son after spending some time with ER and her friends at the cottage: "Eleanor is so happy over there that she looks well and plump, don't tell her so, it is very becoming, and I hope she will not grow thin."

Val-Kill enabled ER to separate from her mother-in-law. Even in the environs of Hyde Park, ER was now physically removed from her constant gaze, daily intrusions, and frequent criticisms. This defused the immediate power struggle between them regarding the children. Although that struggle never really ceased, it was no longer the dominant factor in their daily relations.

Moreover, ER was free for the first time to invite her own guests to a home where she felt in control. The humiliation of having to ask permission to invite anybody home, knowing that Sara never really did approve of her friends, was over. Marion Dickerman flattered herself that SDR's politeness to her represented fondness. But Eleanor knew that Marion deluded herself. Privately, Sara never missed an opportunity to scorn all her friends. Marion Dickerman and Nancy Cook were tolerated by SDR—they were the daughters of educated, old-family, affluent, Protestant New Yorkers. Rose Schneiderman—who ER never dared to invite to Hyde Park, for example—was an ardent unionist, a working-class Russian immigrant, committed to her class and her Jewish heritage. SDR disliked them all and resented their presence in her family circle. She disdained their style, their ideas, and their habits; loathed their presumptions, their knickerbockers, and their politics.

Eleanor's removal to Val-Kill loosened her mother-in-law's grip, and transformed their tug-of-war for FDR's affections. ER had removed herself from the game—or at least from her former and subservient place on the game board. This left SDR temporarily distressed and worried about the future. Eleanor wrote Franklin from Campobello during the summer of 1925: "I wish you could read Mama's last letter to me. She is afraid of everything. . . . Afraid of your going over bad and unfrequented roads, afraid I'll let the children dive in shallow water & break their necks, afraid they'll get more cuts! She must suffer more than we dream is possible!"

But as SDR came to understand that Eleanor and Franklin were both now fully embarked on a path to which they were committed, she too shifted gears, with remarkable grace. When she saw that FDR intended to remain active in business and politics, she became his most ardent and generous promoter. Eventually she also acknowledged the importance of ER's activities, and appeared with her at political luncheons and dinners sponsored by such organizations as the League of Women Voters and the Women's City Club.

Gradually, Sara became a patron of almost all ER's activities— whether or not they helped to promote Franklin's career. Although SDR did not share her son and daughter-in-law's ambitions, and continued to detest their friends and associates, she was entirely proud of their achievements. If she could no longer dominate their lives, she could at least participate fully in them. Moreover, by supporting them financially and publicly she retained a semblance of control.

But for ER and FDR, the 1920s were not about control. They were about convalescence and independence and homes of their own. Out of their joint but separate paths toward greater health and fulfillment emerged a vision of a complex future that was to unite them in work and action as never before, while allowing each a full measure of autonomy.

~

As ER planned her home at Val-Kill, FDR planned his center at Warm Springs. At first ER disapproved of Warm Springs, located, coincidentally, in Bullochville, Georgia, the home of her paternal grandmother, Mittie Bulloch Roosevelt. Her fond memory of the many stories told her by her father and her aunts did nothing to dispel the reality of the gloomy, ramshackle place she saw when she and FDR first visited it in 1924. ER found the Georgia countryside even less appealing than Florida. The healing, bubbling springs that shot out of the rocks and the pool were magnificent, but all the buildings of the former spa, now owned by FDR's friend the philanthropist George Foster Peabody, were shabby and depressing. All the windows needed to be replaced, and there were cracks and holes in the roof and siding: "It won't be practical in the winter for a long time if it ever is." FDR was immediately drawn to the warm healing waters, in which he felt as if he could walk again. He dreamed of establishing and administering a modern therapeutic center, and purchased the facility from Peabody in 1926 for $195,000.

FDR planned to invest two-thirds of his entire trust into what ER at first dismissed as a chimera. When she expressed her reservations, FDR exploded in anguish. It was the first and only time ER witnessed the depth of her husband's "discouragement" and "bitterness" about his condition. FDR made it clear that he was willing to spend any amount of money on the chance that he might "not be quite such a helpless individual."

After this encounter, ER assured FDR that she would support any decision he made; she wanted him to do whatever he thought best. She also encouraged him to keep the houseboat, which he felt he must surrender for financial reasons: "Don't worry about being selfish, it is more important that you have all you need and wish than anything else and you always give the chicks more than they need and you know I always do just what I want!"

Until his outburst, ER, Louis Howe, his mother, and even his law partners had been united in their opposition to Warm Springs.

ER wrote Marion Dickerman that FDR was hurt and dispirited by everybody's lack of appreciation for what he was trying to do. He thought it was "a big thing which may be a financial success and a medical and philanthropic opportunity for infantile and that all of us have raised our eyebrows and thrown cold water on it. There is nothing to do but to make him feel one is interested. . . ."

In the spring of 1926, ER went to Warm Springs, willing to help. After she left, she wrote: "I know how you love creative work, my only feeling is that Georgia is somewhat distant for you to keep in touch with what is really a big undertaking. One cannot, it seems to me, have *vital* interests in widely divided places, but that may be because I'm old and rather overwhelmed by what there is to do. . . . Don't be discouraged by me; I have great confidence in your extraordinary interest and enthusiasm." That autumn, the *Larooco* was destroyed in a hurricane, and once that source of diversion was gone, FDR devoted all his energy to his own physical therapy and the center at Bullochville, now renamed Warm Springs.

With FDR preoccupied by his new healing center, the partners of Val-Kill spent most of their time together. They seemed inseparable until 1932, when their friendship was eclipsed by changing circumstances, especially the appearance of new friends in ER's life whom Marion and Nancy actively disliked, and who disliked them—Lorena Hickok in particular. But the germs of their growing estrangement were planted earlier. ER knew during the 1920s that she needed and wanted intimate friends whose loyalty she could count on for herself alone, as she could with Esther Lape and Elizabeth Read.

But from the beginning, Marion Dickerman especially was dazzled by FDR, and her loyalties were divided. "Never in [her] life," Marion

Dickerman recalled, had she "met so utterly charming a man." It seemed to her "only right and natural that people should devote themselves heart and soul to him and his career." Nancy Cook too saw her political future in terms of FDR's rising star. ER's first mention of Nancy Cook in her correspondence with FDR, dated 29 June 1922, had included the premonitory sentence: "Spent a long time with Miss Cook and agreed to get up a tea with you at once."

Eventually Marion Dickerman and Nancy Cook began to consider themselves the bridge between Eleanor and Franklin, and began to fancy their diplomacy equally appreciated. ER tended to live at the Big House when FDR was actually in residence. But on one occasion they argued so vigorously that Eleanor "closeted" herself at Val-Kill for three days, maintaining her old-style silence. Only after Nancy Cook persuaded Franklin to drive himself over in his hand-controlled auto did ER reluctantly go out to him. They talked for over two hours in the car and then returned to Springwood. Cook and Dickerman took credit for great diplomacy, but their bridge work developed a perilously stretched quality. In time, it tilted too far over to FDR's side, swamping the entire friendship between ER, Dickerman, and Cook.

~

ER SAW HER OWN STRUGGLE FOR INDEPENDENCE AS connected to the wider struggle for full economic and political power for all women. And she fully appreciated that the path to victory involved networks of friendship and support that enabled women to forge their demands from a position of strength and unity. Politics for ER was never a theoretical adventure. She understood politics as she understood her own life: There were things that needed to be done because they were good, and right, and decent.

In August 1923, during her first trip to Campobello since FDR's illness, while reading aloud one evening to Nancy Cook, Marion Dickerman, and Rose Schneiderman, ER repeated several times one particular sentence from *The Countryman's Year* by David Grayson (the pen name of Ray Stannard Baker): "Back of tranquility lies always conquered unhappiness." She referred to that phrase often over the years. During the 1920s, ER conquered unhappiness, and moved beyond it.

14. ER, Political Boss

ELEANOR ROOSEVELT BEGAN HER CAREER AS THE FORE-most political woman of the twentieth century convinced that women and men enter politics for different reasons: Men enter politics to pursue their own careers; women are motivated by a desire to change society, to improve the daily conditions of life. Impressed by the women she worked with, she came to believe that women's public activities would determine America's national future. Not a prewar suffragist herself, she fully appreciated the suffragists' century of struggle, and the grass-roots strategy that ultimately triumphed.

She believed that fundamental change required active and committed women who were willing to go door to door, block by block, and educate people on an individual basis about the real needs and conditions of society. She saw the need for newsletters and information bulletins. ER was one of the first women activists to realize that little would be achieved without a mimeograph machine, and persuaded New York's League of Women Voters to purchase one on 3 October 1922. Above all, ER understood that information and organization required local clubs and political centers, a network of women active in every town and village connected to one another through meetings, debates, round-table discussions, luncheons, dinner parties, and personal friendships.

During the 1920s, there were four centers of political power for women in New York State: the League of Women Voters, which was dominated by Esther Lape, Elizabeth Read, Eleanor Roosevelt, Narcissa Vanderlip, Margaret Norrie, Carrie Chapman Catt, Agnes Brown Leach, and Helen Rogers Reid; the Women's Trade Union League (WTUL), largely in the hands of Rose Schneiderman, Maud Swartz, and Mary Elizabeth Dreier; the Women's Division of the New York State Democratic Committee, which was dominated throughout the 1920s by five intimate friends, Nancy Cook, Marion Dickerman, Caroline O'Day, Elinor Morgenthau, and Eleanor Roosevelt; and the Women's City Club, an umbrella organization dedicated to social reform and municipal affairs. Most of the two thousand members of the club were professional women—attorneys, physicians, educators, consumer activists, unionists, businesswomen, writers, artists, advertising agents, architects, engineers, printers, accountants, volunteer activists, saleswomen, office workers, and bankers—and many of them were active also in the WTUL, and the League of Women Voters. Here ER met and worked with every activist political woman in New York—social workers like Lillian Wald, Mary (Molly) Dewson, and Mary Simkhovitch; labor reformers such as Frances Perkins and Belle Moskowitz; Marie Jennie Howe, the Unitarian minister who created the women's social club Heterodoxy.

There were many and labyrinthine connections. But a small number of women really pulled the network together. They served on the governing councils of each organization and decided on policy and strategy. ER rapidly became a leader of this group, which was made up largely of her own circle of Democratic women. She helped to raise funds, edited newsletters, moderated panels, participated in debates, presented information, toured the state on behalf of candidates and causes, and represented New York at national conventions of political women. To pursue the women's agenda, for six years ER, Nancy Cook, Marion Dickerman, Elinor Morgenthau, and Caroline O'Day went "Trooping for Democracy." In every weather and in every season, they toured New York State in their Democratic blue roadster, which they had bought together, or in O'Day's chauffeured Packard. They toured every county to demand an expanded public-housing program, improved sanitation and sewerage control, frequent and comfortable public transit, new parks and public playgrounds, school lunches and nursing facilities, unemployment insurance, workers' compensation, occupational-safety-and-health legislation, the eight-hour day, protective laws for women workers, mandatory-education laws, child-labor legislation, pure-food-and-milk legislation, the right of women to serve on juries, and equal representation of women on all committees of the Democratic Party.

At first public speaking was an ordeal for ER. But once she became comfortable at the podium, she was grateful for each opportunity to convey the messages she considered so urgent. Louis Howe was her tutor. Initially, he accompanied her when she spoke. He sat in the back of the room and monitored her every move. When her hands shook, he told her to hold the podium, not the paper. When she felt nervous, he recommended that she smile and breathe deeply. She laughed and even giggled inappropriately—at the wrong time, with the wrong sound. That was, he assured her, the worst thing she could do: It sent the wrong message. Howe's advice was specific: Be prepared. Know what you want to say. Say it. And sit down. Never appear nervous.

ER's gifts as a speaker were ultimately the result of her great love for people. Because she cared about her audience, she knew that it mattered to make eye contact and to connect directly with everybody in the room. Subsequently she hired voice trainers in an effort to control her pitch and her register. She was soon in demand as a speaker.

Throughout the 1920s, articles about ER and her political work appeared almost weekly in *The New York Times*. She was the subject of news accounts, columns, editorials, profiles in the Sunday *Magazine* section, and letters to the editor. Her public appearances were national news. Because she spoke candidly, her major statements were frequently quoted in full. On 7 August 1922, for example, ER denounced New York's Republican Governor Nathan Miller as a reactionary:

> He has shown himself affected with the hopeless moral blindness of the man who, losing his sight in early youth, finds it impossible to visualize in his mind anything but the sights and surroundings of the world as he saw it long ago.
>
> This moral blindness is the distinguishing characteristic of the "standpatter." It is quite as dangerous to our country as downright crookedness. The crooked politician is at least anxious to make a

showing of progressiveness in public reform, but the hopeless reactionary is a stumbling block in the march of civilization.

Women are by nature progressives. . . . It is impossible to be both a Republican and a progressive under the leadership of Governor Miller. . . . [So] [t]he women of this State have . . . decided to go forward with the Democrats to better things rather than remain with the Republicans, futilely digging among the war-destroyed ruins of ancient standards of civilization for some charred bits of salvage with which to build a pitiful imitation of our old industrial structure. . . .

Ironically, in her memoirs ER called the chapter devoted to the 1920s, the decade of the most robust political activity she undertook on her own, "Private Interlude." Since she could hardly have meant by that an absorption in private or domestic affairs, one must conclude that this period in her life seemed in retrospect private in the sense that it was hers to do with as she pleased. She neither campaigned for FDR nor served as his surrogate. He was preoccupied with recovery; she was preoccupied with politics. She became famous not as FDR's wife, but as a major political force to be reckoned with.

Yet, the more she achieved, the more she was acclaimed and celebrated in her own right, the more she sought to reassure FDR that she was doing it all for him. On 6 February 1924, for example, ER wrote him a long, rambling letter full of detail about her activities. But she concluded by reminding her husband that she was merely his temporary stand-in. She had been asked to sponsor or attend several memorial services for President Wilson, who died on 3 February. She agreed, though she understood they only wanted FDR's name. She aimed neither to compete with her husband nor to upstage him. Only slowly and with considerable reluctance did ER admit that she was genuinely pleased by her public activities. Much more often she professed a selfless lack of interest in her own work, and her own career, and thereby contributed to our distorted image of her public self. While she was First Lady, she wrote that she was pushed into politics reluctantly—and solely in support of her husband. She never acknowledged her own joy in the game, or her own skills at manipulating the cards.

One of the myths that ER seemed actively to encourage was that she was naïve politically. Not insignificantly, several people who harbored that illusion were actually victims of ER's political intrigue and opposition. The fact that they saw her as a "dim bulb" rather than as their enemy is probably the greatest testimony to her political style and maneuvering. ER's gracious manner often obscured intense emotions, including disapproval and dislike. She tended to avoid confrontations and occasionally walked away from angry words, but never from the battle. She did not play politics transcendentally—somewhere above the fray. She walked hard edges, made tough decisions, and followed her principles wherever they led.

Nowhere was this more clear than in her part in the Bok Peace Award controversy, which caused her to be attacked as a subversive. The Bok Peace Award was established in 1923 by Edward Bok, the former publisher and editor of the *Ladies' Home Journal,* who offered a prize of $50,000 to the plan that would "provide a practicable means whereby the United States can take its place and do its share toward preserving world peace, while not making compulsory the participation of the U.S. in European wars if any such are, in the future, found unpreventable." It might be "based upon the present covenant of the League of Nations or may be entirely apart from that instrument." A fortune equivalent to over $1 million in contemporary currency, the prize was headline news throughout the United States. It was featured in news columns, editorials, and cartoons; Will Rogers joked about it; it appeared in the "Mutt and Jeff" comic strip.

Esther Lape agreed to administer the prize on the condition that Eleanor Roosevelt and Narcissa Vanderlip work with her. The contest created a stir in academic circles, and was taken seriously among leading American internationalists, especially businessmen who hoped for an expanding economic future free of both war and the current hysteria that rejected all European "entanglements"—including "foreign" trade. The former Secretary of War and Secretary of State, Elihu Root, agreed to be jury chair; Judge Learned Hand, Henry Stimson (to become Hoover's Secretary of State and FDR's Secretary of War), and Roscoe Pound (dean of the Harvard Law School) were dedicated members of the committee. The jury also included Colonel Edward M. House, Wilson's former confidant; Wellesley College President Ellen Fitz Pendleton; William Allen White, editor of the Emporia *Gazette;* General James G. Harbord, formerly General John J. Pershing's chief of staff, then president of the new Radio Corporation of America; and Brand Whitlock, the novelist and progressive politician who served as Wilson's ambassador to Belgium.

Lape considered it "deeply significant that none of the law experts" considered the campaign "a superficial popular activity." In fact, a great optimistic mood regarding the possibility of outlawing war and achieving world peace through rational discourse prevailed during the 1920s. Thousands of plans were submitted to the jury from noted legal scholars, businessmen, former and current public officials, including FDR.

FDR worked hard on his plan, a variation of the current League, which he called a Society of Nations (heralding the United Nations). The range of submissions was vast: Harvard's President Charles W. Eliot, for example, saw the path to world peace through increased "family discipline." M. Carey Thomas, Bryn Mawr's longtime president, called for a "Declaration of Interdependence" to outlaw war and create a "Council of Vigilance and Inquiry" to resolve global tensions. Some wanted a national referendum in case of war; many sought means by which war, and the production of weapons for war, would be made unprofitable; one called for an army of hypnotists to drive warlike thoughts from the mind. Many ascribed war to propaganda, misinformation, and packaged hatred, and called for the creation of schools for international ethics and understanding. Hundreds of plans focused on the need for an equitable distribution of raw materials and natural resources; the restructuring of global markets and prices; the creation of a world economic council. The U.S. section of the Women's International League for Peace and Freedom called for a conference to consider the cancellation of the devastating wartime debt; the stabilization of European currencies; a reconsideration of the Treaty of Versailles, especially the evacuation of the Ruhr by the French; and general disarmament.

Of the 22,165 plans submitted, the committee chose a very simple plan by Charles E. Levermore, an academic, who recommended the United States' immediate adherence to the Permanent Court of International Justice and cooperation with (though not membership in) the League of Nations.

Esther Lape selected twenty of the most interesting plans for publication, and introduced them with her analysis of the different *Ways to Peace.* Published by Scribner's, the book sold well and was critically acclaimed. The *New York Times* reviewer considered Lape's essay "better worth a $50,000 prize than any of the plans we have seen." And the New York *Herald Tribune* editorialized that Lape's book was the "best thing that came out of the Peace Award."

The winning plan stimulated Bok, Esther Lape, ER, and their allies to promote U.S. entrance to the World Court. Senate isolationists were outraged and called for an investigation into the un-American and potentially treasonous nature of the Bok Award. They condemned it as propaganda that encouraged "foreign entanglements" and "communistic internationalism."

On 17 January 1924, the veteran Democratic Irreconcilable James Reed called for the Senate Special Committee on Propaganda to investigate charges that the American Peace Award was the tool of "foreign governments or foreign institutions," for the purpose of unduly and improperly influencing or controlling public opinion and legislative action, specifically regarding the "foreign policy of the United States."

The Senate committee accused Edward Bok of conspiracy: He had attempted to manipulate public opinion with untold sums of money in behalf of the League and international peace, creating thereby "a moral menace." Unruffled by threats of contempt charges, Bok refused to disclose the cost of the contest. He insisted that the money he donated to the American public was his affair and that he intended to spend the rest of his life giving his money to worthy causes.

According to *The New York Times,* the Senate committee room "was filled by over 700 men and women peace advocates" who hissed and booed the investigators and cheered Bok and Lape, who appeared as key witnesses.

Lape was particularly brilliant under fire. Although the Irreconcilable investigators sought to discredit and demean her, their questions were so insistent and their tone so assaultive that two senators, Frank Greene of Vermont and Thaddeus Caraway of Arkansas (the only pro-

Leaguer on the committee), frequently interrupted Reed's harangues to "go to the aid of the witness." (Reporters assured their readers, however, that Esther Lape did not require such chivalric services.)

Lape created the greatest flurry when she named ER and Narcissa Vanderlip as the two most significant members of the policy committee. The New York *Herald* took this as the signal to emphasize that the award was a plot by unscrupulous women, influenced by foreign radicals and their bipartisan henchmen (Root and Stimson were Republicans), to ensnare the United States into membership in that un-American organization the League of Nations. "The great Bok peace prize," said the *Herald*, "was managed by two matrons of social distinction [ER and Narcissa Vanderlip] and a highly educated and most efficient young unmarried woman." Lape was in fact older than ER, but unmarried women were generally perceived to be young—or at least younger than matrons of distinction. Nevertheless, the *New York Times* editorial "These Women" praised the skill and wisdom of Esther Lape and her "fellow conspirators."

The Bok hearings were suspended on the news of President Wilson's death, and then simply allowed to expire; but government isolationists pursued Bok's Foundation and punished it by administrative fiat. The IRS removed the Foundation's tax exemption. Its "education work" was declared "political" lobbying, in behalf of that un-American idea: international law.

Eleanor Roosevelt's first specifically "un-American" activity resulted in the first document entered into her voluminous FBI file (only recently declassified through the Freedom of Information Act). Dated 15 February 1924, and heavily deleted, it is part of the FBI's "General Investigation" of the American Peace Award. "Recorded and Indexed," with three copies sent to Washington and routed to J. Edgar Hoover, who signed it, the document itself is bizarrely innocuous: "The other number used by the American Peace Award, namely Murray Hill 4278 was contracted for and signed for by Mrs. *Anna Roosevelt.* This is presumably Mrs. *Franklin D. Roosevelt,* as 'Who's Who' indicates that *Franklin D. Roosevelt* married *Anna Eleanor Roosevelt* of New York on 17 March 1905."

However criticized and harassed, ER, Lape, and the other supporters

of the Bok Foundation were undaunted. They continued to work for
the League, and for U.S. entrance into the World Court. In 1925, the
House voted for U.S. participation, and ER urged a women's crusade
to achieve Senate approval.*

In addition to her work in behalf of international peace, ER spent
some part of every day planning strategy for the New York State Democratic Party. In her 6 February 1924 letter to FDR where she minimized
her activities, she reported that she, Caroline O'Day, and Nancy Cook
had been to a "remarkable dinner" of "600 women from Albany and
nearby and all workers!" They saw Governor Al Smith, who asked them
to lobby for his new reform program, and ER spent several days in
Albany, working out the details. But there was still one piece of additional news, she noted almost as an afterthought: Cordell Hull, the
Democratic Party's National Committee chairman in 1924, had invited
ER—currently finance chair of the Women's Division—to head a platform committee for women to present their demands at the June convention in New York. She was delighted, though she gave no hint of
that to FDR: "I'm up to my eyes in work for the convention preparations
and trying to raise our budget which is going to be an endless job."

ER even rejected FDR's praise for her work, the words of which
are now lost along with most of his correspondence during this period:
"You need not be proud of me dear. I'm only being active till you can
be again. It isn't such a great desire on my part to serve the world and
I'll fall back into habits of sloth quite easily! Hurry up for as you know
my ever present sense of the uselessness of all things will overwhelm
me sooner or later! My love to Missy, and to you, Devotedly, ER."

When one considers the disparity between ER's denial and the reality
of her daily activities, one pauses to wonder what motivated her decision
to trivialize both her work and her commitment to it. Her need to
minimize her efforts and to reassure her husband that she was in fact
no threat, and no competition to his primary place in the political arena,

* It lasted for over a decade and in 1935 resulted in failure. The World Court was only a
first and rather tiny step on the long road toward international peace, she acknowledged
wherever she spoke: But remember: "All big changes in human history have been arrived
at slowly and through many compromises."

is a sturdy testimony to the proverbial double standard that was and remains the burden of political women.

Despite her modest denials, however, ER increasingly went about her own business, whether or not it served FDR, with or without his approval. On 9 April, she wrote that she planned to attend a two-day "convention of women" on law enforcement, specifically as it related to Prohibition, in Washington: "I know you will probably feel with Louis [Howe] that it is politically wrong to come but I do believe in it." It was indeed politically wrong, as ER was quick to realize, and acknowledge.

The Women's Democratic Law Enforcement League was one expression of the 1924 alliance between "dries" and Dixiecrats that ended Prohibition as a cause for social reformers. At this time the alliance between populists and religious fundamentalists (led until his death by William Jennings Bryan), and the reinvigorated Ku Klux Klan, which dominated Dixiecrat politics, focused on the crusade for a dry America, and influenced partisan politics until 1932. ER had hoped that Prohibition might result in "less drinking now among young people than there was among our fathers." But she would not be allied with a reactionary group who opposed progressive politicians like Al Smith because he was a "wet," a Catholic, and a reformer.*

ER was embattled on several fronts in 1924. On 9 April, she wrote FDR that she wished he were at home to advise her "on the fight I'm putting up on a delegate and 2 alternates at large." The fight was classic: Would the female or male party leaders get to name the women delegates? Forty-nine county chairwomen had already selected and endorsed their representatives when Tammany boss Charles Murphy claimed it his privilege to name the delegates. ER, resolute and ready for a fight, wrote: "I imagine it is just a question of which [Murphy] dislikes most—giving me my way or having me give the papers a grand chance for a story by telling [all] at the women's dinner . . . and by insisting on recognition on the floor of the convention & putting the names in nomination!" Clearly, ER had already decided to do full battle: "There's

* See pages 374–75.

one thing I'm thankful for—I haven't a thing to lose and for the moment you haven't either."

The New York Times featured ER's fight for women's equality at the state convention in an article titled "Women Are in Revolt." It was the "only inharmonious note" of the convention: the women supported Smith, but demanded their right to choose their own representatives. "Mrs. Franklin D. Roosevelt . . . slated to be one of the four delegates-at-large, led the fight for the women." She said:

> We have now had the vote for four years, and some very ardent suffragists seem to feel that instead of gaining in power the women have lost. . . .
>
> I have been wondering whether it occurs to the women as a whole that, if they expect to gain the ends for which they fought, it is not going to be sufficient simply to cast a ballot. . . . They must gain for themselves a place of real equality and the respect of the men. . . . The whole point in women's suffrage is that the Government needs the point of view of all its citizens and the women have a point of view which is of value to the Government. . . .

ER was in the vanguard of those feminists who protected and promoted women's issues and the equal representation of women within the party's committees. She demanded that women be represented on county committees "in equal numbers" and be listed among those nominated for office in all primary elections:

> It is disagreeable to take stands. It was always easier to compromise, always easier to let things go. To many women, and I am one of them, it is extraordinarily difficult to care about anything enough to cause disagreement or unpleasant feelings, but I have come to the conclusion that this must be done for a time until we can prove our strength and demand respect for our wishes. . . .
>
> We will be enormously strengthened if we can show that we are willing to fight to the very last ditch for what we believe in.

ER's efforts were victorious. She was named chair of a committee that negotiated the women's right to name their own delegates and alternates. Their meetings with Smith and other party leaders "established a precedent," and ER felt encouraged: "We go into the campaign feeling that our party has recognized us as an independent part of the organization."

But it was only a preliminary victory. The women's political movement had become a significant element within the Democratic Party. It was feminist and bold. And the entrenched male power brokers hated it. They sought at every turn to set up roadblocks, brake its momentum, and destroy it. A daily and nasty battle ensued, fought meanly and through subterfuge. For example, women who finally achieved membership status on a committee often found the doors to the meetings locked, or the meetings moved to secret places. Other apparent victories were no sooner announced than betrayed.

In March 1924, the Democratic National Committee proudly announced that it was "the first political group to seek women's views on important questions of peculiar interest to them so that these social legislation planks as incorporated in the national Democratic platform may represent their ideas." And, with considerable public relations fanfare, the leadership announced it had asked Eleanor Roosevelt to chair the women's platform committee.

ER agreed, and determined to base the recommendations for needed social-welfare legislation on the "requests of all women's organizations in the country." She appointed a panel of activist experts, including Dorothy Kirchwey Brown of Massachusetts, Margaret Norrie of Dutchess County, Elinor Morgenthau, Maud Swartz, Gertrude Ely (a noted philanthropist from Bryn Mawr who was one of ER's closest friends), Charl Williams of Tennessee (who was credited with lobbying the final vote needed for the ratification of the suffrage amendment), and Patti R. (Mrs. Solon) Jacobs of Alabama. The committee endorsed the League of Nations, and called for the creation of a federal department of education, equal pay for women workers, and the ratification of the child-labor amendment. It called for a forty-eight-hour workweek, wages commensurate with the cost of living and health care, the creation of employment bureaus and the means to ensure "healthy and safe working conditions."

But in June, their three months' effort was rudely rebuffed by the Resolutions Committee at the convention. For hours ER and her co-workers sat outside the locked doors of the all-male Resolutions Committee and waited to be heard. At dawn the men voted twenty-two to eighteen, for the third and last time, to reaffirm their refusal even to hear the women's proposals. ER wrote that at the convention of 1924 she saw "for the first time where the women stood when it came to a national convention. I shortly discovered that they were of very little importance. They stood outside the door of all important meetings and waited." She spent most of her time during the deadlocked, heat-filled convention—every day the temperature topped one hundred degrees Fahrenheit—trying to seem calm. "I sat and knitted, suffered with the heat and wished it would end." One day, Will Rogers noticed ER and asked: "Knitting in the names of the future victims of the guillotine?" ER was tempted to respond that she was "ready to call any punishment down on the heads of those who could not bring the convention to a close."

~

THE 1924 CONVENTION WAS A SETBACK FOR THE WOMEN, AND a disaster for the Democrats. But for the Roosevelts 1924 represented another turning point. Both ER and FDR were widely perceived as the most significant contributors to the Democratic convention. The women's political community acknowledged ER as a major leader. Personally, she was informed and toughened by her new understanding of the way male bastions of power actually work. And during the convention, FDR's reputation as a national figure soared. In fact, the only bright moment of the divided and frequently violent convention—a convention dominated by Al Smith and his chief opponent, William Gibbs McAdoo, who was now frankly associated with the Ku Klux Klan—occurred when FDR presented the nominating speech for Smith.

His first major public appearance since he was stricken, FDR had practiced for weeks in order to be able to walk erect on his heavy steel braces, supported only by one crutch and the arm of his sixteen-year-old son, James. According to Marion Dickerman, who sat with ER, SDR, and Nancy Cook, it had been a gray, cloudy day. But as FDR reached the podium, drew himself upright, and smiled "a rather remote smile . . . as if he smiled to himself amid the thunderous applause and cheers," at that very moment the clouds parted "and through the skylight came a burst of sunlight." The entire crowd that filled the great hall of Madison Square Garden cheered with joyous relief and high regard as he walked the distance from platform to podium. His unforgettable triumph represented three years of agonizing effort.

Naming Al Smith "the Happy Warrior of the political battlefield," FDR called in dramatic and resonant phrases for party unity in the face of all differences. "You equally who come from the great cities of the East and the plains and hills of the West, from the slopes of the Pacific and from the homes and fields of the Southland, I ask you . . . to keep first in your hearts and minds the words of Abraham Lincoln—'With malice toward none, and charity for all.' "

The crowd cheered for an hour and thirteen minutes. But FDR's courageous eloquence lifted the spirit of the convention only temporarily. It was deadlocked for 102 ballots. According to the New York *Herald Tribune,* as "the results of the futile balloting droned on," there was "in the exact center of the great hall the one man whose name would stampede the convention were he put in nomination. . . . From the time Roosevelt made his speech in nomination of Smith, which was the one great speech of the convention, he has been easily the foremost figure on floor or platform." From that moment on, FDR was considered the real "Happy Warrior."

Finally, the Democrats agreed on a compromise candidate, a Wall Street lawyer associated with the House of Morgan, John W. Davis. Politically indistinguishable from the Republican nominee, Calvin Coolidge, Davis inspired nobody. Almost five million Americans voted for the third-party candidate as Progressives. Even party stalwarts like Caroline O'Day supported the new Progressive Party's candidate, Wisconsin Senator Robert La Follette. FDR returned to his business ventures, with frequent vacations in warm Southern waters. And ER agreed to help run Al Smith's campaign for re-election as New York's governor—against Republican nominee Theodore Roosevelt, Jr.

ER's willingness to support Al Smith in the face of the continued rebuffs and indignities experienced by the organized political women throughout 1924 was more than a testimony to her belief that Smith was serious about social reform. It was a demonstration of her own conviction that women needed to work systematically and earnestly within the power structure if they were to achieve political change. Votes for women could be rendered meaningless unless women organized to take over specific areas of party activity, specific areas of real power. Now was the time "to prove our strength and demand respect."

ER appreciated that this meant working under duress with frequently hostile allies, who would attempt to undermine every victory. She spoke directly of male hostility to women in politics. In an interview in *The New York Times* published on 20 April 1924, she described male contempt for politically involved women. Men would say: "You are wonderful. I love and honor you. . . . Lead your own life, attend to your charities, cultivate yourself, travel when you wish, bring up the children, run your house. I'll give you all the freedom you wish and all the money I can but—leave me my business and politics." This, ER urged, women must not allow. "Women must get into the political game and stay in it." Women together must build up new institutions of alternative power "from the inside."

She had seconded Smith's nomination at the New York State convention with vigor, and with a thrust at her cousin TR, Jr., that finally and forever alienated the two branches of the family. How could Smith not win, she asserted, since the Republicans, by their useless nomination of TR, "did everything to help him"? She campaigned throughout the state in an extraordinary vehicle rigged up with a steam-spouting teapot to signify TR, Jr.'s involvement in the Teapot Dome scandal. In county after county she systematically dismissed her cousin as a reasonably nice "young man whose public service record shows him willing to do the bidding of his friends."

ER was appealing, vigorous, and dramatic on the stump. She attacked Republicans as "stupid or dishonest public servants" who were unwilling to deal with what she called the real issues: a reciprocal trade agreement, membership in the League of Nations, and economic security. She urged women who wanted improved economic conditions to register to vote. They, especially, had "a great deal at stake" in these elections. ER campaigned for a massive voter-registration drive: "It is because so many who should register and vote fail to do so that we often have what amounts to minority rule . . . [by] sophisticated politicians of the self-interested type." "A full vote in every community is the most direct way of combating undesirable political forces."

ER believed that only a fully participatory democracy would lead to honesty in government. Harding's administration had been a carousel of corruption. Fraud, graft, and a general abuse of power characterized every Cabinet department. But no single scandal better represented the triumph of greed than did "Teapot Dome": the giveaway to private oil interests of the United States' vast oil reserves, which had been for decades jealously guarded by the Department of the Navy.

When FDR was Assistant Secretary of the Navy, he and Josephus Daniels monitored all efforts to capture Wyoming's rich oil lands called Teapot Dome, owned by the United States in trust for the nation. They deemed it an essential stockpile critical to navy operations in case of emergency. Daniels and FDR stayed up all night to oppose the one serious congressional effort to grab these lands for private development interests in Wilson's administration.

But during Harding's presidency, Edwin Denby, Secretary of the Navy, and his assistant secretary, TR, Jr., who then occupied this seemingly traditional Roosevelt position, were less vigilant. When Albert B. Fall, Secretary of the Interior, maneuvered to wrest control of Teapot Dome from the navy, along with California's vastly rich oil lands at Elk Hills, nobody stopped him. Fall prepared for Harding's signature an executive order for the transfer of the lands from Navy to Interior, and everybody acquiesced. After Harding signed, Fall exchanged a lease for Elk Hills to the Pan-American Petroleum and Transport Company, headed by Edward Doheny, for $100,000. He awarded Teapot Dome to Harry Sinclair for $300,000 and some negotiable bonds.*

When Harding died suddenly, evidently of a cerebral hemorrhage, while campaigning on 2 August 1923, the Senate decided to investigate

---

* These scandalous dealings surfaced again during the Nixon administration, which passed along Elk Hills to private developers. The real value to the nation in 1920s currency was over $200 million. Elk Hills alone in 1975 was conservatively valued at $50 billion.

Teapot Dome. Although he was not directly implicated in the scandal, TR, Jr., had been employed by Harry Sinclair, and his brother Archibald continued to be. Ultimately, Fall became the first Cabinet officer to go to jail for taking bribes, but the damage was done: private speculators owned the national oil reserves.

TR, Jr., resigned his post as Assistant Secretary of the Navy in 1924 in order to run for governor. He was succeeded by Aunt Corinne's son Theodore Douglas Robinson, thereby keeping the position in the family. In 1924, sprayed by the steam of ER's automotive teapot team, which frequently included her friends Nancy Cook, Marion Dickerman, and Elinor Morgenthau and her daughter, Anna, TR, Jr., lost by a landslide—almost a million votes behind the victorious Calvin Coolidge. ER admitted that the teapot had been a "rough stunt."

ER was delighted by Smith's victory, and entirely pleased with the success of her "rough stunt." Indeed, she was so proud of the teapot, which was of her own design, that she drove it to Connecticut, evidently to give her Aunt Bye a glimpse of what the fuss was all about. Aunt Bye, who had not joined in Oyster Bay's FDR-bashing efforts in 1920, was now frankly dismayed by her niece's unseemly display of raw political muscle: "Alas and lackaday! Since politics have become her choicest interest all her charm has disappeared, and the fact is emphasized by the companions she chooses to bring with her. . . ."

∼

HOWEVER MUCH ER'S POLITICAL VIGOR, NEW FRIENDS, AND public prominence might disturb the older members of her family, she herself greeted every new controversy with verve. Eleanor Roosevelt had become a feminist. She fought for women's rights steadfastly and with determination; she championed equality in public and private matters; and she herself used the word "feminist." But during the 1920s, the bitterly divisive Equal Rights Amendment ripped the women's movement apart, obscuring for decades the full dimensions of historical feminism—and ER's leadership role within it.

The vision that inspired the ERA was neither new nor frivolous. On 31 March 1777, Abigail Adams wrote to her husband, John Adams: "I desire you would remember the ladies and be more generous and favorable to them than your ancestors. . . . If particular care and attention is not paid to the ladies, we are determined to foment a rebellion, and will not hold ourselves bound by any laws in which we have no voice or representation." Still, Adams and his friends ignored the ladies. Thomas Jefferson opined: "Were our state a pure democracy there would still be excluded from our deliberations women, who, to prevent deprivation of morals and ambiguity of issues, should not mix promiscuously in gatherings of men."

After the Civil War women were specifically excluded from the benefits of the Fourteenth and Fifteenth Amendments. The Fourteenth Amendment inserted the word "male" for the first time into the Constitution, making it clear that the benefits of "due process" and "equal protection" excluded women. Consistently the courts endorsed this situation. In 1873, the Supreme Court upheld an Illinois statute that prohibited women from practicing law. In *Bradwell* v. *Illinois,* the Court decided:

> The harmony, not to say identity, of interests and views which belong, or should belong, to the family institution is repugnant to the idea of a woman adopting a distinct and independent career from that of her husband. . . .
>
> The paramount destiny and mission of women are to fulfill the noble and benign offices of wife and mother. This is the law of the Creator.

The Equal Rights Amendment was introduced in 1923 by the organized militants of the National Woman's Party, led by Alice Paul and over a hundred other women who used civil-disobedience methods to campaign throughout the war years "for suffrage—first." From 1917 until the suffrage amendment was passed in Congress and finally ratified by the states in August 1920, they were the women who kept the suffrage-amendment issue in the headlines. They had picketed the White House, demonstrated against Wilson everywhere he spoke with banners criticizing him and cauldrons in which to burn the hypocritical words he had used to celebrate democracy while they were being arrested, jailed, brutalized, and force-fed. Largely isolated during the war, assailed as

"madwomen," "petticoat Bolsheviks," and traitors, they remained undaunted.

Immediately after suffrage was won, Alice Paul and the militant
warriors of the National Woman's Party sought a new amendment,
which they believed would erase all the laws that discriminated against
women. Paul's original Equal Rights Amendment, as introduced in Congress in December 1923, was as simply worded as its successor during
the 1970s: "Men and women shall have Equal Rights throughout the
United States and every place subject to its jurisdiction."*

One of Paul's most vigorous supporters, Crystal Eastman, believed
that "this was a fight worth fighting even if it took ten years," and
recognized that its importance could be measured by the intensity of
all the opposition to it. And the opposition was immediate: Within
twenty-four hours after it was introduced, every member of Congress
received a passionate protest against it—signed by the leaders of the
seven other major women's-rights and suffrage groups, most notably
the social feminists, identified with the League of Women Voters; and
settlement-house reformers, associated with Florence Kelley, Dr. Alice
Hamilton, and Jane Addams, who supported protective legislation for
women and children. Their goal was to isolate Paul and her movement;
Paul's goal was to dismiss them as antifeminists: humanitarians solely
concerned with "family welfare."

Entirely allied with the social feminists of the League of Women
Voters, and with the effort to achieve protective legislation for women
workers, ER and many of the most radical suffragists, women who had
devoted their lives to fighting social evils, poverty, racism, cruelty of
every kind, now opposed the ERA. They feared it was politically pre-
mature and would serve only to destroy the few laws that served to
protect women and children in the industrial workplace that they had
been able to achieve.

Initially, the political and geographic range on both sides of the
battle included Republicans, Democrats, and socialists; Southern and
Northern sensibilities. The equal-rights feminists, led by Alice Paul,

* After more than fifty years of effort, the text of the ERA, defeated again in 1982, was:
"Equality of rights under the law shall not be denied or abridged by the United States or
by any state on account of sex."

Southern and conservative by any standard, were joined by Crystal Eastman, Doris Stevens, and Lavinia Dock, radical and socialist by any standard. On the protectionist side, Jane Addams was a liberal social reformer, Florence Kelley was a radical socialist who called herself a Marxist, Narcissa Vanderlip was a rather conventional Republican, and Eleanor Roosevelt represented the progressive wing of the Democratic Party.

The tragedy of the split was that it represented a genuine and irreconcilable difference in strategy in behalf of a shared goal: the improved economic and political condition of women, the achievement of power by women. Feminist activists dominated the battle on both sides.

The ERA-protectionist division resulted from a conflicting understanding of what was possible in an unrestrained capitalist economy. In 1923, despite years of progressive action, there was still no limitation on the number of hours or the conditions of work for women *or* men; and ER and the protectionist feminists—all of whom wanted protective legislation for all—sincerely believed that it was possible to achieve a fair and just administration of a forty-eight-hour workweek by demanding it for women *first*. Equal-rights feminists sincerely believed that shorter hours for women first would result in the loss of jobs for women, who were not as valued as men workers and were not paid on a par with them, and who were therefore required by economic need to work longer hours merely to survive. Although both sides agreed that women worked in a brutal economy that achieved profits by demanding the longest possible hours for the least possible pay, the battle between them raged in bitter tones of acrimony. The protectionists believed the ERA women were elitists and careerists who cared only for privileged and professional women and were ignorant of and unconcerned about the poor. The ERA activists believed the protectionists were old-fashioned reformers who refused to see that, until women were acknowledged equal in law, all reforms to protect women were frauds that could only work against them.

On 16 January 1922, Dr. Alice Hamilton, the United States' leading authority on industrial medicine, wrote a letter to explain her position to the editor of the National Woman's Party journal, *Equal Rights,* Edith Houghton Hooker:

I could not help comparing you as you sat there [over a "friendly cup of tea"], sheltered, safe, beautifully guarded against even the ugliness of life, with the women for whom you demand "freedom of contract." The Lithuanian women in the laundries whom the Illinois law . . . permits to work seventy hours a week on the night shift; the Portuguese women in the Rhode Island textile mills, on long night shifts . . . the great army of waitresses and hotel chambermaids, unorganized, utterly ignorant of ways of making their grievances known, working long hours and living wretchedly. To tell them to get what they should have by using their right of contract is to go back to the days of the Manchester School in England, when men maintained that there must be no interference with the right of women and children to make their own bargains with their employers in the cotton mills or at the pitheads. It is only a great ignorance of the poor as they actually are, only a great ignorance as to what is possible and what is impossible under our supposed democracy and actual plutocracy, that could make you argue as you do. . . . [If] you succeed in rescinding all the laws in the country discriminating against women and do it at the expense of present and future protective laws you will have harmed a far larger number of women than you will have benefited and the harm done to them will be more disastrous. . . .

Remember, when you think me over-strenuous, that I have lived for twenty-two years among the poor and that for twelve years I have studied trades employing all sorts of labor. . . . The working woman is a very real person to me. . . .

For the next twenty years, Eleanor Roosevelt shared Alice Hamilton's analysis. She too tended to consider the ERA proponents self-serving aristocrats who cared little and understood less about the needs of the poor. She was drawn toward the vision of reform created by that earlier generation of community activists, unionists, and radicals led by Florence Kelley, Jane Addams, Lillian Wald, Rose Schneiderman, and Dr. Alice Hamilton. Although she was the same age as many of the ERA activists, and was indeed two years younger than Crystal Eastman,

ER understood society the way her earlier mentors in the settlement-house movement did. Above all, ER believed that one utopian constitutional amendment, however virtuous, was virtually meaningless in the real political world, and she opposed the idea of a separate woman's party. Even after 1937, when unionism and collective bargaining caused her to doubt the need for continued opposition to the ERA, she continued to take direction from the Women's Trade Union League.

ER's position began to change after the passage of the 1938 Fair Labor Standards Act, which provided protective laws that covered women and men alike. Although she was ready to endorse the ERA in 1941, she still hesitated because of WTUL leader Rose Schneiderman's continued opposition. But she became impatient with the fight. In 1944, she consented to the Democratic Party's endorsement of the ERA, and finally, in 1946, at the United Nations, she publicly withdrew her opposition.

ER's allies were the social activists who long before suffrage had created such abiding institutions of successful reform as the settlement houses, the National Consumers' League, and the Women's Trade Union League. They had pioneered such improvements as public playgrounds, school lunches, medical care in public schools, the visiting-home-nurse service, sanitation removal, and minimum-wage and maximum-hour laws for women. They regarded the ERA as a fantasy that endangered their life's work.

They were practical women who worked vigorously on the margin of politics, where they were allowed to perform. They did domestic housekeeping for the neighborhood, the community, the city, state, and nation. It was that arena to which they were restricted. The health of women and children, the health of the state was considered women's work. And they accepted it. They had not waited for the vote. They did not wait for the ERA. They did what they could to counter the ills of a wretched, mean-spirited society where children were allowed to starve to death; where mothers and infants routinely died unnecessarily; and where acres and acres of tenements, unfit for dwelling, stunted growth and happiness. To do other than what they did every day would have been to accept powerlessness. They had none of the power and prestige of men, but they were not powerless. They were earnest and bold and committed to the long and arduous process of creating fundamental change.

In her first book, *It's Up to the Women* (1933), ER would write that she was not interested in the abstract idea of equality with men. It "sounded so well," but it only enabled women to compete more successfully with men for jobs. It did not really improve women's ability to change society. Of course she wanted women to run for office, to be accorded the dignity and titles, the power and prestige, reserved for male politicians. But in the meantime, she would fight directly for decent conditions for women workers.

~

IN 1925, HER ENERGIES WERE FOCUSED ON THE FORTY-EIGHT-hour workweek: "Aside from all the so-called sob stuff which we have heard here this afternoon," she said at a legislative meeting, "I am convinced that a great majority of the workingwomen of this State are really in favor of this bill. . . . I can't understand how any woman would want to work fifty-four hours a week if she only had to work forty-eight and could receive the same rate of wages."

At the same hearing, the equal-rights feminists Doris Stevens and Rheta Child Dorr opposed ER's interpretation, and argued that the male-dominated labor unions supported the bill so that women would not be able to compete with men. They urged instead that the forty-eight-hour law cover both women and men, so that women would not be unfairly hobbled. In every competitive job, where women had worked with equality during the war years, women were now fired—as, for example, the women workers of the Brooklyn and Manhattan Transit Company, who testified that all laws intended to put women on "easy street" merely put them resoundingly on the street.

The fight in the New York State legislature for the forty-eight-hour bill for women workers became bipartisan when, in 1926, the bill was denied even the courtesy of a vote and Republican Club women protested. ER considered "the courage and independence" the Republican women demonstrated by "refusing to abide by the mandates of their legislative leaders . . . a vindication of the value of women in politics."

She also congratulated the Republican women on the "fairness and scientific accuracy" of their six-month-long investigation of labor conditions, which revealed that 95 percent of all women workers favored the forty-eight-hour legislation.

ER believed that a great political bonus resulted from bipartisan unity on the forty-eight-hour bill: It revealed the power of voting women to remind men that they would no longer be allowed to sidestep promises made simply to catch votes, or to "neglect party platforms" so solemnly crafted. ER deplored this "final act of the farce-drama" male politicians "have conducted . . . for many years. I know of no more open, cynical and reckless defiance of definite platform and campaign promise than the refusal even to allow a vote on the 48-hour legislation."

~

THE FORTY-EIGHT-HOUR WEEK, AND SUBSEQUENTLY THE battle for a five-day week, seem ordinary and tame demands today. But until the end of the 1930s and the general acceptance of unionism, U.S. workers, women and men, were without real protection of any kind, and routinely worked twelve to fourteen hours a day, six—frequently six and a half—days a week. According to the WTUL's Rose Schneiderman, employers believed that endless toil kept women "out of mischief and that shorter hours would endanger their morals." They believed also "that if working people had rooms with baths they would use the bathtubs in which to keep the coal. . . ." Workers were not supposed to have "leisure" time, and reformers who insisted on maximum-hour and minimum-wage laws were regarded as radical or "parlor pink" if not clearly "Bolshevik."

The disregard for workers' needs and the ordinary dignity of working people, women especially, moved ER to support the activities and principles of the Women's Trade Union League. In April 1929 ER debated the five day week at a well attended Town Hall meeting sponsored by the WTUL. ER's primary opponent was the chairman of New York State's Economic Congress, Merwin K. Hart. He argued that any law for a five-day week would limit individual freedom. Arguing as if workers actually controlled their time and their pay, he declared that people do not like to be told when and for how long they may work. There was, he assured the audience, a "natural desire of the individual to control his own efforts." Whereupon he turned to ER and smugly remarked that she, for example, "would not want to be told you could work only five days a week."

ER agreed: Her work was her life. But she was an independent and affluent woman, who chose her work. She was not an industrial worker: "Repeating a single motion throughout the day in a factory was not like doing work which one enjoyed."

~

AS ELEANOR ROOSEVELT'S INFLUENCE GREW, AND AS HER confidence increased, she threw herself into a range of social initiatives aimed at strengthening government protection for women and children. She fought for the Child Labor Amendment, increased support for the Children's Bureau and the Women's Bureau, and worked to raise state matching funds for the $1.25-million Sheppard-Towner Act to establish maternity and pediatric clinics, and a health-care program for mothers and infants. A great victory for social feminists, who had campaigned for years to decrease the grim rate of infant mortality in the United States, the Sheppard-Towner Act was attacked as "Sovietism," and a dangerous precedent leading to birth control and governmental programs of "social hygiene." ER and Narcissa Vanderlip were among the leaders of New York's crusade to raise the enabling funds.

To charges that the law was unconstitutional and not economical, Vanderlip countered: "If it is constitutional to use federal funds to save hogs from cholera, and cows from tuberculosis, it is constitutional to use them to save babies and their mothers from death."

Every issue involving women was of concern to ER. In April 1925, she went on the radio to describe the significance of the Women's City Club, which she termed a "clearing house for civic ideals." The club conducted its own research on all issues, and held debates and informative lectures. To investigate the issue of outlawing dance halls, for example, the club's members went to numerous dance halls, not as "investigators, but as participants." They discovered, ER noted, "the fascination, the dangers and the surprisingly low percentage of disaster to the girls" despite the "unwholesome surroundings." ER never supported the effort to outlaw dance halls.

She called for equal political education for girls and for boys, and noted with pride that "Girls nowadays may be rivals of their brothers in school, sports, and business." But ER lamented they "lag behind in a knowledge and interest in government." She gave as examples her own daughter, Anna, and Governor Smith's daughter Emily, whom she had overheard complaining that politics dominated their fathers' conversations. ER contrasted this attitude with the one that prevailed among "flappers of politically prominent families in England. British daughters not only take a keen interest in their fathers' careers but go out to help in the political battle." She cited the good works of Ishbel MacDonald and Megan Lloyd George in particular, and concluded that, if "our American girls are not to be left behind, something must be done to stimulate their interest in civic responsibilities." She thought that daughters of politicians should at least want to be able "to outtalk their fathers."

Eleanor Roosevelt's own sense of responsibility took her beyond strong words to vigorous deeds. In 1926, she made headline news when she participated in a mass picket demonstration of three hundred women in support of striking paper-box makers. Eight notable women "of prominence" were arrested for ignoring a police order "to move on," and charged with "disorderly conduct," including ER, Margaret Norrie, Mrs. Samuel Bens, Marion Dickerman, Evelyn Preston, and Dorothy Kenyon.

ER was proud of the achievements of women. She honored their daring, and their vision. She considered women flyers marvelously courageous, and she promoted women in flight. She herself wanted to fly, and she did. ER was one of the first women to fly at night, and she logged more hours in the air during the 1920s and 1930s than any other woman passenger. But she remained a passenger, much to her regret. FDR's only known vigorous opposition to any of ER's efforts was when she decided to become a pilot. Her friend Amelia Earhart gave her preliminary lessons, and ER actually took and passed the physical examination. But FDR persuaded her that he had sufficient worries without her flying above the clouds at top speed. FDR's opposition to flying was genuine. In 1920, he was horrified when his mother flew from London to Paris, and asked her never to go aloft again. Evidently both women acquiesced to his fear; but ER always regretted not becoming a pilot, because, she said, she liked to be in control of her own mobility.

Increasingly, ER's interests became international. In October 1927, she hosted a meeting of four hundred women at Hyde Park to launch a women's peace movement and support the Kellogg-Briand Treaty to outlaw war. Carrie Chapman Catt was the keynote speaker, and again she stirred ER with her call for a crusade against war as mighty as the antislave crusade, as mighty as the suffrage crusade: We must find a way to "end this awful menace to civilization, the disgrace to this century, called war."

For the next ten years, ER was to be one of the most prominent antiwar women in the United States, associated with both Jane Addams's Women's International League for Peace and Freedom, and Carrie Chapman Catt's National Conference on the Cause and Cure of War.

ER devoted considerable space in the *Women's Democratic News* to issues of war and peace. In July 1926, she wrote an editorial calling for bold, spontaneous, anonymous demonstrations for peace by American women: "Have you noticed that in England there have been lately big pilgrimages of women for peace converging on London?" ER was impressed that they seemed spontaneous, and no individual women or groups took credit for their creation. "Of course, English women and European women generally feel more deeply than we do, the horrors of war. They have lost their husbands and sons in great number." But, she asked: "Cannot we women here even interest ourselves enough to study the possible ways open to us in the world today of eliminating the causes of war and then get behind all the movements furthering these ends with some demonstrations of our own?"

Throughout the early months of 1927, ER's editorials focused on Central America, Nicaragua in particular. In January, she wrote "Our Foreign Policy—What Is It?" Since "we do not wish to be entangled in European difficulties, our government's only concern is to collect what money is due us." We seem not even to consider any "constructive effort to build up good feeling," as if it "is too much trouble since we have an ocean to protect us."

But even in this hemisphere, she protested presciently, "we do nothing constructive to build up good feeling, and we drift into a very difficult situation." When Mexico nationalized its oil properties, for example, the United States sent out "a little notice that 'our Marines are being issued tropical kits.' " In contrast to FDR's 1920 bravura over the Caribbean and Central America, ER now asked: "Can it be that we 'the big brother of all nations on this side of the Atlantic' are playing the part of the bully? That is not a part usually admired by our people."

The Coolidge administration's unwillingness to discuss the growing military situation in Nicaragua created additional problems, ER noted: "With the Mexican question is tied up the Nicaraguan question. Just what we are doing there it is hard indeed to understand from the conflicting reports . . . and no matter what happens in both Mexico and Nicaragua we have not shown our Central and South American neighbors a very reassuring picture of a disinterested and magnanimous neighbor. . . ."

In March, ER featured a front-page article in the *Women's Democratic News,* "Banks and Bayonets in Nicaragua," with the banner headline: "Do We Deserve the Hatred of the World?" The article protested the increase of U.S. military forces in Nicaragua to over five thousand, "larger than either of the contending Nicaraguan forces."

Wherever she went, or whatever her announced topic, whenever ER spoke as the decade of the 1920s drew to a close, she spoke at least in part about world peace. Long before the war clouds gathered her message was urgent: "The time to prepare for world peace is during the time of peace and not during the time of war."

~

BY 1928, THE YEAR FDR RAN FOR GOVERNOR OF NEW YORK, Eleanor Roosevelt had become a major political force. For six years, she had served as finance chair of women's activities of the New York Democratic State Committee. She was vice-chair of the Woman's City Club of New York, chair of the Non-Partisan Legislative Committee, editor and treasurer of the *Women's Democratic News,* a member of the board of directors of the Foreign Policy Association and the City Housing Corporation.

In fact, in 1928, ER was one of the best-known and highest-ranking Democrats in the United States. She was named director of the Bureau of Women's Activities of the Democratic National Committee, and in July asked to head a Woman's Advisory Committee, to develop Al Smith's presidential campaign organization.

In 1928, ER held, therefore, the most powerful positions ever held by a woman in party politics. In matters of "turfing," which we now recognize as more than symbolic, she demanded and received equality for the women political organizers: Their offices had the same floor space their male counterparts had, and equal comfort. There were windows, carpets, plants; the accommodations were light and airy. *The New York Times* reported that the space allotted to women in the national headquarters of the Democratic party was "said to be the largest headquarters ever occupied by a women's political organization." ER's rooms and those of John J. Raskob, then Democratic national chairman, were "identical in size and location."

Throughout the 1920s ER worked to insure that this equality involve more than floor space. In September 1926, after a bitter struggle for equal representation for women within the New York State Democratic Party, the party convention elected Caroline O'Day vice-chair of the State Committee, and women were voted equal representation with men in 135 of 150 Assembly districts. On a "day of triumph and celebration," ER delivered the convention's banquet speech and hailed the victory as "the breaking down of the last barrier" to equality within the Democratic Party.

But she quickly realized that equal representation had as yet very little to do with equal power. Increasingly distressed by the manipulations of her male colleagues, ER argued that women needed to take tougher, more direct measures.

In April 1928, she published a boldly feminist article in *Redbook.* "Women Must Learn to Play the Game as Men Do" was a battle cry that urged women to create their own "women bosses" in order to achieve real power:

Women have been voting for ten years. But have they achieved actual political equality with men? No . . . In small things they are listened to; but when it comes to asking for important things they generally find they are up against a blank wall. . . .

Politically, as a sex, women are generally "frozen out" from any intrinsic share of influence. . . .

The machinery of party politics has always been in the hands of men, and still is. Our statesmen and legislators are still keeping in form as the successors of the early warriors [who gathered] around the camp-fire plotting the next day's attack. . . .

ER's tone was outraged and unrelenting: Women went into politics with high hopes and specific intentions. They were courted and wooed. But when they demanded and expected real power, they were rebuffed. ER noted: "Their requests are seldom refused outright, but they are put off with a technique that is an art in itself. The fact is that generally women are not taken seriously. With certain exceptions, men still as a class dismiss their consequence and value in politics, cherishing the old-fashioned concept that their place is in the home."

Although, only a few years before, ER had contended that women did not go into politics for personal gain, or the customary party reward for their work, by 1928 she expressed dismay that the hardworking women who devoted their time and energy to the political game continued to go unrewarded: "Men who work hard in party politics are always recognized, or taken care of in one way or another. Women, most of whom are voluntary workers . . . are generally expected to find in their labor its own reward. . . ."

Then there was the matter of political office. Party leaders "will ask women to run for office now and then, sometimes because they think it politic and wise to show women how generous they are, but more often because they realize in advance their ticket cannot win in the district selected. Therefore they will put up a woman, knowing it will injure the party less to have a woman defeated, and then they can always say it was her sex that defeated her. Where victory is certain, very rarely can you get a woman nominated. . . ."

ER was proud of the many women throughout the United States

who had been elected to public office. And there were at the time three women in Congress. There had been two women governors, and several women had been elected to the various statehouses. But, ER asked: "Does this indicate any equal recognition or share in political power?" She answered with a resounding no: There were instead infinite "examples . . . of women who were either denied a nomination or who were offered it only when inevitable defeat stared the party leaders in the face."

ER suggested a reason for this situation: Public men dislike women in public life. "Beneath the veneer of courtesy and outward show of consideration universally accorded women, there is a widespread male hostility—age-old perhaps—against sharing with them any actual control."

To alter this, she urged women to "elect, accept and back" Women Bosses on every level of party management, in "districts, counties and states. Women must organize just as men organize." ER did not believe in a separate woman's party. "A woman's ticket could never possibly succeed. And to crystalize the issues on the basis of sex-opposition would only further antagonize men, congeal their age-old prejudices, and widen the chasm of existing differences." Rather, within the party, women needed to select, promote, and elect women bosses to positions of leadership and authority—where they could, with equality and independence and above all the assurance that they had the backing of their women's constituency, fight it out with the men who routinely denied power to women.

ER was aware that the word "boss" might "shock sensitive ears." She did not mean by "boss" some sleazy and easy-to-buy politician, but, rather, a "high-minded leader." And she chose the word deliberately, "as it is the word men understand." She explained in detail her conviction that, "if women believe they have a right and duty in political life today, they must learn to talk the language of men. They must not only master the phraseology, but also understand the machinery which men have built up through years of practical experience. Against the men bosses there must be women bosses who can talk as equals, with the backing of a coherent organization of women voters behind them."

Tough-minded and direct, ER was also critical of women who refused to take the business of politics seriously or to consider their own political work a matter of fundamental urgency and significance: "If we are still a negligible factor, ignored and neglected, we must be prepared to admit in what we have ourselves failed." ER believed that too many women refused to work; to take themselves and their visions seriously; and too many women lacked knowledge and refused to "take the pains to study history, economics, political methods or get out among human beings."

She cited male contempt for learned women and acknowledged the misogynist tradition that mocked sophisticated and ambitious women. She quoted an "old politician" who "objected" to the type of political women she hoped to encourage: "Don't you think these women lose their allure, that the bloom is just a little gone? Men are no longer interested?"

ER responded, "Frankly, I don't know. I imagine the answer is individual. It was once said that men did not marry women who showed too much intelligence. In my youth I knew women who hid their college degrees as if they were one of the seven deadly sins. But all that is passing, and so will pass many other prejudices that have their origin in the ancient tradition that women are a by-product of creation."

ER explained, in conclusion, that women could only achieve real power by serious organization, unlimited study, endless work. Male hostility to women was only partly responsible for women's failure to achieve power. Women seemed to ER reluctant to claim power. She dismissed the attitude of those women who professed "to be horrified at the thought of women bosses bartering and dickering in the hard game of politics with the men." She was cheered by the fact that "many more women realize that we are living in a material world, and that politics cannot be played from the clouds." She understood that the task was hard and that the role of women in public life was difficult. Women's lives, to begin with, ER noted, were always "full of interruptions." There was the home, the children, the meals to prepare, the dinner parties to arrange. She was aware of the double standards, and the double-job burdens. And so, she argued, women have to be more organized, more methodical, and, yes, more hardworking than men.

She was adamant: "Women must learn to play the game as men do."

ER's earlier years in Albany and Washington, and her lifelong association with politicians and their ways, had accustomed her to the vagaries and strategies of power. Silence on the sidelines never achieved a thing, and was always interpreted as consent. The more she spoke out, the more she recognized her impact. She was ready to become—indeed, had already become—the very "political boss" about whom she wrote.

ER's *Redbook* article hit the stands with rather a splash. It resulted in several *New York Times* articles, including a *Magazine* interview by S. J. Woolf, "A Woman Speaks Her Political Mind," in which ER was credited with having "a wider experience and a richer political background than most." "Few women in politics today are in a better position to speak" on women's lack of political equality, said Woolf. The article was entirely favorable to ER, as well as to women in politics. Nevertheless, S. J. Woolf's emphasis revealed an ever-present double standard: ER was a mother, a teacher, and a homemaker, Woolf wrote, who never allowed her public or political activities to

interfere with her devotion to her home, nor has she sacrificed her private life in any respect to her public activities. She is the mother of five children and their upbringing has been her first consideration. She believes that a woman fitted to serve her community or her country can show that fitness best in the management of her own home. . . .

Mrs. Roosevelt is tall and has an engaging smile. There is something about that smile that is reminiscent of her illustrious uncle, while the droop in the outer corner of her eyes likewise reminds one of the former President. There is nothing about her that marks her as a woman in public life. Her manner is that of the young suburban mother. She is the strongest argument that could be presented against those who hold that by entering politics a woman is bound to lose her womanliness and her charm.

She is the type of mother that Booth Tarkington has so well described, a woman interested in civic betterment, who believes that that finds its beginning in the home.

Woolf's article was a clear indication of what was expected of ER if she were to maintain credibility and acceptance as a woman in public life. Among her colleagues and friends, she might depart from such prescriptions. But publicly ER understood and always worked within the limitations of her time, and her marriage. Publicly she denied to the end of her life that she ever had, or ever wanted, real political power. She acknowledged that she worked for those issues that she believed in, but not once did she profess to enjoy the game. She never publicly acknowledged that it satisfied her own interests, served her own needs, or that she delighted even in the rough-and-tumble of the deals and battles. Nevertheless, she did express dismay whenever she or other women were bypassed or blithely ignored and men took credit for their efforts and ideas. And she hated it when she was given no specific job to do, or was not encouraged to participate in a way she deemed appropriate—as in the case of the 1928 Democratic Party convention, which finally nominated Al Smith for president.

~

THE YEAR 1928 WAS AN INAUSPICIOUS ONE FOR A DEMOCRATIC victory. The 1920s, years of "Republican prosperity," practically ensured the election of Herbert Hoover. Still, many believed that Al Smith, the popular four-term governor of New York State, could make a difference, and ER was one of Smith's most vigorous boosters. In January, she responded to charges that as a Roman Catholic Smith was un-American, more loyal to Rome than to Washington, by citing two letters in her possession that her Uncle Theodore Roosevelt had written while president. He believed then that someday the United States would fulfill its democratic mandate by electing a Catholic or a Jew to the country's highest office. Now, ER attacked religious bigotry as un-American, and "hoped for the day when presidential candidates might be selected solely on the basis of their ability to serve the people."

In April, ER seconded the New York State party's resolution to nominate Al Smith with a rousing speech:

We crave a man with an understanding and human heart, who will make of government not merely a perfectly running machine,

but an instrument to contribute to the greater well-being and happiness of the whole people.

Democratic women . . . do not want the economy which refuses
to help those who need and deserve the help of the State, nor do
we want the kind of economy which saves a little today and loses
thereby much opportunity for the future. We do not want a purely
Wall Street, Aluminum Trust prosperity, a prosperity of invested
capital as against several millions of unemployed. The human values
mean more to us than the money values. . . .

Throughout the spring, ER worked with Belle Moskowitz, Smith's
political-staff leader, to put together one of the most efficient campaign
organizations in political history. As the convention drew nearer, the
list of players included a number of Eleanor's closest associates. Elinor
Morgenthau was ecstatic at being named delegate-at-large. ER wrote
FDR that both Henry and Elinor Morgenthau were "like children in
their joy. . . . I never realized any one could care so much and only
hope nothing happens to change the minds of the mighty!" Caroline
O'Day went as a delegate, and Marion Dickerman as her alternate. FDR
was again asked to nominate Smith. But ER, who headed the Women's
Committee for all preconvention activities, was given no particular assignment at the 1928 Houston convention despite all her work. Nor
did she ask for one, or even assign herself a task—which she surely
might have done. Had she resented not being named a delegate? Or
did she not want to compete with Franklin?

With no explanation she decided to remain at home. James and
SDR were on tour in Europe. Everybody else except the two younger
boys, who were with her at Hyde Park, was at the convention. ER's
decision represented a major Griselda relapse, which she quickly regretted. Aware that she had miscalculated, she wrote FDR, "it is horrid,
rainy weather and I am quite unreasonably depressed." She would listen
to the activities on the radio, "and expire if it doesn't work!"

Years later, ER insisted: "I had no desire to take part in the hurly-
burly of a convention—the 1924 convention had given me all I wanted
of that type of experience. In addition, our two younger boys, Franklin,
Junior, and John, were at Hyde Park and I had to stay with them." But

when Eleanor had gone to the station to see off her friends, Marion Dickerman noticed "how forlorn she looked, standing on the platform in the rain, waving, as the train pulled out."

Listening to the proceedings in Houston from Hyde Park, Eleanor pictured the scene, and the heroic fact that Franklin had dispensed with his crutches. He leaned on his son Elliott's arm and, with a cane, walked across the stage to deliver his nominating speech. It was another resounding triumph, even surpassing his "Happy Warrior" speech of four years earlier, and the convention united behind Smith, who was nominated on the first ballot. ER never again repeated her decision to stay home alone by her radio, while all her friends and loved ones went jubilantly off to participate in the most intense festival of the political game. From then on, she assigned herself a task, whether as a reporter or a troubleshooter. And she always understood that on most occasions she would have to create the assignment for herself.

After Smith's nomination, ER dedicated herself to the effort of getting him elected. With Wyoming Governor Nellie Tayloe Ross, she served as codirector of the National Women's Committee of the Democratic Party. Governor Ross toured the country, while ER was in charge of headquarters. She put together a staff that would remain with her in one way or another for decades to come. During the 1928 campaign, Malvina Thompson (called "Tommy") became her personal secretary. Efficient and charming Grace Tully, who had been New York's Cardinal Hayes's secretary, also worked in the office and later became FDR's secretary; hardworking Alice Disbrow became Caroline O'Day's secretary during her congressional years. New Jersey Congresswoman Mary Norton ran the speakers' bureau, and witty June Hamilton Rhodes, whom ER remembered as the one who "made us laugh and relax," ran the publicity department. ER also drafted Molly Dewson to run the Midwestern region, which established Dewson as a major figure in the organization of the Democratic Party.

It was a congenial, committed group and, ER recalled, there was throughout the long day much laughter and pleasure. Whatever ER may have thought about the eight-hour day for other women, her staff worked—as she did—twelve-to-sixteen-hour days on a regular basis. ER arrived at her offices "early in the day" every day "and started immediately to prepare a plan for the organization of women throughout the country." Every bureau was under her direct supervision.

On the campaign trail, ER pulled few punches. In a far-seeing reference to what we now call "trickle-down economics," she said that she did not believe that American women wanted merely "the prosperity of the great industries from which prosperity will flow in a more moderate amount to other members of the community." She believed American women wanted "the emphasis to be laid on things which deal with the greatest good for the greatest number of people." "Governor Smith recognizes the necessity of business prosperity, but his mind is not a single-track mind. . . ."

On a radio program, ER expressed pity for the poor Republican campaign workers who had to bolster their lackluster candidates from Calvin Coolidge to Herbert Hoover—whose vision no longer seemed progressive: "The life of a consistent Republican was hard. First, he must for seven years be enthusiastic over an iceberg and now he must transfer his enthusiasm to an adding machine."

Although ER preferred to emphasize the positive—Smith's support for the women's reform agenda, and his opposition to "trickle-down" economics—she could not ignore the bigotry that permeated the campaign. Smith's opposition continually returned to his Catholicism, and the thorny issue of Prohibition. ER recalled that "the kind of propaganda that some of the religious groups . . . put forth in that campaign utterly disgusted me. I think by nature I am a fairly liberal person, without intense prejudice, but if I needed anything to show me what prejudice can do to the intelligence of human beings, that campaign was the best lesson I could have had."

ER indicated that her own position on Prohibition was complex. Although she had supported it earlier, she now believed the United States faced more critical issues. In 1928, ER exacerbated a major split among Democratic women when she publicly refused the invitation of the National Woman's Democratic Law Enforcement League to attend its annual convention by writing that she considered it just as important to enforce the Fourteenth and Fifteenth Amendments, guaranteeing the vote to African-Americans, as it was to enforce the Eighteenth Amendment. And, ER wrote, if the League failed to recognize the importance of the Fourteenth and Fifteenth Amendments, it should change its name to the "National Woman's Dry Enforcement League."

Mrs. Jesse W. Nicholson, head of the League, countered that ER was emulating "reactionary Republicans in dragging in the 14th and 15th Amendments." Her reference was to those civil-rights Republicans who continued to support voting rights for blacks, as their ancestors, known as Radical Republicans, did during Reconstruction.

In Democratic circles before Southern blacks voted, Dixiecrats set the racial agenda, and ER never once during the 1928 campaign actually spoke out in opposition to the growing violence that accompanied the disenfranchisement of black citizens in the South. In an unpublished fragment dated 1928, she admitted, "I have never attacked the South for its attitude toward the Negro," and when directly challenged by Mrs. Nicholson to state Smith's views on race, ER waffled. Nicholson wrote: "I note that you [merely] . . . inferentially deny the suggestion that 'Governor Smith believes in equality among the blacks and whites.' We do not feel quite willing to accept your denial on a point which is important to Southern women and their children."

Whereas race was for most whites a nonissue, religious bigotry and Prohibition ripped party unity to shreds, and were among Democratic women just as divisive as the equal-rights issue was among feminists. In July, Mrs. Clem Shaver, the wife of the retiring Democratic National Committee chairman, astounded party regulars by denouncing Al Smith "as a charlatan and a faker" and a "booz-o-crat." She announced that, "regardless of what Democratic leaders from top to bottom may do, we dry Democratic women will not support the dripping wet ticket." ER responded by disparaging Mrs. Shaver and "the little group of women represented by the Women's Democratic Law Enforcement [League] of Baltimore." Their articles were fraudulent, she said; their assertions, false. ER argued that they considered the "enforcement of the Volstead Act more important than truth or fair play," or any other issue.

In an editorial, "When Greek Meets Greek," *The New York Times* breathed a chivalric sigh of relief that two women were exchanging political punches. Unlike Britain, the United States was unaccustomed to open political divisions "within families," and "Mrs. Shaver's original statement struck Washington like a thunderclap," which her husband was called upon to explain. "Are you married?" he asked of all who demanded his opinion. His political cronies were silenced by confusion or amazement, if not quite chivalry. "But a woman is not so circumstanced," noted *The New York Times,* "and Mrs. Roosevelt has replied with all the heat which many men have felt but do not venture to express. The debate may now proceed on its merits. It is in proper hands. It is politically safe. The greatest hazard of the Nineteenth [Suffrage] Amendment has been passed."

If ER's controversies impacted on her husband's own campaign for New York's governor against Albert Ottinger, the popular Republican state attorney general, neither referred to them. Although ER distanced herself from FDR's race and campaigned exclusively for Smith, she had played a critical part in FDR's nomination. If ER had not encouraged him to run, he would not have done it. FDR had refused all entreaties for months, believing that he needed two more years of serious exercise at Warm Springs to walk again. (Also, he had invested over $200,000 of his capital in Warm Springs and wanted to make it work.) He resisted even after the Democratic national chair, John J. Raskob, offered to pay all his debts and contribute significantly to the center at Warm Springs; and he resisted after Herbert Lehman offered to run as lieutenant governor and promised to take over whenever FDR wanted to return to Warm Springs. His family and advisers opposed his candidacy—Louis Howe considered it premature, and Missy LeHand dreaded it. Only FDR's daughter, Anna, was positive: "Go ahead and take it," she wired. FDR wired back: "You ought to be spanked."

ER was never certain what FDR's return to public office would mean to her own life; but when she appeared for the opening ceremonies of the New York State convention in Rochester on 1 October, Smith and Raskob "begged" her to call her husband. He had avoided them all day, refused all their calls. They were told he was out, and he never returned their messages. There was no doubt what her call would mean, and there is no evidence that she hesitated.

That evening, ER was put through to her husband within minutes. FDR told her, "with evident glee," that he had kept "out of reach all day and would not have answered the telephone if I had not been calling." She replied that she was with Smith and Raskob, and without apology handed the phone to Smith and fled to catch her train for New York City. In 1949, ER wrote, "I can still hear Governor Smith's voice saying: 'Hello Frank,' as I hurried from the room. . . . I did not know until the following morning when I bought a newspaper that my husband had been persuaded finally to accept the nomination."

Although ER never took credit for her role in FDR's decision, Esther Lape believed that "the most wonderful thing Eleanor did was to encourage him to run in 1928 when most people thought he was not up to it."

ER's loyalty to FDR, and to what she truly believed was best for him, involved her perception of his physical progress, which had reached its limit, and her conviction that his return to political life would enhance his health and well-being. After seven years of struggle, he had learned how to walk short distances supported by canes and braces, and the strong arms of his sons and associates. But his legs had no real mobility, no actual strength. Moreover, it was her lifelong belief that one must do "what comes to hand," which did not reflect a careless regard for fate but, rather, her sense of obligation and responsibility to the mysteries and vagaries of opportunity. It would be wrong, ER believed, to disregard destiny, when it so specifically called.

There was considerable confusion and some heavyhearted soul-searching at Warm Springs on 2 October, when FDR was nominated by acclamation and decided not to decline. Nobody was pleased. Missy LeHand wanted FDR free to concentrate on his health; Louis Howe believed the Republicans would win and wanted to avoid another personal defeat for the man he wished to help make president. Howe wired: "BY WAY OF CONGRATULATIONS DIG UP TELEGRAM I SENT YOU WHEN YOU RAN IN SENATORIAL PRIMARIES"—a reference to FDR's misguided attempt to run for the U.S. Senate in the 1914 primary.

According to his mother, Warm Springs went into instant mourning until "Franklin's cheery voice was heard to remark, 'Well, if I've got to run for Governor, there's no use in all of us getting sick about it!'"

Once FDR decided to run, he ran with vigor, and all his allies rallied to support his decision. His mother wrote that, no matter what, "I do not want you to be defeated!" She assured him that "all will be well whatever happens." And, with a mother's commitment that tells us much about the origins of FDR's unrivaled sense of security, she wrote: "Now what follows is *really private.* In case of your election, I know your salary is smaller than the one you get now. I am prepared to make the difference up to you."

ER publicly distanced herself as far as possible from her husband's decision, and told the press that she was "very happy and very proud, although I did not want him to do it. He felt that he had to. In the end you have to do what your friends want you to. There comes to every man, if he is wanted, the feeling there is almost an obligation to return the confidence shown him. . . ." When asked if it were because of her last-minute phone call that he changed his mind, she denied it all: "I never did a thing to ask him to run. Franklin always makes his own decisions."

ER answered questions about her own role in FDR's campaign: "I have plenty to do with the job I am handling now for the national campaign. . . . I do not think I will change my plans, but I may make a few speeches later for my husband. If I can be of any help I shall be glad to give it."

As ER had anticipated, FDR was energized and delighted by the excitement of his nonstop campaign. He told his mother: "If I could campaign another six months, I believe I could throw away my cane."

But the election of 1928 was such a total disaster for the Democrats on every level that ER and FDR left party headquarters at midnight convinced that he too had been defeated. They had been watching the returns in New York City's great armory with Al Smith, who had lost not only the nation but also New York: Bigotry and Prohibition, no less than the celebrated Republican era of prosperity, had ensured his overwhelming defeat. Herbert Hoover went on to win 444 electoral votes to Smith's eighty-seven, and Florida, North Carolina, Texas, and Virginia voted Republican for the first time in history. "Well," Smith said that evening, "the time hasn't come yet when a man can say his beads in the White House."

Only Franklin's mother refused to believe that her son could actually lose. She sat and waited through the night for the final upstate returns to come in, even though they represented districts that had been devoted to Ottinger. FDR and Edward J. Flynn, the colorful "boss of the Bronx," had telephoned upstate sheriffs threatening to investigate their suspiciously tardy returns. But Flynn also left before they arrived. Only Sara Delano Roosevelt sat through the early-morning hours as the votes trickled in. She sat in a darkened corridor, alone with a few party stalwarts and the counting staff, until 4:00 A.M., and was the only member of the family who heard the tally that announced her son's election. Governor Franklin Delano Roosevelt carried New York State by 25,564 votes, even though Smith lost it by 103,481.

~

ER's INITIAL RESPONSE TO SMITH'S DEFEAT AND FDR'S VICtory was complex. For over nine months, she had worked daily and imaginatively for the Smith campaign. ER hated to lose. It was not merely Smith's personal loss, or her own, but the continued defeat on the national level of all the social programs she championed. ER understood that progressive Democrats needed to regroup and reorganize. They would all have to try again in four years, and she urged all her co-workers to begin immediately.

ER was eager to continue the battle, but in terms of her own work, she considered FDR's victory a mixed blessing. She feared that FDR's election to office meant that she would have to withdraw from public life. To reporters, her remarks were restrained, even ungracious: "If the rest of the ticket didn't get in, what does it matter?" "No, I am not excited about my husband's election. I don't care. What difference can it make to me?" In retrospect, she wondered if she had "really wanted Franklin to run. I imagine I accepted his nomination and later his election as I had accepted most of the things that had happened in life thus far; one did whatever seemed necessary and adjusted one's personal life to the developments in other people's lives."

There was in 1928 no accepted place for a political wife, except in the background. ER had grown accustomed to a different role. She was a publisher, an editor, a columnist; she debated on the radio and before large audiences; her opinions were forthright and specific. She had a following, and people relied on her views and depended on her leadership.

~

THE ROLE OF SILENT AND SUPPORTIVE WIFE HAD BEEN LEFT in Rock Creek Cemetery contemplating *Grief.* There was no turning back. Yet neither was there any precedent for this new reality. History presented no other couple similarly equal in spirit, commitment, and ambition—giant personalities, powerful egos, inspiring and commanding presences. Was ER seriously meant to become again the dutiful wife at home with the children, silent by the radio, while her husband and all their friends were engaged in the work she most enjoyed? It was impossible. She could not abide the thought. She resented even contemplating it. And so the Roosevelt partnership departed yet again from tradition. ER never did withdraw from the public sphere.

15. New York's First Lady, Part-Time

ALBANY HAD BEEN ELEANOR ROOSEVELT'S FIRST POLIT-ical home. There, in 1911, she learned the nuances of political survival, the obligations and expectations of public wifery. Now, after seventeen years, she returned to Albany a very different woman in very different circumstances.

At midlife, ER was a teacher, writer, and public activist. Her husband was governor, her children were grown, she had become a grandmother, and she liked her life. Although she did not think of herself as a politician—nor did she encourage anybody else to think of her as one—everybody in her circle understood that she had a considerable amount of raw political power. Still, she regarded the return to Albany with dreary foreboding, until she and FDR made a deal: She would do it all—she would be the governor's wife, and she would pursue her own agenda.

ER now consciously recognized that only an activist's life served her needs and temperament. By May 1927, she had already published an article, "What I Want Most Out of Life," in *Success Magazine,* in which she urged mature women to enter politics in order "to guard against the emptiness and loneliness that enter some women's lives after their children are grown." She was persuaded that women needed to have "lives, interests and personalities of their own apart from their house-holds." "And," she concluded, "if anyone were to ask me what I want out of life I would say—the opportunity for doing something useful, for in no other way, I am convinced, can true happiness be obtained."

In 1928, ER took a giant step along the road that confirmed her career as the most nontraditional wife in American politics. She would continue to support her husband's goals, and she would continue to pursue her own interests. When they disagreed, as they did frequently, they disagreed fully. They would always have different priorities and different emphases. Over the years, the World Court, the League of Nations, civil rights, equal rights, and a great variety of social issues were far more important to Eleanor than to Franklin. But one of the most remarkable aspects of the Roosevelt marriage is the sense of mutual respect that marked their public partnership. They consulted each other, and they influenced each other. FDR never did insist that his wife drop anything she personally cared about to become exclusively the first lady of the Empire State. At a time when financially solvent wives rarely worked outside the home, ER juggled several careers as well as her position as one of America's most public wives and mothers.

On 10 November, *The New York Times* ran a headline: "Mrs. Roosevelt to Keep on Filling Many Jobs Besides Being the 'First Lady' at Albany." Half the week she would be "mistress of the Executive Mansion," the rest of the week she would continue to teach history, literature, and public affairs at Todhunter, and to serve as the school's associate principal. "In spare moments she also will help run a furniture factory, serve on a few committees and boards of directors and keep up with current history in which she is keenly interested. And all the time, as the mother of four boys away at school, she will be on call. . . ."

However unconventional their arrangement, both Roosevelts understood that public appearances mattered. They were and remained discreet. After FDR's election, Eleanor announced that she would remove herself from the most visible political forums. She resigned as editor of the *Women's Democratic News,* and refused several lecture offers. On 16 November 1928, she wrote Franklin that Henry Morgenthau had invited her to attend "his agricultural meeting next week but I've written him that I'm not going to any meetings that savor of politics. I have also been asked by four upstate [women's] committees to come to dinners . . . and I've refused them all, so you see I'm being most discreet!" On 1 December, ER wrote that she attended her classes, had students for dinner, and presided at the Consumers' League banquet "because I promised long ago but it is my last appearance as a speaker on any subject bordering on politics!"

When she resigned as editor of the *Women's Democratic News* in November 1928, her friends and closest associates on the paper—Caroline O'Day (president), Elinor Morgenthau (vice-president), Nancy Cook (business manager), and Marion Dickerman (secretary)—testified in a farewell editorial to their appreciation of all that she had contributed to politics and history since women achieved suffrage:

> In this difficult undertaking and through the struggle of succeeding years, one woman has stood out preeminent because of her brilliant political sense, inherited from her long line of ancestors, distinguished in statesmanship, because of her unfailing energy and blithe courage, because of her understanding of human nature and her sympathy and patience with its failings.
>
> This woman is Eleanor Roosevelt whose resignation lies on the desk before us. . . .
>
> Courageous, unselfish, untiring, and with a sense of humor that has helped us over many a rough place, we love Mrs. Roosevelt for these qualities but I think we love her most because of her unswerving loyalty to women and to the high ideals of women from which expediency has never swayed her.

Elinor Morgenthau also resigned from the *News* at this time, but her resignation represented strained personal circumstances between the five friends. They were not quite the five of hearts: ER supported her friend Elinor Morgenthau, but she was intimate with Nancy Cook and Marion Dickerman, and Marion Dickerman in particular was close to Caroline O'Day. Moreover, there always existed some tension—some rivalry, actually—within this circle for ER's attention. Elinor Morgenthau, always correct and less flamboyant than the others, had evidently criticized Nancy Cook, who seemed to her overbearing, occasionally rude, abrupt, and self-serving. ER wrote Elinor Morgenthau that she did not wish to discuss her criticisms of Nancy Cook:

> I am devoted to her & it will be wiser for you not to talk to me about it as you cannot expect me to agree with you or to be influenced by your feelings. . . .
>
> I have worked more years than you have with Caroline, Nan & Marion & enjoyed it & had no real difficulties & I resign now with regret, only because I know if I take any part in politics everyone will attribute anything I say or do to Franklin & that wouldn't be fair to him. . . .
>
> I have always felt that you were hurt often by imaginary things & have wanted to protect you but if one is to have a healthy, normal relationship I realize it must be on some kind of equal basis, you simply cannot be so easily hurt, life is too short to cope with it! Cheer up & forget about it all, do what you enjoy doing & be happy! I'll be home for lunch tomorrow & Thursday at 1:30. . . .
>
> Much love dear,
Devotedly,
Eleanor

Despite ER's public resignation, however, she remained active behind the scenes. Within weeks, she returned to her old post at the *News:* she continued to write most of the editorials, raise most of the money, and do most of the trouble-shooting. Only the masthead changed. Neither ER's nor Elinor Morgenthau's name now appeared on it—officially, after 1928, Caroline O'Day served as editor. But ER commuted from Albany to New York, to her classes at Todhunter and to the little office of the *Women's Democratic News* at 15 East 40th Street, every week. ER had not removed herself from the fray; she merely removed herself temporarily from the appearance of being always at its center. Her commitment to the cause of Democratic women, to the work she had begun in 1920, remained absolute. Moreover, she retained control of every detail and continued to preside over the contents and format of each issue of the *Democratic News.*

On 6 March 1929, for example, she wrote to Frances Perkins:

Could you and Nelle Swartz write me an article for the Women's Democratic News telling of the work of the Labor Dept. and any particular things which you would like the women of the state to appreciate and have brought to their notice?

I would like to have this . . . by next Tues. . . . Are there any new appointments in the Dept. you would like mentioned? Also I would like a photograph of Nelle.

Frances Perkins, always a much less intimate friend than ER's colleagues on the *News,* nevertheless shared their assessment of her, especially during the Albany years. Perkins wrote that during this time ER "was a very easy woman to know." She

was very much a woman's woman. She talked with another woman on the frankest, pleasantest terms. There wasn't any of this waiting for the men to come in. . . . What she had to say, she was delighted to say to you. . . . Some women don't open up or show off at all until the gentlemen come in from dinner. Some quite brilliant women have nothing to say while the ladies wait in the drawing room. They won't say a word. They're brilliant, witty, entertaining the minute the gentlemen come in. . . . It's all right, but you notice that that particular kind of woman doesn't care a hoot what you say or what you think. You're just another woman. There are very few men who won't open up except before women. Men talk much more freely, show themselves and strut their stuff before men much more than women do.

Like many other women, Frances Perkins noticed a physical charm about ER that the cameras rather consistently failed to capture. During the Albany years,

Mrs. Roosevelt was perhaps as handsome as I have seen her. Her dress and her way of dress for the street and for ordinary circumstances was not very elaborate or charming or interesting, but her evening clothes . . . were perfectly magnificent. . . . Her hair was still quite blonde, so light that you were aware of the blondeness. . . .

> It was an extraordinarily heavy head of hair, but with a natural wave or braids around her head or piled up on top of her head. . . . She was so big and tall that this big head of hair was becoming. It fitted her shape, size and height.

ER also wore unique and impressive jewelry. Perkins particularly remembered the tiger's-tooth necklace ER's father had mounted "with beautifully wrought gold links and balls." ER wore it frequently, and it was so large it "would have been dreadfully unbecoming to most women." But ER had "a very long neck, very sloping shoulders, with a large expanse around the collar bone area," and she could carry it beautifully.

Other, more casual observers also noticed the complexities of ER's attractiveness. One reporter, Helena Huntington Smith, wrote that people tended to see in Mrs. Roosevelt "an almost austere streak of responsibility, of duty, which is very Rooseveltian and a shade British." But that emphasis camouflaged more interesting qualities. While Eleanor seemed to cultivate a careless if not random style, and her everyday clothes were loose, long, and unflattering, one needed to see beyond the camera's vision of her. According to Huntington Smith, the camera's emphasis was "very unjust." "It misses her immaculate freshness of appearance, her graciousness, and the charm of a highly intelligent, forceful, and directed personality."

Subsequently, Lorena Hickok, the highest-paid woman reporter with the Associated Press, made much the same observation. She described a costume Eleanor wore during a 1928 luncheon debate with a "self-possessed, witty and always beautifully dressed" Republican society matron:

> Mrs. Roosevelt that day, had she searched the world over, could hardly have found a more unbecoming costume. Her black skirt was longer than those worn by most women. She had on a knitted silk kind of jumper, very long, of a shade of green that made her skin look gray. Her hat, set squarely on top of her tightly netted hair, looked like a black straw pancake.

"You poor thing!" I thought. "It will be murder for you at that luncheon."

But Hick was surprised. ER was radiant and generous in debate, and for the first time she "became interested in Mrs. Roosevelt on her own account," noticing that although ER could look "rather awkward and ungainly" while standing still, "when she moved it was with the grace of a fine athlete. Her carriage was magnificent." Later, when Hickok saw ER in evening clothes, she was "amazed at the change in her appearance." Her gown was long, of a sensual white chiffon: "Tall and slender and erect, she looked like a queen. . . . I decided that she was as some English women are said to be—they may look rather dowdy in daytime clothes, but in evening clothes they are beautiful." Hickok decided at that moment—as others had before her—that the first lady of New York State deserved closer scrutiny.

∼

DURING FDR'S TERM AS GOVERNOR, ELEANOR ROOSEVELT'S impact was felt not only in her own sphere, but in her husband's as well. Both Eleanor and Franklin always denied the true extent of ER's influence on his daily activities, his policies, and his selection of advisers and associates. But even the most cursory reading of their correspondence indicates its primary significance. Soon after the election, on 16 November, ER wrote: "If I were you Franklin, I would keep personal publicity and state committee publicity more or less apart. Don't let Mrs. Moskowitz get draped around you for she means to be and it will always be one for you and two for Al!"

In 1928, FDR was slow to decide what to do with Smith's people. Smith, after all, had made much of FDR's political life possible. The retention of Robert Moses (as secretary of state) and Belle Moskowitz (as personal secretary to the governor) was the only favor Smith had asked of FDR.

Eleanor had had a friendly association with Belle Moskowitz, and greatly respected her organizing talents: a respect that intensified her conviction that FDR would do well to end Moskowitz's leadership role. Strategist and speech-writer, she was Al Smith's Louis Howe—and there was simply no room in FDR's entourage for both Howe and Moskowitz. The Albany team would be Howe and FDR, or Moskowitz fronting for Smith. They represented different circles and competing interests. ER was consistently clear about who would serve her husband's interests and who would not.

ER distrusted both of Al Smith's closest advisers—Belle Moskowitz and Robert Moses. Though she had just fought a vigorous battle against prejudice, her remarks about them were bluntly bigoted: "By all signs I think Belle and Bob Moses mean to cling to you and you will wake up to find R.M. Secretary of State and B.M. running Democratic Publicity at her old stand unless you take a firm stand. Gosh, the race has nerves of iron and tentacles of steel!" Anti-Semitism was rife when it came to references to Smith's intimate advisers—a popular jingle began "Moskie and Proskie [Joseph Proskauer] are the brains of Tammany Hall"—but Eleanor's distrust of Moskowitz was motivated more by political turf than by bigotry. Whether she was called Mrs. Moskowitz, Lady Belle, or Moskie, Smith's chief adviser was one of the most powerful women in the United States. As governor, Smith did nothing without her advice. And ER saw her as a stalking-horse for Smith's interests.

Eleanor credited her with all the significant social-reform and educational programs Smith's administration introduced or supported. Indeed, ER and Belle Moskowitz had worked together for many of Smith's policies, most of which FDR would try to build upon and encourage a reluctant Republican legislature to fund. Under Smith, New York supplemented the Sheppard-Towner federal program for maternal and infant health; pursued a worker-compensation system; opposed censorship and teachers' loyalty oaths; sought an improved educational system, greater labor-management conciliation, a better health-care program, a coordinated housing program, a public-parks and road-building program, and a public water-power development system.

Belle Moskowitz was a remarkable public-relations pioneer and social reformer—a brilliant politician, who knew whom to talk to and when to deal. As an early "industrial counsellor," she had developed the field of public-relations motion pictures, subsequently called "commercials." Her first film, made in 1920, publicized the New York–New

Jersey Port and Harbor Development Commission, the Port Authority.

She worked on that project with Al Smith, one of the Port Authority's chief proponents. But her relationship with Al Smith began in 1918, when as governor-elect he appointed Moskowitz to head a new commission to reorganize the state's administration and implement his social-reform program.

The year 1918 was the first time women could vote in New York State, and Smith wanted advice about how to attract the new electorate. Belle Moskowitz volunteered, despite his association with Tammany and his well-known contempt for women, especially women do-gooders, whom he then called "crackpots." Their first connection occurred when Moskowitz arranged a luncheon for Smith at the Women's University Club. He attended reluctantly, afraid that he would be dismissed as an uneducated boor, a Tammany hack. As he sat at the dais and regarded his elegant and very wary audience, he turned to Moskowitz:

" 'What the hell am I going to say to a bunch of women like this?' he growled.

" 'If you're smart,' " Moskowitz replied, " 'you'll make the same speech you'd make to a bunch of businessmen.' "

He spoke about the economic issues of the campaign, and noticed that Moskowitz's strategy worked. The women were not only attentive but enthusiastic. Smith never went anywhere without Moskowitz again. They were inseparable, and her influence prevailed. It was her idea to form a Commission for Reconstruction, Retrenchment and Reorganization to reform New York's entire administrative machinery.

Moskowitz always preferred to work in the background, and "without portfolio." However discreetly she worked, from 1918 to 1928 her power throughout New York State was simply absolute; and her commission was the determinant of all changes and policies.

Moskowitz selected Dr. Robert Moses—a Ph.D. from Oxford University, then working at the Bureau of Municipal Research, where his arrogance and his brilliance were equally remarked upon—to be the commission's chief of staff. Although Belle Moskowitz and Robert Moses disagreed frequently and vehemently, their partnership was invincible. Moreover, Moses learned most of what he learned about the political game from Belle Moskowitz, and he was a lean and hungry student.

Robert Moses came from an assimilated and affluent German-Jewish family that had joined the nondenominational Ethical Culture Society before he was born. He had no training or education as a Jew, had participated in no Jewish ceremonial rite of passage—he was neither circumcised nor bar mitzvahed—and he never considered himself Jewish. But in the anti-Semitic era that preceded the Holocaust, Robert Moses was considered a Jew. And in 1928 he was perceived by Eleanor Roosevelt as a Jew first.

~

ER'S ANTI-SEMITISM WAS IMPERSONAL AND CASUAL, A FRAYED raiment of her generation, class, and culture which she wore thoughtlessly. She did not quite remove it until the era of the Holocaust caused her to consider deeply, actually to study, her own feelings. Eleanor Roosevelt was not a bigot, and she opposed prejudice in public life. She never assessed worth or quality on the basis of religion or race. She was revolted by the anti-Catholic hatred in part responsible for Smith's defeat, and deplored the Ku Klux Klan's anti-black, anti-Jewish, anti-Catholic practices which played so large a role in politics during the 1920s. Yet, however much ER opposed bigotry in public life, she had very few Jewish friends until World War II; Elinor and Henry Morgenthau were notable exceptions. Even Bernard Baruch—who over time became one of Eleanor's most intimate friends—was viewed disparagingly during the 1920s. Indeed, when ER met Baruch—at a 1920 Navy party in his honor, to celebrate his contributions to the war effort—she wrote her mother-in-law: "The Jew party was appalling."*

As with her wariness about Belle Moskowitz, it was not specifically Robert Moses's Jewish ancestry that caused ER to distrust and dislike him. ER had more personal, and political, motives. Robert Moses had insulted Louis Howe and ridiculed her husband. Smith had appointed FDR chair of the Taconic State Park Commission, and Moses head of the Long Island State Park Commission in 1924. In those capacities, they were equal in authority. But Moses monopolized all monies through his control of the State Parks Council, and he refused to appoint Louis

---

* See the chapter on ER and the Jews in Volume Two of this biography.

Howe secretary to FDR, as FDR had requested. Moses publicly announced that, if FDR needed a "secretary and valet," he could hire one. Moses would not spend one state cent for the services of that ugly creature he called "Lousy Louie."

As Smith's secretary of state, and chief creator of Long Island's parks and parkways, Robert Moses worked to sabotage all FDR's efforts in behalf of the Taconic State Parkways. He continually denounced FDR as an untrustworthy playboy and a lightweight. He could not believe that Smith had backed FDR for governor, over himself. Moses frequently denounced both Eleanor and Franklin, in rude and sensational terms. Many of his remarks got back to the Roosevelts, including his snide dismissal of FDR as "a pretty poor excuse for a man." As Roosevelt's popularity in Smith's circle grew, Moses's attacks became more and more outrageous—until finally they were "vicious," and ER was among the first fully to perceive that he was a thoroughgoing cad, a bully and liar.

ER's distrust of Belle Moskowitz was more impersonal. FDR told Frances Perkins:

Eleanor said to me, "Franklin, Mrs. Moskowitz is a very fine woman. I have worked with her in every campaign. I never worked with anybody that I liked to work with better. She's extremely competent. She's extremely able. She's far-sighted. She's absolutely reliable. What she says she'll do, she does. You can count on that. I think a great deal of her and I think we are friends. But I want to say this to you. You have to decide, and you have to decide it now, whether you are going to be Governor of this state, or whether Mrs. Moskowitz is going to be Governor of this state. If Mrs. Moskowitz is your secretary, she will run you. It won't hurt you. It won't give you any pain. She will run you in such a way that you don't know that you're being run a good deal of the time. Everything will be arranged so subtly that when the matter comes to you it will be natural to decide to do the thing that Mrs. Moskowitz has already decided should be done. That is the way she works. That is the kind of person she is. She doesn't do it in any spirit of ill will. It's simply that her competence is so much greater than anybody else's that even with Al Smith, as much as she loves him, she still ran him in that same subtle way."

Eleanor phrased her advice to Franklin carefully. She did not actually tell FDR not to reappoint Belle Moskowitz. She left the decision entirely up to him, with a warning: "If you decide to take Mrs. Moskowitz it will be all right. She will make good decisions. She's a capable woman, she knows and she will make them in the direction of the welfare of the people of New York. . . . But they will be her decisions, not yours."

Ultimately, Moses and Moskowitz were the only significant members of Smith's staff FDR dismissed—a move that enabled him to assert his independence from Smith, and prepare for his journey to the White House with his own team.

FDR, for so long under his mother's thumb, resented any direct advice from his wife; but he never turned away from her counsel. He always sought her opinions, her perceptions. He trusted her, above all other reporters he sent out into the field, to return not only with the details, but with the nuances and hidden meanings. Still, he rarely credited her with a job well done, or with any substantial contribution to his decisions. And she tempered her advice with rather disingenuous assurances that she was not giving any advice at all. Neither he nor she ever acknowledged her influence on his appointments.

On 22 November 1928, for example, ER wrote to FDR: "I hope you will consider making Frances Perkins labor commissioner. She would do well and you could fill her place as chair of the Industrial Commission by one of the men . . . and put Nell[e] Swartz (now Bureau of Women in Industry) on the Commission so there would be one woman on it. These are suggestions which I am passing on not my opinions for I don't want to butt in!"

Subsequently, after Eleanor became critical of Perkins and relations between them soured, Perkins denied ER's role in her appointments, both at the state and federal levels. "It has been said that ER urged FDR to appoint me. I don't know if that was true, and I wouldn't know. She certainly never said anything to me about it. I doubt that he said something to her about it, though she may have broached the subject. I really wouldn't know whether she initiated the idea." "I always knew him better than I knew her." Reluctantly, after intensive questioning, Perkins admitted that FDR had told her that he had in fact consulted ER, Nancy Cook, and Caroline O'Day on her appointments.

The fact is that in 1928 Perkins was appointed because ER and her associates thought it would be a good idea; and women were appointed to several other key positions because of the activities of the women's committee which ER did so much to develop. Indeed, increasingly influenced by his wife and her colleagues, FDR celebrated women politicians as the wave of the future in a 1928 essay for the election issue of the Women's City Club *Quarterly,* "Women's Field in Politics":

> It is my firm belief that had women had [an] equal share in making the laws in years past, the unspeakable conditions in crowded tenement districts, the neglect of the poor, the unwillingness to spend money for hospitals and sanitariums, the whole underlying cynical attitude towards human life and happiness as compared to material prosperity, which has reached its height under the present Republican administration, would never have come about. . . .
>
> I have always believed in giving women an equal share in the making of our laws. I have regarded their entry into politics—for they must enter politics if they are to have a voice in our legislative halls—the most noteworthy step toward securing greater happiness and greater prosperity for the individual that we have ever taken.

Those were virtually the same words ER had been using for eight years. Louis Howe shared that vision, and FDR now publicly affirmed his agreement. Still, whatever their shared convictions, ER's public role as first lady of New York State was confined to those domestic chores traditionally reserved exclusively for women. Her very first task was to arrange the sprawling Gothic edifice that was to be their household.

While FDR was in Warm Springs, she rearranged the rooms, redesigned the servants' quarters to make them more spacious, removed the greenhouses to replace them with a swimming pool for Franklin, and made certain that the departing Smiths would be accompanied by their entire zoo of bear cubs, goats, six dogs, three monkeys, assorted elks, foxes, a raucous family of raccoons, and at least one tiger.

She did it all on a one-day inspection tour with Nancy Cook, and wrote FDR that she was "appalled at the number of people who go with the Executive Mansion." She hoped the size of the staff could be reduced dramatically since the household monetary allowances were all insufficient. Nevertheless, "the head man" seemed "nice and all will be comfortable."

For FDR she selected "the grandest sunny room," which boasted "a bathroom and closets so palatial that you can get lost in them." She thought the library would "be a grand den and work room for you and the old office the Governor had upstairs can be made into a family sitting room or Mrs. Smith's dressing room can be made into one." But the latter was "the only single room in the house and I thought we might want to give it to Missy so we will talk that over."

For herself, ER chose a sitting room and study, but not a proper bedroom. ER considered her time too divided for her actually to require a really pleasant bedroom. Although she wrote nothing about her own space to FDR, during one evening when Frances Perkins was invited to stay over after a late-night party ER explained her willingness to give up her room whenever the house got crowded.

According to Frances Perkins, "you have no idea how many people they used to ask to stay when there'd been some big occasion." Then ER would give up her room and move into a servant's room on the third floor with Perkins or some other friend. On one such occasion, Perkins complimented Eleanor on the "wonderful . . . way you casually disturb yourself and move out of your room . . . and adapt yourself to camping out with me." ER replied: "I'm so glad you're here and I can do it, but as a matter of fact, it isn't something for me. You know, this isn't my home. That isn't my room that I sleep in down there. You know, I've never had a home of my own. First I lived with my relatives. . . . Then I lived in a boarding school. Then I came home and still lived in somebody else's house. . . ." In Eleanor's account, as she made the rounds of her aunts and grandmother, she was reluctant "to ask for anything because, after all, they were taking her in."

Then I married Franklin and . . . Franklin's mother took us right in. . . . Nothing could ever be even said about it. . . . She went and bought new carpets, rugs and furniture. . . . I've never bought so much as a tea cup for myself. . . . I never had anything.

Then we moved up here to the Executive Mansion. This doesn't belong to us. This isn't my house. It belongs to the State of New York. It's furnished by the State of New York. It's furnished in the official taste of the State of New York. Even the servants are civil servants hired by the State of New York. Nothing belongs to me except my maid. . . . I've been living in other people's houses and now I'm living in a public institution. So I don't mind giving up my room. That's nothing.

After FDR was elected president, Perkins once reminded ER of that Albany evening. ER laughed. "Isn't it funny? My next move was into a museum."

~

BY 1928 ER DID HAVE A HOME SHE CONSIDERED HER OWN, AT Val-Kill. And work of her own, which she loved. ER co-owned, was vice-principal of, and taught at Todhunter. Her schedule was extraordinary. She left Albany Sunday afternoon of each teaching week to travel to New York City and meet her classes: 9:00–1:00 on Mondays, 9:00–5:00 on Tuesdays, 9:00–11:00 A.M. on Wednesdays. In New York City, her afternoons and evenings were given over to a variety of activities, most of them political. On Wednesday at noon, she returned to Albany, where she presided over the social whirl demanded of the governor's wife. There were Cabinet dinners, afternoon teas, legislative dinners, formal and informal meetings of all variety; lectures and columns; interviews and investigations; and correspondence without end. ER answered every letter sent to her. And there was always her concern for the needs of her children.

About the children, ER noted shortly after the election that Anna and her husband, Curt, were to leave "for a week of shooting in North Carolina"; and the news from Groton was "pretty good." Franklin, Jr., troubled with "a bellyache on the right side," was recovering, and it was not appendicitis. John, who had hurt his knee in an accident, would "be on crutches for a month. Poor Lamb!" Elliott was well, although he threatened to irritate an old stomach rupture by his insistence on playing football. James, a junior at Harvard, was to become secretly engaged to Betsy Cushing. ER was sorry to see her eldest son rush into marriage before graduation, much as she and FDR had. But, she wrote her husband after meeting the Cushings, Betsy "is a nice child, family excellent, nothing to be said against it. . . . Perhaps it will be a good influence & in any case we can do nothing about it."

Above all, during the state house years, ER's central concern and primary focus was the Todhunter School for Girls. ER had always wanted to teach, to be part of that honored community that celebrated intellectual stimulation and public responsibility. She saw teaching as a vehicle through which she might communicate feminist and life-enhancing principles that would help empower future generations of American women. And she had no intention of abandoning this mission because her husband had been elected governor.

Above: During the first years of their courtship and marriage, ER and FDR were supremely happy. They traveled widely, shared many interests, and had fun together. Relaxing at Hyde Park, she holds his drink; he holds her knitting.

Right: On their honeymoon in Scotland, August 1905, ER is seen smoking a cigarette. She smoked occasionally over the years, although never habitually.

*From 1906 until 1916, ER felt forever with child. For ten years, she wrote, she was
either pregnant or recovering from pregnancy: "My family filled my life." This family portrait was taken in Washington, c. June 1918, before "the bottom dropped out"
of ER's world. Seated, left to right: Franklin, Jr., FDR, Eleanor, John, and Elliott;
standing: Anna and James.*

Right: While raising her family, ER had few friends, except her baby nurse, Blanche Spring, shown here at Campobello with Elliott in 1911.

Below: Her other companions were Bob Ferguson, a former Rough Rider, and Isabella Selmes, ER's young friend, whom he married in 1905. This photo of Bob Ferguson, ER, Martha Flandreau Selmes (Isabella's mother, partially hidden by log), and Isabella Selmes Ferguson was taken during the visit ER and FDR made to Cat Canyon, near Silver City, New Mexico, May 1912.

Left: In December 1918, the Roosevelts reviewed the United States fleet on its return from Europe aboard the SS Aztec.

After ER read Lucy Mercer's letters to her husband in September 1918, she offered him a divorce. FDR refused, and they made every effort to rebuild their partnership. But for months ER could not eat, looked emaciated, averted her face from the camera.

Above: During the summer of 1919, even Campobello failed to heal ER's heart. She was frequently comforted by her mother-in-law during this period, and several pictures of the family show SDR's hand around ER's shoulder, or, as here, upon her knee.

Left: ER found solace, however, during the many hours she spent within the holly grove at Rock Creek Cemetery in Washington, contemplating Saint-Gaudens's statue erected in memory of Henry Adams's wife, Clover, who committed suicide. ER called the monument Grief.

Not until ER actively engaged in politics were her spirits reconstituted. Louis Howe, the man most responsible for ER's involvement in FDR's political activities after 1920, was unique among their friends. He earned and maintained the trust and devotion of both ER and FDR.

FDR and his mother, after he was nominated Democratic vice-presidential candidate, July 1920, at Hyde Park.

After 1921, Esther Everett Lape and Elizabeth Fisher Read became ER's political mentors and the first intimate women friends of her adult years. She considered that "Providence was particularly wise and farseeing when it threw these two women together, for their gifts complement each other in a most extraordinary way."

Above: Esther Lape's portrait, c. 1925.

Right: Esther Lape and Elizabeth Read, c. 1930. This picture, taken at Saltmeadow in Westbrook, Connecticut, always hung on ER's wall.

*ER and Esther Lape appear for
the Senate hearings.*

In January 1924, the Senate Special Committee on Propaganda investigated the Bok Peace Award, over which Esther Lape presided with Eleanor Roosevelt and Narcissa Vanderlip. Charged with conspiracy to manipulate America's "foreign policy," creating thereby a "moral menace" during the height of the Red Scare, ER was the subject of a vast FBI file, whose first entry (dated 15 February 1924) refers to these events.

In 1924, ER became prominent in national and state Democratic Party circles for her own activities.

For the national convention, she was named chair of the women's platform committee. But in the end, the male politicians refused to consider the platform, which nevertheless became the liberal agenda for the next decade. Iced out of all proceedings, ER spent tedious convention hours knitting, and in anguish.

She was far more successful at the state level, where her steaming "teapot" campaign car clogged her cousin Teddy Roosevelt's efforts against Al Smith. At a victory meeting in her 49 East 65th Street home, ER and Howe celebrate with their team (including Belle Moskowitz on the left and Josephine Sykes Morgenthau on the right), and the "singing teapot" posters at the rear.

In addition to Democratic Party politics, ER was active in the League of Women Voters, the Women's City Club, and the Women's Trade Union League, where she met Hilda Smith. Dean Hilda Smith directed the Summer School for Working Women in Industry established at Bryn Mawr College in 1921, which ER made every effort to visit over the years.

Above: Hilda Smith sent this photo of herself and ER, taken c. 1930, to Dagmar Schultz of Berlin in 1972.

For several years after 1925, ER was closest to Nancy Cook. With her, Marion Dickerman, and Caroline O'Day, ER built the "honeymoon cottage" on the Val-Kill, bought the Todhunter School and the Val-Kill furniture reproduction factory, and edited the Women's Democratic News. *According to Marion Dickerman, ER "loved Nan much more than she did me." Right: Nancy Cook at the furniture factory.*

*Marion Dickerman on the
stone-and-wood bridge
over the Val-Kill.*

*Above: ER shocked her family, including
Aunt Bye, by appearing with her friends in
knickerbockers—as well as matching
brown tweeds, very dapper and quite
British, which she had ordered made for
herself and Nancy. This photo was taken
during a July 1926 camping trip with
Marion Dickerman, ER, Nancy Cook, and
Marion's sister Peggy Levenson, who
taught French at Todhunter.*

*Right: In the 1920s and '30s, Elinor
Morgenthau was also part of ER's personal
and political circle. During the White
House years, they rode together in Rock
Creek Park virtually every morning before
breakfast. This photo was taken on
21 March 1933.*

Left: Between 1925 and 1932, (left to right) ER, Nancy Cook, Caroline O'Day, and Marion Dickerman worked most closely on the Women's Democratic News, *and at New York Democratic State Headquarters, pictured here in 1929.*

Below: With Todhunter students, principal Marion Dickerman and associate principal ER, third and forth from left, c. 1929.

Left: Dockside with the boys, c. 1925.

Below: Wrestling with Anna at Val-Kill, Caroline O'Day on the left, Anna's dog to the right, c. 1925.

During the 1920s, ER, now in control of her own life, also took charge of family matters. She felt particularly liberated in relationship to her children, with whom she felt closer.

Left: ER was happy to see FDR, Jr., off to a tour of Europe with his Groton class, July 1932.

The boss of women's political activities during the 1920s, ER worked vigorously in behalf of every major reform issue.

Above: Elinor Morgenthau, ER, and Jane Addams while on a visit to Lillian D. Wald, founder of the Henry Street Settlement, who was ailing and at home in Westport, Connecticut, 1929.

Right: ER, Mary Garrett Hay, and Carrie Chapman Catt at a peace conference in Hyde Park to establish a women's movement to support the Kellogg-Briand pact to outlaw war, October 1927.

Unlike Louis Howe, who served as a bridge between ER and FDR, after 1928 Earl exclusively championed Eleanor. Earl Miller and FDR, c. 1925, at the swimming pool in Warm Springs, Georgia.

During FDR's years as governor, Earl Miller was assigned to be ER's bodyguard. They traveled together for four years, and remained devoted to each other. According to his close friend Miriam Abelow, Miller was "large, handsome, athletic and brazen."

Earl Miller and ER at Chazy Lake, New York. Their intimate friendship annoyed some of ER's friends, who claimed he "manhandled" her, put his hand on her knee, draped his arm around her shoulders, and in other ways was too demonstrative in public. Here, however, her hand is on his knee.

Left: Lorena Hickok, the Associated Press's highest-paid woman reporter, in 1932. When Hick first met ER in 1928, she wanted very much to know Mrs. Roosevelt. "But she always held me at arm's length—and her arms were very long." After 1932, Lorena Hickok became ER's special friend, and for almost a decade eclipsed the First Lady's affections for Earl Miller.

Below: ER liked this 1933 portrait, and inscribed it to Hick, bottom right.

Below: Because Lorena Hickok destroyed most of ER's private correspondence between 1932 and 1933, and all of Earl Miller's correspondence has vanished, we have no details about this candid snapshot of Hick and Earl, evidently taken by ER, which reads on the back, "Trip to New York–Canada with ER. July 1933."

Left: FDR's first inaugural: ER, FDR, son James, 4 March 1933.

Below: Unlike FDR and Herbert Hoover, who rode to the ceremony together in frosty silence, ER and Lou Henry Hoover, one of America's most underrated First Ladies, remained cordial.

Below: ER was radiant at the inaugural balls, 4 March 1933.

16. Teaching and Todhunter

ER'S TEACHING CAREER BEGAN WHEN SHE AND MAR-
ion Dickerman purchased (with Nancy Cook and evidently
Caroline O'Day) the Todhunter School for Girls at 66 East
80th Street in New York in 1927. A finishing school "of broad cultural
aim," including college preparation, it attracted the privileged young
women of New York who lived generally between Park Avenue and
Central Park.

When, in 1926, the British-born and Oxford-educated Winifred
Todhunter decided to return to England, she offered her school to her
vice-principal, Marion Dickerman. Short of cash, Dickerman turned to
ER for advice and support. ER, who had longed to teach ever since she
left Allenswood, enthusiastically gave or loaned Marion Dickerman the
capital needed, and agreed to teach. But she hesitated to assume the
title of associate principal because she lacked a college education and
what she considered the necessary training.

On 7 February 1926, ER wrote Dickerman: "I think you ought to
take the 1st place [as principal] for the first year with the understanding
that you have no financial responsibility. It will be easier for you to
settle in that way & when Miss Todhunter and Miss Burrell depart then
I'll slip in & do all I can for you but I feel strongly that you have to
find out gradually what I can do. . . . But associate principals for the
good of the School should have college degrees & I think I'd better be

something less high sounding!" ER also felt that she should receive no salary the first year, "as I would consider that I was being paid in experience and the next year if we assumed joint financial responsibility then we could arrange some percent of profit after your salary & all expenses were paid. I think it will be quite thrilling for it is your gift & it would be a crime for you not to use it & I know you can make a great success."

ER's own success as a teacher was so rapid and thorough, and her popularity so intense, that, her profound modesty notwithstanding, even she had to acknowledge it. For the first time in her adult life, ER was able to take full credit for her work, and to acknowledge its excellence and significance. Despite all her political success, she took unique pride in her teaching career—the fulfillment of her Allenswood ambitions.

After one year of teaching, she would never again feel about herself as she did when she wrote to Marion Dickerman in 1926: "It is going to be such fun to work with you & Nan & you are dear to let me join in it all for I'd never have had the initiative or the ability in any one line to have done anything interesting alone!"

Together, ER and Marion Dickerman, "stately figures in tailored dark red gowns and low-heeled oxfords like those the girls are required to wear," presided over the daily ceremonies that opened the school day. A hundred uniformed girls ranging in age from five or six to eighteen marched to the cadence of a piano tune into the assembly room, which had once been a mid-Victorian parlor; there, behind a long well-polished table, ER and Marion Dickerman waited to receive them. Announcements, songs, and the school prayer followed:

> O God, give us clean hands, clean words, clean thoughts. Help us to stand for the hard right against the easy wrong. Save us from habits that harm. Teach us to work as hard and play as fair, in Thy sight alone, as though all the world saw us. Keep us ready to help others and send us chances every day to do a little good and so grow more like Christ. Amen.

Although Marion Dickerman, Nancy Cook, and ER co-owned Todhunter, and Marion was the principal, Eleanor's influence prevailed.

She wrote the articles in magazines and school newsletters, raised the funds, and attracted the students. Nancy Cook was largely involved with the Val-Kill furniture business, and appeared at Todhunter only occasionally. Marion Dickerman was very much present, but many of the students considered her less progressive, and rather less appealing, than ER. Both Annis Fuller Young (Crystal Eastman's daughter, adopted by Agnes Brown Leach, also ER's close friend) and Patricia Vaill (class of 1936) remembered Dickerman as dour, frosty, a traditional snob. There were other teachers at Todhunter—excellent instructors of art, music, geography, dramatics, languages, and athletics. But, like Marie Souvestre at Allenswood, ER eclipsed all others and dominated the landscape.

ER loved Todhunter. She loved young people. And she loved to teach. It gave her a forum for her vision and a new dimension of confidence and of real pleasure. That portion of her personal journey which she had begun at Allenswood in 1899 was resumed triumphantly at Todhunter. In 1930, she told a reporter that she meant to continue as a teacher, "because it is one thing that belongs to me." And in 1932, she told another reporter: "I like it better than anything else I do."

ER was a natural, enthusiastic, and exciting teacher. Her students adored her—she made them work, and she made them think. To Patricia Vaill, she made history and every character in it come alive—"And I never forgot a damn thing she ever taught me." Every week, on the train to and from Albany, ER did her own homework. She read voraciously, prepared imaginative lesson plans, graded papers with long, thoughtful, sympathetic comments. Her message to her students was: Be Somebody. Be Yourself. Be All You Can Be.

As a teacher, ER consciously modeled herself after Marie Souvestre: Her own experiences with that great teacher caused her to believe profoundly that the main thing in education "is the interest aroused in a young mind by a stimulating, vivid personality." ER assigned her students research projects that would enable them to analyze controversial subjects from several perspectives, and to begin to develop their own points of view, their own theories about truth and fraud, decency and dishonor, morality and immorality—in politics, history, and private life.

As progressive as were some of Todhunter's educational methods,

ER supported a traditional system of tests, midterm and final examinations, reports and grades. She and her colleagues believed, ER explained, "that the girls will have to take certain hurdles in life and that hurdles in school are an important preparation. We try, however, not to compare one child with another. And each girl plots a graph of her own term marks to demonstrate to herself whether she is gaining or losing."

ER's standards were high, and she was occasionally disappointed. Her senior girls were sometimes spoiled and indolent, sometimes impossibly unprepared. She wrote FDR on 2 February 1928, after her first semester at Todhunter: "I can't say I am set up by the exams my children did. I only flunked one but the others were none too good." Ever mindful of her own educational gaps as a young woman, ER was gentle but diligent.

She never forgot that dreadful moment of embarrassment during her honeymoon when she visited the Fergusons. Alone with Lady Helen at tea in the garden, surrounded by rhododendrons and tranquillity, ER was "basking in contentment" until suddenly Lady Helen asked her to explain the structure of the U.S. government. ER repeated that story frequently, and as a teacher dedicated herself to several specific tasks: No student of hers would ever feel so unprepared or politically illiterate. More than that, she wanted her students to be as concerned about the great events of state and their solution as the finest spirits of England, like Lady Helen Ferguson: "a lovely and a brilliant woman, typical of the alert Englishwoman who knows the politics of the hour to the last detail."

All of ER's history and government students were prepared to answer a variety of questions on their final exams:

> What is the difference between a citizen and a subject?
> What is meant by a "public servant"?
> List the ways in which your government touches your home.
> Do you know of any way in which the Government protects women and children?
> How does the family income affect the standards of living?
> What is the difference between civil and political liberty?

What is the object today of inheritance, income and similar taxes?

Why is there a struggle between capital and labor?

Into what three different parts are our national and state governments divided by our constitution? What is the function of each?

What is a tariff?

What is the World Court?

Who is Mahatma Gandhi?

Who is John Brown?

What were the causes of the Mexican War?

What was the Dred Scott case?

What were the causes of the Civil War?

How did you feel about the solution of the Indian problem in the Southern states during [Andrew] Jackson's term of office?

Give your reasons for or against allowing women to participate actively in the control of government politics and officials through the vote, as well as your reasons for or against women holding office in the government.

How are Negroes excluded from voting in the South?

Who is the dominant political figure in Soviet Russia?

Write an account of any article or series of articles on a subject you have read with most interest. . . .

ER's teaching methods were personal and informal. But, like Marie Souvestre, she held her students strictly accountable and suffered neither idlers nor parrots with notable patience. Although she did not encourage her students to become traitors to their class, she did promote responsible citizenship and urged her girls to challenge authority. "That is what the book says," she repeatedly admonished. "Now how would you put it?"

Above all, ER prepared her students to lead productive, cultured, and thoughtful lives: "Education only ends with death," she said repeatedly. Her own appetite for learning, for understanding the complexities and contradictions of the human spirit and society in all its forms, was what she most sought to communicate. Less concerned with an isolated fact or date, she wanted to pass on to her students the tools they needed to make their lives an ongoing adventure in learning and understanding. For ER, the two primary tools were: curiosity and vision.

~

IN 1930, ER WROTE "WHAT KIND OF EDUCATION DO WE WANT for Our Girls?" for *The Woman's Journal:*

"Vision means imagination and is absolutely necessary to the fostering of curiosity. . . ."

ER hoped that children would receive such usable tools in school, "so that they may not only want information, but know where to go to find it." ER wished especially that "we could give to all young people" a "real joy in books. If they find some kind of reading in which they can lose themselves, it will help them through many difficult times in their future lives." Ultimately, education for ER meant the "habit of reading" combined with the opportunity to know "many different kinds of literature."

ER's literature classes were much like the literature classes she most loved at Allenswood, and she relied on her old notebooks, and her own daily readings to engage her students. The authors covered ranged from Aeschylus to Zola. Although she never "forgot the ladies," they represented a very short list. Indeed, except for her inclusion of Jane Austen, Maria Edgeworth, George Eliot, and such transcendentalists as Margaret Fuller and Elizabeth and Sophie Peabody, most of ER's references to women were found in her category "Minor Fiction Writers," which included Miss Sedgwick, Miss Jewett, Miss Wilkes, Sarah Hale, and Lydia Child. Nevertheless, ER's sense of literature was eclectic and nonexclusive. It ranged and rambled from Aristophanes to the medieval ("How did mystery and miracle plays develop?" "What was 14th Century Theatre?") to Oscar Wilde (listed with "minor poetry writers"). A good deal of time was spent on the classics. Shakespeare ("Who was your favorite character in *Midsummer Night's Dream* and in *Twelfth Night?*"), Charles Dickens, Robert Browning, Henry David Thoreau, and Walt Whitman were clearly among her favorites. She spent hours on the pastoral writers of the South, as well as the reformers of New England. Her students in world, British, and American literature were treated to a plentiful and rather democratic feast.

ER's philosophy as an educator reflected the broader political beliefs she had defined during the presidential campaign of 1928 in an article called "Jeffersonian Principles: The Issue in 1928."

> The outstanding issue today is much as it was in Jefferson's day—trust in the people or fear of the people. . . .
>
> Is the Government to be in the hands of the aristocrats . . . or shall it again be in the hands of the people who may make more mistakes but who will be free, responsible citizens . . . ?

ER deplored the fact that Republican policies protected "big business and industry," not the individual on the farm or in the family store. She had no quarrel with big business . . . "we need business, big and little, for prosperity." But, she asserted, the Democrats did not "want one group to prosper as the result of Government favor while another languishes as the result of Government neglect."

Politically, "our desire is to see . . . [a] more human outlook," a commitment to "the interests of all the people" and their "health, education, labor conditions, opportunities for joyous living."

Education, ER concluded, was the essential foundation upon which all democratic institutions rested. Throughout the gubernatorial years, she called for a greater commitment to public education. Public schools were responsible for "training the great mass of our students." But public school teachers were undervalued and underpaid. ER emphasized that women teachers especially were underpaid. Only when their work was justly rewarded, would we know that our society had affirmed its commitment to real education.

As an educator, there was a contradiction between ER's theory and practice. ER had a theory of education as an experiment in social democracy in which children of all classes and groups would know one another and learn to appreciate the exciting richness and variety of our complex society. But her school was expensive and restricted. She believed, abstractly, that public education for all would greatly benefit each individual child, and society as a whole. She even entertained the idea of mandatory public education for all children.

But even by her own example, ER's challenge was contradictory.

Her entire family attended private schools, while she increasingly deplored the insularity of the private school. It was unfortunate, she said, that so many children were "closely confined amongst the little groups of people which form their immediate circle of family and friends. . . . To bring children up with a conception that their own particular lives are typical of the whole world is to bring up extraordinarily narrow people. . . ."

ER was particularly critical of parents who were concerned only about the prestigious aspects of a school and failed even to "inquire how well that school stands scholastically." It amazed her that parents still emphasized almost exclusively their daughters' entrance into "that strange thing called 'society.' " ER dismissed "that magic word 'society.' " "There was a time," she noted, when "perhaps there were really only four hundred people who could afford the gaieties and elegant leisure of the society of that day, which was represented by an old lady in a magnificent house who gave remarkable parties to a few people, many of whom, while they may have belonged to the society of the 'four hundred,' scarcely can have been said to have either ornamented or elevated its standing in the greater social organization we call civilization." But today, ER insisted, "there is no such thing in this country . . . as any one group which may be called 'society.' "

There were too many people, too many interests, too many occupations, too many groups for any one group to monopolize that idea. There "is no such thing possible in this country as an aristocracy of society based on birth." We have now "set up a material basis as the final criterion of social eligibility." But that involves excellence, achievement, success. Many "who arrive at the top are found to have very simple backgrounds. . . ."

So why this insistence, when we are looking for an education, on the school's providing also "society," which in the old sense does not exist at all; and in the new sense can only be entered through the acquiring by the individual of the qualities which make for success in the world at large.

I am hoping that as we grow a little older our schools and our parents will cooperate to impress on our youth that there are many types of success, that one may be lacking in many material things . . . and yet be an outstanding success because of some outstanding service to mankind. Madame Curie is feted over here, she is received everywhere with respect and recognition for the services which she and her husband have through years of patient study rendered to mankind, but the material returns have been very, very small.

I would like to see our schools and our parents cooperate in teaching the younger generation . . . that the point of real education is an ability to recognize the spirit that is in a real human being, even though it may be obscured for a time by lack of education or opportunity to observe certain social customs. . . .

ER believed that educational policies determined the direction of a democratic society; and her goals as an educator were embodied in Todhunter's statement of purpose, sent to all prospective applicants: A "state is the most civilized which has the greatest proportion of happy, healthy, wise and gentle people." Todhunter existed to "educate for such a state. . . ." "In a community of one hundred every one counts 'but none too much'; thus each girl begins to appreciate her importance not only as an individual but also as a member of a group. Because she has a responsibility, the way she lives becomes important, what she is doing is significant not only for herself but for others. . . ."

For ER, Todhunter's methods were "a combination of the old and the new." There were small group discussions, and every student was encouraged to participate in "vivid, first-hand experiences." Museums, theatres, and foreign-language films were regular sources of instruction. Formal textbooks were replaced by a great variety of readings in newspapers and magazines. ER believed that a good teacher started with her students' own interests and led them "into an enlivened understanding of every possible phase of the world into which they are going." It was the teacher's "function to manage this relating process, to seize all opportunities, however unpromising, to make history and literature and the seemingly barren study of the machinery of government somehow akin to the things the pupils are doing in their daily life."

During the first years of what was to become the Great Depression, ER's students were taken to visit courthouses and tenements, state agencies and settlement houses. She introduced them to the work of the Henry Street Settlement, the Neighborhood Playhouse, and the Women's Trade Union League. ER was particularly concerned that her senior girls continue their studies—especially regarding social issues. She urged them to do community service, specifically to join the Junior League, and she offered a course for recent graduates who wanted to carry on and intensify the efforts they had begun at Todhunter. On 9 April 1930, ER wrote to her friend Jane Hoey, who directed the Welfare Council:

> I am very anxious to send a class which has been studying with me this winter of young women, some of them married, all of them out of school for a year or more, on a trip some morning to see the various types of tenements in New York City. . . . I would like them to see the worst type of old time tenement. They need to know what bad housing conditions mean and then I would like them to see as model a tenement as possible in a bad neighborhood and on up to something really good in the way of houses for the moderately salaried groups. . . .

Despite the contradictions between her educational theories and the private-school environment of Todhunter, ER's impact as a teacher was generative and everlasting. She persuaded her students to develop their talents, to be responsible for their lives, to seek opportunity and achieve success, to care about and work for their communities. By the force of her own example and encouragement, she demonstrated that there was nothing they could not do, no interest they could not develop. She argued continually that in their future "there will be nothing which is closed to women because of sex."

~

FOR FOUR YEARS, ER COULD BE SEEN RUNNING DOWN THE length of the train station at the last possible minute, her briefcase and large pocketbook filled to capacity. Train conductors knew her schedule and often held the train. ER never ceased to be surprised to see the conductors smiling and waiting patiently. According to Frances Perkins, ER thought "it odd that a great, tall woman like herself, who towered over everybody in Grand Central Station, would be recognized when she ran for a train and that they would hold the train for her. It never occurred to her to ask to have the train held for the Governor's lady. She was utterly without the quality of presuming upon her privileges. . . ."

En route to New York City every Sunday evening, ER read in preparation for her lessons and lectures. Every Wednesday afternoon, returning to Albany, she graded papers, wrote letters, and drafted the speeches she would give that week somewhere in New York State. Nor did she slight her Albany responsibilities. She took the social reins from Missy LeHand by four-thirty each Wednesday afternoon, just in time to preside over the regularly scheduled midweek tea. The social life of the Executive Mansion intensified with her arrival. The Albany household was enormous, and every one of the nine guest rooms was filled virtually every weekend. There were seventeen servants, and countless household demands. ER generally took it all in stride: "Everything is done for me. I simply give the orders."

But there were times when demands piled up; moments of petty tensions, political failures, exhausting emotional chores. ER had lifelong mood swings. Opposition and imperfection tended to depress her. She would become tired, disgruntled; cold and withdrawn. Those closest to her understood that, when ER expressed fatigue or irritation, something was seriously amiss.

In 1931, Anna wrote her mother: "Father's letter to me was mostly about trying to persuade you to go to Warm Springs for a week with him. He feels you are tired, & ought to 'slow up'—he thinks you could get a substitute for your classes for three days & he seems so very anxious to have you go with him. . . . Pa thinks one week would 'put you in fine shape for the winter.' . . . I had thought you were quite harassed—more than tired—about 3 or 4 weeks ago." Anna urged her mother to vacation, "cut out a few of the meetings, and some of the speeches (which you swore last summer you were not going to make!) and if you think it would give you any rest at all to go to Warm Springs—do go. Pa seems to want you there so badly. . . ."

However accurate her family's sense of her fatigue, the prescription was ignored. ER never vacationed when she felt emotionally or physically exhausted. She worked harder, as if each new task was a potential source of new energy. Moreover, she never sought a substitute for her classes. That was the one realm she could always rely upon to lift her spirits, and enhance her well-being.

17. ER at Forty-five

D URING FDR'S TWO TWO-YEAR TERMS AS GOVERNOR, Franklin and Eleanor's life together seemed to have achieved a sustained compatibility. They understood each other, respected each other, and protected each other from the barbs of the outside world. But they were also fiercely protective of their own needs and their own interests; and these were guarded in turn by their respectively devoted inner circles.

In these years, there was a pattern to Roosevelt family life. ER and FDR and their staffs spent Christmas and the early winter months in Albany, Hyde Park, and New York, with Eleanor commuting between the Executive Mansion and Todhunter. FDR, Missy LeHand, and assorted associates spent April and May in Warm Springs—with occasional but infrequent visits from ER and Louis Howe. The summer months were generally spent in Albany and Hyde Park. In the autumn, and always for Thanksgiving, FDR returned again to Warm Springs, where ER joined him for at least a week.

Crowded and unconventional, the Roosevelt household was generally full of fun, purposeful activity, and countless friends and politicians who came and went, day and night. The statehouse, like the White House after 1933, was rather like Grand Hotel. But there were no separate tables, and there was only one purpose: to advance and promote the policies and visions of FDR, and to entertain him and each other.

So much entertaining occurred at home because it was impossible for FDR to get around. He hated the inconvenience of restaurants, and it was easier to bring a film to him than for him and his entourage to go out. FDR's friends went to great lengths to keep him entertained, and were largely successful. Besides card games and parties, there were theatricals and performances—frequently directed and master-minded by Louis Howe. And every meal was either a meeting or ceremony, or some kind of organized frolic. ER was always mindful of FDR's needs. She participated in the hilarity as fully as she could, given that his entertainments frequently did not represent her preferences. When her work took her elsewhere, she arranged for his friends to be there and to be well received and cared for in her absence.

The Roosevelts were charming and informal. They tended to transform their households into an extended family unit that generally pulled in one direction. Still, formal distinctions were maintained between upstairs and downstairs, between servants and served, staff and leadership. Moreover, during the Albany years, their respective circles became increasingly distinct.

In addition to Esther Lape, Elizabeth Read, Marion Dickerman, Nancy Cook, Elinor Morgenthau, Caroline O'Day, and Louis Howe, ER's primary domain expanded to include her lifelong secretary Malvina ("Tommy") Thompson. Efficient and political, with wartime experience in the Red Cross, Tommy had worked diligently in the 1928 campaign and was devoted to her boss.

During the gubernatorial campaign of 1928, several other people were also added to Eleanor's permanent network of political allies and intimate friends: the delightful publicity director June Hamilton Rhodes; Mary Norton, a New Jersey labor reformer, subsequently elected to Congress; and that spectacular strategist of all reforms dedicated to empowering women in public life, Molly Dewson. They each admired ER's gifts as a leader and considered themselves ardent members of her loyal brigade.

Within FDR's personal sphere, Missy LeHand, always the mistress of Warm Springs, now moved into the statehouse with the family and became more routinely and entirely FDR's companion. Her assistant, Grace Tully, also joined the inner circle. Originally Eleanor's secretary in the Women's Division during the Al Smith campaign, she moved on to FDR after his election. ER was gracious to both women, and always regarded Missy LeHand with particular warmth. ER worried about her fragile health, monitored her cigarettes, and repeatedly urged her to get more sleep. They shopped together, and took long walks in the countryside and along the river. If ER was ever jealous of Missy LeHand, she never showed it.

Franklin's team also included Lieutenant Governor Herbert Lehman, a banker who had been one of Smith's chief financial supporters; Edward J. Flynn, known since 1922 as the Boss of the Bronx, whom FDR named secretary of state; James Farley, a Democratic Party stalwart, contractor, and state boxing commissioner; Frances Perkins; Henry Morgenthau; FDR's law partner Basil ("Doc") O'Connor; and speech-writer and counsel Sam Rosenman. They talked politics, played cards, went fishing, and were in a variety of ways entirely available to the "Boss."

Only Louis Howe, who spent the gubernatorial years as FDR's business representative in New York and worked out of his law office to enhance the Boss's national political visibility, was actually a member of both Eleanor's *and* Franklin's networks. By 1930, ER and Howe had virtually divided the gubernatorial campaign committees between them. ER, now with Molly Dewson, ran the Women's Division, and Howe ran publicity as never before—with enhanced radio and movie coverage. When ER and Howe were both at home on East 65th Street, they made special time for each other: to plan strategy, to have fun. They both enjoyed the same quiet local restaurants, and delighted especially in the theatre. Howe spent only occasional weekends in Albany between 1928 and 1932.

Marion Dickerman and Nancy Cook also considered themselves at home in both camps, although their primary friendship was with ER. But at some point, charmed by the seduction of influence and the beacon of office, they began their slow slide toward that dangerous abyss they considered neutrality.

Although the final and tragic break in their friendship did not occur until 1938, Eleanor became increasingly disenchanted with Marion Dickerman and Nancy Cook. In addition to their mercurial sense of loyalty—now to ER, now to FDR—there were occasional breaches of what for Eleanor mattered significantly: propriety and *gentillesse*. It was not about "good manners" in any conventional sense but, rather, an emotional carelessness, a lack of sensitivity. When, for example, ER's adolescent sons called her "Muddie," she did not like it but recognized it as part of their adolescent nonsense. But when Marion Dickerman called her "Muddie" at Todhunter with students present, ER was stunned. It was not only disrespectful or unkind: It was unprotective. And that, for ER, was unacceptable.

Still another aspect of the tensions that emerged between ER and her Val-Kill partners was that ER tended to move on: Once her work was done in one area, she selected another. Once she was satisfied in one way, she turned her attentions elsewhere. She was searching, endlessly curious—and restless. She sought and made new friends, who represented different classes. They looked and behaved differently, and they were increasingly unacceptable to Nancy Cook and Marion Dickerman. Whether or not they were merely snobs who did not share ER's interests in working people, recent immigrants, and members of America's various minorities, or they were simply jealous, the fact is that Dickerman and Cook did not like ER's new friends.

It happened gradually and, for a time imperceptibly—but their interests diverged. During the summer of 1929, ER undertook what was to be her final vacation trip with Marion Dickerman, Nancy Cook, and two of her sons—John (thirteen) and FDR, Jr. (fifteen). Throughout the 1920s, the three friends, with assorted children, had spent several weeks of each summer together. They had hiked and camped and motored throughout the countryside, thoroughly enjoying one another's company. But the two months they spent in Europe between July and September 1929 were almost entirely disagreeable. In many ways, this trip ended an era.

The trip began amid an agony of misunderstanding. ER had wanted to hike and camp in Europe with her friends and two younger sons—now adolescents—much as they had in the States: alone in their own automobiles, without chauffeurs or formal clothes. When they discussed their trip at dinner one night, FDR seemed quite satisfied with the plans. But SDR objected vehemently: Her grandchildren should not travel like vagabonds across the capitals of Europe. Moreover, they were no longer private citizens. It was unseemly and impossible for the governor's wife to drive her own car. The family had standards to maintain, appearances to consider.

Unfortunately, FDR, Jr. (called Brother), chose that moment to support his grandmother, and mock his mother. Yes, he agreed; besides, Mother would probably land the car in a ditch, or smash a gatepost, as she was wont to do. ER turned for support to FDR, who said, as usual, nothing. Never once had he taken his wife's side against his mother. Marion Dickerman and Nancy Cook, immobilized by the tension that swelled the air, said nothing. ER, who had relied especially on Brother as an ally in their many adventures, felt particularly betrayed. Coldly, without apparent emotion, she addressed her mother-in-law: Your grandchildren will travel in the manner you deem appropriate. And then she stood up, threw her napkin on the table, and stormed out of the room. Only then did FDR order Brother to apologize, and persuade ER to return to the table. He did apologize when he saw his mother in tears, and he did persuade her to return. But the trip was doomed.

In suits, stiff collars, and ties, the boys sat with ER behind liveried chauffeurs in rented limousines. They wanted to sit in front, or accompany Marion Dickerman and Nancy Cook, who toured in the car ahead—their own Buick roadster, with the top down. But Eleanor was adamant. Marion Dickerman recalled with a sigh, "Brother paid very dearly for that remark. Eleanor could be very hard."

Formally and decorously they toured Ireland, England, Belgium, Germany, and France. Despite the many cultural sights, the warm visit with older brother James, now married to Betsy Cushing, also vacationing in Ireland; despite several good horse shows, and the beauty of the Lake Country, nobody enjoyed the trip very much, least of all ER. There were pleasant moments: Everybody had a good lunch at Rumpelmeyer's; there was a delightful dinner in Soho at a restaurant Marion and Nan had frequented during the war, where "the food was excellent"; and they all enjoyed some splendid shopping, especially at Harrod's: "I assure you I am ruined but [the boys] are swank and very happy!" She also bought FDR "some silk pajamas & 2 lovely soft pleated silk shirts all very expensive but very good & I hope you like them as well as I do." For herself, ER bought a raincoat and hat at Burberry's. And then proceeded to Liberty's, where she "bought presents, 2 cute dresses for [her granddaughter] 'Sisty' & a knit suit for Missy."

There were excursions and exhibitions. Nan and Marion enjoyed their wartime friends "& they say so far none of their old friends have been a disappointment which is remarkable after ten years!" The boys went to a motorcycle race, and a cricket match—which they found "too dull for description." ER thought the boys had "a good time," but she felt "too old" to enjoy the unexpected. And she resented particularly "the constant care & supervision" the boys required. Although she wrote that they had "been very good," they found countless ways to burst out of their enforced restraints, especially by battling each other. Daily they tested their mother's endurance. She tried to keep them walking, and they climbed to the top of every mountain and tower in sight. Her hope was that, if they were tired at night, they would sleep. But they fought anyway. It was all "rather wearing," ER admitted.

London was crowded, and ER had never seen so many "tourists in my life." And then there was a "tragedy." When John went to buy a tiepin for Franklin, Jr.'s birthday, he discovered his purse had been stolen. "Tears & desperate sorrow! I've made it up to him but it was a good lesson for I had told them to keep their purses in their inner pockets & he put his in his outer coat pocket."

After England, the party proceeded to Bruges, Ghent, Antwerp, Brussels, Cologne, Coblenz, and Luxembourg. They visited "Roman remains," in which "the boys seemed much interested." Franklin, Jr.'s birthday was toasted with local champagne. ER wrote FDR: "The others had some champagne . . . for dinner & drank your health & wished you were present. I joined in [with] Evian water! FJr has had a taste of everything and likes it but I won't let him have it as a rule!" In Verdun they visited the battlefields, and then went to Rheims and Paris, where they were joined again by James and Betsy. En route to Cherbourg, from which they would sail for home, they visited Chartres and Mont-Saint-Michel. The boys had been fighting, and Eleanor left them at their hotel in Mont-Saint-Michel to take a long and tranquil walk through the Gothic splendor and peacefulness for which she was by then positively parched. As she returned to the hotel, she saw that a crowd had gathered, their heads back; people shouting and pointing up: Franklin, Jr., had pushed John out of the window and held on to him, precariously, by his ankles, as he faced death.

For ER, the trip had been an unbearable ordeal. They returned on 15 September, and Eleanor vowed that she would never travel that way again. In fact she never again traveled for any length of time with her sons, nor did she, Marion Dickerman, and Nancy Cook ever again resume their traditional summer holiday excursions.

In other significant ways, an era was ending. On 24 October, the New York Stock Exchange plunged in the crash that ushered in the Great Depression. In the coming years, both ER and FDR would address profoundly new and difficult challenges. Although Al Smith had left the state in efficient working order—in his six years as governor, he had introduced almost every one of those controversial social ideas that came to define progressive politics in America—it was up to FDR to see them through a Republican and reluctant state legislature. Every major issue and policy subsequently associated with the New Deal was advanced during FDR's governorship.

In his gubernatorial inaugural address on 1 January 1929, FDR had introduced his vision of the future. It would become an American crusade:

> To secure more of life's pleasures for the farmer; to guard the toilers in the factories and to insure them a fair wage and protection from the dangers of their trades; to compensate them by adequate in-surance for injuries received while working for us; to open the doors of knowledge to their children more widely; to aid those who are crippled and ill; to pursue with strict justice, all evil persons who prey upon their fellow men; and at the same time, by intelligent and helpful sympathy, to lead wrongdoers into right paths—all of these great aims of life are more fully realized here than in any other State of the Union.

FDR's 1929 inaugural included unemployment relief through public-works projects, minimum-wage and maximum-hour laws, the development of public utilities and the regulation of private utilities and banks, farm relief, reforestation, conservation, urban planning, homesteading, prison reform, rural electrification, the use of public funds for housing, education, and support of the handicapped.

But Roosevelt presided over an opposition legislature dominated by "stand-pat" Republicans. The enactment of a progressive vision depended on new elections, and a sense of urgency for needed social legislation that only emerged as the Depression deepened.

The Roosevelts were slow to appreciate the significance of enormous changes that threatened Europe during the 1920s: The struggle between socialism and capitalism, the emergence of fascism, and the intensity of racism and anti-Semitism. During the winter of 1925, for example, when Sara Delano Roosevelt took Anna to Europe, she prearranged their visit to Rome so that they might have audiences with both the Pope and Il Duce. Anna was surprised, about the audience with the Pope since SDR "had grown up a Unitarian and became a *low* church Episcopalian only when she married my grandfather." Her decision to "pull strings" for a "private audience" with Mussolini was even more mysterious. Anna attributed it to "Granny's intellectual adventurousness," and noted that she was vastly impressed with the dictator who seemed since 1923 to have cured unemployment and arranged for the trains to run on time.

Subsequently, she and her husband, Curtis, left their two-year-old daughter with ER and embarked on a European tour that heralded momentous events. On 24 March 1929, Anna Roosevelt Dall wrote to her parents from Vienna that she and Curtis "have fallen in love with Vienna":

> We had a letter of introduction to a Countess Hoyos, and she and her family have been very nice to us. . . . The old lady is Granny's age and very keen, but a stickler for the old customs and manners, and very much the "grande dame." Her son and daughter-in-law seem to be more or less lost in this day & generation. . . . They are delightful, however, and know their history. . . . They, of course, want a king, and firmly believe it is only a matter of time before nearly every country in Europe will be a limited monarchy. They say Vienna itself is very Socialistic but the country districts

are not. Of course, they are frightfully bitter over the way Austria was cut up after the war. . . . The old Countess' second daughter married Bismarck's eldest son. They think nothing of Emil Ludwig's [biography of Bismarck]. . . . Ludwig is a Jew & dropped the name Cohen, which was his family name, when he became a biographer! By the way, here in Vienna Jews are taboo. They are the only really wealthy people and have the most beautiful houses & gardens in Vienna. However the younger Countess said "We regard the Jewish question here as you regard your negro question in America!" It is considered frightful for a gentleman to marry even a Jewess of the best family. The Rothschilds were received at court so they are grudgingly accepted. It seems to me that the truth is they fear the Jews, who are clever & hard workers & very powerful & wealthy. They are very numerous and have a very large Society of their own. . . .

Regarding the "Negro question in America," FDR seemed as indifferent as he was to the rise of fascism. He refused to act against Robert Moses's discriminating policies in the management of the state's park system, which made it difficult for poor people, and especially black people, to benefit from the new beach parks, particularly Jones Beach. Moses accomplished this by prohibiting the use of public transportation to Long Island's parks and beaches. Then other deliberate policies were introduced to discourage people Moses considered the "dirty" and the "riff-raff": There were very few black lifeguards, and they were assigned to the most remote and least developed beaches. In addition, since "Moses was convinced that Negroes did not like cold water . . . the temperature at the pool at Jones Beach was deliberately icy to keep Negroes out." Protests were filed. Legislators were addressed. The press was notified. Civic groups were aroused. At this point, FDR ordered an investigation, which confirmed the allegations, and the governor sent Moses a letter of inquiry. When Moses denied everything, however, FDR did not press the issue—not even when Moses imposed a fifty-cent public parking fee to discourage poor patrons further, at a time of mounting unemployment and worsening depression. FDR wrote to ask Moses to reconsider the fee, but when he refused (to do so would alter the "entire character of the place"), FDR backed off. When, in response to one of the most vigorous public outcries against discrimination in New York history, the legislature actually passed a bill to prohibit fees in state parks, FDR vetoed it.

Although both FDR and ER had continually expressed concern about rising unemployment and the farm crises that preceded the Great Depression by almost ten years, when the stock market actually crashed on "Black Thursday" it seemed a remote situation to Franklin. By 15 November, the lists of the New York Stock Exchange had fallen in value by 40 percent, a paper loss of over $26 billion. But on 1 December, FDR advised Louis Howe to go to the Anderson Galleries for "the final liquidation sale" of a late, lamented friend: "It is just possible that the recent little Flurry down town will make the prices comparatively low. I have marked several items." Both FDR and Missy LeHand were also interested in an auction of "Chinese things." FDR sent Howe a check and urged him to "do some Christmas shopping of your own . . . for the things might go fairly cheap."

Always more deeply involved with working people, especially women workers associated with the Women's Trade Union League, ER responded to the Depression more personally. She intensified her own work with the WTUL, and as chair of the Finance Committee, initiated efforts to fund new projects, and to pay off the mortgage for the WTUL clubhouse.*

Before the disaster unfolded, ER and her committee raised the

---

* ER's finance committee included her longtime friend Dorothy Payne Whitney Straight, who first introduced ER to Rose Schneiderman and the work of the WTUL at a tea in her home; and Mrs. Thomas Lamont, who had rented the Roosevelts' 65th Street house during the war years. A partner with J. P. Morgan, Thomas Lamont figured prominently in a banker's consortium of the "Big Six" that speculated vigorously during the first week of the stock market's collapse. In an effort to revive confidence, they bought up endless quantities of sagging stock, with considerable fanfare. Lamont and Richard Whitney (vice-president of the Exchange) appeared on the floor themselves, ostentatiously bought significant shares, and dismissed the implications of what Lamont called "a little distress selling." But they evidently unloaded their bargains quickly and quietly, found few new words of confidence with which to greet the press, and only served to create greater panic. When Herbert Hoover denounced unprincipled speculation, Lamont criticized the president, eliciting Hoover's famous rejoinder: "The only trouble with capitalism is capitalists. They're too damn greedy." But few believed in the winter of 1929 that the collapse would be long-lasting.

$30,000 to retire the WTUL mortgage, and then the money needed for remodeling, rewiring, and painting. The women owned their five-story townhouse at 247 Lexington Avenue outright by June 1929, the WTUL's twenty-fifth-anniversary year; and a feeling of optimism and confidence in the future prevailed. The WTUL leaders planned a party to celebrate their anniversary—and Sara Delano Roosevelt, who increasingly supported her daughter-in-law's political work with a new personal extravagance—sent an invitation to the entire League, offering to host the party at Hyde Park.

ER persuaded the governor to attend, telling him "you are the pièce-de-résistance." Mary Dreier wrote a pageant, which was well rehearsed and artfully produced. And on 8 June, over two hundred factory workers, "shop-girls," secretaries, union leaders, and their philanthropic allies chartered a boat for the journey up the Hudson for the party, highlighted by FDR's remarks, dinner on SDR's terrace, and the $35,000 check raised by ER's committee.

~

AS THE "ROARING TWENTIES" GROUND TO A HALT FINAN-cially, ER was not alone in her conviction that there really was opportunity and productivity enough for all. There was no reason technologically or materially for women to be denied access to or advantages in work; no reason for poverty, deprivation, or exclusion. There was enough for everybody. The machine age changed everything, except the consciousness of those who ruled. To deny that reality was willful and wrong. ER was among the first to protest loudly and specifically against the continued outrages that barred women from rewarding work and new opportunities.

In October 1929, ER keynoted the eighth annual Exposition of Women's Arts and Industries. Countless displays filled the rooms of the grand old Hotel Astor with the activities and achievements of women in business, politics, and the arts. In her address, ER assailed Henry Ford's contention that women were too "imprecise" for industrial work, and that in any case their "proper place" was limited to the home, as narrow-minded, old-fashioned silliness.

ER proudly noted: "The best answer to Mr. Ford is this exposition." "All women are seizing the ever-increasing opportunities which are being opened to them." The advances of "the machine age [are] changing the education and achievement of women so that in the future" women, no less than men, would have every opportunity for gratification, success, and fulfillment.

ER herself was regarded as one of the new breed of women industrialists. Her furniture-reproduction factory at Val-Kill was the subject of considerable attention—one *New York Times* interview with ER bore a headline that termed her "Woman-Run Factory" a "Feminine Industrial Success" where ER, and her partner Nancy Cook, directed a large crew of "expert craftsmen." "As one of the few factories . . . in the country initiated, built, managed and owned entirely by women, it is in a sense a milestone on woman's industrial highway." But ER saw it as only the beginning. "There is no reason why we should not have a female Henry Ford. I am hopeful for women in industry. They will have to overcome prejudice . . . which will disappear as soon as they prove themselves capable industrial heads."

Just days into the greatest economic collapse the world had yet seen, ER encouraged women to be bold: to borrow money, invest in ventures and industries that previously barred them. "There are many small factories throughout the country that could be run successfully by women. Some could in fact be run better by women than by men." And throughout the Eastern states many of these were closed and for sale at "ten times" below their value. ER believed that women had to give up their peculiar reluctance "to borrow money" in order to expand industrially.

ER urged women to face the business future as she had urged them to face the political future: They needed to play the game as men do. Her own experience emboldened her. The Val-Kill plant had expanded from six workers to thirty; it had grown in size and services. Profits were used for expansion, and Val-Kill "weathered the Wall Street crash and its subsequent unemployment crisis without having to lay off one workman."

~

AS DEPRESSION CONDITIONS WORSENED, ER CONTINUED TO insist on women's right to work, to educate themselves for gainful employment, and to resist the growing demand that in hard times women should not compete with men but should return with docility, if not joy, to the role of homemaking. Rising unemployment created understandable opposition to college-trained women who did not need to work, or married women who worked only for "pin money."

ER urged comfortable parents to keep their children in school and out of the labor market as long as possible, and suggested that affluent women serve their communities through volunteer services. She considered it "not an utterly unreasonable attitude that women not driven by compelling necessity refrain from entering into competition with women who must have a job to live." But, she insisted: "It is a different matter to insist that as a permanent truth married women should stay out of the gainful occupations. The contention that they create unemployment will not hold. It happens that in good times there is work enough for everybody, however large the labor supply, and in times of depression there is idleness, no matter how small the supply."

She worked with the Junior League leadership, which sought to contribute solutions to the problems of unnecessary competition during this tense time. In November 1930, ER agreed to write an article entitled "What the Country Expects of the Junior League in the Unemployment Crisis" for the League's magazine. ER called for equality in ambition and career goals. And she urged affluent and privileged girls to give of their time and talent creatively, to create jobs in the process of pursuing their own interests:

> Now there has never seemed to me to be any question but what the girl had the same right to work that the boy had. A college boy, from the same type of family from which the membership of the Junior League is drawn, may take any job if he is not trained in some profession but he knows and his employer knows and his co-workers know that he is only gaining experience. It is an accepted premise that he is aiming for and will achieve an executive position, something where he creates work for others. Why should not this same conception hold for the girls?

ER did not accept the notion that affluent girls should be reduced to "elegant idleness." Some will be happy in volunteer work, in philanthropy or the arts. But, ER wrote, the measure of success in the contemporary world was work—"financially profitable" work. "A girl having had great opportunities should realize that her job is to create, to make work for others." Such girls might start new businesses with the money they would have spent on clothes or parties. "I wish," ER concluded, "that I could make every Junior League girl see that her greater opportunities put on her greater obligations."

ER understood the tensions between "factory girls" and "business girls," and deplored them. She sought dignity and justice for women workers, and wanted to add a recreational program and a course in "body rhythmics" to the activities the WTUL sponsored. Rose Schneiderman, president of the Women's Trade Union League, agreed that such an undertaking was welcome, since "industrial girls" did "not mix easily with the group to be found in the Y.W. and the League of Girls' Clubs," where factory workers were often patronized. ER agreed to send fund-raising letters for the effort and wrote Schneiderman: "I am deeply interested. . . . Why is it that we must be divided into strata?"

As the Depression worsened, ER campaigned for better living conditions for workingwomen, and keynoted a two-day conference sponsored by the Association to Promote Proper Housing for Girls, Inc. She called for imaginative ways to end unemployment, and a wage scale to end the perpetuation of dreadful and unsanitary housing conditions. ER considered unionization the key to all economic security for working women.

While union organizers were being harassed and arrested for their activities, Eleanor publicly supported strike efforts. When 450 women struck for a decent contract between the International Ladies' Garment Workers' Union and the Fifth Avenue dressmaking firm of Hattie Carnegie, ER sent a message of support from Albany in praise of "the movement which has as its object improvement of conditions for those women workers in the dressmaking establishments where, up to this time, the women workers have not been organized."

Referring to these activities, *The New York Times* explained that ER was "noted for her sympathies toward organized labor, and especially toward women in industry." Over the years, ER consistently reaffirmed her conviction that it was not unionism, or strikers, or radicals, or even communists that concerned her: it was unemployment and the economic devastation that mocked our pretenses at civility and decency. In March 1930, she told a meeting of two hundred representatives of the Southern Women's Democratic Organization that she was "not excited about the Communists" but, rather, the "great number of people . . . who cannot get work."

By 1932, Eleanor had become convinced that there was something fundamentally wrong with a system and a civilization that tolerated the cruel conditions so many Americans faced. In January, she told the New York City League of Women Voters that there was a need for "something more than temporary alleviation of suffering through emergency aid" or "charity." Emergency relief was simply not enough, for it did nothing to alleviate the real problem. "It is nice to hand out milk and bread. It gives you a comfortable feeling inside. But fundamentally you are not relieving the . . . reasons why we have to have this charity." ER urged women to become dissatisfied with temporary, superficial solutions. It was time to "face the fact that we may have to have great changes, . . . new solutions. So we must be prepared to meet things with open minds and go to the roots of questions as they come up. We can't go on drifting."

Over and over again, in all the speeches ER made during the early years of the Depression, she called for new and bold solutions, a revolutionary level of courage and imagination equal to these critical times: "A spirit which is not afraid of new difficulties and new solutions, nor afraid to stand hardships." ER believed that women especially could create fundamental change, if they organized.

In an address to hundreds of women of the Congress of States Societies, representatives from women's groups in twenty-eight states, ER said: "We are not only a part of the government, but we are the government, and on each one of us devolves the responsibility of trying to help solve these economic problems. The women together can do a great deal. Therefore, let us realize that it is not just for pleasure that we have met and let us try to unite at a time quite as serious as war."

In her increasingly visible attacks on the status quo, Eleanor now ran afoul of one of the members of FDR's inner circle—the attorney, speech-writer, and former state assemblyman Sam Rosenman, who had moved into the executive mansion with his wife, Dorothy. An outsider with pretensions of power and a sense of self-assurance some considered arrogance, Rosenman was not warmly received by Louis Howe. As Rosenman described it: "Like a faithful watchdog he showed his teeth at anyone who came near Roosevelt, and if a person was welcomed too heartily or got too close, Howe became his jealous enemy. He did not really like me from the very start—and he liked me less the more work Roosevelt gave me to do."

Rosenman was impatient with ER's ideals and frankly annoyed at FDR's willingness to listen to his wife's views on all issues. By 1932, Rosenman had joined the ranks of those who, whether for misogynist or political reasons, sought to "get the pants off Eleanor and on to Franklin." Rosenman considered ER too assertive, even aggressive: He personally preferred Missy LeHand's quiet, more deferential manner. In 1960, he recalled the happy Albany days, especially those days when ER was away: "Miss LeHand was the hostess, and she could preside at a table and direct servants and the general conduct of a social gathering with even greater efficiency than Mrs. Roosevelt could. In addition to that, she could sit at the table and entertain guests, lead the conversation, and charm them with her gracious manner."

Eleanor's position in the extended Roosevelt household was now frequently embattled, since she represented liberal positions that FDR was only occasionally willing to include in his program and actually fight for. Many of his advisers resented her influence, her activities, and indeed her presence. The increased criticism prompted her to write a series of articles disclaiming any power, influence, or even interest in her husband's affairs.

In "Wives of Great Men," she wrote: "Even if a woman has the most definite ideas, she must never try to persuade her husband to do anything he does not consider right. . . ."

ER believed that a political wife was always entitled to her opinions. She had a right to maintain them, and to announce them. But "she should never nag her husband . . . ; nor need she make [their differences] public." ER drew a very distinct line.

I say what I believe, but I will not stump against my party, regardless of its program. I will not sit on the platform where the subject of the speeches is one upon which I differ with my husband and his party; nor will I issue statements about it. . . .

There are few avenues of life where men and women agree on everything. In politics they differ along very definite lines.

Men tend to look at things from a legalistic point of view; women from a practical one. . . .

Women generally are more interested in reforms than in tax laws. Consequently, if a bill dealing with maternal and infant welfare is before the legislature a wife is quite likely to consider it the most important measure. . . . Her husband might disagree, insisting that income tax revision should take priority. Here there is no adjustment of opinion. Each must keep his own. The approach is fundamentally different.

ER considered it *"impossible for husband and wife both to have political careers."* "It requires all the energy and united effort of an entire household to support one." There might be negotiation about who should be the chosen and agreed-upon candidate in the household. She pointed with pride to Nancy Astor in England as the obvious case where a woman "had such an intense interest and love of politics, and such an obvious flair for it, that her husband withdrew from any family competition. He helps her, instead." She also gave examples of women and men who shared the political game in equal measure. But, ER concluded, every politician needed "a conscientious, competent wife. Matrimony in official life is no small job." And the wife's responsibilities were important. "She must do her official entertaining heartily and graciously. Her work is practically a career in itself."

Happily, she explained, she and FDR agreed on most issues. They agreed on the tariff, on the need for customs reduction. They agreed that the United States had been "too completely absorbed in our own materialistic gains. . . . A state ruled wholly by the self-interest of a few cannot be just." "Governor Roosevelt and I both have great confidence in the judgment of the average [person]. . . . The more power resides in the people as a whole, the better we think it is for each of them and for the nation." Also, they agreed "heartily in our liberal views on foreign relations, although I tend to be somewhat more radical than he." And despite her wifely effort not to disagree publicly, ER evidently could not resist the temptation to make the feminist point: "This is a common phenomenon in this realm, where women have no heritage or national inhibitions, no obsolete credos taught in youth to obstruct their views."

However much ER might secretly have envied Lady Astor, she assured her readers that she had no intention of emulating her: A political wife may have her own opinions, "but she must keep them to herself." Despite her protestations, however, she found it impossible to ignore affairs of state. In the Roosevelt household there were always two politicians. On 2 October 1930, for instance, ER wrote FDR: "Miss Perkins came to see me today and she has a *secret* offer which will be made if you agree. The commission she got together to look into the public employment department will recommend if you are agreeable that a commission similar to the old age pension one be appointed." There were discussions about private-foundation funding, and ER was very enthusiastic about the proposal: "It looks good to me for it would take into account middle aged and physically handicapped, etc., and you would get the jump on Hoover, but they won't move till you let me know what you think."

Although ER and FDR differed in emphasis and political timing, especially regarding such issues as civil rights and the World Court, they were able to transcend the pettier power games, and remained united by a sense of basic decency and principle. Moreover, they served each other's political needs.

On election night 1930, when FDR amassed the greatest vote any Democrat had ever received in New York State, Eleanor cabled him: "Much love dear and a world of congratulations. It is a triumph in so many ways dear and so well earned. Bless you and good luck these next two years."

~

ON 11 OCTOBER 1929, ELEANOR ROOSEVELT CELEBRATED HER forty-fifth birthday. Being forty-five impressed ER. She talked about it and she wrote about it. Serene and in many ways content, she did not experience a midlife crisis but, rather, a midlife liberation. She marked the year, assessing her life to date. And when she felt unexpected, yet familiar chemical emotional stirrings, the kind women in menopause know are much like those metabolic sensations first ignited during adolescence, she determinedly denied them—for a while.

At the end of that year she wrote a rhapsody to self-awareness, "Her Forty-fifth Birthday!," for *Vogue*. She summarized her childhood, her years as a young mother. All that was behind her. Her children were grown, she "was quick and executive. . . . She enjoyed books, she liked people and she had many interests." She celebrated her new ability: "To be as an old French Lady once put it 'in the front line trenches of life. . . .' "

ER believed that by forty-five certain things ought to be well learned—especially the fact that "happiness does not come from the seeking, it is never ours by right." She wrote of responsibility, discipline, and self-control. She never referred to self-denial, but she noted that

> you must learn to love without criticism, to see things as others see them, even though it may be a point of view alien to your own. If you have learned these things by forty-five, if you have ceased to consider yourself as in any way important, but understand well the place that must be filled in the family, then the role will be easy. Your years up to now have been well spent and you can go on to the next step, the building up of an individual life and personality which will make you happier in yourself, and more interesting to all those who come in contact with you. . . .

At forty-five, ER no longer needed to nag her children or brood "over her deserted state." She had kept "an open and a speculative mind," and was now "ready to go out and try new adventures, create new work for others as well as herself, and strike deep roots in some community where her presence will make a difference to the lives of others."

> Forty-five has many compensations, the storm and stress bound up with the emotional life of youth is over, one can no longer be

interested in oneself, but one is thereby freed for greater interest in others. . . . Nature means more to us, a blue sky, a flight of birds, a sunset, all become part of the infinite goodness of God and we learn to say with Stevenson "the world is so full of a number of things I think we should all be as happy as Kings."

ER was glad to have the "storm and stress" of her emotional youth behind her. She did not anticipate the reappearance of *Grief*'s counterpart: the kind of excitement and joy awakened by romance and passion. The young girl who longed for her father to return and be different, who yearned for her mother to love her just a little, seemed to have moved far beyond *Grief*. But there lingered a memory, if not a longing, for those passionate feelings of her past—part romance, part expectation—that could delight or devastate her soul.

Consciously, ER emphasized her commitment to a life of responsibility. She talked endlessly to reporters about discipline, duty, and self-control. After long and thorough interviews, Helena Huntington Smith wrote that ER was

a personality ruled by reason. As to emotion, she probably rather dislikes it. A visitor once referred carelessly to her "passionate interest" in welfare legislation; Mrs. Roosevelt smiled her quick smile and interposed:
"Yes, but I hardly think the word 'passionate' applies to me."

Nevertheless, from 1928 until her death in 1962 the word "passionate" did apply to Eleanor Roosevelt. Her politics were the politics of passionate intensity. And her affections, as she was soon to learn, were to be woven in new fabrics of surprising and romantic design.

18. Earl Miller: A Champion of Her Own

WHEN ER WROTE WITH RELIEF THAT THE "STORM AND stress" of her emotional life were behind her, she could not have foreseen that she was about to embark on a series of intimate relationships that would involve passion, excitement, and occasional upheaval.

ER greeted the romantic passions of her mature years with a new freedom. Having worked so hard to be free, she refused to be fettered. ER did not want to possess another, or to be possessed. Her definition of love was very specific: simply to want the best for the one you love.

Earl Miller was the first romantic involvement of ER's middle years. A state trooper, Corporal Miller had been assigned to the executive mansion during Al Smith's administration. FDR was delighted to see Miller in Albany. They had first met in 1918, when FDR was Assistant Secretary of the Navy, touring battle areas in England, France, and the North Sea, and Earl Miller was a chief petty officer assigned to guard the visiting dignitary. Although Miller was one of a "12-Man detail," he became FDR's "#1 escort." One suspects that his robust and appealing charm had something to do with his privileged position, but Miller credited his special status to his having recently won the U.S. Navy's Atlantic Middleweight Boxing Championship.

Tall and handsome, with a warm and affectionate manner, Miller was primarily interested in athletics. A circus acrobat, an award-winning swimmer, horseman, and marksman, he had also been an alternate boxer on the U.S. Olympic team at Antwerp—as well as a member of the floor-and-horizontal-bar gymnastics team, until his professional-circus past disqualified him from actually performing, "after weeks and months of gym training for the event." Before his political assignments, he taught judo and boxing at the New York State Police Academy.

In 1929, FDR assigned Earl Miller to the First Lady of the Empire State as her bodyguard. When ER refused to be driven in the state-appointed limousine, insisted on her right to drive her own car, and especially rejected the presence of a chauffeur (except during official ceremonies), FDR insisted on a bodyguard.

Earl Miller and Eleanor Roosevelt were in odd ways well-suited to each other. To begin with, they were both orphans. ER, orphaned at ten, had a ready sympathy for Earl, who had become homeless at twelve, then wandered about finding odd jobs—as a contortionist, stuntman, and circus acrobat. Generous, flirtatious, and sentimental, he had a great gift for friendship; but he was often unlucky in love. ER sensed his loneliness and encouraged him to tell her his story. They confided in each other and remained for over thirty years intimate and profound friends.

Many of ER's other friends considered him showy, self-absorbed, just a touch too vain about his body, which he kept in perfect shape. But he charmed Eleanor Roosevelt. And he was charmed by her. With him she was relaxed, frequently carefree and frolicsome. With her he was unfailingly attentive, and chivalrous. She was forty-four and he was thirty-two, with a reputation among his barracks buddies as a womanizer generally in pursuit of very young women. They were surprised by his attentiveness to that "old crab," but he called her "the Lady" and turned aside all teasing remarks with protestations of adoration.

They laughed together, journeyed for weekends through the countryside and along the shore. At night, in front of the fire, ER frequently read aloud—poetry, stories, novels. With friends, especially Miller's show-business friends Mayris Chaney and Eddie Fox, they often sang around the piano. Earl Miller loved to play the piano and sing, much as her father had. ER particularly cherished those evenings.

In ER's several volumes of autobiography, she referred substantially to Earl Miller only once. In *This I Remember,* which she wrote more as a memorial to FDR than as a personal memoir, she tells us virtually nothing about Earl Miller or his place in her heart. She tells us only of his kindness to children, the gift he made to her of riding lessons and her horse Dot, and the fact that, at Warm Springs over Thanksgiving, "Gus Gennerich and Earl Miller . . . used to play the piano for the children by the hour, to the great joy of them all."

Earl's ability to bring music and song back into her life meant a lot to ER. In 1943, when she moved into a new apartment on Washington Square in Greenwich Village, her friend John Golden, the Broadway producer, offered to buy her a piano. But she refused. She would not be using the apartment sufficiently "to warrant such expense." Besides: "I'd rather have Earl's [piano] in the future for purely sentimental reasons."

Physically, Earl Miller re-energized ER by reintroducing her to long-forgotten sports and activities that she had enjoyed before her marriage—before her husband had discouraged her participation in such things. Earl not only gave her a chestnut mare named Dot, which she rode daily at Hyde Park and later in Washington; he regularly coached her tennis game, and later built her a deck tennis court at Val-Kill for daily practice. He presented her with a growling but well-trained police dog for protection, and taught her to shoot a pistol so successfully that she actually came to enjoy target practice, especially in the country, on an open range, where she wore a holster and shot from the hip.

Then there was her obsession with diving. ER was determined to dive. It took her almost ten years to dive gracefully, with form and an observable spring off the board. But Earl Miller was there every step of the way. Her sons ridiculed her; others were uninterested, or worse; but Earl encouraged her. Every day. Every dive. The head, the arms, the hands, the legs, the toes. After countless belly-flops and much messy splashing, ER learned to dive. She was pleased. For some reason it had mattered, and Earl understood that.

Above all, Earl Miller protected and defended ER. He was an antidote to the petty insults, the ways in which she was taken for granted, the frequency with which her ideas were appropriated without attribution by Franklin. Earl Miller let everybody know that that was his

Lady's idea, his Lady's policy. She had said it first, argued for it—and there it was. ER appreciated that. Even when her car went off the road because a curve came up too fast while she was talking about something really important, Earl said it wasn't her fault: She was one of the best drivers in America, and, like all good drivers, she preferred to drive fast. ER appreciated that too. He made her feel comfortable, and she was secure in his friendship. She could always depend on it; she learned to trust him absolutely.

Earl Miller served her faithfully in her efforts to keep family agonies from the press or public. He knew what to do to hide or remove her brother, Hall, if his alcohol consumption during a dinner party or a public ceremony seemed to make him too garrulous or abusive. Miller was imaginative and assertive in the most difficult situations.

On 12 July 1930, ER wrote to her Aunt Maude Hall Gray about a dreadful confrontation at the family home in Tivoli with her alcoholic Uncle Vallie, several family members, and Vallie's friends, including one particularly disreputable young man who was "working for Vallie and bringing in stuff to drink. Vallie was not drinking very hard but was in rather a weepy stage. I found there was a good deal against [the young man]." He had been arrested twice, once for the rape of a ten-year-old girl, and Earl Miller "decided that he could put up a bluff. We took Vallie off into his room and talked to him for three quarters of an hour. Corporal Miller took charge of [the young man] and saw him pack and depart. . . . He followed him out of the county and told him that if he returned to the county, he ran the risk of arrest. He admitted everything. We had no warrant for him if he had put up any fight. I think now that Vallie will straighten out. . . . I reminded him of the consequence three years after a rather more violent spree, and on the whole he took it quite meekly. . . ."

Throughout the Albany years, ER was accompanied by Earl Miller on regular inspection tours of state hospitals, prisons, public projects. She wrote that, because FDR could not walk through an institution to see how it was actually administered, she agreed to do so. During her first tour, she read the daily menu, which seemed to her nutritionally adequate. But FDR asked if she had looked into the pots, and whether the food corresponded to the menu: "I learned to notice whether the beds were too close together, and whether they were folded up and put in closets or behind doors during the day, which would indicate that they filled the corridors at night; I learned to watch the patients' attitude toward the staff," to watch for signs of tension, confusion, or fear. ER became an insistent and diligent investigator. She also learned to appear unannounced, a trick Earl Miller suggested. And to return unexpectedly. Issues of food, medical care, overcrowded conditions, hostile and careless treatment of the ill and the elderly, of the orphaned and infirm mattered to ER and FDR, and to Earl Miller. When she arrived unannounced with Earl Miller in full dress uniform, they made a formidable team.

Earl Miller hated to see his Lady taken in, cheated, or bamboozled in any way. He thought she was too trusting. People could be a lot meaner than she was willing to acknowledge, and they were a lot more dishonest. During the summer of 1929, when the family was away, there were only three people living at the mansion, and the bills were enormous. Miller became suspicious, and went through each bill with each vendor—item by item. He went to the butcher and checked every purchase for three months: "They must have eaten a ton of filet mignons while we were not there. I don't know whether they ate them or whether they were being charged and splitting. That made me check the gasoline pumps. When we left 1400 gallons. When we came back 300. I made out a detailed report, and it knocked the lady right out of her chair." Earl Miller realized that just the name Roosevelt inflated all prices. He became the unofficial purchasing agent, and for decades monitored household expenses and ER's every philanthropic penny.

Earnest squire, dedicated athletic coach, reliable companion, Earl Miller was also a delightful minstrel. ER's leisure time with him was filled with laughter, music, pranks, and surprises. They made silly home movies of high jinks and adventure like *The Pirate and the Lady,* in which Earl Miller dressed as a pirate (in bathing suit, rolled-up pirate shirt, painted-on mustache and goatee, bandanna, and eye patch), kidnapped ER, by then the president's wife. He bound her wrists, tied a blindfold around her eyes, and carried her off into the sunset. There were other characters in the film: Earl's friend, dancer Mayris Chaney ("Tiny," who subsequently became one of ER's great friends), and her dance partner, Eddie Fox; Nancy Cook, who sat on a porch imitating the First Lady. She took the curious role of rocking and knitting and waiting for ER's demise so that she might replace her and inherit her mantle. At last, two state troopers appeared in a canoe through the mists of Chazy Lake during the last minutes of the 450-foot film to rescue the Lady, left by her pirate tied to a rock.

Some of ER's friends, notably Marion Dickerman and Nancy Cook, were distressed that Earl Miller "manhandled" her, and deplored what they considered his indiscretions, his familiarities. There was his arm around her waist and then around her shoulder, even when they were both in bathing suits. There was his hand in hers. Above all, there was his hand on her knee, in that time-honored expression of intimacy. And there was her hand on his knee, just casually there as they talked, knee to knee, at poolside. Then there were those meals she prepared especially for him, and her special Christmas parties just for him—and, in the 1930s, one for him and one for Lorena Hickok.

ER was criticized by her friends because she seemed to cater to his every whim, and on more than one occasion got down on her hands and knees and scrubbed his kitchen floor. Occasionally he was rude; occasionally he was gruff. Her friends considered him spoiled and demanding. And she never reproached him or seemed to disapprove. Then, too, they were disconcerted that she kept a room for him wherever she was—whether at Val-Kill, in the apartment she rented during the 1930s in Esther Lape's and Elizabeth Read's 11th Street house in Greenwich Village, or in the White House.

One evening, Esther Lape went upstairs to the 11th Street apartment to visit unannounced. After she rang the bell, she heard ER hurry to the door. Dressed elegantly for very special company, ER flung open the door with an uncommon enthusiasm. Her great warm smile disappeared instantly, Esther Lape recalled: ER could hardly conceal her disappointment. She said, "Oh, I was expecting Earl, but do come in." Esther Lape left quickly, convinced that ER was a woman waiting for a lover. Unlike Dickerman and Cook, Esther Lape was more impressed than disapproving. Later, Lorena Hickok also disapproved. But she was more specifically jealous.

ER's son James Roosevelt believed that ER and Earl Miller were more than boon companions, more than devoted friends:

> I believe there may have been one real romance in mother's life outside of marriage. Mother may have had an affair with Earl Miller. . . .
>
> Mother was self-conscious about Miller's youth, but he did not seem bothered by the difference in years. He encouraged her to take pride in herself, to be herself, to be unafraid of facing the world. He did a lot of good for her. She seemed to draw strength from him when he was by her side, and she came to rely on him. When she had problems, she sought his help. . . . He became part of the family, too, and gave her a great deal of what her husband and we, her sons, failed to give her. Above all, he made her feel that she was a woman.
>
> If father noticed, he did not seem to mind. Curiously, he did promote a romance between Miller and Missy, but that did not last. Miller, who'd had an unhappy first marriage, later married a cousin of his first wife, and that ended the gossip about mother and him. But this was not a happy marriage either. . . .
>
> All the while, Miller had continued to see mother and frequently was a guest at Val-Kill. He saw other women, too, and she encouraged his romances. He married a third time in 1941, though he continued to see mother regularly. This marriage was a failure too. . . . Maybe because of mother. Their relationship deepened after father's death and ended only with mother's death. . . .

James Roosevelt believed that to diminish Miller's role in ER's life, "as though to protect her reputation," was a great "disservice to her" and only suggested "that because of her hang-ups she was never able to be a complete woman."

ER's friendship with Earl Miller has been and remains an amazing study of denial and lost documents. No other friendship has been so well covered up. Although there are photographs and home movies, there are no diaries, no memoirs, no letters to detail their relationship, or to help us characterize or appreciate its precise nature. There are rumors that a voluminous correspondence between Earl Miller and ER was anonymously purchased and destroyed, or purchased and locked away. Without those letters, the inevitable questions loom larger still: Who was responsible, and what was the need to bury those letters? What would they have told us? Without them, what can we know? In the absence of any significant contemporary account, we have only the fact of the cover-up to fuel our speculations and theories.

In 1971, Joseph Lash wrote in *Eleanor and Franklin:* "Eleanor wrote him faithfully, letters full of warmth and affection." But in 1982, in *Love, Eleanor,* Lash referred to "Eleanor's many letters to Earl, which have disappeared."

The only other reference to specific letters relates to the 1947–48 divorce proceedings between Earl and his third wife, Simone Miller, in which a packet of "endearing" letters was introduced and evidently sealed by the court. Whatever their contents, and whoever their author, Mrs. Miller was awarded a considerable but undisclosed settlement and custody of their two children—Earl, Jr., age six, and Anna Eleanor, three. ER was godmother to both children. The rather sensational divorce proceedings received a flurry of press attention. On 13 January 1947, New York *Daily News* columnist Ed Sullivan noted: "Navy Commander's wife will rock the country if she names the co-respondent in her divorce action!!!"

Earl Miller told several different versions of his marital troubles. According to one, it was true that he got married in 1932 and again in 1941 to quell rumors about himself and ER. After 1929, they had become constant companions; they were seen everywhere together; the gossip abounded. "Mrs. R was going to stick with [the] Governor until he was elected and then she and Sergeant were going to get married. That's why I got married in 1932 with plenty of publicity. I got married with someone I wasn't in love with. Same with second marriage. But I was never successful in killing the gossip."

According to Miller, even his affair with Missy occurred in order "to run interference for the lady." Earl Miller evidently told Joseph Lash that he played a courtly role: "When I heard that story of Lucy Mercer my heart went out to her—that he should have hurt her so."

Then, when ER told him "about the situation" with Missy LeHand, "I said I would break it up": "I played up to Missy—carried on an affair with her for two years. At that time she was not having anything to do with the Governor. Missy had me put on night duty so that I could come to her room [at Warm Springs]. My main purpose in playing up to Missy was because I knew the lady was being hurt."

But Miller had not counted on Missy's becoming deeply involved with him. When she found out that he was also "playing around with one of the girls in the Executive Office," she took to her bed and cried for three days. ER, dismayed by Earl Miller's behavior toward Missy, "made me go up to her room and see her and make amends."

Earl Miller told a different version of the story to his friend Miriam Abelow in 1972:

> I squired Missy for all the time FDR was Gov. up until I married at Hyde Pk late in 1932. It was common knowledge to all. I admired Missy very much & was attracted to her by her devotion to family as I was. Missy & I spent our free time together wherever we were with the family & both the "Boss" & Lady encouraged. I suppose that could be misconstrued also. When I told the Lady I had fallen in love with Ruth she was concerned for Missy as she felt that Missy was in love with me. I had no such conviction. . . . But Lady had impression our relationship was more serious than it actually was. I had already written Missy in Washington of my [engagement] plans. Her reply was most gracious. But it wasn't until Missy didn't attend the wedding at Hyde Pk that I realized she had concealed her real feelings. I only saw her casually after 1932 when I visited the W. House. She was then going with Bill Bullitt. . . .

Whatever version was true, the downstairs staff had a busy time trying to figure out the doings of the upstairs folk. Lillian Rogers Parks, then a White House maid, recalled that they

> sometimes thought backstairs, that Missy was going to try to have a life of her own away from FDR. For a time she dated Earl Miller, who we heard was romantically involved with Eleanor. . . . For a

time, Missy also dated the wealthy William Bullitt, whom FDR made the first Ambassador to Russia and later appointed Ambassador to France.

We wondered if FDR engineered these romances just so Missy would see how much better off she was with him. Some speculated that FDR used Missy to get Earl away from his wife, just for his own amusement. It gave us a lot to think about.

Scattered facts and fragmentary letters, conjecture and gossip, give us only hints of the texture of a relationship between two passionate and complex people that lasted for over thirty years. It is perhaps enough to say that countless images preserved through snapshots and home movies give us ample evidence that they enjoyed each other's company. With Earl Miller, ER developed a capacity for fun and relaxation only suggested before. We have the contours and the time frame of their relationship, but not the songs they sang, or the poets they read aloud; nor do we have the details and the dailiness of their correspondence. To date, not a single letter from ER to Earl Miller has surfaced.

Among the widely scattered facts are some unexpected characteristics: Earl Miller loved to cook, to bake, and to keep house. He adored Julia Child, and after 1963 watched her faithfully on TV. He collected spices, and lined them up "militarily" in his enormous spice rack. One of Earl Miller's few letters to ER that survived, buried among her daughter's papers, written in October 1951—long after the most intense years of their friendship—concerns food and house fixtures. We know too that he was profoundly political, progressive, and forthright about his convictions. He had a great sense of public relations, and of timing.

When FDR began to consider the possibilities of becoming a presidential candidate, Earl Miller believed that photographs of him on a horse would silence all the Republican propaganda that dismissed the governor as too sick to be taken seriously. He also believed that FDR's leg muscles might benefit from riding. After the appearance of local Georgia editorials mocking FDR's health, and suggesting that if elected in 1932 he would not last through the first term, "I had him atop a horse and invited the Atlanta Journal reporter and photographer in. They spread it in the Rotogravure brown section full page. We rode 4 miles that day (at walk of course) but they didn't follow and didn't know he didn't trot or canter. It was enough to stymie the health angle."

Miller was also mindful of ER's public appearance, and encouraged her to project a positive and warm image if journalists were around. When she was being posed, he stood behind the photographer making ridiculous faces until she smiled, relaxed, laughed. After 1928, ER's rigid unhappy glances and strained looks away from the camera were replaced by a direct gaze and a gracious smile.

And what of Earl Miller? This greathearted squire who adored his Lady? Personally, he appreciated her more completely than any other man ever had. Miller believed that ER "would have made a better president" than FDR, and he resented FDR's lack of appreciation for her work, her visions, her contributions. "Her influence with him was great." But "I don't think he ever gave her credit to her face—ever." Miller thought that, whereas FDR went off looking for "a return in the voting booth," ER was more dedicated and "had a keener insight into what people of the country needed. . . . She had a helluva time on the child labor business. He thought he might antagonize important groups. Only thing he didn't pull any punches on was Wall Street."

Politically, Earl Miller and ER agreed on many issues and had more actual "sympathetic understanding"—the kind that mattered to ER for "happy companionship"—than has ever been realized. Everything ER considered important, and every one of FDR's policies introduced from 1929 on, were also important to Earl Miller, and were condemned as radical, Miller wrote to his friends decades later. Today, "Old Age Insurance, Social Security, etc [are] accepted as normal." But in 1929 they were attacked as "just too far advanced." "Anyone that took up the cudgels for the underdog was a pink or radical."

Earl Miller took pride in what he was able to do in behalf of the "underdog," and was particularly proud of his efforts to combat the most revolting aspects of racism. Assigned by FDR to inspect prisons in Georgia and Florida, he was, ironically, accompanied by Lucy Mercer Rutherford who was now a highly regarded philanthropist. Earl Miller thought it significant that Lucy Mercer "copied" ER in her political interests, and she had become "quite the 'all-out' worker & giver of her time & money to many underprivileged." Together Miller and Rutherford made "many tours through the Georgia countryside to check on living and factory conditions." According to Miller, Lucy Mercer even asked questions the way his Lady did, and sounded "like her former boss." He concluded: "A person could just *not* be associated with the Lady without much of her 'do-good' rubbed off on you."

Miller recalled his role during the Roosevelt administration in exposing prison conditions "after that boy died in a 'Sweatbox' in Fla. for not saying '*sir*' to his White Trash Guard." He worked vigorously to end the violent brutality of Southern prisons: "I got a conviction and abolishment of the boxes in Ga. & Fla." And Lucy Mercer wrote him that "she was proud that she was part of it."

ER was impressed by Earl Miller's insights, patience, and tact. In some ways he was a lot like Louis Howe: purposeful and blunt. He understood the press, and he worked every angle. His advice, and his activities, irritated Louis Howe. According to Miller, Howe resented his presence in ER's life, in the household, and at the dining-room table. Earl Miller represented something new at the Roosevelt hearth. His loyalties were not divided. For him, ER came first. With him, she had a champion of her own.

Competition and jealousy were, over the years, to become recurring themes among ER's friends. Gossip and criticism abounded, in and out of press range. For the most part, Earl Miller kept his opinions strictly to himself until decades later, when he confided his feelings only to his intimate friends. In 1965, for example, Miller wrote to his friend Miriam Abelow that Joseph Lash "leaned a little too much to the right and at times I felt he influenced the Lady in that direction." And he criticized Lash and all the others who wrote about his Lady. To the end of his life, Miller sought to protect ER, according to his best lights. He told his friends that he had many stories—but "I don't cash in on my friends." After the divorce publicity, he considered it "more important than ever that I remain in the background." He wanted his friends to know that, during all the interviews, "Joe didn't get anything from me along that line, I'd rather die first."

Forever chivalric, Earl Miller never provided any details of his friendship with ER. He did talk to Joseph Lash about his affair with Missy LeHand. He referred frankly to his wives and his troubles. But even in his last years, faced with cancer and chemotherapy, Miller remained silent about Eleanor, or discreet and ambiguous. Because we are not playing with a full deck, only theories are possible. Partly for personal reasons, Joseph Lash has interpreted ER's friendship with Earl Miller in mother-and-son terms. He used as evidence his own mother-son relationship with ER. While it is certainly true that ER loved Joseph Lash, and that he, more than any of her intimate friends, was the dutiful and devoted son she so longed for, his insistence on comparison does not result in an equation. First of all, Lash tells us that he was not attracted to Mrs. Roosevelt. More than that, he asserts that men generally did not find her attractive, and that ER "underestimated the strength of the sexual drive. Or perhaps it was the inability of men to desire her sexually." "She carried an aura of greatness that set her apart. Neither Earl nor David [Gurewitsch] nor I was able to call her 'Eleanor.' " For Lash, ER's deepest affections never seemed to be more than "exercises in altruism." She "was unable to let herself go."

There are two stereotypes at play here: Frumpy older women do not have sex—because they cannot; aristocratic women do not—because they will not. Beyond the stereotypes, we are reassured that Joseph Lash did not find ER sexually or physically alluring: He was and remained a proper, dutiful, and devoted son. But that tells us little about Earl Miller. He never did call ER "Mrs. Roosevelt." He called her "Lady," and "Dearest Lady." And Earl Miller was not a dutiful son. He was a wild child who lived continually on the edges of danger, where passion is routinely known to reside. Contradictory and appealing, he was flirtatious and rude, physically boastful and charming. He pranced and he preened, and involved ER in all of his doings. She dismayed some of her friends by her evident ability to enjoy his company and even encourage his antics.

Loyal and silent, Earl Miller confounded history. Without correspondence or testimony, one of the most enduring relationships in ER's life remains a mystery. And so, as one explores the vagaries of a woman's life, one searches for and entertains alternative historical questions, such as: Why not? ER's friends deplored the fact that Corporal Miller seemed unable to keep his hands off his "Dearest Lady." And then there are all those photographs and films—carousing moments of play and obvious intimacy. Also, when ER was not working she wanted to enjoy herself. And there were very few people in her life who were as loving or as playful as Earl Miller.

What then is the nature of romance, of love and passion? What are the varieties of lust and love, of physical and emotional contentment, excitement and satisfaction, in a woman's life? Historically, in the courtly love story between the squire and his Lady, the intensities of passionate romance dance outside or just beyond the fields of lust. In this very modern saga, did lust remain on the outskirts of love? There are many ways in which a fully eroticized romance between two intimate and caring adults may emerge. ER had a private life. She risked censure and criticism on a daily basis—in order to be alone with her chosen friends, to fulfill her needs and wants as she experienced and understood them. It is obvious that ER and Earl Miller had a romantic friendship, a life-enhancing relationship. Whatever rules they agreed upon, they were two mutually consenting adults who were engaged in a discreet relationship that took them frequently into rustic cabins, high atop the Adirondack Mountains, and occasionally into remote seaside villages along the East Coast. There they sought privacy, relaxation, and comfort and did—whatever they agreed to do.

~

IN 1931, AT THE HEIGHT OF WHAT WAS THE MOST INTENSE phase of her friendship with Earl Miller, ER wrote an article called "Ten Rules for Success in Marriage." Written for money during the early years of the Depression, it is a reassuring column of advice to those women who had no interest in stepping outside convention but were faced with new and complex choices. The article tells us much about ER's life, as well as her concerns and hopes for her children's marriages. It also reveals what she longed for, and found, beyond the confines of her own marriage. She emphasized socially acceptable solutions, while acknowledging the growing availability of free choice. At once, and in the same article, ER called for greater stability in marriage, condoned divorce, and celebrated "the new freedom between the sexes which is characteristic of our time."

ER wrote that a marriage failed because the couple lacked ideals or purpose; because one party or the other lacked imagination; because the wife had "no stimulating interests of her own" and her home had become "an exceedingly dull place." She concluded with ten rules for success:

1. Have a plan, some central idea, as definite a pattern for your life as possible, and a clearly understood object for the joint project.
2. Remember that sooner or later money is apt to be a cause of friction. [ER counseled keeping a budget.]
3. Apportion your time and energy, allowing each [partner to] share joint homemaking duties, as well as individual responsibilities.
4. Let neither husband nor wife strive to be the dominating person in the household. A victory for either . . . means failure for the partnership.
5. Expect to disagree. Two people may hold entirely different views on many subjects and yet respect and care for each other. . . .
6. Be honest. [With yourself, and with each other.]
7. Be loyal. Keep your differences to yourselves. The less said about your married troubles, except between yourselves, the better. The feeling that many young married people have, that they can complain to their parents when things do not go just right is bad for them and brings more serious trouble later on.
8. Talk things over. When hurt do not keep it to yourself, brooding over it. Meet every situation in the open. Troubles that seem momentous quickly vanish when frankly dealt with.
9. Avoid trivial criticisms. Grumbling and complaints use up the vital forces of man or woman.
10. Keep alive the spirit of courtship, that thoughtfulness which existed before marriage. Look for traits in the other that can be admired and praised. You can accomplish much by stimulating self-confidence in your partner. . . .

ER also had words of advice for parents and "in-laws." "Offer as little advice to the newly married as possible, preferably none." ER wrote very firmly about this: "I have known many promising marriages to be wrecked because the young people began their life together in the home of their parents or had parents come to live with them."

ER opposed hasty marriages, and suggested a long, intimate engagement, where you see your intended for weeks at a time, preferably at breakfast and in a variety of difficult ordinary living situations. "Do not misunderstand me! I am not advocating trial marriage! I mean that, short of trial marriage itself, the engaged couple should have almost constant association" to see if "they can really stand the jars and jolts and routine of life together."

ER discussed trust, independence, equality, and values. "It has always been accepted as a truism that boys should be encouraged to be independent and to take the initiative. I think it is equally important in the education of the girl." Indeed, ER had the bold belief in 1931 that a girl should be independent by fifteen, and "not be kept under the control of her mother too long."

Regarding love specifically, ER recommended caution. It was a dangerous state: "We all know that when two people are in love they are easily carried away by their emotions. Some psychologists go so far as to say that love is a kind of sickness owing to the abnormal mental and psychological reactions it produces."

ER believed that "the new freedom between the sexes which is characteristic of our time" was useful in determining one's emotional truth. When combined with "character" and proper training, ER was "convinced that the greater freedom of our young people today . . . will eventually lead to happier lives."

> Between the freedom of youth today and the restraints which surrounded older generations the difference is indeed vast. Our young people "play around," as we say. . . . They talk about all sorts of topics . . . —morality from different aspects, differences in the economic standards of different classes of people, the freedom of the man and the woman, and the development of individuals. . . . On the whole it is a splendid thing.

On the specific issue of divorce, ER took both sides of the argument. "Many of us lack the stamina to face and see uncomfortable situations through. Today many seem to think that marriage is like a position in employment, which one can leave when everything does not go well. We should think of it as a permanent, lifetime job."

On the other hand, before exhaustion, depression, and malaise set in, ER counseled divorce. "It is far better for two people who cannot get along to separate than to lead a quarrelsome life." Especially if there were no children, divorce seemed to her appropriate when either party found that life together had "ceased to have any real spiritual value." With children, it was more problematic. But in the end, she considered it "better that a home should be broken than that the children should live where the father and mother are continually pulling against each other."

Ultimately, for ER happy companionship did not depend on class affinities, economic privilege, or "mere physical attraction which at the best could last but a short time." Rather, there was something more indefinable, some unconscious sense of character that might be called "good taste," which really mattered—and which transcended class lines and the boundaries of the family circle:

> There is something which no real fellow can do without, whether the fellow be boy or girl, namely the feeling which we call good taste, which makes us know instinctively when we meet people, no matter what their outer shells may be, whether they are real people, with that kernel of gold which is the one requisite for a deep and true relationship.
>
> A man and a woman may come from different backgrounds, they may not have had the same opportunities, and therefore they may lack certain knowledge and education in social customs and habits, but if, at bottom, they are the right kind of people, if the kernel of gold is there, then good taste will recognize and claim unswervingly its mate for friendship and for love with very little chance for future disappointment.

However much Earl Miller, and subsequently Lorena Hickok, possessed that "kernel of gold," marriage for ER retained its own sanctity. She had offered FDR a divorce in 1918, and renewed rumors of divorce shocked her circle in 1932. When FDR decided to run for the presidency, her most intimate friends feared that she wanted to flee.

ER faced the prospect of the White House with foreboding. From all accounts, she hated the idea. She had seen firsthand what it had done to Aunt Edith, Uncle Ted's wife. She feared that she would have no life of her own. Her closest friends—Nancy Cook, Marion Dickerman, and Earl Miller—all referred in later years to the rumors that ER wanted to leave FDR after the election and marry Earl Miller. The only evidence we have for that rumor is a letter, an almost "hysterical" letter, ER was alleged to have sent Nancy Cook in Chicago with the nominating team. She, in a mild panic, showed it immediately to Louis Howe. He promptly tore it to shreds, warning Cook and Dickerman: "You are not to breathe a word of this to anyone. Not to *anyone*."

FDR biographer Kenneth Davis, who interviewed Marion Dickerman at length, gave her version of what ER wrote in the letter: ER could not "bear to become First Lady!" Her entire being rebelled "against the prospect of being a prisoner of the White House, forced . . . onto a narrow treadmill of formal receptions, 'openings,' dedications, teas, official dinners. . . . She won't do it! She'll run away with Earl Miller—never mind the fact that Earl has just become engaged to Ruth Bellinger and that Eleanor has been arranging, against her mother-in-law's contemptuous disapproval, a wedding ceremony for him at Hyde Park. She'll flee with Earl, who loves and respects her as Franklin never did, nor her sons. She'll file suit for a divorce. . . ."

When Joseph Lash asked Earl Miller about the accuracy of this version of the letter, he dismissed it breezily—"She may have been down in the depths." He warned Lash never to trust anything Dickerman ever said. Lash agreed. The jealousies in ER's crowd were "phenomenal."

ER referred to this episode only obliquely, and with a vastly different emphasis: "The night before my husband was nominated, we sat up until morning in the Executive Mansion. All the newspaper people, among them Lorena Hickok, whom I was later to know well, spent most of the night in the garage. Finding them still there the following morning when I came down, I invited them to come in and have breakfast with me on the porch." Two days later, the family flew to Chicago, where, in an unprecedented departure, FDR accepted the nomination in person—rather than wait through the summer months to be notified at home by the "notification committee." The flight included ER, FDR,

Missy LeHand, Grace Tully, Gus Gennerich, and Earl Miller. ER wrote: "For Earl Miller this was the last trip with my husband. When Franklin left Albany, Earl Miller went into the Department of Correction and became personnel director."

Perhaps ER's initial panic and reluctance to become First Lady involved, in some part, her impending geographic separation from Earl Miller—mentioned so casually in her memoir. She had not been consulted in FDR's decision to take Gus Gennerich with him to Washington but not Earl Miller. Perhaps FDR did in fact intend to separate his wife from her companion, not only when he decided to leave Miller in New York, but also when he encouraged Miller's romance with Missy LeHand.

Possibly Earl Miller preferred to remain in New York, and had no interest in moving to Washington with the Roosevelts. In any case, unlike Louis Howe, who succeeded in demonstrating absolute impartiality between ER and FDR, Earl Miller's primary allegiance was to ER. They had become inseparable, until Earl Miller was summarily wrenched from the family circle.

For a time, ER was inconsolable. She dreaded Washington, the White House, and all the changes that seemed so completely beyond her control. Lorena Hickok noticed that ER was unusually quiet, and amidst all the political excitement seemed disheartened. "Hick" was the first seriously to seek the reasons, and played a very large part in the restoration of ER's equilibrium.

19. Assignment ER:
Lorena Hickok and the 1932 Campaign

WHATEVER EMOTIONAL TURBULENCE ER FELT DURING the heady months preceding the 1932 Democratic convention in Chicago, outwardly she maintained her composure, and seemed as always poised and correct. Few noticed her mood swings, and since she never "bothered" anyone about them, nobody needed to pause from the relentless demands of a political campaign to acknowledge her distress.

There was so much pressing business, so many deals to be made, and so many galling opponents—as well as surprising new enemies to deflect, most notably FDR's former booster Al Smith.

Lorena Hickok was the first political reporter to focus on the bitter rivalry that had emerged between Al Smith and FDR. Smith, who would always believe he had created FDR, now sought to crush him, and portrayed FDR as a thoroughly ungrateful wretch who had betrayed him. Not only had he not reappointed Moses or Moskowitz, throughout Roosevelt's gubernatorial years, Smith had been exiled to a meaningless land without power or patronage, a land without consultation or respect. Politics was Smith's world, the center of all things meaningful and pleasurable. Hick recalled that during his years of exile in "big business" he became "a lonely, embittered old man. The warmth of his greeting, when any of us political reporters would drop in to see him, was almost pathetic."

ER did not participate in the Smith-Roosevelt conflict, although she "must have been disillusioned and disappointed" when, just before the convention, following a long and apparently unfruitful conversation with FDR, Smith allied himself to the House of Morgan and other conservative political and financial interests. Years later, Hick showed ER "two dents" in the pavement on 65th Street, implanted by Hick's "two feet, standing out there with the rest of the gang, waiting for Al Smith to come out and tell us what he and your husband had been talking about." The press was told, "We were talking about our grandchildren." But it was by then brutally clear that the legacy of FDR's 1928 and 1930 New York victories was one of the most bitter political rivalries in Democratic Party history, culminating in the divided convention of 1932.

Before the convention, Louis Howe, hoping for a major human-interest story, arranged for Lorena Hickok to tour the Roosevelt home at Hyde Park. Intent on cultivating her support, the Howe publicity machine went all out: She was met at the Poughkeepsie station by a state trooper and driven to the Big House for tea. Hick recalled that during her first visit to Hyde Park she sat in front of an open fire listening to politics and family lore while ER sat on a couch knitting: "I don't recall that she said much."

After tea, FDR was carried by two state troopers to his specially equipped car, and he drove her down the steep hill behind the house, where he had coasted as a boy in winter. Proudly he pointed out the stand of virgin timber, the working farm, his Christmas-tree business, and the details of all eleven hundred acres of his and his mother's estate—including Val-Kill, and the place atop the nearby hill where he later built his own hideaway cottage.

When he showed Hick Val-Kill, he said: "I built that for my Missis. I was my own contractor, and the design was mine, although I did have the help of an architect. It's supposed to be a reproduction of a Dutch colonial cottage." FDR seemed to Hick "immensely proud of the cottage," and she noted that, "set in beautifully landscaped grounds, it

really was lovely." ER, with her friends Nancy Cook and Marion Dickerman, "awaited us there." FDR asked ER to show Hick "through the
place." ER was "cordial and friendly—in an impersonal way—as she
always was. We talked about furniture, but I don't recall anything else
she said."

Indeed, in the four years Lorena Hickok had covered New York
State politics for the Associated Press, ER had been far less concerned
about the reporter's presence than Louis Howe or FDR, who had both
courted her. ER did once invite Hickok to tea at the 65th Street house
when she was first assigned to interview the First Lady of the Empire
State in 1928, which surprised Hick: "It was most unusual for a reporter
calling for an interview with a woman in Mrs. Roosevelt's position to
be served tea! It had never happened to me before." "I watched with
fascination the graceful way she manipulated the tea things with her
long, slender hands. She was wearing a lace-trimmed hostess gown,
considerably more becoming than the things I had seen her wearing
around headquarters. But the hairnet was still there. . . ."

They talked more about dogs than about politics. Anna's police dog,
Chief, was much like Hick's police dog, Prinz; and "curled up at Mrs.
Roosevelt's feet was a little black Scotty, named Meggie. . . ." Regarding
politics, ER "seemed much more distressed over Governor Smith's
defeat than elated over her husband's victory. . . ." But ER was "reticent"
and her remarks were "guarded." Hick "felt that she didn't trust me,
cordial as she was in her reception of me." "I failed to get much news
out of her, but I was so impressed with her graciousness and her charm
that I ended my story with this sentence: 'The new mistress of the
Executive Mansion in Albany is a very great lady.'"

Still, Hick made no effort to interview ER again. Like most women
journalists, who struggled to be taken seriously in the profession, Hick
"had a strong aversion" to the "women's page stuff." And Hick was
proud that, throughout FDR's years as governor, she was part of his
ever-present press entourage when he was in town. "Since I was always
the only woman in the group of political writers, I came in for a good
deal of good-natured ribbing from him." Later, ER told her that she
was the only woman reporter FDR or Louis Howe knew when Franklin

became president. "Women just did not cover men in politics in those days."

Nevertheless, Hick recalled, "I wanted very much to know Mrs. Roosevelt. But she always held me at arm's length—and her arms were very long."

ER did not seem actually to take much notice of Hick until the Chicago convention was under way. Representatives of FDR's team—including Louis Howe; his campaign manager, Jim Farley; and three of the Roosevelt children, Anna, Franklin, Jr., and James—were in Chicago. FDR, ER, Missy LeHand, Earl Miller and Gus Gennerich, Sam Rosenman, Grace Tully, Elliott, and John waited in Albany. The situation was tense. Al Smith had gone to Chicago determined to stop FDR. With six serious contenders and several favorite sons, nothing was certain. The press corps in Albany had set up shop in the executive garage. Surrounded by typewriters and practically hidden by cigarette and cigar smoke, they were hooked up to Chicago by radio, telephone operators, and telegraph wires. The Roosevelts were cozy in FDR's study, beside the radio. FDR smoked ceaselessly, and smiled for one and all, while ER knitted. At midnight, she sent out coffee and sandwiches to the press corps. The AP was represented by Hick and Elton Fay of the Albany bureau, who were the last to leave the garage in the morning, after the first deadlocked ballots threatened to destroy Roosevelt's entire effort.

The Democrats' two-thirds rule had destroyed the party's most popular candidates before. Some held it responsible for the Republicans' twelve-year triumph. Now, although FDR led the majority with 666¼ ballots, he needed 770. Al Smith was second with 201¾, and Jack Garner of Texas, the popular Speaker of the House, held on to the 90 critical votes of Texas and California. New York's delegation was split, with 65½ for Smith and 28½ for FDR.

After the first ballot, as the long, grueling hours of 30 June melted into the bleary-eyed morning of 1 July, ER seemed actually to recognize Hick for the first time, and noticed that, after a long night's work, she was hungry. Hick recalled that as she and Fay left the garage they saw ER "looking very clean and crisp in a light summer dress, getting ready for breakfast on a screened side porch." As they approached, ER "hur-ried to the door" and invited them to join her and her young companion, Bobby Baker, Louis Howe's grandson. "She gave us a good substantial meal—we were both famished."

But Hick noticed something more:

> Impressed as we were by her hospitality and grateful for it, Elton and I were both a little puzzled by her attitude. Not that she wasn't cordial and solicitous for our comfort, but she seemed rather withdrawn—shut up inside herself. She showed little interest in the night's proceedings, appeared unwilling to discuss the subject. That was perhaps natural. But there was something else—something I couldn't define or understand.
>
> "That woman is unhappy about something," I told Elton as we drove away.

On the afternoon of 1 July, FDR held a press conference. He was "fresh, buoyant, confident, laughing and joking with us even more than usual." That evening, during the fourth ballot, the reason for his mood became clear. To avoid a deadlocked convention and a successful stop-Roosevelt move, some very swift deals had been made. Jim Farley ap-pealed to Garner's campaign manager, Sam Rayburn. Joseph Kennedy, a Roosevelt supporter and well-known power broker, contacted William Randolph Hearst to report his impression: The convention choice would be either Newton D. Baker or Franklin Delano Roosevelt.

Hearst hated Baker, the most outspoken Wilsonian internationalist. And FDR had at least fudged for years on the League of Nations and the World Court. Hearst had hoped he could get a more malleable compromise candidate, like Maryland's more conservative Governor Albert Ritchie. But Kennedy insisted: FDR or Baker. Hearst could live with FDR, and Howe telephoned to negotiate the deal: Hearst wanted Texas's favorite son, John Nance Garner, for vice-president, along with assurances that FDR would never support the League of Nations or the World Court. Howe called FDR with the terms of the deal, and FDR called Hearst. Whatever else ER may have felt that morning, she was certainly "unhappy" about that deal; she never accepted without a struggle FDR's willingness to sacrifice principles for pragmatism.

That morning, Hearst's Washington correspondent informed "Cactus Jack" Garner that "the Chief believes nothing can now save the country but for him to throw his votes to Governor Roosevelt." The message reached Garner at 11:00 A.M., and Garner released his delegates. He would be vice-president; William Gibbs McAdoo would control California patronage and maintain a veto over the decision for secretaries of state and treasury. By 8:00 P.M., the deal was solidified, and the fourth ballot began.

William Gibbs McAdoo asked to speak from the platform—a significant request. The hall quieted as he strode down the long corridor. A hush fell as he boomed over the airwaves of America: "California came here to nominate a president of the United States." California "did not come here to deadlock this convention, or to engage in another desolating contest like that of 1924. . . . And so, my friends, California casts forty-four votes for Franklin Delano Roosevelt."

The storm broke. Pure pandemonium went on for what seemed like hours as the Democrats shouted themselves into a wild frenzy, to the tune of "Happy Days Are Here Again." The other delegations fell into line in rapid procession. Except for Smith diehards, it was an enthusiastic landslide for Roosevelt. Against the greatest odds, and in less than twelve hours, the Roosevelt team had pulled out an amazing victory.

~

MUCH OF THE CREDIT FOR FDR'S VICTORY WOULD ALWAYS GO to Louis Howe. Perhaps his chief contribution in Chicago was his infallible good sense of what worked, what stirred people, what they wanted to hear, to see, to remember. FDR's convention demonstrations had been lackluster. The mood was vague and unfocused; the speeches were uninspiring or positively dull. The most vigorous noises belonged to Al Smith's boo-ers. Their hoots and jeers seemed to dominate all thirty thousand seats in the gallery. And they were dedicated to one purpose: anyone but Roosevelt.

Moreover, FDR's preferred theme song fell flat. His own choice was "Anchors Aweigh." It drove Howe mad. Throughout the convention, he listened as his radio blasted the doings into his tiny, steamy, crowded room (Room 702, better known as "operations central"). Over and over there was that familiar college-football fight song, "Anchors Aweigh." Sweating, sick, gasping for breath, flat out on the floor, Howe wheezed into Ed Flynn's ear: "For God's sake, tell 'em to play something else." But the theme song was important—the banner, the metaphor—and FDR had chosen it. Howe insisted, and introduced the new theme: "Happy Days Are Here Again." It worked to change the mood, the beat, and the metaphor.

Breaking with all tradition, FDR decided to accept the nomination in person in Chicago, the very next day. Customarily, the candidate had awaited formal notification of his nomination for two months, the amount of time personal travel might take by horse and wagon from an eighteenth-century convention site to the candidate's country home. But FDR decided that, in the midst of America's most grievous depression, he would acknowledge the facts of twentieth-century technology: instant communication through radio, telephone, telegraph; rapid transit by airplane. FDR became the first flying candidate.

The press had noticed a new three-motored plane waiting at the Albany airport, and asked him if that was his Chicago transport. The Associated Press reporters Hickok and Fay reported his answer:

> "Now, I'll tell you what I'm going to do. . . . I'm going to bicycle out to Chicago.
>
> "I'm going to get one of those quinters—you know, five bicycles in a row.
>
> "Father will ride in the first seat and manage the handlebars. Jim will ride the second, then Elliott, then Franklin, Jr. and then John.
>
> "Sam (referring to speech writer and aide, New York's Supreme Court Justice Samuel I. Rosenman) will follow—on a tricycle."

If anybody noticed FDR's omission of his wife's pedaling position, nobody mentioned it. The entire Albany household flew into mighty headwinds for nine hours so that FDR might personally announce his determination to fight for a new future in the midst of America's gloom-

iest malaise. He was greeted with a spontaneous outpouring of celebration, a standing ovation of hope.

Smiling and confident, FDR pledged a bold but balanced crusade
against poverty and discontent: "Ours must be a party of liberal thought,
of planned action, of enlightened international outlook, and the greatest
good to the greatest number of our citizens." "We will break foolish
traditions and leave it to the Republican leadership, far more skilled in
the art, to break promises." While he warned against radicalism, he also
warned against "those who squint at the future with their faces turned
to the past."

~

THERE WAS A LITTLE SOMETHING FOR EVERYBODY. BERNARD
Baruch—who originally supported Ritchie, and had even arranged an
alliance luncheon between McAdoo and Smith—now pledged $50,000
to the Roosevelt campaign. Wall Street and workers were to greet the
sunrise together. FDR's charisma, and his personal triumph in the face
of his own physical adversity, made it all work. His unprecedented flight
and his dramatic thirty-minute speech were received with tumultuous
enthusiasm. In conclusion, he outlined his political philosophy:

> Never before in modern history have the essential differences
> between the two major parties stood out in such striking contrast
> as they do today. Republican leaders not only have failed in material
> things, they have failed in national vision, because in disaster they
> have held out no hope, they have pointed out no path for the people
> below to climb back to places of security and of safety in our
> American life.
>
> Throughout the Nation, men and women, forgotten in the po-
> litical philosophy of the Government of the last years, look to us
> here for guidance and for more equitable opportunity to share in
> the distribution of national wealth.
>
> On the farms, in the large metropolitan areas, in the smaller
> cities and in the villages, millions of our citizens cherish the hope
> that their old standards of living and of thought have not gone
> forever. Those millions cannot and shall not hope in vain.

I pledge you, I pledge myself, to a new deal for the American people. Let us all here assembled constitute ourselves prophets of a new order of competence and of courage. This is more than a political campaign; it is a call to arms. Give me your help, not to win votes alone, but to win in this crusade to restore America to its own people.

For the American public, that speech signaled a new era. For Roosevelt's inner circle, it also signaled the end of an old order. It was written by various members of his new advisory team, "the Brain Trust," and Louis Howe hated it. He too had written a speech, but only the first page of it was used. Feelings about that speech ran so high that years later, ER sought to settle the matter in her memoirs: Columbia University professor "Raymond Moley has stated that he wrote the acceptance speech. I feel sure he was never aware of some of the things that happened in connection with it." In fact, FDR and Sam Rosenman wrote and rewrote one draft of the team speech in Albany. Columbia professors Rexford G. Tugwell and Adolf A. Berle and FDR's law partner, Basil ("Doc") O'Connor, also worked on a version of the speech. Then Howe, contemptuous of all the team drafts, wrote an entirely new speech—confident that his version would be used. But FDR and Sam Rosenman spent most of the nine-hour flight from Albany to Chicago revising and rewriting the speech altogether.

And their revision was the one he read. He included Howe's first page and some additional paragraphs from Howe's version. But the "New Deal" was pure Sam Rosenman, written sometime after three in the morning, after the disappointing first ballot. Rosenman went into the kitchen to boil some frankfurters, for himself and the newspaper people in the garage. While off by himself in the small, informal dining room, munching on frankfurters, he wrote almost casually the words that would become the permanent symbol for FDR's presidency: the call for "bold, persistent experimentation . . . I pledge you, I pledge myself, to a new deal for the American people."

Louis Howe, the man most responsible for FDR's political career, the chief conductor of the preconvention orchestra, now shared his authority and influence with newcomers he neither liked nor respected.

Although he personally had chosen Edward Flynn and James Farley, they were strategists—responsible for the votes, the tactics. He had had nothing to do with the formation of the new idea department called the Brain Trust. And that shop was entrusted to Sam Rosenman's men—the professors, with whom Howe had little in common. They seemed to Howe progressive idealists who knew nothing and cared less about the game, the business, the very stuff of politics. And Howe astounded them with the allies he sought, the tactics he used. They were especially dismayed when he welcomed aboard financial and political conservatives such as Bernard Baruch and Virginia's Governor Harry Byrd.

Ironically, the moment Howe had fought so hard for was, for him, bittersweet. The long struggle he had waged, the years of strategy and preparation for this presidential moment, was precisely the moment that he was eclipsed, by other needs and other advisers.

ER was also eclipsed. But she had known all along she would be. She had feared and hoped for this moment, and now felt profoundly ambivalent. FDR had never consulted her about his decision, had never even bothered to tell her when he decided to run for the presidency. It was not a secret, precisely. For two years, every speech, every activity had one aim: There had been only one purpose in the Roosevelt household for months. The organization, the speeches, the team were all carefully prepared. But there was no family discussion about the decision. Nor was ER consulted about any issue or subject relating to the campaign.

When FDR actually fulfilled his part of the Hearst-Garner deal and repudiated the League of Nations in a speech to the New York State Grange, and then went further to imply that he would disassociate himself from the World Court, which ER cared so fervently about, she was aghast. For the first time in years, she turned away from Franklin in that almost forgotten cold and silent Griselda mode.

FDR invited ER's friend Agnes Brown Leach, a philanthropist and an activist they both respected, to lunch, in the hope that she would agree that politics required these pragmatic moments: "Eleanor is very fond of you and you can make peace between us. She hasn't spoken to me for three days." But Agnes Brown Leach, a longtime internationalist and peace advocate who had supported both the American Union Against Militarism and the Woman's Peace Party during World War I, was also appalled: Yours "was a shabby statement," she noted: "I just don't feel like having lunch with you today."

When ER heard of the exchange, she was delighted: "Agnes, you are a sweet, darling girl. I hear you upset Franklin very much. I didn't know you had it in you."

Whatever the dimensions of her personal anguish, ER was a team player. She not only rallied publicly, but sought to protect FDR from her deepest misgivings: "I did not want my husband to be president. . . . It was pure selfishness on my part, and I never mentioned my feelings on the subject to him." What would she be able to do? How much of her life would she have to abandon? What of her teaching at Todhunter? What of her friends, her weekends, those private, quiet entertainments that meant so much to her? What of her own political work? The Statehouse was one thing. The White House quite another.

ER did not work directly in her husband's campaign. Nevertheless, wherever she went and whenever she spoke, she made terrific copy. She was at all times and under all circumstances an asset. Whatever her own feelings or forebodings, she never refused to travel with the campaign party when asked, or to speak when called upon. Moreover, she spoke more eloquently than most other public figures regarding the needs and hopes of Americans as they faced the worst economic calamity in the history of the nation. Men as well as women from every walk of life and from every corner of the country responded to her integrity, her earnest commitment to improve the situation for each and every individual. Empathic, spontaneous, and warm, ER inspired a rare outpouring of affection and trust. She, as much as any member of FDR's team, represented the purpose and the essence of the New Deal.

Eleanor Roosevelt was a new phenomenon in American politics. The AP's most astute political reporter, Lorena Hickok, recognized that ER was different from other candidates' wives and merited coverage of her own. In those days candidates' wives "were supposed, like children, to be seen and not heard." Hick persuaded the AP to assign a regular journalist to cover ER. She did not seek the job for herself, and actually "did not want it." She much preferred her old job, and had fully enjoyed all the perks and privileges that went with her assignment to FDR.

Hick was relieved when the assignment went to Katherine Beebe, the only other woman on the AP's news staff in New York, and she was allowed to maintain her assignment on FDR's campaign trail. But Hick soon noticed that Kay Beebe had disappeared from sight. Later, she was told that Beebe had resigned and moved to San Francisco. As a result, throughout most of the campaign Hick remained the only woman reporter. The AP simply assumed that, if an interesting story concerning ER emerged, Hick would report it, in addition to her other tasks.

During September, Hick traveled on FDR's first whistle-stop campaign train through seventeen Western states, including stops in Chicago, Topeka, Salt Lake City, Seattle, Portland, and San Francisco. ER met the train in Arizona, as it headed home. At Prescott, the train pulled off to a siding while the Roosevelts took the day off to visit ER's friend Isabella Selmes Ferguson Greenway.* The reporters were told it was a social affair: "There would be no news, and we were not invited." But when the press corps discovered that one reporter had been invited, they were outraged.

Years later, and evidently still peeved, Hick wrote that the exception was "a young man considerably below the professional stature of most of the writers on the train, and he had become friendly with Anna and Jimmy." He was the Chicago *Tribune*'s John R. Boettiger, with whom Anna had fallen in love. Boettiger and Anna R. Dall both divorced their respective spouses to marry each other within months of this trip. Hick and the other correspondents "cooling their heels on a railroad siding" considered the incident "probably the worst job in public relations ever inflicted on any candidate." "I was so indignant that I sought out Mrs. Roosevelt . . . and told her about it."

ER surprised Hick by being "more approachable than usual," and by inviting her to join the expedition to one of the largest cattle ranches

* Bob Ferguson had died in 1927, and Isabella married Jack Greenway—a family friend and also a former Rough Rider. See notes, page 560.

in the United States. "The story didn't amount to much. I saw some cowboys roping steers and trying to stay on bucking broncos, and I ate some barbecued beef. But Mrs. Roosevelt came and sat with me for quite a long time in the car and told me about her girlhood friendship with Isabella Greenway."

After that conversation, Hick returned to the train—where she was met by an indignant Marvin McIntyre, FDR's public-relations man. He was as furious at her as she had been at Boettiger. But Hick decided that, since she was the only woman in the press corps, ER had a right to invite her. After all, "Mrs. Roosevelt was a Roosevelt, too, and she also had the right to invite someone if she chose to do so, and she had invited me." The fact is that if there was a story to get Hick got it.

ER evidently spent that evening talking with Tommy about Hick, and also with Louis Howe. Since they both admired her political sense, ER decided during that trip she could trust Hick, and more regularly invited her company. As the train returned eastward through Colorado and Kansas and into Chicago, Hick's stories for the AP frequently focused on ER. Mostly she wrote about ER's stamina: "I recall puffing, panting, and perspiring as I followed her through a cornfield somewhere in Nebraska or Iowa. She moved swiftly, coolly and as easily as though she were accustomed to striding through a cornfield every day of her life. With despair I watched her glide nimbly through a barbed wire fence into an adjacent pasture. When I tried it I got tangled up in the wires, ruined a pair of silk stockings (nylons had not been invented in 1932) and had to be helped."

ER's vigor seemed to Hick matched only by her calm and her courage. In Chicago, during a vast torchlight procession around the Loop, highlighted by brass bands, flares, fireworks, and thousands of cheering citizens—who frequently broke through the police lines—a mounted policeman lost control of his horse. The horse reared, and it looked as if the front hoofs would come down in the open car carrying the Roosevelts. Hick, a short distance behind—in another open car, which was carrying several reporters—could see "through the smoke and the flashes of light . . . Mrs. Roosevelt, sitting perfectly erect, apparently unperturbed!"

The next morning, ER invited Hick to join her. Hick, still "surprised when she allowed me to accompany her those days," asked ER if she hadn't been frightened "when that horse reared over you last night?" ER replied that it had all happened so fast, there was no time "to get frightened," and added: "If I had been frightened, I'd have been frightened for Franklin. I can move quickly, but he can't."

Hick's growing admiration for ER was peppered with a certain amount of amusement. There were things in life that mattered to Hick that ER dismissed: baseball, for example. FDR's Chicago campaign stop included one of the greatest World Series games in history. The entire family went to see the Yankees and the Chicago Cubs go at it. Not to attend would have been positively un-American. ER sat between her husband and son Jimmy. The place was packed, and "she could not have fallen over even if she had collapsed." But Hick was amazed to see ER's head drop ever so slightly forward. Later, Jimmy told Hick that ER had slept through the entire game, even though "Babe Ruth and Lou Gehrig each hit two home runs!" Hick got more mileage out of that event than any of her other columns to date; and especially appreciated ER's ability to laugh at herself and enjoy Hick's story.

By October, it seemed clear that FDR was going to be elected. The AP then assigned Hick to cover ER on a regular basis. It had, after all, been her idea to begin with. After Hick returned from covering the Republican state convention in Buffalo, she was told by Bill Chapin, the AP's city editor: "She's all yours now, Hickok. Have fun!"

Hick felt "diffident" the day she went over to ER's office to tell her of her new assignment. "It means that I shall have to follow you around all the time, everywhere," she explained. ER was not thrilled. Hick assumed that Louis Howe and FDR had both prepared her for this eventuality and that they considered the publicity valuable. But ER preferred her privacy. She frowned and sighed, and looked generally disgruntled. Still, she was more resigned than rude to her new reporter-companion, and said: "I'm afraid that you won't have much to write about. I'll not be doing anything very interesting. I do realize that it's your job, of course, and you may go with me whenever I do anything publicly."

Coincidentally, this conversation occurred on 11 October 1932, ER's forty-eighth birthday. Which, ER told Hick, partly added to her somewhat unsettled mood: "I'm a middle-aged woman. It's good to be middle-aged. Things don't matter so much. You don't take it so hard when things happen to you that you don't like."

For weeks Hick kept ER in sight. She went everywhere with her, recorded her every word, noticed every nuance, observed every detail. Very often there was simply no story. Days on end would go by when ER said nothing of significance and lived her life privately, with Hick cooling her heels, waiting for a tidbit outside her office, or outside campaign headquarters, or occasionally in some office at Todhunter. She wondered if her assignment was worth the AP's money. But her boss, Bill Chapin, was supportive, and when Hick despaired, he'd say, "Stay with it, kid," and inquire: "How are you fixed for cash?" Running around with ER required loose change: mostly for taxis, trolley cars, buses, trains. Fortunately, ER never made poor copy. Even on dull days, Hick was impressed. On one day without any particular news, Hick wired the AP that there was no story but, for the record, "THE DAME HAS ENORMOUS DIGNITY. SHE'S A PERSON."

In her effort to remain herself, ER was confronted by mounting criticism. She traveled by public conveyances. She bought apples from men on street corners. Her clothes were too plain. Her hats looked as if "she had rushed in and bought them while her bus waited for the traffic light to change." And, her critics explained, she did all of these ordinary things because she was really a publicity hound.

ER considered the wildest attacks against her positively funny. As their friendship developed, Hick was particularly impressed by ER's sense of humor and her ability to face serious emergencies with the most extraordinary calm. One morning, at breakfast, their conversation was interrupted by ER's cook, who rushed up from the kitchen in terror. FDR's valet, Irvin McDuffie, had a drinking problem. Just then he was wildly drunk, and Reynolds, the butler, was "going after him with a carving knife!" Without saying a word, ER arose from the table and went down to the kitchen. When she returned, she sat down wordlessly and resumed her breakfast. Finally, Hick broke the silence:

"Well, what did you do with them?"

"I took the knife away from Reynolds and sent McDuffie to bed. . . ."

Hick was equally fascinated by ER's frugal eating habits. "Unless she is taking some one to lunch—and she likes to take people to lunch—she may usually be found eating her lunch at some drugstore counter." The first time Hick was invited to ER's home for a Sunday-night supper, she was surprised by the menu: scrambled eggs with little sausages, cold sliced chicken and cold meats, salad, and dessert. Since the Wilson years in Washington that Sunday-night supper was a tradition, and ER always scrambled the eggs herself, "at the table in a chafing dish." It was the only cooking ER ever did. Hick considered it odd, and thought that perhaps FDR "liked to watch her do it."

ER had other frugal habits. She wore formless "ten dollar dresses." When she traveled alone, she always rode a day coach or, at night, simply a lower berth. "And all this is true," Hick pointed out, despite the fact that ER really spent "a good deal of money and holds salaried jobs because she needs more than her private income."

" 'I don't know where it goes, exactly,' she says with a smile, 'but I know I have a lot of fun doing things with money.' " Throughout her life, ER gave most of her money away. She spent as little as possible on herself, in order to spend as much as possible on others. ER "likes people, all sorts of people, and loves to have them around. She has intimate friends among people of all ages and all circumstances in life." And, like her father, she gave every one of them the most thoughtful gifts on every conceivable occasion.

Also, ER liked to entertain. "Every afternoon in the executive mansion at Albany, at Hyde Park, or at the Roosevelt town house in New York, wherever she happens to be, tea is served—a good substantial tea, usually with chocolate cake. Whoever is about is invited in." Reporters and family members, secretaries and staff, intimate friends, state troopers, distinguished guests, visiting royalty. No one was excluded.

Hick found ER interesting when she talked politics. And interesting when she refused to talk politics. But "the candidate's wife who doesn't talk politics" had an odd way of talking politics most of the time. In

1932, she worked for the state ticket, and campaigned arduously for Herbert Lehman's race for governor. Wherever she spoke, ER took the opportunity to defend FDR's record: Only the Democrats cared about the poor in this long moment of crisis.

At one campaign dinner in Syracuse, for example, ER assailed Lehman's opponent, Colonel William J. Donovan.* Like all Republicans, she chided, he continually "grieved over extravagance" in government. But it was really they who were extravagant; their economies were foolhardy, useless, and cruel. They were willing to cut $21 million out of the Department of Public Works, 80 percent of which went to pay for labor. Economy, ER explained, "can be made to appear a very wonderful thing. And yet it can do a great deal of harm." The Republicans were willing to fire "thousands of young engineers, draughtsmen, and laborers" employed in public works, and were then willing to appropriate "$126,774,000 for extras over and above the governor's budget for running the state," including many millions for additional public relief. ER asked: "Now which would have been better—to pay that money out in salaries for labor on public works, or to pay it in unemployment relief." Their so-called economy, ER concluded, created "a situation far more serious than before, with people far more desperate than they have been up to now." "If you and I were hungry, I doubt whether we'd be so patient as these people have been so far."

On 27 October, on the way to Syracuse, ER took time off from the campaign to visit Earl Miller and his new wife, Ruth Taylor Bellinger, who was a cousin of his first wife's. They were married at Hyde Park on 8 September 1932, amid a great deal of fanfare, with the Roosevelt children in attendance. Anna Roosevelt Dall was matron of honor; Elliott Roosevelt was best man. The Roosevelts gave them "a piece of land at Hyde Park."

Earl Miller's second marriage was almost immediately in trouble. Her parents arranged an annulment, in November 1933, on the grounds that Ruth "was under 17 when married and did not have their consent."

ER was dismayed and wrote Nancy Cook:

---

* During World War II, FDR appointed "Wild Bill" Donovan to head the Office of Strategic Services, forerunner of the CIA.

Things have come to a head & Ruth has told him she is going out with another boy & having a good time & felt she gave up too much in marrying so she wants ½ of everything, an annulment! of her marriage & $50 a month for 3 years. Isn't it strange to be so calmly mercenary? She asked him *after having* told him this, for her birthday present ahead of time as she wanted to buy a jewelled sorority pin & she took $25 from him! She also wishes to be friends & feel she can depend on him & retain all his friends!

Earl intended to set up his own household immediately, and ER asked Nancy Cook to "order the mattress & springs & 2 pillows for Earl," and additional furniture from their Val-Kill factory: "He wants the simplest possible bookcase to go with his furniture 5 ft high 24 in. wide & 9 inches deep & has his desk & chair. I'll give him those things for Xmas & birthday so send the bill to me!"

The Roosevelts' adult children Anna and Elliott were also in the throes of marriage crises between 1932 and 1933. But discussions of divorce, however fiercely they swirled around the family table, were kept out of the press. To the extent that Lorena Hickok now had privileged information, she ignored it. Daily she let the scoops go, and emphasized instead ER's political strengths, determined vision, and amazing stamina.

On 30 October, Hick reported on ER's five-day journey into the center of New York. Hick was with her every mile of the way, and she counted "50 hours on trains since she left." Hick's report of one day during their New York State trip chronicled ER's feats of endurance: She arose "at 5:45, put in the forenoon on a train between Binghamton and Albany and the afternoon on another train between Albany and Boston." She "spent the evening with her husband's secretary [Missy LeHand] whose mother had died that day." She arrived "at the hotel after 11, gave an interview, posed for photographs, ate her dinner, sent off a dozen telegrams, talked on the telephone with the Governor in Albany, and finally got to bed well after 1 A.M."

She is never hurried, apparently never harassed, and is seldom, her secretary says, even slightly irritable.

"She doesn't ever really get cross," the Secretary, Miss Malvina Thompson, who has been with her 10 years, said. "The only thing I notice is that sometimes if she's bothered about something—or perhaps tired—she gets sort of remote. But she always has time to talk to people and listen to them."

The next day, ER drove herself twenty miles through "a misty rain" in a borrowed roadster, having waved aside a "state trooper escort," and took a "brisk walk through a cow pasture." Hick reported that she drove up a little country road beside the Saint Lawrence River, stopped the car, and beckoned Hick: " 'Come along. I want to show you something.' Striding swiftly down through a cow pasture—while the cows stared at her mistrustfully—she led the way to Little Sou Rapids, explaining that here was to be a part of the international water power project," and a canal to connect the Atlantic Ocean with the Great Lakes.

Hick's effort to keep up with ER during one of her country excursions, whether for politics or pleasure, was to become a subtheme in their rapidly unfolding friendship—and in Hick's stories about her. In another column, Hick reported:

Much of the time she walks with a long, swinging stride. She does most of her walking alone. Even when she is wearing high heels it is difficult to keep up with her. Her friends say that at Hyde Park, when she puts on a pair of golf shoes and starts off, it is practically impossible.

She likes to go places alone and hates being recognized. Very often she is not. While she was on the western campaign trip with the Governor a few weeks ago, she spent a whole morning going about Chicago accompanied only by a couple of friends, and not a soul recognized her, although the night before she had ridden in a car behind her husband in one of the biggest parades the loop ever saw.

She is, to use the expression of one of her friends, "a whirlwind." She gets along perfectly on five or six hours' sleep a night and apparently does not know the meaning of the word "fatigue."

During the last weeks of the campaign, the relationship between ER and Hick was transformed from that of a journalist with her subject to an intimate friendship. The very first note from ER to Hick that has survived is dated 26 October 1932. Formally addressed to "Dear Miss Hickok," it is an invitation to "drive down together" to New York. "Will you come up for breakfast at 8:30 anyway." It was signed "Affectionately, Eleanor Roosevelt."

On 30 October, when ER accompanied Missy LeHand to her mother's funeral, Hick traveled with them. As she reported:

> There was only one drawing room available on the train that night, and Mrs. Roosevelt gave that to Missy. She and I found two lower berths in the car outside. Early in the morning the train stopped at a station. . . .
>
> When I had finished dressing . . . , I found Mrs. Roosevelt seated, her berth made up for the day, and set out on Pullman towels on the seat opposite her were cardboard containers filled with coffee and orange juice and some rolls.
>
> She had remembered that there was no diner on the train and had got up in time to get dressed and buy them at the station.
>
> "I thought you'd like some breakfast," she explained.

Hick did not go to the funeral. But ER "looked me up at the restaurant where I was having lunch. She had borrowed an automobile and asked if I'd like to go for a drive." That was when ER took Hick to see the projected Saint Lawrence Seaway. ER commented that she did not "see so many Democratic posters around. . . . Franklin is going to be dreadfully disappointed if he loses this election. For awhile he won't know what to do with himself."

That night, a stormy, rainy night, there was only one drawing room available on their return home.

> All the berths were filled. During the Depression, the railroads ran only as many cars as were needed, and they were usually filled.
>
> To my embarrassment, Mrs. Roosevelt insisted on giving me the

lower berth and taking for herself the long, narrow couch on the other side of the drawing room.

"I'm longer than you are," she said when I protested.

"And," she added with a smile, "not quite so broad!"

It was early, neither of us was sleepy, and so we started talking. It was then that she told me that I could thank Tommy for the fact that she had accepted me and permitted me to follow her about. . . .

"It was hard for me at first. I was brought up by a very strict grandmother, who thought no lady should ever have stories written about her, except in the society columns.

"To be frank with you, I don't like being interviewed. And that applied especially to you. For Franklin used to tease me about you. He'd say: 'You'd better watch out for that Hickok woman. She's smart.' He wasn't criticizing you in any way—he likes you. He was only teasing me."

During that trip home, as heavy rains streamed across the window, ER told Hick her life story. She told of her "odd sort of childhood"; of her school days with Marie Souvestre, "my first taste of freedom. Not that I was at all rebellious. . . . But it did arouse my interest. I wanted to know people—all kinds of people." She told of her work at the Rivington Street Settlement, the early years of her marriage, the nurse she had for all her children—who taught her so much about nursing. ("From her I learned what a lot of fun work could be.") ER also detailed the first years in Albany, when the men would talk and smoke "under the nursery, until finally the smoke got up into the nursery, and I had to move the children. I used to sit and listen by the hour, fascinated. But it never occurred to me to enter into it." She told of the years in Washington, when for four years ER did more entertaining and calling than any other woman in town. And then came the war— "my emancipations and my education." When FDR went to Europe during the summer of 1918, ER sent the children to their grandmother in Hyde Park and lived alone in Washington with one servant. "After that—well, you can see what would happen, can't you? When we first came back to New York in 1921 I was pretty restless. . . ."

ER flew by the postwar years, ending with her entrance into women's politics through the League of Women Voters, "and the rest—I think you know," she concluded.

Then ER "smiled and picked up a book." Rather firmly ending the conversation, she said: "I think I had better get to work on next Monday's History. If the teacher is not well prepared, you know, the children very quickly catch on."

Hick asked if she might use some of what ER told her; "she said softly, 'If you like. I trust you.'"

More than a political interview, that evening on the train was the beginning of the most intimate friendship of their adult years. ER had by then shared her life story with a very select number of friends, each of whom was special to her and occupied a specific place in her heart. To tell of her childhood had become for ER an almost routine prelude to deep affection and friendship. Perhaps, in the telling of her early life, she freed herself to move beyond that constrained emotional place, and into a new relationship. Occasionally, as with Frances Perkins, she told her life story to somebody who for one or another reason did not become close. But until she wrote her autobiography, she never told it casually or to strangers. And those who became her intimate friends understood the trust and the tenderness expected in return. That had been the pattern with Esther Lape and Elizabeth Read, Louis Howe, Marion Dickerman and Nancy Cook, with Earl Miller, and now with Lorena Hickok.

Shortly after their train ride to New York, Hick was given a major scoop by George Akerson, one of her good friends from the Minneapolis *Tribune*, who now handled publicity for the Republican National Committee: ER's Aunt Edith, Uncle Theodore's widow, was to introduce President Hoover that night. Hick was stunned. Edith Roosevelt had never before spoken at any political event. But she had been moved to action when she received congratulatory telegrams regarding the nomination "of her son Franklin." Her appearance that evening "was a big secret," recalled Hick. No other reporter had been told. An extraordinary murmur passed through the crowd as TR's widow, dressed entirely in black, emerged out of more than a decade of seclusion and walked onto the rostrum at Madison Square Garden. "Unforgettably dramatic" as she "stood there before that wildly cheering audience, gesturing with her black-gloved hands," she completely overshadowed President Hoover.

Hick left immediately after Edith Roosevelt's speech to meet ER, who had arranged to pick her up in a taxi near the Garden and take her to a meeting. But Hick had to return to the AP office to write her story. As she got into the cab, she said:

> "What do you suppose your Aunt Edith did tonight?"
> Mrs. Roosevelt looked surprised and shook her head.
> "I can't imagine," she said.
> "Well," I told her, "she introduced Herbert Hoover at Madison Square Garden!"
> "How very interesting," ER said quietly.
> And that was all she said.

ER became more and more reliant on Hick's presence in her life. She welcomed Hick's shrewd advice, comforting directness, and sharp political insights. She was charmed by her pungent and often startling sense of humor, her quick and robust capacity for fun. Hick became a fixture in the Roosevelt family circle, and FDR simply took her presence for granted.

On the night before the election, ER accompanied FDR to a rally in Poughkeepsie that ended toward midnight. After his speech, ER announced that she intended to drive to New York to teach as usual the next morning. FDR objected. It was late, and rainy; the roads were wet and slippery. He was afraid that if she drove alone she might get drowsy, as she sometimes did down those winding and dangerous black-top roads.

Finally, he agreed, on the condition that she "take Hick along to keep you awake." Pleased to be alone with Hick, ER defended and preserved the moment: That night they became aware that other press syndicates had finally hired women to cover ER. As they approached the car, a reporter asked to go along. ER refused. Her blue convertible had room only for two. " 'Can't I ride in the rumble seat,' " she persisted. ER shook her head no and quickly took off, "leaving the woman standing in the parking lot."

Astounded by ER's determined getaway, and her willingness even to seem rude, Hick told ER that she wasn't " 'going to be able to do that sort of thing' " in the future. " 'That girl is furious, and I can't say I blame her.' " ER retorted, " 'She'd only get soaked to the skin. I couldn't crowd her in here with us. It's not a very good night for driving, and I'll need elbow room. And besides what makes you so sure Franklin is going to be elected?' "

~

ER RETURNED TO HYDE PARK AFTER HER MORNING CLASSES in time to vote; then everybody went back down to New York for the campaign party at the Biltmore Hotel, where the returns were monitored by special telegraph, telephone, and radio hookups connected to a big board in the grand ballroom. Before the party, ER hosted a buffet supper for relatives, friends, and several newspaper people at 65th Street.

ER, resplendent in a flowing white chiffon gown, greeted Hick at the door, "and when I came in, she kissed me and said softly: 'It's good to have you around tonight, Hick.' "

That night's party was an ordeal for ER. Hick, who joined the other reporters in the jubilant crowd, occasionally caught a glimpse of ER. "She was smiling and gracious as she greeted people," but whenever she was alone her expression became sober, thoughtful, "a little sad," Hick thought. During her first press conference as the prospective First Lady, she held her head very high. It was a gesture Hick had already learned to suspect. "Through it all," Hick reported, "she kept smiling, but once she looked directly at me. She shook her head, ever so slightly, and the expression in her eyes was miserable." It was a mob scene, and Hick was "reminded of a fox, surrounded by a pack of baying hounds"—including Hick. "But she carried it off as best she could— and that was good enough."

In any case, the election results overshadowed all other realities. A vast majority of the American electorate voted for the man who declared: "Ours must be a party of liberal thought, of planned action, of enlightened international outlook." On 8 November 1932, FDR carried forty-two states. Only Connecticut, Delaware, Maine, New Hampshire, Vermont, and Pennsylvania voted Republican. FDR's unprecedented Democratic victory was enhanced by a congressional sweep. The Senate was now Democratic by 59 to 37, the House of Representatives by 312 to 123.

The day after the election, ER invited Hick to go with her to Todhunter, where she attended ER's current-events class for senior girls. The discussion was informal and relaxed, although quite spirited on such issues as "What makes people commit suicide?" and the "Need for brains and ambition" when in pursuit of a career. The election was not mentioned until the class ended. One student said: "We think it's grand to have the wife of the president for our teacher." But ER protested: "You mustn't think of me that way."

ER was adamant: There was not going to be any "First Lady" after 4 March; there was "just going to be plain, ordinary Mrs. Roosevelt." She refused secret-service protection, and sent all uniformed protectors away whenever they appeared to escort her: "Nobody is going to hurt me. I'm not important enough." And she would not, under any circumstances, consent to "being trailed around that way."

ER told Hick, for publication, that she hated the gossip that went about, stirred by people who claimed to know, that "my ambition for myself drove him on—even that I had some such idea in the back of my mind when I married him. I never wanted to be a President's wife, and I don't want it now. You don't quite believe me, do you? Very likely no one would—except possibly some woman who had had the job." ER was "sincerely glad" for FDR, but as for herself: "Now I shall start to work out my own salvation." She understood the difficulties. "I know what Washington is like. I've lived there. I shall doubtless be criticized. But I can't help it."

Hick, of course, did believe ER's protests. She also shared her misgivings about giving up her own work, work that she loved above all. ER would continue as the editor of a new magazine of advice for mothers called *Babies—Just Babies,* but she announced her intention to discontinue her work at Todhunter:

> I wonder if you have any idea how I hate to do it. I've liked it more than anything else I've ever done. But it's got to go.
>
> For one thing, it might not be fair to the pupils. . . . I realize that my job in the White House will make heavier demands than my job in the Executive Mansion ever made.
>
> I'm going to keep my interest in the school, though. I hope to get up here every two or three weeks and meet and talk with the parents, as I've always done. And perhaps occasionally some of the girls can come down to see me in Washington. . . .*

Until the inauguration, Hick's Associated Press columns on ER were syndicated throughout the United States on a regular basis. ER and Hick fully shared in the creation of ER's new press image. Together they decided on the emphases and the public persona, and co-authored some of the myths that emerged during the campaign of 1932 and were to be repeated forever after. Inevitably, some of the emphases and press accounts were not ER's or Hick's.

Individual newspapers decided which of Hick's columns to use, and which of her words to feature. Some newspapers, including *The New York Times,* chose to delete all the passages in Hick's column on ER's ancestry and childhood that described her wealthy and aristocratic forebears. Hick began with "her great-great-great grandfather, who administered the oath of office to George Washington . . . Chancellor Robert R. Livingston." And then she went three generations back to "another Robert Livingston, founder of one of America's first great families, who held by royal grant from George I of England 163,000 acres of land . . . along the Hudson river between Albany and Poughkeepsie and extending east to the Massachusetts and Connecticut boundaries." And back again "among the Livingston kinsfolk," "Mary

---

* Subsequently, ER worked out a schedule that allowed her to continue teaching at Todhunter, and she retained a close connection with her school, at least until 1936.

Livingston, who went to France as lady-in-waiting to the beautiful young Mary Stuart. . . ."

Instead, many newspapers emphasized only the poor-little-rich-girl aspect of ER's heritage, "an orphan growing up in the home of her mother's people;" and *The New York Times* headlined her "Girlhood Path at Tivoli. . . . Carrying Cane Under Arms to Keep Shoulders Straight."

But, whatever individual newspapers did to Hick's stories, together she and ER agreed on the presentation and created several specific images: the perfect wife, who did everything she did for her husband and children; a woman who was herself unconcerned about politics and whose interests were entirely circumscribed and dictated by her husband's needs and interests. For example, Hick reported that ER "likes to do things for herself. She built a cottage near the furniture factory [at Val-Kill] in order that the children might learn to live without servants. 'The little boys,' she says, 'used to fight Sunday mornings over who was going to make the cocoa.' "

ER was perfectly willing to craft a public image appropriate to the demands of her new position. She was prepared to give up some of the work that most satisfied her. But she was unwilling to be influenced by the kind of criticism that called upon her to dissolve entirely into the background of First-Ladyhood. In February 1933, she directly addressed the growing opposition to her public activities. After 4 March, she would "curtail somewhat her activities." But not because of the criticism. "What some people do not seem to understand is that I am really not doing anything that I haven't done for a long time. It's only Franklin's position that has brought them to the attention of people." In addition to Todhunter, ER would give up her radio programs, which required her to endorse products—programs that were paid for by commercials. She also returned several writing contracts, and announced that she would in the future "make very few speeches." Moreover, she would not lend her "name to anything that might be used for advertising promotion." She supposed she had made some mistakes, "but saw no reason why I should make a fuss about it." And she would continue to write, but not "about politics or Franklin's position. I like to write, and I've done a good deal of it in the last few years," she explained. "It may be true that Franklin's name does help to sell my articles. It is also true that I wrote and sold magazine articles before that element entered in. I've had rejection slips in my day—and I expect to have more. I don't mind them."

~

WHATEVER COMPROMISES ER WAS WILLING TO MAKE REGARD-ing her public life, she was unwilling to give up her friends, and the privacy she needed in order to live the kind of life she had so carefully crafted. There would be no secret service, and no intrusive press detail. Almost immediately after the election, however, ER was made aware of the kind of struggle required if she was to live her life unobserved and unattended.

Within days after the election, ER made a date to dine with Hick at her apartment. She took an early train from Albany on Sunday evening, and to Hick's surprise arrived late "and very much annoyed." A young woman reporter, assigned to cover the First Lady–elect, had been trailing her everywhere: hanging out in front of the executive mansion, waiting for her in train stations, dogging ER's every step. On this particular Sunday, she had waited for ER in the Albany station and followed her onto the train. But the train was crowded, so she waited until ER got off at Grand Central and then cornered her. According to Hick, the following conversation ensued:

> Girl reporter: "Where are you going, Mrs. Roosevelt?"
> Mrs. Roosevelt: "I'm dining with a friend."
> Girl reporter: "Who is your friend?"
> Mrs. Roosevelt: "I'm sorry, but I cannot tell you. It's a purely private and personal engagement."
> Girl reporter: "May I follow you and wait outside?"
> Mrs. Roosevelt, emphatically: "You may not! I told you it's a private, personal dinner engagement. There will be no story about it."
> Girl reporter: "But I *have* to follow you, Mrs. Roosevelt."
> Mrs. Roosevelt, beginning to get really annoyed: "I'm sorry, but you *cannot* follow me. If you insist, I shall spend the rest of the

evening right here in the station. But I am *not* going to be followed—by you or anybody else."

The reporter finally gave up. And ER taxied to Hick's apartment. Hick wondered why ER did not simply confide in her: "It might have satisfied her, and she'd have left you alone." ER took Hick's advice, and reporters generally honored her confidences.

Still, both Hick and ER experienced several wild times when they tried to remain anonymous. The first time Hick met FDR's Aunt Kassie was, for example, a positive ordeal. Invited to 65th Street for lunch, Hick was casually seated next to "an elderly woman" whom ER introduced only as Mrs. Collier, and who was much annoyed at the excessive publicity ER seemed to attract. Hick, "chief perpetrator of the crime," did not confess her identity, but tried to explain that it was "very difficult" for one in ER's position "to avoid publicity."

"Nonsense!" Mrs. Collier exploded. "I have never talked to a newspaper reporter in my life!"

Hick "nearly choked" over her soup, and spent the rest of the lunch "in mortal terror lest, in the general conversation, it might come out that I was [the] reporter."

FDR "roared with laughter" over the incident, and for weeks thereafter repeatedly asked Hick: "Have you seen my Aunt Kassie again? Has she found out about you?"

20. The First Lady's First Friend

FOR YEARS—FOR DECADES, ACTUALLY—NEITHER AUNT Kassie nor anybody else outside the magic circle "found out" about Lorena Hickok. The fact of ER's closest woman friend during the White House years was erased, distorted, and demeaned. Even photographs of intimate family dinners were cropped before publication to delete Hick. When included, she was not identified. More recently, when identified, she was framed by the most insulting stereotypes.

Hateful stereotypes aside, attractiveness—that mysterious chemical element that draws one to another—is after all in the eyes of the beholder. To her detractors, Hick was "without sexual attraction. She was five foot eight but weighed almost two hundred pounds." She smoked cigars, cigarettes, and pipes. She acted and looked like "one of the boys. . . . In any case she was no vamp."

In contrast to the stereotypes that have ridiculed her face and mocked her girth, Hick appealed to women and men. She may have acted and looked like "one of the boys." She was, after all, the only woman in a very jealously guarded male environment. Because of her humor, her professionalism, and her warmth, her colleagues became her lifelong friends. She would have been very lonely if she were not "one of the boys." Instead, she was surrounded by people who not only enjoyed her company but seemed not to mind that for over twenty years she was frequently given the best stories to cover. With them, she smoked, played poker, and drank—mostly bourbon on the rocks. She frequented saloons, enjoyed coffeehouses, and liked to entertain at home, to bake, and to cook.

Hick was fun to be with. Smart and generous, she told a good story; loved to listen to a good story; and was passionate about politics, sports, and music. She was a pro, who played the game to succeed; and she understood the need for costumes. She preferred trousers, flannel shirts, and high work boots, but only wore them in the country. At all other times she dressed for the occasion, and she dressed well. For concerts and the opera, she painted her nails, wore dangling earrings, coiffed her hair (which she generally wore long and pulled back), and applied makeup, especially bright-red coral lipstick—which she wore most of the time. In the office, she rolled up her sleeves to type. But she usually wore long, bright silk scarves to set off her dress or suit when she was out on assignment. She was portly, and frequently dieted. She also wore stockings and girdles—the old-fashioned kind that worked, and hurt. Her eyes were alert, warm, and frequently filled with merriment and mischief, as the most casual glance at photographs taken during the 1920s and 1930s shows. She had a strong, smiling face and was full-breasted; even into the 1950s, pictures of Hick in shorts highlighted truly shapely legs.

Since friendship and love are rarely about straight teeth or bony clavicles, one must pause to ask how it has served history to caricature Lorena Hickok, and why she was for so long disregarded. Like the disappearance of ER's correspondence with Earl Miller, the answer in retrospect seems evident: Today, our generation continues to cringe and turn away from cross-class, cross-generational, or same-sex relationships. In this instance, however, both Eleanor Roosevelt and Lorena Hickok saved their correspondence, although Hickok typed, edited, and then burned the originals of ER's letters between 1932 and 1933 and many more of her own letters over the years. For all the deletions and restraint, the thousands of letters that remain are amorous and specific.

ER repeatedly ended her ten-, twelve-, fifteen-page daily letters with expressions of love and longing. There are few ambiguities in this correspondence, and a letter that was defined as "particularly susceptible to misinterpretation" reads: "I wish I could lie down beside you tonight & take you in my arms."

After a long separation, during which both ER and Hick counted the days until their reunion, Hick noted: "Only eight more days . . . Funny how even the dearest face will fade away in time. Most clearly I remember your eyes, with a kind of teasing smile in them, and the feeling of that soft spot just north-east of the corner of your mouth against my lips. . . ."

The fact is that ER and Hick were not involved in a schoolgirl "smash." They did not meet in a nineteenth-century storybook, or swoon unrequitedly upon a nineteenth-century campus. They were neither saints nor adolescents. Nor were they virgins or mermaids. They were two adult women, in the prime of their lives, committed to working out a relationship under very difficult circumstances. They had each already lived several other lives. They knew the score. They appreciated the risks and the dangers. They had both experienced pain in loving. They never thought it would be easy or smooth. They gave each other pleasure and comfort, trust and love. They touched each other deeply, loved profoundly, and moved on. They sought to avoid gossip. And, for the most part, they succeeded. They wrote to each other exactly what they meant to write. Sigmund Freud notwithstanding: A cigar may not always be a cigar, but the "north-east corner of your mouth against my lips" is always the northeast corner.

The romantic and passionate friendship between ER and Hick was neither idyllic nor perfect. Actually, it was a very bumpy ride. It was simply there—inevitable and undeniable. Alone in a sea of unknown and uncontrollable events, they were drawn to each other. Theirs was a powerful attraction, in the beginning based on work and political interests. ER admired Hick's independence, her single-minded dedication as a journalist. They shared a world-view, and were ardently engaged by the political game.

Hick may have been "one of the boys," but she was no man-hater. Like Eleanor Roosevelt, she was a team player, content to work for and with men—although she consistently promoted the interests of women.

If she was perceived as a lesbian by those who knew her, FDR and Louis Howe nevertheless encouraged and appreciated her company and professional support. ER came to rely upon it.

In the fulfillment of their desire to be with each other, ER and Hick risked publicity, discovery, national scandal. Over the years, for three decades, they created a rare and loving friendship of absolute trust and amazing generosity. Their relationship passed through phases, some more distant than others. There were storms and hurt silences. But there was also laughter, pleasure, and respect.

~

WHO, THEN, WAS THIS WOMAN WHO TOUCHED ER SO PRO-foundly? Self-created and self-defined, Lorena Alice Hickok was the foremost woman reporter in the United States, and one of the great American journalists of either sex. Her words and her work were highly esteemed. Her bylines were bigger, her salary was larger, and her reputation was greater than those of many of her contemporaries. She won awards, and front-page space. She was one of the most popular writers on the syndicate trail—popular especially in all those small towns throughout the country that were so like the ones in which she grew up.

The daughter of a butter-maker, she was born on a dairy farm in East Troy, Wisconsin. Her father, an abusive and violent man, continually searching for work, moved the family to a dusty little corner of South Dakota when she was ten. For the next three years, they lived in a succession of prairie towns, "each a little more forlorn than the last."

Like ER, Hick turned to books and fantasies in order to deal with her childhood situation—which seemed to her "a confusing, kaleidoscopic series of strange neighborhoods, different schools, new teachers." She was always the new girl in town and had to make friends over and over again. For a time she considered herself an "introvert," and sought refuge in an "enchanted" fantasy world where people rarely appeared. "The only fellow-human who ever really gained admittance was my sister Ruby. That was because she was so determined." But there were always horses, dogs, cats, and assorted farm animals. Hick loved animals, and always believed they "could and did talk among themselves." And she knew they loved her no matter how tall she grew, or how "round-shouldered" she became in order to seem shorter. By thirteen, Hick was the tallest in her class and was often "miserable." Still, she knew, "cats and dogs didn't care whether you were pretty or not!" But she was an excellent student who loved the theatre, and music most of all.

The first words of her unpublished autobiographical manuscript, written toward the end of her life, described her connection with music:

> The first thing I remember is light—warm, yellow light, probably shining through a window.
>
> With the light I have a fainter memory of a swaying motion and a soft, humming sound, a kind of formless music. And a feeling of drowsy contentment.
>
> I could not have been more than a year old, perhaps less. . . . I may have been making the music myself. I have been told that I tried to carry a tune before I could talk. Ever since I can remember, through almost every waking hour, music has run through me, somewhere in the back of my throat. Old hymns, dance music, fragments of symphonies and operas, my own improvisations on familiar tunes . . .
>
> I think I was perhaps three when I first experienced ecstasy. As I awoke from my afternoon nap, a breeze played through the branches of a tree outside the window, making the loveliest sound I had ever heard. I can still feel the sharp, almost painful thrill of pleasure that went through me.

Hick's mother hated the continual moves, and was isolated and lonely in a dreadful place called Bowdle, "the dustiest and dreariest" of all the towns, which, Hick thought, "must have fitted to perfection my mother's idea of hell." Raised in southern Wisconsin, she longed for trees, hills, and especially lakes. When she heard that there actually was a lake in a nearby town, she persuaded her husband to rent a team of horses and a surrey for a Sunday picnic at that lake. "Instead of a lake, however, we found only a mud hole filled with rushes and surrounded by a grove of cottonweeds. Sitting there in the surrey, with the reins in her hands, she broke down and cried as though her heart were breaking." She died that September, when Hick was twelve.

But Hick loved the prairie:

> To me those wide, treeless spaces offered the promise of infinite and intoxicating freedom. You could run all the way to the very rim of the world if you wanted to! If I close my eyes, I can still feel the wind on my face and feel again the exhilaration, the sense of physical well-being it used to give me. The pale, tender green of the prairie in spring, with furry lavender crocuses nestling the grass, the deep blue—almost black—of the little ponds and water holes under an April sky, those golden autumns, the sunsets—now and then all my life I've had an acute nostalgia for them.

Long before her mother's death, Hick's father had been abusive. He whipped Hick cruelly, killed her dog, smashed her mother's kitten against the barn "and dashed its brains out." He was in many ways a maniacal brute. All through her childhood until her mother died, Hick wondered "why my mother, who was a grown-up, too, and just as big as my father, let him do the things he did." Hick "learned very early not to look to my mother for protection. . . . At times she tried. . . . After one bad whipping I heard her remonstrating with him—he had beaten me with a stave out of a butter keg, and I had black and blue stripes all over my back and legs. . . ."

Hick was puzzled until much later in life as to why her mother "always wept when he went away on one of his job-hunting trips and was so happy when he came back." From the moment of Hick's first memory of him, she disliked her father. Eventually her dislike grew "into bitter hatred." He vowed "to break my temper. I wasn't afraid of him. I only resented him." As she grew older, "the whippings grew progressively more severe," and Hick always said: " 'You wouldn't dare do this to me if I were as big as you are.' "

After her mother died, Hick managed to send herself to school while working as a "hired-girl" in rooming houses and boarding houses, or as a live-in and unpaid servant girl, or, worst of all, for "an old lady" who needed a temporary cook for a crew of twelve threshers. She was shown "a kitchen on wheels, a kind of miniature caboose" with "a big stove that burned soft coal," was "handed an alarm clock set for 3 a.m.," and was to have the crew fed by five. Hick tried it for three days, but it was impossible:

> I was a squirrel in a sweltering cage, running frantically round and round. . . . Dripping perspiration in clouds of steam and smoke and soot that caked on my skin and smarted in my eyes and nostrils, I struggled along . . . through an agonizing routine of boiling, baking, frying, through bushels of grimy potato peelings, through sliding avalanches of greasy dishes, with never enough soap or hot water, shoving hunk after endless hunk of filthy soft coal into that stove that never got enough. My mistress did not berate me. She only growled and, when I got too far behind, grudgingly gave me a hand.

During those years, she saw her father only sporadically. Once she accidentally saw him on a train when she was fifteen, and he berated her for being "an ungrateful daughter." She left him on the train and never saw him again.

For the rest of her life, Hick's childhood experiences enabled her to understand the needs and wants of people without power, without money or prestige. Though she retained a pious faith in the vast possibilities of "rugged individualism" and never acknowledged the reality of absolute powerlessness, she also believed that everybody sooner or later might need help. Since she herself had survived as a child because she had generous friends, she never refused to help anybody who came to her in need, whether friend or stranger.

Hick had nine jobs in the two years between the ages of fourteen and sixteen. But whenever she managed to stay in one place long enough actually to attend school, she was quickly seen to be a very special student. She won essay contests and was selected to represent Bowdle High School in a region-wide "declamatory contest," in which she had also to sing. Her last job was with eccentric Mrs. O'Malley, "who was held in low esteem by the good women of Bowdle." Married to the town's less respectable saloon-keeper, she wore flamboyant costumes, painted her face, and drank. Hick considered her a seventy-year-old "bird of paradise" who stalked "defiantly about a barnyard populated by little brown hens." She was gentle and kind, paid Hick a good salary, encouraged her to attend school, and made her dresses and hats, blouses and suits, many with laces, ribbons, and other fine trimmings. And she probably saved Hick's life.

Mrs. O'Malley wrote a letter to Hick's favorite relative, her mother's cousin, "Aunt Ella." "I still thought of Aunt Ella as the loveliest person I had ever known, but I doubted if she could take me to live with her." Hick had not seen her since her mother died, three years before; and she had failed to answer Aunt Ella's letters, which soon stopped. But as soon as Aunt Ella received Mrs. O'Malley's message, she sent a check to pay for Hick's railroad fare to Chicago. Hick finally had a home, and was happy with Aunt Ella, who sent her to high school in Battle Creek, Michigan. From there she went to Lawrence College in Wisconsin. But Hick was too old and too independent to be happy in such a sorority-obsessed environment, and quit to begin her career as a reporter.

Over the years, she tried to finish college, and attended the University of Minnesota while working at the Minneapolis *Tribune*. But the more her work absorbed her, the less involved she became with classes. Moreover, the dean of women insisted that she live in a college dormitory the year she became Sunday editor of the Minneapolis *Tribune*. She quit, and never graduated—which had no effect on her career.

Although Hick's rise in journalism was rapid, she was not unique in the Midwest during the first years of the twentieth century: She aspired to be as successful as Edna Ferber, and by 1910 she was on her way. She went from her first job as a $7-a-week cub on the Battle Creek *Journal* to society editor for the Milwaukee *Sentinel* within a year. She was twenty-one. Hick loved Milwaukee. She loved the people she worked with, the operas she attended, the Viennese-style coffeehouse she frequented, and the thrill of having her first byline. In Milwaukee she met divas and politicians, suffragists and feminists.

She delighted a wide audience with her interviews of the remarkable and famous: The great pianist Ignacy Paderewski; Lillian Russell; and Nellie Melba, Britain's premier contribution to grand opera's golden age. (Allegedly, the British were so proud of the prima donna of Covent Garden that they named the ice-cream dessert "peach Melba" for her.)

Hick also wrote an unforgettable account of her attempt to interview Geraldine Farrar, certainly the most temperamental and perhaps the only slender diva of the *fin de siècle*. An American by birth, Farrar began her operatic career in Berlin in 1901. By the time Hick sought her interview, Farrar practically owned the roles of Madame Butterfly and Tosca; and was, for fifty-eight performances, the New York Metropolitan's most enduring Carmen. Hick was intrigued:

> I always did admire prima donnas. . . . Yes, even though I know that genius is capricious. . . . Somebody told me that prima donnas were harder to reach than kings, ladies in harems or murderers about to be hanged.
>
> Now I believe it.
>
> After splashing through exactly 163 puddles of water and plowing through an acre or so of nice, rich mud, most of which clung to my best shoes, I arrived at the private car of the peerless Geraldine.

But the diva would not see Hick, who wore a new suit trimmed in monkey fur for the occasion. Her colleague Abe Altrowitz described the scene: "On the way she was caught in a downpour of rain." As she waited in the foyer, Wiggles, the temperamental diva's frisky pet terrier, began "to chew all the fur from my Sunday suit. He also kissed me— oh, the thrill of it! To be kissed by Geraldine Farrar's dog!" But, the longer she waited, the more unbearable the situation. Her inexpensive suit trimmed with monkey fur began to dry, and to shrink. "And then she sensed an odor and realized that the monkey fur as it dried was giving off a most undesirable scent. . . ." When Hick returned to her office, she "sat down at her typewriter and pounded out a scorcher."

As the city editor started reading the story he exploded with laughter. He laughed long and loud and when he'd finished reading and laughing he told Hick such a crackerjack of a piece hadn't come across the desk since Fido was a pup. The story was printed as written. . . .

Later in the day the city desk telephone rang. The call was for Hick. She picked up the telephone.

At the other end was Miss Farrar's manager.

He said Miss Farrar had enjoyed reading her story and would be very happy to see her between acts at the opera that night.

For answer Hick snapped into the telephone:

"You tell Miss Farrar for me to go to hell!"

And then she banged down the receiver.

What a gal she was!

Hick's personal life in Milwaukee was also momentous—highlighted by her great friendship with another diva, the legendary Ernestine Schumann-Heink. One of the greatest contraltos in history, Schumann-Heink was vastly admired; her "great and dear friend" Johannes Brahms wrote his *Lullaby,* his *Rhapsody,* and his *Sapphische Ode* "most especially for you." When she visited Brahms during his last illness, he said: "I wrote them for you, and now I give them to you. They are yours. . . ." For decades Madame Schumann-Heink rarely gave a concert or cut a record without including Brahms's *Sapphische Ode.* Her triumphant career took her to Bayreuth, Covent Garden, New York's Metropolitan Opera House, and finally into radio and films.

Ernestine Schumann-Heink was married three times, had seven sons, traveled widely, and, according to one biographer, led "a colourful private life." At some point, she met Hick. About that meeting there is only a sentence in the table of contents for Hick's autobiographical proposal: "I begin long friendship with Ernestine Schumann-Heinck." We also know that Schumann-Heinck gave Hick a sapphire ring surrounded by diamond chips to be worn on her little finger. It was that ring that Hick gave to ER in 1933, and which she wore until her death.

Evidently Hick left Schumann-Heink when she left Milwaukee for the Minneapolis *Tribune,* on her twenty-third birthday, 7 March 1917. According to Hick, Tom Dillon, the *Tribune's* editor—whom she called "The Old Man"—taught her "the newspaper business, how to drink, and how to live." Tom Dillon and his wife, Clarissa, called Riss, became two of Hick's closest and lifelong friends. She would always call Minneapolis her home, and remained close with her *Tribune* colleagues throughout her life. After her death, Hick's colleague Abe Altrowitz celebrated her days at the Minneapolis *Tribune:*

> She was endowed with a vast body, beautiful legs and a peaches-and-cream complexion.
>
> When she was pounding out a sob-story (tear-jerker), we'd see tears streaming down her cheeks. When it was a humorous piece, her entire vast body rippled with merriment. And she could write both kinds—and the straight news variety, too—with an excellence few could surpass, then or now.

During the *Tribune* years, Hick lived with Ella (Ellie) Morse, a part-time reporter on the society page. Ellie, petite and physically fragile, was two years older than Hick, and heir to a wheat-futures-and-real-estate fortune. She adored Hick—and always called her "Hickey Doodles." Hick and Ellie lived together for eight years in one of Minneapolis's most elegant residences, where they entertained often and lavishly. For a time, they both took literature classes at the university while working at the *Tribune* at night. But all the while, Hick wrote feature stories that achieved more and more attention. She specialized in murder trials and political scandals; she interviewed Sinclair Lewis and the "rather frowsy Queen of Romania." She became the first woman sports reporter, and won the admiration of all Minnesota's football players. She traveled with them, and played some of the best poker. She was, moreover, loyal. Win or lose, they could count on her for a great story. In 1923, the Associated Press awarded her its best-feature-story-of-the-month award, for an article on President Warren G. Harding's funeral train.

Nobody wanted her to leave the *Tribune* in 1926, when she and Ellie decided that, because of Hick's recently diagnosed diabetes, they would go to San Francisco for a rest, and then maybe to Europe. Hick was thirty-two and had been working endless hours, practically nonstop, since she was fourteen. Ellie urged Hick to rest and write a novel. The 1920s were, after all, a period of new opportunities, new forms of expression, adventure, and travel.

Hick agreed to take a leave for one year. But in San Francisco Ellie met and eloped with a childhood friend, Roy Dickinson. Hick was devastated, although they remained friends and corresponded every week until Ellie's death. Hick could not bear to return to Minneapolis alone, and decided to go to New York City, where she landed a job at the New York *Mirror*. Then, on 8 August 1928, *Variety* announced: "Lorena Hickok, byline sobbie on the *Mirror* is going to the Associated Press." One of the most dazzling feathers in the AP's cap, Hick was assigned the hottest features, the most scintillating beats. In addition to getting the top political stories, in 1932 she was selected to cover the Lindbergh baby kidnapping case.

When ER first met Hick, the reporter had friends, prestige, and money. She was happy, secure, and able to acknowledge frankly that she was one of the best. Tough and competitive, she nevertheless loved to laugh, and could laugh at herself. Most of Hick's friends and colleagues remembered her laugh first: contagious and uncontained, her laughter simply warmed up a room. It was the mark of her personality.

Initially, ER was impressed by her reputation, her dedication to her work, and her discipline. As with Earl Miller, she identified with Hick's triumph over a grim childhood. ER respected Hick; she appreciated her political savvy, and she enjoyed her passion, enthusiasm, and spontaneity. She could trust Hick, who never bothered with duplicity or flattery.

But there was one thing more. Hick was totally loyal to and entirely involved with ER. She was protective and encouraging, and, like Earl Miller, championed ER and promoted her best interests. Unlike Earl Miller, Hick devoted herself exclusively to ER, and for years put even her own professional needs to the side. Subsequently, ER wrote: "Every woman wants to be first to someone sometime in her life & [that] desire is the explanation for many strange things women do. . . ."

For ER, "that desire" was for a time fulfilled by Hick. She wrote Hick during their first days of separation after the inauguration that she enjoyed nobody else's company so much, missed nobody so much. On 7 March 1933, Hick's fortieth birthday, ER wrote: "Hick darling, All day I've thought of you & another birthday I *will* be with you, & yet tonite you sounded so far away & formal. Oh! I want to put my arms around you. I ache to hold you close. Your ring is a great comfort. I look at it and think she does love me, or I wouldn't be wearing it."

ER had never felt loved in this way before. Hick made demands— more demands than ER was prepared to fulfill. Hick was jealous and willful, tempestuous and difficult, intensely emotional, and expressive. With Hick there was no reason to pine and long. That was a new experience for ER; she was no longer the one left lonely. She was wanted, and pursued. It was pleasant and yet frightening. Hick was exciting, rambunctious, uncontrollable. ER never knew what might happen next. Did she mind? Not really, at first.

ER's friends were always amazed that she never told Hick to speak more softly, behave more decorously. It never occurred to her. Esther Lape and her circle considered Hick "a bit rough and tumble," but were delighted and pleased that she made ER happy. ER's other friends either grudgingly accepted or disapproved of Hick. Nancy Cook and Marion Dickerman particularly resented her company and deplored her presence. They never mentioned her in their reminiscences, oral histories, or their interviews. Hick's presence at picnics and around the dining-room table they all shared was simply ignored. Most of ER's friends, both old and new, spoke and wrote for decades as if Hick simply did not exist.

Throughout their lives, their relationship was stormy, unpredictable, and somehow rather grand. The period of passion soared and mellowed, and did not last very long, though longer than either would have predicted. Still, their happiness seemed worth all the trouble. And their friendship ended only with death.

ER learned a lot from Hick. She sought her advice and welcomed her suggestions. It was Hick who recommended that ER hold press conferences restricted to women reporters. At the height of Depression unemployment, ER's decision caused veteran journalist Ishbel Ross to observe: "Never was there such a gift from heaven for the working press." It was Hick who suggested that ER publish the "diary" portion of her daily letters. Every day, ER sent Hick ten-, twenty-page letters filled with hourly details of her workday. Hick said they were wasted on her; the entire nation would be interested in ER's experiences and observations. "My Day," ER's popular daily column, began in 1936 and was syndicated to scores of newspapers throughout the United States.

The most intense phase of their relationship coincided with FDR's election, and ER's first published reference to Hick concerns their first postelection visit to Washington, in January, when ER went to make inaugural preparations and White House living arrangements: "I remember that trip very clearly. I had gone down with Lorena Hickok, who was then a reporter for the Associated Press and assigned to 'cover' me, and had spent the night at the Mayflower Hotel. In the morning we walked down Connecticut Avenue and then parted." As ER walked the remaining steps alone to the White House portico, she "thought of the days when my husband was Assistant Secretary of the Navy and I used to drive by the White House and think how marvelous it must be to live there. Now, I was about to go there to live, and I felt it was anything but marvelous."

According to Hick, they took the midnight train with Louis Howe and Elliott, and went to the Mayflower for breakfast and several meetings. ER's first meeting was with FDR's cousin (Aunt Kassie's son) Warren Delano Robbins, then the State Department's chief of protocol. He arrived with his wife to offer ER a ride to the White House in his State Department car, since she had spurned the White House car Mrs. Hoover had offered. Hick noted that Warren Delano Robbins was aghast when ER announced firmly that she intended to walk to the White House:

"But Eleanor, darling, you can't do that! . . . People will recognize you! You'll be mobbed!"

"Oh, yes, I can. Miss Hickok is walking over with me."

Hick and ER walked down Connecticut Avenue and through Lafayette Park, and crossed Pennsylvania Avenue to the northwest gate to the White House. There Hick waited for ER while she was shown about the house by Ike Hoover, the head usher and resident of the place since the days of William McKinley and TR. ER's visit with First Lady Lou Henry Hoover was brief but cordial. In record time, ER assigned rooms and considered the decorative changes needed to accommodate her large and active sons. She rejoined Hick in less than an hour, pausing for a photographer who snapped her picture as she emerged. ER later inscribed that photograph to Hick: "We were only separated by a few yards dear Hick & I wonder which of us felt most oddly!"

The rest of the day was equally rushed. They had a late lunch with Elliott and Louis Howe, where they discussed assassins and crises. When ER was asked what she would do if an assassin took aim at FDR, she replied: "I'd step in front of him, of course." Elliott thought that a poor idea, since they would both be shot. But ER said, "Oh, but I have a weapon," and exhibited from the interior of her handbag what looked like a bulky fountain pen. "You press this little thing here, and it shoots out tear gas," she explained as she pointed it at a rapidly ducking Elliott. Hick wondered if ER had been looking for assassins throughout the campaign. She had noticed that whenever FDR spoke ER continually turned "her head this way and that, as if she were looking for something." ER explained that she always looked for fire exits. "If a fire had broken out in one of those places, and the crowd started to panic, it would have been almost impossible to get Franklin out. Without his leg braces, two men can pick him up and carry him easily and quickly. But when he is wearing his leg braces, he is so awkward and unwieldy! He can't move himself or be moved quickly."

Later that afternoon, ER met with Ettie (Mrs. Jack) Garner, who asked ER if she might continue to be her husband's secretary when he became vice-president, as she had been for all the years he had been senator, when she had cooked his lunch on an electric grill in his office. ER had replied that she "most certainly" thought it a good idea.

Indeed, the idea inspired ER. On her return to New York, she asked FDR if she could have a "real job and take over some of his mail." It was ER's only attempt to suggest some substantial work beyond the formal requirements of White House hostessing. But FDR only looked at her "quizzically." He reminded her that Missy did his mail, and thought that she might feel that ER "was interfering." It never occurred to ER that she would have far more mail of her own to worry about, and many other tasks as well.

In the beginning, neither ER's role nor her place in the White House was clear. It was up to her to create them—a task made more complex by the emotional realities of her marriage, and the fact that FDR had invited Lucy Mercer Rutherford to the inauguration. He arranged a car for her, and she evidently spent some time in the White House on Inauguration Day. Perhaps she and FDR had some quiet time together when ER and the children attended the various inaugural balls. Perhaps ER knew nothing of the visit; or perhaps that was why it was so important to her to take Hick out to the statue of *Grief* at 7:45 A.M. the day before the inauguration.

To dash secretly about Washington that morning required some planning, and ER told Hick "to meet her with a cab at a side entrance to the Mayflower that opened into a little foyer off the main lobby [where] there was an elevator that went up to the presidential suite. . . . 'There will be Secret Service men there,' she said, 'but I'll tell them you're coming, and I'll try to be just inside the door when you drive up. I don't want to be followed, and that early in the morning I don't think we shall be.'"

ER was there waiting, and "slipped out the entrance" as soon as Hick's cab appeared. She instructed the driver to go out along R Street, to show Hick where they had lived, but there was "a large sign on the lawn: 'Former Residence of Franklin D. Roosevelt.' Hurriedly she told the driver to move on" to Rock Creek Cemetery. ER sat silently during the long drive across Washington, "wrapped up in her own thoughts— and memories."

Once inside the protected sanctuary of the holly grove, ER and Hick sat on the curved stone benches before the statue of *Grief* in silence. Hick pondered ER's mood, and the power of that statue:

> As I looked at it I felt that all the sorrow humanity had ever had to endure was expressed in that face. I could almost feel the hot, stinging unshed tears behind the lowered eyelids. Yet in that expression there was something almost triumphant. There was a woman who had experienced every kind of pain, every kind of suffering . . . and had come out of it serene—and compassionate. Whatever bitter unhappiness, whatever agony of body or soul the viewer might be going through that woman had known. . . .

When ER finally broke the silence, she spoke in hushed tones, "as though she were in church": " 'In the old days, when we lived here, I was much younger and not so very wise. Sometimes I'd be very unhappy and sorry for myself. When I was feeling that way, if I could manage it, I'd come out here, alone, and sit and look at that woman. And I'd always come away somehow feeling better. And stronger. I've been here many, many times.' "

No longer alone, the First Lady–elect, accompanied by her First Friend, contemplated the past, and the monumental challenges of the White House.

That evening, ER telephoned Hick, who had been alone in her room at another hotel, from the presidential suite at the Mayflower: "Franklin is tied up. There's a continuous stream of people coming and going. . . . Jimmy and Louis are with him. The other children are all out, and I'm alone. Would you mind coming over and dining with me?"

Dinner was sent up, but nobody was hungry. Jimmy and Louis Howe brought in the latest reports from around the country. "They were all bad." The United States' credit structure was paralyzed. All that week, in state after state, banks closed and locked their doors. Fear mounted as the savings of millions of Americans—workers, farmers, small-business families—seemed to be locked behind iron gates. The savings of countless others had simply evaporated as eighty-five thousand businesses failed. The national income in the United States had fallen from $81 billion in 1929 to $41 billion in 1932. Over thirteen million Americans were unemployed, more than 25 percent of the entire work force. Great cities began to default on their payrolls, including New York and Chicago. The Federal Reserve Board reported that a quarter of a billion dollars in gold had poured out of the system in the week before FDR's inauguration.

On 2 March, the Federal Reserve reported that during the previous week the amount of money in circulation had risen $732 million and the Treasury gold reserves had declined $226 million. There was a $100-million loss attributed to hoarding. Panic began, and bank runs. By the evening of 3 March, twenty-seven states had limited withdrawals or closed their banks. President Hoover wanted FDR to issue a joint statement with him to end the panic. There were several possibilities: The federal government could guarantee bank deposits; issue bank certificates, or scrip; use the war power emergency act to control withdrawals, by declaring a bank holiday.

All that week, Hoover had made overtures to FDR. But FDR refused to act jointly with the lame-duck president, whose popularity was at an all-time low. FDR pointed out that Hoover could act alone until 4 March, and did not need his cooperation. At 11:30 P.M., with only thirty minutes left to his administration, President Hoover made one last effort to persuade FDR to issue a joint statement. He called FDR on the telephone at the Mayflower. But FDR urged him to do nothing, and allow the governors of each state to close their banks as necessary. As the clock chimed the midnight hour, Hoover told his aides it was all over, there was nothing more they could do.

Then FDR announced his plan: He would close the banks. Hoover never spoke to him again. The icy inaugural drive down Pennsylvania Avenue the next morning was an ordeal of silence and anguish.

During the discussions that preinaugural evening, ER worried: "Anything could happen." "How much can people take without blowing up?" FDR sent in the final version of his inaugural speech before it went to the mimeographers. ER considered it "a good speech, a courageous speech. It has hope in it."

> This is a day of national consecration. . . . This is preeminently
> the time to speak the truth, the whole truth, frankly and boldly.
> Nor need we shrink from honestly facing conditions in our country
> today. This great Nation will endure as it has endured, will revive
> and prosper.
>
> So, first of all, let me assert my firm belief that the only thing
> we have to fear is fear itself—nameless, unreasoning, unjustified
> terror which paralyzes needed efforts to convert retreat into
> advance. . . .

A friend of ER's had given her a copy of Thoreau, which she gave FDR. "Nothing is so much to be feared as fear," Thoreau wrote. FDR had it with him in his room at the Mayflower when he revised his speech.

It was a vigorous speech. It aimed at the unemployed, the hard-working, the frightened and angry citizens who easily agreed that the breakdown of the nation's banking system was caused by the "practices of the unscrupulous money changers." Those men lacked vision. "When there is no vision the people perish." "The money changers have fled far from their high seats in the temple of our civilization. We may now restore the temple to the ancient truths. The measure of the restoration lies in the extent to which we apply social values more noble than mere monetary profit."

FDR called for an end to crude standards of "material wealth," "pride of place and personal profit." There were other values—spiritual, ethical, and creative values—that needed to be nurtured and would ensure more meaningful success: Family farms must be protected; foreclosures must be prevented. Work must be created; unemployment must end. The banking and investment systems must be regulated; a sound national economy must be established.

FDR introduced a new international policy: "I dedicate this Nation to the policy of the good neighbor." Above all, FDR promised bold, strong executive action to move the nation out of its decline, to end despair, and to prevent upheaval. He would ask Congress for broad emergency powers to end the economic chaos, "to wage a war against the emergency, as great as the power that would be given to me if we were in fact invaded by a foreign foe."

Hick had a preview of it all. She was in Washington, after all, on assignment. She had arranged with FDR and Louis Howe to do the first Inaugural Day interview with a First Lady in United States history. That evening, Hick bore witness to the biggest story of her career and simply passed it by: With a single phone call, she could have scooped the bank holiday, or Hoover's call, or any paragraph of FDR's stirring speech. Later, she realized the enormity of her own situation, the change that had occurred at that moment in her life. There "I was, a newspaper reporter, right in the middle of what that night was the biggest story in the world. And I did nothing about it. . . . scoops and my career did not seem important that night, even to me. . . . My suffering, my sense of guilt came later."

Shortly after that pre-inaugural night, Hick confided her dilemma to Louis Howe. But he was hardly comforting: "A reporter," he advised, "should never get too close to the news source." Hick never discussed her situation with anybody else. But she realized: That night, the night before FDR's inauguration, "Lorena Hickok ceased to be a newspaper reporter."

The next day, her long-anticipated interview with ER seemed to Hick something of a disaster. Constrained by the fact of their friendship, her words were confined and she failed to write her customarily fresh and dynamic story. ER described the scene: "Soon after the inauguration ceremonies Lorena Hickok, to whom I had promised an interview, came up to my sitting room." ER was sure that Hick would write "a friendly and discreet story," since "we had become warm friends and I felt that she would always be fair and truthful." ER did not remember what she told Hick, "but I do remember that we were interrupted so often that we finally retired to the bathroom to finish the interview."

Years later, Lillian Rogers Parks, a White House maid, wrote that just how close Lorena Hickok and Mrs. Roosevelt "already were became obvious to some servants on the very day of the inaugural ceremonies. Eleanor and Hicky, as we were soon calling her, spent a lengthy time together in Eleanor's bathroom and came out claiming that was the only place they could find privacy for a press interview." The staff considered it "hardly the kind of thing one would do with an ordinary reporter. Or even with an adult friend."

Such momentary lapses aside, through twelve years in the White House ER and Hick were discreet and self-protective. But that interview and her lapse as a reporter tormented Hick with the specter of her career at an end. Journalism had given Hick pride, prestige, self-respect. Without it, she would be lost. For several months, she continued to work at the AP, assigned to important front-page stories. But increasingly she was torn. She had privileged information she would not use, sources of information she no longer pursued.

ER encouraged her to leave the AP and join her in Washington. She suggested that Hick could do a series of magazine articles, or a book. Or ER would find her work, good and meaningful work. They would be together. Hick did not want to leave the AP, or her colleagues and friends in New York, but she regularly refused assignments that concerned the First Lady. Her position as a journalist became increasingly untenable, and her heart was in Washington with ER.

They wrote daily, and spoke on the telephone. They made plans to see each other regularly. Nothing was simple. ER's long daily letters to Hick began the first evening after the inauguration, on 5 March 1933, when Hick returned to New York, and ER felt quite alone in a completely guest-filled White House:

Hick my dearest—

I cannot go to bed tonight without a word to you. I felt a little as though a part of me was leaving tonight. You have grown so much to be a part of my life that it is empty without you, even though I'm busy every minute.

These are strange days & very odd to me but I'll . . . try to plan pleasant things & count the days between our times together.

To begin my diary, after you left I went to supper taking F Jr and John Mama & Betsy & we were followed by FDR & James just before the boys left. I went to the station with them & left the Secret Service man at home. (1st assertion of independence!) Saw the boys on train. [Massachusetts's Governor Joseph B. Ely, a Smith supporter] took the trouble to come up to me & tell me he thought F's speech was great. Quite a change! Returned, had a short talk with FDR James & Betsy, read Proclamation. Tommy came & we arranged tomorrow's work. At ten Meggie & I took her to the gate & I thought of you & Prinz. [Tommy] seemed very happy & said everyone had had a good time, also that you looked "stunning" dressed up! I then went back and devoted ¾ of an hour talking to Mama, then listened to FDR broadcast, sorted mail & am now preparing for bed. So endeth my first Sunday.

I'll call you tomorrow night. . . .

Oh! darling. I hope on the whole you will be happier for my friendship. I felt I had brought you so much discomfort and hardship today & almost more heartache than you could bear & I don't want to make you unhappy—All my love I shall be saying to you over thought waves in a few minutes

> *Good night my dear one*
> *Angels guard thee*
> *God protect thee*
> *My love enfold thee*
> *All the night through*
>   Always yours
>   ER

Discomfort. Hardship. Heartache. ER and Hick struggled to work out the boundaries and limits of their friendship in the uncongenial environment of the White House. After all, theirs was not an equal situation. ER had, in addition to position and authority, all the privileges of marriage and family. She was a mother and a grandmother. They lived on different levels of emotional security, and Hick's affections were more vulnerable. Although both ER and Hick denied it for many months, the reality of the White House changed everything. It was a very public place, and ER had personal, public, and social obligations to perform.

~

ER PREPARED FOR HER NEW LIFE IN WASHINGTON WITH A determination that masked her sense of dread. It had been for her a town filled with bitter memories. Now she was expected to preside over its most formal events, adhere to its rigid customs, celebrate its ongoing traditions. At the height of the Depression, she was expected to please the cliff-dwellers, those rare birds who lived permanently in the big houses with their fossilized views and commitment to a society she had long since abandoned. She was expected to give up her teaching, her editorial position—indeed, all her public works—and become the nation's First Wife. It seemed unbearable. In fact, it was impossible.

ER felt a need to fortify herself. Between the election and the inauguration, she began work on two books, which enabled her to face her new position with a new freedom. The first was a tribute to her father: *Hunting Big Game in the 'Eighties: The Letters of Elliott Roosevelt, Sportsman.* The second was an assessment of her understanding of the role of women in public life, and a rallying call to political activism:

It's Up to the Women! In that book, ER reached out to the women of America to join her in a crusade for change and decency.

Within months, ER involved most of America in that crusade. She wrote articles, gave interviews and radio talks, and dashed about the country "here, there, and everywhere, literally from the depths of the earth to the heights of the clouds," on behalf of that crusade. At first her detractors were many, and veteran journalists like Rita S. Halle considered ER's omnipresence "evidence of a ruthless craving for personal publicity." Halle, like other critics, gradually experienced a "complete change of heart."

ER's performance during a September 1933 conference "to plan ways and means of helping the needy . . . through the coming winter" changed Halle's mind. The First Lady presided over the dinner meeting and "made the most heart-tearing speech" Halle had ever heard. It seemed unrehearsed, and unprepared:

> Perhaps it was really as it seemed, the spontaneous outpouring of her heart, for she used no notes. . . . Her audience was exhausted by a long, hot, busy day. Several others had spoken before her. Then Mrs. Roosevelt rose. Despite a lithe, graceful figure, she is not beautiful. She does not charm by her personal appearance. Yet, as she spoke, the wearied audience uncurved its collective spine until, all over the large room, men and women were sitting forward on their chairs in intent response to the magnetism of her simple sincerity.

ER "spoke of the needs of the common people, needs that could not be delayed for the unwinding of red tape, needs that she had seen with her own eyes, touched with the antennae of her own heart." Somebody had told ER that "she was too sentimental about human want . . . poor people did not suffer as she would . . . because they were used to less." And she declared:

> When I heard that, I could not but think of the mother I had seen . . . whose child had just died. He had died because he had slept on a cold, wet bed. He had slept on that kind of bed because there

were no panes in the windows and the rain came in. They lived in that sort of a place because a few days before they had been evicted from the home they could no longer keep, with the father out of work. When the Sheriff had come to evict them, she had pleaded with him to let them stay until her baby was better. But he had replied: "I ain't here to nurse your goddam kids! . . . I'm here to put you out." And he did. And the baby died. Yet people say that the poor do not suffer. People who say that just don't think and don't know. . . .

Halle reported that after that speech, "even at the hard-boiled press table there was an emotional and spiritual response such as I have never before witnessed at a public gathering." And Halle herself left the meeting "profoundly stirred." She heard the comments of others as well, and understood the full dimensions of Eleanor Roosevelt's commitment: Despite all criticism, she "had the courage to be herself and to do the things which seems right to her." As one Gloucester fisherman was heard to say: "She ain't dressed up, and she ain't scared to talk!"

The White House had never been used as a platform from which the First Wife expressed bold, dissenting political ideas. But Eleanor Roosevelt was to transform the position of First Lady as her sense of responsibility and political urgency continually grew. Throughout the White House years, ER juggled her public responsibilities, her ever-increasing political activities, and her complicated private life.

Notes

In the notes I refer to the Franklin Delano Roosevelt Library in Hyde Park, New York, as FDRL; Eleanor Roosevelt's memoir *This Is My Story* as *TIMS*; and Elliott Roosevelt's edition of *FDR: His Personal Letters*, 4 vols., as *Letters*.

Introduction

1–2 *"Her very presence":* The quotations are from various people around the United States—students and friends, members of ER's extended family, and critics who prefer to remain anonymous.

An encounter with Eleanor Roosevelt remains one of the most vivid experiences in the lives of many people. Her friends, the general public, relatives, members of the press, people who met her casually or only once have stories to tell. During the decade I researched this book, and wherever I spoke about my research, interested people have given me their memories, their version of Eleanor Roosevelt.

For the quotations above or in the forthcoming Volume Two of this biography, I am particularly grateful to Jane Marcus, who sent me Eleanor Roosevelt jokes, and a sense that every woman in Boston and Cambridge of a certain age and disposition modeled herself on Eleanor Roosevelt; Audre Lorde, whose mother went to business, and managed money, and "carried herself regally, straight and high, and wore Eleanor Roosevelt hats. Eleanor Roosevelt was the only visible positive image for women that existed. Did you ever see Mary McCleod Bethune in the [New York] Daily News?"; and Robin Morgan, Arthur Blaustein, Carolyn Heilbrun, Connie Murray, Marion Harmon, Estelle Linzer, people who chose to remain anonymous, and people whose names are lost, especially the woman ER helped onto the Fifth Avenue bus, who told me the story at the *Darlinghissima* book party.

3 *Many judge her naïve:* Some of those who dismissed Eleanor Roosevelt as stupid, silly, and naïve turned out to be political women, or daughters of political women, whom ER specifically opposed. In 1985, Elizabeth Thompson (Betty) Babcock (vaguely related to ER through her grandmother, Angelica Livingston Hoyt—Mrs. William Dare Morgan) told me that her mother and her aunts always liked ER but considered her gullible and usable. Among the leading suffragists and reformers of Dutchess County,

Betty Babcock's mother, Geraldine Livingston Morgan Thompson, and her aunts, Margaret Lewis Morgan Norrie and Ruth Morgan, were allied during the early years of the League of Women Voters with ER's enemies. Indeed, Margaret Norrie and Mary Garrett Hay were the leaders of the group ER opposed. ER instead supported the women who were to become her closest friends: Esther Lape, Elizabeth Read, and Narcissa Vanderlip;. Although ER admired Margaret Norrie's progressive campaign in behalf of the Sheppard-Towner Act and other causes to protect women and children, and subsequently worked frequently with peace activist Ruth Morgan, they were during the 1920s rivals for power, and represented opposing factions. If Geraldine Thompson and her sisters thought ER naïve because her actions benefited Lape and Vanderlip, it was in part because they did not know the intensity of ER's primary loyalties—or her willingness to play rough political games.

3 *vast FBI file:* Eleanor Roosevelt's FBI file is now open, as a result of the Freedom of Information Act. It consists of more than 3,000 pages, and constitutes a running record of her work in behalf of dignity, decency, and justice, with an emphasis on her opposition to segregation and lynching; fascism in Europe; her support for civil rights, workers' rights, and unionism; human rights, international peace, and a sane nuclear policy.

5 *associate with spirituality:* As I contemplated ER's journey in terms of her spirituality (see Volume Two), I benefited from conversations with Rabbi Marshall Meyer, Honor Moore, Shula Konig, and Dorothy Norman, who began her memoir, *Encounters*, with the words of Rainer Maria Rilke: "Religion is something infinitely simple, ingenuous. . . . It is a direction of the heart."

5 *working in politics:* "Good Advice from Mrs. Roosevelt," *Democratic Digest*, July 1936, p. 3.

6 *her last book:* ER, *Tomorrow Is Now* (Harper & Row, 1963); see esp. ch. 9.

8 *"Learning and living":* ER, *You Learn by Living* (Harper & Brothers, 1960), p. 3.

8–9 *these new feminists:* Esther Lape to Anna Roosevelt Halsted, n.d. [1971], Esther Lape Papers, FDRL.

9 *"a . . . poor teacher":* ER, *This Is My Story* (Garden City Publishing, 1937), pp. 108–9 (hereafter *TIMS*). ER continued insistently to minimize her influence and power in *This I Remember* (Harper & Brothers, 1948) and *On My Own* (Harper & Brothers, 1958).

10 *"world . . . split open":* Muriel Rukeyser, "Käthe Kollwitz," from *The Speed of Darkness* (1968), in *The Collected Poems of Muriel Rukeyser* (McGraw-Hill, 1978), pp. 479–84. See Louise Bernikow, ed., *The World Split Open: Four Centuries of Women Poets in England and America, 1552–1950* (Vintage, 1974).

10 *caters to her own presentation:* See Joseph P. Lash, *Eleanor and Franklin* (W. W. Norton, 1971), and *The Years Alone* (W. W. Norton, 1972).

10 *"tyrannies and servilities":* Virginia Woolf, *Three Guineas* (Harcourt, Brace & Co., 1966 [1938]), p. 142.

11 *asexual spinsters:* See Blanche Wiesen Cook (hereafter BWC), "Female Support Networks and Political Activism: Lillian Wald, Crystal Eastman, and Emma Goldman," *Chrysalis*, Autumn 1977, reprinted in Linda Kerber and Jane De Hart, eds., *Women's America: Refocusing the Past* (Oxford University Press, 1987, 1990).

12 *Born in 1884:* For the continued imprisonment of ER in a Victorian "cage," see William H. Chafe, "Biographical Sketch," in Joan Hoff-Wilson and Marjorie Lightman, *Without Precedent: The Life and Career of Eleanor Roosevelt* (Indiana University Press, 1984), p. 18. For alternative understandings, see especially Ethel Spector Person, *Dreams* *of Love and Fateful Encounters: The Power of Romantic Passion* (W. W. Norton, 1988), p. 20 ("Love is an act of the imagination. For some of us it will be the great creative triumph of our lives"); Carroll Smith-Rosenberg, *Disorderly Conduct: Visions of Gender in Victorian America* (Alfred A. Knopf, 1985); and Carolyn Heilbrun, *Writing a Woman's Life* (W. W. Norton, 1988).

Eleanor Roosevelt wrote frequently and with clarity about love: "It takes courage to love, but pain through love is the purifying fire which those who live generously know. We all know people who are so much afraid of pain that they shut themselves up like clams in a shell and, giving out nothing, receive nothing and therefore shrink until life is a mere living death." ("My Day," 1 April 1939.)

ER also believed that "women know not only what men know, but much that men will never know. For, how many men really know the heart and soul of a woman?" ("My Day," 6 March 1937).

15 *"subject is highly controversial":* Virginia Woolf, *A Room of One's Own* (Harcourt, Brace & World, 1957 [1929]), p. 4.

15–16 *In February 1942:* ER to Fannie Hurst, Hurst Papers, University of Texas at Austin.

17 *Eleanor Roosevelt devoted her life:* See A. Glenn Mowrer, *The United States, The United Nations, and Human Rights: The Eleanor Roosevelt and Jimmy Carter Eras* (Greenwood, 1979); BWC, "Eleanor Roosevelt and Human Rights: The Battle for Peace and Planetary Decency," in *Women and American Foreign Policy*, ed. Edward Crapol (Greenwood, 1987); and BWC, " 'Turn Toward Peace': ER and Foreign Affairs," in Hoff-Wilson and Lightman, *Without Precedent*.

17 *"consciences grow so tender":* ER, "The Importance of Background Knowledge in Building for the Future," *Annals of the American Academy*, July 1946, pp. 9–12.

18 *"to save the U.S. from Eleanor Roosevelt":* Eisenhower on ER in *The Diary of James Hagerty*, ed. Robert Ferrell (Indiana University Press, 1983), 11 Jan. 1954, p. 6.

18 *"Where . . . do . . . human rights begin":* ER's 1958 speech, "Challenges in a Changing World," ER Papers, Box 3058, FDRL.

19 *"wonderful to feel free":* ER to reporters as she left for London, 3 Jan. 1946, quoted in Lash, *A World of Love: Eleanor Roosevelt and Her Friends, 1943–1962* (Doubleday, 1984), p. 209.

19 *"never turn one's back":* ER, *Tomorrow Is Now* (Harper & Row, 1963); see especially "The Individual and the Revolution," pp. 119–30.

19 *TV commercials:* See Thomas L. Stix, "Mrs. Roosevelt Does a TV Commercial," *Harper's*, Nov. 1963, pp. 104–6; and Abram L. Sachar, *A Host at Last: Chancellor of Brandeis University* (Atlantic–Little, Brown, 1976), passim for ER at Brandeis. I am grateful to Eleanor Pram for this reference.

19–20 *needs of this planet:* "My Day," 14 Sept. 1962.

20 *"honor the word* free*":* ER, *Tomorrow Is Now*, p. 138.

I. Ancestry and Heritage

21 *"My mother":* All quotations from Eleanor Roosevelt in this section are from *This Is My Story* (Garden City Publishing, 1937), pp. 1–5ff. See also *The Autobiography of Eleanor Roosevelt*, a one-volume compendium, recently reprinted (Harper & Row, 1958, 1978; G. K. Hall, 1984, with a new introduction by John Roosevelt Boettiger).

According to Virginia Woolf, "We think back through our mothers if we are women" (*A Room of One's Own* [Harcourt, Brace & World, 1929 (1957)], p. 79). See Jane Marcus, "Thinking Back Through Our Mothers," in *New Feminist Essays on Virginia*

Woolf, ed. Jane Marcus (University of Nebraska Press, 1981), pp. 1–30; and Jane Marcus, *Art and Anger* (published for Miami University by the Ohio State University Press, 1988).

21–22 *"maternal grandmother:"* Family materials relating to the Halls, Livingstons, and Ludlows are in Eleanor Roosevelt Family Papers at the FDRL. Lorena Hickok's interview with Eleanor Roosevelt shortly after the election of 1932 took ER's Livingston connection all the way back to Mary Livingston, "who went to France as Lady-in-Waiting to the beautiful young [Queen] Mary Stuart." (AP wire, Dec. 1932, Lorena Hickok Papers, FDRL.)

22 *after the Civil War:* For Ward McAllister in the context of Knickerbocker Society, see Cleveland Amory, *Who Killed Society?* (Harper & Brothers, 1960); for Sarah Van Brugh Livingston (Mrs. John Jay), pp. 114–15.

For issues of society in extended context, see G. William Domhoff, *Who Rules America?* (Prentice Hall, 1967), and *The Higher Circles: The Governing Class in America* (Vintage, 1971); E. Digby Baltzell, *The Protestant Establishment: Aristocracy & Caste in America* (Vintage, 1966); and Stephen Birmingham, who wrote: "Roosevelts always were and always will be Real Society" (*The Right People: A Portrait of the American Social Establishment* [Dell, 1958], p. 10).

23 *"My father":* ER on her father's democratic impulses, *Autobiography of ER*, pp. 4–5.

ER emphasized her vision of her father's egalitarianism in several of her writings. When she edited her father's letters for publication in 1933, she prefaced, for example, a letter of congratulations on her birth from one of Elliott's servants, Harry Hewitt, his horse trainer at the Meadow Brook Club, by explaining: "I include the following letter because it shows the sympathy which existed between Elliott and many different types of people. He loved people for the fineness that was in them and his friends might be newsboys or millionaires. Their occupations, their possessions, meant nothing to him, only they themselves counted." (ER, *Hunting Big Game in the 'Eighties* [Charles Scribner's Sons, 1933], 15 Oct. 1884, pp. 157–58.)

23–24 *a religious zealot:* For Valentine Hall's business and theological interests, see Eleanor Roosevelt Family Papers, FDRL; and Joseph P. Lash, *Eleanor and Franklin* (W. W. Norton, 1971), p. 15.

24 *Oak Terrace:* I am grateful to Karen Greenberg for a tour of Oak Terrace at Tivoli, and nearby environs.

25 *"pining for excitement":* Correspondence between Elliott Roosevelt and Anna Livingston Ludlow Hall are in Eleanor Roosevelt Family Papers, Box 1, FDRL. Elliott Roosevelt's writings are in Box 5, FDRL, and in the Roosevelt Family Papers in the Houghton Library at Harvard University (hereafter Houghton).

25–26 *Oyster Bay branch:* For Roosevelt family background I have relied upon Allen Churchill, *The Roosevelts: American Aristocrats* (Harper & Row, 1965); Nathan Miller, *The Roosevelt Chronicles* (Doubleday, 1979); Lash, *Eleanor and Franklin*; and especially David McCullough, *Mornings on Horseback* (Simon & Schuster, Touchstone, 1981).

27 *Cobb County, Georgia:* For the removal of the Creek, Cherokee, and other Indians from Georgia lands and its impact on American life, see Angie Debo, *The Road to Disappearance* (University of Oklahoma Press, 1941); BWC, "In Pursuit of Property: The Dispossession of the American Indian," in BWC et al., *Past-Imperfect: Alternative Essays in United States History*, vol. 1 (Alfred A. Knopf, 1973), pp. 195–204; Michael Paul Rogin, *Fathers & Children: Andrew Jackson and the Subjugation of the American Indian* (Alfred A. Knopf, 1975), esp. ch. seven; Richard Drinnon, *Facing West: The Metaphysics of Indian-Hating and Empire-Building* (New American Library, Meridian, 1980); and Dee Brown, *Bury My Heart at Wounded Knee* (Holt, Rinehart & Winston, 1970).

28 *At Bulloch Hall:* Clarence Martin, *The History of Bulloch Hall and Roswell, Georgia* (Historic Roswell, Inc., 1973). I am grateful to my colleague Howard Umansky for this reference.

I am also grateful to Darden Asbury Pyron of Florida International University, for sending me the manuscript of his biography of Margaret Mitchell, *Southern Daughter* (Oxford University Press, 1991); and several out-takes, including his description of Margaret Mitchell's interview with the last surviving bridesmaid in the Bulloch-Roosevelt wedding party at Bulloch Hall. Mrs. William Baker particularly emphasized the vast quantities of food served: There was baked ham, "shaved so thin it curled like a lady's hair," chicken and turkey and roasted meats, and all manner of sweets; icing parties preceded the feast for days so the cakes would be pretty. (Peggy Mitchell, "Bridesmaid of 87 Recalls Mittie Roosevelt's Wedding," 10 June 1923; and "Across Covered Bridge to Bulloch Hall," 20 July 1924; Darden Pyron to BWC, with notes, 3 Sept. 1991.

28 *"little black shadow":* For the story of Daniel Elliott's murder of a slave child, see McCullough, *Mornings on Horseback,* p. 45.

28–29 *Civil War was devastating:* The descriptions of Civil War tensions within the Roosevelt-Bulloch hearth are derived from McCullough, *Mornings on Horseback*; and Lilian Rixey, *Bamie: Theodore Roosevelt's Remarkable Sister* (David McKay, 1963), pp. 10–12.

29 *the famous* Alabama *raider:* Built and outfitted in England, the *Alabama* destroyed fifty-eight commercial vessels during its two years at sea. When it was finally torpedoed off Cherbourg, the crew, including Irvine Bulloch, were rescued by a British ship. On 10 Sept. 1863, abolitionist Senator Charles Sumner of Massachusetts, chair of the Senate Foreign Relations Committee, vowed revenge on Britain and France for their diplomatic support of the Confederacy. In a monumental four-hour speech, Sumner sneered at Queen Victoria, that "virtuous lady," who embraced the South, civilization's last "bordello" of slavery, and served to extend the Civil War for years.

Coincidentally, Senator Charles Sumner pressed the *Alabama* claims just as the Roosevelts arrived in England in 1871 for their first European family tour. The demands were front-page news. Sumner wanted $100 million from Britain for its perfidy; the British press clamored for war to protect its version of neutrality and freedom of the seas. Ultimately the Treaty of Washington demilitarized the U.S.-Canadian border; the Crown apologized; the crisis passed. But the turmoil meant little to the Roosevelt children, who gloried in the heroism and of their Confederate relations.

For the Bullochs' connection to the *Alabama,* see McCullough, *Mornings on Horseback*, pp. 44, 64, 73–76; for Charles Sumner's agitation against England, and the diplomatic negotiations involved—all of which were referred to as the *Alabama* Claims, see David Herbert Donald, *Charles Sumner and the Rights of Man* (Alfred A. Knopf, 1970); and Adrian Cook, *The Alabama Claims: American Politics and Anglo-American Relations, 1865–1872* (Cornell University Press, 1975).

29–30 *hired a substitute:* Although there is some disagreement about what contribution Theodore Roosevelt, Sr., actually made in behalf of the Union effort, he was away for months at a time during a two-year period. He is reported to have persuaded Abraham Lincoln to adopt a salary allotment plan to protect the pay sent to troops in the field so that their families, and not gamblers or gangsters, received their pay. Invited to Washington by his friend John Hay, TR was associated with the U.S. Sanitary Commission, precursor of the Red Cross.

According to Jeanie Attie's work on the U.S. Sanitary Commission, TR's name appears as an associate member of the Commission after March 1864. Jane Turner Censer, ed., *The Papers of Frederick Law Olmsted* (vol. 4): *Defending the Union: The Civil War and the U.S. Sanitary Commission, 1861–1863* (The Johns Hopkins University Press, 1986), credits the idea for the family allotment plan to Olmsted, who lobbied Congress and the War Department for a "system that would allow soldiers to forward their military pay to their families" (p. 7). (Attie to author, private conversation, and letter, 28 Nov. 1990.)

29–30 *New York City draft riots:* One result of the conscription law during the Civil War, whereby the rich hired the poor, was the violent New York City draft riots of 1863. See Adrian Cook, *The Armies of the Streets: The New York City Draft Riots of 1863* (University of Kentucky Press, 1974).

30 *fanatic about cleanliness:* Bamie described to Alice Roosevelt Longworth Mittie's fastidious bathing habits and horror of dirt during and after the Civil War. See Alice Roosevelt Longworth, *Crowded Hours* (Charles Scribner's Sons, 1933), p. 20; Rixey, *Bamie*; and McCullough, *Mornings on Horseback*.

31 *"beggars came round":* Theodore Roosevelt, *Diaries of Boyhood and Youth* (Charles Scribner's Sons, 1928), 14 Dec. 1869, pp. 122–23.

31 *"Father tossed pennies":* Ibid., 4 Jan. 1870, pp. 155–56. See also 18 Dec. 1869: "The beggars are becoming worse . . ." (pp. 131–32). (I have corrected TR's spelling.)

32 *enjoyed . . . bodybuilding:* McCullough, *Mornings on Horseback*, p. 35.

32 *"As athletes we are about equal":* Quoted in Edmund Morris, *The Rise of Theodore Roosevelt* (Coward, McCann & Geoghegan, 1979), p. 116. The competitive theme between Elliott and Theodore, highlighted by Morris, has been especially emphasized by Howard Umansky, whose unpublished conference paper, "Mourning Patterns of Theodore Roosevelt," is compelling and provocative.

32 *much-treasured overcoat:* On Elliott's gift of his new overcoat, see McCullough, *Mornings on Horseback*, p. 35, and ER, *Hunting Big Game*, pp. viii–x.

Eleanor Roosevelt edited and published her father's letters shortly after her husband's election to the presidency, to keep Elliott Roosevelt's memory alive for her own children and grandchildren: "They will read much in many books of their uncles and their aunts . . . , but no less important in our daily lives are the things and the people who touch us only personally." "He was the one great love of my life as a child," she wrote; and she considered his outstanding characteristic the "generosity [that] actuated him. . . . With him his heart always dominated." (Pp. viii–x.)

Eleanor Roosevelt seems to repeat for purposes of historical memory the tones of competition between the brothers. Referring to her father's first years on the Texas frontier, she wrote: "These early camping and shooting experiences added to the love of all sport which seems to have been inborn in my father." Years later a friend who lived "on a ranch near Uncle Ted's in the bad lands of the Dakotas told me she remembered my father well and the surprise he occasioned among the cowboys by his shooting and riding. It seemed to be natural to him, whereas Uncle Ted acquired his skill through persistence and against great odds, for he was delicate as a boy and shortsighted all his life." (P. 33.)

32 *spectacles and his gun:* McCullough, *Mornings on Horseback*, p. 118, 120, 124.

For TR's descriptions of his "great enjoyment from the shooting," see letters to Aunt Annie Bulloch, 26 Jan. 1873; Henry Davis Minot, 11 July 1877; and especially to his sister Anna ("Darling Bysie") Roosevelt, 20 Sept. 1884, concerning the big game he bagged in Wyoming, which eclipsed birds forever: "I came out after two weeks, during which time I killed three grizzly bear, six elk . . . and as many deer, grouse and trout as we needed. . . . I was more anxious for the quality than the quantity. . . . I have now a dozen good heads for the hall." (Elting, Morison et al., eds., *The Letters of Theodore Roosevelt*, vol. 1 (Harvard University Press, 1951).

33 *"What will I become":* Elliott to his father, 19 Sept. 1873. Correspondence in Houghton; and quoted in McCullough, *Mornings on Horseback*, pp. 144–46.

34 *"It came from overexcitement":* TR, Sr., to Mittie Bulloch Roosevelt, 9 Nov. 1874, and 14 Nov. 1874. Ibid.

34 *"afraid to leave [Elliott]":* TR to Teedie, 23 Nov. 1874. Ibid.

34 *"funny, my illness":* Elliott to Teedie, 22 Nov. 1874. Ibid.

34–35 *Saint Paul's School:* Elliott's letters from Saint Paul's were "homesick and unhappy." Although he fought "against it," his attacks left him nervous. "But I am all well now so don't worry," he wrote his father. "You told me to write you everything or I would not bother you with this, but you want to know all about me don't you? . . . Don't forget *me* please and write *often.*" (ER, *Hunting Big Game*, 1 Oct. 1875, pp. 10–12.)

35 *"brother came up":* Quoted in McCullough, *Mornings on Horseback*, p. 147.

35 *sent off to Texas:* Elliott's letters to his mother, "Dear little Muz," and "My Dear Father," from Houston and Fort McKavett, 8 Jan.–22 Feb. 1876, in ER, *Hunting Big Game*, pp. 15–29; and McCullough, *Mornings on Horseback*, p. 148. Elliott's Texas notebooks, filled with pen-and-ink drawings, stories, and verse, several of which include references to himself as a hero and a woman, are in the FDRL.

35 *"the great Southern herds":* Theodore Roosevelt's dedication is in *Hunting Trips of a Ranchman (Works*, vol. 1 [Charles Scribner's Sons, 1926]). For the slaughter of the great herds, see ibid., p. 192; see also p. 459.

36 *"curious habits":* Cecil Spring-Rice quoted in Sylvia Jukes Morris, *Edith Kermit Roosevelt: Portrait of a First Lady* (Coward, McCann & Geoghegan, 1980), p. 136.

36 *"avoided . . . the New York fellows":* TR to Bamie, 15 Oct. 1876, quoted in McCullough, *Mornings on Horseback*, p. 165.

36 *"Elliott gave unstintedly":* Corinne Roosevelt Robinson, *My Brother Theodore Roosevelt* (Charles Scribner's Sons, 1921), p. 104.

36 *Afterward, Elliott agonized:* For Elliott's anguish over Theodore's absence during their father's last hours, Umansky, "Mourning Patterns." Umansky's emphasis on the fact that Theodore was not called by Elliott, who had promised to do so, encourages speculation on the path of their relationship from that point forward.

36 *"Tell Teedie and Ellie":* On 20 July 1873, after visiting the site of his last enthusiasm, the Museum of Natural History, he wrote his wife: "I think without egotism this really would never have been carried through without my aid. Three things that I can recall with pride are my connection with this [museum], the 18th Street Lodging House, and the Orthopaedic Dispensary. . . . Tell Teedie and Ellie. . . ." (TR to Mittie, 20 July 1873, quoted in Umansky, "Mourning Patterns," p. 25.)

37 *"ruled the world":* Corinne to Douglas Robinson, 18 March 1881, quoted in McCullough, *Mornings on Horseback*, p. 30.

The belief that Anna Roosevelt Cowles, Aunt Bye, would have been a great leader continued for generations. In 1953, Nicholas Roosevelt wrote: "Had she been a man in seventeenth-century Europe it would be easy to imagine her as a successful and highly capable minister of state or perhaps a cardinal, unquenchable in zeal and effective in guile. She charmed all by her wit and astonished them by the wide scope of her knowledge of men and affairs and by the acuteness of her intellect. In many ways hers was the best mind in the family, and her personality one of the most dominant and fascinating." (Nicholas Roosevelt, *A Front Row Seat* [University of Oklahoma Press, 1953], p. 33.)

Although the Roosevelt women are as fascinating as their brothers, they have been neglected by scholars. We await the new work by Betty Boyd Caroli, who is now researching all the Roosevelt women.

2. Elliott and Anna

38 *"secure golden world":* Lash, *Eleanor and Franklin*, p. 25.

39 *left standing:* Although the details of Eleanor's abandonment at the Knickerbocker Club have become hazy with time, she evidently waited all day, and presumably spent part of the time walking about with the dogs and waiting under the canopy. ER wrote about being left "in the dog room" of the Knickerbocker Club at the age of six in the last article she wrote for her monthly column in *McCall's*. Called "I Remember Hyde Park," it was published in Feb. 1963, several months after her death (pp. 71–73, 162). See also Lash, *Eleanor and Franklin*, pp. 51–52.

39 *a splendid jaunt:* TR to Anna ("Darling Bysie"), 22 Aug. 1880, Houghton.

40 *"Elliott revels":* TR to Corinne ("Darling Pussie"), 12 Sept. 1880, in *Letters of TR*, ed. Morison, vol. 1, p. 46.

40 *serious heart trouble:* McCullough, *Mornings on Horseback*, p. 229.

40 *elephants and tigers:* Ibid.

40–41 *Sara Delano and James Roosevelt:* See ibid, p. 226.

41 *Elliot began his journey:* For Elliott's travel adventures, political observations, and introspections while in India, see ER, *Hunting Big Game*, pp. 35–144.

42 *"to buy pretty things":* Elliott to "My Dear Little Mother," 17 May 1881, ibid., p. 88. "I have enjoyed great opportunities for seeing the way of living and governing of both natives and Europeans . . ." (Ibid., 3 Feb. 1881, p. 53.) For his letter from Ceylon, see p. 124.
    During his time in India, Theodore sent his brother his rifle and snow shoes, and was encouraging and generous: "This is your last great hunt, so stay as long as you wish . . ." (6 Dec. 1880, ER Family Papers, Box 5, FDRL.)

42 *"My Love":* Elliott fell in love with Anna Rebecca Hall, and they announced their engagement in June 1883. His diary essay, "My Love," is dated Feb. 1883 and is in Houghton.

43–44 *"All my love and ambition":* Anna Hall to Elliott, 8 Aug. [1883], in ER, *Hunting Big Game*, p. 149.

44 *"This happiness of yours":* Aunt Ella Bulloch to Elliott, 1 July 1883, ER Family Papers, Box 1, FDRL.

44 *"Ellie is very ill":* Aunt Annie Gracie journal, TR Collection, Houghton.

44 *"You must be very pure":* Aunt Annie Gracie to Elliott, 1 July 1883, FDRL.
    See other congratulatory letters in ER, *Hunting Big Game*, pp. 150–55.

44–45 *"Roosevelt-Hall Wedding":* *New York Times*, 2 Dec. 1883.

44–45 *Edith Wharton:* See *The Age of Innocence* for a glimpse of Knickerbocker society during the 1870s and 1880s (Charles Scribner's Sons, 1968 [1920], with introduction by R. W. B. Lewis).
    Born Edith Newbold Rhinelander Jones, Edith Wharton was a contemporary and neighbor of Eleanor Roosevelt's parents' generation in New York and Newport. Since ER's Aunt Pussie (Edith Livingston Hall) was thought to be the model for Lily Bart, see especially *The House of Mirth* (Bantam, 1984 [1905]); also Wharton's *Summer* (Berkley Books, 1981 [1917] and *Old New York* (Berkley Books, 1981 [1924]), both with splendid introductions by Marilyn French.

45 *"a curse on this house":* 12 Feb. 1884, quoted in McCullough, *Mornings on Horseback*, p. 283.

45 *double funeral service:* "The Double Funeral of Alice Hathaway Roosevelt and Martha Bulloch Roosevelt," *New York Times,* 17 Feb. 1884.

46 *"a miracle from heaven":* Autobiography of ER, p. 5.

46–47 *"my hand is shaking":* Regular correspondence, mostly from Anna to Elliott, generally undated, chronicles their lives during these years. Because there are so few letters from Elliott to Anna, we can only presume she destroyed them.

47–48 *"I am . . . not the same strong girl":* 21 Aug. [N.Y.]. *"Poor old Nell":* n.d. [Nov. 1887]. *"Have you had any doubts":* n.d. Anna's letters to Elliott are in ER Family Papers, Box 4, FDRL.

47 *"Amateur Comedy Club":* Biographical information, references to Anna Hall's Amateur Comedy Club and other activities in a memoir by "Three Friends," *In Loving Memory of Anna Hall Roosevelt* (pamphlet, privately printed, 1892), FDRL; and *New York Times* obituary, 8 Dec. 1892.

48 *The first day out:* For the devastating account of the *Britannic* disaster, see New York *Herald,* 23 May 1887; New York *World,* 23–24 May 1887 (clippings in FDRL); see also Lash, *Eleanor and Franklin,* pp. 29–30; Geoffrey C. Ward, *Before the Trumpet: Young Franklin Roosevelt* (Harper & Row, 1985), pp. 268–69; and ER, *Hunting Big Game,* pp. 158–61.

49 *Browning asked:* See Lash, *Eleanor and Franklin,* p. 23, and McCullough, *Mornings on Horseback,* p. 249.

49 *Elliott wrote again to Bye:* 8 July, on the success of the Hall sisters, in ER, *Hunting Big Game,* pp. 158–61; and Houghton.

50 *the spring of 1888:* TR to "Darling Bysie," 17 June 1888, in *Letters of TR,* ed. Morison, vol. 1, pp. 140–41. ("Elliott has had a really hard illness during this last week. He has had two abscesses on his neck; they prevented him from swallowing, and drove him nearly mad with pain; . . . he got a severe attack of rheumatism. He looks ghastly . . . and has been kept much under the influence of anodynes. . . . Aunt Annie is with him. . . .")

50 *"I do hate his Hempstead life":* Ibid., 24 June 1888.

50 *"I don't grudge the broken arm":* TR to Henry Cabot Lodge, Oct. 1886, quoted (along with details of the hunt) in E. Morris, *Rise of TR,* pp. 315–16.

51 *Alice ran in horror:* Alice Roosevelt Longworth's memory of her father in Michael Teague, *Mrs. L: Conversations with Alice Roosevelt Longworth* (Doubleday, 1981), p. 42.

51 *almost deadly rivals:* On the Meadow Brook–Oyster Bay polo accident, see S. J. Morris, *Edith Kermit Roosevelt,* p. 116.

52 *"Newport has been very gay":* Elliott's and Anna's correspondence during Aug. 1888 (and especially Anna to Elliott, 25 Aug., and n.d.. ["Halfway Nirvana"]), FDRL.

52 *"everybody loved her":* Elliot to Bye on Eleanor's birthday ("The funny little tot had a happy little birthday"), 13 Oct. 1888, in ER, *Hunting Big Game,* p. 162.

52–53 *"broke his nerves":* ER on the accident at Larry Waterbury's (who subsequently married and divorced ER's Aunt Maude), TIMS, p. 8.

53 *"Under Anna's ready hand":* Elliott to Bye, 13 June 1889, in ER, *Hunting Big Game,* pp. 163–64.

53 *Totty is flourishing":* Pussie to Elliott, n.d. [Oct. 1889], FDRL. Elliott, Jr., was born on 29 Sept. 1889.

54–55 *"Please don't worry"*: Anna to Elliott, along with all Thanksgiving- and Christmas-season correspondence, n.d., ibid.

55 *"a perfect nightmare"*: TR to Bye, 24 Jan. 1890, Houghton.

3. Childhood of Tears and Loss

56–57 *"poor old Nell"*: TR to Bye, 30 April 1890, Houghton.

57 *"Half measures simply"*: TR to Bye, 2 May 1890, Houghton.

57 *"For Bye only"*: Elliott to Bye, 21 July 1890, Houghton.

58 *"first in his heart"*: TIMS, pp. 8–9.

58 *"Dear Anna's Mother"*: Elliott's letters to Mrs. Hall from Venice, FDRL.

58 *"given a donkey"*: TIMS, p. 9.

ER returned to this episode of her life with her father in Sorrento, and her efforts to conquer fear, frequently, most notably in her March 1939 article, "Fear," published as "Conquer Fear and You Will Enjoy Living," *Look*, 23 May 1939; original typed manuscript in Lorena Hickok Papers, FDRL.

But ER wrote nothing of her father's unraveling. Venice was full of temptations, old friends, and drinking partners. Elliott wrote to "Dear Anna's Mother" on 20 Oct. 1890: "Our stay in Venice has been made very agreeable by the Curtis's, Edens and Brownings—whose invitations . . . would have filled the winters. As it is I think that we are now bound for Florence then Naples or Sorrento, as Anna desires (Because it is warmer—she says . . .). " (FDRL.)

59 *"a perfect angel"*: Anna to Bye, 15 Oct. 1890, Houghton.

59–60 *"something dreadful awaiting us"*: Elliott Roosevelt Mann was born on 11 March 1891; Gracie Hall Roosevelt was born on 28 June 1891.

60–62 *"go into an asylum"*: TR to Bye, Bye to TR and Edith Roosevelt, and other correspondence concerning Catherine (Katy) Mann, from March to May 1891, is in Houghton. Elliott and Anna to Bye, in FDRL.

62–63 *hopes of protecting Eleanor*: On the convent school, her mother's warning, and the house in Neuilly, TIMS, pp. 11–12.

The effort to educate Eleanor, no matter what tensions swirled about, evidently continued from Germany to Graz, Austria, to Italy, to France. Indeed, during their first stay in Graz, Elliott wrote his brother: "Tell Alice that Eleanor takes French lessons every day and tries hard to . . . write so she won't be far behind her when we return. Eleanor is learning to skate too, quite well. She has some little German friends with whom she coasts and plays snow balling all day. She really talks German very well." (20 Jan. 1891, Houghton.)

64 *an idyllic time*: Elliott to Mrs. Hall, n.d. 1891, 2 June 1891, FDRL.

64–65 *"My own dearest sister"*: TR to Bye, 7 June 1891, Houghton.

65n. *Katy Mann settlement*: Edmund Morris, the first to deal with the Katy Mann affair, wrote that Katy Mann "mysteriously" faded from history, and assumed that she was paid "her price [of] $10,000." "The scandal never broke. Evidently the girl [sic] got her money, although how much, and when, and who paid it, is unknown." (See E. Morris, *Rise of TR*, pp. 437–41.) After the publication of his book, Elliott Roosevelt Mann's daughter, Eleanor Mann Biles, wrote to Morris that whatever trust money existed was presumed stolen (quoted in Joseph Lash, *Love, Eleanor* [Doubleday, 1982], pp. 11–12). Elliott Roosevelt Mann died on 13 April 1941. See John Allen Gable, ed., "The Roosevelt Family in America: A Genealogy," *Theodore Roosevelt Association Journal*, Spring 1990, pt. 2, pp. 52, 75.

65–66 *TR was now unrelenting:* TR to Bye, 17 June, 2 July, 12 July 1891, Houghton.

66 *divided the family:* The Gracies tried to get TR to pull back. On 21 July 1891 (ibid.), TR wrote Bye that Corinne and Douglas stayed with them for several days; "and I have had some dextrous steering and hard fighting to do. . . ." Anna also continued to hesitate, dreading the legal suit.

66 *her own tooth powder:* On Edith Roosevelt, see S. J. Morris, *Edith Kermit Roosevelt*, p. 140.

66–67 *stood virtually alone:* Anna to Bye, n.d.; Anna to Bye, June and July 1891, FDRL.

68 *tried to derail the suit:* James King Gracie's efforts were met by TR's anguish: "Uncle Jimmie has certainly played the fool. I fear we have an ugly fight ahead. . . ." (TR to Bye, 22 Aug. 1891, Houghton.)

ER remained emotionally close to those who fought for her father. She corresponded with and visited the Bullochs in England during and after her school years, and felt particular warmth for Uncle Gracie until his death in 1903.

In 1951, she wrote to Helen Gracie Lowrie: "In answer to your letter, my grandmother's half sister, a Miss Bulloch from Georgia married Mr. James King Gracie. . . . The house they lived in . . . is now the official residence of the Mayor of New York City. I imagine you read about my visit to the house. I am sorry I do not know the genealogy of the Gracie family." (ER Papers, Box 3912, FDRL.)

69 *"I slept in my mother's room":* TIMS, pp. 12–13.

69 *"Sometimes I woke":* Ibid., pp. 15–16.

70 *martinet named Madeleine:* Ibid., p. 18.

70–71 *"disgracing my mother":* Ibid., pp. 16–18.

71 *wanted life to go on:* Anna to Bye, n.d., FDRL.

71 *"nobody told me anything":* Autobiography of ER, p. 8.

72 *to spell the simplest words:* Lash, *Eleanor and Franklin*, p. 42.

72 *"a great trial to my mother":* TIMS, p. 14.

72 *"I fear":* TR to Bye, 2 Sept. 1891, Houghton.

72 *a preventive war:* John Hay to Henry Adams in E. Morris, *Rise of TR*, pp. 443–44.

72–73 *"Won! Thank Heaven":* TR to Bye, 21 Jan. 1892, Houghton.

73–74 *On 28 January:* Evidently Florence Bagley Sherman sent her diary entry and several letters to Corinne Roosevelt Robinson, who gave the documents to ER, and they are now in the ER Family Papers, FDRL.

74–75 *"Was Miss Vedder an Adventuress?":* Elliott's thirty-one-page typed story is in the ER Family Papers, Elliott Roosevelt's writings, Box 5, FDRL.

75 *"both wicked and foolish":* TR to Bye, 22 Feb. 1892, Houghton.

75–76 *Desperate to prove himself:* Elliott to Bye, 25 Feb. 1892, FDRL.

76 *"Try and think lovingly":* Elliott to Bye, 5 March 1892, FDRL.

76 *Her fears were "groundless":* 12 June 1892, FDRL.

77 *Anna lay dying:* On Robert Munro Ferguson, TIMS, p. 18. See also Rixey, *Bamie*, pp. 63–66.

77–78 *Anna's final struggle:* Elliott to Mrs. Hall, 23 Nov., 26 Nov., 7 Dec. 1892, FDRL.

78 *"my mother was dead":* TIMS, p. 19.

4. Years of Dreams and Longing

Most of Elliott Roosevelt's letters to his daughter are published in ER, *Hunting Big Game*. His other letters, especially those to Anna Hall Roosevelt and Mrs. Hall, are in ER Family Papers, FDRL. Several of Eleanor Roosevelt's letters to her father are in Joseph P. Lash's recently opened collection, Box 12, as are other previously unavailable or presumed lost letters and several of ER's school essays.

80 *"With my father"*: TIMS, pp. 17–21.

81 *Society mourned:* All Anna Hall Roosevelt's memorial and obituary notices are in ER Family Papers, FDRL.

81 *"tragedy of utter defeat"*: TIMS, p. 19.

82 *Elliott wrote . . . to Mrs. Hall:* FDRL.

82–85 *wrote to Eleanor:* 20 Jan. 1893 (on education), 6 April 1893 (on generosity), 20 Aug. 1893 ("a very trying time") in ER, *Hunting Big Game*; 26 May 1893 ("We bury little Ellie), FDRL.

All through 1893, Elliott worked vigorously to restore a semblance of financial security. On 22 Sept., he wrote Mrs. Hall that he had traveled three states in an effort "to protect my interests. All of western Virginia went under, including the coal fields. . . . I have lost heavily dear lady and am in great distress and sorrow, for I was doing well. . . . I hope to pull out allright."

And he was desperate not to become completely erased from his children's memory: "I love them with all my heart. . . . [Do] try and make them love my *name* at least as *'father'* . . ."

According to Abingdon-area newspaper accounts written in 1933, when Eleanor Roosevelt as First Lady visited her father's last home, Elliott's ventures were relatively successful during the Panic of 1893. Though he lost over $30,000 in an effort to save his bank, he bailed out other mining, lumbering, and land-development ventures, "launched the Coeburn Land Development Company," "worked desperately for the relief of the starving miners," and enabled the interests of the Douglas land company to thrive. "Elderly Southwestern Virginians Remember the Father of Mrs. Roosevelt, Who Once Lived at White Top [Mountain], Washington County, Was Liberal to the Needy, Won Friends Quickly, and Was a 'Sport.' " (Clippings in ER Family Papers, Box 3, FDRL.)

85 *"in a dream world"*: TIMS, pp. 20–21.

86 *Washington was rhapsodic:* TR to Bye, 11 Oct. 1893, Houghton.

86 *"Eleanor saw him driving"*: Corinne to Bye, 11 Oct., ibid.

86–87 *a spirited hunter:* TIMS, pp. 19–20.

87 *"high points"*: Ibid.

ER wrote of these events in "My Father and I," an article written for Leonard White, who asked eleven American celebrities "to share with the world their most vivid recollection of their fathers," in honor of Father's Day, for *The New York Times*, 16 June 1946.

87 *"the children of my dear Friend"*: ER, *Hunting Big Game*, 2 Feb. 1894, p. 178.

By the summer of 1894, only Corinne was trying to see Elliott. TR wrote to Bye on 29 July: "I do wish Corinne could get a little of my hard heart about Elliott; she can do, and ought to do, nothing for him. . . . Poor fellow! If only he could have died instead of Anna!" (Morison, ed., *Letters of TR*, vol. 1, p. 392.)

87 *"my love to the puppies"*: 24 June 1894, FDRL.

87 *"Brudie wears pants"*: 5 July 1894, FDRL.

87 *"lessons with Grandma"*: 30 July 1894, in Lash Papers, Box 12, FDRL.

87–88 *On 13 August:* Elliott's last letter to Eleanor, in ER, *Hunting Big Game.*

88 *"Elliott died suddenly"*: Corinne to Bye, 15 Aug. 1894, Houghton.

88–89 *"frightful drinking"*: TR to Bye, 18 Aug. 1894, Houghton. According to TR, "for the last few days he had dumbly felt the awful night closing in on him." But he would not allow the family "to come to his house, nor part with the woman, nor cease drinking for a moment, but he wandered ceaselessly . . . , wrote again and again to us all. . . . He was like some stricken, hunted creature. . . ."

After Elliott's death, TR lost some of his own interest in the hunt. On 4 April 1901, he wrote to Hamlin Garland: "As I grow older I find myself uncomfortable killing things without a complete justification, and it was a real relief this year to kill only 'varmints,' and to be able to enjoy myself in looking at the deer, of which I saw scores or hundreds every day and never molested them." (Morison, ed., *Letters of TR*, vol. 3, p. 40.)

But, more immediately, on 25 Aug., he wrote Bye of the ongoing business ends of Elliott's demise:

"Freddy Weeks has been in charge of Mrs. Evans and poor Elliott's affairs generally; and he has now closed them all out, without a scandal. We narrowly missed one, too; for Mr. Evans arrived on the scene and threatened both his wife and Fred with a loaded revolver! but finally left, pacified. Freddy has behaved like a trump, as he always does in such emergencies!

"Emlen and Harry Weeks, the executors, have not behaved at all well, wishing to refuse to pay Mrs. Evans her claim of $1250.00, writing Corinne to pay it! They say they do not see that the interests of the children are concerned! She has a fair claim to it, and it is *not* our affair, but the children's; and I have written them very sharply that they ought to pay at once." (Houghton.)

89 *The Halls were . . . overlooked:* Corinne wrote Bye a twelve-page letter detailing Elliott's last days and funeral, which she had arranged. She chose "Just As I Am" for the first hymn: "I felt as if God would surely hear and accept our poor Elliott that way, and then I had 'Jesus, Saviour of My Soul,' and 'Rock of Ages,' those hymns we sang so often with Aunti & Mother" (Houghton). According to Corinne, Theodore "came to me at once" after Elliott's death "and we did together the things always so hard to do connected with the death of those we love." (C. Robinson, *My Brother Theodore Roosevelt*, p. 156.)

89 *"Elliott loved flowers"*: Mrs. Hall to Corinne, 25 Aug. 1894, in Lash Papers, Box 12, FDRL.

89 *Elliott's funeral followed the pattern:* TR to Corinne, 29 Aug. 1894, in *Letters of TR*, ed. Morison, vol. 1, p. 397. ("There is one great comfort I already feel; I only need to have pleasant thoughts of Elliott now. He is just the gallant, generous, manly boy and young man whom everyone loved. I can think of him now . . . the time we were first in Europe . . . and then in the days of the dancing class, when he was distinctly the polished man-of-the-world from outside, and all the girls, from Helen White to Fanny Dana to May Wigham used to be so flattered by any attentions from him. Or when we were off on his little sailing boat for a two or three days trip on the Sound; or when he first hunted; and when he visited me at Harvard. . . .")

90 *"wondering about his children"*: Florence Bagley Sherman to Corinne Roosevelt Robinson, n.d. [Aug. 1894], and 17 Aug. 1895, ER Family Papers, Box 1, FDRL. Evidently Corinne Robinson gave Mrs. Sherman's letters to her niece, who kept them with her papers.

90–91 *book of poetry:* Corinne Roosevelt Robinson, *One Woman to Another and Other Poems* (Charles Scribner's Sons, 1914), pp. 1–6.

91–92 *from Bar Harbor:* Mary Livingston Ludlow Hall to Corinne, 25 Aug. 1894, in Lash Papers, Box 12, FDRL.

92 *"in constant dread":* Edith Carow Roosevelt to her sister, Emily Carow, 10 Aug. 1894, Houghton.

92 *"never wished Alice to associate with Eleanor":* Edith to her mother, Gertrude Carow, 4 Nov. 1893, Houghton. On Edith's father's alcoholism and business difficulties, see S. J. Morris, *Edith Kermit Roosevelt*, p. 15; and Teague, *Mrs. L*, pp. 30–31. Although Edith did not want the cousins to consort, she hoped above all, that the "poor little soul," who looked so "forlorn" in the "makeshifts" she was made to wear, would be sent to "a good school." (Edith to Bye, n.d. [1892], Houghton; S. J. Morris, *Edith Kermit Roosevelt*, p. 137.)

Alice Roosevelt Longworth wrote of the closeness between the Roosevelt-Robinson cousins, the frequent children's parties at both Sagamore Hill in Oyster Bay and the Robinson place in Orange, New Jersey. Aunt Corinne and Aunt Bye were both central to the children's lives: "Aunt Corinne was as much of a companion with her children and nieces and nephews as Father was. She took part in everything we did. . . . She could stand on her head and turn cart-wheels better than any of us. . . . [She] was the moving spirit in everything that went on." But Eleanor and Hall rarely took part. Grandmother Hall was against it, and Edith Roosevelt was against it too. (Alice Roosevelt Longworth, *Crowded Hours*, pp. 30–31.)

Aunt Bye sent ER a set of Shakespeare for Christmas 1894; on 27 Dec., ER wrote a note of gratitude, saying, "I have already begun it." (Houghton.)

93 *the nurse Madeleine: Autobiography of ER*, pp. 16–17.

93 *Mrs. Overhalse:* Ibid., pp. 15–16. Madeleine the martinet caused ER "many tears," and ER was "desperately afraid of her." Nevertheless, she wrote of her in 1933: "Madeleine was my little brothers' Alsatian nurse. Very strict with me but adoring them. She talked French and German with us and taught me to sew and to darn. I thought her very hard when I had darned a heel and she took her scissors and cut it all out . . . , but now I think she was probably very good for me." (ER, *Hunting Big Game*, p. 170. On Mrs. Overhalse, see also *TIMS*, pp. 21–23.)

94 *wear short skirts:* On ER's old-fashioned, inappropriate, and ungainly clothes, and her friends' protective reactions, see Lash, *Eleanor and Franklin*, pp. 60–61, 63; and *TIMS*, p. 36 ("All my clothes seem to me now to have been incredibly uncomfortable!").

94 *young aunts and uncles:* On ER's adventures with her uncles, especially Vallie, who taught her to jump horses and shoot rifles, see *TIMS*, pp. 31, 360, and passim.

94 *corrective steel brace:* ER recalled that steel brace as "vastly uncomfortable and prevented my bending over." (*TIMS*, p. 28.)

95–96 *ER especially esteemed: TIMS*, pp. 22, 360–61, and passim.

96–98 *the Roser schoolroom:* Manuscripts of ER's stories—including "The Flowers," "Gilded Butterflies," and "Ambition," poetry, and pages from her "headache journal" written during her Roser years are in Lash Papers, Box 12, FDRL.

ER had no particular interest in Mr. Roser, something of a prig, and certainly a bore. He was "fashionable," but ER considered him hardly "remarkable." His assistant, however, Miss Tomes, evoked ER's "admiration." "She taught us well and thoroughly." (*TIMS*, p. 17.)

98–99 *reading and dreaming:* Over the years, ER wrote several articles about what she had liked to read as a child and gave advice about the importance of books in the lives of young people: "The great thing for the child of today is to form the habit of reading so that they may escape sometimes from their surroundings into different ages and different moods." (ER to Henry Canby, for *The Saturday Review*, 6 Nov. 1929, Box 15, FDRL. Quotations from "Article for *Children: The Magazine for Parents*," 1941.)

99–100 *Dodsworth's . . . dance classes:* TIMS, p. 47.

100 *Eleanor loved the theatre:* On Eleanora Duse, see *Autobiography of ER*, p. 18.

100 *"attention or . . . admiration":* TIMS, pp. 22.

100–1 *Marie Souvestre:* To Mrs. Hall, FDRL. Marie Souvestre's correspondence with Anna Roosevelt Cowles and Corinne Roosevelt Robinson and her daughter Corinne Robinson Alsop, in Houghton. I am grateful to Judith Friedlander and Naomi Holoch, who helped me translate Souvestre's French script.

101n. *Aunt Bye . . . married:* For Anna Roosevelt Cowles's marriage, see Rixey, *Bamie*, pp. 86–87; S. J. Morris, *Edith Kermit Roosevelt*, pp. 160–61.

5. Allenswood and Marie Souvestre

102 *sailed for England:* For ER on Aunt Tissie, see TIMS, p. 53. The Mortimers' Roslyn house is described in Steven M. L. Aronson, "A Life in the Country: Patrician Bohemians Barbara and Stanley Mortimer Look Back . . . ," *House and Garden*, April 1984, pp. 168ff; I am grateful to Barbara Guest for this article.

Too little is known about ER's Aunt Tissie, Elizabeth Hall Mortimer, who impressed generations of Roosevelts by her ability "to walk the moors all day and play poker . . . far into the night" (ER, *This I Remember*, p. 10). For information on her British circle of friends, see Jane Abdy and Charlotte Gere, *The Souls* (London: Sidgwick & Jackson, 1984).

103 *not an ordinary finishing school:* In 1899, Henry James wrote William James that Marie Souvestre "is a very fine, interesting person, her school holds a very particular place (all Joe Chamberlain's daughters were there and they adore her), and I must tell you more of her" (quoted in Lash, *Eleanor and Franklin*, p. 74). Although there is to date no study of Marie Souvestre, or her schools, for the impact of her life on the women she taught, see especially Michael Holroyd, *Lytton Strachey*, vol. 1, *The Unknown Years, 1880–1910* (Holt, Rinehart & Winston, 1967), esp. pp. 36–41; and Elizabeth French Boyd, *Bloomsbury Heritage: Their Mothers and Their Aunts* (London: Evelyn Adams & Mackay, 1968), pp. 64, 87.

Souvestre's influence on men was equally significant. According to Michael Holroyd, although Lytton Strachey was often fierce in his criticism, *"cette grande femme,"* as he called Marie Souvestre, "was almost unique in that, throughout his often drastic and belligerent correspondence, he never once mentions her in a derogatory manner."

104 *She also wrote* Olivia*:* Dorothy Strachey Bussy wrote *Olivia* in 1933, but it was not published until 1948. All quotations herein are from the Arno Press Reprint, 1975. On the Stracheys, see Holroyd, *Lytton Strachey*; for a more sympathetic portrait of Lady Strachey, see Virginia Woolf, "Lady Strachey," *The Nation & Athenaeum*, 22 Dec. 1928, reprinted in Virginia Woolf, *Books and Portraits*, ed. Mary Lyon (Harcourt Brace Jovanovich, 1977), pp. 208–11.

See also Martha Vicinus, "Distance and Desire: English Boarding School Friendships, 1870–1920," in *Hidden from History: Reclaiming the Gay and Lesbian Past*, ed. Martin Duberman et al. (New American Library, Meridian, 1989), pp. 212–29; and BWC, "Women Alone Stir My Imagination: Lesbianism in the Cultural Tradition," *Signs*, Summer 1979, pp. 718–39, in which I first suggested that Laura was based in part upon Eleanor Roosevelt—not only because of the obvious similarities in character, but because of the peculiar chronological circumstances of the year when Dorothy Strachey Bussy was moved to reconsider her own school years, as pupil and teacher, and the little girl she knew as "Totty," who had just become America's First Lady. Nor is it irrelevant that Laura was portrayed as the daughter of England's "leading statesman." During ER's years at Allenswood, her Uncle Theodore was elected vice-president of the United States on 6 Nov. 1900. (He and William McKinley defeated William Jennings Bryan and Adlai E. Stevenson, Sr.) On 22 Sept. 1901, TR succeeded to the presidency when McKinley died of an assassin's bullet.

For a scene remarkably reiminiscent of the meeting between Laura and another school "favorite" in *Olivia*, see ER's account of her meeting with Beatrice Chamberlain, in my opinion the other model for Laura, in *TIMS*, p. 75.

104–5 *giant cucumbers:* Woolf, *A Room of One's Own*, p. 65.

105 *Beatrice Webb:* For Webb on Souvestre, see Norman and Jeanne MacKenzie, eds., *The Diary of Beatrice Webb*, 2 vols. (Harvard University Press, 1982), esp. vol. 1, p. 277; vol. 2, pp. 340–41; and passim.

105–6 *Marie Souvestre in action:* Dorothy Strachey Bussy descriptions in *Olivia*.

106 *"far and away":* For ER on Souvestre, Allenswood, and her schoolmates, see *TIMS*, ch. 3.

All Allenswood records are in ER Papers, Boxes 1 and 3, FDRL, except for several of her devoirs, report cards, and letters from Marie Souvestre, which are in Lash Papers, Box 12, FDRL.

106 *Helen Gifford:* Quoted in Lash, *Love, Eleanor*, p. 27.

106–8 *became confident:* TIMS, p. 58.

108–9 *"Jane":* Ibid., pp. 60–63.

109–10 *Souvestre wrote Mrs. Hall:* n.d., 1899, FDRL.

110 *ER's scholarship ranged:* Report cards and notebooks, ER Papers, Boxes 1 and 3, FDRL.

111 *Classes were compulsory:* TIMS, pp. 59–60.

111 *Souvestre's library:* According to Rixey, the "rather startling" nudes of Pierre Puvis de Chavannes "overpowered" some of Marie Souvestre's students (*Bamie*, p. 15).

111–12 *Souvestre read aloud:* TIMS, ER on Souvestre, pp. 64–65.

112–13 *"gets terribly mad":* Corinne Robinson to her mother, Alsop Family Papers, Houghton: quoted in Lash, *Love, Eleanor*, p. 29.

113 *Heroines were few:* ER's notes and essays on Christine de Pisan and other notables are in her French-literature notebook, summer 1901, Box 1, FDRL. I am grateful to Judith Friedlander, who helped me translate these essays. See also Charity Cannon Willard, *Christine de Pizan: Her Life and Works* (Persea Books, 1984).

114–15 *At Alassio:* For ER's travels with Marie Souvestre, see *TIMS*, ch. 3. For a discussion of Marie Souvestre's curiously complex friend Mary Augusta Ward, see Virginia Woolf, "The Compromise (Mrs. Humphry Ward)," a review of *The Life of Mrs Humphry Ward* by her daughter Janet Penrose Trevelyan, *The New Republic*, 9 Jan. 1924, reprinted in *Virginia Woolf: Women and Writing*, ed. Michele Barrett (London: The Women's Press, 1979), pp. 169–72; see also Vera Brittain, *Women at Oxford* (London: George G. Harrap, 1960), pp. 41–46; and Jane Marcus, *Virginia Woolf and the Languages of Patriarchy* (Indiana University Press, 1987), esp. pp. 70–71.

115 *"I lose a dear friend":* Souvestre to Mrs. Hall, [1901], Lash Papers, Box 12, FDRL.

115–16 *encounter with her Aunt Pussie:* TIMS, pp. 89–90.

116 *"after much begging and insistence":* Ibid.

116 *"beloved by everybody":* Corinne Robinson quoted in Lash, *Eleanor and Franklin*, p. 84.

116–19 *when they meet:* Quotations are from *Olivia.* On Dorothy Strachey Bussy and *Olivia*, see Holroyd, *Lytton Strachey*, vol. 1, pp. 36–41, 46.

119 *Decades of biographical denial:* For the view that Eleanor Roosevelt did not quite comprehend *Olivia* and was ashamed of Marie Souvestre's life, see Lash, *Love, Eleanor*, ch. 2.

It is significant that ER and Virginia Woolf were contemporaries (Woolf was born in 1882), since so much of ER's life has been attributed to her alleged "Victorianism," and so many of her papers are lost. Woolf's accounts provide us with a vivid understanding of the relationships between women of that generation that were a daily and lifelong aspect of women's experience in ER's culture. Woolf explained that she was attracted to such lesbian friends as Vita Sackville-West and Dame Ethel Smyth because "these Sapphists *love* women." Friendship with them "is never untinged with amorosity." She was not being metaphorical or whimsical, or imprecise.

In 1937, the same year ER wrote *This Is My Story*, Virginia Woolf wrote a New Year's Day letter to Dorothy Strachey Bussy: "London was the usual scrimmage. I saw too many people—among them, tell Janie [Dorothy Bussy's daughter], La Princesse de Polignac, née Winnie Singer, but whatever she was born she's grown into the image of a stately mellow old Tory, and to look at her you'd never think she ravished half the virgins in Paris, and used, so Ethel Smyth tells me, to spring upon them with such impetuosity that once a sofa broke." (Virginia Woolf to Dorothy Strachey Bussy, 1 Jan. 1937, in Nigel Nicolson and Joanne Trautman, eds., *The Letters of Virginia Woolf* [Harcourt Brace Jovanovich, 1980], vol. 6, p. 100.)

120 *"She wrote me lovely letters":* For ER on Marie Souvestre, see *TIMS*, p. 97. In the 1960 *Autobiography of ER*, p. 35, we find it repeated: "She wrote me lovely letters which I still cherish. They show the kind of relationship that had grown up between us and give an idea of the very fine person who exerted the greatest influence, after my father, on this period of my life."

120–23 *Souvestre wrote:* Typed translations of Marie Souvestre's letters to ER, 7 July 1902, 17 Aug. 1902, 5 Oct. 1902, are in ER Papers, Box 3, FDRL.

124 *In October 1905:* Marie Souvestre's obituary is in London *Times*, 1 April 1905, pp. 1, 6; the 5 April 1905 Memorial Service book is in Lash Papers, Box 12, FDRL.

6. Coming Out and Courting

125 *"Protect yourself":* Marie Souvestre to ER, 7 July 1902, ER Papers, Box 3, FDRL.

126 *Three locks:* For this information I am grateful to Geoffrey C. Ward, who interviewed Laura Chanler White when she was over 100. A family friend, and Stanford White's daughter-in-law, Laura Chanler White asked ER why there were so many locks on her door, when she stayed over one night during their adolescence. ER replied simply, "to keep my uncles out." (Ward to author, 23 April 1991. See Ward, *Before the Trumpet: Young Franklin Roosevelt, 1882–1905* [Harper & Row, 1985], ch. 7.)

Because we have only recently considered seriously the frequency and impact of emotional and sexual abuse in the lives of young women, we have tended to ignore or trivialize many of the most significant moments in a woman's emotional development. Whether or not ER's "lurching" uncles ever succeeded in molesting her or were sexually abusive cannot now be known. But that she recognized the need to create physical barriers to their presence indicates a far more embattled adolescence than we have heretofore understood. See especially Louise De Salvo, *Virginia Woolf: The Impact of Childhood Sexual Abuse on Her Life and Work* (Beacon Press, 1989).

126–27 On *Leonie Gifford:* and other visitors to Tivoli, see *TIMS*, pp. 97–99.

127 *Hall to Groton: Autobiography of ER*, pp. 36–38.

127–28 *alone in New York City:* Ibid.

128 *"Odious comparisons":* Alice Roosevelt quoted in Teague, *Mrs. L*, p. 36.

128–29 *"really rather attractive":* Ibid., p. 154.

129–30 *Ellen ("Bay") Emmet:* TIMS, pp. 102–3.
After her marriage (in 1911) to William Blanchard Rand, there was more financial security; but throughout her life Ellen Emmet Rand painted for both love and money. Henry James once wrote her: " 'You're quite right—it's a world in which one must beg away for one's self and count on nothing and nobody. Lucky for you that you've such a splendid little self to count on. . . .' " By the time of her sudden death in 1941, Bay Emmet had painted more than 800 portraits, including most notable American leaders, and, in 1934, the official presidential portrait of FDR. (See Martha Hoppin, *The Emmets: A Family of Women Painters* [Berkshire Museum, 1982], p. 31 and passim. I am grateful to Honor Moore for this reference.)

130–31 *Madison Square Garden:* Franklin's diary entry, quoted in Ward, *Before the Trumpet*, pp. 307–9. Lash, *Eleanor and Franklin*, notes that FDR was not mentioned in the press coverage of the horse show (p. 92).
Throughout 1902, ER's name was regularly mentioned in New York's society columns, and society's most popular gossip weekly, *Town Topics*. Since there were five Roosevelt cousins ("Princess" Alice, Christine, Dorothy, Elfrida, Eleanor) involved (Alice had come out the year before), and Eleanor attended most of their parties, as well as several hosted specifically for her—including a much-celebrated theatre-dinner-dance party at Sherry's given by Aunt Tissie (the play was *The Cavalier*, with Julia Marlowe)—one is left with a breathless sense of activity during this season of "social dissipation." All the Roosevelt debutantes seem to have been invited to the famous Assembly Ball at the Waldorf Astoria on 11 Dec. 1902 (which ER attended with the Parishes). (See Lash, *Eleanor and Franklin*, pp. 92–93.) But of the cousins, only Eleanor Roosevelt's name appears on the list of guests at Mrs. Astor's still more exclusive evening.
If Eleanor was indeed the only Roosevelt debutante of the 1902–3 social season invited to Mrs. Astor's annual ball, as press coverage indicates, it was because of the ongoing vigor of her mother's connections. However much ER disparaged the event, Mrs. Astor's remained in Jan. 1903 the "one large entertainment to which all that is representative in society in New York . . . stands first. . . . An invitation to Mrs. Astor's ball carries with it an absolute cachet as to social position." (See *New York Times*, 13 Jan. 1913, p. 3, and list of "some of the guests.")
In many ways ER did her mother proud: she was dressed elegantly by the best Paris designers, and she was remembered as unfailingly gracious, and sophisticated. But there was a tone of disapproval, even rather a snide quality, to some of the press commentary, the worst appearing in *Town Topics*: "The debut of Miss Eleanor Roosevelt, daughter of the late Mrs. Elliott Roosevelt, also recalls the brilliant days of New York Society in the late eighties. Mrs. Roosevelt and Mrs. Barclay [who died in 1894, and whose daughter was also coming out in 1902] were in the limited definition of that day 'leaders,' a term which now has no special significance." (*Town Topics*, Nov. 1902, p. 4; see also 11 Dec., 18 Dec. 1902.)

131–32, n. *"utter agony":* For ER's memory of great misery during 1902–3, see *TIMS*, pp. 100–1; Lash, *Eleanor and Franklin*, pp. 92–93; Duncan Harris to ER, 1937, quoted in Ward, *Before the Trumpet*, p. 306.

132 *"E is an Angel":* See Ward, *Before the Trumpet,* ch. 7.

133 *"addressed as 'Granny' ":* TIMS, pp. 103–4.

133 *Rosy gave a "very jolly!" dinner party:* Ward, *Before the Trumpet,* p. 254.

133 *Alice Sohier:* Ibid.

134 *"made many friends":* TIMS, pp. 105–7.

134–35 *most gratifying hours:* For ER on her settlement work and the Consumer's League, see ibid., pp. 107–9. For information on Mary Harriman and the founding of the Junior League, see Persia Campbell, "Mary Harriman Rumsey," *Notable American Women,* ed. Edward James, Janet Wilson James, and Paul Boyer (Harvard University Press, 1971), vol. 3, pp. 208–9; and Rhoda Aderer, on the Junior League's sixtieth anniversary, *New York Times,* 12 March 1961, p. 90.

Originally called The Junior League for the Promotion of Settlement Movements (1900–1907), and "organized by the debutantes of the winter 1900–1901," the group worked to improve neighborhood conditions, built coalitions with other settlement workers, and worked to interest college women and debutantes in their efforts. See Robert Woods and Albert Kennedy, eds., *Handbook of Settlements* (Russell Sage Foundation, 1911), esp. pp. 190–95.

134 *Jane Addams:* See Allen F. Davis, *American Heroine: The Life and Legend of Jane Addams* (Oxford University Press, 1973).

134 *Lillian Wald:* See especially Clare Coss, *Lillian D. Wald: Progressive Activist* (The Feminist Press, 1989); and Doris Groshen Daniels, *Always a Sister: The Feminism of Lillian D. Wald* (The Feminist Press, 1989).

134 *Gladys Vanderbilt:* Quoted in Amory, *Who Killed Society?,* p. 219.

135 *"There was no clubhouse":* For ER on the League, see "Interview with Eleanor Roosevelt—Charter Member, New York Junior League, 1940," reprinted in *50th Anniversary Commemorative Anthology Issue, 1927–1971* (Association of the Junior Leagues, Spring 1971), pp. 53–54.

135–36 *"nicest part of the day":* ER to FDR, 6 Jan. 1904, FDRL. Most of ER's letters to FDR during this period are in the Family Papers Donated by the Children, Boxes 13–16, FDRL. Unfortunately, ER destroyed all of FDR's courtship letters, presumably after she learned of his affair with Lucy Mercer in 1918.

137–38 *also inspired by her Aunt Bye:* For ER on Washington, Uncle Ted's campaign, and Aunt Bye, see *TIMS,* pp. 112–15.

139 *"a great curiosity":* ER's engagement to her fifth cousin once removed, *TIMS,* p. 111.

139 *"Oh! darling":* ER to FDR, 6 Jan., 24 Jan. 1904, FDRL.

140 *The next week:* ER to FDR, 24 Nov. 1903, FDRL.

140 *"with my darling":* For FDR's proposal and diary entry, see Ward, *Before the Trumpet,* p. 313.

140 *James King Gracie died:* On 23 Nov. 1903; *New York Times* obituary, 24 Nov. 1903. *TIMS,* p. 112.

140–41 *"I am going to write it out":* ER to FDR, 24 Nov. 1903, FDRL.

141–42 *subject of tension:* ER to FDR, 1 Dec. [1903], FDRL.

142–43 *"Boy darling":* ER to FDR, [6 Dec. 1903], FDRL.

143–44 *so cold, so disapproving:* Although there is to date no full-length biography of Sara Delano Roosevelt, see especially Rita Halle Kleeman, *Gracious Lady: The Life* of *Sara Delano Roosevelt* (Appleton-Century, 1935); Clara and Hardy Steeholm, *The House at Hyde Park* (Viking, 1950); Eleanor Roosevelt, "I Remember Hyde Park," *McCall's*, Feb. 1963, pp. 71–73, 162–63; and Sara Delano Roosevelt (as told to Isabel Leighton and Gabrielle Forbush), *My Boy Franklin* (Long & Smith, 1933).

ER named her mother-in-law as one of "The Seven People Who Shaped My Life," *Look*, 19 June 1951, pp. 55–58: "My mother-in-law was a lady of great character. She always knew what was right and what was wrong. She was kind and generous and loyal. . . . But it was hard to differ with her. . . . She dominated me for years."

144–45 *sin of human carelessness:* For Squire James's political values, see Ward, *Before the Trumpet*, pp. 154–56.

145 *"Franklin is a Delano":* SDR quoted by James MacGregor Burns, *Roosevelt: The Lion and the Fox* (Harcourt, Brace & World, 1956), p. 7.

145 *very serious stables:* ER wrote of Gloster in *FDR and Hyde Park: Personal Recollections* (Washington, D.C.: U.S. Government Printing Office, 1949), pp. 4–5. See also Ward, *Before the Trumpet*, p. 53.

146 *Little Lord Fauntleroy:* Alice Longworth in Teague, *Mrs. L*, p. 46.

146 *"my bath alone":* FDR to his father, quoted in Burns, *Lion and Fox*, p. 4.

146 *Groton:* On FDR at Groton and Harvard, see Ted Morgan, *FDR: A Biography* (Simon & Schuster, 1985), ch. 4, pp. 239ff.

147 *Taddie . . . eloped with . . . Dutch Sadie:* Ibid., p. 75.

147 *"disgrace to the name":* FDR to "My Darling Mama and Papa," 23 Oct. 1900, FDRL. These are the sentences deleted from FDR's published *Letters*, vol. 1, pp. 429–30. (Elliott Roosevelt, ed., *FDR: His Personal Letters* [Duell, Sloan and Pearce, 1947; Kraus Reprint, 1970], hereafter *Letters*.)

Ironically, Theodore Roosevelt—always so afraid of scandal—was inconveniently besmirched, since the headlines occurred during his campaign for the vice-presidency. But the entire family pulled together, and on 30 Oct. 1900 FDR marched through Cambridge in his crimson cap and gown in the Republican torchlight parade.

148 *a model Grotonian:* Ward, *Before the Trumpet*, chs. 5, 6; Burns, *Lion and Fox*, pp. 13–21.

148 *something of an outsider:* Joseph Alsop, *FDR: A Centenary Remembrance* (Viking, 1982), pp. 35–36.

148n. *"my friend":* Endicott Peabody quoted in Baltzell, *Protestant Establishment*, p. 249.

148–49 *"those* squaws*":* Morgan, *FDR*, pp. 68–69.

149 *"How about Teddy Robinson and Eleanor":* FDR to "Dearest Mama and Papa," 11 Dec. 1898, in *Letters*, vol. 1, pp. 243–44. This was FDR's first mention of ER.

149 *failure to make Porcellian:* William Sheffield Cowles, Jr., quoted in Alsop, *Centenary Remembrance*, pp. 36–37.

150 *"I know what pain":* FDR to SDR, 4 Dec. 1903, in *Letters*, vol. 1, p. 518.

150 *"Dearest Cousin Sally":* ER to SDR, 2 Dec. 1903, in ibid., p. 517.

150–51 *Caribbean cruise:* SDR's Caribbean effort was a failure. After the trip, FDR wrote his mother, "It is horrid to be back after such a perfect trip—if it only could have lasted longer without being *very* far away from N.Y.!" (14 March 1904 in *Letters*, vol. 1, p. 527.)

151–52 *the Delano "clan":* TIMS, pp. 118–22.

152–53, n. *Howard Cary: TIMS*, p. 110; Lash, *Eleanor and Franklin*, pp. 134–37. On Cary's suicide, see W. A. Swanberg, *Whitney Father, Whitney Heiress* (Charles Scribner's Sons, 1980), p. 239.

153–54 *Nicholas Biddle:* Biddle and Lyman Delano on ER, the Delanos' enthusiasm, and Grace Tully in Lash, *Eleanor and Franklin*, pp. 136–37; congratulatory letters in FDRL.

154 *"by no means good enough for her":* Corinne Robinson Alsop's papers and her unpublished diaries are now available at Houghton; quoted in Alsop, *Centenary Remembrance*, p. 36.

154 *"I like 'Fear nothing' ":* ER to FDR, 18 Nov. 1903, FDRL.

154 Sonnets from the Portuguese: ER to FDR, 18 Dec. 1903, FDRL.

155 *"learn to love me":* ER to FDR, 3 Dec. 1903, FDRL.

155 *consulted Cousin Susie:* ER to FDR, 6 Dec. 1903, FDRL.

155 *master's degree:* ER to FDR, 7 Oct. 1903, FDRL.

155–56 *promoted all his activities:* 19 Dec. 1903, FDRL.

156 *"not worth it":* ER to FDR, 17 Dec. 1903, FDRL.

157 *"just as well":* ER to FDR, 12 Feb. 1904, FDRL.

157 *"Women have served":* Woolf, *A Room of One's Own*, pp. 35–37. It is a situation, Virginia Woolf concluded, that leads "to such curious notes in the margin of the private mind."

157–58 *five weeks of separation:* ER's letters to FDR during his Caribbean trip, 16 Dec. 1903; 7 Jan., 18 Jan., 27 Jan. 1904; 6–11 Feb. 1904, Box 14, FDRL.

158 *diverting, even entertaining:* Lash, *Eleanor and Franklin*, pp. 124–26.

158–59 Candida: All quotations from *Candida: A Mystery*, in Bernard Shaw, *Complete Plays with Prefaces* (Dodd, Mead, 1963), vol. 3, pp. 199–268. For "propagandistic" tour with *A Doll's House*, Shaw's preface, p. 112.

159–60 *"Don't let her feel":* ER to FDR, 23 May 1904, FDRL.

160 *"adopt her fully":* Sara's pre-Christmas letter to FDR quoted in Ward, *Before the Trumpet*, pp. 323–24.

160 *momentous times:* For the Roosevelt-Robinson wedding and FDR's graduation, see ibid., p. 333.

160 *Mrs. Hartman Kuhn . . . wrote Eleanor:* quoted in Lash, *Eleanor and Franklin*, p. 135.

161 *"high life lady":* ER to FDR, 17 May 1904, FDRL.

7. Franklin and Me, and Sara Makes Three

162 *17 March 1905:* All greetings, congratulatory letters, gift listings, and other wedding memorabilia are in Family Papers Donated by the Children, Box 20, FDRL.

162–63 *"beautiful," "regal":* Bridesmaids' and ER's gown, and the fullest description of wedding, in *New York Times*, 18 March 1905.

163 *Aunt Pussie:* Lash, *Eleanor and Franklin*, p. 140.

164 *"more claim to good looks":* However complimentary, *Town Topics* was also disapproving: "Miss Helen Cutting and Miss Eleanor Roosevelt have elected to be married in Lent, and, moreover, Miss Roosevelt has chosen a Friday (St. Patrick's Day) for her nuptials" (9 March 1905).

Helen Cutting was to marry Lucius Wilmerding; Isabella Selmes, who was to become ER's closest confidante during the early years of her marriage, had been staying that year with her mother, Martha Flandrau Selmes, at Cousin Susie's. A Southern aristocrat and Western adventurer, Mrs. Selmes was particularly close to TR and Aunt Bye, and was Cousin Susie's great friend. *Town Topics* rhapsodized over "Miss Isabella Selmes, the charming Louisville beauty, who is spending the winter with Mrs. Parish" (9 March 1905).

164 *Aunt Bye replied:* Anna Roosevelt Cowles to ER, 19 Dec. 1904, Box 20, FDRL.

164–65 *"We are greatly rejoiced":* TR to FDR, 29 Nov. 1904; Aunt Edith to ER, 28 Dec. 1904; cf. TR to ER, 19 Dec. 1904, Box 20, FDRL.

165 *"Really you are a saint":* For the notion that Alice was "downright jealous" of TR's offer to ER, see Carol Felsenthal, *Alice Roosevelt Longworth* (G. P. Putnam's Sons, 1988), p. 77.

165 *"in Bobbie Goelet's auto":* ER to FDR, 30 Jan. 1904, FDRL.

165–66 *"so pleased with your gift":* Autobiography of ER, p. 49.

ER was indeed pleased with many of her gifts. Although there were many conventional silver trays and ornate vases, there were also many considerably selected gifts: carved and interesting clocks, and leatherbound first editions of Ralph Waldo Emerson, Jane Austen, the Brownings, and Christina Rossetti. ER cherished particularly Bay Emmet's portrait of Aunt Bye. She never referred to Aunt Edith's present, a small watercolor of children wading, framed by Fischer, originally a gift to TR from a Dutch genre painter named Blommer. Edith Roosevelt was glad to be rid of it. She wrote her sister, Emily: "It is really good of its kind, but a kind which I don't happen to care for."

(Gift lists and memorabilia, Box 20, FDRL. Edith Roosevelt quoted in S. J. Morris, *Edith Kermit Roosevelt*, p. 289.)

166 *"scuttled" into New York:* TR wrote his son Kermit, "I paid a scuttling visit to New York on Friday to give away Eleanor at her marriage, and to make two speeches" (in Joseph Bucklin Bishop, ed., *Theodore Roosevelt's Letters to His Children* [Charles Scribner's Sons, 1919], p. 18).

167 *"the lion of the afternoon":* TIMS, pp. 124–26. The New York *Tribune* headlined: "President's Flying Visit / Gives Niece Away . . . , Speaks at Two Dinners and Whisks Back to Capital." The *Tribune* story was the least critical: "The residence of Mrs. Henry Parish, Jr., is one of the most attractive in New York, and is especially well adapted to a large wedding. . . . Miss Roosevelt, who is a tall girl, made a handsome bride, and the bridesmaids looked uncommonly well also."

The New York *Sun* called the wedding "a simple one." Detailed and neutral, *The New York Times* noticed that ER was "considerably taller than the head of the nation, suggesting to many present her beautiful mother. . . . She has much of that simple grace that characterized her mother."

(All newspaper accounts are dated 18 March 1905.)

168–69, n. *"the most perfect wedding":* SDR to "My precious Franklin & Eleanor," quoted in Morgan, *FDR*, p. 103.

Nobody (not even SDR, who seemed to enjoy the fact that Franklin missed the first bars of the "Wedding March" from *Lohengrin* when she related the story in *My Boy Franklin*) referred to the egregious wedding review in *Town Topics*, 23 March 1905:

"The Henry Parishes, the Livingston Ludlows and the other relatives of Miss Eleanor Roosevelt received as much advertising out of the wedding as did Mrs. Goelet and Mrs. Oliver Belmont out of the ducal alliances of their daughters. The event was characterized by pathetic economy and the guests were not overly conservative in discussing it. To begin with, the food was supplied by an Italian caterer, not of the first class, and one man said he got only a fleeting glimpse of a bottle of champagne. . . ." (Since, to date, nobody has discovered a picture of the wedding party, one might add: And no photographer was hired for the occasion.)

"The street in front of the Parish house was jammed with a typical St. Patrick's Day crowd, noisy and full of an exuberance of spirits that was embarrassing. . . . The police had been ordered to let no one through the lines . . . and the guests who were unwise enough to leave their carriages before reaching the house ran against a solid bank of bluecoats. . . . Mrs. Alexander nearly lost her overskirt and had considerable difficulty readjusting her bonnet. Colonel Latrobe, of Baltimore, had a much worse time. . . . Mrs. I. Townsend Burden and Miss Gwendolyn had the distinction of being mistaken for Mrs. [Theodore] Roosevelt and the little daughter of the President . . . and their open carriage was surrounded. . . . Mrs. Norman Whitehouse arrived . . . and some woman in the crowd took such a fancy to her that she threw a bunch of violets at her. . . . The President fooled the crowd in leaving . . . by the Fifth Avenue end. . . . The uninvited spectators failed to notice the bridal couple, who went away unobserved in a closed cab. . . ."

Until FDR completed his semester at Columbia, the couple lived in a small apartment in the Hotel Webster, at 40 West 45th Street. (*TIMS*, p. 126.)

169 *three-month European honeymoon:* TIMS, pp. 127, 135; Lash, *Eleanor and Franklin*, pp. 146–47.

169 *"a* wonderful *sailor":* FDR to SDR, 25 July 1905, in *Letters*, vol. 2, pp. 46–47.

169–70 *Franklin had nightmares:* Ted Morgan, *FDR*, pp. 104–5.

170–71 *"we did things":* TIMS, p. 135.

171–72 *hike up the Faloria:* Ibid., p. 130; Lash, *Eleanor and Franklin*, p. 148.

ER's subsequent hiking and climbing feats give one pause as one considers the Dolomites, and Franklin's failure to encourage his wife even on their honeymoon. Indeed, Lake Roosevelt, high above the Tuolumne Meadows of Yosemite National Park, near the base of Mount Connes, was named for Eleanor Roosevelt. She had helped to stock it with rainbow trout in 1934. Moreover, with Ranger Forrest Townsley, she "climbed up an elevation of some 13,000 feet. When they came down, I thought the ranger was going to have a stroke." But Lorena Hickok thought ER looked as if she had returned from "a stroll in Central Park." (Shirley Sargent, *Yosemite's Famous Guests* [Flying Spur Press, 1970], p. 34. I am grateful to ranger and naturalist Carl Sharsmith for his memories of ER during her second visit to Yosemite in 1942. See Volume Two.)

172 *Aunt "Doe":* TIMS, pp. 131–32.

172 *"prolonged bat":* FDR to SDR, 14 Aug. 1905, in *Letters*, vol. 2, p. 66.

172–73 *"extremely 'French play' ":* TIMS, p. 131; and ER to SDR, 16 Aug. 1905, in *Letters*, vol. 2, p. 69.

173 *time with Marjorie Bennett:* TIMS, pp. 131–32.

173 *"brought home the loss":* Ibid., p. 132.

173 *Scotland . . . with . . . the Fergusons:* Ibid., pp. 134–37; Lash, *Eleanor and Franklin*, p. 150; Rixey, *Bamie*, pp. 63–65.

173–74 *"sweet . . . together":* "It is impossible to imagine how sweet she and Bob are together for I would not know him for the same man." ER to SDR, "Dearest Mama," 30 Aug. 1905, in *Letters*, vol. 2, p. 80. In this letter ER also noted that they had met Beatrice and Sidney Webb at Novar: "Franklin discussed the methods of learning at Harvard with the husband while I discussed the servant problem with the wife!" (Ibid.)

174–75 *a home and a family:* See ER, "I Remember Hyde Park."

175 *sought Sara's advice: Autobiography of ER*, p. 61.

175 *"just the sweetest, dearest":* ER to SDR, 7 June 1905, in *Letters*, vol. 2, p. 4.

176 *"no plans to make": TIMS*, p. 138.

177 *"For ten years": Autobiography of ER*, p. 62.

178 *Bound by custom: TIMS*, p. 142. On Alice's wedding, and Edith Carow Roosevelt to Alice Roosevelt Longworth, see Felsenthal, *Alice Roosevelt Longworth*, pp. 104–7.

178 *"I had never had any interest": TIMS*, p. 142.

178–79 *a trained nurse:* For ER on childrearing, see ibid., pp. 145–46, 151; and ER, "I Remember Hyde Park." On the tensions and cruelties of the nursery, see also James Roosevelt, with Bill Libby, *My Parents: A Differing View* (Playboy Press, 1976); and Bernard Asbell, *Mother and Daughter: The Letters of Eleanor and Anna Roosevelt* (Coward, McCann & Geoghegan, 1982).

179n. *Decades later: TIMS*, p. 145.

179 *Society for the Prevention:* Ibid., p. 151.
Even at the time, ER acknowledged that she was considered "a fussy mother" by her contemporaries, but she wanted to be both correct and protective: "Anna and Brother [James] are very well but Cousin Susie tells me if I keep them up on the roof so much I will ruin all their chances for growing up with any imagination and so I have bought Brother a carriage and he and Anna will spend occasional afternoons in the park 'to cultivate their imaginations and see other children'! It strikes me as a little ludicrous to worry so young about these things but I suppose that is because I am so 'matter of fact'!" (ER to Isabella Ferguson, 28 Dec. 1908; 8 Jan. 1909. All letters from ER to Isabella Selmes Ferguson Greenway are in the Greenway Collection, Arizona Historical Society, Tucson [hereafter Tucson]).

180, n. *"Griselda" moods: TIMS*, pp. 149–52. My discussion of Griselda has been informed by Judith Bronfman's splendid Ph.D. dissertation, "The Griselda Legend in English Literature," New York University, 1977; and Robert Dudley French, *A Chaucer Handbook* (Crofts, 1947).

180 *"I never talked to anyone":* ER to Lorena Hickok, 1933, Hickok Papers, FDRL. See Volume Two.

181 *only one horse:* Lash, *Eleanor and Franklin*, p. 156.

181–82 *summer of 1908: TIMS*, pp. 157–59.

182 *Mrs. Hartman Kuhn:* Lash, *Eleanor and Franklin*, p. 163.

183 *cried and cried: TIMS*, pp. 162–63. Whether the new house reminded her of her mother's last home in the same neighborhood, or the Ludlow-Parish twin houses of her godmother and great-aunt, or whether it was the lack of privacy, ER did not want to live in the house that Sara built: "I had nothing to do with getting it and it is not the kind of house I would have got. I hate it." (Quoted in Alfred Steinberg, *Mrs. R: The Life of Eleanor Roosevelt* [G. P. Putnam's Sons, 1958].)

183 *"E. brave and lovely":* SDR quoted in Lash, *Eleanor and Franklin*, p. 166.

183 *Eleanor Roosevelt blamed herself: TIMS*, pp. 164–65.
Baby Franklin was born on 18 March 1909. On 14 April, ER noted with dismay that her baby "is very flourishing but I've already stopped nursing him so I don't expect him to gain much for a little while though the food agrees with him finely." On 25 Oct., she wrote, "Anna and James are very well but baby Franklin is not as fine as I would like, however I hope he will improve. . . ."
The baby was buried on 7 Nov., and ER was in a state of emotional depression for

months thereafter, the record for which is almost entirely in her letters to Isabella Selmes Ferguson, Tucson. On 12 Nov., she wrote: "Sometimes I think I cannot bear the heartache which one little life has left behind but then I realize that we have much to be grateful for still, and that it was meant for us to understand and sympathize more deeply with all life's sorrows."

Almost three years later, when Teddy and Helen Robinson Roosevelt lost their month-old infant, ER wrote again: "No matter how little one's baby is, something of one's self dies with it I think and it leaves an empty place in one's heart which nothing can ever fill again. . . . Oh, well I suppose there is a reason for it all & we can but try to take it in the best way. . . ." (ER to Isabella Selmes Ferguson, 7 March 1912, Tucson.)

184 *"I miss you dreadfully":* ER to FDR, 23 Sept. 1910, quoted in Lash, *Eleanor and Franklin*, p. 166.

184 *Franklin's habits:* TIMS, p. 149.

184–85 *opportunity not only knocked:* Osborne to FDR, 8 Oct. 1910, quoted in Alfred B. Rollins, Jr., *Roosevelt and Howe* (Alfred A. Knopf, 1962), p. 16.

In 1908, TR, having regretfully announced that he would not run again, vacated the White House for his hand-picked successor, William Howard Taft. But Taft tilted toward reaction, and horrified Roosevelt Republicans, who called themselves Progressives. Progressivism among New York Democrats was also on the agenda. In his letter to FDR, Osborne observed that TR was "trying to make his party radical, which is impossible; don't let us be forced into the mistake of trying to make our party conservative, which is equally impossible."

185 *"I'll take it":* FDR to Perkins, quoted in Morgan, *FDR*, p. 112.

185–86 *first political campaign:* Rollins, *Roosevelt and Howe*, pp. 17–22.

8. Eleanor Roosevelt, Political Wife

187 *a congenial house:* TIMS, pp. 168–71.

After the death of baby Franklin, the move to Albany seemed ER's salvation. Both the State Street house, and later the house at 4 Elk Street, appealed to her: "You don't know how I am looking forward to the winter there. It is all so quiet, no crowd, no rush just stately houses overlooking a broad street with occasional passers by, really, I feel one might have time to live there."

The State Street house was a "square brownstone . . . only two blocks from the capitol so F can be home for lunch. It is quite a big house with a piazza and a big yard . . . and built more like a country house. . . ." (ER to Isabella Ferguson, 26 Nov. 1910, Tucson.)

187–88 *She experimented:* On her first days in Albany, and the wet nurse, see TIMS, pp. 168–71.

188–89 *"very, very busy":* ER to Isabella Ferguson, 11 Jan. 1911, Tucson.

189–90 *now a political wife:* ER's thoughts and activities during the Albany years, the political books she read and commented upon, and her occasional criticisms of Franklin's speeches are found scattered throughout her correspondence to Bob and Isabella Ferguson, Tucson. Her appeal to the Tammany reformers is derived from Frances Perkins's Oral History, Columbia University. Although she invariably supported her husband's position in private as well as public, her own reactions were occasionally those of an entertained observer: "We went to the opening of the Senate and Bob would have enjoyed hearing a dreadful Senator Newcomb attack the Governor's message and then Senator Grady, who is a reprehensible character but a delightful speaker, get up and defend it. I thought they would come to blows and it certainly was not a dignified argument but Grady had the whole room laughing before he had been speaking five minutes and I could not help being sorry for any one who tried to oppose him!" (ER to Isabella, 11 Jan. 1911, Tucson.)

190–91 *anti-Tammany "Insurgents":* For FDR and the Insurgency, see Rollins, *Roosevelt and Howe,* pp. 25–33. The ten-week struggle led to a compromise candidate, James O'Gorman, and both sides claimed victory.

192 *charmed by State Senator Tom Grady:* TIMS, pp. 172, 176.

192 *Tom Grady wrote ER:* Quoted in Lash, *Eleanor and Franklin,* p. 173. ER discussed those politicians who interested her in a letter to Isabella, 30 Jan. 1911, Tucson.

192 *poor Jewish children:* FDR's letter to ER, written on Carter, Ledyard and Milburn stationery, is undated, and presumably written, therefore, after 1907. (ER Papers, Box 3, FDRL.)

192–93 *After 1910:* TIMS, p. 181.

193 *a "damn fool":* Al Smith on FDR, quoted in Matthew and Hannah Josephson, *Al Smith: Hero of the Cities* (Houghton Mifflin, 1969), p. 95.

Those, like FDR, interested less in social legislation and more in good government were at this time frequently called "goo-goos."

193 *Tim Sullivan:* Quoted in Frances Perkins Oral History; Frances Perkins, *The Roosevelt I Knew* (Viking, 1946), pp. 11–12.

193–94 *In 1911, Franklin was not the reformer:* Perkins, *Roosevelt I Knew,* p. 14; Morgan, *FDR,* pp. 125–27; Rollins, *Roosevelt and Howe,* pp. 43–44; Arthur M. Schlesinger, Jr., *The Age of Roosevelt: The Crisis of the Old Order, 1919–1933* (Houghton Mifflin, 1957), pp. 334–38. See, most recently, Geoffrey C. Ward, *A First-Class Temperament* (Harper & Row, 1989), ch. 4; and Frank Friedel, *FDR: A Rendezvous with Destiny* (Little, Brown, 1990). (The latter two works appeared after this book was written.)

For Frances Perkins's career, see especially her 5,000-page Oral History, Columbia University; Charles Trout, in Barbara Sicherman, et al., eds., *Notable American Women: The Modern Period* (The Belknap Press of Harvard University Press, 1980), pp. 535–39; and George Martin, *Madame Secretary: Frances Perkins* (Houghton Mifflin, 1976).

The publicity given to the lives of the Triangle Fire victims, and the mean conditions under which they toiled, fortified the emerging suffrage campaign among working women and their allies, and intensified labor-reform activity—led in Albany by the vigorous activities of Frances Perkins. See especially Elizabeth Dutcher, "Budgets of the Triangle Fire Victims," *Woman Voter,* June 1912, pp. 14–16; and Dutcher's vivid description of Perkins's last-minute chase to find Christy Sullivan and his cousin "Big Tim" Sullivan, who supported the fifty-four-hour bill on behalf of his hardworking mother and sister.

Their votes were crucial, but they were en route to New York City when the bill came up. When they received Perkins's message, they dashed off the ferry, ran up the hill, and arrived as the roll call was taken: A "mighty roar" greeted their arrival, "right hands raised," shouting their votes. The Senate "was swept by a tidal wave of emotion. . . . Callous old politicians, who had long forgotten what a tear was, were weeping. . . . And at the back of the chamber, clinging to the brass rail, beyond which she might not go, Frances Perkins was weeping too."

According to Dutcher, after the vote "Senators engulfed" Frances Perkins with praise and congratulations. She named several, but FDR was not among them. (Elizabeth Dutcher, "Frances Perkins: Doctor of Politics," *Woman Voter,* Sept. 1912, pp. 12–13.)

194–95 *invited Gifford Pinchot:* FDR on desertification, quoted in Schlesinger, *The Crisis of the Old Order,* p. 335.

195 *Of those first years in Albany:* TIMS, pp. 180–81.

195 *"an anti-suffragette"*: Lash, *Eleanor and Franklin*, pp. 238–39.

The only indication, cited repeatedly, that ER actively opposed suffrage is a letter from her brother, Hall, written from Groton on 31 Jan. 1908: "You seemed surprised that Auntie Pussie is a suffragist (ette). I told you that the day I went to lunch with her. The most surprising part to me is that she is trying to convert you of all people!" (Hall Roosevelt to ER, FDRL.)

But, to date, there is scarcely one contemporary word from ER directly on the subject. Subsequently, she analyzed her belated evolution as a feminist who embraced enfranchisement, equality, and the full empowerment of women: "In my grandmother's home politics were never mentioned and I think she was rather ashamed to acknowledge that even by marriage anything so contaminating as a government official was related to the family." At Allenswood, "I came in contact . . . with the first women I had ever known who were really intellectually emancipated, and I found this experience extremely stimulating." But here one must pause to recall that Marie Souvestre was eager to introduce the impressionable sixteen-year-old Eleanor to her great friend Mrs. Humphry Ward, Britain's leading antisuffragist.

As a debutante and young matron, ER "still heard with amusement and horror in the early nineteen-hundreds of the early fighters for suffrage who had worn trousers and walked around the streets of New York in them." ER dated the real change in her views, and the views of her society, with World War I, and noted: "I had my first contact with the suffrage movement rather late, and consider myself lucky to have heard Anna Howard Shaw speak and to have known Carrie Chapman Catt before she was widely recognized as the great leader of women in the struggle for equal political rights." (ER, "Women Have Come a Long Way," *Harper's Magazine*, Oct. 1950, pp. 74–76.)

195–96 *In 1912:* Jane Addams speech, *New York Times*, 8 Aug. 1912. See also, A. F. Davis, *American Heroine*, pp. 186–97.

On 5 Nov. 1912, TR wrote to Jane Addams: "I prize your action, not only because of what you are and stand for, but because of what it symbolized for the new movement. In this great National Convention of a new party women have thereby been shown to have their places to fill precisely as men have, and on an absolute equality." (Quoted in Melanie Gustafson, "Women's Partisanship and the Progressive party of 1912," unpublished paper presented to the Eighth Berkshire Conference on the History of Women, June 1990, p. 23. I am grateful to Melanie Gustafson for sending me this paper.)

196 *refrained from any public support* (of TR): *TIMS*, p. 189.

197 *"F is . . . well satisfied"*: ER to Isabella and Bob Ferguson, 24 July 1912, Tucson.

197 *Her brother, Hall: TIMS*, pp. 186–87, 193.

197 *Margaret Richardson:* The granddaughter of architect Henry Hobson Richardson (noted for Trinity Church and the Hay-Adams houses in Washington), she was an enthusiastic sportswoman, and a celebrated Boston belle. On 14 Jan. 1912, the Boston *Herald* noted that she was "one of the most strikingly good looking girls of her set," and that Gracie Hall Roosevelt was "foremost in her train." I am grateful to Honor Moore for this reference.

197–98 *ER and FDR were separated frequently:* FDR to ER, 14 April 1912, FDRL. (FDR's correspondence with SDR during his Panama trip is in *Letters*, vol. 2, pp. 180–90.)

198 *New Mexico:* ER planned the visit with the Fergusons for months. (Tucson correspondence.)

198 *"love at first sight"*: On the Democratic convention, see Morgan, *FDR*, p. 139; Josephus Daniels, *The Wilson Era: Years of Peace, 1910–1917* (University of North Carolina Press, 1944). Privately, ER wrote Isabella, her heart was with the Progressives. (24 July 1912, Tucson.)

199 *"You must have a fever"*: SDR quoted in Lash, *Eleanor and Franklin*, p. 178.

199–200 *Louis McHenry Howe:* For descriptions of Howe, see Burns, *Lion and Fox*, p. 44; Morgan, *FDR*, p. 132; Rollins, *Roosevelt and Howe*, ch. 1; *TIMS*, p. 193.

Daniels and Root are quoted in Burns, *Lion and Fox*, p. 50, Morgan, *FDR*, p. 143.

As the election neared, ER wrote several letters to Bob and Isabella Ferguson expressing hope that Uncle Ted would "win." On 28 Sept. she wrote Isabella: "Uncle Ted's Progressive ideas have fired so many of the young men to real work in this state that even if he doesn't win this time I feel a big work will have been accomplished." (Tucson.)

On 2 Nov. 1912, ER wrote that even if TR did not win "this time he will four years from now." (Tucson.)

200 *During the inauguration:* ER's observations on the suffragists, Wilson, and the new First Lady, Ellen Axson Wilson, are in letters to Isabella Ferguson, 12 March 1913, 11 April 1913, Tucson.

200 *"nice fat ladies"*: ER's curious note failed to give any hint of the excitement of the day. *The New York Times* devoted a full page to the event, and described in detail both the march ("the capital saw the greatest parade of women in its history"), and the "wonderful allegory" on the Treasury steps:

"Over 5,000 women passed down Pennsylvania Avenue. . . . Floats . . . illustrated the progress the woman's suffrage cause had made in the last seventy-five years. Scattered throughout . . . were the standards of nearly every State in the Union. It was an astonishing event."

Over 500,000 persons watched the march: "Imagine a Broadway election night crowd. . . . Imagine that crowd surging forward constantly, without proper police restraint. . . . It was necessary many times to call a halt while the mounted escort and the policemen pushed the crowd back."

(Washington's failure to monitor the crowd was insulting to the suffragists, who had their own escorts, and with their own restraint and horsemanship managed the affair. Subsequently, Dr. Anna Howard Shaw demanded an investigation.)

"Through all the confusion and turmoil the . . . paraders marched calmly, keeping a military formation. . . ."

Mounted on a white horse, Inez Milholland led the parade "in a white broadcloth Cossack suit and long white-kid boots. From her shoulders hung a pale-blue cloak, adorned with a golden maltese cross."

At the rear, equally honored, was General Rosalie Jones and the women who had hiked from New York to Washington. "Carrying her yellow pilgrim staff and a great bunch of roses, Gen. Jones walked in front of the line of women," all in brown, who had made the trip on foot.

The first section marched under the banner "Women of the World, Unite!" and was led by the Marysville, Missouri, band of thirty-five, "wearing the yellow color of the suffragist cause," and followed by delegations from twenty nations.

The floats of the second section told the story of the suffrage fight from 1840 to the present, and included several men "representing 'male supremacy' [who] seemed rather ashamed of themselves." The float called "Today" was limited to women, in college gowns, followed by a troop of women cavalry from Baltimore.

The third section portrayed women's various callings: farmers, housekeepers, patriotic workers, and "floats for all the occupations," including one representing the interior of a sweatshop, followed by delegations of women. "The clergy was represented by six sedate, rather elderly women in black gowns." The educational division included "thirty-two colored women from Howard University," all in caps and gowns. The businesswomen "marched 400 strong in blue. The writers . . . wore white gowns. Artists were in pink, and musicians in red." Actresses, attorneys, librarians, social workers, housewives, physicians all followed, delegation, by delegation, wearing "gowns of like color."

After the parade, "one of the most impressively beautiful spectacles ever staged in this country" occurred on the steps of the Treasury Building. "It was a triumph for the women who came here to play an unprecedented part in the festivities attending the inauguration. . . ."

The elaborate allegory, featuring brilliantly colored costumes and the most stirring music, "illustrated those ideals toward which both men and women" continued to struggle: Columbia, upon hearing the trumpets of march as it made its way up Pennsylvania Avenue, "summoned to her Justice, Charity, Liberty, Peace and Hope, to review with her the 'New Crusade' of women." Columbia, in velvet-and-silken robes of red, white, and blue, waited while Justice, "clad in richest purple and attended by maidens robed in all the violet shades came down the long flight of steps. . . ." "The triumphal march from AIDA served to herald the coming of Liberty, a girl in trailing veils of rose color, who . . . danced across the stage, an unfettered being, beautifully free." As the band "struck into the opening strains of the *Lohengrin Overture*," Peace, robed in white, stood motionless—and then lifted her arms to free a white dove, which "sprang joyously into the air, circled down over the crowd and away."

The "bare legs" of the participants, which ER had commented upon, were also a subject of interest in the *Times'* celebration:

"The raw, biting wind . . . was not suited to the almost diaphanous costumes that served to adorn most of the figures . . . and most of them presented bared arms to the cold that was enough to make the men in the crowd glad that they had brought their heaviest fur coats." Though the wind "served to whip and turn and flutter the drapery most attractively, it did not serve to allay the concern for the health of the participants that could be heard expressed. . . . But the real suffragists said it was heroic."

("5,000 Women March / Beset by Crowds," *New York Times*, 4 March 1913.)

9. The Roosevelts in Wilson's Washington

201 *Eleanor was not with him:* FDR to ER, 17 March 1913, FDRL.

201 *second letter:* Correspondence between FDR and his mother, 17 March, 18 March 1913, in *Letters*, vol. 2, pp. 199–200.

202 *ER spent the summer:* On the aftermath of Josie Zabriskie's death, and SDR's reaction to ER's guests at Campobello, ER to FDR, quoted in Lash, *Eleanor and Franklin*, pp. 180–81.

203 *"I have a little more milk":* ER to Isabella, Sept. 1914, Tucson.

203 *She gave a party:* Lash, *Eleanor and Franklin*, p. 194. On John Aspinwall's birth, see *TIMS*, p. 239.

203–4 *Wilson's most radical allies:* Daniels's 1 Oct. 1912 editorial, on "the subjection of the negro," in the *News and Observer*, quoted in Morgan, *FDR*, pp. 147–48.

On Wilson, darling of the Dixiecrats, see especially Kathleen Wolgemuth, "Woodrow Wilson and Federal Segregation," *Journal of Negro History*, April 1959, pp. 158–73. According to Wolgemuth, the impetus for the unprecedented segregation of federal workers came from Postmaster General Albert Burleson, Secretary of the Treasury William Gibbs McAdoo, and Josephus Daniels. See also Nancy Weiss, "The Negro and the New Freedom: Fighting Wilsonian Segregation," *Political Science Quarterly*, March 1968, pp. 61–79; Rayford W. Logan, *The Betrayal of the Negro from Rutherford B. Hayes to Woodrow Wilson* (Macmillan, Collier Books, 1965 [1954]); and Harry N. Scheiber, *The Wilson Administration and Civil Liberties, 1917–1921* (Cornell University Press, 1960).

W. E. B. Du Bois was stunned by Wilson's executive order that mandated segregation in office buildings, cafeterias, and toilets throughout the federal city. In his editorials in *The Crisis*, Du Bois had urged African-Americans to support Wilson in 1912: "We sympathize with those faithful old black voters who will always vote the Republican ticket. . . . We can understand those who, despite the unspeakable Theodore Roosevelt, accept his platform which is broad on all subjects except the greatest—human rights. . . . [But] we sincerely believe that even in the face of promises disconcertingly vague, and in the face of the solid caste-ridden South, it is better to elect Woodrow Wilson. . . ." ("The Last Word in Politics.")

Six months after Wilson's inauguration, W. E. B. Du Bois wrote "An Open Letter to Woodrow Wilson," full of disbelief that Wilson (who in 1912 had said he wanted to see "justice done to the colored people . . . ; and not mere grudging justice, but justice executed with liberality and cordial good feeling") even knew "of the gravest attack on the liberties of our people since emancipation."

"Public segregation of civil servants in government employ, necessarily involving personal insult and humiliation, has for the first time in history been made the policy of the United States government.

"In the Treasury and Post Office Department colored clerks have been herded to themselves as though they were not human beings. We are told that one colored clerk who could not actually be segregated on account of the nature of his work had consequently had a cage built around him to separate him from his white companions of many years. Mr. Wilson, do you know these things? Are you responsible for them? . . ." (*The Crisis*, Sept. 1913.)

204 *Daniels expressed horror:* For ER on Josephus Daniels, see Jonathan Daniels, *The End of Innocence* (J. B. Lippincott, 1954), p. 80.

204–5 *Ellen Axson Wilson's crusade:* See ibid., pp. 85–86, 125, 136; Edith Elmer Wood, "Four Washington Alleys," *The Survey*, 6 Dec. 1913, pp. 250ff; Mrs. Ernest P. Bicknell, "Home-Maker of the White House: Mrs. Woodrow Wilson's Social Work in Washington," *The Survey*, 3 Oct. 1914, pp. 10ff; and "Mrs. Wilson's Death and Washington's Alleys," *The Survey*, 3 Oct. 1914, pp. 515ff.

Charlotte Everett Hopkins was president of the board of the Home for Incurables, and chaired the women's department of the National Civic Federation. She waited only several weeks to engage ER in her crusade for decent housing in 1933. See Volume Two of this biography for ER's efforts in behalf of public housing after 1933.

205 *"next step will be Socialism":* ER to Aunt Maude, [1912], quoted in Lash, *Love, Eleanor*, p. 63.

206 *respect for Mrs. Daniels:* Jonathan Daniels, *End of Innocence*, p. 38.

206 *unruffled by the 1912 breach:* TR to FDR, 18 March 1913, Family Papers Donated by the Children, Box 20, FDRL.

206 *in Aunt Bye's home:* For ER's assessment of her friends and allies in Washington, see TIMS, pp. 198–99, 234–37.

When Sir Cecil Spring-Rice was recalled to London during the war, ER felt a personal loss, and was outraged that he had been so shabbily treated by his government. He was replaced by Lord Reading, who was considered more knowledgeable about the war, and better able to get along with Wilson. ER wrote Bob Ferguson: "We were all very sorry to see the Spring Rice's go & it seemed very sudden & inconsiderate but I suppose governments can't bother about anyone's conveniences now. What a change in British policy to send a politician, isn't it? Franklin says he is very clever and able and of course is close with the present government. Sir Cecil never was well known by many people in this country . . . but those who knew him, loved him & will miss him and his wife." (23 Jan. 1918, Tucson.)

ER also wrote Isabella that, when she asked Henry Adams how he felt about Spring-

Rice's sudden departure, he said: "Jews are trumps just now!" His comment presumably referred to Rufus Isaacs, Earl (later Marquess) of Reading, and it appears ER did not at the time disagree. (ER to Isabella, 11 Jan. 1918, Tucson.)

Although Sir Cecil left the United States in good health, he was stunned by his recall, given no other appointment, and died suddenly on 14 Feb. Henry Cabot Lodge believed he "died of a broken heart." ER wrote, "We were truly grieved about Sir Cecil," and sent Isabella a note Florence Spring-Rice had written so that Isabella might see her "particularly brave and unselfish" qualities (ER to Isabella Ferguson, 24 Feb. 1918, Tucson). (Henry Cabot Lodge quoted in S. J. Morris, *Edith Kermit Roosevelt,* p. 418.)

206–7 *curmudgeon Henry Adams:* Oliver Wendell Holmes quoted in Jonathan Daniels, *End of Innocence,* p. 83.

207 *"loved to shock his hearers":* TIMS, pp. 236–37.

207 *"very interesting":* ER to SDR, 9 Jan. 1919, *Letters,* vol. 2, p. 445.

Within a month after Sir Cecil's death, during the night of 26 March 1918, Henry Adams died in his sleep. During the early years of Wilson's administration, ER shared Henry Adams's views on certain issues, most notably his antagonism to Jews in high places. For a discussion of the development of her social thought on issues of bigotry and race, see Volume Two.

207 *tradition of "calling":* ER's journals for this period (FDRL) are filled with daily lists of whom she called upon, who was home, where she merely left her card. They are also filled with seating arrangements for weekly official and unofficial dinner parties given for ten to forty people.

207–8 *"dreariness and waste":* ER to Isabella, 21 June 1916, Tucson.

208 *Two Sundays a month:* On "The Club," Mrs. Leavitt, and other Washington friends, see TIMS, pp. 198–99; Lash, *Eleanor and Franklin,* pp. 190–91.

208–10 *Franklin K. Lane:* For ER on Lane, see TIMS, pp. 256–58. Lane's 1920 letter to ER is quoted in Lash, *Eleanor and Franklin,* p. 260; Lane to FDR on his behavior toward Josephus Daniels is quoted in Jonathan Daniels, *End of Innocence,* p. 129. On Josephus Daniels's amazing patience with his frequently impertinent subordinate, see Schlesinger, *Crisis of the Old Order,* p. 345; Jonathan Daniels, *End of Innocence,* passim.; and Rollins, *Roosevelt and Howe,* pp. 117–19 and passim.

210 *a uniquely devoted . . . couple:* On Washington's perceptions of ER, and her own sense of reality, see TIMS, p. 238; Jonathan Daniels, *End of Innocence,* p. 246.

211 *"her really brilliant mind":* FDR to Aunt Maude, quoted in Lash, *Eleanor and Franklin,* p. 182.

211 *beginning of the war:* ER on TR and William Jennings Bryan in TIMS, pp. 230–32.

212 *"All one's thoughts":* ER to FDR, 7 Aug. 1914, FDRL.

212 *"seemed the least bit excited":* FDR to ER, 2 Aug. 1914, in *Letters,* vol. 2, p. 238.

On 1 Aug., FDR had written his wife: "Germany has declared war against Russia. A complete smash-up is inevitable. Mr. [Daniels] totally fails to grasp the situation. . . . These are history-making days. It will be the greatest war in the world's history. All well." (Ibid., p. 233.)

Despite the outbreak of war, FDR decided to run in the Democratic primary for the U.S. Senate in 1914. ER wrote the Fergusons: "He doesn't stand a chance of winning but I hope he'll run well to encourage them [the party leadership] for future battles." (28 Sept. 1914, Tucson.)

For the activities of that segment of the peace movement spearheaded by women and men who were later to become ER's political friends and allies, see BWC, "Woodrow Wilson and the Antimilitarists, 1914–1917," Ph.D. dissertation, The Johns Hopkins University, 1970; BWC, "The Woman's Peace Party," in *Peace and Change,* March 1972; BWC, "For Peace and Democracy in England and the United States, 1914–1918," in Charles Chatfield, ed., *Peace Movements in America* (Schocken, 1973); C. Roland Marchand, *The American Peace Movement and Social Reform, 1898–1918* (Princeton University Press, 1972); Barbara Steinson, *American Women's Activism in World War I* (Garland, 1982); and, most recently, John Whiteclay Chambers, ed., *The Eagle and the Dove: The American Peace Movement and United States Foreign Policy, 1900–1922* (Syracuse University Press, 1991), which includes excellent bibliography and documents.

212–13 *Mexico, and Haiti:* On the successful effort to avert war with Mexico, which U.S. oil interests and Republican "jingoes" allied with TR agitated for in 1914 and 1916, see BWC, "Woodrow Wilson and the American Union Against Militarism"; Chambers, ed., *Eagle and Dove,* pp. 76–87; Frederich Katz, *The Secret War in Mexico: Europe, The U.S., and the Mexican Revolution* (University of Chicago Press, 1981); and Arthur S. Link, *Woodrow Wilson and a Revolutionary World, 1913–1921* (University of North Carolina Press, 1982).

On 14 July 1914, FDR dispatched 700 Marines and two ships to the U.S. naval base at Guantánamo in Cuba to be prepared for all exigencies in the area, and went himself on a fact-finding mission at the end of the year. ER wrote the Fergusons that she would have the "very interesting book" they had sent her for Christmas "to read in the very lonely evenings when F goes to Haiti, San Domingo and Guantanamo, a three weeks trip which is to begin the 21st." (Tucson.)

The United States occupied Haiti in 1915. Negotiations to purchase the Danish West Indies (now the United States Virgin Islands) also began in 1915, and were completed in 1917. See William Boyer, *America's Virgin Islands: A History of Human Rights and Wrongs* (Carolina Academic Press, 1983).

Although more cautious about intervention than FDR, Josephus Daniels was not a pacifist or an anti-imperialist when it came to Haiti, or other areas in the Caribbean. Rather, he called for "the complete pacification of Haiti," if the Haitian government and leadership refused to sign the treaty which established U.S. control. By 1917, Haiti's National Assembly was dissolved and Haiti was ruled by the Marines, under direct authority of Daniels and FDR. When FDR toured Haiti in 1917, he was so well pleased by the effects of martial law, he considered investing in the area's tourist future. If he saw any of the brutal excesses later so graphically reported, he wrote nothing of them after his journey to what he called the "Darkest Africa of the West Indies."

In 1919, FDR urged the navy "quietly to take title" to an "unused" Caribbean island, and then to "slip the matter" into an appropriations bill later. For FDR's 1917 trip, see especially Morgan, *FDR,* pp. 176–77. On his investment interest in Haiti, see Rollins, *Roosevelt and Howe,* p. 173. On FDR's 1919 suggestion, see Rollins, p. 121.

FDR at first boasted and then denied that he wrote Haiti's new constitution. Contemporary sources fully credit him with having done so, including the most hated and resisted clause, which gave Americans ("foreigners") the right to own Haitian lands. The treaty with Haiti was signed on 16 Sept. 1915, and ratified with speed by the Senate on 28 Feb. 1916.

See especially Emily Greene Balch, ed., *Occupied Haiti* (Garland Publishing, 1972 [1927]); Major General Smedley D. Butler, "War Is a Racket," in *Three Generals on War,* ed. John Whiteclay Chambers (Garland, 1973 [1935], an expansion and revision of Butler's *Forum* article of the same title, Sept. 1934, pp. 140–43; Rayford Logan, *Haiti and the Dominican Republic* (Oxford University Press, 1968).

213 *she wrote with dismay:* ER to FDR, 5–6 Aug. 1914.

213 *"I'm glad Bryan is out":* ER to FDR, 10 June 1915, Box 15, FDRL.

On 11 June 1915, ER wrote Isabella Ferguson: "We are all much excited politically since Mr. Bryan's resignation. . . . My new governess has three brothers at the front, one wounded, so we feel the war rather close. . . ." ER also shared FDR's feelng about preparedness in 1916: "Our chief interest now," she wrote Isabella, were the "National Defense Bills. F does not think them adequate—but the question seems to be, 'will Congress give even this'? . . ." (14 Nov. 1916, Tucson.)

213–14 *World War I destroyed the progressive alliance:* For the wartime breach between the Wilson-Hughes suffragists, see BWC, ed., *Crystal Eastman on Women and Revolution* (Oxford University Press, 1978). For the demise of the Jane Addams–TR alliance, see A. F. Davis, *American Heroine,* p. 223. See also Allen Davis, ed., *Jane Addams on Peace, War, and International Understanding, 1899–1932* (Garland, 1976).

214 *TR was desperate:* TR to ER, 15 March 1915, Family Papers Donated by the Children, Box 20, FDRL.

214 *"a bitter blow":* TIMS, pp. 249–50.

214–15 *Hall and . . . Quentin . . . enlist:* TIMS, p. 252.

215 *the war meant new work:* TIMS, pp. 245–46; 254–65.

216 *Washington's night life:* ER to Bob Ferguson, 16 Sept. 1920, Tucson.

216 *Livy . . . Davis:* ER wrote most frequently about Livy Davis to her mother-in-law; see especially ER to SDR, 8 Feb. 1919, in *Letters,* vol. 2, p. 467.

216 *"gay and glamorous":* On Davis, see Jonathan Daniels, *End of Innocence,* pp. 252–54; and Morgan, *FDR,* pp. 202–3.

217 *first . . . mention of Lucy Mercer:* ER to FDR, 23 July 1916, Family Papers, Box 15, FDRL.

217–18 *"goosy girl":* FDR to ER, 16 July 1917, in *Letters,* vol. 2, 347.

Many of ER's letters, beginning in 1915, have a hurt, angry, resigned quality. On 15 Oct. 1915, she wrote: "Not a word from you wretch!" On 10 July 1916: "The infantile paralysis is terrible and I am thankful to have the children here." (Family Papers, Box 15, FDRL.)

218 *"Such a funny party":* FDR to ER, 25 July 1917, in *Letters,* vol. 2, p. 352.

218–19 *"food-saving program":* New York Times, 17 July 1917, and FDR to ER, 18 July, are both in ibid., pp. 349–50.

219 *"it was horrid":* ER to FDR, 24 July 1917, FDRL.

219 *"nothing I ask for appears":* Ibid.

219 *"My threat was no idle one":* ER to FDR, 15 Aug. 1917, FDRL.

220 *another jolly outing:* FDR to ER, 20 Aug., in *Letters,* vol. 2, p. 358.

220 *"Isn't she perfectly lovely":* For the conversation between Alice Roosevelt Longworth and FDR on Lucy Mercer, and her oft-repeated string-bean story, see Teague, *Mrs. L,* pp. 157–58, 160; also Alsop, *Centenary Remembrance,* p. 67; and Felsenthal, *Alice Roosevelt Longworth,* p. 137.

220 *her own marriage disintegrated:* Alice told her family as early as 1912 that she wanted a divorce, but they persuaded her that the public scandal would be too terrible (Teague, *Mrs. L,* p. 158).

221 *"look up in the chandelier":* On the rivalry between Alice Longworth and Cissy Patterson for Senator Borah, see Ralph G. Martin, *Cissy: The Extraordinary Life of*

Eleanor Medill Patterson (Simon & Schuster, 1979), p. 189; Felsenthal, *Alice Roosevelt Longworth*, pp. 135, 147, 149. Cf. Eleanor Gizycka, *Glass Houses* (Minton, Balch, 1926).

Despite their rivalry, Alice always considered Cissy Patterson a "great friend": "Cissy was an enchanting creature." (Teague, *Mrs. L*, pp. 174, 176.)

222 *"she wanted to be Eleanor Roosevelt":* Cissy Patterson on ER, R. Martin, *Cissy*, p. 324; cf. Alice Albright Hoge, *Cissy Patterson* (Random House, 1966).

Although Alice could barely abide her husband, they remained politically allied. For their relations, see Felsenthal, *Alice Roosevelt Longworth*, ch. 8; on destruction of his papers and violin, see p. 168.

According to composer Mary Howe, who frequently played with Nicholas Longworth, his violin was an "excellent Stradivarius," and the congressman was very serious about his music. "It was almost incongruous in his apparently hard-boiled make-up." (Mary Howe, *Jottings* [Washington, D.C., privately printed, 1957].) I am grateful to Dorothy Indenbaum for this reference.

222–23 *"most unjust to poor May Ladenburg":* On the Bernard Baruch–May Ladenburg caper, see Teague, *Mrs. L*, pp. 162–63; Alsop, *Centenary Remembrance*, pp. 66–68; Felsenthal, *Alice Roosevelt Longworth*, pp. 137–39.

223 *"terribly disappointed":* ER to FDR, 5 Nov. 1917, FDRL.

223–24 *"Dearest Honey":* ER to FDR, n.d. [1918], Box 15, FDRL.

224 *her canteen . . . co-workers:* especially Mary Astor Paul Munn; she and her husband (the "Charlie Munns") were members of the set that FDR and Lucy Mercer partied with. See, for example, FDR to ER, 25 July 1917, in *Letters*, vol. 2, p. 352.

224 *"I loved it":* ER to Lorena Hickok, Oct. 1932, AP Release, Hickok Papers, FDRL.

224 *"asked me to go":* ER to FDR, 20 July 1918, Box 15, FDRL; see also ER to SDR, 17 July 1918, Box 13, FDRL.

ER was restless. In her 20 July letter, she had noted that "life is very quiet here." "I feel as though you had been gone years." On 1 Aug. 1918, she wrote: "Dearest honey, I got your letter from the Azores. . . . It was wonderful to hear only I hate not being with you and seeing it all! Isn't that horrid of me!"

225 *letters of gratitude:* Letters to ER quoted in Lash, *Love, Eleanor*, pp. 216, 218–19; and FDRL.

225 *to raise money:* TIMS, pp. 255, 259.

225 *Theodore Roosevelt decided:* On TR's gift to ER, see S. J. Morris, *Edith Kermit Roosevelt*, p. 422.

225 *ER had also learned:* "I went in bathing with the chicks on Friday and had a rope on and I think Butler may succeed in teaching me to swim . . . and all the chicks [are] learning to swim too . . . Elliott with the best stroke of all" (ER to FDR, 4 Aug. 1919, Box 15, FDRL).

226 *"Is F paying any attention":* Hall to ER, 26 July 1912, FDRL.

226 *"many quiet evenings":* ER to Isabella, 13 Nov. 1917, Tucson.

226–27 *"noblesse oblige":* SDR to "Dearest Franklin and Dearest Eleanor," 14 Oct. 1917, in *Letters*, vol. 2, pp. 274–75. SDR's own affirmations were strained as the world she knew teetered around her. She concluded this letter with the observation: "When I *talk* I find I usually arouse opposition, which seems odd, but is perhaps my own fault, and tends to lower my opinion of myself, which is doubtless salutary. . . ."

227 *"how lucky we are":* ER to SDR, 22 Jan. 1918, FDRL.

227 *"I love you dear":* ER to SDR, 18 March 1918, FDRL.

228 *the "bottom dropped out":* Lash, *Eleanor and Franklin,* p. 221.

There is no record of ER's feelings between FDR's return in Sept. 1918 and their trip to Europe together in Jan. 1919.

Although her brother, Hall, was a regular correspondent, his letters for this period are not among his papers. And to the Fergusons ER wrote at a great slant: On 13 Nov. 1918, ER wrote Bob Ferguson: "Franklin had a horrid time but is quite well again." She apologized for not writing for so long, because the war's end had left everything so uncertain: "We've lived in suspense from day to day never knowing what would happen next and no one making any definite plans so I put off even writing till things settled down a bit!" (Tucson.)

Ironically, Josephus Daniels's son was the first to write of the Lucy Mercer affair. See Jonathan Daniels, *The Washington Quadrille: The Dance Beside the Documents* (Doubleday, 1968).

228–29 *Lucy Mercer's Catholicism:* According to Joseph Alsop, Lucy Mercer's "extra-strict" Catholicism prevented not only divorce but any consummation of an affair with a married man (*Centenary Remembrance,* pp. 68ff). But Lucy Mercer evidently told family and friends that she would have married FDR if Eleanor had only been "willing to step aside." (Jonathan Daniels, *Washington Quadrille,* p. 145.)

Although Lucy Mercer was educated at a convent school in Austria, her mother was divorced when she married her Roman Catholic father. See Kenneth S. Davis, *FDR: The Beckoning of Destiny, 1882–1928* (Random House, 1971), pp. 484–85.

229 *"Lucy Mercer married Mr. Wintie":* ER's life was frequently intersected by one of history's most interesting women, Alva Erskine Smith Vanderbilt Belmont. Her husband, O. H. P. Belmont, was a friend of Elliott's, who sent him a terrier for company during his exile in Abingdon. In 1905, *Town Topics* compared ER's wedding to her daughter's. On the ERA, they were political opponents, although there is no evidence that they ever confronted each other.

The woman who donated Belmont House in Washington to the feminist cause, and became an outstanding leader of the equal-rights movement internationally, began her public life when she prevented her daughter from marrying Winthrop Rutherford. Famous as the most dominating mother in American society, Alva Erskine Smith was the daughter of fabulously wealthy cotton planters in Alabama and Kentucky. She married William K. Vanderbilt in 1875, and divorced him in 1895 on grounds of adultery. She married Oliver Hazard Perry Belmont, recently divorced from Sarah Whitney, in 1896. But her own marital history was as nothing compared with the cruelty of her daughter's fate. At seventeen, Consuelo Vanderbilt fell in love with Winthrop Rutherford, a bachelor of thirty, and they became secretly engaged. Alva Belmont would not have it: "She made me leave the country." "She intercepted all letters my sweetheart wrote and all of mine to him. She caused continuous scenes. She said I must obey. She said I knew very well I had no right to choose a husband, that I must take the man she had chosen."

And at her daughter's hearings before the Rota, the Vatican's Ecclesiastical Court in Rome, where Consuelo applied for an annulment in 1926, Alva Belmont agreed with her daughter's testimony: In 1895, she had chosen for her daughter the ninth Duke of Marlborough. (To arrange the marriage had cost the Vanderbilts a fortune estimated at $10 million.) Her daughter had no right to choose her husband. "I have always had absolute power over my daughter. . . . I ordered her to marry the Duke."

Her daughter and the Duke separated in 1908—ironically, the same year Alva Belmont, influenced by Anna Howard Shaw, became one of America's most militant and generous feminists. Evidently her first move was a reconciliation with her daughter. In 1909, she agreed to pay the rent for the new headquarters of the New York State Suffrage Association and the entire expenses of the National Association's press department, and to finance the Political Equality League, which she organized.

By 1919, she supported virtually every suffrage and feminist activity, including the

Southern Woman's Suffrage Conference and the Women's Trade Union League. She also contributed thousands of dollars to Max Eastman's radical journal *The Masses*. She cared little for partisanship, she insisted, only for victory.

Her heart, she wrote, belonged to women the world over. There was "a common ground" between the richest woman on earth and the poorest "peasant woman." After suffrage, she became the international leader of equal-rights feminists and worked ardently for women until her death in France in 1933.

In 1926, she spoke to the International Alliance of Women in Paris as president of the United States' National Woman's Party: "Have courage in your own judgment; trust yourselves; do not listen to the voice of fear; speak out. . . . Let us all together bear witness . . . that we will not cease for a single day until all women are completely emancipated."

(The Rota testimony is quoted in Amory, *Who Killed Society?*, pp. 233–34; Belmont's speeches in BWC, *Crystal Eastman*, pp. 207–9. Although there is to date no biography of Alva Belmont, see Christopher Lasch in *Notable American Women*, ed. James et al., pp. 126–28.)

230 *"My husband did not seem"*: TIMS, p. 268.

230 *"I think I learned"*: Ibid., pp. 259–60

232 *Mother never slept with Father*: Elliott Roosevelt and James Brough, *An Untold Story: The Roosevelts of Hyde Park* (G. P. Putnam's Sons, 1973); J. Roosevelt with Libby, *My Parents*, pp. 101–2. ER's granddaughter said she remembered her mother's words exactly. Anna told her own daughter that upon her marriage (in June 1926) ER told her that sex "was an ordeal to be borne." (Eleanor Seagraves to author.)

232 *a second honeymoon*: With few exceptions, the letters from both ER and FDR to Mama and the children during the European tour of 1919 are in *Letters*, vol. 2, pp. 444–70.

232–33 *death of her Uncle Theodore*: ER to SDR, 9 Jan., in ibid., p. 445; *TIMS*, p. 275.

ER did not write with emotion about her uncle's death. Nor did she associate it with his months of evident agony over Quentin's death. Indeed, when Quentin was killed, his plane shot down over enemy lines, ER wrote Bob Ferguson that he had died instantly "by two bullet holes in the head so he did not suffer and it is a glorious way to die; but I know Aunt Edith and Ethel are suffering." (28 July 1918, Tucson.)

It seems, however, that the bellicose warrior was shattered. A light faded, his friends noticed; "the boy in him had died." (S. J. Morris, *Edith Kermit Roosevelt*, p. 428.)

TR wrote his son Kermit that Edith had been wonderful in crisis. "Mother has . . . the heroic soul." They went for a row "out on the still, glassy water towards the sound; there was a little haze, and it all soothed her poor bruised and aching spirit; then we took a swim; and as we swam she spoke of the velvet touch of the water and turning to me smiled and said, 'there is left the wind on the heath, brother!' " (S. J. Morris, *Edith Kermit Roosevelt*, p. 425.)

Six months later Theodore Roosevelt was dead.

ER wrote with tenderness about her Uncle Douglas Robinson's death on 12 Sept. 1918. Her Aunt Corinne's husband had been her father's mentor and business partner, and she "joined the family and friends" for his funeral at Herkimer, the family compound, "a very sweet place," in bird-filled woods, "nine miles up the mountain." "Of all the cemeteries I know, it is the least lonely place to leave someone you love." (*TIMS*, p. 267.)

233 *a transforming experience*: ER to Isabella, 11 July 1919, Tucson.

233 *Astounded by the devastation*: TIMS, pp. 278–88.

233 *grieved not to be with FDR*: ER to SDR, 31 Jan. 1919, Box 16, FDRL.

234 *"fascinated by Lady Scott":* ER to SDR, 11 Feb. 1919, in *Letters,* vol. 2, p. 469.

234 *"the scandals":* Ibid.

234 *nobody referred to the Lucy Mercer affair:* ER's glancing comment about her "breathless, hunted year" contrasts with the long, detailed letters she wrote to Isabella and her mother-in-law about the dissipations of her cousins in Paris. She worried especially about Aunt Corinne's son Munro, who behaved much as her father had. When he returned to the United States, his behavior worsened "and [he] is now in Bloomingdale's. . . . I confess to rather a hopeless feeling as to the future unless they can send him where he must work hard physically as well as mentally." (ER to Isabella, 11 July 1919, Tucson.)

235 *lost her appetite:* ER to FDR, May 1919, quoted in Lash, *Eleanor and Franklin,* p. 244.

235 *Clover Adams committed suicide:* Eugenia Kaledin, *The Education of Mrs. Henry Adams* (Temple University Press, 1981).

236 *the poem Cecil Spring-Rice had written:* Quoted in Lash, *Love, Eleanor,* p. 237.

10. 1919–20: Race Riots and Red Scare, Grief and Renewal

237 *The Russian Revolution:* ER considered Russia "certainly a baffling problem and one can't help feeling sorry for those poor people." (ER to Bob Ferguson, 24 Feb. 1918, Tucson.)

Neither ER nor FDR viewed the secret Allied intervention into Russia with concern. On 8 Aug. 1918, ER wrote FDR: "the news continues good and I imagine you are glad to be in Europe. . . . I'm sorry General Glover and not General Wood goes in command of Siberia. . . ." (FDRL.)

237 *Women demanded the vote:* The radical suffragists of the Woman's Peace Party of New York hailed the revolution with "mad, glad joy." (*Four Lights,* 24 March 1917.)

238 *"There is no life":* Emmeline Pethick-Lawrence quoted in BWC, *Crystal Eastman,* p. 11. On Anglo-American suffragist militancy and the war, see Midge Mackenzie, *Shoulder to Shoulder* (Alfred A. Knopf, 1975); Jane Marcus, ed., *Suffrage and the Pankhursts* (Routledge & Kegan Paul, 1987); and J. Stanley Lemons, *The Woman Citizen: Social Feminism in the 1920s* (University of Illinois Press, 1973), ch. 1.

238 *"terms must please you":* ER to Bob Ferguson, 13 Nov. 1918, Tucson.

239 *Red Scare:* William Preston, Jr., *Aliens and Dissenters: Federal Suppression of Radicals, 1903–1933* (Harvard University Press, 1963; Harper Torchbooks, 1966); Robert K. Murray, *Red Scare: A Study in National Hysteria, 1919–1920* (McGraw-Hill, Paperback, 1964); Stanley Coben, *A. Mitchell Palmer: Politician* (Columbia University Press, 1963); and Joan Jensen, *Army Surveillance in America, 1775–1980* (Yale University Press, 1991).

The demand for political repression against "un-Americans" predated communist revolution, and was not limited to Wilsonians. It began with a crusade against immigrants and workers' rights after the Civil War, and intensified mightily during World War I. In April 1917, Theodore Roosevelt gave a speech at Oyster Bay on the "Duty of Every American." This introduced his frequently quoted line "No man can serve two masters," and was a rallying cry against radicals, conscientious objectors, and dissenters of all persuasion: "The American who is not now heart and soul . . . in favor of fighting this war . . . is a traitor to this country and a traitor to mankind. He is unfit to live in America. He is unfit to be a free man, for his soul is the soul of a slave. . . ." The neutralist should be sent "to some other neutral country." The seditionist "should be shot." (Quoted in Chambers, ed., *Eagle and Dove,* pp. 126–27.)

240 *Alice Wadsworth and Eleanor Roosevelt lunched:* On Alice Hay Wadsworth and the antisuffragists, see Lemons, *Woman Citizen,* pp. 11–13; 35–36.

240 *the "Palmer Raids":* New York Times, 9 Nov. 1919. See also Robert W. Dunn, ed., *The Palmer Raids* (International Publishers, 1948).

240–41 *the first "Red Ark":* On the cruelty and illegality of the deportations, see "The Buford Widows," *Survey,* 10 Jan. 1920; Louis F. Post, *The Deportations Delirium of 1920* (Charles Kerr, 1923).

241 *"boast of a superior liberty":* Max and Crystal Eastman quoted in New York State Legislature, Joint Committee Investigating Seditious Activities, Clayton R. Lusk, chair, *Revolutionary Radicalism: Its History, Purpose and Tactics,* 4 vols. (J. B. Lyon, 1920), vol. 1, *Propaganda,* pp. 1254–55. See BWC, ed., *Toward the Great Change: Crystal and Max Eastman on War and Revolution* (Garland, 1979).

241 *Palmer's descriptions:* A. Mitchell Palmer, "Extent of the Bolshevik Infection Here," *Literary Digest,* 17 Jan. 1920, quoted in Preston, *Aliens and Dissenters,* p. 193.

241 *"Like a prairie-fire":* A. Mitchell Palmer, "The Case Against the Reds," *Forum,* Feb. 1920, p. 179.

241–42 *democracy seemed limited:* Theodore Roosevelt, Jr.'s commitment to civil liberties, in Miller, *Roosevelt Chronicles,* p. 296. On Berger, Debs, and the New York State five, see BWC, "The Socialist Party Convention," in *Crystal Eastman,* pp. 349–56; Paula Eldot, *Governor Alfred E. Smith: The Politician as Reformer* (Garland, 1983), pp. 314–24.

Arrested for obstructing the draft, and sentenced to ten years in prison, Debs addressed the court: "Your honor, years ago I recognized my kinship with all living beings, and I made up my mind that I was not one bit better than the meanest on earth. I said then, and I say now, that while there is a lower class, I am in it; while there is a criminal element, I am of it; while there is a soul in prison, I am not free." Harding released him after 32 months. (See Ray Ginger, *The Bending Cross: A Biography of Eugene Victor Debs* (Rutgers University Press, 1949.)

243 *As a member:* On the DAR and "Spider Web," see Lemons, *Woman Citizen,* pp. 223–24.

243 *ER was appalled:* Women's Democratic News, July 1927, p. 6. Carrie Chapman Catt wrote that all those under attack were opposed "because all have expressed the hope:

"That peace will one day supplant war

"That children will be taken from factories and sent to school.

"That mothers and babies will not die by preventable causes.

"That this country may at least have as high a percent of literacy as that of Japan. . . ."

ER printed and distributed the article to all her friends.

243–44 *progressive change was the answer:* ER to Bob Ferguson, 16 Sept. 1919, Tucson.

244–45 *Palmer's house was dynamited:* ER to SDR, 3 June 1919, FDRL.

245 *"thought happiness did not matter":* ER to Trude Lash, 1940, in Lash, *Love, Eleanor,* p. 66.

245–46 *In that sanctuary:* Clover's life was known to ER. Whatever version of the stories she had been told, her family was for generations connected to the Hay-Adams circle. During the Civil War, for example, ER's grandfather Theodore Roosevelt was brought down to Washington by John Hay, and worked, as did Clover Hooper (Adams), with the U.S. Sanitary Commission. For Clover Adams's life, I have relied on Kaledin, *Education of Mrs. Henry Adams.*

246–47 *"I shall dedicate"*: Henry Adams to Elizabeth Cameron, 1884, quoted in ibid., p. 183.

There remains a curious unwillingness to consider Elizabeth Cameron (also Clover's best friend) a serious factor when one contemplates Clover Adams's suicide. In the most recent work on the subject, Patricia O'Toole's *The Five of Hearts: An Intimate Portrait of Henry Adams and His Friends* (Clarkson N. Potter, 1990), filled with much new research and detail, one is encouraged yet again to disregard Elizabeth Cameron on that day Clover took her life. It is a Sunday, and we are told Henry Adams left his wife in the afternoon because he had an appointment with his dentist. That Friday, Clover and Henry visited Elizabeth Cameron, who was not feeling well. Later we learn that she was pregnant with Martha, with whom Henry had a lifelong attachment of rare affection. When Henry died, Aileen Tone and Elizabeth Cameron went through his desk. In the top drawer they found the partially empty bottle of potassium cyanide that had killed Clover so quickly. "And in the kneehole hung a sign, hand-lettered in red ink on white paper, . . . MME. MARTHE, MODISTE." The sign had never been removed in thirty years from that place where little Martha Cameron played so often; she was Uncle Henry's "first adopted niece." (P. 399.) And still we are told that Clover Adams's depression and suicide were due entirely to her father's death—without even a pause to consider circumstance and chronology.

247 *a howling letter of protest*: Henry Adams to the American Historical Association, in Kaledin, *Education of Mrs. Henry Adams*, pp. 169–70.

Henry James, however, did appreciate the "intellectual grace" as well as the irreverent manner of his friend, and called Clover Adams the "genius of my beloved country." Ibid.

249 *Grandmother Hall died*: TIMS, pp. 299–301. Cf. Mrs. Valentine G. Hall, *New York Times* obituary, 16 Aug. 1919; and Mary Livingston Ludlow Hall, of 20 Gramercy Park, in "Wills for Probate," *New York Times*, 25 Aug. 1919.

250 *replaced all her servants*: TIMS, pp. 295–96.

251 *the colored race*: Ibid. "Amid a world of people who are having fearful domestic trials, I seem to be sailing along peacefully, having acquired on my return from England . . . a complete darky household." (ER to Isabella Ferguson, 26 Oct. 1919, Tucson.)

251 *"a ton of bricks"*: ER to FDR, 23 July 1919, FDRL. On her dinner with Mama, see Lash, *Eleanor and Franklin*, p. 244.

252 *race riots*: ER to FDR, 23–25 July 1919, FDRL.

252 *"It is surely a rainy time"*: FDR to ER, 22 July 1919, in *Letters*, vol. 2, pp. 479–81.

252 *"The riots seem"*: FDR to ER, 23 July 1919, in ibid, p. 481.

253–54 *"gave birth to the new Negro"*: Arthur Waskow, *From Race Riot to Sit-in* (Doubleday, 1967), p. 25 and passim. For a day-to-day account of the riots, see Adrian E. Cook, "At the Gates of the White House: The Washington, D.C., Race Riots of 1919," in R. Jeffreys-Jones and B. Collins, eds., *The Growth of Federal Power in American History* (Edinburgh: Scottish Academic Press, 1983).

254–55 *His plans were vague*: FDR to ER, 25 July 1919, in *Letters*, vol. 2, pp. 480–81.

255 *party at Chevy Chase*: See Teague, *Mrs. L*, 160.

255 *"My family filled my life"*: TIMS, pp. 173, 177, 189.

256 *"feats of endurance"*: Ibid., pp. 203, 208.

256 *"don't know what I want"*: ER to FDR, 28 Sept. 1919, FDRL.

256 *"I should be ashamed"*: ER to FDR, 3 Oct. 1919, FDRL.

257 *letter of apology:* ER to SDR, 6 Oct. 1919, FDRL.

257 *On 11 October:* ER was alone on her birthday, while FDR was with Livy Davis and Commander Richard E. Byrd, in the Canadian woods, hunting moose. (Lash, *Eleanor and Franklin,* pp. 242–43.)

258 *her first contact:* ER on the International Congress of Working Women, see *TIMS,* p. 304.

Margaret Dreier Robins's husband, Raymond Robins, had particularly appealed to ER when she heard him at a Progressive Party "goodbye dinner for Uncle Ted" in 1913. "Uncle Ted made a splendid speech . . . absolutely clear & logical & yet very amusing. . . . A Mr. Robins from Illinois also spoke well. . . ." (ER to Isabella Ferguson, 4 Oct. 1913, Tucson.)

On the International Congress and Margaret Dreier Robins, see Philip S. Foner, *Women and the American Labor Movement* (Macmillan Free Press, 1979), pp. 273–76. This congress led to the creation of the International Federation of Working Women in Geneva in 1921. In 1922, Robins resigned as president of the National Women's Trade Union League and became president of the International Federation, declaring that the first task of women was to declare "war against war." She called for an end to the manufacture of armaments, and a political struggle for full employment: "When we are hungry and homeless and idle or slaughtering our brothers or killing our sons, let us vote against the government without regard to party." (Foner, *Women,* pp. 275–76.)

On the early relations between these activist women and the International Labor Organization, see Carol Riegelman Lubin and Anne Winslow, *Social Justice for Women: The ILO and Women* (Duke University Press, 1990).

258 *"Women had no direct share":* Margaret Dreier Robins, quoted in Foner, *Women,* pp. 273–74.

259 *unusual marital partnership:* Elizabeth Anne Payne, *Reform, Labor, and Feminism: Margaret Dreier Robins and the Women's Trade Union League* (University of Illinois Press, 1988), p. 31 and passim.

259 *A businessman and an adventurer:* On Raymond Robins, see William A. Williams, *American-Russian Relations, 1781–1947* (Rinehart, 1952), much of which is derived from Williams's important, but unpublished, Ph.D. dissertation on Robins.

259 *Leonard Woolf:* Introduction to Elizabeth Robins, *Raymond and I* (Macmillan, 1956).

259–60 *opponent of the Allied Intervention:* Robins believed that it was the secret military intervention against the Soviet Union, not the first stirrings of revolution, that threatened the Treaty of Versailles, and the future:

"Bolshevik Russia, blockaded, starved, attacked by Finns and Poles and Serbs and Czecho-Slovaks and French and Italians and British and Americans and Senegalese, cries Bolshevism now with a doubled voice. It cries . . . to every working-class in the world to rally to the rescue of the world's only working-class government, beset by the world's capitalism. . . .

"The deeper the Allies go into Russia, the deeper they go into the class war at home. . . ."

(William Hard, *Raymond Robins' Own Story* [Harper & Brothers, 1920], pp. 216–17.)

260 *League opponents:* Ralph Stone, *The Irreconcilables: The Fight Against the League of Nations* (W. W. Norton, 1970); Robert James Maddox, *William Borah and American Foreign Policy* (Louisiana State University Press, 1969).

260 *never quite warmed to . . . Wilson:* TIMS, pp. 289–91; Lash, *Eleanor and Franklin,* pp. 233–35.

261 *"Colonel of Death":* Felsenthal, *Alice Roosevelt Longworth,* p. 141; Teague, *Mrs. L.*

262 *Cousin Susie Parish:* ER wrote most candidly about her godmother, Cousin Susie Livingston Ludlow Parish, to Isabella Ferguson, whose mother was her lifelong friend (13 Nov. [1916], 16 Sept. 1919, 11 Jan. 1920, Tucson). Hall occasionally wrote ER anguished letters about Cousin Susie: During the 1920s she became so critical, he threatened never to see her again, and considered her views those of a "Klanner."

262 *The Delano women:* ER to FDR, Dec. 1920, quoted in Lash, *Eleanor and Franklin,* p. 245.

263 *"I cannot bear any funeral parlor":* TIMS, pp. 307–9. According to the *New York Times* obituary, 5 Feb. 1920: "Mrs. Edith Morgan, wife of W. Forbes Morgan, . . . and her two daughters, Barbara, 14 years old and Ellen, 10, died of suffocation in their burning house at 52 West Ninth Street. . . . [They] were alone in the house, because the mother recently had been doing most of her own work, owing to the difficulty in getting servants." Neighbors tried unsuccessfully to call the fire company, and called for an investigation of the long delay.

263 *"Pussie might have been":* TIMS, p. 360.

263–64 *"the horror":* ER to Isabella, 10 Feb. 1920, Tucson.

264 *"needed and wanted":* TIMS, pp. 307–9.

II. The Campaign of 1920 and Louis Howe

265 *ugly political scandals:* The scandals had been seething for years. The Newport scandal first hit the press in June 1917. (Rollins, *Roosevelt and Howe,* p. 152.)

265–66 *Admiral William Sims:* For the Sims charges, see FDR's 1 Feb. 1920 Brooklyn Academy speech, and Livy Davis to FDR, 5 Feb., in Morgan, *FDR,* pp. 216–17. See also charges in *Letters,* vol. 2, p. 487.

266–67 *deep financial distress:* FDR to SDR, 11 Feb. 1920, in *Letters,* vol. 2, p. 486.

267–68 *Newport sex scandal:* Lawrence R. Murphy, *Perverts by Official Order: The Campaign Against Homosexuals by the United States Navy* (Harrington Park Press, 1988), is the best researched and most detailed source for these events.

268 *Drag shows . . . popular:* ER on drag shows and Captain McCauley's "happy ship" in TIMS, pp. 290–91. See also ER's correspondence with her mother-in-law during the Jan. 1919 voyage: "The crew gave a play with wonderful 'ladies' and we all have had a wonderfully comfortable and entertaining trip" (ER to SDR, 3 Jan. 1919, in *Letters,* vol. 2, p. 445). And FDR to his mother: "You would all have loved the sailors dressed up as chorus girls! This is what we call in the Navy a 'Happy Ship' from Capt. McCauley down—and it makes a lot of difference to one's comfort and satisfaction" (FDR to SDR, 10 Jan. 1919, in *Letters,* vol. 2, p. 448).

268–69 *"She is the daintiest":* Sims quoted in Murphy, *Perverts by Official Order,* p. 8.

269 *took it upon himself:* On FDR and the creation of Section A, see ibid., pp. 16–17, 72–75, 102.

269–70 *The clergy petitioned:* Ibid., pp. 156–57.

270 *FDR appeared before the Dunn Board:* Ibid., pp. 233–35.

270–71 *Dunn Board presented its findings:* Ibid., pp. 242–45.

271 *"restrooms for the girls":* ER to Isabella, June 1920, Tucson. ER wrote to Isabella that she thought FDR wanted to run again for the U.S. Senate, but FDR confided to another friend that he thought "being in the Senate 'stupid.' " In May 1920, an Albany newspaper hailed him as its presidential contender. (See Rollins, *Roosevelt and Howe*, p. 154.)

271–72 *three major contenders:* During the balloting, FDR cast his votes for Smith until he withdrew, then for McAdoo, and voted with Tammany against prohibition. (Rollins, *Roosevelt and Howe*, p. 155.)

272 *"Mama is very proud":* ER to FDR, 3 July 1920, FDRL.

273 *"glad for my husband":* Autobiography *of ER*, p. 107.
On 6 Aug., FDR officially resigned as Assistant Secretary of the Navy.

273 *internationalism and progressivism:* FDR's notification speech and local press reaction are in *Letters*, vol. 2, pp. 499–508.

273–74 *sympathy for her mother-in-law: TIMS*, p. 312.

274 *"for I believe":* ER's interview with the Poughkeepsie *Eagle News*, 16 July 1920, quoted in Lash, *Eleanor and Franklin*, p. 252.

274–75 *Harding held . . . "Respectable Women's Day":* Lemons, *Woman Citizen*, pp. 87–101.

275 *Carrie Chapman Catt:* See Jacqueline Van Voris, *Carrie Chapman Catt: A Public Life* (The Feminist Press, 1987).

275–76 *Anne Martin:* Martin and Alva Belmont quoted in Lemons, *Woman Citizen*, p. 109. See also Christopher Lasch on Alva Belmont; and Kathryn Anderson on Anne Martin, in *Notable American Women: The Modern Period*, ed. Sicherman et al.

276 *"sad about politics":* ER to Isabella Ferguson, 10 Jan. 1920, Tucson.

276 *hoped that Herbert Hoover:* ER to Isabella Ferguson, 11 Jan. [1919], Tucson.

276–77 *" 'Back to Normalcy!' ":* Quoted in Felsenthal, *Alice Roosevelt Longworth*, p. 144; and Longworth, *Crowded Hours*, pp. 324–25. See also Francis Russell, *The Shadow of Blooming Grove: Warren G. Harding in His Times* (McGraw-Hill, 1968).

277 *William Allen White:* Quoted in K. Davis, *Beckoning of Destiny*, p. 611.

277 *"The chief business":* Coolidge quoted in Schlesinger, *Crisis of the Old Order*, p. 57.

277–78 *"Mrs. Harding was divorced":* FDR quoted in Morgan, *FDR*, p. 228.

278 *"I miss you":* FDR to ER, 17 July 1920, in *Letters*, vol. 2, p. 494.

278 *FDR was "a maverick":* Churchill, *American Aristocrats*, pp. 268–71, 291; and Morgan, *FDR*, pp. 229–30.

278 *"some kind of diary":* FDR to ER, 15 Aug. 1920, in *Letters*, vol. 2, pp. 509–10.

278–79 *four-week train trip:* On the campaign train, see ER to SDR, 19 Oct. 1920, quoted in Lash, *Eleanor and Franklin*, p. 256.

279–80 *"the big brother":* FDR quoted in *New York Times*, 19 Aug. 1920. See Rollins, *Roosevelt and Howe*, p. 160; K. Davis, *Beckoning of Destiny*, p. 621. On FDR's role in Haiti, see Balch, *Occupied Haiti*, pp. 24, 146.
During 1920, *The Nation* ran several articles that revealed the violence of U.S. policies in Haiti—including "America's Ireland: Haiti—Santo Domingo," 21 Feb. 1920, and Herbert J. Seligman's "The Conquest of Haiti," 10 July 1920. FDR's boast coincided with the liberal journal's three-part series on Haiti by James Weldon Johnson, "Self-Determining Haiti," 28 Aug., 11 Sept., 25 Sept. 1920. According to Oswald Garrison Villard, Warren Harding used the charges and facts first printed in *The Nation*, and "unsealed the lips of Washington officials" (see Villard, " 'Pitiless Publicity' for Haiti,"

The Nation, 6 Oct. 1920, reprinted in *Oswald Garrison Villard: The Dilemmas of the Absoulte Pacifist in Two World Wars*, ed. Anthony Gronowicz [Garland, 1983], pp. 148–49).

280 *"hyphenated Americans":* FDR quoted in Geoffrey C. Ward, *A First-Class Temperament: The Emergence of Franklin Roosevelt* (Harper & Row, 1989), p. 544.

280–81 *Centralia:* See Murray, *Red Scare*, pp. 183–84; and Louis Adamic, *Dynamite: The Story of Class Violence in America* (Peter Smith, 1963 [1934]), pp. 292–305.

281 *"pilgrimage to the very graves":* FDR on the four martyred Legionnaires quoted in Morgan, *FDR*, p. 231.

281 *"Belittlement is the worst":* ER to FDR, 27 Aug. 1920, FDRL.

282–83 *"an ambidextrous genius":* See Rollins, *Roosevelt and Howe*, p. 7 and passim.

283 *"rather extraordinary eyes":* ER on Howe, and the campaign train, in *TIMS*, pp. 315–19.

284 *Niagara Falls: TIMS*, pp. 318–19. ("Louis proved to be a very pleasant person wtih whom to sight-see, silent when I wished to be silent and full of information on many things of which I knew nothing.")
  Her first political friend, Louis Howe remained one of ER's most considerate companions: "Years later I remember Louis Howe taking me out to dinner at a restaurant, sitting at a table he did not like, and eating food he did not like, simply because he said he knew I would be uncomfortable if he made me conspicuous by getting up and changing to another table or complaining about the food." (P. 229.)

284–85 *Howe was an artist:* Rollins, *Roosevelt and Howe*, pp. 168ff.

285 *"stand much teasing": TIMS*, p. 319.

285 *"young and pretty":* ER, *This I Remember*, p. 28.

286 *"ladies of Thibet":* ER, "Politics Here and Elsewhere," ER Papers, Box 3022, FDRL.

286–87 *business-boom parade:* After the election, FDR worried about money. In Dec., he wrote a friend, "I am honestly a fit candidate for a receiver," and he and Howe embarked on several speculative business projects. "They wanted to get rich—and quickly." (See Rollins, *Roosevelt and Howe*, pp. 173–75.)

12. ER and the New Women of the 1920s

288 *"an impossible mode":* Autobiography of ER, p. 112.

289 *Narcissa Cox Vanderlip:* ER supported Vanderlip in the League of Women Voters' first factional struggle. When she prevailed, ER wrote: "Dear Mrs. Vanderlip, I've been meaning to write and congratulate you on your wonderful work and the persistence which finally let you succeed. . . . I wish I could tell you how much warm admiration and respect and affection I have for you." (ER to NCV, May [1921], Narcissa Cox Vanderlip Papers, Box 8, Frank Vanderlip Collection, Columbia University.)

289 *a "useful adjunct":* Lape to Vanderlip, Mon., n.d., ibid.

289 *Attractive and athletic:* Hilda R. Watrous, *Narcissa Cox Vanderlip* (Foundation for Citizenship Education, 1982); Hilda R. Watrous, *In League with Eleanor: Eleanor Roosevelt and the League of Women Voters, 1921–1962* (Foundation for Citizenship Education, 1984). I am grateful to Hilda Watrous, historian of the New York State League of Women Voters, for the thoroughly researched biographical pamphlet on Vanderlip, and other references.

290 *"Vanderlip is a Bolshevist"*: Doheny on Frank Vanderlip quoted in Schlesinger, *Crisis of the Old Order*, p. 49.

290–91 *annual convention*: On the New York League's Jan. 1921 Albany convention, see Lemons, *Woman Citizen*, pp. 98–99.

291 *"The people in this room"*: Catt quoted in Van Voris, *Carrie Chapman Catt*, p. 164.

291–92 *"very interesting day"*: ER to FDR, 11 April 1921, FDRL.

292 *A scholar and an attorney*: In 1923, Elizabeth Read wrote Narcissa Vanderlip, then vacationing on her 16,000-acre ranch in Palos Verdes: "California sounds lovely. I should have been born out there. My father went west over the plains in 1850, and had a ranch . . . in the Sacramento valley—and a mine . . . ; he went back east in 1870, and married there, expecting to go back at once; but they were induced to wait, on account of my grandmother's health, until—he died before grandmother did! And we were all born in the effete east." (24 Feb. 1923, Vanderlip Papers.)

292–93 *"felt humble and inadequate"*: TIMS, pp. 324–25. ("My mother-in-law was distressed" because of all the time ER gave to her new friends, "and felt that I was not always available, as I had been when I lived in New York before.")

293–96 *the "New Women"*: See Estelle Freedman, "The New Woman: Changing Views of Women in the 1920s," *Journal of American History*, Sept. 1974; BWC, "Feminism, Socialism, and Sexual Freedom: The Work and Legacy of Crystal Eastman and Alexandra Kollontai," in *Women in Culture and Politics: A Century of Change*, ed. Judith Friedlander et al. (University of Indiana Press, 1986); Christine Fauré, "The Utopia of the 'New Woman' in the Work of Alexandra Kollontai," ibid; Esther Newton, "The Mythic Mannish Lesbian: Radclyffe Hall and the New Woman," in *Hidden from History: Reclaiming the Gay and Lesbian Past*, ed. Martin Duberman et al. (New American Library, Meridian, 1990); and Carroll Smith-Rosenberg, "The New Woman as Androgyne: Social Disorder and Gender Crisis, 1870–1936," in Smith-Rosenberg, *Disorderly Conduct*. On the women of Greenwich Village, see also Susan Ware, *Partner and I: Molly Dewson, Feminism, and New Deal Politics* (Yale University Press, 1987); Caroline F. Ware, *Greenwich Village, 1920–1930* (Harper Colophon, 1965 [1935]); and Judith Schwarz, *Radical Feminists of Heterodoxy: Greenwich Village, 1912–1940* (New Victoria, 1986).

296–97 *Lape and . . . Read lived together*: I am grateful to Esther Lape's friends Margaret (Peggy) Bok Kiskadden, Olga Bendix, Harold Clarke, Bert Drucker, Michael Sonino, and Patricia Spain Ward for their descriptions of the Lape-Read homes in Saltmeadow and New York, and a vivid sense of their style. I am particularly grateful to Peggy Kiskadden, who gave me a sense of their political enthusiasm, personal integrity, and warm hospitality, and showed me several costumes made for Lape by her designer and tailor—whom ER also used for formal wear.

Esther Lape's unpublished memoir, "Saltmeadow: From the Perspective of a Half Century," and copies of the weekly bulletin *City, State and Nation* are in the Lape Collection, FDRL; copies of *Weekly News*, the publication of the League of Women Voters of New York State, are in the Vanderlip Collection.

Lape wrote that "the financial support of [*City, State and Nation*] was assumed by Helen Reid [former treasurer of the New York State Suffragist Party; later owner and publisher of the New York *Herald Tribune*], Narcissa Vanderlip and Eleanor Roosevelt." (Lape, "Saltmeadow," p. 22.)

298 *balance in life*: Elizabeth Read to Narcissa Vanderlip, 24 Feb. 1923, Vanderlip Papers.

298 *" 'toujours gai' "*: Esther Lape asked Maureen Corr, ER's last secretary and Esther Lape's friend, to repaint the doormat. She told me the story during our tour of Saltmeadow.

298 *"Providence was . . . wise"*: TIMS, p. 325.

299–300 *"She made me go there"*: Asbell, *Mother and Daughter*, pp. 33–34. See also Anna to ER, 12 Aug. 1924, FDRL.

300 *"College for me"*: Asbell, *Mother and Daughter*, p. 39.

13. Convalescence, Marital Unity, and Separate Spheres

302–3 *he encouraged her work:* FDR coached ER and her friends on political games-manship "con amore." (Lape, "Saltmeadow," pp. 20–22.)

303 *Coolidge's attack against women's colleges:* ER's resolution defended Vassar College Professor Winifred Smith, who had been named a dangerous heretic after she spoke against the United States' stifling climate of intellectual "narrowness." ER insisted that Professor Smith was a "public-spirited and devoted citizen," and condemned "all thoughtless aspersions" in times of "public excitement." (See Lash, *Eleanor and Franklin*, pp. 263–64.)

303 *Most startling:* ER, "Common Sense Versus Party Regularity," [League] *News Bulletin*, 16 Sept. 1921, Vanderlip Papers.

304–5 *He drank more:* On FDR's "uproarious" behavior at Margaret Krech-Sheffield Cowles's wedding, and on ER mixing cocktails at Campobello (for Elizabeth Bibesco, Herbert Asquith's daughter), see Lash, *Eleanor and Franklin*, pp. 265–66.

305 *"LIBELLOUS REPORT"*: *New York Times*, 23 July 1921.

306 *"I know it worries you"*: ER to FDR, 22 July 1921, FDRL.

306 *"no papers have taken it up"*: FDR to ER, 21 July 1921, in *Letters*, vol. 2, pp. 516–18.

307 *"None of this worries me"*: Ibid., pp. 519–22.

307 *"he looked tired"*: Missy to ER, 5 Aug. 1921, quoted in Morgan, *FDR*, p. 247.

307–8 *FDR arrived:* For the events preceding polio, see TIMS, pp. 328–30.

308–9 *"very anxious few days"*: ER to Rosy Roosevelt, 14 Aug. 1921, in *Letters*, vol. 2, pp. 523–25.

309 *"skilled nursing"*: TIMS, pp. 328–33; See also Lash, *Eleanor and Franklin*, pp. 268–69. The fullest description of this period is Ward, *First-Class Temperament*, which was published after this book was written. In any case, he interprets ER meanly, and credits her with very little. He opines that for Franklin "this unavoidable business must have been especially disagreeable" since they were no longer "intimate," and Eleanor was always "too humorless, too admonitory, too easily aggrieved, too unwilling to relax," for her husband to abide her (pp. 587, 678). Ward's theme is "the bottomless solicitude of [FDR's] mother and the incessant prodding of his wife." (P. 668.)

310 *"Franklin has been quite ill"*: ER to SDR, 27 Aug. 1921 in, *Letters*, vol. 2, p. 527.

310 *"their glorious example"*: SDR to her brother, quoted in Lash, *Eleanor and Franklin*, pp. 270–71.

310 *"Your letters have amused him"*: ER to Missy LeHand, ibid.

310 *"really very remarkable"*: TIMS, p. 334.

311 *"beloved invalid" husband:* Quoted in K. Davis, *Beckoning of Destiny*, pp. 668–69.

312 *"too busy to need a room":* TIMS, p. 337.

312 *"the most trying winter":* For ER on Anna and SDR's manipulations, see *TIMS*, pp. 334–38.

312 *Miss Chapin's:* Asbell, *Mother and Daughter*, pp. 30–31.

312–13 *ER broke down: Autobiography of ER*, pp. 119–20.

313 *"gossipy old Cousin Susie":* Lash, *Eleanor and Franklin*, p. 274; Asbell, *Mother and Daughter*, p. 40.

313–14 *"a blessing in disguise":* TIMS, p. 342.

315 *"somewhat negligee existence":* FDR to SDR from his houseboat, 5 March 1923, in *Letters*, vol. 2, pp. 535–36. (And see editor's note, p. 534, stating that neither ER nor the children saved FDR's letters from the 1920s.)

Frances Appleton Dana de Rham, who accompanied FDR several times during these years, was unhappily married. Beautiful, stylish, and sporty (she shopped at Brooks Brothers and "started the fashion for wearing men's shirts"), she married Henry Casimir de Rham, one of FDR's most social classmates, on 25 Jan. 1905. Given to parties and frolics, they were never particularly happy. Seven months after their marriage, their first child was born, weighing over eleven pounds. Henry never found work he enjoyed, and refused to allow Frances to do work she wanted to do. He was remembered as both "stuffy and fierce," with a violent, brutish temper. She felt trapped, wanted a divorce, sought diversions elsewhere, traveled frequently across Europe. Although her grandchildren remembered her as their delightful "dancing grandmother," she committed suicide on 6 Oct. 1933. (Rosamond Wild Dana, "Privileged Radicals: The Rebellious Times of Six Dana Siblings in Cambridge and New York," unpublished master's thesis, City University of New York, 1991, pp. 56–61. I am grateful to Rosamond Dana for this source, and our many conversations.)

315 *"eerie and menacing":* TIMS, pp. 345–46. See also logbook of the *Larooco*, excerpts by FDR in *Letters*, vol. 2, pp. 537–60, 570–77. Unfortunately, for the period between 24 Feb. and 24 March 1925, including the period of ER's tenth-anniversary visit, the log was kept by others and not therefore printed. See *Weona* and *Larooco* logbooks, FDRL.

315 *"utterly splendid person":* Esther Lape to Narcissa Vanderlip, 1 March 1923, Vanderlip Papers.

315 *"most attentive and thoughtful":* TIMS, p. 334.

315–16 *sturdy valet:* Whatever difficulties FDR's black valet, LeRoy Jones, may have faced as FDR cruised the Florida keys, the New York yacht broker who rented the *Weona* accepted him aboard with the four-man crew after he ascertained that he was "not impregnated with the present so-called 'rights,' and is of the willing kind." (Ward, *First-Class Temperament*, p. 660.)

316 *"I haven't told Mama":* ER to FDR, 24 Feb. 1924, FDRL.

317 *"Nan spent the night":* ER to FDR, 1 March 1924, FDRL.

317–18 *major source of tension:* For FDR's expenses and investments, see especially Rollins, *Roosevelt and Howe*, passim; and K. Davis, *Beckoning of Destiny*, pp. 697–710.

In 1922, FDR became head of the American Construction Council, a bipartisan organization promoted by Herbert Hoover to promote cooperation between business and government, an unsalaried post. United European Investors was more immediately lucrative: In Aug. 1924, when it was liquidated, investors had "an announced profit of 200 percent." (K. Davis, *Beckoning of Destiny*, p. 706.)

318 *"almost matriarchal style":* On ER's fiscal independence, see *Autobiography of ER*, p. 135.

318 *"No form of love":* Margaret Kennedy, *The Constant Nymph* (Virago Classic, 1984 [1924]), p. 130.

318–19 *"I was always on the go":* ER to FDR, 27 Feb. 1925, FDRL. ER's resumed activities are described in the same letter.

319 *"a touch of that sadness":* ER to FDR, 26 March 1925, FDRL.

319–20 *Nancy Cook:* See Marion Dickerman Oral History, Columbia University; Kenneth Davis, *Invincible Summer: An Intimate Portrait of the Roosevelts Based on the Recollections of Marion Dickerman* (Atheneum, 1974), p. 13.

The exchange of violets between women intensified in the popular culture during the 1920s in part because of an internationally acclaimed play, Edouard Bourdet's *La Prisonnière*, which took Europe by storm after it first opened in Paris. Translated into *The Captive*, it opened on Broadway in 1926. *New York Times* critic Brooks Atkinson called it a "loathsome" play of "warped infatuation" and lamented its "vastly popular" existence. The play's theme was a simple triangle, unusually resolved. The "captive" left her male lover for a mysterious, captivating woman (who never appeared on stage). The captivator plied her with gifts—notably violets—and stole her heart. Although the play ends tragically, the moralists were so incensed by it, and others like it which appeared during the 1920s, that they successfully lobbied the New York legislature to outlaw the treatment of "sexual perversion" on the New York stage for several decades.

The theatre censorship law remained on the books until 1967, supplemented by other censorship decrees which annually banned dozens of works for "indecency." Booksellers and librarians were arrested throughout 1924 and 1925 for selling or lending the greatest variety of books, ranging from serious works of literature to simple-minded trash. Librarians and publishers fought back against the "Society for the Suppression of Vice" by suing for false arrest. Occasionally the libertarians won. A salesclerk won a $2,000 judgment for false arrest, for example, when Gautier's *Mademoiselle de Maupin* was judged decent. (*New York Times*, 26 Feb. 1925.)

ER and her friends stood solidly behind the freedom to read, deplored censorship in the theatre, and editorialized against the Society for the Suppression of Vice.

320 *"an attractive woman":* ER, *This I Remember*, p. 32.

321 *Endell Street Hospital:* For a fictionalized account of women volunteers in England during the Great War, with a provocative afterword by Jane Marcus, see Helen Zenna Smith, *Not So Quiet* (The Feminist Press, 1989, [1930]).

321 *Women's Joint Legislative Conference:* Papers are in Marion Dickerman Papers, Boxes 2 and 6, FDRL.

321–22 *Marion Dickerman . . . could defeat him:* On her campaign for New York State Assembly, see Dickerman Oral History, Columbia.

322 *She "loved Nan much more":* Ibid., p. 351; quoted in Lash, *Love, Eleanor*, p. 96.

Kenneth Davis referred to "the intimate correspondence" he saw between Marion Dickerman and Nancy Cook, and with ER (*Invincible Summer*, p. viii). He also wrote: "Of Eleanor Roosevelt's feminism, her embittered revolt against masculine domination, her letters to Marion and Nancy during these years give abundant evidence." ("Symbolic Journey," *Antioch Review*, Summer 1979, p. 275.)

But in the FDRL, one finds only scattered letters, and scattered typed copies of letters. It is particularly odd, given what we now know of ER's letter-writing habits, that the sampling of ER's letters that have survived are addressed to Dickerman, and there is virtually no correspondence with Nancy Cook.

323 *"forget the . . . world existed":* ER to Marion Dickerman, 27 Aug. 1925, Dickerman Papers, Box 4, FDRL.

323 *"I wish you were here"*: ER to Dickerman, 5 Feb. 1926 (from Florida), 18 May 1926 (from Massachusetts), ibid.

323–24 *Caroline O'Day:* See her biography (written by Marion Dickerman) in *Notable American Women: The Modern Period*, ed. Sicherman et al.

324 *"secret of The Cottage"*: Caroline O'Day, *Women's Democratic News*, Nov. 1925.

325 *"build a shack"*: FDR to Elliott Brown, 5 Aug. 1924, in K. Davis, *Invincible Summer*, p. 35.

325–26 *"The Honeymoon Cottage"*: Dickerman Oral History, Columbia; K. Davis, *Invincible Summer*, pp. 35ff, and ch. 5.

326 *"So what is it all about"*: FDR to Dickerman, in K. Davis, *Invincible Summer*, p. 59.

326–27 *"If you build it that way"*: FDR to "Dear Nan—also Marion," 6 March 1925, with P.S. from Missy LeHand, Dickerman Papers, Box 5, FDRL.

327–28 *"Mother burst into tears"*: TIMS, p. 348; see also Lash, *Eleanor and Franklin*, p. 275. SDR took Anna to Europe several times (see Asbell, *Mother and Daughter*, pp. 34–38).

328 *"Where are your husbands"*: Lash, *Eleanor and Franklin*, p. 298.

328 *"still serene"*: TIMS, p. 350.

328 *"Father the 'Cascaret' "*: quoted in K. Davis, *Invincible Summer*, pp. 45–47.

328 *"I won't be slandered"*: ER to FDR, 25 July 1925, Box 15, FDRL.

329 *"Elliott tells me"*: ER to FDR, 22 Sept. 1926, FDRL.

329 *"feeling quite impotent"*: ER to Marion Dickerman, typed from original by "MBS," Dickerman Papers, Box 4, FDRL.

330 *"further than she meant"*: ER to FDR on Anna's engagement, 29 July 1924; 12 Aug. 1924, FDRL; and Asbell, *Mother and Daughter*, pp. 32–41.

330 *"three nights drunk"*: ER to FDR, 25 Oct. 1927, FDRL.

330 *to cancel it:* ER to FDR, 28 March 1927, FDRL. Mindful of her own desire to create her own home, ER had decided not to interfere or try to supervise Anna's plans. But: "Mama says I'm cruel to leave the poor child alone! . . . [She] has done nothing but get in little side slaps today." ER was relieved to return to Val-Kill "for a quiet evening with Nan. I've written two editorials and three letters and we have had supper and the peace of it is divine. . . ."

330–31 *"a run in with Mama"*: ER to FDR, 31 March 1927, FDRL; SDR's letter of apology is quoted in Lash, *Eleanor and Franklin*, p. 301.

331 *"send me money"*: ER to FDR, n.d. [Sept. 1927], FDRL.

331 *"you hate to be bothered"*: ER to FDR, 25 Oct. 1927, FDRL.

331 *"real business proposition"*: ER to FDR, 10 April 1926, FDRL.

332 *"Please send Nan a check"*: ER to FDR, 8 Feb. 1928, Box 16, FDRL.

332 *"I am glad"*: ER to FDR, 18 April 1928, FDRL.

333 *"I have 'moods' "*: ER to Marion Dickerman, 18 May 1926, Dickerman Papers, Box 4, FDRL.

333 *"happy . . . and plump"*: SDR to FDR, quoted in Lash, *Love, Eleanor*, p. 200.

334 *"She is afraid of everything"*: ER to FDR, ibid.

335 *"discouragement" and "bitterness":* TIMS, p. 335.

If ER considered the irony of FDR's purchase of a healing center in Bullochville/ Warm Springs, there is no record of it. She did, however, write of the disparity between the plantation stories she had been told by her Great-Aunt Annie (Mrs. James King Gracie), and the current realities of the place: "She had made me feel that life in the South must be gracious and easy and charming. . . . It was a disappointment to me to find out for many, many people life in the South was hard and poor and ugly, just as it is in parts of the North." (ER, *This I Remember*, p. 27.)

FDR signed the agreement to purchase the resort, "its thermal springs and pools, its ramshackle hotel, its cottages, and some 1,200 acres of land," on 29 April 1926 (K. Davis, *Beckoning of Destiny*, p. 798. See also Hugh Gregory Gallagher, *FDR's Splendid Deception* (Dodd, Mead, 1985); and Theo Lippman, Jr., *The Squire of Warm Springs: FDR in Georgia, 1924–1945* (Playboy Press, 1977).

336 *"Don't worry about being selfish":* ER to FDR, 4 May 1926, FDRL.

336 *"a big thing":* ER to Marion Dickerman, 24 April 1926, in K. Davis, *Invincible Summer*, p. 61.

336 *"Don't be discouraged":* ER to FDR, 29 June 1926, FDRL.

336–37 *"should devote themselves":* Marion Dickerman quoted in K. Davis, *Invincible Summer*, p. 17.

337 *"Back of tranquility":* ER quoting David Grayson, ibid., p. 42.

14. ER, Political Boss

338 *mimeograph machine: Weekly News*, 22 Oct. 1922. Published by the New York League of Women Voters, in 1922 *Weekly News* was edited by Eveline Brainerd, and co-owned by Caroline Slade, Florence Canfield Whitney (Mrs. Caspar Whitney), Eleanor Roosevelt, and Dorothy Payne Whitney Straight. It provides a running record of ER's activities between 1922 and 1924. In 1923, ER was elected vice-chair of the League.

339 *many and labyrinthine connections:* On ER and the Women's City Club, see Elisabeth Israels Perry, "Training for Public Life: ER and Women's Political Networks in the 1920s"; on the larger network, see Susan Ware, "ER and Democratic Politics: Women in the Postsuffrage Era," both in *Without Precedent*, ed. Hoff-Wilson and Lightman, pp. 28–45, 46–60. See also Schwarz, *Radical Feminists of Heterodoxy: Greenwich Village, 1912–1940*. Although many of ER's colleagues attended Heterodoxy meetings, she never did, nor did Lape and Read or Cook and Dickerman. It serves, therefore, as a signpost to indicate the political and social boundaries of their network.

339–40 *"Trooping for Democracy":* This became a regular column in the *Women's Democratic News*, reporting their activities monthly.

340 *Never appear nervous:* ER, *This I Remember*, p. 32.

340 *"hopeless moral blindness":* ER in *New York Times*, 7 Aug. 1922.

341 *"Private Interlude [1921–1927]":* ER, *This I Remember*.

341 *temporary stand-in:* ER to FDR, 6 Feb. 1924, FDRL.

342 *Bok Peace Award:* Edward Bok wanted the contest to raise abiding questions: "Is there a part America must play in the prevention of future wars? . . . "Can we have a fundamentally changing Europe without a changing America? . . ." (Minutes of Meeting of Policy Committee of the American Peace Award, 27 June 1923 in Lape Papers, FDRL; Lape, "Saltmeadow," pp. 52–62.)

342–44 *"Mutt and Jeff":* Lape to Vanderlip, 8 Aug. 1923, Vanderlip Papers.

All papers relating to the Bok prize are in the Lape Papers, FDRL; there is also significant correspondence in the Swarthmore College Peace Collection, the Vanderlip Papers, and the Helen Rogers Reid Papers, Library of Congress.

See Charles DeBenedetti, "The $100,000 American Peace Award of 1924," *Pennsylvania Magazine of History and Biography*, April 1974, pp. 224–49.

344–46 *Senate Special Committee on Propaganda:* Press coverage of ER, Lape, and the hearings on "foreign relations" was extensive and daily. See especially *New York Times*, 21, 22, 24, 25 Jan. 1924. At the end of Jan., however, the pace of the hearings subsided when all Washington's attention turned to another issue. On 31 Jan. *The New York Times* headlined: "Committee Slowness Irks Bok Witnesses / Inquiry Is Being Held Up by Teapot Dome Flurry." "Peace plans, Bolshevism and all other things which concern Senators" were submerged by Teapot Dome and the Elk Hill scandals.

See ER, "The American Peace Award," *Ladies' Home Journal*, Oct. 1923, p. 54.

346 *"an endless job":* Cordell Hull asked ER to chair the Women's Platform Committee (ER to FDR, 6 Feb. 1924, FDRL).

347 *"politically wrong":* ER to FDR, 9 April 1924, FDRL.

347 *"I imagine":* Ibid.

348 *"Women Are in Revolt":* New York Times, 15 April 1924.

348 *"disagreeable to take stands":* ER quoted in "Democratic Women Win," ibid., 16 April 1924.

349–50 *Democratic National Committee . . . announced:* Ibid., 31 March 1924.

To seek women's views, ER also organized an advisory committee and invited Carrie Chapman Catt, a Republican, to serve on it: "Besides the Democratic women . . . I am having an advisory committee on each of the following subjects which is entirely nonpartisan in character. Women in Industry, Public Health and Child Welfare, Foreign Relations, Law Enforcement, Education, Removal of Civil Disabilities, Prison Reform and Public Control of Natural Resources." (ER to Catt, 14 April 1924, Catt Papers, Box 1, New York Public Library.)

Catt was unable to serve, but wrote ER to "congratulate you upon the brave stand you took in the Democratic Convention. . . . I do not think the politicians were made happy by the conduct of the women, but the old suffragists were and I want to pat you on the back for it." (Catt to ER, 22 April 1924, Box 1, Catt Papers.)

350 *rudely rebuffed:* On ER's committee and June efforts, *TIMS*, pp. 354–55. See "Women Democrats Offer a Platform," *New York Times*, 11 June 1924; and Anne O'Hagan Shinn, "Politics Still Masculine Convention Women Discover," *New York Times*, 23 June 1924.

351 *"burst of sunlight":* Marion Dickerman quoted in K. Davis, *Invincible Summer*, p. 30.

351 *The crowd cheered:* On the reaction to FDR's "Happy Warrior" speech, see *Letters*, vol. 2, p. 562.

352 *"prove our strength":* ER quoted in *New York Times*, 14 April 1924.

352 *"leave me my business and politics":* Interview with ER by Rose Feld, "Women Are Slow to Employ Power of the Ballot," *New York Times*, 20 April 1924.

ER emphasized the difference beteween U.S. and British women: In England "the work of government [is] alive and vital to them. . . . It is not because English women are superior to American women. . . . It's because Englishmen haven't shielded them from the 'rough, dirty game of politics.' It's because Englishmen in social intercourse haven't felt that they must talk down to the intelligence of their wives. . . .'"

352 *"bidding of his friends":* ER in *New York Times*, 27 Sept. 1924.

352 *"dishonest public servants":* ER in ibid., 6 Oct., 10 Oct., 2 Nov. 1924.

353 *"Teapot Dome"*: See Miller, *Roosevelt Chronicles*, pp. 296–300.

Kenneth Davis notes that several members of Wilson's administration, including FDR, were involved with Doheny: "ex–Secretary of Interior Lane, who died in June 1921; ex–Secretary of War Lindley M. Garrison; Ex–Attorney General Thomas W. Gregory" were all employed by Doheny. War propagandist George Creel was briefly employed as his publicist; and William Gibbs McAdoo was Doheny's "principal attorney."

On 13 April 1922, FDR wrote McAdoo on behalf of Fidelity and Deposit's West Coast branch: Doheny "is a good friend of mine and I feel sure he will be very glad to have you place the [surety bonding] business our way." (K. Davis, *Beckoning of Destiny*, pp. 696–97.)

354 *"rough stunt"*: ER, *This I Remember*, pp. 31–32. ("In the thick of political fights one always feels all methods of campaigning that are honest are fair, but I do think now that this was a rough stunt and I never blamed my cousin when he retaliated in later campaigns against my husband.")

354 *"Alas and lackaday"*: Anna Roosevelt Cowles to Corinne Alsop, Alsop Family Papers, Houghton; quoted in Ward, *First-Class Temperament*, p. 701n.

354–57 *Equal Rights Amendment*: The controversy over ERA has resulted in a great historical confusion: a misunderstanding that labeled protectionists antifeminist, and equal-rights feminists callous and unconcerned about workingwomen. During the 1920s, before the right to bargain collectively in labor unions was achieved, there was profound disagreement over tactics and priorities, and all suffragist unity was destroyed in the battle between the feminists who insisted on protection for women first, because that was politically feasible; and the feminists who insisted on protection for women and men alike—because protection for women alone classed them with children and suggested that they were biologically inferior and socially dependent.

In the beginning, ER's circle of Lape-Read-Vanderlip was closer to the National Woman's Party than has ever been appreciated. In Feb. 1923, when Esther Lape was with ER in Florida, Elizabeth Read decided to answer a letter Vanderlip had sent Lape which concerned Read's efforts with the League of Women Voters' "Equal Laws Committee." The committee had worked for months to achieve compromise legislation in Albany that both the League and the Woman's Party could agree upon, and sponsor jointly. They agreed to ten principles, and four pieces of social-welfare legislation.

But League factionalism ended their efforts. Caroline Slade accused Read of trying "to sneak in" four Woman's Party bills, which were actually League bills. ER served as a mediator between Slade and Read, and called legislators directly to discover the source of very complex machinations. "Mrs. Roosevelt learned an awful lot that day!" Read's committee "agreed to make another attempt to combine with the Woman's Party, and all of us except the industrial groups were willing to back the WP bills on our accepted principles." Belle Moskowitz was consulted, and she "was for them." And so Read was sure a congenial state senator could be found who would introduce "bills backed by working women and rich women, Catholics and Jews, . . . etc." But additional internal bickering occurred, and it was agreed to "drop the whole thing for this year . . . which is what Hay and Slade and Moskowitz want."

Elizabeth Read felt bitter about League leadership: "As a matter of fact, I do not see any working group a decent woman could belong to, in NY, except the Woman's Party at present.

"I worked as long as there was any use, and longer, in trying to carry out the Conference Committee and Equal Laws Committee mandates,—but when your side decides to quit fighting, you certainly are discharged. Hay et al. would rather see nothing good be accomplished. . . . As I wrote [Esther Lape] the other day, the cause of women in NY is at a dead stand-still till some one slugs Mary Garrett Hay over the

head. . . . It might be possible to start a compact chosen little band of scrappers who really want to get something done. . . ."
(Read to Narcissa Vanderlip, 24 Feb. 1923, Vanderlip Papers.)
After the ERA became the Woman's Party's exclusive issue, all efforts at compromise failed.

On 12 Nov. 1924, Crystal Eastman, whose work as an attorney had pioneered worker-compensation laws, and health and safety legislation for the protection of all workers, and who was one of the four authors of the ERA, wrote a letter to the editor of *The Nation*, called "Feminists Must Fight," to challenge ER's position.

She agreed with ER's idea "that the battle for 'recognition,' political and official, will have to be fought inside party lines. If women want to be in politics they must be politicians, . . . choose their party and play the political game from the ground up. But it seems to me most emphatically not true that the battle for 'equal rights' must be fought within party lines. It can never be won there. It must be fought and it will be fought by a free-handed, nonpartisan minority of energetic femininsts to whom politics in general . . . will continue to be a matter of indifference so long as women are classed with children . . . so long as even in our most advanced States a woman can be penalized with the loss of her job when she marries. . . .

"The principle of the Equal Rights Amendment is supremely important. The very passion with which it is opposed suggests that it is vital. To blot out of every law book in the land . . . that centuries-old precedent as to woman's inferiority and dependence and need for protection, to substitute for it at one blow that simple new precedent of equality.

"That is a fight worth making if it takes ten years."
The differences between feminist activists were not about reactionary vision, or style—as some have insisted. Joseph Lash, for instance, claimed that "the embattled females of the Woman's Party . . . were too masculine for Eleanor's taste." (*Eleanor and Franklin*, p. 290.)

357–58 *Dr. Alice Hamilton:* Alice Hamilton to Edith Houghton Hooker, 16 Jan. 1922, in Barbara Sicherman, *Alice Hamilton: A Life in Letters* (Harvard University Press, 1984), pp. 254–56.

On 22 May 1952, Dr. Alice Hamilton also publicly withdrew her opposition to the ERA in a letter to the New York *Herald Tribune*. After thirty years of opposition, it now "seems best for our country to join in the effort of the United Nations to adopt such a principle internationally."

359–60 *"sounded so well":* ER, *It's Up to the Women* (Frederick A. Stokes, 1933), pp. 201–2. On the ERA, see Mary Frances Berry, *Why ERA Failed* (Indiana University Press, 1986); and Joan Hoff-Wilson, ed., *Rights of Passage: The Past and Future of the ERA* (Indiana University Press, 1986).

360 *forty-eight-hour workweek:* ER and Doris Stevens in debate, *New York Times*, 26 Feb. 1925.

361 *power of voting women:* ER's letter of support to Grace Davis Vanamee, chair of the State Affairs Committee of the Women's National Republican Club: "I cannot tell you how pleased we all are at your announcement at the Consumers' League" that, by a vote of four to one, Republican women "would not accept the rebuff given the women on the 48-hour week."

While ER celebrated the unity of women, she condemned male politicians for their "open, cynical and reckless defiance of definite platform and campaign promises." (*New York Times*, 22 March 1926.)

361 *"rooms with baths":* Rose Schneiderman to ER, 21 May 1936, FDRL.

361–62 *five-day week:* ER's WTUL-sponsored debate covered in *New York Times*, 9 April 1929.

362 *"hogs from cholera":* Vanderlip on Sheppard-Towner, quoted in Watrous, *Narcissa Vanderlip*, p. 31.

362 *Women's City Club:* New York Times, 7 April 1925.

362–63 *dance halls:* ER, in ibid. For the controversy, see Elisabeth Israels Perry, *Belle Moskowitz: Feminine Politics & the Exercise of Power in the Age of Alfred E. Smith* (Oxford University Press, 1987), pp. 42–57.

363 *equal political education:* New York Times, 26, 27 May 1927.

363 *"disorderly conduct":* Ibid., 9 Dec. 1926.

363–64 *She herself wanted to fly:* As First Lady of New York State, ER would christen a plane only if she were taken aloft: "No flight, no christening." (Ibid., 1 June, 6 June 1929.)

364 *"menace to civilization":* Catt called for conferences in every community, and announced: "War will disappear from the earth when women decide the time has come." (Van Voris, *Carrie Chapman Catt*, p. 207.)

364 *"pilgrimages of women":* ER, *Women's Democratic News*, July 1926.

364–65 *"Our Foreign Policy—What Is It?":* Women's Democratic News, Jan. 1927.

365 *ER featured a front-page article:* The March 1927 issue's banner headline, "Do We Deserve the Hatred of the World? Under Wilson We Were Regarded as the Unselfish Idealists of the World—Under Coolidge They Call Us 'Money Grabbers'—Why?," was followed by a long two-full-page article, "Banks and Bayonets in Nicaragua."

365 *"to prepare for world peace":* ER quoted in *New York Times*, 15 Oct. 1927; 8 Dec. 1927; 2 Nov. 1929.

366 *same floor space:* Ibid., 19 July 1928; 4 Aug. 1928.
Achieving equal space with John J. Raskob of General Motors, Al Smith's great friend, was no small item. Vice-president of DuPont, Raskob was one of the Democratic Party's richest contributors. In 1929, he and Pierre S. DuPont announced a new corporation to erect a 102-story office building on the site of the old Waldorf-Astoria, where for so many years society's Assembly Balls had been held. The Empire State Building would be 200 feet higher than the Chrysler Building. (Kenneth S. Davis, *FDR: The New York Years, 1928–1933* [Random House, 1985], p. 139.)

366 *elected Caroline O'Day:* ER's speech in *New York Times*, 28 Sept. 1926.

366–70 *feminist article:* "Women Must Learn to Play the Game as Men Do," in *Redbook*, April 1928, pp. 71–72ff.
ER wrote as a realist: "Personally, I do not believe in a Woman's Party. A woman's ticket could never possibly succeed. And to crystallize the issues on the basis of sex-opposition would only further antagonize men, congeal their age-old prejudices, and widen the chasm of existing differences." (P. 141.)

370–71 *S. J. Woolf:* In *New York Times Magazine*, 8 April 1928.

371 *attacked religious bigotry:* New York Times, 25 Jan. 1928.

371–72 *"We crave a man with . . . human heart":* Ibid., 19 April 1928.

372 *"like children":* ER to FDR, 27 April 1928, FDRL.

372 *"I am quite unreasonably depressed":* ER to FDR, 22 June 1928, FDRL.

372–73 *"I had no desire":* ER, *This I Remember*, p. 38.

373 *"how forlorn":* Marion Dickerman on ER, and on FDR's walk without crutches, in K. Davis, *Invincible Summer*, p. 81.

373 *She put together a staff:* ER, *This I Remember*, p. 41.

On 26 Oct. 1948, June Hamilton Rhodes wrote ER: *"Time* magazine said 'you are the greatest woman in the world' I knew that in 1928." (ER Papers, Box 4566, FDRL.)

374 *On the campaign trail: New York Times*, 19 July 1928, 4 Aug. 1928.

374 *"The life of a consistent Republican:* Ibid., 22 Sept. 1928.

374 *"without intense prejudice":* ER, *This I Remember*, p. 39.

374–75 *her own position on Prohibition: New York Times*, 30 Jan. 1928 (also on Fourteenth and Fifteenth Amendments).

375 *"National Woman's Dry Enforcement League":* ER to Jesse Nicholson, 28 Jan. 1928, in Lash, *Eleanor and Franklin*, p. 313.

375 *"I have never attacked the South":* ER's unpublished 1928 notes on race are in James Kearney, *Anna Eleanor Roosevelt: The Evolution of a Reformer* (Houghton Mifflin, 1968), p. 61.

375 *"We do not feel quite willing": New York Times*, 10 July 1928.

375 *Mrs. Clem Shaver:* ER, in ibid., 7 July 1928.

375–76 *"When Greek Meets Greek":* Ibid., 9 July 1928.

ER was personally ambivalent about Prohibition. In her own family, alcoholism continued to ravage lives. ER wrote Elinor Morgenthau that she went to Tivoli because "the woman who lives with my uncle [Vallie] wrote me he'd been drinking for a month and something must be done. . . . I'm wondering how I can get the place raided as not only Vallie but some young boys on the farm under 20 whom he influenced are getting drunk constantly and their mother has tuberculosis and is at her wit's end! Isn't it too annoying! Tonight I want the Volstead law enforced unmodified and I want to get rid of all the state police who connive with bootleggers!" (29 April 1927, Elinor Morgenthau Papers, FDRL.)

376–77 *"with evident glee":* ER, *This I Remember*, p. 45.

377 *"the most wonderful thing":* Esther Lape quote in Lash, *Eleanor and Franklin*, p. 318.

377 *Nobody was pleased:* Rollins, *Roosevelt and Howe*, p. 235.

377 *"no use . . . getting sick":* SDR, *My Boy Franklin*, p. 110; Burns, *Lion and Fox*, p. 101.

378 *"what follows is really private":* SDR to FDR, 2 Oct. 1928, quoted in Lash, *Eleanor and Franklin*, p. 317.

378 *"an obligation to return":* ER, *This I Remember*, pp. 46–47.

378 *"plenty to do":* ER, in *New York Times*, 3 Oct. 1928.

378 *"throw away my cane":* FDR to mother, *My Boy Franklin*, p. 110.

378–79 *Only Franklin's mother:* Frances Perkins was one of the few witnesses to Sara Delano Roosevelt's lonely vigil (Perkins Oral History, Columbia). On the vote tallies, see *Letters*, vol. 2, p. 649.

379 *"If the rest of the ticket":* ER to press Quoted in Lash, *Eleanor and Franklin*, p. 320;

379 *In retrospect:* ER, *This I Remember*, p. 46.

There was evidently considerable tension between ER and FDR during the two campaigns. ER wrote Elinor Morgenthau that she was "neither very tired, nor especially happy or depressed." "I felt Gov. Smith's election meant something but whether Franklin spends two years in Albany or not matters as you know comparatively little. . . ." (13 Nov. 1928, Elinor Morgenthau Papers, FDRL.)

ER had inspired the women she worked with during the presidential campaign, and she received countless letters of praise, gratitude, and hope. Dorothy Kirchey Brown, who headed the Massachusetts campaign, wrote: "You must know without being told that working with you was a very great pleasure and satisfaction. . . . I never cease to marvel at your capacity for work and your serenity and poise through it all. . . ." (27 Nov. 1928, FDRL.)

15. New York's First Lady, Part-Time

381 *"What I Want Most Out of Life"*: Success Magazine, May 1927. Quoted in Lash, *Love, Eleanor*, p. 104.

382 *"Filling Many Jobs"*: New York Times, 10 Nov. 1928.

382–83 *"being most discreet"*: ER to FDR, 16 Nov. 1928, 1 Dec. 1928, FDRL. See also Lash, *Eleanor and Franklin*, ch. 32.

383 *"In this difficult undertaking"*: Women's Democratic News editorial to ER, Nov. 1928, p. 6.

383–84 *criticized Nancy Cook:* ER to Elinor Morgenthau, 13 Nov. 1928, Elinor Morgenthau Papers, FDRL (transcribed by Maureen Corr).

Although ER was devoted to Elinor Morgenthau, she also considered her unreasonably sensitive: "To say that your letter amazed me would be mild somehow I always forget how tragic things seem to you. . . . As to your saying you had a 'rotten deal' I don't know what you mean. You and Nan have not worked well together this autumn why, heaven knows, but those things happen and if you want to resign, that is your choice but no one has forced you to do it. . . . Caroline is a fine person to work with or for and I think you must realize it when you think it over."

384–85 *"write me an article"*: ER to Frances Perkins, 6 March 1929, Frances Perkins Papers, Reel 4, Columbia.

385–86 *"a woman's woman"*: Perkins Oral History, Columbia, vol. 3, pp. 266, 290, 531.

386 *"an almost austere streak"*: Helen Huntington Smith, "Profiles: Noblesse Oblige," New Yorker, 5 April 1930.

386–87 *"black straw pancake"*: Lorena A. Hickok, *Eleanor Roosevelt: Reluctant First Lady* (Dodd, Mead, 1980 [1962]), pp. 10–11, 58.

387 *"If I were you"*: ER to FDR, 16 Nov. 1928, Box 16, FDRL.

388–89 *"Belle and Bob Moses mean to cling"*: ER to FDR, 13 Nov. 1928, FDRL.

The most powerful political woman of the era, Belle Moskowitz was widowed and left to support three children when Charles Israels, her architect husband, died in 1911. She married social-reform leader Henry Moskowitz in 1914. According to Elisabeth Israels Perry, her biographer and granddaughter, the entire field of public relations, commercial and political propaganda, was largely created by Belle Moskowitz. From the very beginning, she worked with Edward Bernays, in a variety of projects that sought with "conscious and intelligent manipulation" to change the "habits and opinions" of people. (Perry, *Belle Moskowitz*, pp. 140–41.)

389 *" 'to a bunch of women' "*: Perry, *Belle Moskowitz*, p. 119; Robert Caro, *The Power Broker: Robert Moses and the Fall of New York* (Alfred A. Knopf, 1974), pp. 94–96.

390 *"The Jew party"*: ER to Sara Delano Roosevelt, 16 Jan. 1918, FDRL.

391 *Moses publicly announced:* Caro, *Power Broker*, pp. 287–98.

By 1928, however, both ER and FDR publicly deplored religious bigotry. Sam

Rosenman, who wrote many of FDR's speeches in the campaign against Ottinger, noted that FDR himself wrote the passage blasting religious bigots in politics: "May God have mercy on your miserable souls." (Morgan, *FDR*, p. 293.)

391–92 *" 'a very fine woman' ":* Perkins Oral History, Columbia, vol. 3, pp. 13–14, 21–22.

392 *"I hope you will consider":* ER to FDR, 22 Nov. 1928, Box 16, FDRL.

392–93 *"I wouldn't know":* Perkins Oral History, Columbia, vol. 2, p. 720; see also pp. 169–70.

393 *"It is my firm belief":* FDR, "Women's Field in Politics," *Women's City Club Quarterly*, 1928, quoted in Lash, *Love, Eleanor*, p. 109.

394 *"go with the Executive Mansion":* ER to FDR, 1–2 Dec. 1928, Box 16, FDRL.

394–95 *According to Frances Perkins:* ER's story in Perkins Oral History, Columbia, vol. 3, pp. 530–39.

395–96 *"a week of shooting":* ER to FDR, 1–2 Dec. 1928, FDRL.

396 *"a good influence":* ER to FDR, 22 Nov. 1928, FDRL.

16. Teaching and Todhunter

397–98 *"less high sounding":* ER to Marion Dickerman, 7 Feb. 1926, Marion Dickerman Papers, Box 4, FDRL.
ER wrote this letter aboard the *Larooco*, and noted: "Franklin has just heard that the [Oswald] Mosleys [subsequently the leader of England's fascist party] are coming in so we are going to be quite crowded . . . & I may try to leave Thursday night, the day Missy arrives as I don't know where she will sleep if I don't. I'm sleeping on deck."

398 *"O God, give us clean hands":* Materials relating to Todhunter, descriptive brochures, school publicity, and exams, are in ER Papers, Box 7, and in Marion Dickerman Papers, Box 4, FDRL.

399 *"belongs to me":* Smith, "Noblesse Oblige," *New Yorker*, 5 April 1930.

399 *"better than anything":* ER to Eunice Fuller Barnard, "Mrs. Roosevelt in the Classroom," *New York Times Magazine*, 4 Dec. 1932.

399 *students adored her:* I am grateful to Annis Fuller Young and Patricia Vaill for their memories of Todhunter.

400 *"others were none too good":* ER to FDR, 2 Feb. 1928, FDRL.

400 *"basking in contentment":* ER on Lady Helen, *Autobiography of ER*, pp. 54–55. "Wives of Great Men," *Liberty*, 1 Oct. 1932.

400–1 *final exams:* Class tests are in ER Papers, Box 7, FDRL; these questions are from a history exam, April 1931, and a current-events final, May 1931.

401 *"what the book says":* Smith, "Noblesse Oblige," *New Yorker*, 5 April 1930.
ER expected "full cooperation in every phase of school work, from Latin grammar to tennis." And "every girl . . . is held to strict accountability with reports and marks."

402 *"Vision means":* "What Kind of Education Do We Want for Our Girls?," *Woman's Journal*, Oct. 1930.

403 *"The outstanding issue":* ER, "Jeffersonian Principles: The Issue in 1928," *Current History*, June 1928.

403 *"training the great mass":* From address to Women's Division of Federations for Support of Jewish Philanthropies, quoted in *New York Times*, 20 Feb. 1929.

404–5 *"closely confined amongst the little groups":* "Ideal Education," *Woman's Journal,* Oct. 1930.

405 *"the most civilized":* Todhunter: Its History and Philosophy, n.d., ER Papers, Box 7, FDRL.

406 *"old time tenement":* ER to Jane Hoey, 9 April 1930, ER Papers, Box 12, FDRL.

406 *"nothing . . . closed to women":* New York Times, 10 Oct. 1929.

406–7 *"a great, tall woman like herself":* Perkins Oral History, Columbia, vol. 3, p. 389.

407 *"Everything is done for me":* Lash, *Eleanor and Franklin,* p. 326.

407 *"Pa seems to want you there":* Anna to ER, n.d. [1931], in Asbell, *Mother and Daughter,* pp. 50–51.

17. ER at Forty-five

410 *spectacular strategist:* On Molly Dewson and the Women's Division, see Ware, *Partner and I.*

411 *ER and Howe had . . . divided:* see Rollins, *Roosevelt and Howe,* p. 287.

412 *called her "Muddie":* Patricia Vaill to author. The boys called her Muddie, so Dickerman imitated them. Little things; but noticeable, and snide.

412–13 *agony of misunderstanding:* ER had "cold feet" about leaving all spring. "It seems such a fearful effort," she wrote FDR on 19 May (FDRL). Marion Dickerman, however, attributed "her reluctance" to her new friendship with Earl Miller. (See Kenneth S. Davis, "Symbolic Journey," *Antioch Review,* Summer 1979, p. 265. The article recounts the trip from Dickerman's point of view.)

The voyage over was, nevertheless, something of a personal triumph for ER: She did not get sea sick; and she and FDR, Jr., were "the only two to make breakfast. . . . The food service is excellent. . . . I walk three miles daily. . . ." (ER to FDR, 27–29 July 1929, FDRL.)

413 *"the food was excellent":* ER to FDR, 14 Aug. 1929, FDRL.

414–15 *"Tears & desperate sorrow":* On pickpockets and fights, see ER to FDR, 25 Aug. 1929, Box 16, FDRL. See also K. Davis, "Symbolic Journey."

415–16 *gubernatorial inaugural address:* FDR quoted in Burns, *Lion and Fox,* p. 105.

416 *"private audience" with Mussolini:* Asbell, *Mother and Daughter,* p. 35.

416–17 *"We had a letter of introduction":* Anna to parents, 24 March 1929, in ibid., pp. 48–49.

417–18 *the "Negro question":* Caro, *Power Broker,* pp. 317–19.

Moses specifically prohibited the Long Island Railroad's proposal to create a shuttle to Jones Beach, and he barred buses from creating routes to the park. He went so far as to build bridges too low for buses to pass beneath. Charter buses had to obtain "permits." According to Caro, "buses chartered by Negro groups" rarely received permits.

418 *recent little Flurry":* FDR to Howe, 1 Dec. 1929, in *Letters,* vol. 3, pp. 92–93.

On the crash, Thomas Lamont, and Richard Whitney, see K. Davis, *New York Years,* pp. 144–48; Nathan Miller, *FDR: An Intimate History* (Doubleday, 1983), pp. 235–39.

418–19 *to retire the WTUL mortgage:* In Lash, *Eleanor and Franklin,* pp. 328–29; Rose Schneiderman with Lucy Goldthwaite, *All for One* (Paul Erickson, 1967), pp. 150–63, 175–76.

419–20 *Exposition of Women's Arts:* ER's keynote in *New York Times*, 10 Oct. 1929.

420 *"Woman-Run Factory":* *New York Times Magazine*, 16 Nov. 1930.
   ER looked "forward to an industrial world as familiar to women as it now is to men. . . . The woman studying mass production, with original ideas, drive, force, vision, capable of heading hundreds of workmen is bound to come. . . ."

421–22 *As depression conditions worsened:* "What the Country Expects from the Junior League," Nov. 1930; article and letter, Edith G. Lindley to ER, 20 Nov. 1930, Box 12, FDRL.

422 *"factory girls" and "business girls":* Schneiderman to ER, 8 July 1930, Box 16, FDRL.

422 *"divided into strata":* ER to Rose Schneiderman, 9 June 1930, Box 16, FDRL.

422–23 *supported strike efforts:* *New York Times*, 18 Nov., 19 Nov. 1930.

423 *"cannot get work":* *New York Times*, 4 March 1930.

423 *"can't go on drifting":* Ibid., 13 Jan. 1932.

423 *"We are not only":* Ibid., 15 Jan. 1932. See also 14 Dec. 1932.

424 *"a faithful watchdog":* Sam Rosenman, *Working with Roosevelt* (DaCapo Reprint, 1972 [1952]), p. 25.

424 *"greater efficiency":* Rosenman on Missy LeHand, Oral History, Columbia, p. 108.

424–26 *"should never nag":* ER, "Wives of Great Men," *Liberty*, 1932.

426 *"get the jump on [Herbert] Hoover":* ER to FDR, 2 Oct. 1930, FDRL.

426–28 *"Her Forty-fifth Birthday!":* *Vogue*, ms. in Box 10, sent 23 Dec. 1930.

428 *"the word 'passionate' ":* Smith, "Noblesse Oblige," *New Yorker*, 5 April 1930.

18. Earl Miller: A Champion of Her Own

This is the only chapter of ER's life for which there are no letters by her to document the facts, or establish the texture of the reality. All the letters by Earl Miller available to date were written to his friends the Abelows during the 1960s and 1970s. There are, however, photographs and films. Their times together are referred to most frequently in ER's letters to her daughter, and to Lorena Hickok. Esther Lape, Marion Dickerman, Joseph Lash, and ER's children present different versions of their friendship.

429 *Middleweight Boxing Championship:* Earl Miller's naval boxing matches were conducted by Walter Camp, who originated All-American football and was "the Daddy of Physical Fitness" during World War I (Miller to Miriam Abelow, 6 Dec. 1962). Concerning his activities, Miller to "dear folks," 4 Sept. 1972, Abelow Collection, FDRL.

430 *"old crab"* . . . *"the Lady":* On Miller's attentiveness and his barracks reputation, see Lash, *Love, Eleanor*, p. 117.

431 *"used to play the piano":* ER, *This I Remember*, p. 28.

431 *"I'd rather have Earl's":* ER to John Golden, 1943, quoted in Lash, *A World of Love: Eleanor Roosevelt and Her Friends, 1943–1962* (Doubleday, 1984), p. 68.

432 *"Corporal Miller took charge":* ER to Maude Hall Gray, 12 July 1930, ER Papers, Box 2, FDRL.

432–33 *inspection tours:* ER, *This I Remember*, p. 56.

433 *"check the gasoline":* Quoted in Lash, *Love, Eleanor*, p. 120; and letters to the Abelows, FDRL.

433–44 The Pirate and the Lady: Evidently filmed by Nancy Cook, in FDRL.

434 *"manhandled" her:* Marion Dickerman Oral History, Columbia.

434 *"I was expecting Earl":* I am grateful to Peggy Kiskadden and Maureen Corr for their memories of Esther Lape's conversations regarding ER and Earl Miller.

435 *"one real romance":* J. Roosevelt with Libby, *My Parents,* pp. 110–11.

436 *"Eleanor wrote him faithfully":* Lash, *Eleanor and Franklin,* p. 481. On the disappearance of letters, Lash, *Love, Eleanor,* p. 116.

Lash noted: "Some of her friends were puzzled by her attachment to this 'cop,' but if Franklin could make Missy a part of his household, she could do the same with Earl." (*Eleanor and Franklin,* p. 481.)

436 *sealed by the court:* Lash, *A World of Love,* p. 297. See Volume Two of this biography.

436 *"will rock the country":* Ed Sullivan, New York *Daily News,* 13 Jan. 1947.

436 *his marital troubles:* Lash, *Love, Eleanor,* pp. 118–19. See these same pages for Miller on Missy LeHand.

436–37 *"to run interference":* Lash, *Eleanor and Franklin,* pp. 117–19.

437 *"I squired Missy":* Miller to the Abelows, 7 Jan. 1972, FDRL.

437–38 *"sometimes thought backstairs":* Lillian Rogers Parks, with Frances Spatz Leighton, *The Roosevelts: A Family in Turmoil* (Prentice Hall, 1981), p. 185.

438 *Miller loved to cook:* Earl Miller to ER, Oct. 1951, in Anna Roosevelt Halsted Papers, FDRL.

438–39 *"I had him atop a horse":* Miller to Miriam Abelow, 12 June 1965, FDRL.

439 *"would have made a better president":* On ER as president, see Lash, *Love, Eleanor,* p. 121.

439 *"pink or radical":* Miller to the Abelows, 12 June 65, FDRL.

439–40 *Lucy Mercer "copied" ER:* Miller to the Abelows, 22 Aug. 1966, FDRL.

440 *"White Trash Guard":* Ibid.

440 *"leaned a little too much to the right":* Miller to Miriam Abelow, 12 June 1965, FDRL.

440 *"Joe didn't get anything from me":* Miller to Abelow, 19 Oct. 1971, 7 Jan. 1972.

441 *mother-and-son terms:* Lash, *Love, Eleanor,* p. 123.

441 *"unable to let herself go":* Lash, *A World of Love,* pp. 340, 347–48.

442–45 *ER wrote an article:* "Ten Rules for Success in Marriage," *Pictorial Review,* Dec. 1931.

446 *marry Earl Miller:* On ER's shredded letter to Nancy Cook, see K. Davis, *The New York Years,* pp. 329–30.

446 *"down in the depths":* Quoted in Lash, *Love, Eleanor,* p. 119.

446–47 *"The night before":* ER, *This I Remember,* p. 70.

19. Assignment ER: Lorena Hickok and the 1932 Campaign

449 *cultivating her support:* Lorena A. Hickok, *Eleanor Roosevelt: Reluctant First Lady* (Dodd, Mead, 1980 [1962]), pp. 29–30.

450 *"It was most unusual":* Ibid., pp. 13–15.

451 *"her arms were very long":* Ibid., pp. 17, 21.

452 *" 'That woman is unhappy about something' ":* Ibid., pp. 31–33.

452–53 *FDR called Hearst:* On this deal, see Morgan, *FDR,* pp. 351–53.

453–54 *"Happy Days Are Here Again":* Rollins, *Roosevelt and Howe,* p. 342.

454 *the first flying candidate:* Rosenman, *Working with Roosevelt,* p. 74.

455–56 *"a party of liberal thought":* Quoted in ibid., pp. 67–79.

456 *"Raymond Moley":* ER, *This I Remember,* pp. 69–71.

456–57 *the man most responsible:* On Howe's eclipse, see Rollins, *Roosevelt and Howe,* pp. 338–48.

457–58 *"a shabby statement":* Agnes Brown Leach to FDR, and ER to Leach, quoted in Lash, *Eleanor and Franklin,* p. 347.

458 *"I did not want my husband to be president":* ER, *This I Remember,* pp. 65, 69.

459 *ER's friend:* Isabella Selmes Ferguson Greenway was elected to Congress in 1932.
During ER's years of grief in Washington, she wrote Isabella frequently that her courage was a guide:
"You mean more to me each year, and your life and the way you have faced it and all you do and are doing has meant so much to me in example and inspiration.
"Someday when much lies behind us both and we have time to be together . . . there is going to be real joy for both of us I hope."
(ER to Isabella, 16 Sept. 1919, Tucson.)

459–60 *"more approachable":* Hickok, *Reluctant First Lady,* pp. 37–39.

460 *"I recall puffing":* Ibid.

461 *World Series:* Ibid., pp. 41–42.

461 *"She's all yours":* Ibid., pp. 43–44.

462 *publicity hound:* On this and other press attacks, see ibid., p. 62.

462–63 *" 'I took the knife away' ":* Ibid., p. 68.

463 *"Unless she is taking":* Ibid., pp. 66–67.

464 *Like all Republicans:* ER in *New York Times,* 29 Oct. 1932.

464–65 *"Things have come to a head":* On Miller's divorce, see ER to Nancy Cook, quoted in Lash, *Love, Eleanor,* p. 170.

465–66 *ER's five-day journey:* AP wires, Hickok Papers, FDRL.

467 *The very first note:* ER to Miss Hickok, 26 Oct. 1932, Hickok Papers, FDRL.

467–69 *"There was only one drawing room":* Hickok, *Reluctant First Lady,* pp. 48–49. See also AP interview, published 10 Nov. 1932, Hickok Papers, FDRL.

469–70 *a major scoop:* On Edith Roosevelt's speech, see Hickok, *Reluctant First Lady,* pp. 50–51.

470–71 *" 'That girl is furious' ":* Ibid., pp. 53–54.

471 *ER hosted a buffet supper:* Ibid., pp. 57–59.

472 *"We think it's grand":* AP wire, 8 Nov. 1932, Hickok Papers, FDRL.

472 *"I'm not important enough":* ER never wanted to be a president's wife, AP wire, 9 Nov. 1932, Hickok Papers, FDRL.

473 *ER's new press image:* AP wire, 17 Dec. 1932.

473–74 *Some newspapers: New York Times*, 17 Dec. 1932.

474 *"likes to do things for herself":* AP wire, 12 Nov. 1932, Hickok Papers, FDRL.

474–75 *"curtail . . . activities":* AP wire, 4 Feb. 1933, Hickok Papers, FDRL.

475–76 *"and very much annoyed":* Hickok, *Reluctant First Lady*, pp. 64–65.

476 *"seen my Aunt Kassie":* Ibid., p. 67.

20. The First Lady's First Friend

477 *insulting stereotypes:* See Doris Faber, *The Life of Lorena Hickok: ER's Friend* (William Morrow, 1980). The first researcher to see Hickok's correspondence, Faber wrote that she was so horrified by what she read, she urged William Emerson, then director of the FDR Library, to close the collection until at least the year 2000. That being impossible, she decided to beat out that "summer's tide of assistant professors" and scholars who were certain to discover the significance of the material. But Faber was so distraught that she decided to ignore all "political or social issues," lest she give "an unjustifiable pretension of importance to Lorena Hickok and her relationship with Eleanor Roosevelt." (Pp. 332, 335.)

477–78 *"no vamp":* Lash, *Love, Eleanor*, p. 126. For fuller descriptions of Hick, I am grateful to Hick's friend Howard Haycraft and to Doris Dana, Bill Dana's daughter, who knew Hick during the years she lived in the "little house" on her father's Long Island estate in Mastic. Bill Dana was one of Hick's great friends. I am also grateful to Doris Dana and Anne Farr for a tour of Hick's favorite home.

479 *"take you in my arms":* ER to Hick, quoted in Faber, *Life of Lorena Hickok*, p. 176. We are further informed by Faber that "there can be little doubt" that ER's wish "could not mean what it appears to mean."

479 *"north-east of the corner":* Quoted in Faber, *Life of Lorena Hickok*, p. 152.

479 *not . . . a schoolgirl "smash":* See Nancy Sahli, "Smashing: Women's Relations Before the Fall," *Chrysalis*, no. 8, 1979, pp. 17–22.

480–85 *daugher of a butter-maker:* All quotations and biographical information in this section are from Hickok's letters, memorabilia, and her chs. for an autobiography, Hickok Papers, FDRL.

485–86 *"did admire prima donnas":* In Abe Altrowitz, "Memories of Her Abound: Lorena Hickok's Newspaper Career Was Colorful, Vital," Minneapolis *Star*, 16 May 1968. I am grateful to Anne Farr for this reference.

486 *Ernestine Schumann-Heink:* Henry Pleasants, *The Great Singers from the Dawn of Opera* (Simon & Schuster, 1981), pp. 279–83.

Neither her thrilling voice nor her theatrical genius protected Ernestine Schumann-Heink from the misogyny that enables history to empasize her appearance: "Homely." "Unattractive." "Fat." One of opera's major "ugly ducklings." Some of us might consider her large and handsome, but, as in the case of Hick, that is not how she has been portrayed. Her own defense was her great wit. Once, upon leaving the stage, she had trouble getting through the orchestra. The first violinist suggested she go sideways. She stared at him for a moment and snapped: "Young man, don't you see? I have no sideways!" (I am grateful to Sadonia Ecker Wiesen and Lili Engler for their memories of Schumann-Heink.)

488 *warmed up a room:* I am grateful to Doris Dana and Howard Haycraft for their memories of Lorena Hickok's laugh and personality from the 1930s to the 1950s; and to her last editor, Allen Klots, who had similar memories of Hick even at the end, when she was near death.

488 *"Every woman wants to be first"*: ER to Lash, quoted in *A World of Love*, p. 116.

488–89 *"Your ring is a great comfort"*: ER to Hick, 7 March 1933, Hickok Papers, FDRL.

489 *"a bit rough and tumble"*: Peggy Kiskadden to author.

489 *disapproved of Hick:* For example, ER's daughter, Anna, was particularly close to Hick. But any evidence that she was knowledgeable about the nature of their relationship, or—conversely—that there was anything to be knowledgeable about, has been dismissed, with rhetorical flourish: "Both Anna and John [Boettiger] would have considered lesbianism not nice, a form of morbidity." (Lash, *Love, Eleanor*, pp. 175–76.)

Nevertheless, both ER and Hick saved most of their thirty-year-long correspondence. After ER died, Hick destroyed some of ER's letters and many of her own. One weekend at Esther Lape's in Westbrook, she sat before the fire for hours and burned letter after letter. And she sanitized others. The first year of their relationship, the period from Election Day to the inauguration and for months beyond, was simply revised by Hick. She typed each letter to preserve ER's public and political record, deleted all personal references and endearments, and donated the transcriptions to the FDRL.

Subsequently, Hick wrote to Anna that she burned entirely only fifteen of ER's letters. But it is clear that she burned many more of her own. Presumably, the letters that her sister Ruby Claff burned after Hick's death were the original versions of the typed letters that chronicled that first year. After she read them, Ruby Claff threw them into Hick's fireplace and told Anne Farr, "This is nobody's business." (Farr to author.)

490 *"Oh, yes, I can"*: On this visit to the White House, see ER, *This I Remember*, pp. 75–76; Hickok, *Reluctant First Lady*, pp. 71–77.

491 *"I have a weapon"*: Hickok, ibid.

492–93 Grief . . . *before the inauguration:* Ibid., pp. 80–92.

493–95 *The national income:* On this, and also on FDR and Hoover, see especially Frank Freidel, FDR: *Launching the New Deal* (Little, Brown, 1973), pp. 1–45; and Kenneth S. Davis, *FDR: The New Deal Years, 1933–1937* (Random House, 1986), pp. 1–42.

495–96 *"My suffering"*: Hickok, *Reluctant First Lady*, pp. 94–96. For ER on the interview, see ER, *This I Remember*, p. 78. For Hick on the interview and on Howe, see Hickok, *Reluctant First Lady*, p. 104.

496 *"became obvious to some servants"*: Parks with Leighton, *The Roosevelts*, p. 5.

497–98 *"All my love"*: ER to Hick, 5 March 1933, Hickok Papers, FDRL.

499–500 *"She ain't dressed up"*: Rita S. Halle, "That First Lady of Ours," *Good Housekeeping*, Dec. 1933, pp. 20–21, 193–94.

Selected Bibliography

(See Volume Two for full bibliography.)

Most of the primary source materials for this book are in the Franklin Delano Roosevelt Library (FDRL), in Hyde Park, New York. They include: Eleanor Roosevelt's Papers, Gracie Hall Roosevelt's Papers, the Roosevelt Family Papers Donated by the Children, the Hall Family Papers—including correspondence with ER's father, Elliott Roosevelt—and FDR's Papers. Many of FDR's letters to his family were printed in *FDR: His Personal Letters*, 4 vols., edited by Elliott Roosevelt et al., (Duell, Sloan and Pearce, 1947; Kraus Reprint, 1970).

In addition to family letters, photograph albums, home movies, and miles of film footage, the FDRL houses the collections of Marion Dickerman, Anna Roosevelt Halsted, Lorena Hickok, Louis Howe, Esther Lape, Elinor Morgenthau, and Miriam and Robert Abelow's letters from Earl Miller.

Newly opened materials in the Theodore Roosevelt Collection and the Alsop Family Papers at the Houghton Library, Harvard University, in Cambridge, Massachusetts, were particularly useful for ER's paternal family history. Before his death, Joseph Alsop graciously gave me access to his papers. The Joseph and Stuart Alsop Collection at the Library of Congress is now opened, as are the family papers at Houghton. Another collection at the Library of Congress used for this volume is the Helen Rogers Reid Papers, which includes Esther Lape's correspondence with Reid. I have also benefited from the Esther Lape Papers in the private collection of Harold Clarke and Bert Drucker in Phoenix, Arizona.

ER's correspondence with Robert Munro Ferguson and Isabella Selmes Ferguson Greenway (King) is in the Greenway Collection, Arizona Historical Society, Tucson.

In addition to the Eleanor Roosevelt Oral History Project at the FDRL, other collections used include: Marion Dickerman Oral History, Frances Perkins's Papers, and her Oral History, Columbia University, New York City; Narcissa Cox Vanderlip Papers, in the Frank Vanderlip Collection, Columbia University; Carrie Chapman Catt Papers, New York Public Library; and the Fannie Hurst Papers, University of Texas at Austin.

City, State, and Nation, the *Weekly News* of the New York League of Women Voters, *The New York Times*, *The Crisis*, *The Nation*, *Town Topics*, and the *Women's Democratic News*, which merged with the *Democratic Digest* during the 1930s, were particularly useful sources for this volume.

During ER's centennial year, R. David Myers, Margaret L. Morrison, and Marguerite

563

D. Bloxom compiled and annotated *A Bibliography of Selected Material by and About Eleanor Roosevelt.* (Library of Congress, 1984).

By Eleanor Roosevelt

BOOKS

The Autobiography of Eleanor Roosevelt, New York: Harper & Row, 1958, 1978; New York: G.K. Hall, 1984, with a new introduction by John Roosevelt Boettiger.
Hunting Big Game in the 'Eighties: The Letters of Elliott Roosevelt, Sportsman. Edited by His Daughter. New York: Charles Scribner's Sons, 1933.
It's Up to the Women. New York: Frederick A. Stokes, 1933.
On My Own. New York: Harper & Brothers, 1958.
This I Remember. New York: Harper & Brothers, 1949.
This Is My Story. New York: Garden City Publishing Co., 1937.
Tomorrow Is Now. New York: Harper & Row, 1963.
You Learn by Living. New York: Harper & Brothers, 1960.

ARTICLES

"As a Practical Idealist." From series "Why Democrats Favor Smith," in *The North American Review,* November 1927.
"Building Character." *Parents Magazine,* June 1931.
"Conquer Fear and You Will Enjoy Living," *Look,* 23 May 1939.
"Her 45th Birthday!" Article written for *Vogue,* sent 23 December 1930, ER Papers, Box 10, FDRL.
"I Remember Hyde Park." *McCall's,* February 1963.
"Ideal Education." *The Woman's Journal,* October 1930.
"The Importance of Background Knowledge in Building for the Future." *The Annals of the American Academy,* July 1946.
"Jeffersonian Principles: The Issue in 1928." *Current History,* June 1928.
"The Seven People Who Shaped My Life." *Look,* 19 June 1951.
"Ten Rules for Success in Marriage." *Pictorial Review,* December 1931.
"What I Want Most Out of Life." *Success Magazine,* May 1927.
"What Kind of Education Do We Want for Our Girls?" *Woman's Journal,* October 1930.
"Wives of Great Men." *Liberty,* 1 October 1932.
"Women Have Come a Long Way." *Harper's Magazine,* October 1950.
"Women Must Learn to Play the Game as Men Do." *Redbook Magazine,* April 1928.

PAMPHLET

Franklin D. Roosevelt and Hyde Park: Personal Recollections of Eleanor Roosevelt. Washington, D.C.: Government Printing Office, 1949.

Other Sources

Alsop, Joseph. *FDR: A Centenary Remembrance.* New York: Viking, 1982.
Amory, Cleveland. *Who Killed Society?* New York: Harper & Brothers, 1960.
Asbell, Bernard. *Mother and Daughter: The Letters of Eleanor and Anna Roosevelt.* New York: Coward, McCann & Geoghegan, 1982.
Balch, Emily Greene, ed. *Occupied Haiti.* New York: Garland, 1972 [1927].
Baltzell, Digby E. *The Protestant Establishment: Aristocracy & Caste in America.* New York: Vintage, 1966.
Barnard, Eunice Fuller. "Mrs. Roosevelt in the Classroom," *New York Times Magazine,* 4 December 1932.

Beasley, Maurine. "Lorena Hickok: Journalistic Influence on Eleanor Roosevelt," *Journalism Quarterly*, Summer 1980.

Bellegarde-Smith, Patrick. *Haiti: The Breached Citadel*. Boulder, Colo.: Westview Press, 1990.

Bellush, Bernard. *Franklin D. Roosevelt as Governor of New York*. New York: Columbia University Press, 1955.

Bernikow, Louise, ed. *The World Split Open: Four Centuries of Women Poets in England and America, 1552–1950*. New York: Vintage, 1974.

Berry, Mary Frances. *Why ERA Failed*. Bloomington, Ind.: Indiana University Press, 1986.

Birmingham, Stephen. *The Right People: A Portrait of the American Social Establishment*. New York: Dell, 1958.

Bishop, Joseph Bucklin, ed. *Theodore Roosevelt's Letters to His Children*. New York: Charles Scribner's Sons, 1919.

Boyd, Elizabeth French. *Bloomsbury Heritage: Their Mothers and Their Aunts*. London: Evelyn Adams & Mackay, 1968.

Brittain, Vera. *Women at Oxford*. London: George G. Harrap, 1960.

Bronfman Judith. "The Griselda Legend in English Literature." Ph.D. diss., New York University, 1977.

Burns, James MacGregor. *Roosevelt: The Lion and the Fox*. New York: Harcourt, Brace, & World, 1956.

Bussy, Dorothy Strachey. *Olivia*. New York: Arno Press Reprint, 1975, [1948].

Caro, Robert. *The Power Broker: Robert Moses and the Fall of New York*. New York: Alfred A. Knopf, 1974.

Chambers, John Whiteclay, ed. *The Eagle and the Dove: The American Peace Movement and United States Foreign Policy, 1900–1922*. Syracuse, N.Y.: Syracuse University Press, 1991.

Churchill, Allen. *The Roosevelts: American Aristocrats*. New York: Harper & Row, 1965.

Coben, Stanley A. *A. Mitchell Palmer: Politician*. New York: Columbia University Press, 1963.

Cook, Adrian Edward. *The Alabama Claims: American Politics and Anglo-American Relations, 1865–1872*. Ithaca, N.Y.: Cornell University Press, 1975.

———. "At the Gates of the White House: The Washington, D.C., Race Riots of 1919." In *The Growth of Federal Power in American History*, edited by R. Jeffreys-Jones and B. Collins. Edinburgh: Scottish Academic Press, 1983.

Cook, Blanche Wiesen. "Eleanor Roosevelt and Human Rights: The Battle for Peace and Planetary Decency." In *Women and American Foreign Policy*, edited by Edward Crapol. New York: Greenwood, 1987.

———. "Female Support Networks and Political Activism: Lillian Wald, Crystal Eastman, and Emma Goldman." *Chrysalis*, Autumn 1977. Reprinted in *Women's America: Refocusing the Past*, edited by Linda Kerber and Jane De Hart. New York: Oxford University Press, 1987, 1990.

———. "Feminism, Socialism, and Sexual Freedom: The Work and Legacy of Crystal Eastman and Alexandra Kollontai." In *Women in Culture and Politics: A Century of Change*, edited by Judith Friedlander et al. Bloomington, Ind.: University of Indiana Press, 1986.

———. "Women Alone Stir My Imagination: Lesbianism in the Cultural Tradition." *Signs*, Summer 1979.

———, ed. *Crystal Eastman on Women and Revolution*. New York: Oxford University Press, 1978.

———, ed. *Toward the Great Change: Crystal and Max Eastman on War and Revolution*. New York: Garland, 1979.

Coss, Clare. *Lillian D. Wald: Progressive Activist*. New York: The Feminist Press, 1989.

Dana, Rosamond Wild. "Privileged Radicals: The Rebellious Times of Six Dana Siblings

in Cambridge and New York." Master's thesis, City University of New York, 1991.
Daniels, Doris Groshen. *Always a Sister: The Feminism of Lillian D. Wald*. New York: The Feminist Press, 1989.
Daniels, Jonathan. *The End of Innocence*. New York: J. B. Lippincott, 1954.
———. *The Washington Quadrille: The Dance Beside the Documents*. Garden City, N.Y.: Doubleday, 1968.
Daniels, Josephus. *The Wilson Era: Years of Peace, 1910–1917*. Chapel Hill, N.C.: University of North Carolina Press, 1944.
Davis, Allen. *American Heroine: The Life and Legend of Jane Addams*. New York: Oxford University Press, 1973.
———, ed. *Jane Addams on Peace, War, and International Understanding, 1899–1932*. New York: Garland, 1976.
Davis, Kenneth S. *FDR: The Beckoning of Destiny, 1882–1928*. New York: G. P. Putnam's Sons, 1971.
———. *FDR: The New Deal Years, 1933–1937*. New York: Random House, 1986.
———. *FDR: The New York Years, 1928–1933*. New York: Random House, 1985.
———. *Invincible Summer: An Intimate Portrait of the Roosevelts Based on the Recollections of Marion Dickerman*. New York: Atheneum, 1974.
———. "Symbolic Journey." *The Antioch Review*, Summer 1979.
De Salvo, Louise. *Virginia Woolf: The Impact of Childhood Sexual Abuse on Her Life and Work*. Boston: Beacon Press, 1989.
Domhoff, William G. *The Higher Circles: The Governing Class in America*. New York: Vintage, 1971.
———. *Who Rules America?* Englewood Cliffs, N.J.: Prentice Hall, 1967.
Donald, David Herbert. *Charles Sumner and the Rights of Man*. New York: Alfred A. Knopf, 1970.
Dunn, Robert W., ed. *The Palmer Raids*. New York: International Publishers, 1948.
Dutcher, Elizabeth. "Budgets of the Triangle Fire Victims." *The Woman Voter*, June 1912.
———. "Frances Perkins: Doctor of Politics." *The Woman Voter*, September 1912.
Eldot, Paula. *Governor Alfred E. Smith: The Politician as Reformer*. New York: Garland, 1983.
Erikson, Joan M. "Nothing to Fear: Notes on the Life of Eleanor Roosevelt." *Daedalus*, Spring 1964. Reprinted in *The Woman in America*, edited by Robert Jay Lifton. Boston: Houghton Mifflin, 1967.
Faber, Doris. *the Life of Lorena Hickok: ER's Friend*. New York: William Morrow, 1980.
Felsenthal, Carol. *Alice Roosevelt Longworth*. New York: G. P. Putnam's Sons, 1988.
Flemion, Jess, and Colleen O'Connor, eds. *Eleanor Roosevelt: An American Journey*. San Diego, Calif.: San Diego State University Press, 1987.
Foner, Philip S. *Women and the American Labor Movement*. New York: Macmillan, Free Press, 1979.
Freedman, Estelle. "The New Woman: Changing Views of Women in the 1920s." *Journal of American History*, September 1974.
Freidel, Frank. *FDR: Launching the New Deal*. Boston: Little, Brown, 1973.
———. *Franklin D. Roosevelt: A Rendezvous with Destiny*. Boston: Little, Brown, 1990.
Gable, John Allen, ed. "The Roosevelt Family in America: A Genealogy." *Theodore Roosevelt Association Journal*, Spring 1990, pt. 2.
Gallagher, Hugh Gregory. *FDR's Splendid Deception*. New York: Dodd, Mead, 1985.
Ginger, Ray. *The Bending Cross: A Biography of Eugene Victor Debs*. New Brunswick, N.J.: Rutgers University Press, 1949.
Halle, Rita S. "That First Lady of Ours." *Good Housekeeping*, December 1933.
Hard, William. *Raymond Robins' Own Story*. New York: Harper & Brothers, 1920.
Hareven, Tamara. *Eleanor Roosevelt: An American Conscience*. Chicago: Quadrangle, 1968.

Heilbrun, Carolyn. *Writing a Woman's Life*. New York: W. W. Norton, 1988.

Hickok, Lorena A. *Eleanor Roosevelt: Reluctant First Lady*. New York: Dodd, Mead, 1980 [1962].

Hoff-Wilson, Joan, ed. *Rights of Passage: The Past and Future of the ERA*. Bloomington, Ind.: Indiana University Press, 1986.

Hoff-Wilson, Joan, and Marjorie Lightman, eds. *Without Precedent: The Life and Career of Eleanor Roosevelt*. Bloomington, Indiana University Press, 1984.

Hoge, Alice Albright. *Cissy Patterson*. New York: Random House, 1966.

Holroyd, Michael. *Lytton Strachey: The Unknown Years, 1880–1910*. New York: Holt, Rinehart & Winston, 1967.

Hoppin, Martha. *The Emmets: A Family of Women Painters*. Pittsfield, Mass.: Berkshire Museum, 1982.

James, Edward, Janet Wilson James, and Paul Boyer, eds. *Notable American Women*. 3 vols. Cambridge, Mass.: Harvard University Press, 1971.

Johnson, James Weldon, "Self-Determining Haiti." *The Nation*, 28 August, 11 September, and 25 September 1920.

Josephson, Matthew and Hannah. *Al Smith: Hero of the Cities: A Political Portrait Drawing on the Papers of Frances Perkins*. Boston: Houghton Mifflin, 1969.

Kaledin, Eugenia. *The Education of Mrs. Henry Adams*. Philadelphia: Temple University Press, 1981.

Katz, Jonathan. *Gay American History: Lesbians and Gay Men in the U.S.A.* New York: Thomas Y. Crowell, 1976.

Kearney, James. *Anna Eleanor Roosevelt: The Evolution of a Reformer*. Boston: Houghton Mifflin, 1968.

Kelly, Joan. "The Doubled Vision of Feminist Theory." In *Women, History and Theory: The Essays of Joan Kelly*. University of Chicago Press, 1984.

Kleeman, Rita Halle. *Gracious Lady: The Life of Sara Delano Roosevelt*. New York: Appleton-Century, 1935.

Lash, Joseph P. *Eleanor and Franklin*. New York: W. W. Norton, 1971.

———. *Love, Eleanor: Eleanor Roosevelt and Her Friends*. Garden City, N.Y.: Doubleday, 1982.

———. *A World of Love: Eleanor Roosevelt and Her Friends, 1943–1962*. Garden City, N.Y.: Doubleday, 1984.

Lemons, J. Stanley. *The Woman Citizen: Social Feminism in the 1920s*. Urbana, Ill.: University of Illinois Press, 1973.

Leuchtenberg, William E. *Franklin D. Roosevelt and the New Deal*. New York: Harper Torchbooks, 1963.

Lippman, Theo, Jr. *The Squire of Warm Springs: FDR in Georgia, 1924–1945*. Chicago: Playboy Press, 1977.

Logan, Rayford W. *The Betrayal of the Negro from Rutherford B. Hayes to Woodrow Wilson*. New York: Macmillan, Collier Books, 1965 [1954].

———. *Haiti and the Dominican Republic*. New York: Oxford University Press, 1968.

Longworth, Alice Roosevelt. *Crowded Hours*. New York: Charles Scribner's Sons, 1933.

Lorde, Audre. "Uses of the Erotic: The Erotic as Power." in *Sister Outsider: Essays and Speeches by Audre Lorde*. Crossing Press, 1984.

Lubin, Carol Riegelman, and Anne Winslow. *Social Justice for Women: The International Labor Organization and Women*. Durham, N.C.: Duke University Press, 1990.

McCullough, David. *Mornings on Horseback*. New York: Simon & Schuster, Touchstone, 1981.

MacKenzie, Norman and Jeanne, eds. *The Diary of Beatrice Webb*. 2 vols. Cambridge, Mass.: Harvard University Press, 1982.

Mackenzie, Midge. *Shoulder to Shoulder*. New York: Alfred A. Knopf, 1975.

Maddox, Robert James. *William Borah and American Foreign Policy*. Baton Rouge, La.: Louisiana State University Press, 1969.

Marcus, Jane. *Art and Anger*. Columbus, Ohio: Ohio State University Press, 1988.

————. "Thinking Back Through Our Mothers." In *New Feminist Essays on Virginia Woolf*. Lincoln, Neb.: University of Nebraska Press, 1981.

————. *Virginia Woolf and the Languages of Patriarchy*. Bloomington, Ind.: Indiana University Press, 1987.

Martin, George. *Madame Secretary: Frances Perkins*. Boston: Houghton Mifflin, 1976.

Martin, Ralph G. *Cissy: The Extraordinary Life of Eleanor Medill Patterson*. New York: Simon & Schuster, 1979.

Miller, Nathan. *FDR, An Intimate History*. Garden City, N.Y.: Doubleday, 1983.

————. *The Roosevelt Chronicles*. Garden City, N.Y.: Doubleday, 1979.

Morgan, Ted. *FDR: A Biography*. New York: Simon & Schuster, 1985.

Morgenthau, Henry, III. *Mostly Morgenthaus: A Family History*. New York: Ticknor & Fields, 1991.

Morison, Elting, John Blum, et al., eds. *The Letters of Theodore Roosevelt*. Vols. 1 and 2. Cambridge, Mass.: Harvard University Press, 1951.

Morris, Edmund. *The Rise of Theodore Roosevelt*. New York: Coward, McCann & Geoghegan, 1979.

Morris, Sylvia Jukes. *Edith Kermit Roosevelt: Portrait of a First Lady*. New York: Coward, McCann & Geoghegan, 1980.

Mowrer, Glenn A. *The United States, The United Nations, and Human Rights: The Eleanor Roosevelt and Jimmy Carter Eras*. New York: Greenwood, 1979.

Murphy, Lawrence R. *Perverts by Official Order: The Campaign Against Homosexuals by the United States Navy*. New York: Harrington Park Press, 1988.

Murray, Robert K. *Red Scare: A Study in National Hysteria, 1919–1920*. New York: McGraw-Hill Paperback, 1964.

New York State Legislature. Joint Committee Investigating Seditious Activities, Clayton R. Lusk, chair. *Revolutionary Radicalism: Its History, Purpose and Tactics*. 4 vols. Albany, N.Y.: J. B. Lyon, 1920.

Newton, Esther. "The Mythic Mannish Lesbian: Radclyffe Hall and the New Woman." In *Hidden from History: Reclaiming the Gay and Lesbian Past*, edited by Martin Duberman, Martha Vicinus, and George Chauncey. New York: New American Library, Meridian, 1990.

O'Toole, Patricia. *The Five of Hearts: An Intimate Portrait of Henry Adams and His Friends*. New York: Clarkson N. Potter, 1990.

Palmer, A. Mitchell. "The Case Against the Reds." *Forum*, February 1920.

————. "Extent of the Bolshevik Infection Here." *Literary Digest*, 17 January 1920.

Parks, Lillian Rogers, with Frances Spatz Leighton. *The Roosevelts: A Family in Turmoil*. Englewood Cliffs, N.J.: Prentice Hall, 1981.

Payne, Elizabeth Anne. *Reform, Labor, and Feminism: Margaret Dreier Robins and the Women's Trade Union League*. Urbana, Ill.: University of Illinois Press, 1988.

Perkins, Frances. *The Roosevelt I Knew*. New York: Viking, 1946.

Perry, Elisabeth Israels. *Belle Moskowitz: Feminine Politics and the Exercise of Power in the Age of Alfred E. Smith*. New York: Oxford University Press, 1987.

Person, Ethel Spector. *Dreams of Love and Fateful Encounters: The Power of Romantic Passion*. New York: W. W. Norton, 1988.

Preston, William, Jr. *Aliens and Dissenters: Federal Suppression of Radicals, 1903–1933*. Cambridge, Mass.: Harvard University Press, 1963; Harper Torchbooks, 1966.

Pyron, Darden Asbury. *Southern Daughter: A Biography of Margaret Mitchell*. New York: Oxford University Press, 1991.

Rich, Adrienne. "Compulsory Heterosexuality and Lesbian Existence." In *Blood, Bread, and Poetry: Selected Prose, 1979–1985*. New York: W. W. Norton, 1986.

Rixey, Lilian. *Bamie: Theodore Roosevelt's Remarkable Sister*. New York: David McKay, 1963.

Robinson, Corinne Roosevelt. *My Brother Theodore Roosevelt*. New York: Charles Scribner's Sons, 1921.

————. *One Woman to Another and Other Poems*. New York: Charles Scribner's Sons, 1914.

Rollins, Alfred B. *Roosevelt and Howe*. New York: Alfred A. Knopf, 1962.

Roosevelt, Elliott, and James Brough. *An Untold Story: The Roosevelts of Hyde Park*. New York: G. P. Putnam's Sons, 1973.

Roosevelt, James, with Bill Libby. *My Parents: A Differing View*. Chicago: Playboy Press, 1976.

Roosevelt, Nicholas. *A Front Row Seat*. Norman, Okla.: University of Oklahoma Press, 1953.

Roosevelt, Sara Delano (as told to Isabel Leighton and Gabrielle Forbush). *My Boy Franklin*. New York: Long & Smith, 1933.

Roosevelt, Theodore. *Diaries of Boyhood and Youth*. New York: Charles Scribner's Sons, 1928.

————. *Hunting Trips of a Ranchman*. New York: Charles Scribner's Sons, 1926.

Rosenman, Sam. *Working with Roosevelt*. New York: DaCapo Press Reprint, 1972 [1952].

Rukeyser, Muriel. "Käthe Kollwitz." In *The Collected Poems of Muriel Rukeyser*. New York: McGraw-Hill, 1978.

Russell, Francis. *The Shadow of Blooming Grove: Warren G. Harding in His Times*. New York: McGraw-Hill, 1968.

Sargent, Shirley. *Yosemite's Famous Guests*. Yosemite, Calif.: Flying Spur Press, 1970.

Scharf, Lois. *Eleanor Roosevelt: First Lady of American Liberalism*. Boston: Twayne, 1987.

Scheiber, Harry N. *The Wilson Administration and Civil Liberties, 1917–1921*. Ithaca, N.Y.: Cornell University Press, 1960.

Schlesinger, Arthur M., Jr. *The Age of Roosevelt: The Crisis of the Old Order, 1919–1933*. Boston: Houghton Mifflin, 1957.

Schneiderman, Rose, with Lucy Goldthwaite. *All for One*. New York: Paul Erickson, 1967.

Schwarz, Judith. *Radical Feminists of Heterodoxy: Greenwich Village, 1912–1940*. Norwich, Vt.: New Victoria, 1986.

Seligman, Herbert J. "The Conquest of Haiti." *The Nation*, 10 July 1920.

Sicherman, Barbara. *Alice Hamilton: A Life in Letters*. Cambridge, Mass.: Harvard University Press, 1984.

Sicherman, Barbara, et al., eds. *Notable American Women: The Modern Period*. Cambridge, Mass.: Harvard University Press, 1980.

Smith, Helen Huntington. "Profiles: Noblesse Oblige." *The New Yorker*, 5 April 1930.

Smith-Rosenberg, Carroll. *Disorderly Conduct: Visions of Gender in Victorian America*. New York: Alfred A. Knopf, 1985.

Steeholm, Clara and Hardy. *The House at Hyde Park: Together with Sara Delano Roosevelt's Household Book*. New York: Viking, 1950.

Steinberg, Alfred. *Mrs. R: The Life of Eleanor Roosevelt*. New York: G. P. Putnam's Sons, 1958.

Stone, Ralph. *The Irreconcilables: The Fight Against the League of Nations*. New York: W. W. Norton, 1970.

Swanberg, W. A. *Whitney Father, Whitney Heiress*. New York: Charles Scribner's Sons, 1980.

Teague, Michael. *Mrs. L: Conversations with Alice Roosevelt Longworth*. Garden City, N.Y.: Doubleday, 1981.

Umansky, Howard. "Mourning Patterns of Theodore Roosevelt." Unpublished paper.

Van Voris, Jacqueline. *Carrie Chapman Catt: A Public Life*. New York: The Feminist Press, 1987.

Vicinus, Martha. "Distance and Desire: English Boarding School Friendships, 1870–1920." In *Hidden from History: Reclaiming the Gay and Lesbian Past*, edited by Martin Duberman et al. New American Library, Meridian, 1989.

Villard, Oswald Garrison. " 'Pitiless Publicity' for Haiti." *The Nation*, 6 October 1920. Reprinted in *Oswald Garrison Villard: The Dilemmas of the Absolute Pacifist in Two World Wars*, edited by Anthony Gronowicz. New York: Garland, 1983.

Ward, Geoffrey C. *Before the Trumpet: Young Franklin Roosevelt*. New York: Harper & Row, 1985.

———. *A First-Class Temperament: The Emergence of Franklin Roosevelt*. New York: Harper & Row, 1989.

Ware, Susan. *Partner and I: Molly Dewson, Feminism, and New Deal Politics*. New Haven, Conn.: Yale University Press, 1987.

Waskow, Arthur. *From Race Riot to Sit-In*. Garden City, N.Y.: Doubleday, 1967.

Watrous, Hilda R. *In League with Eleanor: Eleanor Roosevelt and the League of Women Voters, 1921–1962*. New York: Foundation for Citizenship Education, League of Women Voters, 1984.

———. *Narcissa Cox Vanderlip*. League of Women Voters' pamphlet. New York: Foundation for Citizenship Education, 1982.

Weiss, Nancy. "The Negro and the New Freedom: Fighting Wilsonian Segregation." *Political Science Quarterly*, March 1968.

Williams, William A. *American-Russian Relations, 1781–1947*. New York: Rinehart, 1952.

Wolgemuth, Kathleen. "Woodrow Wilson and Federal Segregation." *Journal of Negro History*, April 1959.

Wood, Edith Elmer. "Four Washington Alleys." *The Survey*, 6 December 1913.

Woolf, S. J. "A Woman Speaks Her Political Mind." *New York Times Magazine*, 8 April 1928.

Woolf, Virginia. "The Compromise (Mrs Humphry Ward)." Review of *The Life of Mrs Humphry Ward* by her daughter Janet Penrose Trevelyan in *The New Republic*, 9 January 1924. In *Virginia Woolf: Women and Writing*, edited by Michele Barrett. London: The Women's Press, 1979.

———. "Lady Strachey." In *The Nation & Athenaeum*, 22 December 1928. Reprinted in *Books and Portraits*, edited by Mary Lyon. N.Y.: Harcourt Brace Jovanovich, 1977.

———. *A Room of One's Own*. New York: Harcourt, Brace & World, 1957 [1929].

Youngs, William J. *Eleanor Roosevelt: A Personal and Political Life*. Boston: Little, Brown, 1985.

Index